Electric Shock

From the Gramophone to the iPhone –

125 Years of Pop Music

Also by Peter Doggett

The Man Who Sold the World:
David Bowie and the 1970s

You Never Give Me Your Money:
The Battle for the Soul of the Beatles

There's a Riot Going On:
Revolutionaries, Rock Stars and the
Rise and Fall of '60s Counter-culture

The Art and Music of John Lennon

Are You Ready for the Country:
Elvis, Dylan, Parsons and the Roots of Country Rock

Abbey Road/Let It Be

Lou Reed: Growing Up in Public

As Rufus Lodge

F**k: An Irreverent History of the F-Word

As contributor

The 1960s Photographed by David Hurn

Art Kane

Separate Cinema: The First 100 Years of Black Poster Art

Tom Kelley's Studio

Mario Casilli

Hollywood Bound

Electric Shock

From the Gramophone to the iPhone –

125 Years of Pop Music

Peter Doggett

THE BODLEY HEAD
LONDON

1 3 5 7 9 10 8 6 4 2

The Bodley Head, an imprint of Vintage,
20 Vauxhall Bridge Road,
London SW1V 2SA

The Bodley Head is part of the Penguin Random House group of companies
whose addresses can be found at global.penguinrandomhouse.com.

Penguin
Random House
UK

First published in Great Britain by
The Bodley Head in 2015

www.vintage-books.co.uk

A CIP catalogue record for this book
is available from the British Library

ISBN 9781847922182

Typeset in Adobe Caslon by Palimpsest Book Production Limited,
Falkirk, Stirlingshire

Printed and bound by
Clays Ltd, St Ives plc

Penguin Random House is committed to a sustainable future for our
business, our readers and our planet. This book is made from
Forest Stewardship Council® certified paper.

MIX
Paper from
responsible sources
FSC
www.fsc.org
FSC® C018179

For Rachel

Contents

Introduction

I

If, in 1973, you mailed a postal order for £2.50 to a box number on Merseyside, you might receive a record in an unmarked sleeve, processed-egg yellow or smoked-salmon pink. Or your money might vanish, all subsequent letters ignored.

Two times out of three, my parcel arrived; poor odds for an impecunious schoolboy, except that the prize justified the risk. It was illicit, occult, an experience unavailable from the ill-stocked record shop in my home town, where some of my schoolmates pilfered singles from the half-price box at lunchtime. Although I was too moral, or scared, to join them, I was still prepared to steal from corporations and millionaires. So I wrote to the mysterious people who made their living from selling illegal LPs – bootlegs, as they were known – via obliquely worded ads in the back pages of the London music papers.

That was how, at the age of 16, I first heard a recording of Bob Dylan and the future members of the Band, performing at the Royal Albert Hall in 1966. Or so it said on the yellow photocopy tucked inside the cover, the only validation of its contents.

By purchasing *Royal Albert Hall*, against the wishes of the artist and his record company, I was buying my way into a secret society: insider trading, if you like, in the mythology of rock 'n' roll. I was already aware that this recording was regarded by many as the artistic pinnacle of Dylan's career, and its aesthetic worth was multiplied for me by its exclusivity. What I hadn't anticipated was its sonic force, delivered with the fury and contempt of a man who sounded as if he were staring an apocalypse in the eye.

The album's climax has become a piece of 1960s folklore. It documents a confrontation between audience members who had convinced themselves, against all aural evidence, that Dylan was only valid with an acoustic guitar; and a man who had staked his sanity on living with extremes, among them the crushing volume of an electric band. 'Judas', someone called from the stalls. Dylan drawled a contemptuous response, before leading his musicians into 'Like a Rolling Stone'.

Adjectives wouldn't begin to convey the effect of immersing myself in that moment, and that music, over the months ahead. As I slid towards a teenage nervous breakdown, it offered me not salvation, exactly, because my fate was sealed; not transcendence, because when it was over I still had to face my own existence; but recognition, the hint that I might not be entering the darkness alone; that one could go down into the pit defiantly, self-righteously; that someone else had been there before. Later, after the apocalypse, bemused to have survived, I gathered from that same performance the hope of renewal, just as Dylan had weathered the storm (in another mythological tale) to find respite in a Woodstock basement.

Thirty years later, returned to the scene of my adolescent collapse by a surreal sequence of romantic circumstances, I wandered through the air-conditioned limbo of my home town's shopping centre, digesting impressions old and new. Amidst the echoing chatter was the distant sound of music: intended to ease our consumerist footsteps into chain stores or fast-food merchants; to smooth our passage, without being heard. But I can never register the presence of music without wanting to recognise it; and as I concentrated, I realised I had heard this sound before. For the contraband of 1973 was now legal tender: remixed, remastered, repackaged (and relocated in the interests of historical accuracy from London to Manchester's Free Trade Hall). It was offered by a multinational corporation as an authentic and fully authorised slice of rock history – still transcendent, but robbed of its underground lustre. The soundtrack for my own descent into the inferno was now being piped at almost subliminal volume through a soulless mall. Music which I would once have chosen to represent my identity, by an artist at the end of his own fraying rope, at war with his psyche and his society, had been rendered in perfect sound quality, at last, so it could serve as background for the sale of burgers and jeans. The music was the same, but its status had changed as radically as the now middle-aged man who was struggling to comprehend what it might all signify.

If the soundtrack of psychological decay and clinical depression could become muzak, then surely nothing was immune to a metamorphosis as shocking and, perhaps, comic as the fate of Kafka's Gregor Samsa. Another scene came to mind. London's Dominion Theatre, in 1991: a bill promising three 1960s hitmakers, the Merseybeats, Herman's Hermits and the Byrds. Or, to be precise, half of the original Merseybeats; some vintage Hermits, but no Herman; and a Byrds line-up assembled by their first drummer, alongside two men who must have been in short trousers when the group had made their initial visit to Britain in 1965.

They were merely the backdrop for a bizarre clash of cultures. The musicians masqueraded unconvincingly as the elite of 1965, in front of an audience dominated by teenagers clad in recreations of the Carnaby Street fashions once worn by their parents. The youngsters responded to this ersatz nostalgia by throwing themselves into a display of hippie dancing which they can only have learned from vintage newsreels. The collage was surreal: music, motion and clothing utterly out of sync. It signalled a vain quest for a golden age, from a generation who had been bottle-fed on the superiority of the 1960s to any other era of human history.

Or, again, an incident repeated daily: I'm queuing to pay for petrol, and over the loudspeakers comes 'The Game of Love' by Wayne Fontana and the Mindbenders. I relax into its familiarity, sing along in my head, and suddenly awaken to what's happening. In 2015, music that is almost fifty years old provides a constant soundtrack to our financial transactions and consumerist obsessions. Above our heads, it is always 1958, or 1965, or 1972, and the music of the rock 'n' roll revolution – two decades of radio hits, from Bill Haley to Fleetwood Mac – is universal currency so stripped of its value that it signifies nothing, evokes no surprise, triggers nothing more than a sense of belonging, whether or not we are old enough to remember when it was new and stood for something. Now it is culturally empty, but familiar to children and parents alike: as constant and faithful an ingredient of our daily lives as the logos of McDonald's or Tesco's. In 1965, 'The Game of Love' was a No. 1 hit. In 1966, it was forgotten, swept away by relentless waves of novelty. In the early 1970s, friends thought I was strange – and I was – because I supplemented my diet of new music with battered 1960s hits from junkshops. I was keeping the past alive, but I needn't have bothered: it was never going to die. It's easy to imagine returning to whatever will serve as a collective space in the twenty-second century, and still hearing 'Walk On By', 'Lola' and, yes, even 'The Game of Love' in the air, just loud enough to calm the fears and aid the impulse-buying of our great-grandchildren.

II

Somewhere amidst those eerie encounters with the musical past lie the seeds of this book. For most of the last half-century, I have been an active consumer of popular music, in increasingly varied forms. For perhaps 70% of that time, I have been writing about the same subject; or, at least, a blinkered representation of it. Fortunate enough to have been paid to investigate pop history for several decades, I have been compelled to experience music that lay far beyond my personal aesthetic.

But I have still imposed that aesthetic judgement on everything I've heard; defined myself as someone who, for example, loves Bob Dylan but not Tom Waits; Crosby, Stills & Nash but not Emerson, Lake & Palmer; Sonic Youth but not the Smiths; soul but not metal; some MOR but not most AOR – a vast Venn diagram of choices and prejudices, at the interlocking heart of which stands just one man, constructed upon the music he loves.

As my experience in the local garage suggests, we live in a world where people like me have created an approved canon of popular music which is open to constant minor revision, as the latest issue of your favourite heritage rock magazine offers 'The Greatest Albums You've Never Heard' or slips a choice obscurity into the 'Best 100 Punk Singles of All Time'. There is an authorised list of momentous events in musical history, which we all agree to recognise, from Elvis Presley at Sun Studios in 1954 to, yes, Bob Dylan and 'Judas' in 1966 and on and on; a gallery of classic albums, life-changing singles, vital genres, halcyon eras, eternally fresh, eternally ripe for discovery.

Yet this is also an age in which all sense of a critical consensus and a carefully curated heritage has been demolished, almost at a stroke, by the catch-all expansiveness of the Internet. Anyone with a broadband connection can access almost every recording made since the invention of recorded sound. True, Beyoncé's music enjoys a higher profile on YouTube, iTunes and Spotify than her early twentieth-century equivalents, such as Mamie Smith or Marion Harris. But all that separates us from the music of 1920 is the same click of the mouse, or swipe across the tablet, which brings us Beyoncé. The choice is entirely ours.

So this is a unique moment: for the first time, modern technology allows us to construct our own route through documented history. But it also strips that history of its context. Streaming and download sites offer you the music, but no hint of when or why it was made; and who it was made for. Also missing is any sense of why we enjoy the music we choose; how we have learned, down the generations, to react as we do when the hailstorm of contemporary media fires jazz or hip hop or punk in our direction.

III

The invention of recorded sound transformed music from an experience into an artefact, with physical and psychological consequences which reverberate to this day. It imposed a distance between the moment when the music was made and when it was heard. It allowed for endless repetitions of what would once have been a unique performance. And it facilitated the creation of an entire industry, now global in its span, devoted to the making, selling and disseminating of recordings, and the invention of technology to carry that music around the world.

This revolution in the nature of music-making has altered everyone and everything touched by it – the performer, the audience, and the music itself. The nature of that change has been far-reaching: it has left its mark on the way we think, the way we feel and even the way we move. (It's even loosened our underwear, or so the horrified commentators of the 1920s recounted, as young women unfastened their corsets to dance the Charleston.) The most powerful changes have been those which involve a change in the rhythms that govern our lives, from the syncopation of ragtime and jazz to today's unrelenting computerised dance beat. They have altered the way we deal with each other; the language of love, the rhetoric of hate. They have enabled races to communicate and assimilate more easily; and provided the fuel that could engulf those relationships in flames.

At each step of the way, music has represented modernity, at odds with convention and tradition: the new world perpetually bullying and hectoring the young. But one of the qualities of music, regardless of its origins, is that its delights are inexhaustible. Each musical revolution has altered the soundtrack of the age, but left all its predecessors intact. Yesterday's mainstream becomes tomorrow's carefully guarded memory, reviving our individual and collective past every time that the listener pulls a favourite record off the shelf (or opens the appropriate download).

Technology and music have altered in tandem: revolutions in one field spurring changes in the other, backwards and forwards, to the point where it is difficult to tell Pavlov from his dogs. The development of new recording techniques in the 1920s allowed crooners to whisper their sweet nothings into our ears, raising the stakes for any mere mortal who wasn't Bing Crosby, but found himself with a girl in his arms. The invention of the Walkman and the iPod allowed us to become living enactments of the music we loved, parading down the road to the glorious rebel-rousing of metal, punk or hip hop. Before the advent of modern technology, music was made in the home, or witnessed in the concert hall or theatre. Now it can be omnipresent to the extent that we barely recognise its existence. It is literally the soundtrack of our lives – both the badge of our identity, and a background wash of noise whenever we turn on the TV, or walk through a supermarket. And that is one of the dominant themes of this book: what has changed is not just the music, and the technology, but the role that the combination of those two unstable elements plays in our lives.

This is also the tale of how a world devoted to the lusty pleasures of the Victorian music hall and vaudeville was captivated by the African-American rhythms of ragtime, the first in a long line of musical genres which have entered our lives as if from outer space. Each arrival has been greeted as an outrageous threat to the sanity and sanctity of innocent women and children, while being instantly accepted by the young as a symbol of joyous independence from parental and adult authority. The invader is gradually accepted and tamed, just in time for the cycle to begin again. One generation's revolutionary becomes the conservative of the next; every musical innovation is both the death of civilisation as we know it, and the dawning of a multidimensional new world.

IV

The era of universal accessibility to the past and the present deserves a history that is open, not blinkered. In the arts as in politics, there is nothing more dangerous and deceptive than unanimity, which can easily become tyrannical. There is tyranny, too, in listening only to the masses, as anyone condemned to a world where music was defined by TV talent contests might agree. But it pales alongside the arrogance of a coterie of critics pronouncing that only they are capable of deciding what is worthy of everyone else's attention. As someone who has been part of that coterie, I know the seductiveness of offering up one's own artistic tastes for universal acceptance.

In my previous incarnation as a music journalist, I was as guilty as anyone of forcing my taste upon my readership, of using fancy language to justify aesthetic choices which were, ultimately, both arbitrary and entirely personal. But gradually the hypocrisy of my stance became inescapable. Politically, I was a radical (and hardly alone in that, among the rock or jazz critics of the past century). But culturally, I was a snob. One hand held a placard screaming 'Power to the People'; in the other was a more discreet sign, on which was written 'Why Do the People Have Such Terrible Taste?'

So my first task in writing this book was to throw away decades of prejudice, however well argued and intelligently phrased; and to return to a series of deceptively simple questions – what were people listening to? Where did it come from? Why did they like it? And what did it bring to their lives? Approaching music in a spirit approximating genuine democracy offered me something of a blinding revelation. If I removed my blinkers and opened up my ears, I could find pleasure in music which had previously brought me none. For a cynical and opinionated critic (are there any other kinds?), it was something akin to being born again. That is how I found myself, for the first time in my life, hearing (to seize some names at random) Bing Crosby, Glenn Miller, Mantovani, Queen, Kylie Minogue and Metallica with genuine appreciation, rather than closing my mind as soon as I saw their names.

It wasn't enough to adjust my focus. I also had to retreat far enough to be able to view the entire landscape. Various fault lines cut through the history of twentieth-century music, but the widest of them equates the arrival of rock 'n' roll with a revolution that is musical, social and psychological. The exact co-ordinates of this great divide are open to debate, and refugees from either side of the border are often ushered across enemy lines. But the significance of this moment is apparent from the two rival narratives most commonly employed to explain pop's progress through the century. The first harks back to the 1930s – the era of Cole Porter and Rodgers and Hart, Benny Goodman and Louis Armstrong – as a golden age, and views the teenage cacophony of the mid-1950s as a sorry falling-away from paradise. The second depicts rock 'n' roll as salvation from years of genteel boredom: a triumph of youthful excitement over decades of parental repression.

Setting out to chronicle popular music and its eternal quest for modernity, I knew where the story would end, in the here and now, but where should I begin? With Elvis Presley? Frank Sinatra? Louis Armstrong? There was a valid case to be made for each. But the more I listened, and plunged into the strange panorama of the past, the more I realised that the two most revolutionary moments in the life of twentieth-century music actually pre-dated that century. They were the creation of recorded sound as a commercial artefact, and the birth of ragtime; and they coincided in the 1890s. That was the moment when African-American rhythms first seized hold of popular entertainment, and spread across the Atlantic; when the anthems of youth first confronted and appalled older generations; when music was transformed from a kind of entertainment into a business that would eventually touch all of our lives, in ways that would have been unimaginable when ragtime was born. That was where the modern world began: with two concussions so profound that we can still feel their echoes shaking the ground beneath our feet today.

One final set of prejudices and assumptions had to be discarded, like a rock critic's uniform. Writing this book, I no longer believed, automatically, that confrontational music is always better than comforting music; that experimental always trumps conventional; that rough beats smooth; that spontaneity towers over contrivance; that elitist counts for more than populist. This doesn't mean that I have entirely abandoned my aesthetic preferences; merely that, as much as possible, I have tried to excise them from this book, to tell a popular story rather than a personal one. But at the same time, this is a very personal book: it's based on years of my research, and my intense listening; my mental leaps to make connections between apparently disparate subjects; my experience of more than a century's music from all our yesterdays.

The first requirement of popular music, surely, is that it should be popular (and musical, although the precise definition of that quality is buried beneath festering cans of worms). Much as I admire the cunning of the New York rock critic Robert Christgau in identifying the term 'semi-popular music' to describe the music he loves, the tastes of a mass audience tell us something about a society that the preferences of an elite may not. So this book is unashamedly about music that has proven to be popular – globally, racially, generationally – rather than that which has since been judged, by critics and other fools, to have the richest aesthetic value.

This is also, unashamedly, a book with a British perspective, about a world and a history that has increasingly been dominated by the music and culture of the United States of America. The accident of a (mostly) shared language has made it easy for American sounds, images and ideas to infiltrate and then dominate our lives. But one of the themes of this book is that the same process of almost invisible colonialism has been taking place around the world, speeding to its inevitable climax in the final decades of the last century. If you had travelled the world as the First World War broke out, visiting cities selected at random from every continent on earth, you would have been exposed to a multiplicity of sounds and sensations that would have seemed dazzling. Each country begat and cherished its own culture – or cultures, to be exact, as the centuries before the advent of rapid transportation ensured that every region on the planet owned its distinctive vision of the world, with a soundtrack to match.

Now you can stand on a street corner in Europe, South America, Africa, Asia – and hear Jay-Z, or Rihanna; Elton John or the Rolling Stones; or, perhaps, their local equivalents, sublimating their national traditions in favour of the all-conquering rhythms of hip hop or stadium rock, Broadway musicals or Hollywood theme songs. Religious and cultural differences may be as savage as ever, and the means of transporting them around the world has carried the problems of each continent into all its neighbours. But the global network of multinational marketing, and the worldwide web, ensures that the dominant icons and events of the world's entertainment headquarters are transmitted instantly across the planet. Almost every nation may be in conflict or at risk; but when it comes to culture, we are finally one world – not the universal brotherhood envisaged by the creators of the United Nations, perhaps, but a race linked by the ubiquity of our heroes, and the rhythm of our lives.

That global heritage of popular music is the product of 125 years of artistic and scientific innovation. It represents a constant quest for modernity, which must be endlessly renewed. This is the story of that quest: of the musicians, the generations that they delighted and divided, and the technology which captured their music in the moment of its creation, and preserved it for our collective enjoyment and amazement. This is their story; and ours.

Two Near-Apologies

1. Recounting the history of popular music entails the use of language that is, and was, disrespectful and insulting towards African-Americans (and sometimes other races too). Racism has always been as entrenched in popular culture as in any other area of life. But omitting or censoring that language would only obscure that racism, and present a misleading account of our collective past.

2. It is quite possible that your favourite artists or recordings are not mentioned in the book. Before you rise up in protest, please remember this: neither are most of mine.

Speaking of the Past

There are towns where one can enjoy all sorts of histrionic spectacles from morning to night. And, we must admit, the more people hear lascivious and pernicious songs, which raise in their souls impure and voluptuous desires, the more they want to hear.
   Fifth-century saint

Such tunes, although whistled and sung by everybody, are erroneously supposed to have taken a deep hold of the popular mind . . . [but] they are hummed and whistled without musical emotion . . . they persevere and haunt the morbidly sensitive nerves of deeply musical persons, so that they too hum and whistle them voluntarily, hating them even while they hum them . . . such a melody breaks out every now and then, like a morbid irritation of the skin.
   John S. Dwight, journalist and composer of hymns, 1853

The California beetle cannot stand [recorded] music. It kills him. Three playings of a slow piece like 'Home Sweet Home' put him out of misery, but ragtime will kill him in a few bars. The deadly tarantula falls into a stupor. Butterflies are not affected. The bumble-bee flies into a nervous fit. Wasps suffer from wing paralysis and are unable to fly again, though otherwise unaffected. Worms try to crawl nearer the phonograph horn, as though pleased. They evidently want to do the latest wiggle.
   Amateur entomologist, California, 1913

[The 79-year-old music professor] listened for a few minutes to a jazz band playing at furious pace and turned to his nephew, declaring: 'That isn't music! Stop it!' Then he swayed and fell dead.
   Daily Mirror, 1926

Jazz is born of disorder in the nervous system. Heart tests have shown that the original composers of jazz music suffered from irregular heartbeats.
   American neurologist, 1929

Music begins to atrophy when it departs too far from the dance.
   Ezra Pound, *ABC of Reading*, 1934

'In time we may all get our music by mechanical means.'

Daily Mirror, 22 December 1903

CHAPTER 1

THE
VOICE
OF THE
DEAD

'And the tunes that mean so much to you alone –
Common tunes that make you choke and blow your nose,
Vulgar tunes that bring the laugh that brings the groan –
I can rip your very heartstrings out with those ...
I, the everlasting Wonder-song of Youth.'

Rudyard Kipling, 'The Song of the Banjo', 1895

It is a matter of honour among judges that they should pretend ignorance about all matters of popular culture – even if the oft-repeated remark, 'Who *are* the Beatles?', was never actually uttered in the High Court. Not that such comments were unknown: Mr Justice Bicknill, officiating in a divorce hearing of 1903, enquired of one of Britain's most celebrated music-hall performers, Miss Vesta Victoria: 'May I ask what is it you *do*? Do you *sing*?'

Judges of the Edwardian era delighted in their disdain for popular entertainment. In May 1904, Mr Justice Darling was called to adjudicate upon the ownership of a long-forgotten song, 'Oh Charlie, Come to Me'. Miss Gracie Grahame, aged 29, esteemed for her vivacity and golden curls, had applied to the King's Bench Division of the London courts for an injunction. She wished to prevent a fellow performer – Miss Katie Lawrence, seven years her senior, long linked in the public memory with the song 'Daisy Bell', and its bicycle made for two – from singing 'Oh Charlie', claiming that it was her own original composition. Mr Justice Darling did not attempt to hide his derision: 'anything less distinguished' than the song in question 'I cannot imagine', he complained. He proceeded to mock the song's rhyming scheme, scansion and grammar, before pronouncing that 'it is rather a melancholy state of things that legal copyright should exist in such rubbish', and finding against Miss Grahame.

The case had a tragic denouement. A week after her appearance in court, Miss Grahame topped a variety bill at her husband's theatre, the Empress in Brixton. Her act was brought to an abrupt end when she launched impromptu into the chorus of the disputed song, whereupon her husband called for the curtain to be brought down. It was, Miss Grahame declared later, 'the worst thing that can happen to an artist. I felt they had taken my very livelihood away.' Gracie then set out with her fellow theatricals for a hostelry near Waterloo Bridge, but broke away from her friends, ran down the steps that led to the mudflats, and jumped headlong into the water. It was low tide, and the Thames was no more than three feet deep; but Miss Grahame's voluminous skirts helped to drag her beneath the surface – until she was pulled clear by a constable who had witnessed her desperate plunge.

Miss Grahame was removed to a local infirmary, where she was found to have suffered no ill effects. She spent the night awaiting an inevitable court appearance on the charge of attempted suicide. Perhaps magistrates looked more kindly upon the music hall than did their senior legal peers, as Mr Fenwick examined the pathetic circumstances of the case, and declined to impose the standard prison sentence. Instead he demanded £20 (equivalent of £2,000 today) from the accused, to be held against proof of her good behaviour for six months, and required her to promise that she would not venture on to the mudflats again.

The copyright dispute left its mark upon the victor, too. Within days of the press reporting upon Miss Grahame's vain efforts at self-harm, Miss Katie Lawrence took the stage of the Bedford Music Hall in Camden. She was greeted as the villainess of the affair, with a chorus of boos so prolonged that she was unable to begin her act. She could, she felt, have won the audience round had she been able to state the facts of the case, but the show's producer had strictly forbidden her from speaking. Miss Lawrence died less than a decade later, remembered today only as the subject of a portrait by Walter Sickert in 1887.

Only the most celebrated or notorious entertainers could hope to survive in the collective memory beyond their lifetime. Likewise the material stuff of their performances. It is safe to assume, for example, that neither 'Good Morning Carrie' nor 'It's Up To You Babe' is remembered today. They were the subject of another copyright dispute, heard by Judge Lacombe in the New York Circuit Court in 1902. The two songs were both described as 'ragtime', about which a *New York Times* editorial declared: 'Its systematic lack of harmonic coincidence suggests to the musical ear that this way madness lies . . . as a habit, it ranks with cocaine and morphine.' The paper added that ragtime songs should be restricted to 'the banjo, and other parodies of musical instruments'. This would ensure that anyone carrying a banjo could, like the possessor of burglar's tools, be treated as offering '*prima facie* evidence of the intent to commit crime'.

What differentiated this case from all previous legal rulings on the subject of musical copying was the evidence offered to the court. Lawyers brought forward phonograph records of both songs, to prove the similarity – or dissimilarity, as it might be – between them. Judge Lacombe laughed these artefacts aside, declaring that his time was too precious to be wasted by a 'musical concert, however good'. When a legal clerk offered to provide a violin on which the melodies could be demonstrated, Lacombe packed away his papers and scampered from the court.

The *New York Times* heartily congratulated the judge on his actions: nobody whose nerves were comprised of a substance less than steel, it declared, would be able to tolerate a ragtime song on a phonograph. In its cynicism, the newspaper overlooked the significance of the phonograph and its rivals. These machines not only offered an instant solution to a debate about musical copyright, but ensured that both performers and their compositions would endure beyond their natural lifespans. More important still was their role in democratising the distribution of music, which was now available in the home of anyone – regardless of their musical ability – who could afford to purchase a phonograph record or cylinder.

> You can study the great artistes. It is not mere mechanical music – it is the living voice of the singer.
>   Gramophone advertisement, 1904

> In your own home, miles and miles away from London, during the long dark evenings that are with us now, for a small outlay, you can be seated comfortably round your fire listening to the Best Songs, the Best Bands, and the best of the World's Musical Talent.
>   Anglophone advertisement, 1904

The birth of recorded sound, no matter how crude its early manifestations, represented a profound shift in the nature of human existence; as profound, it could be argued, as the representation of human speech and thought on papyrus, parchment, paper or, in due course, computer screen. Thomas Edison intended his invention as a means of documenting conversation or debate, or preserving the speeches and bons mots of great men, or as a vehicle for education of the young. He might have been amused to learn that his phonograph was used in 1903 by a suspicious wife to record conversations between her husband and another woman, which were introduced as evidence during their divorce proceedings.

Even before his device reached the public, an American scientist anticipated its ability to conjure up the past: 'How startling it will be to reproduce and hear at pleasure the voice of the dead!' Edison himself believed that 'The Phonograph will undoubtedly be liberally devoted to music. A song sung on the Phonograph is reproduced with marvellous accuracy and power.' Yet he appears not to have considered a more philo-sophical consequence of his machine: that a musical performance would not only be captured and held, but would thereby be changed in essence and in form.

The composer Claude Debussy reflected upon the strangeness of this transformation in 1913: 'In a time like ours, when the genius of engineers has reached such undreamed of proportions, one can hear famous pieces of music as easily as one can buy a glass of beer. It only costs ten centimes, too, just like the automatic weighing scale! Should we not fear this domestica-tion of sound, this magic preserved in a disc that anyone can awaken at will? Will it not mean a diminution of the secret forces of art, which until now have been considered indestructible?' Instead, it was performances that were now indestructible, as long as the artefact on which they were stored remained undamaged.

Those artefacts were often fragile, and assumed many forms. Edison's first phonograph, invented in 1877, was exhibited across the United States as 'The Miracle of the 19th Century ... The Talking Wonder'. At its heart was a metal cylinder, wrapped in a layer of tin foil, which was 'inscribed' as a recording was made. A stylus was then used to retrieve the sound from the cylinder as it was turned by hand. Audiences flocked to see it in action, but the novelty was soon exhausted, and Edison abandoned the device to concentrate on the electric light. Alexander Graham Bell and Charles Tainter contrived a rival machine, the grapho-phone, in 1887, substituting wax for the tin foil. Edison countered by adding an electric motor; and in 1888 a company was formed to market both models.

In a preview of the 'format wars' that would mark each stage of technological development ahead, Thomas Edison's phonograph and cylinder were soon pitched into battle with Emil Berliner's gramophone. Berliner's recording was captured on a disc – originally made of metal, although he soon created a cheaper alternative from hard rubber. The cylinder was, in its virgin form, unique: each example represented an indi-vidual performance, and the musician who wished to make commercial capital out of his or her skills would have to reprise their piece as often as the market required. Faced with Berliner's gramophone record, which allowed for multiple duplicates of an original performance, Edison's team were forced to concoct their own mass production, at some cost to the already dubious audio quality of their machine.

The gramophone record thereby seized a commercial advantage which would survive, through metamorphoses of recording technique, disc format and musical content, until the brief triumph of the cassette tape and then the more crushing dominance of the digital compact disc. Berliner's success imposed a crucial limitation on the preservation of music, however. Edison's cylinder method allowed anyone to play existing recordings, and also to make their own. Salesmen would carry their demonstration phonograph door to door, so that awestruck customers could hear the sound of their own voices, caught in one moment, replayed faithfully in the next. The gramophone of Herr Berliner, on the other hand, ensured that the making of records would remain a professional affair, imposing divisions between performer, distributor and consumer which seemed not only natural but inevitable to anyone born between 1900 and 1960.

In one field alone, Edison's technology remained triumphant. In the earliest days of the cylinder, many leading performers refused to waste their time on travelling to a distant studio to create something as ephemeral as a record. Instead, they insisted on being visited in their own homes, allowing the engineer to ensnare nature raw and in its own habitat: the earliest in a long tradition of what would become known as location recordings.

Without the cylinder, we would not have the earliest recording of a papal voice. Pope Leo XIII was captured at the age of 92, in 1903, chanting a frail 'Ave Maria' and 'Benediction'. These two recordings – neither longer than a minute – were issued in 1905 on cylinders, and later discs, at the cost of eight shillings apiece: the equivalent of a working-man's daily wage. The manufacturer conceded that 'The Pope was aged and feeble when the records were made', but insisted: 'To Collectors Their Value Is Almost Priceless.'

The religious impulse was channelled that same year into what are believed to be the earliest known musical recordings by African-Americans: recordings of 'Negro Shouts by Dinwiddie Colored Quartet: These are genuine Jubilee and Camp Meeting Shouts sung as only negroes can sing them.' What's striking, more than a century later, about these spirituals, with their unaffected balance between leader and harmonised support, is their sense of existing beyond time, as if, recording deficiencies aside, they might have been performed hundreds of years ago – or today.*

---

* The melody of one of these 1903 recordings, 'Poor Mourner', reappeared sixty years later in Bob Dylan's 'I Shall Be Free', a striking example of the folk process in action.

Those deficiencies convinced 'people of sensitivity [that] the Gramophone was merely an instrument which made objectionable noises'; while Edison's cylinder was 'not then capable of producing any music that was not blatant or vulgar'. Those more generous in spirit were prepared to concede that recordings could deliver a faithful reproduction of the shape and duration of a musical piece; but one journalist remarked that 'You will find that the effect of any song upon a record is immensely improved if you play over the accompaniment from the music upon the piano, while it is being played upon the machine.'

Aside from its novelty appeal, recorded sound needed to offer substance that would transcend the barbed-wire scratchiness and foggy hiss, the tin-can tone and horizon-distant volume, which afflicted a majority of early discs. In 1894, the Edison Kinetoscope Company augmented its jerky 'peep show' films with cylinder recordings, which required the consumer to peer through an eyepiece and insert stethoscope tubes in their ears. The combination of inadequate sound and indistinct vision was presumably more appealing than either without the other.

Another exploratory venture into the union of science and music involved the earliest experiments with wireless telephony, or 'radio'. In 1906, just five years after Marconi sent his first telephonic message across the Atlantic, a Massachusetts engineer named Reginald Fessenden was able to 'broadcast' his own rudimentary violin solos, and readings from the New Testament, to ships just offshore. Fessenden also antici-pated the role of the disc jockey by beaming a gramophone record of Handel's 'Largo' aria to his handful of listeners. (Lee de Forest of New York subsequently claimed this achievement for himself, after he broad-cast the *William Tell* overture from the city's Parker Building in 1907; his hubris was rewarded when the entire building burned to the ground a few weeks later.)

Almost a century before a broadband connection was assumed to be a key requirement of civilised life, telephone subscribers in Wilmington, Delaware were offered a 'dial up' phonograph service: 'Attached to the wall near the telephone is a box containing a special receiver, adapted to throw out a large volume of sound into the room ... At the central office, the lines of musical subscribers are tapped to a manual board attended by an operator. A number of phonographs are available, and a representative assortment of records kept on hand ... When it is desired to entertain a party of friends, the user calls the music department and requests that a certain number be played. He releases and proceeds to fix the megaphone in position. At the same time the music operator plugs up a free phonograph to his line, slips on the record and starts the machine. At the conclusion of the piece the connection is pulled down, unless more performances have been requested.' Miraculous though this service must have appeared in 1909, any aesthetic value must have been trumped by its prestige as a status symbol.

One man can claim to have brought recorded music a lustre that none of these technological schemes could match. In a recording career that stretched almost twenty years, he became – to borrow a term from later decades – the first 'superstar' produced by the music industry, and the highest-paid entertainer in the world. His fame arose not from sentimental ballads or comic monologues, the staples of the era; but from unadulterated pieces of what we now call 'classical' music, arias from the world's most famous operas.

Enrico Caruso was 29 years old in 1902, when he left his native Naples for America, preceded by his reputation as Europe's finest operatic tenor. His first US recording for the Victor company – 'Vesti la giubba' (1904), from Leoncavallo's opera *Pagliacci* – carried such unfeigned passion that it established the name of Caruso as a vocal superlative. Eight years later, he would surpass this epic performance with his portentous reading of Sir Arthur Sullivan's lament for his late brother, 'The Lost Chord', staring down grief with a courage that still defies the listener to remain unmoved. By his death in 1921, Caruso was guaranteed an annual income of $100,000, topped up by a generous royalty on record sales.

Victor could afford to reward the Neapolitan so handsomely because he had enabled them to transform the gramophone from a curiosity into a mark of sophistication and wealth. Caruso became the focal point of the company's Red Seal records – mostly one-sided, and therefore featuring only one piece of less than four minutes' duration. Whereas Victor's standard, two-sided records of ephemeral popular songs retailed for 75c, the Red Seal offerings cost anything up to $7 apiece – the differential justified not just by the musical content, but also by the social prestige conferred by ownership of these exclusive items. Opera buffs were not restricted to the wealthy elite, of course, and many less privileged families skimped on essentials for the life-affirming joy of owning a few precious minutes of Caruso in his prime.

Lucrative though Caruso's career was, the infant recording industry could not survive on operatic arias and ballads by distinguished composers alone. For every extract from Puccini or Verdi, there were several dozen songs that were not expected to live beyond the season. Indeed, for the first time in musical history, they were specifically designed to fade after an initial burst of enthusiasm. Thomas Edison himself had experienced the gulf between ephemera and enduring art. While testing his equipment, he selected a recording of a favourite tune in waltz-time. 'We played that waltz all day long', he recalled. 'The second day it began to pall upon us a little. At the end of the fourth day the men began to get dreadfully irritated. At the end of the week they could not stay in the room. I firmly believe that it is this question of reiteration which makes it possible for you to hear Beethoven and Wagner over and over again without getting tired. The music of these great composers is so complicated that it does not weary the nerve centres, while the simpler melody, however tuneful, at last induces dislike and disgust.' His findings would inadvertently inspire a barbaric form of sonic torture a century later in the so-called 'war on terror'.

Nobody involved in the production of self-consciously popular songs – designed to appeal instantaneously, and quickly be replaced by something equally addictive – anticipated that anyone would be foolhardy enough to punish themselves in the manner of Edison's engineers. Nor were they so deluded as to imagine they were creating transcendent art worthy of Caruso. But around 1890, in New York, there arose a self-perpetuating business devoted, like consumer capitalism itself, to creating a desire that the public did not realise it felt, and then satisfying it with such efficiency that the want would mutate into an obsession. The result was the manufacturing of popular songs in a system akin to factory farming. It was the great fortune of this industry that it emerged just as scientific innovation produced a method for distributing products around the world: the two strands of music production and reproduction created a global industry which, over the course of the twentieth century, would colour and transform the everyday lives of generations of eager consumers.

The young men like the popular sentimental song. It helps them very much at the beginning of a courtship. They can sing a popular chorus which may imply much or little to the girl. But it is straight enough to be understood, and oblique enough to be easily and tactfully disregarded if the girl so wishes.

In the thousands of songs that we publish, there are hundreds of

appropriate choruses, which I know friends sing to each other; and
by their means, the girl is often led to 'understand'!
London music publisher, 1912

The public . . . must be very faithful to old ideals, to judge from the
unvarying stream poured out upon it by songwriters and publishers
. . . practically every lyric is on the one theme – love.
Daily Mirror editorial, 1904

The credit for inventing the modern popular song was claimed by Charles
K. Harris, the composer in 1891 of one of the most enduring hits of the
pre-jazz era: 'After the Ball'. Across three lengthy and maudlin verses, each
answered by an equally pathetic refrain, Harris portrayed a lonely old man
who is asked by his infant niece: 'Why are you single? Why live alone?
Have you no babies? Have you no home?' Uncle unveils the sorry tale of
the love he lost because he saw her kissing another man; only to discover,
after her death, that his supposed rival was merely her brother. 'After the
Ball' 'lay upon the shelf for over a year, no singer caring to take it up on
account of its extreme length', Harris recounted. It eventually found its way
to the statuesque Canadian vaudeville artist, Miss May Irwin, and thence
was 'interpolated' – a standard practice, whereby contemporary 'hit' songs
would be added to an existing show – into the touring musical *A Trip to
Chinatown*. It was recorded, to piano accompaniment, by George J. Gaskin,
'the Silver-Voiced Irish Tenor' from Belfast; and then by the noted whistler, John Yorke Atlee. The success of Harris's composition was measured
not in cylinders or records, however, but in sales of sheet music, which were
estimated to run into the millions.

In the era before mass communication, a piano in the home was the
only reliable way for a family to reprise the songs they had heard at a theatre or
music hall. And the music-publishing industry – which can be traced back to
Ottaviano dei Petrucci and his collection of French *chansons* in early sixteenth-
century Venice, through the song-seller in Shakespeare's *A Winter's Tale*, to the
ballad-mongers and broadsheet sellers of Victorian England, and the concentration of publishers' offices in the first of two New York districts designated as
'Tin Pan Alley' in the 1880s – existed to supply (and renew) that demand. By
then, American publishers were copying the recent English trend of paying
stars of variety and music hall to perform their songs, in the hope that lucrative
sheet-music sales would follow.

Before the enactment of strict copyright legislation in the early twentieth century, publishers were plagued by 'music pirates'. Rather than selling counterfeit CDs and DVDs in street markets, as they would a century later, these miscreants gathered outside theatres and halls offering cut-price copies of the songs that had just been performed. In Britain alone, around 60,000 sheets of pirated music were seized every month by representatives of the Musical Copyright Association. The illicit trade gradually forced legitimate publishers to cut their prices by up to 75% – shrinking the earnings of the humble songwriter. The music-hall star Miss Ellaline Terriss registered the success of a new song: 'I think the public like it, for I see the irrepressible "music pirate" is already selling it outside the theatre. I expect one day to find a man standing in the street with a phonograph singing the song in my voice, and advising the public not to pay to go in the theatre when they can hear just as well for a penny outside.'

Between performers such as Miss Terriss, and songwriters such as Harris, existed several tiers of the industry: the publishers themselves, and their arrangers; their demonstrators, who would hope to interest visiting singers in their material; and travelling agents, whose work could involve anything from door-to-door salesmanship, to apparently 'spontaneous' exhibitions of fervour in a public place. In his early teens, the celebrated composer Irving Berlin scraped together an income from busking outside bars, singing in a vaudeville chorus and working as a song plugger or 'boomer'. Publishers hired him to sit in the audience of a vaudeville theatre, and react with exaggerated gusto when a particular song was aired. Experts in this dubious art would encourage their fellow spectators to demand an impromptu encore – and amidst such tactics, a hit song could be born. It was only when Berlin won a job as a singing waiter – a busker *inside* the establishment, rather than hovering outside – that he could demonstrate his ability to compose impromptu parodies of well-known songs, and then showcase his original compositions.

In the 1890s, few people had access to a phonograph or gramophone, and beyond the pages of the sixpenny sheet, music existed only in live performance. There were brass bands, often with military connections, at municipal events or at bandstands in the park (a tradition that survives in Britain to this day); respectable concerts of music light or serious; and comic operas, ranging from the sentimental to the acutely satirical fare of Messrs Gilbert and Sullivan. While W. S. Gilbert skewered the pillars of the Victorian establishment (from MPs in *Iolanthe* to Oscar Wilde's aesthetes in *Patience*), Arthur Sullivan exposed the compositional genius that had enabled him to publish several enduring hymns and anthems before his thirtieth birthday – notably 'Onward Christian Soldiers' and 'It Came Upon a Midnight Clear'. Yet Sullivan was an early victim of the tug of war between popularity and refinement, commerce and art. His forte was sophisticated entertainment, but he was encouraged by his peers to pursue more serious forms of composition, less suited to his genius.

A rung below Gilbert and Sullivan's comic operas were operettas and musical comedies, few of which endured beyond their run in the theatre. One exception was an Austrian import, *The Merry Widow* (*Die lustige Witwe*), by Franz Lehár, which reached London in 1907, Paris two years later, and thereafter spanned the world. The London craze for Austrian works was halted only by the outbreak of the Great War in 1914, in which Herr Lehár's nation unfortunately took the opposing side.

Popular though *The Merry Widow*, *The Pirates of Penzance* and their ilk were, they were far from being the dominant form of musical performance at the end of the nineteenth century. The common people – those who lacked the means to frequent the same venues as dukes and debutantes – visited theatres and music halls for the multifaceted entertainment known as 'the varieties' in Britain (or 'music hall', after the venue for such delights) and 'vaudeville' in the United States.

What began as a potpourri of musical and theatrical elements, from low comedy to extracts from high opera or Shakespeare, was gradually standardised into a method of presentation that varied widely in quality and tone, but was comfortingly familiar to its audience. Offering variety by nature as well as name, music hall or vaudeville bills promised a constant shift of mood and style. At one moment the audience might be guffawing at ribald sexual innuendo; at the next, weeping at the ballad of a dying child; the next, marvelling at the daring and dexterity of knife-throwers or tumblers. Ruling this eclectic gathering was the chairman, rolling many-syllabled boasts and jibes around his rubicund cheeks as he hyperbolised the charms of one act or denigrated the failings of another.* His verbal

---

* For British readers of a certain age, the 'chairman' will inevitably bring to mind Leonard Sachs, the host of BBC television's *The Good Old Days*, which helped to solidify the enduring image of the classic London music hall. The show ran for thirty years, from 1953 to 1983, but as early as 1939, before he had reached his thirtieth birthday, Sachs was introducing a regular programme of old-time music hall at the Player's Theatre in London.

extravagance would provoke cheers – or boos, as appropriate – from an audience who expected to join in the entertainment, raising their voices in a popular chorus or entering into repartee with the comedians and singers. Certain venues, such as the Glasgow Empire, enjoyed a ferocious reputation amongst performers, although few could rival the virulence of a French audience in Marseilles, as the cabaret star Mistinguett recalled: 'A startled, demoralised teenage singer [was] faced with cries of "Higher! Higher, you bitch!", because her voice didn't reach the balcony. She gathered up her skirts till she showed everything she had, shouting, "Is that high enough for you bastards?", before flouncing off the stage in tears.'

The French music hall was an altogether harsher environment than its English equivalent. Likewise its *chansons*, which did not hesitate to confront life at its most bitter. Its compelling stars were *réalistes*, who played out their personal dramas in their songs – perhaps insulting their audiences, perhaps breaking down into tears, while depicting scenarios too vivid for the delicate tastes of London or New York.

What brought audiences to the British or American theatre was not a stark confrontation with reality but the promise of entertainment. The pull was the lustre of a star name: a performer as reliable as Marie Lloyd, Harry Lauder, Albert Chevalier or Harry Champion – or as exotic as the conjoined twins Rosa and Josefa Blažek, who played dulcimer and violin respectively. Much of their appeal lay in their familiarity: Miss Lloyd could be guaranteed to stretch the boundaries of good taste with her risqué humour, Mr Champion to chronicle the traumas of working-class life with such ditties as 'Have You Paid the Rent?' But for fail-safe reputations to endure, the performers also required a constant turnover of material: woe betide the comic who returned with the same parodies and sketches he had offered the year before. Hence the need for the admitted 'hack', the songwriter who could turn out several hundred almost identical comic songs or sentimental ballads every year, each hinged around an instantly accessible and (they hoped) uniquely unforgettable hook or chorus. The themes were perennial – errant husbands, nagging wives, lonely old mothers, faithful lovers – but the variations were endless. One London composer claimed to have penned no fewer than 17,000 music-hall songs, 'writing up to three a day and selling them for a shilling each'.

Once a song had 'settled' with the public, it was assured of a decent lifespan. 'A repertoire such as Florrie Forde would build up lasted her a full year or two,' recalled recording pioneer Herbert Ridout in 1940, 'adding new successes and dropping old ones as she went along. There were no dance bands, as we know them, to adopt them to dance rhythms. No radio to popularise them in a week and kill them in three months or so. No hero-worship of American composers, such as the wireless has brought in its manufactured "build-ups".' For touring performers, there were two key periods: Christmas, when pantomimes would feature the hit songs of the season; and summer, when stars were showcased in 'runs' at seaside resorts – a tradition that was still intact when the Beatles began touring Britain in 1963.

At the height of the music hall, in the late Victorian era, before safety considerations forced the closure of the more nefarious venues, there were nearly 400 theatres, halls and public houses offering variety bills in London alone, and at least one in every town across the country. Those numbers paled alongside the thousands of variety theatres in the United States before the First World War – many of them offering material only suitable for men of the world. The American equivalent of London's classiest music halls was vaude-ville, providing family entertainment with just enough innuendo to satisfy the racier members of the audience.

The vaudeville stage provided much of the early output of the recording industry: Steve Porter's or Dan Kelly's comic Irish monologues; the lugubrious songs of Edward M. Favor (such as 'His Trousers Would Bag at the Knee'); the boldly contemporary ditties of the baritone J. W. Myers ('Come Take a Trip in My Air-Ship') or the tenor Harry Tally ('Come, Josephine, in My Flying Machine'); Harry Lauder's countless re-recordings of his signature tunes, 'Stop Your Ticklin', Jock' and 'Roamin' in the Gloamin''; the more delicate ballads of Leslie Stuart ('The Lily of Laguna' and 'Tell Me, Pretty Maiden'); and hundreds more, some still preserved as national folklore, most squeezed dry of novelty within weeks of their birth.

As arguably the most successful composer of the era, Charles K. Harris published a brief guide to his craft, *How to Write a Popular Song* (1906). 'Only a few years ago a sheet-music counter in a department store was unheard of', he wrote. 'Today in the largest dry goods emporiums and department stores in New York, down to the smallest in every city in the United States, can be found a music counter where all of the popular songs of the day are on sale.' What qualified a song for that status? Its 'ultimate success or failure', Harris determined, rested in the refrain (or chorus), which was 'the kernel of the song'. Equally urgent was an arresting title:

'the shorter and more concise', the better. The mass audience demanded 'a song with a story – a story with a moral'. To that end, the aspiring composer must 'Avoid slang or double entendre. They may seem witty and clever, but they ruin the chances for the song to sell well. Refined people do not care to have songs containing such words or allusions seen in their homes, or used by members of the family.' There was one further restriction: no syllable should command more than one note:* on precise diction and rapid intelligibility did the appeal of a song depend. Harris's pamphlet also made the earliest known attempt to categorise the modern popular song, by themes that were, at turns, timeless or soon destined to seem outmoded:

A – The Home, or Mother Song
B – The Descriptive, or Sensational Story Ballad
C – The Popular Waltz Song (on a thousand and one subjects)
D – The Coon Song (Rough, Comic, Refined, Love or Serenade, etc.)
E – The March Song (Patriotic, War, Girl, Character, etc.)
F – The Comic Song (Topical, Character, Dialect, etc.)
G – The Production Song (for Interpolation in big Musical
    Productions, entailing the use of a Chorus of Men, or Girls, or
    both, and certain novel action, costume, or business)
H – The Popular Love Ballad
J – High Class Ballads
K – Sacred Songs

Harris's delineation of the market took no account of a seismic shift in public taste which had occurred between the writing of 'After the Ball' and the publication of his primer. It would pass into history as the moment when America created its first authentic genre of popular music, and sent it out to conquer the world. This was now, although Harris preferred not to see it, the era of ragtime.

---

* Harris may not have known that the first Book of Common Prayer, issued by the Church of England in 1549, laid down a very similar edict: 'for every syllable a note, so that it may be sung distinctly and devoutly'.

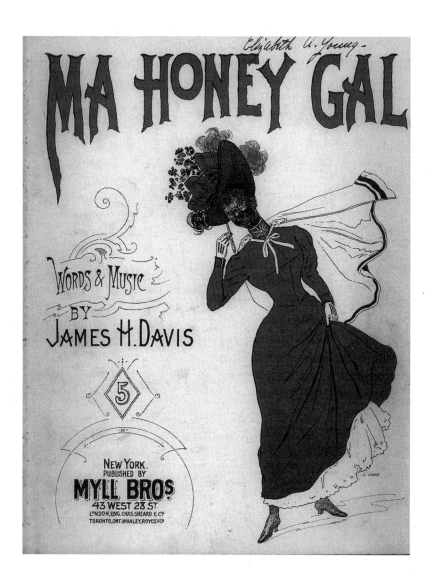

CHAPTER 2

EV'RYBODY'S DOIN' IT NOW

'With regard to ragtime, I do not think the Americanisation
of English music will have any permanent influence at all.
It is merely a passing phase.'

Orchestral conductor Thomas Beecham, 1912

'The ragtime rush is only at its beginning. Every week brings
a fresh consignment of weirdly-named songs that have simply
got to be sung.'

Daily Express, 1913

As an unscientific survey suggests, the word 'ragtime' tends to conjure up one of two pieces: 'Alexander's Ragtime Band', Irving Berlin's hit song of 1911; and Scott Joplin's piano instrumental, 'The Entertainer', written in 1902, and chosen as the main theme of *The Sting* (1973). Of these, the first epitomises the ragtime era, but has little of ragtime about it; the second is genuine ragtime, but not what the citizens of the early twentieth century imagined when they heard the word. Ragtime was an elusive concept, even during its prime. It was also the first genre of popular music to become a pejorative word – a warning of immorality or indecency at large.

Ragtime was both a narrowly prescriptive style of instrumental composition, written for the piano but popularised by the banjo or the brass band; and shorthand for a confluence of influences and impulses which amounted to nothing short of a revolution in American music. To most ears, it appeared shockingly new. It reeked of youthful exuberance, rather than Victorian sobriety; it came unashamedly from the African-American population, even though most of those who exploited ragtime were white (and many of the richest from European immigrant families); and, most startling of all, it was built around a rhythmic device known as syncopation, which recurred throughout the next century of black music and entered the pop mainstream around the world.

Syncopation is not intrinsically black, or American, or indeed popular: examples occur in the music of Bach and Beethoven, Mozart and Handel. It describes any rhythm which throws the accent on to the unexpected, which delays the beat, or suspends it, or falls between it. At its most basic, it transfers a 4/4 rhythm from the on-beat (*one*-two-*three*-four) to the off-beat (one-*two*-three-*four*). Simpler still, syncopation is what makes music swing. It became so natural a part of our lives over the twentieth century, transported from ragtime to jazz to R&B to soul to rock to hip hop and beyond, that only its absence was shocking.

The last champions of unsyncopated popular music were the Victorian ballad singers who survived into the Edwardian era and even beyond the Great War. They sang as soloists, or (if male) in quartets. They were men such as Harry McDonough, a stalwart of the Edison Male Quartet, the Haydn Quartet, the Lyric Quartet, and many more. His operatic training dampened any faint urge he may have felt to swing, or even sway; he specialised in duets with women that were utterly lacking in sensuality; and as late as 1916, when journalists were beginning to suggest that ragtime was being supplanted by jazz, he could still deliver an Irving Berlin tune like 'The Girl on the Magazine' with a stiffness that stifled any erotic intent. Likewise, there was no rhythmic twist in the work of Joe Belmont, the whistler known as 'The Human Bird'; in Henry Burr, arguably North America's most popular balladeer before Bing Crosby; or, heaven forbid, in the voluminous catalogue of the Athlone baritone John McCormack, trained operatically in Italy, a prominent balladeer in America from 1910, and still on hand to lend a steadying voice to Allied morale in the Second World War.

They were the old guard, whose rigid adherence to their station would hold little attraction for the new century. Their audience – like that of the phonograph, ownership of which connoted at least a degree of wealth – was adult, although their music could be enjoyed by the entire family. They never set out to divide that audience, to stake an identity by appealing to an elite; their goal was universal entertainment. What marked out their music was ethnicity: they carried the heritage of Europe in their bones. The participants in the ragtime era, whether they realised it or not (and often they cared not to), performed in a style that was easier, more relaxed. They swaggered rather than marched – and their music bore the irrepressible hallmarks of its origins in black America.

In the ragtime era, several forms of entertainment, pointed and benign, collided; one might even say they were coupled, for much of the panic aroused by the spirit of ragtime was its threat of sexuality and racial transgression, a culturally lethal marriage at the dawn of the twentieth century. Some sense of the tangled racial history of nineteenth-century American society is suggested by the minstrel tradition, which both celebrated African-American culture and simultaneously mocked it in the crudest imaginable way. From minstrels, black and white, came one of the formulae listed by Charles K. Harris: the 'coon song'. Combine the coon song with the syncopation of instrumental 'rags', and you have the ragtime song: the first generation of American pop, and (in both cultural and musical terms) the recognisable ancestor of the tradition running from Al Jolson to Bing Crosby to Elvis Presley – each a champion, in his way, of black American music; each accused of stealing it from its originators.

The nineteenth-century minstrel borrowed the African-American tradition of the singing, comic, cavorting stage performer, who might exaggerate his supposed racial characteristics to please his white 'superiors', and turned it into – well, *what* exactly? Cultural derision, certainly; entertainment, without doubt; affectionate tribute, on occasion. The minstrel show was an event so ambiguous that it required black men to caricature their own culture and accentuate the colour of their skin by adopting 'blackface'. This ensured they would not startle audiences acclimatised to white performers who had adopted the burnt-cork make-up, exaggeratedly painted mouths and curly black wigs which transformed them, to their satisfaction, into authentic 'nigger minstrels'.

The most famous of the white man's minstrel characters was 'Jim Crow', created by Thomas Dartmouth Rice around 1830, and brought to London six years later. But the impulse for white men to paint themselves black can be traced back to the early seventeenth century, when Ben Jonson wrote a masque which would enable England's queen, Anne of Denmark, to don the face paint; while Shakespeare's *Othello* effectively required its leading man to follow suit. In the 1840s, the Virginia Minstrels quartet – white men, on fiddle, banjo, tambourine and 'bones' – set the shape for the white minstrel show, 'with a fast-moving program of songs, jokes, dances and instrumental specialties'. After the American Civil War of the 1860s, this theatrical genre expanded to encompass African-American performers. Racism was so intrinsic to the society from which the so-called 'nigger minstrels' (black or white) came that it was scarcely noticed by those who perpetrated it; and regarded as inevitable by those who endured it.

Among the contortions, moral and physical, required of black performers was a high-stepping dance that became known as the 'cakewalk'. It took its title from the tradition – roots unknown – whereby white spectators would offer the prize of a cake for the most dramatic and energetic display of black dancing. By 1877, this idea was sufficiently entrenched for it to form the basis of a minstrel routine, 'Walking for Dat Cake'. Fifteen years later, the *New York Times* reported on a contest with the 'suspicion that the intention was not to hold out the cake walkers as models for the reverent imitation of the spectators, but to expose them to the derision of an unsympathetic concourse of whites. This is all very wrong.' But the cakewalk did offer some pioneering black performers a vehicle with which to command white attention. The music that accompanied it introduced the art of syncopation to an audience for whom this irregular sense of rhythm was both exotic and strangely compulsive.

> The future music of this country must be founded upon what are called the Negro melodies. This must be the real foundation of any serious and original school of composition to be developed in the United States . . . They are pathetic, tender, passionate, melancholy, solemn, religious, bold, merry, gay, or what you will. It is music that suits itself to any mood or purpose.
> Antonín Dvořák, 1893

> What with 'coon songs', banjo picking and 'cake walks', the white people are picking up what the better class of colored people are trying to get away from. Are the white people degenerating in these tastes?
> *Baltimore Afro-American* newspaper, 1898

Beyond the minstrel shows of the late nineteenth century, African-Americans performed spirituals (the primary cause of Dvořák's admiration), traditional melodies, popular songs, comic monologues; and, on banjo or perhaps piano, syncopated dance tunes which came to be known as 'rags'. When first documented, a 'rag' was often a gathering (usually unruly) rather than a piece of music: a Kansas newspaper in 1891 complained that the weekly 'rags' in a town hall 'are a nuisance and should be abated'. There was an immediate association between 'rags', violence and drunkenness. The *Leavenworth Herald* remarked in 1894 that 'Kansas City girls can't play anything on pianos except "rags", and the worst kind of "rags" at that.' (A dictionary from 1902 defined a 'rag-time girl' as 'a sweetheart or harlot'.) But the same newspaper also referred kindly to 'a country "rag" dance', with its callers, routines and rhythmic clapping of hands, as if it were no more threatening than a quadrille in the days of Jane Austen. The black pianist Blind Boone, renowned as one of the fathers of ragtime, performed piano recitals (occasionally accompanied by a vocalist) through the early 1890s in the politest of society, with a repertoire ranging from light classics (Strauss and Liszt) to improvised 'rags' around tunes which were either traditional or else penned in a comparable style, such as Stephen Foster's 'Old Folks at Home'. (One excited journalist of 1893 described Boone's playing as having been 'clear out of sight'.)

In the hands of Tin Pan Alley, these rags became a commercial property, marketed as an invitation to perform the cakewalk – hence the title of an 1892 instrumental for banjo and piano, 'Kullud Koons' Kake Walk'. It was an era when, as ragtime historians have noted, 'the popular music market was bombarded by a succession of Ethiopian oddities, darky songs, coon songs and plantation songs', and when a professional song-writer, such as the effortlessly adaptable Kerry Mills, could make a lucrative career out of such novelty tunes as 'Rastus on Parade' and 'At a Georgia Camp Meeting'. A former slave, George Washington Johnson, billed himself as 'The original whistling coon and laughing darkey', inaugurating a long tradition of 'laughing' records with his 1891 recording of 'The Laughing Song'. (Charles Penrose's 'The Laughing Policeman' is probably the most enduring of these novelties.) His performance – which he is believed to have repeated some 40,000 times, so that a fresh cylinder could be made from each rendition – was viciously self-mocking, with its casual references to a 'huckleberry nig' and a 'big baboon'.

In the sorry history of racial indignity in popular music, few songs have matched the notoriety of an 1895 composition by Ernest Hogan – a pseudonym hiding the identity of the black entertainer Reuben Crowders. He picked up a chorus from a Chicago saloon, entitled 'All Pimps Look Alike to Me', fleshed it out, and rendered it suitable for decent company as 'All Coons Look Alike to Me'. Soon, as the historian David Suisman noted, 'Whites taunted blacks by whistling the first few notes of the chorus, turning the sounds themselves into a weapon of racial intimidation.' Reuben Crowders was said to have been tormented by his role in the affair, though that did not prevent him from penning an equally cartoonish portrait of his race, 'My Coal Black Lady', the following year. Such songs were purveyed to the masses via music sheets which bore grotesque carica-tures of African-Americans, their features apelike, their expressions untameable.

What's ironic is that these notorious 'coon songs' combined their utterly degrading 'comic' lyrics with music that owed its rhythmic appeal to the adventurous African-American style of the day. Whether these mass-produced novelty tunes were billed as a cakewalk or a coon song, 'Ethiopian' or 'nigger', their accompaniment was invariably syncopated in a style that was described as 'rag' or 'ragtime'. So closely were these two elements linked that the pale-skinned African-American songwriter Ben Harney was able to publish a *Ragtime Instructor* in 1896, in which he claimed to have been 'the Originator of Ragtime', though he was merely one of its best-rewarded exploiters.

As early as 1898, the American magazine *The Etude* had determined that ragtime 'is a term applied to the peculiar, broken, rhythmic features of the popular "coon song". It has a powerfully stimulating effect, setting the nerves and muscles tingling with excitement. Its esthetic effect is the same as that in the monotonous, recurring rhythmic chant of barbarous races. Unfortunately, the words to which it is allied are usually decidedly vulgar, so that its present great favor is somewhat to be deplored.' The style having been identified, its moniker was reliably stated to have come from the ragged state of the clothes worn by its earliest black practitioners; or their ragged, self-taught playing, in which – simple creatures as they were assumed to be – each musician would make the same mistakes; or, more technically, the unpredictably ragged nature of the syncopation around which these melodies were built.

The white audience for coon songs and cakewalk novelties was satisfied by these explanations, and relished the intoxicating effect of the rhythms. To serious black composers, meanwhile, the equation of ragtime and coon songs was 'a libellous insult', said the *Negro Music Journal*. 'The typical Negro would blush to own acquaintance with the vicious trash put forth under Ethiopian titles.' They maintained that the title of 'ragtime' should be reserved for a class of composition that has since been dubbed 'classic ragtime'. It was, inevitably, infiltrated by white imitators, and handled by white publishers. But at its finest, this 'ragtime' tradition was intended to provide not just popular entertainment, but an aesthetic experience comparable to the pinnacles of 'serious' European composition.

> The authors and publishers . . . have succeeded in illustrating for the first time the absolute theory of the now famous 'RAG-TIME' music, which originated with the Negroes and is characteristic of their people. The Negroe in playing the piano, strikes the keys with the same time and measure that he taps the floor with his heels and toes in dancing, thereby obtaining a peculiarly accented time effect which he terms 'RAG-TIME'.
> Introduction to the sheet music of 'Syncopated Sandy', 1897

'Description of Louisiana Niggers Dancing' was the explanation given to those few who, in 1897, purchased the first instrumental rag to be published as a music sheet: Theodore Northrup's 'Louisiana Rag'. More than 300 similar compositions followed over the next twenty-five years, with titles that were alluring ('The Fascinator', 'The Peach'), comic ('Car-Balick-Acid Rag-Time', 'Who Let the Cows Out'), racially demeaning ('Pickaninny Capers', 'Jungle Time') and suggestive ('A Tennessee Tantalizer' and 'St Louis Tickle', for whistling which young men might be slapped in the face or even jailed in the state of Missouri, so carnal were the words that had become attached to it).

To untrained ears, these rags, regardless of their associations, can sound like a random collection of piano themes. But the 'classic ragtime' composition was carefully structured. It contained four (or occasionally three) discrete musical sections, each of sixteen bars' duration. These sixteen bars could be divided again: the first eight bars introducing a theme, but leaving it hanging; the second returning to it, with variations that would 'resolve' the theme (musically and emotionally). In addition, rags would often begin with a four-bar introduction, and similar passages (the 'vamp') might allow the cunning composer to move from one melodic section to the next.

By comparison with, for example, symphonic form, the rag was a simplistic medium. Alongside the popular songs with which the public was most familiar, however, rags appeared much more artful, in every sense of the word: they were crafted, and contrived. 'After the Ball', the song sensation of 1891, had followed each individual verse (we'll call it the 'A' section) with a repeated refrain ('B'). Its structure could therefore be broken down like this: A1; B; A2; B; A3; B. So predictable was this format that the listener would scarcely notice it – any more than the pop fan of the 1960s would be surprised to hear a song that followed the then-standard structure of two verses, a chorus, a 'middle eight', another chorus, a final verse and then a chorus to provide a rousing climax.

Charles K. Harris had insisted that it was the refrain that sold the song, differentiating the 'hit' from the rabble. 'Coon songs', regardless of their supposed links to ragtime, adhered to his rules, with an instantly identifiable chorus. 'Classic ragtime' compositions, however, eschewed such reliance on a single hook. Take the example of Scott Joplin's 'The Entertainer', which follows this structure: Introduction; A; A; B; B; A; A; C; C; vamp; D; D. Midway through the composition, the listener could be forgiven for imagining that the 'A' section was the refrain, or hook; but after its fourth appearance, which is where an orthodox popular song might have finished, the 'A' is jettisoned, and two entirely different themes are introduced, connected almost imperceptibly by a four-bar vamp.

Ragtime was clearly no refuge for those who lacked a gift for melody. Each composition contained sufficient ideas to propel several popular songs, and the composer frequently scored minute variations on his themes as the piece progressed, to deepen the subtlety. In addition, ragtime musicians would often improvise their own revisions to a published score, to the disgust of composers who believed that their work should be handled with the same reverence that would be paid to a Bach concerto. Rags were written *on* the piano, and *for* the piano. The more 'serious' the composer and his ambitions, the more carefully he intended his work to be performed. John Stark, the publisher of Scott Joplin's work, stated baldly that the rags he handled 'cannot be interpreted at sight. They must be studied and practised slowly, and never played fast at any time.' This instruction would often be ignored by subsequent generations.

Perhaps the most famous rag of the age was Joplin's 'Maple Leaf Rag' (1899), for which John Stark awarded Scott Joplin the rare honour of a 1c royalty on each music sheet. A decade later Stark was able to boast that half a million copies had been purchased. Based in Sedalia, Mississippi, Stark amassed a cabal of talented composers around him. He was not only a perceptive and (for the time) non-exploitative businessman, but also arguably the first great entrepreneur of the popular music age – the precursor of Andrew Loog Oldham, Malcolm McLaren and all those non-composing geniuses who turned hyperbole into an art form. Like McLaren, he was a visionary who shaped his clients to his vision; like Oldham, he was a natural ad man, ready to pen purple poems or playlets in his advertising copy. One goal was beyond even Stark's grasp: translating ragtime piano into a commercially viable form of recorded sound. The problem was not economic or artistic, but technical. So primitive were the recording techniques of the period that many musical sounds, including the female voice, the large instrumental ensemble, and the piano, could not be reproduced on disc with any hope of fidelity. Familiar though 'Maple Leaf Rag' was in the early decades of the twentieth century, it was not recorded in its primal form, as a piano piece, until 1923.

This was a serendipitous moment for the purveyors of a musical instrument that might have been designed for ragtime (and vice versa): the player piano. Often known as the 'Pianola' in the same way that a vacuum cleaner is called a 'Hoover', the instrument resembled an orthodox piano, but issued music automatically as a roll of paper (or occasionally metal) was passed through it, having been pre-punched with the appropriate pattern to produce a tune. Manufacturers pandered to their customers' vanity by accentuating the skill that was required to control the tempo of the 'performance' – 'Pianola playing is *real* playing', one boasted – and many models allowed the 'pianist' to vary the volume, sustain notes, and masquerade as a musical artist. What is irrefutable is that a piano roll could bring the sound of a professional musician to everyman's parlour, for close study of the work or pure listening pleasure. Thousands of different tunes were translated into piano rolls before the machine lost its commercial standing after the Great Depression of 1929: everything from the most complex classical sonatas to the most banal and ephemeral of Tin Pan Alley songs. In the case of ragtime, many rolls were 'played' by the composer himself, on to a keyboard that cut the holes in the master roll. Trained assistants were required to correct any errors that might have arisen, or to add flourishes and grace notes beyond the capability of human hands.

The incompatibility of piano and phonograph did not preclude the recording of rag tunes in the 1890s and 1900s. Banjo player Vess Ossman not only accompanied vaudeville star Len Spencer on such choice offerings as 'A Hot Time in the Old Town', but was spotlighted, with light orchestral support, on a series of ragtime tunes – including a gallop through Joplin's 'Maple Leaf Rag', which must have exasperated its composer with its stubborn refusal to follow the correct tempo.

If the fluency of Ossman's banjo-picking could be equated to the manual dexterity of the expert piano player, the other prime outlet for rags depended on an entirely different skill: that of the arranger. By 1900, America was home to an estimated 10,000 brass bands. Their repertoire was dominated by marches, but it could span the musical spectrum from high art to novelty tunes; and their audience quickly grew to relish the rhythmic excitement and sonic propulsion of ragtime in brass. The dominant bandleader of the era was John Philip Sousa. He composed more than a hundred marches, among them 'Stars and Stripes Forever' and 'The Liberty Bell' (latterly the theme to *Monty Python's Flying Circus*). As the conductor of the United States Marine Band until 1892, he was responsible for the most popular recording to come from the industry's baptismal months: 'Semper Fidelis' (1890).

When he assembled his own band two years later, Sousa struggled with the symbols of modernity. He despised what he called 'canned music', and allowed his trombonist and arranger, Arthur Pryor, to conduct the Sousa band in his stead when they were called upon to record. Pryor also introduced Sousa's ensemble to syncopation, and it was his arrangements of cakewalk and ragtime tunes that became the highlights of the band's public appearances. So much in demand were these contemporary offerings that Sousa learned to hold them back until after the intermission, to ensure that his audience would not depart before the more 'serious' items in his repertoire – operatic themes and classical overtures – could be aired.

Sousa was not alone in his reticence to enter fully into the commercial spirit of the age. Like Sir Arthur Sullivan in London, Scott Joplin – widely regarded as the most elegant composer of the piano rag, although his own pianistic skills were mediocre – was not content to master a popular idiom. In his sights was a higher summit: nothing less than the first ragtime opera. He had learned his trade in bordellos, and married a brothel-keeper; in his youth, he contracted the syphilis that would eventually rob him of the ability to play the piano, and even to speak, before claiming his life at the age of 49. An introvert adrift in a wild man's milieu, he escaped the rowdy clubs of Sedalia in his 30s. In New York, his writing gathered sophistication, but lost its connection with common taste. His compositions became cloaked in significance, like the 'Wall Street Rag' in which he portrayed the power of music to dispel the worries of stockbrokers. Other, less talented men now commanded the marketplace.

Joplin's initial attempt at an opera was staged briefly, then forgotten, and finally lost when he had to skip out on his landlord, who was demanding backdated rent. In New York, he assembled the score for what he intended as his masterpiece: *Treemonisha*. But nobody would bankroll either its publication or its performance; and his efforts to achieve these aims ended in debilitating failure. A year after the ragged bones of *Treemonisha* received their first inadequate airing, he was consigned to an asylum as his illness took hold. After his death, his wife tantalised potential bidders with tales of suitcases stuffed with unpublished manuscripts, but when she too had gone, thirty-three years after Joplin, all the papers had vanished. Scott Joplin suffered the bittersweet agony of being adored for something he could do almost without effort, and scorned for daring to extend himself. Many others to come – Stan Kenton and Artie Shaw, Joni Mitchell and Elvis Costello – would likewise find themselves stretched between the demands of their audience and the irresistible tug of their creativity.

There were more comfortable ways for a black man to move through the golden years of ragtime. Selling themselves as 'The REAL Coons', dancer George Walker and singer Bert Williams were able to infiltrate the upper echelons of the vaudeville circuit. They came to personify the cakewalk for white New Yorkers, and charmed them with Williams's original ragtime songs. They even carried the cakewalk to Britain, where the novelty value of their appearance was reinforced by their grandiose billing as 'the Tobasco Senegambians'. Their willingness to caricature themselves tarnished their reputation among their own race, while Walker gradually exhausted himself in his efforts to secure more humane conditions and fairer wages for African-American performers. Williams soldiered on alone, writing and recording comic songs and ballads, the most enduring of which was 'Nobody' (1906). In his lugubrious voice and lazy, self-assured phrasing, it's possible to hear the premature echoes of later black artists who would employ street smarts, humour and savage intelligence to enchant a potentially hostile white audience – Chuck Berry, to name the most obvious example. There is a clear line of descent from Bert Williams's sly drawl on 'He's a Cousin of Mine' (1907) to the equally knowing but browbeaten narrators of the Coasters' vignettes of African-American urban life in the 1950s. Sadly, this pre-modernist died of pneumonia in 1922 at the age of 47, three years short of the technological innovations that would have enabled future generations to appreciate his talent.

These silly dances are physically bad as well as morally bad. The turkey trot, the bunny hug, the tango and all other dances of the ragtime species are the cause of poor figures, while they also cause deformities. The positions of the hips throw them into all sorts of attitudes, and thereby encourage superfluous flesh, as well as displacing the internal organs. They throw the whole body out of poise. The moral is: if you wish to have a good figure, don't tango, and refrain from ragtime dances. Ragtime and tango dances would demoralise the figure of a Greek goddess, and transform her to the shape of a sack of potatoes.

American doctor Maude Dunn on 'Englishwomen', 1914

To imitate a grizzly bear or a turkey cock – that is comic, grotesque
if you like, but beautiful? – never! They are not dances for any
young girl to dance. They are, to put it frankly, provocative dances.
They are the outcome of the present-day need for excitement, like
telephone, car, photography, cinemas. We are becoming incapable
of subtle sensations. We need excitement.
    Russian ballerina Anna Pavlova, 1913

So accustomed were white audiences of the music hall and vaudeville to
minstrel routines and blackface comics that they rarely expressed qualms
about the appearance on stage of Bert Williams, any more than they
objected to a white man billing himself 'The Famous Chocolate-Coloured
Coon', as did G. H. Elliott. Complaints on racial grounds would only
surface when black performers no longer agreed to caricature their race.
What aroused the public's interest, disquiet and sometimes outrage on the
eve of the First World War was the spectacle of a young generation
flinging itself around the dance floor to the syncopated pulse of ragtime.
Despite frequent suggestions from the press that youth's enthusiasm for
ragtime was about to fade, and that the waltz would soon be reinstated as
the natural rhythm of the dance-floor, music publishers poured out novelty
tunes designed to accompany a bewildering variety of new steps. Within
short succession in 1912 and 1913, the formality of the ballroom
succumbed to such dangerously exotic exhibitions as the bunny hug, the
grizzly bear, the turkey trot, the dog bite, the hitchy-koo, the London
lurch, the fish walk and the style that would outlast and eventually encompass them all: the foxtrot. Some emerged from backstreet bars in Chicago
or Harlem; others were the invention of songwriters or publishers in New
York or London.

   No longer did young men and women flit from one partner to the
next to avoid the slightest hint of immorality. Now they were encouraged
to pair up for the evening, and even press their bodies tight in a manner
that would previously have been reserved for married couples, and then
only in the privacy of their homes. The Manhattan editor of the *Ladies'
Home Journal* was so appalled to discover that his female typists were
devoting their lunch hours to ragtime dancing that he fired fifteen offenders
on the spot.

   None of the so-called 'ragtime' dances was as controversial as the
tango. It had arrived in France around 1900, infiltrating both Paris high

society and the brothels of Marseilles. Even a nation that had withstood and accommodated the fleshy revelations of the can-can chose to be appalled by this carnal innovation. 'The tango is a pseudo-dance that should be censored!', one critic railed. 'It is truly impossible to describe with precision what one is seeing in Paris. However it could be said that the tango resembles a double belly-dance, where lasciviousness is accented through exaggerated contortions. One believes oneself to be watching a Mahometan couple under the effects of opium.' So potent was its name that 'tango' was soon used to describe every dance of exotic origin.

In Germany, the Kaiser warned his military to shun families who indulged in the dance. The British royal family let it be known that Queen Mary did not approve, and a magazine with the comforting title of *The Gentlewoman* described it as 'The Dance of Moral Death'. The Archbishop of Paris wrote a newspaper column denouncing the tango's moral failings. A middle-aged man in Philadelphia was arrested after severely beating his 35-year-old son. 'If I catch him cutting up any more with the tango,' he said defiantly, 'I'll repeat the dose.' There was no awareness of the dance's origins in the brothels and cafes of Argentina and Uruguay, or its status there as a dramatic exploration of male sensuality and female subversion. By the time it reached Britain, it was merely another demonstration of what Lady Helmsley called 'nigger-dance characteristics'.

Fortunately, British society found a way to accommodate and smooth out the lascivious traits of the tango. A woman named Gladys Beattie Crozier wrote a book of etiquette entitled *The Tango, and How to Do It*. The Queen's Theatre in London launched 'tango teas', at which patrons watched calmly from their tables as an exhibition of dancing was followed by a fashion parade. Other prestigious restaurants highlighted an equally enticing Brazilian dance, the maxixe, performed to music that shared the four-part structure of ragtime.

Married couple Vernon and Irene Castle had been hired to demonstrate the latest dances at the Café de Paris in the French capital. After moving to the sister restaurant in New York, they opened a dancing school, and then a chain of salons across America. The Victor label inaugurated a series of dance records under the Castles' name, with black bandleader James Reese Europe providing suitable music for the turkey trot and the rest.

Western civilisation, it seemed, had gone 'dance crazy'. The hottest theatre ticket in London – where it was possible at Christmas 1912 to buy a wind-up 'nigger ragtime doll' – was for a revue entitled *Hullo Ragtime*, originally intended for the pantomime season, but so popular that its run was extended for two years. (One of the stars of its all-white cast was named Bob Dillon.) Every few months a 'new edition' of the show would be announced, replacing the songs that had become stale. Eventually the revue closed, but only to be replaced by the remarkably similar *Hullo Tango*. There were now syncopated songs on every imaginable subject, including 'Ragtime Suffragette' and 'Let's Have Free Trade Amongst the Girls' to mirror pressing political controversies. The playwright George Bernard Shaw, always eager to reflect society's whims, had his two leading characters in the 1913 play *Androcles and the Lion* dancing to ragtime. The following year, he staged *The Music-Cure*, a satire on the country's preoccupation with this American import.

The likely consequences of this ceaseless 'ragging' were hotly debated. Ragtime was blamed for the arrest of a young man who was found drunk and disorderly in North London, clinging to a lamp post while he bellowed a current hit. It was reported that bands in top restaurants would break into ragtime when the establishments were preparing to close, to encourage the diners to eat more quickly. That the hypnotic, unsettlingly irregular rhythms of ragtime would affect the psyche, there seemed no doubt. The actor Gerald du Maurier declared that all the ragtime movements were 'only forms of the oldest dance in the world, St Vitus' Dance'. There was talk of dancers being 'inoculated with the ragtime-fever'; of a 'virulent poison', a 'malarious epidemic'; of ragtime being 'syncopation gone mad', which 'can only be treated successfully like the dog with rabies, namely, with a dose of lead'. These various accusations were neatly summed up by one critic: 'when taken to excess, it overstimulates; it irritates'. Thinly veiled beneath these dismissive verdicts was a fear that the impulse most vulnerable to this overstimulation would be immorality. The twitching rhythms, convulsive dance steps and physical contact occasioned by dancing to ragtime would be sure to lead to licentiousness; to freedom; to, as one American commentator thundered, 'falling prey to the collective soul of the negro'.

There were those, however, who welcomed the jolt of ragtime as a long-overdue awakening from cultural stasis, an adrenaline surge that could be guaranteed to set 'the nerves and muscles tingling with excitement'. Ragtime historian Edward Berlin uncovered one account of exposure to the music, which shares the evangelical fervour of those who first experimented with psychedelic chemicals: 'Suddenly I discovered that my legs were in a condition of great excitement. They twitched as though charged with electricity and betrayed a considerable and rather dangerous desire to jerk me from my seat. The rhythm of the music, which had seemed so unnatural at first, was beginning to exert its influence over me. It wasn't that feeling of ease in the joints of the feet and toes which might be caused by a Strauss waltz, no, much more energetic, material, independent, as though one encountered a balking horse, which it is absolutely impossible to master.' Independence that was impossible to master: it was exactly this quality of syncopated youthful rebellion that struck fear into adult hearts.

> Along Atlantic Coast resorts and in summer parts, etc., it is the song everybody is singing and whistling.
> *Edison Phonograph Monthly*, 1911

> As they would say in the States, 'Alexander's Ragtime Band' is *it*. We have ragtime hits every season now, but this catchy number would seem to be by far the biggest thing of its kind ever introduced over here.
> *Phono Trader & Recorder*, 1912

Catchier even than 'All Alone' ('the great telephone song'); or that 'Hebrew' ragtime novelty, 'Yiddle on Your Fiddle', 'Alexander's Ragtime Band' swept rapidly across the English-speaking world in 1911–12. It was introduced in vaudeville by Emma Carus, then taken up by the leading recording artists of the day – Billy Murray, sounding decidedly aged at 34; Arthur Collins and Byron Harlan, affecting to be a male and female duet team; and Billy Fay, who attracted a review so laden with racial stereotyping that it bears repeating in full: 'One of the Children of Ham, as light-hearted as he is dark-visaged, endearingly apostrophises his ebony inamorata as "Ma Honey" many times repeated, from which one may gather that our "cullud brudder" must be very much in love with his sooty Dinah or Chloe, as the case may be. Very cleverly sung by Mr Fay, who hits off the negro idiom of vernacular as if to the manner born.'

The song originated not from a 'cullud brudder' but from a young man of Jewish descent who was named Israel Baline by his parents in Russia, though his identity was anglicised as Irving Berlin. We met him earlier as a singing waiter working for 'Nigger Mike' Saulter (another Russian Jew, awarded his affectionate nickname because of his dark complexion). Berlin oozed melody and invention, though he wrote his songs solely on what he called the 'nigger keys' of the keyboard. When he became successful, he purchased a transposing piano, which allowed him to change key with a flick of a switch, rather than learn to utilise the 'white' notes as well. For more than four decades, he consistently turned out hit songs. Many of them are still instantly recognisable today, 130 years after his birth: 'White Christmas', 'God Bless America', 'Let's Face the Music and Dance', 'Puttin' on the Ritz' and 'Anything You Can Do, I Can Do Better'. Born before the launch of the gramophone as a commercial enterprise, he lived long enough to hear Madonna and hip hop, although as early as 1962, when he was a mere 74 years old, he already knew that his time as a commercially viable songwriter had passed: 'You don't have to stop yourself. The people who have to listen to your songs tell you to stop.'

More than half a century earlier, his irrepressibly bubbly, almost unfailingly optimistic songs extolled the joy of music-making. He first caught the public's imagination with 'My Wife's Gone to the Country' – 'Hooray! Hooray!', ran the chorus – before revising a familiar strain from the classical repertory as 'That Mesmerizing Mendelssohn Tune'. But it was 'Alexander's Ragtime Band' that reached even the people who had managed, in those days before mass communications, to ignore the previous fifteen years of the ragtime craze. Berlin was an astute critic of his own work: 'The lyric, silly though it was, was fundamentally right. Its opening words, emphasised by immediate repetition – "Come on and hear! Come on and hear!" – were an invitation to "come", to join in and "hear" the singer and his song. And that idea of inviting every receptive auditor within shouting distance became a part of the happy ruction – an idea pounded in again and again throughout the song in various ways – [and] was the secret of the song's tremendous success.'

Within a few months, he had fashioned an equally exhilarating sequel, 'Everybody's Doin' It Now', the precise nature of 'it' left to the listener's imagination. Besides all else, 'it' definitely involved dancing, which is how Berlin became associated with the Castles, cementing his reputation as the king of the dance tune. Like Scott Joplin before him, he lost his first wife within a few months of their marriage in 1912. From his grief came a ballad devoid of syncopation, 'When I Lost You', which sold more than a million copies as a music sheet. A decade later, Berlin penned two songs that drew on his grief, 'What'll I Do?' and (another) 'All Alone' – thereby inaugurating a strand of lonely-in-my-room songs which would spark the 1960s and 70s cliché of the 'bedsitter balladeer'. The only ambition that defeated him was one he shared with Joplin: his determination, expressed in a 1913 interview which credited him with writing 'Five Tunes a Day', to create 'a grand opera in ragtime . . . a real opera on a tragic theme'.

The performer who best expressed the joy of Berlin's songs was slightly older than him; Jewish, though Lithuanian rather than Russian; anglicised for public consumption, too, from Asa Yoelsen to Al Jolson. His reputation has been scarred by the blackface make-up he first adopted in his late teens, although he always claimed – stretching the truth a little – that 'a Negro dresser' had told him he'd get more laughs that way. Spike Lee's barbed show-business movie satire *Bamboozled* (2000) drove the final stake through the heart of this dubious ritual, but to dismiss Jolson, a genius of entertainment, because he followed a thoroughly orthodox tradition is imposing modern values on a century-old milieu.

Jolson's innovations were lasting. He was the first popular singer to realise that his audience demanded a *show*, which shone from start to finish. He was the first to build a company, and carry it from town to town, showgirls, lighting, orchestra and all. He sang around the beat, carrying it forward, holding it back, acting out every song as if it was gushing from his heart. As with the compulsive improvisers of the rock era, such as Bob Dylan and the Grateful Dead, 'there was the anticipation of discovering how he was going to sing his songs', his biographer Michael Freedland recounted. 'Even when he repeated songs in subsequent performances, he changed the way he delivered them. The Winter Garden regulars played games with each other – spotting the changed lyric, the different treatment of a chorus, the substituted phrase.'*

So ebullient was Jolson, so charged with energy, that when he was first asked to record, in 1912, he skipped around in front of the Victor recording horn as if he were still under Broadway lights. 'In the end,' Freedland wrote, 'they placed a coat around him, buttoning it at the back like a straitjacket, sat him on the chair and told him to sing without

---

* On consecutive nights in 2005, I watched Bob Dylan, his voice reduced to a husk of its former range and power, deliver three renditions of 'Positively 4th Street' so different in tone and emotional impact that it was difficult to believe they were the same song. I like to imagine Jolson smiling in recognition, though perhaps not in blackface.

moving.' The result was 'That Haunting Melody', delivered with a pizzazz and satirical edge that must have been startling to his peers – and which anticipated the barnstorming performances to come.

The joint efforts of Jolson and Berlin seem to have loosened the spine of the American recording industry (then, as now, dominating the release schedules in Britain as well). Exuberance was the spirit of 1912–13: 'Everybody Two-Step', 'Ring-Ting-a-Ling', 'The Gaby Glide' (yet another dance), 'Ragtime Cowboy Joe', 'Ragtime Jocky Man', 'In Ragtime Land' – the permutations were endless. Collins and Harlan teased out the potential for sexual innuendo in 'Row! Row! Row!', a comic tale on the theme of infidelity; Jolson decried 'The Spaniard That Blighted My Life'; Elsie Janis, a 22-year-old vaudeville star, pleaded 'Fo' De Lawd's Sake, Play a Waltz', because hearing another rag would send her doolally.

So vibrant was the industry of ragtime, so enlivened the nerves of its aficionados, that a copywriter for His Master's Voice advertised the company's latest wares with what sounded like a plea for the madness to end: 'So nothing is to be sacred to Ragtime's composers, and one awaits only the transformation of an entire Handel oratorio into Ragtime to provide the limit of its shamelessness. Yet it has a great fascination, this syncopated music – its restlessness and lilt have a charm all their own, and there is little doubt that the vogue will be lasting – but one can't help wondering, where will it stop?'

In Europe, it stopped with war. Not that the rag culture could be dulled entirely. It took only a month for a British sailor to boast that 'We had our first battle yesterday . . . we saw them off in ragtime.' But ten weeks into a global conflict which was destined to stretch for four apocalyptic years, a *Daily Mirror* headline stated: 'Homely Songs Stir Nation's Heart. Old-Time Ballads Replace Ragtime and Jingo Songs'. There was little appetite, it seemed, for compositions that ridiculed the Germans or trumpeted British supremacy, such as 'We're Going to Hang the Kaiser under the Linden Tree'. It was nostalgia, family and the comforting memory of hearth and garden and rolling hills that won the hearts of those on the way to the slaughter fields of France, and those left behind: 'Home Sweet Home', rather than the latest sensations from America, such as 'Ballin' the Jack' and 'The Memphis Blues'.

A reporter for the *Daily Mail* described hearing troops in France singing 'It's a Long Way to Tipperary', a pre-war music-hall song, and his account ensured that others followed suit, to the delight of the song's publisher. Other songs won their familiarity more organically, through their ability to tap into the collective mood. 'Pack Up Your Troubles', written for a London revue, failed to spark but then won an American competition to find a wartime marching song. (Its co-creator, Felix Powell, committed suicide whilst wearing his Home Guard uniform in the Second World War.) 'Alexander's Ragtime Band' was rewritten by soldiers as 'Lord Kitchener's Army', one of dozens of familiar music-hall and even hymn tunes that were adapted to serve the sometimes profane needs of the fighting men. As the horror of trench warfare intensified, those in the front line took comfort from the dark humour of 'Hanging on the Old Barbed Wire', or from revising a familiar song: 'If you were the only Boche in the trench, and I had the only bomb'.

Ivor Novello and Lena Guilbert Ford's 'Keep the Home Fires Burning' was a favourite on the home front. It was carried to the troops by concert parties dispatched to heighten morale. Also sent to France, often by the Red Cross, were hundreds of portable gramophones, so that the soldiers – when they weren't enduring savage bombardment or burying the mutilated remains of their comrades – could delude themselves that they were sharing the same culture as their loved ones across the Channel. 'Every YMCA hut, every canteen and every hospital at the front has its gramophone', a major manufacturer boasted in 1917. 'Any padre will tell you that it is one of the greatest influences for good that can be found. In the officers' mess of a regiment that has won many laurels, there is a standing rule that any officer going on leave must bring back with him at least a dozen records of the songs from the current hit "shows".'

There were sufficient Americans of European descent to ensure that the United States took a close interest in the Great War, even before it became enmeshed in the carnage. The American Quartet offered the most popular version of 'Tipperary', which its US publisher promoted as 'The song They sing as They march along' even before that was true. Billy Murray's tongue-twister 'Sister Susie's Sewing Shirts for Soldiers' was presumably intended to be sympathetic. But the internal political battle over whether America should be pulled into the war was also reflected in its songs. The Peerless Quartet's 'I Didn't Raise My Boy to Be a Soldier' aimed for the heart, with its tale of a mother crying for mediation rather than military action. 'Don't Take My Darling Boy Away' tugged at the same delicate strings. The Peerless Quartet switched perspectives by hymning the peace-mongering qualities of their president with 'I Think

We've Got Another Washington (Wilson is His Name)'. It was left to Frederick J. Wheeler in 1916 to sound the battle cry with 'Wake Up America!': 'Let's get ready to answer duty's call . . . America is ready!'

Eventually, on 6 April 1917, the United States declared war on Germany; and Tin Pan Alley *was* ready. 'Let's All Be Americans Now', declared the American Quartet, throwing in a chorus of the Southern anthem 'Dixie' to reinforce the point. Their Peerless colleagues forgot their earlier misgivings by recording what the publisher called 'The Sentiment of Every American Mother': 'America, Here's My Boy'. Suddenly, the recording industry could offer nothing but war songs, from the hopeful ('Say a Prayer for the Boys Over There') to the sentimental ('Somewhere in France is Daddy') and the gloriously confused ('I Don't Know Where I'm Going, But I'm on My Way'). The unchallenged champion of America's war anthems, however, was 'Over There', offered originally by the American Quartet, and welcomed by troops who might not have looked so kindly on the unrealistic comedy of Henry Burr's 'Life in a Trench in Belgium'. Nor might they have appreciated the blithe propaganda of the British papers, which boasted that the Allied troops were 'as happy as sandboys' as long as they could sing the choruses from the latest comic songs and hear a little ragtime.

Back in London, the *Hullo Ragtime* and *Hullo Tango* revues had been superseded by the timely *Hullo America*. Its star was Elsie Janis, and her big number 'When I Take My Jazz Band to the Fatherland'. 'Every Fritz and Hermann', she sang, 'will learn to jazz in German. We're going to say, Now, here's your chance – dance!' The Armistice was declared on 11 November 1918, and those soldiers fortunate enough to have survived the inhuman traumas of the Western Front returned to a world that was both strangely familiar, and eerily changed. Women, those delicate flowers whom the troops had been fighting to protect, were now occupied in manual and professional labour, showcasing their new-found independence, demanding the same rights as men. Just as shocking for British troops was the discovery that their homeland had, in their absence, been invaded: not by the accursed Huns, but by a fresh wave of exotic rhythms from the United States, a frenetic melee of musical excitement and jangling nerves which was known by the puzzling name of 'jazz'.

⚡

CHAPTER 3

Take Me to the Land of Jazz

'Do you jazz-trot? Latest Dance for Men on Leave –
An American Invention.'

Daily Mirror, May 1918

'Officers on leave complain that, having mastered certain
intricate steps, they return a few weeks later to find them
regarded as "bad form" and "out of date". The fancy for
the moment is to dance out of time. It is fascinating to watch
and do. It was introduced by the Americans. Introductions
are dispensed with, eager "jazzers" considering them a
waste of time.'

Daily Mirror, February 1919

4

Jazz, so the *Daily Express* explained a few days after the Armistice treaty was signed, was 'The New Noise That Makes People Gay'. It was syncopated (hence it was danced 'out of time'). It was American, for only such a young and carefree society could have concocted anything so free-spirited. It required a band, if such a name could be applied to the cacophonous assemblage of horns, banjos and random kitchen utensils which were tapped, thumped or crashed together in the search for novelty. And it was, without doubt, a menace to the society that had existed before the war began.

Its effect could be traced on women's bodies, and the way they used them. 'You cannot dance the writhing, wriggling jazz music in the tight, stiff bodices of 1840', one commentator noted. As corsets were cast off, so were the chaperons who had been accustomed to guard a young woman's reputation at a pre-war dance. What mattered after the war was not her good name, but her ability to find a partner. Women would dance together until a suitable man intervened. Even married women were not immune to the dancing fever. Officers newly returned from the front, it was noted, were 'complaining that in her craze for the restaurant, the revue, the tea-dance, the jazz or the foxtrot, they find difficulty in recognising the wife they marched to war for'.

There were now 10% more young women in Britain than young men, and thousands of the latter severely injured or still absent on military service. So any girl who was invited to dance was 'expected to bring with her always her own partner . . . And when he is found, whether he is liked or disliked personally, he is tolerated if only his step is in sympathy with his finder's.' A fresh cast of characters was on display in London society: parlour snakes and lounge lizards; cads and dancing pests; 'the sleek, well-dressed dancing man, with his saponaceous, unctuous suave manner' and 'the girl who is asked everywhere because she dances well'. One observer complained that 'some of these girls have not even good looks to recommend them, and they are obviously out of place in the clubs and hotels where dancing is conducted'. But class, it seemed, no longer mattered: everything had to bow to the dance and the jazz band.

'Dancing', a columnist asserted, 'is the natural sequel to war . . . In a few weeks, when the girls have got used to the boys coming home, dancing will be normal again and only those who love dancing for dancing's sake will fill our halls and ballrooms. The war dancer will recover, and be the sober, sensible citizen that he was before.' As victors of the recent conflict, British youth would be the first to resume a life of tranquillity, psychologists believed. In Munich, however, where defeat had led to revolution, people 'danced night after night into the late hours, when the city has been the scene of anarchy, terror and bloodshed. They have discovered the most potent anaesthetic in life, for dancing kills care, kills worry, kills unhappiness ... Terrified inhabitants of anarchy-stricken towns, not knowing whether they will be dead in a rough grave on the morrow, dance wildly on through the night, snatching an anodyne from care, drinking to the dregs the glorious opiate of oblivion, conscious of shining eyes, conscious of the lilt of the music, conscious of a drowsy intoxication, forgetting, forgetting . . .' In a German satirical newspaper, a cartoon entitled 'The Demoniacs' showed dancers 'jazzing' to the music of a starving peasant and a skeleton. 'In your dance frenzy, you don't see that your musicians are Hunger and Need!', read the caption.

Urban disorder was not sufficient to explain this jazz-induced mania. The music was a 'mental opiate', according to the war poet Paul Bewsher. He courageously located the front line in the war between jazz and civilisation: 'The call of the music hypnotises the body, as it moves in exact answer to every beat of the melody. In some peculiar way the rhythm of the two, meeting in absolute harmony, drugs the senses. At times I have become almost unconscious in the utter physical satisfaction of inspired movement. The brain is dormant. The body alone lives, ruled no longer by the mind but by the external influence of sound.'

Unsurprisingly, guardians of public morals were alarmed by the threat posed by jazz. Canon Drummond told the appropriately titled Maidenhead Preventive and Rescue Association that 'People seem to have lost themselves . . . A nigger dance, to music from every conceivable instrument – not to make music but to make a noise – was a symptom of a very grave disease which was spreading across the country.' A magistrate in West Ham declared that jazz was simply 'a bunch of crazy niggers accompanied by a noise'. Assorted clerics on both sides of the Atlantic assailed jazz as part of a global Bolshevist conspiracy; or, worse, a symbol of the African jungle besmirching the white man's world. The jazz musician was 'an outlaw and a musical bandit. Like the gunman he is running amok and should be relentlessly put down.'

There were unlikely defenders of jazz. The Prince of Wales (the future Edward VIII) and his brother, Prince Albert (George VI), were evidently aficionados of the jazz band; while the latter was 'adept at strumming jazz tunes on the piano', the former rarely resisted the opportunity to assault any drum kit within reach of his syncopated royal fingers. Edward was soon dubbed 'the Jazz Prince', and his attendance was both a badge of honour for any jazz dance, and also a source of acute anxiety. He was prone to approaching bandleaders with exact instructions as to the tunes that should be performed, and any musicians who were asked to accompany him had to adjust discreetly to his accidental changes of tempo.

London's elite appeared to have surrendered to the American invader without the slightest resistance. As early as February 1919, chic dancing establishments in Kensington and Knightsbridge were boasting of their jazz bands, while the Queen of Romania was persuaded to take the floor with the Prince of Wales at a Hyde Park Hotel jazz ball. There were jazz teas; jazz shoes which, at two guineas a pair, wore out more quickly than most girls could afford to replace them; even, at the Dickins & Jones department store, a jazz dress 'of gold and silver tissue'. Soon the fashion notices of the London press were filled with suggestions like this: 'Just one simple, curling natural plume set in a gold or enamel holder makes a jazz fan – and no jazz fiend feels in the mode without one. Aesthetically they are right, for barbarian noises call for barbarian adornments, and an ostrich plume is savage beauty in itself.' By 1920, not only had 'jazz' become a synonym for 'dance', but it was now a multi-purpose term applied to anything bright, jarring, exotic, unexpected – anything, in other words, that was modern. When the ill-fated peace treaty of Versailles was signed in June 1919, London celebrated with 'a jazz night – a mad, jolly night of frolic and dance'. And within a few weeks, the press was reporting confidently that jazz was dead, or dying, or at least fading, and certainly doomed: 'Jazz was overdone during its reign, and all overdone crazes quickly die.' Yet the Jazz Age was just about to begin.

Some of you may wonder what 'Jazz' means. I don't know exactly. The word comes from America, and it means – well, whenever you feel particularly 'dancy' and excited and you don't care if it snows ink, then – you are jazzy.
Children's author 'Uncle Dick', 1919

There are sufficient creation myths attached to jazz to equal those of the world's great religions. Even the name was open to multiple interpretations, and several choices of spelling: jazz, of course, but also jass, or jaz. The first author to pen a historical account of the music, as early as 1926, was forced to concede that, however it was spelled, the word 'has no relations at all in the English language', and must therefore hail from a different culture – Africa, in all probability. Some claimed that there was a musician, perhaps in New Orleans, named Razz, and that a mishearing of 'Razz's band' had resulted in the coining of the term. Others insisted that the musician concerned was Chas Washington, a virtuoso of the drums; or perhaps James Brown, from Dixieland via Chicago, whose given name was commonly abbreviated as 'Jas'. Links were sought with a 'jazzbo', which was either the climax of a vaudeville production, or (on more scholarly evidence) a description of a trumpet with a kazoo tied into its horn. The French verb *jaser*, meaning to chat or to gossip, was commandeered as a potential source. It was perhaps the slang term for 'noise' (members of the various anti-jazz leagues imagined it so). Or, perhaps most convincingly, 'jazz' was (like 'rock 'n' roll' to follow) a term connoting sexual intercourse, in this instance used by black Americans as a code during the slavery era.

If there was little concord about the origins of the word, there was still less harmony when it came to the music it described. Today, we like to imagine we can recognise jazz, in a club or on a film soundtrack: it is a stylistic language that we can decipher easily enough, whether the speaker is mellow (like Wynton Marsalis) or frenzied (like Archie Shepp). But from the late 1910s onwards, no such unanimity could be reached. Indeed, the exact borderlines of jazz were (and still are) hotly debated and contested. The distinction was not just, as the early critics had it, between music that was 'hot' (jazz) or 'sweet' (not jazz); or which was based upon improvisation (jazz) or tightly scored (not jazz, unless . . .). Almost as soon as jazz, whatever it was and is, was invented, it proved to be such a mesmerising concept, provoking such ferocity of ownership and identification, that the classification of music into jazz and non-jazz categories took on the air of a moral crusade.

Jazz was the earliest musical genre to provoke such argument and passion. In that sense, it was the first modern form of popular music: the first to divide and conquer its followers, to be demonised and celebrated in equal measure; to become, by name alone, a badge of pride and a symbol of freedom – artistic, moral and political.

And yet the vast majority of the music that inspired the outrage of clerics and politicians, and prompted such carefree abandonment of reserve amongst dancers in the years after the end of the Great War, was not – by the aesthetic standards of today, or even those of 1930 – jazz. Its creators may have seen themselves as jazz musicians, but subsequent generations have chosen to rob them of that title. While people believed fervently that they were living through the Jazz Age, more accurately, according to the definitions laid down retrospectively, this was the era of the dance bands, some of whom were bold enough to have flirted with 'authentic' jazz music amidst their repeated choruses of what was soon dismissed by critics as 'slush'.

In the year 1915, jazz music burst upon the white population of America with the suddenness of a volcanic eruption.
R. W. S. Mendl, *The Appeal of Jazz*, 1927

Some say the Jass band originated in Chicago. Chicago says it comes from San Francisco . . . Anyway, a Jass band is the newest thing in the cabarets, adding greatly to the hilarity thereof. They say the first instrument of the first Jass band was an empty lard can, by humming into which, sounds were produced resembling those of a saxophone with the croup. Since then, the Jass band has grown in size and ferocity.
Victor catalogue, 1917

Victor's tentative exploration of the origins of jazz was designed to promote the first releases by the musicians who comprised (by common if not unanimous consent) the first jazz band to be immortalised on record: the Original Dixieland Jazz Band, or ODJB. (Illustrating the elusive identity of their music, they were the Original Dixieland *Jass* Band until 1917.) The group's cornet player and co-founder, Nick LaRocca, claimed that 'The invention of jazz was the result of a mistake. It happened because four other guys and I couldn't play what we heard at band concerts in New Orleans because we were unable to read music. We tried to play the tunes as we heard them, but they wouldn't come out.' It's a deliberately naïve account, designed to admit that although the ODJB had borrowed from superior black musicians in their home city, they were still the true originators of jazz.

Not a single historian of jazz would support LaRocca's account, and with good reason. Yet the ODJB startled those who stumbled across them in New Orleans around 1915, as the journal *Talking Machine News* recounted: 'Visitors to the city heard a combination playing dance music of a type they had never heard before, and were fascinated. The players were futurists in music, and they express much the same ideas in noise as the futurists in art express in colour.' In late 1916, vaudeville stars Arthur Collins and Byron Harlan recorded a novelty tune that was surely inspired by the ODJB: 'That Funny Jas Band From Dixieland'. Besides some embarrassingly racist (to modern ears) minstrel by-play, the song talked about 'that harmony queer' and 'mad musicians playing rhythm'. There were even a few seconds of authentic 'hot' jazz playing to emphasise the point. The Collins/Harlan duet can with some merit be claimed as the first commercial record to offer any jazz musicianship, but it clearly had comic rather than pioneering intent.

In June 1917, American record-buyers were able to purchase the Joseph C. Smith orchestra's 'Havanola Fox-Trot', a tightly controlled but eminently danceable piece of ensemble playing. The Prince's Orchestra, a Columbia Records house band named after its founder rather than the jazz-mad Prince of Wales, released 'American Patrol', a march tune which would become a staple of the Glenn Miller Orchestra two decades later. And Victor unveiled the ODJB, with a 78 rpm recording of 'Livery Stable Blues'.

How did it differ from its contemporaries? It suggested a gang of crazed instrumentalists fighting for supremacy, while still managing to add their voices to something greater than themselves. The canon of classical music – such as the opening movement of Bach's first 'Brandenburg' Concerto – was rich in instances of ensemble playing which involved individual musicians throwing themes, and variations upon themes, back and forth (in faithful reading of a printed score, of course). To the unwary, 'Livery Stable Blues' sounded like a free-for-all, a rugby scrum rather than Bach's polite passing of the teacakes.* What's obvious in retrospect is that the ODJB are adhering to an agreed structure as closely as any Bach sextet: they all break at the same moment, hold back to let the clarinet squeal or the cornet squawk, maintain a tight melodic pattern,

---

* The ODJB's trombonist, 'Daddy' Edwards, recalled that the band's records would have been even more explosive had the primitive recording techniques of the day been equal to the sonic punch of Tony Spargo's bass and snare drums.

depart and arrive on perfect schedule. There are moments of spontaneity, when they paint over the lines, though the lines are never dissolved. For anyone unversed in the previously undocumented tradition from which the recording came, however, 'Livery Stable Blues' represented anarchy, not precision. It was a shock of non-recognition that would be repeated whenever popular music jolted into the future, whether with 'Heartbreak Hotel' or 'Anarchy in the UK' or 'Jack Your Body': all those moments when events that have been occurring outside the viewfinder suddenly loom into sharp focus on the screen.

Today it is easier to pull the camera back and reveal the wider canvas. In their home town of New Orleans, the ODJB were able to capitalise upon a blend of influences, black and white, English and European, traditional and brazenly commercial, which by the dawn of the twentieth century evolved into something that we would recognise as jazz. The pianist Jelly Roll Morton insisted on being acclaimed as 'the Originator of Jazz and Stomps', who had invented jazz in 1902. His contemporaries remembered the trumpet player Buddy Bolden as the catalyst, his status all the more mythical because (as far as we know) he was never recorded. Before any of this music was preserved, it had crept out of Louisiana to the West Coast, then up the river to Chicago – which is where club owners persuaded white New Orleans bands to venture in 1915–16, and entertainment journalists began to refer to jazz as 'vaudeville's newest craze'. In January 1917, one of those bands reached New York, with a residency at Reisenweber's restaurant, and within a matter of days they were hired by the Victor label, with the results we have seen. The ODJB was now able to bill itself as America's highest-earning band, and – although exact sales figures for their debut recording aren't available, and have often been wildly overestimated – 'Livery Stable Blues' undoubtedly brought the nascent sound of jazz into several hundred thousand American homes.

Their success prompted immediate litigation: there were well-founded copyright disputes over both sides of their record, leading cynics to mutter that perhaps the Dixieland Jazz Band was not so Original after all. As the jazz composer Gunther Schuller astutely summarised, the ODJB's appeal was rooted in its unoriginality: 'The ODJB reduced New Orleans Negro music to a simplified formula. It took a new idea, an innovation, and reduced it to the kind of compressed, rigid format that could appeal to a mass audience. As such it had a number of sure-fire ingredients, the foremost being a rhythmic momentum that had a physical, even visceral appeal.'

But Schuller concluded that their music exhibited 'none of the flexibility and occasional subtlety shown by the best Negro bands of the period'. Unfortunately, that could not be demonstrated to anyone who didn't witness the 'Negro bands' in person. Jazz legend has it that black cornet player Freddie Keppard was offered a recording contract in 1916, but turned it down, explaining: 'We won't put our stuff on records for everybody to steal.' The honour of making the first black jazz recordings therefore fell not to Keppard, but to Wilbur Sweatman, although ironically there appear to be fewer improvisational passages in his early records than in the ODJB's.

Keppard's conservatism may sound naïve, but it reflected the suspicion and lack of interest with which the process of recording was regarded before the sales boom of the 1920s. Race was also a constant obstacle. As the leader of a black band, Keppard was affected by the closure in 1917 of the red-light district of New Orleans, known as Storyville, which had previously offered plentiful work to jazz musicians. He was barred from seeking the jobs that were open to the ODJB: fraternity week-ends at Ivy League colleges, for example, or a gala dance for the servicemen of the USS *Charleston*. Racial tension in many American cities mounted as white soldiers returned from Europe to find that their jobs had been 'stolen' by African-Americans, and riots ensued from Texas to the nation's capital in 1919.

By not transparently offering their audience 'Negro' music, the ODJB could be enjoyed for the glorious racket they made. Few who heard their records or watched them perform would have been able to distinguish which elements of their sound were improvised, and which were carefully arranged in advance. Jazz music was, to its earliest white adherents, wild, unpredictable and cacophonous. The ODJB's competitors, and there were plenty of college bands keen to follow their example, won their reputations by using kitchen utensils as percussion instruments and adopting madcap costumes. First to win a national audience were Earl Fuller's Famous Jazz Band, whose 'Slippery Hank' (1917) reproduced all the external pizzazz of the ODJB, without a hint of their authentically spontaneous 'jazz' moments. There was a suspicion that unless performers consciously escalated their novelty appeal, their audience would soon tire of them. One jaded observer noted in 1919, 'As the popularity of the dance wanes, the costumes and the music grow louder. A jazz party I attended last night was a picturesque approach to Bedlam. One of the instrumentalists had a weird whistling instrument between his lips, which I was told was Hawaiian; another squeezed a motor hooter.' Such antics symbolised 'jazz' to a public who had no means of comprehending the origins of the music.

Many of the earliest jazz recordings were based soundly on existing rag tunes, although the transition from one melodic element to the next was often hidden beneath the crash and clamour of drums and horns. Others, in a style that became especially identified with New Orleans, seemed to set up an interlocking pattern of instrumental motifs (riffs, as they would soon be known) and then repeat them with rampant displays of energy. Few observers noticed that a proportion of jazz excursions now took place within a structure which would become one of the most familiar song formats of the entire century: the twelve-bar blues.

> The year 1923 has given us – or, more politely, some of us – 'the Blues', which possess undoubtedly an interesting, albeit a monotonous, new rhythm . . . The majority of those whom I have seen dancing it appear to imagine that it is a species of 'slow-motion' foxtrot, which my musical ear, such as it is, tells me it cannot be.
> British critic Harry Melville, 1924

> Blues records long ago ceased to be issued.
> *Gramophone* magazine, 1925

As early as 1904, a ragtime song called 'One O' Them Things' opened not with a four-bar motif, as convention demanded, but with what we would now recognise as a blues chorus of twelve bars. Three years later, the ethnographer Howard Odum carried his explorations of America's 'natural' music into Lafayette County, Mississippi. There, as the blues historian Marybeth Hamilton recounted, 'he found something curious: songs made up of a single line, repeated two or three times . . . [musicians] adapted their songs to suit their mood, and they could stretch them out for what seemed like hours, fusing lines from different tunes to take them straight from one song to another, and sliding a knife or bone along the guitar strings to make the instrument "talk" in response'. So perturbed was Odum by the strangeness of what he heard – described by its creators sometimes as 'rag times', sometimes as 'knife songs' in honour of what we would now recognise as the bottleneck guitar technique, sometimes as 'coon songs' – that he devoted little time to analysing their contents, and eventually destroyed the cylinder recordings he had made, rather than preserving their raw and unsettling contents for posterity. Had those aural documents survived, subsequent scholars of the blues might have lost the pleasure of conjuring up their own creation myths.

To prove that authenticity is at best a precarious concept when it comes to popular music, the process of translating origins into legends began with the man who has passed into history as the Father or Originator of the Blues. It is W. C. Handy, the son of a comparatively well-to-do African-American preacher, whose statue stands by Beale Street in Memphis, and whose face appeared on a US postage stamp in 1969. It was his name that appeared on the 1912 sheet music for 'Dallas Blues', 'Baby Seals Blues' and 'The Memphis Blues' (also known as 'Mr Crump'); and he who was credited as the sole author of one of the most revisited tunes of the twentieth century, 'St Louis Blues'.

Handy was no more the originator of the blues than were Adam and Eve the parents of all mankind. But a musical tradition so glorious demands a father figure, and Handy fitted the bill. The leader of a small dance band, he struggled for tips at a saloon in Cleveland, Mississippi, watching in amazement as a local trio out-earned him ten to one by playing 'one of those over-and-over strains'. In the money, as a good American capitalist, Handy 'saw the beauty of primitive music . . . That night a composer was born, an *American* composer.' That was one strand of Handy's chosen myth. The other found him on a railroad platform in Tutwiler, Mississippi, where he heard an itinerant guitar player perform 'the weirdest music I had ever heard' – a groaning lament made up of short verses of just three lines, the first and second identical. By his account, he stored away this memory until he was commissioned to write a campaign song for a Memphis mayoral candidate in 1909. The result was 'The Memphis Blues', which won a nationwide audience in 1914 via rag-inspired recordings by both Prince's Orchestra and the Victor Military Band. Collins and Harlan, always open to novelties from the black community, recorded a vocal rendition the following year.

'The Memphis Blues' was, according to Handy, 'A Southern Rag'. Of 'St Louis Blues', first publicised as an instrumental by Prince's Orchestra, he wrote: 'My aim would be to combine ragtime syncopation with a real melody in the spiritual tradition.' That 'tradition' was something he acknowledged as his inspiration, stating quite unashamedly that each of his compositions was based upon a strain or a melody that he had retrieved from his past. There was no hint that he imagined himself founding a musical genre; nor, despite the pathetic fallacy that blues equated with sadness, did he see himself as a prince of melancholy. Quite the opposite: of an early performance of 'St Louis Blues', he wrote 'The dancers seemed electrified. Something within them came suddenly to life. An instinct that wanted so much to live, to fling its arms and to spread joy, took them by their heels.'

For the generation who walked backwards through musical history, as they explored the roots of the 1960s rock guitarists, the blues was a signifier of a primal desolation, its origins the cry of a people enslaved and belittled in their homeland. The original audience for the blues, through the 'classic' era of the 1920s and beyond, would not have recognised this description; they would probably have laughed, indeed, at how confused the white man could become. In the words of blues historian Albert Murray, 'The blues as such are synonymous with low spirits. Blues music is not. With all its so-called blue notes and over-tones of sadness, blues music of its very nature and function is nothing if not a diversion. With all its preoccupation with the most disturbing aspects of life, it is something contrived specifically to be performed as entertainment. Not only is its express purpose to make people feel good, which is to say in high spirits, but in the process of doing so it is actu-ally expected to generate a disposition that is both elegantly playful and heroic in its nonchalance.'

Two words leap out of that description as the antithesis to the mythic vision of the blues: 'contrived', and 'entertainment'. The blues, from its gestation, was intended as a commercial music – was fashioned that way, indeed, by W. C. Handy himself. No doubt the true originators of its varied sounds and styles would have a richer, broader tale to relate, but the notion of the blues as the sole property of the haunted troubadour, picking his ragged guitar and keening his misery across the Deep South, is a romantic fiction.

Other misconceptions have long since been abandoned: that all blues songs are based on the twelve-bar structure which both scared and mystified Howard Odum; and that the archetypal blues singer is a black man with an acoustic guitar. There are musicological ways of under-standing and identifying the blues (those 'blue', or sometimes 'worried', notes, the flattened third and the flattened fifth); and it is certainly true that a large proportion of songs by blues performers follow the twelve-bar grid (allowing for the idiosyncratic timekeeping of such mavericks as John Lee Hooker). But as a quick study of 'St Louis Blues' demonstrates, that reassuringly simple pattern is far from being obligatory.

Neither is the caricature of an African-American guitarist meeting the Devil at a Mississippi crossroads remotely definitive. The commercial blues of the 1920s – later designated the 'classic blues', as if to segregate it from what followed – was sung almost entirely by women: by Bessie Smith and Ma Rainey, pre-eminently, but first by the unrelated Mamie Smith. Like Handy, they also did not believe that they were occupying either a blues ghetto or a future pantheon. Many of them, such as Mamie Smith, came out of the vaudeville tradition, most likely the TOBA variety circuit, the initials standing for Theatre Owners Booking Association, which provided acts for a discretely African-American network of venues (although some artists preferred to believe that TOBA actually meant 'tough on black asses'). Others were associated with jazz bands, and it was jazz musicians who provided the accompaniment on the vast majority of 'classic blues' recordings in the 1920s and beyond. Ask Bessie Smith what she was, and after she'd slapped your face for your cheek and ignorance, she'd have said contemptuously: 'I'm a jazz singer.' She and her counterparts would not have wished to be remembered solely for their recordings, which (particularly in the early 1920s) were arranged to reflect the technical limitations of the process. As Bessie's contemporary Lizzie Miles recalled in 1957, 'When singing with raucous bands, I sound like a fish peddler, but that is not true New Orleans music. New Orleans jazz was musical. It had all kinds of pretty fill-ins and figures, beautiful tones and all that. You should have heard the violins . . . the sweetness of those early jazz violins.' Her repertoire stretched from what we'd recognise today as the blues to songs in Creole French, though the latter were never represented in her recordings.

There is one final complication to the accepted story of the blues. Mamie Smith, first of the black 'classic' singers to record, entered the studio for the first time in February 1920, at the age of 36; and then again in August, emerging with 'Crazy Blues', which sold 75,000 copies in its first month, and kept selling. But Mamie, or indeed any of the other female Smiths who littered the 1920s blues market, did not make the first vocal blues records. Just as the ODJB (or Collins and Harlan, depending on your definitions) were responsible for launching jazz on record, the first blues singers preserved for posterity were also white.

In August 1916, when most of her contemporaries were capital-
ising on the American public's passing infatuation with songs about
Hawaii, a 20-year-old vaudeville singer named Marion Harris entered
Victor's recording establishment in New York. 'I Ain't Got Nobody Much'
became the 'plug' side of her debut recording, and by February 1917 it was
one of the biggest-selling discs in America, competing alongside the latest
Broadway show tunes. It was not a twelve-bar blues tune, but it was identical in structure and mood to many of the songs which would be accounted
as 'classic blues'. Moreover, Harris slurred her words and held back her
phrasing in a manner she can only have learned from watching African-
American performers, though she never lapsed for a moment into caricature or comic mimicry. This was as 'authentic' a piece of blues as Elvis
Presley performing 'That's All Right', or Cream, Led Zeppelin or the
Rolling Stones reviving the Robert Johnson songbook, and it predated the
ODJB's first 'jazz' record by several months.

Nor was Marion Harris alone in her unknowing blues crusade,
which would spawn such late 1910s hits as 'Everyone's Crazy 'Bout the
Doggone Blues' and 'Take Me to the Land of Jazz' (Memphis, as it
happens), before she reached her pinnacle with a desolate rendition of
'St Louis Blues' in 1920. Billy Murray, whose prolific recording career
saw him tackle rags, sentimental ballads, a car song ('In My Merry
Oldsmobile') which predated Chuck Berry's by exactly half a century,
comic duets, Hawaiian hula novelties and the most familiar version of
the baseball anthem 'Take Me Out to the Ball Game', reflected the
miseries of the Wartime Prohibition Act with 1919's 'The Alcoholic
Blues' – meant for laughs, of course, but a classic blues conception none-
theless. Al Bernard not only attempted 'St Louis Blues' a full year before
Marion Harris, but belied his Caucasian complexion by singing 'I'm
black as a berry, and for me the gals all fall' on his 1919 hit, 'Nigger
Blues'. Bernard's vocals betrayed none of Harris's familiarity with the
vocal hallmarks of the genre, but his adventures into the mildly exotic
did yield the first known composition to bear the title, 'Shake, Rattle
and Roll'. And then there was Nora Bayes, whose 'Regretful Blues' of
1918 may have misrepresented the genre, but who redeemed herself (bar
her 'blackface' monologue) with 1920's 'Prohibition Blues'.

Small wonder that black artists did not choose to classify themselves as 'blues' singers alone, when the style could so easily be slipped over
the vaudeville costumes of their white counterparts. Indeed, it was only the

persistence of black songwriter Perry Bradford that enabled the African-American 'classic blues' tradition to be born. He had presented his songs to the Okeh Records company, which suggested that they should be given to the cyclonic Russian-born vaudeville star, Sophie Tucker. Instead, Bradford put forward Mamie Smith, having persuaded jazz bandleader George Morrison to lend him some musicians. By Morrison's account, Mamie was a shabby dresser in a ramshackle, fetid house, so he gave her $150 (far more than she would have earned from the recording session) and 'I dressed her from the inside out.' Once she was established as a star, Mamie Smith affected an altogether more dazzling display, as her near-contemporary Victoria Spivey recalled: 'Miss Smith walked on that stage and I could not breathe for a minute. She threw those big sparkling eyes on us with that lovely smile showing those pearly teeth with a diamond the size of one of her teeth. Then I looked at her dress. Nothing but sequins and rhinestones, plus a velvet cape with fur on it. We all went wild. And then she sang – she tore the house apart. Between numbers while the band was playing she would make a complete change in about a minute, and was back in record time for her next selection. Her full voice filled the entire auditorium without the mikes like we use today. That was singing the blues!'

After Mamie Smith established that there was money to be made from black women and the blues, the music industry responded as it did when every other new fad or gimmick found an audience: it soaked the market with her peers, competitors and imitators. There were literally dozens of female blues singers making records in the 1920s, until the Depression of 1929 squeezed the trade almost out of existence. The most famous of them, then and now, was Bessie Smith.* She was, in Columbia Records' words, 'the best loved of all the Race's great blues singers' – 'the Race' evoking a sense of robust identity amongst those who were accustomed to being dubbed 'Negroes' or worse. Bessie Smith and her peers were promoted to the African-American audience, who constituted the vast majority of her buyers, as someone who could understand their lives and voice their emotions, perhaps even take on their sadness as her own. If spiritual music offered consolation, blues represented a defiant refusal to be beaten. 'You'll feel better', Okeh boasted of Margaret Johnson, 'because no one could be so sad and blue

* She died in a 1936 car accident, but not – contrary to popular legend – because the ambulance attending her refused to carry her to a white hospital.

as Margaret.' The same label offered salvation in the form of Victoria Spivey's voice: 'Wanna be happy? Then buy our Blues!' The song in question was 'TB Blues', a chilling account of an illness which was devastating the African-American community during the 1920s.

As a marketing device, 'blues' envisaged a powerfully voiced black woman supported by a jazz band: a style of singing, and also a mood, which would combine to form a musical genre. Bessie, Mamie, Clara and Trixie Smith, Ma Rainey, Johnson, Spivey and the rest were assumed to appeal to a predominantly female audience of 'the Race': when Bessie Smith sang 'Nobody Knows the Trouble I've Seen', she provoked recognition on both ethnic and gender grounds. But the great blues-women of the 1920s were also gathering a secret audience of white devotees, of whom the most eloquent was perhaps the American novelist Carl Van Vechten. In 1926, the same year he published an immensely sympathetic novel about black life in Harlem with an ill-fated title, *Nigger Heaven*, Van Vechten painted a portrait of Columbia Records' 'World's Champion Moaner', which was so vivid that it bordered upon the garish: 'Clara Smith's tones uncannily take on the colour of the saxophone; again of the clarinet. Her voice is powerful or melancholy, by turns. It tears the blood from one's heart. One learns from her that the Negro's cry to a cruel cupid is as moving and elemental as his cry to God, as expressed in the spirituals.'

Van Vechten's was a stray voice, however. Most whites believed that 'the blues' was merely a dance step, one of the bewildering array of movements on display in dance halls and ballrooms. For it was there that people first encountered the new sounds, translated into mainstream entertainment by one of the hundreds of dance bands who would dominate the music industry for the next fifteen years.

$$\frac{\style{}{\text{ϟ}}}{}$$

'Graceful dancing is dead in ballrooms ... We conclude that fox-trot and one-step express our odd and ugly manners, our modern helter-skelter. They show the wheel coming again full circle – back to the Polynesian, round the camp fire, with the tom-tom.'

'Don't the daily cases in the Divorce Court, and elsewhere, lead us to suppose that manners have become uncontrollable, like the fox-trot which images them on the ballroom floor?'

Daily Mirror editorial, 1920

CHAPTER 4

DANCE
-O-
MANIA

'It would be difficult to find in London any hotel or public building that does not hold regular dances. Dancing in the West End begins at three in the afternoon ... The real dance maniacs attend these afternoon affairs and then go to an evening dance – which costs on an average a guinea a head in the West End – and when this is over finish up at one of the many new London night clubs.'

'London's Orgy of Dancing', *Daily Express*, 1919

The psychological and physical impact of the First World War had been so crushing, especially upon the nations of Europe, that the mania for incessant dancing and the blaring of jazz horns was assumed to be an inescapable consequence. Would it die down? Would the etiquette of the pre-war era return, with its sedate tea dances free of syncopation and musical discords? 'The War shattered many of our illusions and brought us nearer to earthy things', the author Stanley Nelson wrote in 1934. 'That is why the artificiality of the Victorians in their dance music was superseded by a dance music which was unashamedly proud of showing its crude emotional stress.'

The music of that proud, crude impulse was always – when it was not being demeaned with blatantly racist epithets – called 'jazz'. Not without confusion, however: *Melody Maker* reviewer Edgar Jackson, who would become one of Britain's most ardent supporters of 'hot' jazz, initially demanded that no one should confuse the artistry of white jazz with its barbaric black equivalent. This cultural superiority came easily in a world where (in Britain) black people were rarely seen and (in America) an entire system of discrimination was ranged against them.

These niceties of distinction were lost on the people who were dancing. 'Jazz' described any music to which young people danced and socialised, and which aroused disquiet amongst their elders. It was recognised not by its degree of syncopation or improvisation, but by its tempo, its percussive clamour and strident use of horns and clarinets. One instrument in particular, previously scorned by classical musicians, came to epitomise jazz. As if starring in a West End farce, a London High Court judge uttered the question of the moment: 'What *is* a saxophone?' In 1927, a club on Merseyside was granted a dancing licence on the strict understanding that saxophones would not be used, for fear of upsetting the neighbours.

There were occasional distractions from trial by saxophone. While young Europeans were being slaughtered on the battlefields of Verdun and the Somme in 1916, their American counterparts were serenading their sweethearts with an instrument, and a sound, that emanated from Hawaii. It took three years for the ukulele to cross the Atlantic, where it was greeted as 'the antithesis of jazz', boasting 'the soft seductiveness and peacefulness of the Pacific isle whence it comes'. It was accompanied by the 'hula dance', ideally performed (by Hawaiian women only, of course) in a grass skirt with enticingly bare limbs. When a ukulele band reached London's Savoy hotel, a porter remarked: '*That's* music. That dashed jazz *isn't*.'

War ensured that Britain and the Continent were late to experience the latest novelties from America. James Reese Europe, musical director for the dancing Castles, led the seventy-piece 369th Infantry Band ('the Hellraisers') to France in early 1918, raising morale among troops and locals alike with their jazz-inflected anthems. (Europe himself was murdered by one of his percussionists the following year, setting the bar high for future intra-band squabbles.) Records by the Original Dixieland Jazz Band had made their way to Britain by 1918, inspiring the first home-grown jazz record: Murray Pilcer's 'I'm All Bound Round with the Mason–Dixon Line', which resembled an explosion in a musical instrument store.

Britain was able to judge the ODJB's merits at first hand in spring 1919, when the band joined the cast of the Hippodrome revue, *Joy Bells*. Their run lasted just one night, after which star comedian George Robey issued a 'them or me' ultimatum. They transferred to the Palladium, where the audience seemed confused as to whether the ODJB were a comic turn, albeit a deafening one: Britain had heard nothing so raucous as their three-horn front line. 'This is the most discordant and uninteresting entertainment I have ever seen at the Palladium', a reviewer lamented. 'The resident orchestra fast asleep could amuse me more. These jazz bandsmen played like a swarm of bees who had lost their hive and found a home at the Palladium. I can see clearly that if I can rattle on any old tin, my future is made.'

The ODJB were followed by the mostly black Southern Syncopated Orchestra, a thirty-piece unit which performed a mixture of classical themes, spirituals and what we would now recognise as jazz. Among their number was the first of the great jazz instrumentalists to perform in Europe: clarinettist Sidney Bechet, whose playing was described as 'astonishing' and 'extraordinary'. The *Daily Express* acclaimed the band as 'Magicians' offering 'High-Art Ragtime', before letting forth with an equally astonishing display of racial stereotyping: 'They are coffee-coloured, with glittering teeth, gollywog eyes on swivels, close-cropped hair, and heads on universal sockets, which will turn any way.' Both bands proved so alarming and abrasive to many listeners that the press mounted a concerted campaign to declare that jazz was on the wane, hopelessly old-fashioned, and probably dead. Such declarations were repeated at almost monthly intervals, with no noticeable result, until jazz became culturally acceptable. The pattern would be repeated for the rest of the century: new music was not to be trusted, was probably immoral, and was surely about to be replaced by something altogether more sedate.

Race, sex, drink and drugs certainly comprised a poisonous cocktail. In October 1916, police raided Ciro's Club behind London's National Gallery, having been alerted that liquor was being sold illegally (on a Sunday night, no less). They discovered 250 patrons, around seventy of whom were 'dancing to the ragtime music of a nigger band'. Chief Inspector Glass was not an aficionado of ragtime: 'It was rather rough. It was not classical. The musicians evidently struck the notes of their own accord.' Such spontaneous music must surely be immoral. The press speculated wildly about the 'eminent persons' who were shepherded away from the scene to avoid arrest, the ubiquitous Prince of Wales being a likely suspect.

Soon, however, London was inundated with dance orchestras and gyrating young aristocrats. The most prestigious venue was the Savoy hotel in the Strand. In 1920, its management recruited the Belgian-born manager of Rector's Club, in Tottenham Court Road, to assemble suitably high-class entertainment. Already ensconced were the Savoy Quartet (a banjo band), to which W. F. De Mornys added a Hawaiian orchestra. This experiment faltered after the leader of the Hawaiians called the resident drummer 'a damn nigger', to which the abused percussionist replied: 'Mr De Mornys, isn't he blacker than I am?' In their stead, De Mornys formed a syncopated combo, the Savoy Havana Band, and added a second, more mellifluous ensemble, the Savoy Orpheans, explaining: 'I am certain that although the British public likes the rhythm, they want to hear the melody and dislike the music too swinging – they want melody and quality of tone.' His original line-up was a mixture of British and American musicians, 'and some of the Yanks had their own ideas about jazz. When they got too "hot" for the Savoy, I sent them over to Claridge's, where they soon had to quieten down. The restaurant manager there went berserk if they played a note of jazz.'

As bandleader Ted Heath recalled, 'Jazz was a novelty, and people wanted to dance and forget the horrors of the First World War. Consequently, any good musician who had a feeling and a flair for playing the new syncopated dance music found himself in a lucrative line of business. Actually, such musicians were in short supply. The music was too new, too strange and somewhat alien to the British temperament.' There was, too, a premium placed upon the involvement of visiting Americans, whose playing was believed to be more authentic than that of their home-grown equivalents.

While London's hotels resounded to the subdued tones of American jazz, the tango and the foxtrot had followed a generation of rich young Americans to France. The beaches of Trouville and the casinos of Deauville reverberated to the rhythm of jazz dancing in the summer of 1920, and the wave swept down to the Riviera, inaugurating the decadent, hedonistic culture portrayed in F. Scott Fitzgerald's novel, *Tender Is the Night*.* Fitzgerald was responsible for coining the phrase 'the Jazz Age', and widely acclaimed as its exemplar, despite his own ambivalent relationship with both the hedonism and its soundtrack. Not that the Jazz Age required a promoter: its momentum was self-generating, stoked by the relief that war was over and its shadow dispelled for generations to come.

In the final weeks of the war, the breakneck rhythm of the ODJB's 'Tiger Rag' presaged the hyperactivity to follow. Dozens of outfits followed in their wake. Variety was provided by the hint of beguiling scents from distant lands, via discs such as 'Arabian Nights' by the Waldorf-Astoria Dance Orchestra, with its hypnotic mock-Turkish melody; and the multi-million-selling 'Dardanella' (alias 'Turkish Tom Toms') by Ben Selvin's Band, its repeated themes from xylophone and banjo anticipating the serial music of half a century hence. The latter's success in January 1920 spawned copycat tunes entitled 'Afghanistan' and 'Alexandria'.

The entire order of American popular music was in flux. With few exceptions, the era of the ballad singer, unchanged since Victorian days, was over. Ragtime had been subsumed into jazz, and vaudeville stars, unless they were frightfully amusing, had to incorporate dance rhythms or the fashionable 'blues' feel to avoid sounding disastrously 'before-the-war'. With 'I'll Say She Does' and then 'Swanee' (by the young George Gershwin), Al Jolson hurled himself at the new order with such elan that rejection was impossible. He was the ultimate song stylist, stamping his personality on everything he recorded, his exaggerated vocal delivery the source of his charm. Effervescence of a similar order came from bandleader

* The French passion for American jazz would lead to the formation of such bands as the Quintet of the Hot Club of France, starring guitar virtuoso Django Reinhardt.

Ted Lewis, who fancied himself the true father of jazz (despite having been sacked from his first orchestra because his clarinet playing was so amateurish), but whose forte was disorderly dance tunes such as 'When My Baby Smiles at Me'. This was not jazz by any scholarly measurement, but its entertainment value was undeniable.

The first stars of the dance-band years were the Art Hickman Orchestra, renowned for their inability to read music (which seemed to boost their jazz credentials), and their reputation for infectious rowdiness. 'The first note plunges you into an hilarious abandon from which there is no rescue 'til the music stops', their record company declared, though few of Hickman's discs were ever quite that thrilling. Like those of his 1920 peers, however, they might have been manufactured with the words 'guaranteed to propel a couple around the dance floor' scrawled across their fragile grooves.

In the late summer of 1920, an orchestra emerged whose leader had greater pretensions. The son of a classical conductor, Paul Whiteman had played violin with the San Francisco Symphony. In his self-aggrandising autobiography, simply titled *Jazz* (1926), he recalled how he had first met this intoxicating music 'at a dance dive on the Barbary Coast. It screeched and bellowed at me . . . my whole body began to sit up and take notice. It was like coming out of blackness into bright light.' His infatuation was consummated in 1919, when he met composer and arranger Ferdie Grofé. Late of Art Hickman's band, Grofé has been credited by scholar James Lincoln Collier as the man who 'came up with the idea of the dance-band "arrangement". Until this time bands had generally played chorus after chorus of the tune in the same way, for as long as was required. It was Grofé's idea to vary the music from chorus to chorus, now poising the saxophones against a trombone line, now allowing the banjo to solo, now pitting the trumpet against the saxes.'

This simple and (in retrospect) obvious innovation transformed the history of twentieth-century popular music. It provided structure where previously anarchy had raged; introduced sophistication to raw ingredients; and allowed each bandleader (and his arranger) to create his own trademark sound and style. Every combination of horns, woodwinds and strings would become as recognisable to aficionados as would a singer's timbre. In collaboration, Whiteman and Grofé made a vital decision: the refinement they had inhaled from their classical training should be applied to the previously impromptu art of the dance band. Their creation, the Paul

Whiteman Orchestra, would beguile America and then Europe, establish the template for the 'sweet' dance sound that dominated the 1920s and 30s, and – in the opinion of subsequent critics and fans – cause lasting harm to the reputation of jazz.

> Those who like his music refuse to patronize a dance hall and mingle with the masses; while dance hall patrons won't pay $2 to get into a Whiteman concert.
> *New York Clipper* newspaper, 1922

> Paul Whiteman was known as the King of Jazz and no one as yet has come near carrying that title with more certainty and dignity. He 'dressed her in woodwinds and strings', and made a lady out of jazz.
> Duke Ellington

It was unfortunate that the self-styled 'King of Jazz' bore a striking resemblance to comedian Oliver Hardy, and that his nickname became the title of a 1930 movie which belittled the race who had given jazz life. Paul Whiteman was certainly not the King of Jazz, or its inventor; nor, despite the crude animations of monkey-like 'natives' in his controversial movie, was he a racist. By his own account: 'All I did was to orchestrate jazz. If I had not done it, somebody else would have.' Whiteman's tragic flaw was combining the trappings of a jazz dance band with acutely tasteful orchestrations. He emerged with a sound that was highly commercial, creative, coherent, filled with gorgeous melodic and harmonic touches – and amounted to a travesty of jazz.

His most successful recordings were his earliest: sides such as 'Whispering', 'Japanese Sandman' and 'Wang Wang Blues', each of which borrowed the novelty elements of the first white jazz bands and coated them with lush romanticism. With his 1921 rearrangement of a Rimsky-Korsakov theme, 'Song of India', Whiteman's work shed even its token allegiance to jazz, and anticipated the purveyors of 'easy listening' music. By 1923, melody had supplanted rhythm as his music's most potent ingredient. Yet Whiteman also introduced two of the most significant American performers of the era: Bix Beiderbecke and Bing Crosby. And as proof of what could be achieved in the abandoned ground between popular music, light music, jazz and classical, there was Whiteman's 1932 recording of Ferdie Grofé's *Grand Canyon Suite*, part overture, part blueprint for one of songwriter Jimmy Webb's most expansive late 1960s ballads.

It was Whiteman's epic grasp of American music that made him perhaps the only possible collaborator for a young man in his mid-20s who, like Whiteman, had been thrilled by jazz, but wanted to paint on a larger canvas. Jacob Gershvin – better known today as the anglicised George Gershwin – was a genius who by his twentieth birthday had recorded hundreds of player piano rolls, and composed the 1919 stage musical *La-La-Lucille!* He wrote 'Swanee', a hit for Al Jolson, and unconsciously echoed Scott Joplin in his ambition to base an opera on 'Negro' music.

Gershwin first met Paul Whiteman in 1922, on the set of a theatrical revue. The following autumn, he staged an ambitious recital in New York at which he mixed contemporary American songs (including his own) with modernist classical pieces by the likes of Arnold Schönberg. Gershwin's fearless presentation inspired Whiteman to pursue his own cross-fertilisation of styles: a concert performance which would demonstrate the validity of music he described as 'symphonic jazz'. The bandleader laid out his argument: 'I intend to point out, with the assistance of my orchestra, the tremendous strides which have been made in popular music from the day of discordant jazz, which sprang into existence about ten years ago from nowhere in particular, to the really melodious music of to-day, which – for no good reason – is still called jazz.'

Gershwin agreed to provide a new 'symphonic' piece for the event, which had been christened 'An Experiment in Modern Music'. He then forgot about the commission until three weeks before the event, whereupon he concocted a medley of themes, which he titled *American Rhapsody*. It was his brother Ira who suggested the more painterly description: *Rhapsody in Blue*.

The debut of this haunting and episodically brilliant union between the serious and the popular followed less than two weeks after the belated American premiere of an even more dramatic intervention in the narrative of twentieth-century music, Stravinsky's *The Rite of Spring*. Yet *Rhapsody in Blue* did not mark a revolution in the language of music, as Stravinsky's work had done: Gershwin was merely toying with its colour, adding distinctively American (and notably African-American) tones to the European concerto form. He remained ambivalent about the nature of his experiment, remarking the following year: 'I do not think that serious music will ever be influenced by jazz, but it is quite probable that jazz will be influenced by serious music.' The reviewer in *Time* magazine was alarmed by the prospect: 'Jazz music is descending into the final pit of banality by becoming serious.' Whiteman was defiant, declaring that jazz was 'the only true American musical art'. Gershwin's 'jazz concerto' was incorporated into his repertoire, and the Whiteman orchestra sold more than a million copies of *Rhapsody in Blue* split over the two sides of a twelve-inch 78 rpm single (though it had to be trimmed and performed at breakneck tempo to fit on to one disc).

Whiteman's New York presentation is now remembered solely for its Gershwin premiere. Yet the bandleader intended it as a radical manifesto: a bid to rescue jazz from its raucous, undignified origins in the brothels and bars of Storyville, and establish his 'symphonic' variation as its natural successor. He began his recital with what was intended to be a mocking revival of the ODJB's 'Livery Stable Blues', and was alarmed when the audience greeted it with enthusiasm. The programme also included two arrangements of Whiteman's first hit, 'Whispering': one wildly syncopated and ragged; the other gentle and sophisticated, violins to the fore. He politely signalled which of these the audience should find more worthwhile.

Composer and critic Virgil Thomson complained that when Whiteman approached jazz, he had 'smoothed its harshness, taught elegance to its rhythms, blended its jarring polyphonies into an ensemble of mellow harmonic unity ... He has suppressed what was striking and original in it, and taught it the manners of Vienna.' He might have added: in Whiteman's jazz, there was little room for the music of black America, except as folklore which could be refined into literature. By sidelining the saucepan-and-can clatter of the ODJB in favour of elegant flourishes and smooth rhythmic transitions, Whiteman had created music that did not unsettle any potential audience. He had, effectively, dressed the youthful rebellion of jazz in sensible adult clothes.

With this move, Whiteman seemed to have repaired a schism that briefly separated young and old. Vaudeville and music hall were intended for adults, but their songs and (with some risqué exceptions) comic routines could appeal to the entire family. The high jinks of the ODJB and their peers were definitely designed to thrill the young, and outrage everyone else. Even amongst the hottest of jazz aficionados, music did not represent an alternative culture or lifestyle; it was merely a diversion, like all forms of entertainment, from the grind of daily life. (For those in the privileged position of not being subject to the indignities of full-time employment, it was the social whirl of jazz dancing, rather than its soundtrack, that constituted their milieu.) In Whiteman's symphonic jazz, however, there was scope for dancing, for casual listening, and even for the concert hall.

His example was followed by hundreds of dance bands across the United States. The leading protagonists had enormous followings in their time, but today their names – the likes of Vincent Lopez, Paul Specht, Leo Reisman, Isham Jones, Nat Shilkret and Fred Waring – are little known. Paul Whiteman loomed large over them, in every sense: besides his lavish personality and physique, he became a genuine celebrity, pursued by crowds of admirers. When he returned from a visit to Europe in 1923, his liner was greeted by a vast gathering of worshipful musicians, some of them even taking to the water to signal their appreciation. Yet his rivals were stars in their own right, profiled in popular magazines, their wives and children regarded with reverent curiosity.

An entire industry was created to promote them, as they crossed America playing one-nighters. Between their dances, variety shows and occasional recitals, they made records – hundreds of them, the top bands often releasing three or four double-sided discs per month. Freshness was everything, as bands required a constant input of songs. During the early 1920s, it was rare for a dance band to make a vocal recording; balancing the sound of an orchestra in the days before electrical recording was challenge enough, without trying to squeeze the human voice into the 'mix'. But on the road, the most promising singers on the bus would be encouraged to set aside their instruments for a song or two and serenade their audience.

Bandleaders also seized upon novelties – clip-clop percussion, horns that mimicked animals (a throwback to the 'Livery Stable Blues' days) or fire sirens, a number that would allow a section of the orchestra to don fancy hats or blow swanee whistles: anything to send the crowd away with a smile. There was no ethos of constant musical progression in this world, no sense of setting a bold course for the future as the pioneers of jazz and rock did in the decades after the Second World War. Any revolution in sound or stagecraft was almost accidental, intended to boost the bottom line at the expense of their competitors. Yet the music did change, most obviously because the average size of a dance band gradually expanded.

The ODJB had thrilled or scandalised people with just six players; by 1926, Whiteman was touring with almost thirty, many of them doubling on a variety of brass and woodwind instruments, and half a dozen offering a sumptuous wash of violins.

Each band had its trademark effects, each arranger his signature blend of instruments. Yet their repertoires were often strangely similar, just as every Liverpool beat band in 1962 worked slight variations on the same material. They would all draw upon the finest songs to emerge from Tin Pan Alley, and a dozen outfits might simultaneously record the key song from a new Broadway musical. Top outfits were inundated with manu-scripts by hopeful publishers, however. Each week, for example, London's Savoy Orpheans were sent several hundred new songs. At any point, the band could reproduce as many as 1,000 different numbers without needing to consult a score. (Among them was Gershwin's *Rhapsody in Blue*, which their leader recalled was 'coldly received'.)

Cast adrift amongst thousands of dance-band records from the 1920s, the unwary listener of the twenty-first century might struggle to locate individuality or any reliable method of assessing quality. Some songs – those still acclaimed as standards, having survived nearly a century – leap out, thanks to their familiarity; the rest blur, unless they offer the qualities of spontaneity or rawness that we have come to expect from jazz and rock. But even when these recordings appear to have been mass-produced from a single blueprint, it's easy to see what held their audience ninety years ago. Each three-minute performance introduces a recognisable melody and a danceable rhythm, and handles both with just enough variety to keep the ear engaged, and feet in motion.

The prevailing mood was, as Selvin's Novelty Orchestra put it in 1920, 'Dance-O-Mania', and by the end of 1921 more than half of America's best-selling records would have been classified as 'jazz'. The remainder spanned an almost unimaginably broad chasm, from Sam Ash's tribute to the late Enrico Caruso ('They Needed a Song Bird in Heaven'), to Zez Confrey's rag piano showcase, 'Kitten on the Keys' – perhaps the first instance of an outmoded style being revived for the sake of a nostalgia-hungry audience. In place of the square-footed balladeers of the Victorian and Edwardian eras, the new entertainers were those with pizzazz. For Al Jolson, every song was an invitation to incite his audience to tears or laughter; Fanny Brice, with 'My Man' and 'Second Hand Rose' in 1922, staked an early claim to Broadway immortality; Sophie Tucker turned blues and jazz into performance art; and Eddie Cantor tripped through his comic songs as if, in the end, nothing really mattered that much. One moment he was pretending to be outraged about immigrants, in 'The Argentines, the Portuguese and the Greeks'; the next, the inanity of Tin Pan Alley itself was in his sights, with 'Yes, I've Got the "Yes We Have No Bananas" Blues'. He even provided some political commentary in 'Oh Gee! Oh Gosh! Oh Golly I'm in Love!', revealing: 'I feel as weak and useless as a German mark'. Not that the market for familiar pleasures had died: there were always comic duets from the likes of Ernest Hare and Billy Jones (whose 'Does the Spearmint Lose its Flavor' lost its own flavour, when it was covered by Lonnie Donegan thirty-five years later) and Billy Murray and Ed Smalle. In the summer of 1923, when jazz and the strange agony of 'the blues' were in keenest vogue, the Irish baritone John McCormack rekindled the mood of his distant youth with a rendition of Sir Arthur Sullivan's 'The Lost Chord' so refined that everything around him must have sounded appallingly intrusive.

Yet it was jazz and the blues that increasingly held sway in America, as record companies struggled to comprehend that the market for their wares was not single-minded. Many college students relished the warmer varieties of jazz, to the extent that Ivy League Cornell in upstate New York banned its prize athletes from dancing, lest they exhaust themselves in all-night frenzies. The soundtrack to these orgies might be provided by the ODJB's 'Bow Wow Blues', on which their dog imitations eventually triumphed over their jazz licks, or the Club Royal Orchestra's homage to the sizzling Valentino film, *The Sheik*; or one of the bands who aimed themselves shamelessly at the college audience, such as Fred Waring's Pennsylvanians. While it was acceptable for young men to rag, jazz and scamper around the dance floor, women needed to heed the warning offered by Henry Burr's 'Just a Girl That Men Forget', in which party-fuelled flappers were advised that when it came to marriage, boys would brush them aside in favour of 'an old-fashioned girl with an old-fashioned smile'.

Burr remained silent on the likely fate of female vaudeville stars, who explored the nascent blues genre with the same gusto their male counterparts displayed when flirting with jazz. Queen of the white blues singers was Marion Harris, whose 'I'm a Jazz Vampire' from 1921 celebrated her intoxication while striking a moral tone that would become familiar in subsequent decades: 'I am all the evil music has'. Irving Berlin offered a pastiche of the style with 'Home Again Blues', which was phrased with authentic blues feeling by Aileen Stanley, and more decorously by Frank Crumit.

None of these performers could hope to rival the African-American blues for emotional commitment and rugged jazz accompaniment. Mamie Smith may have recorded first, and Ethel Waters fused the style with theatrical sophistication, but neither of them matched the presence of Bessie Smith. She debuted with 'Down Hearted Blues' in 1923, accompanied solely by Clarence Williams's piano, and this recording alone would be enough to brand her name indelibly into the history of music. She was a performer at heart, an entertainer without shame; she could walk a high wire over the whirlpools of the heart, letting her audience slip into the maelstrom below. Then, to illustrate that jazz and the blues expressed the same emotions, she ventured into the open melodic terrain of ''Tain't Nobody's Biz-ness if I Do', with such precision that it made her chaotic piano accompaniment irrelevant.

Such spontaneity was a hallmark of African-American jazz. In the summer of 1925, Bessie Smith revived that touchstone of black music, 'St Louis Blues', dragging out the tempo as if she had a slide trombone between her lips and another locked around her feet. Behind her was the melancholy drone of a harmonium; skipping between them, dancing around the melody like a sprite, was a 24-year-old trumpet player named Louis Armstrong. He had first recorded two years earlier with King Oliver's band, as they rampaged like hooligans through the likes of 'Dipper Mouth Blues', and would shortly shape jazz in his own image for eternity. He shared the madcap energy and reckless enthusiasm of his generation: the men in Mamie Smith's or Ethel Waters's bands, for example, who borrowed their leaders' names to make such wild records as 'Royal Garden Blues' (on which every musician soloed at once, like Cream at the Fillmore in 1967) and 'Spread Yo' Stuff'.

Clarence Williams echoed their approach when he returned to ''Tain't Nobody's Biz-ness' a few weeks after Smith. His Blue Five stretched the jazz credo to the limit: rather than laying out the tune, and then repeating it with carefully scheduled variations, like the white bands, they barely alluded to it, and then went their own merry way. Not content with trampling joyously across a song that would become a blues standard, they left room for a rhythmic device which had become a sensation on the dance floor in African-American clubs, and would, when carried into polite society, arouse charges of immorality more heinous than those already raised against jazz itself.

The trouble with the modern girl is that she never knows when to stop, and does not stop to think, but lives in a constant whirl of excitement, turning night into day, until her whole vitality is sapped, and she is reduced to a nerve-wracked neurotic condition.
  Letter to *Daily Mirror*, 1925

We ought to consign jazz to a hotter place than this earth . . . It is bootleg music . . . Let us not try to reform jazz, but to stamp it out – to kill it like a rattlesnake.
  Baptist minister Dr John Roach Straton, New York, 1926

In 1927, Commander Kenworthy, a Conservative Member of Parliament, was defending the rights of moneylenders in the House of Commons. It was true, he admitted, that some people were driven to their graves by the debts they amassed. But he had heard of many instances of death by excessive dancing, and he believed that several fatalities could be attributed to the Charleston alone. (Pause for laughter from the honourable members.)

His political wit was scarcely more outrageous than the other claims made against what was, after all, nothing more than a dance step. What made the Charleston so appalling ('the most disgusting thing I have ever witnessed', so my grandmother was told by her father) was that it encouraged young women – unmarried women – to move their bodies in ways that were positively lascivious. Some even loosened their undergarments before attending a dance, to ensure they could enter fully into the frivolity. From this stemmed every evil that could attend a virgin in such circumstances: not only would she writhe provocatively in front of strange men, but she might begin to experience feelings that were indecent, at best, and should be reserved for those safely committed to matrimony. No wonder that the Charleston was often banned, and that some American universities were said to have prohibited it on architectural grounds, for fear their ancient buildings would crumble beneath a mass display of this monstrous agitation.

The cause of this farrago of exaggeration and myth was nothing more devilish than a melody from a Broadway revue called (appropriately) *Runnin' Wild*. 'The Charleston' was first recorded at the end of 1923 by the black bandleader Arthur Gibbs. Not only was it heavily syncopated, but it was studded with pauses and breaks, which shook the dancer off balance (and on to the off-beat). For anyone raised on the predictability of the waltz, or even the foxtrot, its zigzag rhythm was like altering gravity. Within a year or two, the Charleston was forgotten, as its detractors struggled to come to terms with the next outrage: the black bottom. The stomp was equally maligned: even a sympathetic critic could only describe it as 'a nigger's shuffling step with knees bent'.

This fresh outbreak of aberrations rekindled the opposition of all those who abhorred the African-American (or indeed African) influence. Jazz, said a London columnist, was the noise of 'savages', some of whom 'still live in trees'. The rector of an Oxford college preferred to blame Satan for the 'Nigger music', adding for good measure: 'Our civilisation is threatened by dreadful noises, horrible motor-traffic, Americanisms and jazz music.' It was fortunate that he does not seem to have witnessed the Charleston. According to classical musician Sir Henry Conrad, jazz and its 'attendant immodest dances' threatened the basis of the entire British Empire: 'Coloured races can no longer think the European a super-man, when they find him delighting in the banging of pots and pans and the braying of trombones, and observe him capering with the female of his species to these dissonances. So they cease to respect him and Imperial rule decays.' (The jibe about 'pots and pans' was still being employed against jazz when Hungary relaxed its ban on the genre, after Stalin's death in 1953.)

It was ironic that these sweeping generalisations about black culture coincided with what was known retrospectively as the Harlem Renaissance. This involved a flowering in African-American art, literature, political discourse – every facet that made up a modern culture. The poet Langston Hughes, whose first collection was entitled *The Weary Blues*, wrote: 'We younger Negro artists who create now intend to express our individual dark-skinned selves without fear or shame. If white people are pleased we are glad. If they are not, it doesn't matter. We know we are beautiful. And ugly too.'

The leaders of what was then known as the New Negro Movement were uncertain whether jazz was beautiful, or ugly. While it was at root a form of black folk art, it was troublingly commercial in nature. Did it show off the Negro at his most progressive? The answer, in retrospect, is blindingly obvious, as evidenced by the pianist, bandleader and composer Duke Ellington. For almost half a century, Ellington led an orchestra of various shapes and tones through arguably the most eclectic catalogue of music ever attributed to a single name: dance tunes, ballads which soon became part of the standard pop repertory, celebrations of black identity, jazz suites, film soundtracks, 'sacred' music concertos and exhibitions of jazz musicianship which represented every salient style from 'hot' to swing to bop to cool. Though he ran his band with military organisation, he was a generous leader when it came to spotlighting the talents at his disposal (even if he sometimes pocketed their copyrights). His was not a band of fiery spontaneity, like Clarence Williams's Blue Five or Mamie Smith's Jazz Hounds: he preferred improvisation to occur within the carefully composed intricacies of his scores. A case in point is the record from summer 1927 which introduced him to a mass audience, 'East St Louis Toodle-Oo'. Its selling point was, ostensibly, the muted cornet which seemed to speak to the listener. Only with repetition was it apparent how subtly the orchestra was arranged, and how its other voices were aired within those constraints.

Throughout the late 1920s, the Ellington band were regulars at the Cotton Club in Harlem, an establishment that demonstrated why there were misgivings about the cultural value of jazz. This was no backstreet dive of dubious repute: it could hold 700 customers across two dance floors, and played host to celebrities as diverse as Ernest Hemingway and the Marx Brothers. Unfortunately, all those celebrities were white, there to experience not only the glories of Ellington but also the 'ethnic' trimmings – a backdrop which evoked the Deep South of the slave era, barely clothed (black) dancing girls, and comic skits which reduced the black man to his African roots. Worse still, as one of Ellington's biographers noted, 'The venue's exclusionary policies and excessive prices barred blacks from the club, except for the rich and famous, and even those visits were rare. There existed a separate section for the black families of performers.' This was not so much a renaissance, Ellington aside, as a caricature.

Few ever dared to criticise Ellington for demeaning his black identity (except perhaps after he devoted an album to the songs from the Disney film *Mary Poppins* in the mid-1960s). Sadly, that fate could not be avoided by the jazz performer who was the polar opposite of Duke in almost every sense: Louis Armstrong. His genius was instinctive rather than ordered, like Ellington's; his playing was raucous and sometimes excessive, where Duke's was cool and restrained; his stagecraft was flamboyant and comic, while Ellington was the epitome of genteel dignity. Armstrong was criticised, both by his own race and (especially) by white jazz critics, on all these grounds; he was accused of 'Tomming'* when he showed off by hitting dozens of high notes in succession at the climax of his performances, or mopped his brow constantly between solos, or hammed up his stage dialogue and facial mannerisms. The audience that applauded these antics, so his detractors said, did not appreciate jazz; they simply relished a black man playing the fool. Nor were his critics impressed by his willingness, from the 1930s onwards, to record white pop tunes – somehow failing to notice that what he did to that repertoire was often a living definition of jazz itself.

Others were equally scathing about another facet of Armstrong's work: his scat singing, his pioneering use of his distinctively earthy voice to improvise riffs and runs as eloquent as anything that came from his cornet. And that instrument was the most significant in jazz history. It enabled him to create a new kind of jazz, in which the dense collective interplay of an ensemble would give way to the individual voice of an instrument; jazz as a personal statement, or as a succession of the same, if the musicians were capable of taking up the challenge. The shift was evident on 'Muskrat Ramble', the 1926 hit by his Hot Five which introduced his name to a national audience. Vamping around a melody that would carry a notorious anti-war anthem by Country Joe & the Fish forty years later, Armstrong's quintet collectively laid back while each in turn handled a chorus, a structure that revealed talents and flaws with equal clarity.

This wiped away at a stroke the old ethos of bands in New Orleans, where it was the interlocking of parts and the building of counterpoint that represented the body and soul of the music. It required the refinement of recording techniques (especially the electrical revolution of 1925) to make the change possible. But more than that, it needed an ego large enough to wrest control of the music, and a talent commensurate with that sense of ambition. Armstrong had both. With instrument and voice, he could do anything: improvise with the spontaneity of a child, construct epic solos like an architect, make music into a personal language.

His Hot Five and Hot Seven recordings of the late 1920s – especially

---

* Or being unduly subservient to the white man, after the leading character from Harriet Beecher Stowe's 1852 novel, *Uncle Tom's Cabin*. It did not aid Armstrong's reputation amongst jazz aficionados that he declared his passion for grand opera, and for the sweet sonorities of Guy Lombardo's white-bread dance band. But these choices demonstrated his ability to find pleasure in music beyond his own milieu, with an openness rarely shared by his most ardent followers.

the likes of 'Potato Head Blues', 'Hotter Than That' and the high-wire act of Clarence Williams's tune 'West End Blues' – remain among the most revered jazz recordings of the century. For some, they stand as the summit of the art form; others prefer the smoother but more mature recordings Armstrong made in the following decade. Those were the years when he tore apart 'St Louis Blues' with a ferocity that mixed the promise of Bill Haley's rock 'n' roll from 1954 with the vocal bravado of Bob Dylan from 1966; toyed with Hoagy Carmichael's famous 'Star Dust' melody like a tiger with a mouse; and sauntered through 'Rockin' Chair' (Carmichael duetting at his side this time) and 'Lyin' to Myself' with the insouciance of a king. Along the way, he dropped seeds which grew into swing, R&B, rock 'n' roll, trad jazz, even perhaps bebop, besides providing a role model for everyone from Bing Crosby and Frank Sinatra to Miles Davis and Jimi Hendrix. If Paul Whiteman was the interior decorator of popular music in the 1920s, Louis Armstrong threw open the door to everyone, whether or not they'd wiped their boots clean, or could even afford shoes at all.

The subsequent history of jazz has its moments of seismic shift, one of the most convulsive not occurring until the 1940s. After Louis Armstrong, however, jazz no longer belonged to groups, but to soloists. The virtuoso couldn't usually perform alone (pianists excepted); at the very least, he required a rhythm section. But the artists who commanded the loyalty of an audience, mass or cult, were the mavericks and maestri who could transcend their surroundings within the briefest of solos. Sometimes, as at the height of the swing era, several of those room-busting talents could be contained within a single band. More often, especially after the Second World War, all that the audience required was one instrumental genius: the role of his sidekicks was to set him up, and then keep out of his way.

Armstrong's fluency and daring enabled his peers and even his mentors, such as Fletcher Henderson and rag-piano pioneer Jelly Roll Morton, to cut some of their hottest jazz sides from the mid-1920s onwards. His influence also slipped over the racial border. Within the context of a dance band, for example, Eddie Lang could introduce the guitar as a viable jazz voice on Red Nichols's 'Washboard Blues' and Frankie Trumbauer's 'Singin' the Blues'. His accomplice on the latter was Bix Beiderbecke, a trumpet player who drank himself to death in 1931 at the age of 28. His friend Jimmy McPartland recalled that Bix could never repeat a solo the way he had recorded it. 'It's impossible', he was told. 'I don't feel the same way twice. That's one of the things I like about jazz, kid. I don't know what's going to happen next. Do you?' Bix's unaffected spontaneity won him a coterie of dedicated fans, which transubstantiated into a cult after his early demise. Bix topped the pantheon of white instrumentalists whose contributions, however brief, to dance and jazz records in the late 1920s and early 1930s were relished and debated. Their lustre quickly spread to Britain and Europe, where in the 1950s aficionados would still be arguing over exactly which Paul Whiteman tunes Bix had graced with a few seconds of his magic.

In the early weeks of 1928, some of the most remarkable American music of the era was released simultaneously, like a banquet in which every course appeared on the table at once. George Gershwin was in his prime, serving up such eternal songs as 'The Man I Love'; Jimmie Rodgers was setting out on his first 'Blue Yodel'; Bing Crosby establishing himself as the most mellow of jazzmen; Hoagy Carmichael satirising his own jazz obsession with Paul Whiteman on 'Washboard Blues'; crooners, torch singers (Ruth Etting's 'The Song is Ended' effectively defines that genre), hillbilly harmonisers – the whole gamut of American popular genres raising their flags in unison. Forcing their way to the front of this crowded stage were Bix Beiderbecke and His Gang with 'At the Jazz Band Ball', the leader for once outgunned by the baritone sax of Adriani Rollini, who sounded as if he had seen 1956 on the distant horizon and wanted to attract its attention. But there was another Bix on offer: the piano soloist of 'In a Mist', a composition that leaned upon the ragtime tradition but entered some realm of transcendent beauty which makes analysis irrelevant. Had he lived, he might have explored this landscape again; instead he left only the map for this solitary excursion, a tantalising glimpse of what jazz might have become, had Erik Satie rather than Louis Armstrong been its guiding spirit.

'In a Mist' wasn't just a snapshot of a musical genius in repose; it was also a stunning illustration of everything that technological innovation had made possible. Five years earlier, only the harsh echoes of Beiderbecke's piano would have survived on to disc. By 1928, musicians had entered a world in which sophistication and subtlety no longer had to cede centre stage to cacophony. Three years earlier, engineers had perfected the art of electrical recording, and ushered in one of the most dramatic reversals of mood in the history of popular music.

⚡

'An innovation of this kind must be regarded by the smaller and lesser known dance bands as a serious menace to their existence.'

Gramophone magazine, 1925

CHAPTER 5

WIZARD
OF THE
MICROPHONE

'A cheap dance record that does not sound cheap is what we want. Fox-trots have so short a vogue that we grudge the large sums we have to spend on unnecessarily long-lived records.'

Gramophone magazine, 1923

The innovation was the Academy Gramophone Amplifier, one of a series of transformations in the way that records were manufactured and heard. Not for the last time, an entire generation of comfortingly familiar appliances and discs was rendered obsolete without warning. The Victor and Columbia record companies, who shared the licence for electrical recording via microphones, schemed to keep their new technology a secret from the public until the last possible moment, fearing that consumers would stop buying records while they waited for the revolution to occur. Scientists boasted about their inventions, journalists echoed their self-congratulation, and the public divided between those who leapt towards the future and those who clung loyally to the past. The British novelist Compton Mackenzie, who doubled as editor of *Gramophone* magazine, declared that his wife found the 'new noise' of electrical recording 'quite unbearable', but that he had grown to enjoy it, 'which may or may not be a good thing'. By 1930, he was of the opinion that 'I do not believe any audience could sit still and listen nowadays to hours of electrical recording, and remain sane' – a charge that would be repeated in the digital age.

'Let It Rain, Let It Pour' by the International Novelty Orchestra (featuring operatic tenor turned American folklore balladeer, Vernon Dalhart) is often cited as the first release of the electrical age, but two weeks earlier, in late February 1925, Victor had concocted 'A Miniature Concert', effectively an eight-minute variety show featuring their most popular vaudeville artists, though they delayed releasing it for five months. The biggest stir, in every sense, was aroused by a bizarre but technically superb recording of 'Adeste Fideles' (alias 'O Come All Ye Faithful'), by the Assorted Glee Clubs of America, almost 5,000 vocalists in all. Several hundred thousand Americans hurried to purchase this Christmas carol at the height of summer, a triumph of marketing as well as technology. In Britain, the breakthrough in sonic fidelity was reserved for lighter fare: 'Feelin' Kinda Blue' by the bandleader Jack Hylton in June 1925.

What was the impact of electrical recording? According to an advertisement for Brunswick Records, it offered 'Sound Photographed on to a Record! . . . There are no "gramophony" noises whatsoever. Just pure sound with the value of every voice or instrument reproduced exactly.'

Tones that had been buried or distorted by primitive recording methods, such as instruments at the bass end of the scale or high female voices, were recognisable at last. Listeners were amazed by the 'immense loudness'. No longer would bandleaders or engineers have to restrict their arrangements in servitude to the recording process. Now they could place music at the top of their agenda, and leave the rest to the technicians.

The electrical revolution provoked a more subtle realignment of thinking about music which passed the general public by. Bandleaders were now free to construct a collage of sounds that was not quite artificial – the musicians were there in the studio, after all – but which was certainly a form of fiction, rather than pure documentary. The days had gone when the only concern was to place the musicians so that their contributions could be picked up by the recording horn. (Louis Armstrong remembered that when he made his first recordings, his leader King Oliver would set him ten feet behind the rest of the band, because he played so loudly.) Now the advent of microphones and amplifiers enabled musicians, and what would soon become known as 'record producers', to paint textures of sound that would be almost impossible to replicate, with total fidelity, before an audience. This knowledge came slowly, and, like Eve's fatal bite of the apple, it could not be taken back. There were many in later decades who bemoaned the loss of the old spontaneity, when the alternative was musicians devoting painful hours or even days to tapping a snare drum or striking a single piano note over and again, while engineers tweaked knobs and applied a feather's touch to faders in the hope of achieving the fool's destination of the 'perfect' sound. There was now no such thing as an 'authentic' recording of a musician; every reproduction of a performance was idealised and imaginary, whether or not it matched the expectations of its makers.

The process of manufacture extended beyond the constituent musical parts. The record-makers realised that with a dextrous arrangement of sounds, they could create or enhance a mood that would spark a particular emotional reaction. In later decades, the range of feelings would extend to hatred, disgust and fear, as musicians catered for a youth culture swamped in self-loathing. In the late 1920s and 30s, the emotional aims of the musician and engineer were more positive, if still fabricated: to provoke excitement, joy, romanticism, comfort or the illusion of intimacy. The last of these represented the most striking interaction between music, technology and their willing accomplice, the listener. It introduced the musician, most often a vocalist, as the audience's friend, lover or even potential seducer.

Having been virtually absent from dance band recordings in the early 1920s, singers had begun to slip almost unnoticed into the formularised three-minute dance arrangements that were issued by the dozen every week. Their role was to add variety to a band; they were simply another feature, no more important than a trumpet solo. The vocalist seldom received credit on the label of a dance-band disc; at best, the company might add 'Vocal chorus' in small print as a promise or warning of what was contained therein. To emphasise the singer's lowly position in the proceedings, he or she might have to wait until half of the performance had passed before being allowed a cameo, which would rarely extend beyond a single chorus. (Singers were given more licence on records that bore their name, rather than that of a band.) They didn't emote, but delivered their allotted lines with the restraint of a pre-war BBC announcer, enunciation being considered more important than syncopated phrasing or a jazz sensibility.

After the electrical dawn, microphone technique became part of the singer's toolbox. The vocalist not only had to worry about pitch, timing and being word-perfect; he or she now needed to inspire the appropriate audience response, while infiltrating the ear of the listener without overloading the microphone. Until overdubbing became possible during the Second World War, band and vocalist always recorded together. One of the engineering skills that became most valuable was the knack of presenting a full orchestra alongside a singer who might be whispering the most delicate of sentiments to their imaginary lover, without sacrificing either end of the sonic spectrum. Meanwhile, the singer – once content merely to be heard – came to realise that every note and (potentially) breath issued near the microphone would be reproduced in all-too-graphic detail for millions to hear. Vocal power was no longer the sole requirement for stardom; warmth and dexterity were equally telling, and the purest, most perfectly pitched of singers would lose their audience if they could not connect with them on an individual basis.

In 1924, the American passion for anything redolent of Hawaii resurfaced in the form of a renewed obsession with the ukulele.* For British

---

* To be strictly accurate, the instrument popularised in the Great War was actually an American offspring of the original Portuguese instrument, named the banjulele. It was said to be an especial favourite of the Prince of Wales, who in 1926 was 'particularly partial' to a ukulele ditty named 'Save Your Sorrow'. 'Such a title', a *Melody Maker* reviewer noted, 'is bound to appeal to his sunny temperament.' On such deference was the British Empire built.

listeners, the instrument kindles inescapable memories of George Formby Jr. He was the son of a famous Lancashire comedian whose trademark was a hacking bark, followed by the doleful line: 'Coughing better tonight; coughing summat champion.' (Many music-hall careers were based on less.) After he suffered a fatal throat haemorrhage, Formby Sr's name and repertoire were revived by the younger George. He worked the banjulele into his act and then found that his audiences insisted upon it. By the Second World War, his mock-innocent range of risqué comic songs, all delivered to the ferocious strumming of his 'uke', had made him one of Britain's best-loved film stars and variety turns. The innuendo of his punchlines, mostly revolving around phallic symbolism and voyeurism, concealed the almost jazz-tinged fluency of his ukulele solos, invariably delivered with the grin of a gargoyle. This disguise did not always protect him from censorship: in 1933, 'discretion won the day' when the release of Formby's bawdy 'With My Little Ukulele in My Hand' was abruptly cancelled.

The uke's role in American music was far more restrained. A year before electrical recording was first used, Frank Crumit's 'Say It With a Ukulele' – promising romantic success to anyone who could master the four-string shuffle – brought a new style of vocalist into the popular idiom. Cliff Edwards, otherwise known as 'Ukulele Ike', seized his moment, and prepared for the new era with his whimsical 1924 performance of 'Somebody Loves Me', sounding uncannily like an ancestor of the country-rock pioneer Michael Nesmith. Indeed, a whole parade of late-1960s troubadours – John Sebastian, James Taylor, John Denver – can trace their emotional and musical heritage back to the new melodians of the mid-1920s.

While Edwards stretched himself to imitate horns amidst his playful love songs, his rival Gene Austin (notably on 1925's 'Yearning') demonstrated that it was possible to be a jazz singer without demonstrating the least affinity with African-American music. If one man can be classed as the father of jazz phrasing in white pop, it is not Bing Crosby – who was arguably the master of the art – but Austin, for whom the sometimes derogatory but entirely accurate epithet 'crooner' was invented. He and Edwards sparred their way through the remainder of the decade, offering a mixture of romance, vaudeville showmanship and uncanny vocal control. Edwards's gallop through 'Singin' in the Rain' perhaps showed him to best effect, while Austin's 'Bye Bye Blackbird' epitomised his devastatingly easy charm. Gene Austin had another weapon at his disposal, however: his white spiritual tune, 'End of the Road', was delivered with a tired reverence that was beyond his peers.

America was now awash with singing idols who didn't need to raise their voices to capture an audience – one that was predominantly young, female and avid. There was the cowboy crooner Nick Lucas, who helped to popularise an instrument rarely heard before in popular music. 'Why not learn the guitar?', prompted a British reviewer of Lucas's oeuvre in 1926. 'It is a coming instrument for dance work.' Another exemplar was the 'whispering pianist', Art Gillham, who played a cross between blues and ragtime piano, and anticipated the rampant egotism of rock 'n' roller Jerry Lee Lewis in the way he told himself to 'play it pretty, baby'. He was soon trumped in the barely-breathing stakes by Whispering Jack Smith (not to be confused with his 1960s Whistling namesake). His forte was sounding like a Yankee twin to the British writer and cabaret artiste Noël Coward; his voice was so clipped and hushed that it was as if he were standing behind the record-buyer and mumbling suggestive nothings into her ear. On stage, he adopted 'a really confidential attitude', draping one arm casually over his piano as if he were in the back seat of a cinema, and accompanying himself with a minimum effort of the right hand. There were dozens more of lesser personality, now long forgotten: Chester Gaylord, Charles Lawman, Smith Balleur, Seger Ellis . . . even a British contender or two, such as Sam Browne and Maurice Elvin, who was known on these shores as 'the wizard of the microphone'.

The definition of 'crooner' soon stretched sufficiently to encompass any singer of a romantic disposition. Foremost among those was Arthur Tracy, universally known as 'The Street Singer'. Though he was clearly operatically trained, threatening hearing loss to any modest damsel into whose ear he might roar, he attracted a fervent female following, first in his native America and then in Britain, where he was a regular feature in the popular weekly magazines. He posed for cameras and pen-portraits as a wandering hobo of the accordion, and it seemed not to affect his reputation in the slightest when it was revealed that he had never sung in the streets, and did not actually play the accordion heard on his records.

By early 1927, there was even a female crooner in tow: Vaughn DeLeath (admittedly not the most feminine of stage names for a woman born Leonore Vonderleath).* Like her male rivals, however, DeLeath had

---

* As a demonstration of the importance of understanding the microphone, compare DeLeath's precise control on 'Blue Skies' with the over-modulation of May Alix, Louis Armstrong's duet partner on the contemporaneous 'Big Butter and Egg Man'.

to bow to the paragon of the genre. Paul Whiteman's 'Muddy Water' was a cover of a recent hit by Harry Richman, who was set on stealing Al Jolson's vaudeville crown. After eighty jaunty and uneventful seconds, the melodious waves parted to reveal a 23-year-old singer who gave off a burst of contradictory signals – reticence, sly humour, politeness and an innate sense of jazz timing. This was the solo debut of a young man named Harry Lillis Crosby, who was one half of a vaudeville team called the Rhythm Boys, one quarter of Whiteman's vocal combo, and a performer of whom bandleader Artie Shaw famously said (to the youngster's finest biographer, Gary Giddins): 'The thing you have to understand about Bing Crosby is that he was the first hip white person born in the United States.'

For anyone born in the 1950s or afterwards, it is difficult to square that reckoning of Crosby's talent with the distant memory of a middle-aged entertainer who seemed to lack Sinatra's panache, Presley's physicality or Dylan's insight, to name but three hip white persons from subsequent eras. Bing seemed, to the rock 'n' roll generation, to be a showbiz schmoozer who exhibited a strange distance from his peers, whilst masquerading as their closest friend. Then he died, and various family members testified to his shortcomings as a husband and father. While Sinatra's appeal and presence merely multiplied with age and beyond death, Crosby felt (I don't say 'sounded' because, really, who was listening to him in 1977?) like the most prominent member of a breed that had been rendered irrelevant by the arrival of rock 'n' roll. The rock 'n' roll generation (and this writer, as its guilty representative) didn't know what it was missing. Bing Crosby wasn't merely the ultimate crooner – a category that would soon become the subject of similar derision – but arguably the most influential singer of the twentieth century. His celebrity fans would have concurred: among them Frank Sinatra, Elvis Presley and Bob Dylan.

One of the most enduring of Crosby's achievements was translating scat singing into a tool that could be used by any performer. By 1932, his technique had become so prevalent that the *New York Times* could deplore 'the boys and girls who intersperse the vapid lines of the chorus with a medley of monotonous, meaningless syllables which defy print. These interpolations sound as if the singer had forgotten the words of the ditty and had to fill in with a tra-la. Sometimes they vary it with a whistled bar or two.' So relaxed and inviting was this style that it lent itself to imitation. 'People sing more than they did, and more for their own pleasure than with any thought of an audience', noted a BBC report at the end of that decade. It was now unremarkable to hear someone humming, whistling or scatting a tune in the street, activities that a few years earlier would have made them candidates for an asylum. With a vested interest, the BBC's sociologists declared that the credit for this shift in public behaviour could be claimed not only by the sublime easiness of the crooners – but by the prevalence of the medium that had brought them to the masses: the radio.

Soft, foul, crooner-obsessed Britain . . .
  A. K. Chesterton, propaganda director, British Union of
  Fascists, 1936

Whiners and bleaters defiling the air . . . a degenerate form of singing . . . No true American would practice this base art . . . They are ribald and revolting to true men.
  Cardinal O'Connell, Archbishop of Boston, 1932

At the height of the Second World War – as the first battle of El Alamein raged, and German forces advanced towards the Russian fortress of Stalingrad – the BBC turned its sights on the enemy within. The Corporation believed that the morale of the British public was in its care. The nation's spine needed to be stiffened and straightened. This was not the time for 'flabby' entertainment, which would soften the British will to resist Germany and its allies.

'Male crooners', a senior BBC executive declared, 'are quite divorced from the reality of the times.' Their voices were unmanly, and betrayed homosexual leanings; their songs sentimental and enervating; their demeanour threatened to reduce the British heart to 'slush'. On 21 July 1942, the organisation issued a formal Dance Music Policy, which laid down its guiding principles. At its head was a simple aim: 'To exclude any form of anaemic or debilitated vocal performance by male singers . . . To exclude numbers which are slushy in sentiment.' Several of Britain's leading dance-band vocalists were banned from the airwaves for the duration of the conflict.

Bing Crosby was spared from the BBC's assault. Indeed, his appearance later in the war on the immensely popular radio show *Variety Band Box* was thought to have provided a welcome shot of adrenaline to a public worn down by years of bombing and rationing. It helped that, as his biographer noted, 'Bing's singing was nothing if not virile . . . the Cardinal

O'Connells of the world could never tag him with imputations of effeteness.' Gary Giddins explained the magic of his vocal technique: 'Bing conveyed a chest-tone approach, making full use of his diaphragm.' By contrast, 'Most of his predecessors who were not belters belonged to the genteel school, and sang with effete head tones.'

Foremost among these 'effete' performers was a bandleader whose voice, in the pre-microphone age, had been so slight that he required a megaphone to be heard above the hubbub of his band. In the late 1920s, however, Rudy Vallee* began to appear on a weekly radio variety show in New York, *The Fleischmann Yeast Hour*. In that medium, the delicacy of his vocals became an asset rather than a burden, lending him a sense of intimacy which many listeners found positively erotic – especially his female fans, who could imagine that he was addressing each of them personally. As one historian noted, 'This approach made some people uneasy, and they viewed Vallee and his counterparts as effeminate, as "sissies" who did not project traditional masculinity into the music. But his legions of fans felt otherwise; they loved the image of a man confessing his weaknesses in a romantic relationship.'

Almost immediately, Vallee and his Connecticut Yankees aroused a following that was both fervid and voluble. His fans were almost entirely female, and many of them in their teens, an audience who had never before been targeted with such cunning accuracy. 'Men Hate Him! Women Love Him!', screamed the advertisements for his 1929 film *The Vagabond Lover*. The journalist Martha Gellhorn witnessed this phenomenon as Vallee performed at the Paramount in Brooklyn: 'The audience, except for the few uncomfortable males present, goes mad. A murmur of delight rises like a tidal wave, becomes an envious moan, pants into a yearning sob . . . The woman in the next seat murmurs, "Isn't he the sweetest ever?" Another, behind us, sighs, "That's too lovely to be true" . . . The audience does not slacken in its turbulent enthusiasm. It is enraptured, fanatical . . . He is their darling, their Song Lover.'

---

* His real name was Hubert Vallee, and he adopted his stage name in tribute to a jazz saxophonist, Rudy Wiedoeft. He must surely have calculated the advantages, however, of sharing a name with silent-film star Rudolph Valentino, whose death in 1926 robbed America's young women of their most sexually potent idol. As an aside: one British newspaper declared that Vallee could best be described as a 'blues singer', suggesting that the journalist in question had never heard a blues record.

Such ecstatic devotion was stirred solely by Rudy Vallee's persona on radio, which was now an essential vehicle for anyone who wished to rival his success. Bing Crosby accompanied Paul Whiteman's orchestra on many broadcasts, before winning his own nationally networked Columbia Broadcasting show in 1931. Its success was instantaneous: within weeks he had begun a lengthy season of performances at the Paramount theatres in Brooklyn and on Broadway, where fans were perhaps less frenzied than they had been around Vallee, but proved to be more enduringly loyal. So concerned was the NBC network by the impact of Crosby's CBS programme that they scheduled another crooner showcase, starring Russ Columbo, immediately afterwards. Only a bizarre shooting accident in 1934 cut short the youthful Columbo's advance on Crosby's crooning crown.

The radio technology pioneered by Marconi at the birth of the twentieth century was initially assumed to be an extension of the telephone, transmitting messages to an audience beyond earshot. By 1910, however, records were being broadcast in several major US cities. Within another decade, the first officially licensed transmitter (beaming station KDKA) began broadcasting from East Pittsburgh, and could be picked up by amateur radio enthusiasts across the Atlantic.

Crooning and radio grew in tandem, fuelling each other's rise. More than news or features, the public wanted entertainment. Broadcasters quickly learned that the medium lent itself to a gentler style than that appropriate for a vaudeville theatre. While the airwaves of Britain and the BBC were placed under government control in 1927, America was the home of sponsored broadcasting. Top entertainers would act as the mouthpiece for any company or product that purchased their services. The limitations of technology, and the slightly invasive act of entering people's homes, combined to make certain forms of music more acceptable to the masses than others: hence the popularity of the soft-voiced crooners, who could bring warmth to the most solitary of listeners. To enhance the illusion that they were the audience's friends, they were given affectionate nicknames, so that Little Jack Little was known as the Friendly Voice of the Cornfields and, more exotically, Joe White became the Silver-Masked Tenor, his true identity a secret for many years.

Radio could convince millions that an entertainer was performing for each of them alone; it turned music, and especially the art of the crooner, into a private act of communion. It was more seductive than listening to a record, because not only could the performers be heard to speak, but their voices seemed to come into the room as if by magic – without the fantasy-shattering necessity of winding up a gramophone or placing a needle on a record every three minutes.

Radio could create its own stars, who often had to perform in public under pseudonyms invented by their sponsors – the Mono Motor Oil Twins, for example, or the Interwoven Pair (also known as the Happiness Boys, or in pre-radio days as Billy Jones and Ernest Hare). It also boosted the careers of dance bands, especially after the mid-1920s, when technology made it feasible for live performances to be broadcast; and, from 1928 onwards, these programmes could be heard across the United States, as local stations were 'hooked up' to form national networks. While comedians complained that too much radio exposure killed their prospects as live performers, because audiences had already heard their gags, dance bands competed for airtime, confident that their popularity would be multiplied by the kudos of broadcasting.

It was not enough to be heard on the radio, of course; one had to be enjoyed. Just as crooners provided superior (and 'easier') listening than strident baritones or piercing sopranos, 'sweet' bands were greatly preferred to their 'hot' counterparts. As the head of the Davey radio network explained in 1932, 'The constant jar and rasping of irritating sound that is sometimes called music has a tendency to put the nerves on edge. If one turns his radio on for a whole evening and hears nothing but slam-bang jazz, his nervous system is likely to be in rebellion. It seems to me that one of the most desirable qualities of a radio program is restfulness, which causes one to lean back in his chair and be comfortable while listening to the music. A little stimulant is all right, but modern people need a larger proportion of the soothing qualities of entertainment.' Those who were employed to judge the aesthetic quality of music might often disagree, but the majority demanded smooth, melodious sounds. Radio was in effect an uninvited guest, which had to mind its manners and quell its idiosyncrasies to avoid being asked to leave.

A decade earlier, the French composer Erik Satie had imagined a form of music that would 'mask the clatter of knives and forks without drowning it completely, without imposing itself'. Simultaneously, a former brigadier general from the US Army conceived the idea of music as a form of social control, dampening any urges towards rebellion or subversion. The two thoughts were combined in 1922 when the North American company Wired Music Inc. began to pipe a blend of music and news reports into subscribers' homes. Rather than relying on records, with their risk of aural stimulation, Wired Music assembled its own library of suitably sedated dance music – taking familiar tunes, and rearranging them so that nothing would grab the audience's attention. The company offered its programming to hotels, shops and restaurants, matching the mood of their selections precisely to the ambience it was designed to create. By the mid-1930s, this service had assumed a more recognisable name, coined by combining the words 'music' (for its content) and 'Kodak' (to denote modernism): the Muzak Corporation.

Compton Mackenzie had taken note of radio's changing role. 'There was a time when dance music was played by the BBC under the impression that people danced to it', he wrote in 1934. 'That delusion has long been cured. Dance music has become the staple noise emanating from a loudspeaker.' But BBC radio had another task: adhering to the strict ethical principles of its supremo, director general John Reith. Here there was no commercial criterion to satisfy: listeners might have preferred a constant diet of light music, dance bands and crooning (although the latter two categories would have appalled those who regarded themselves as mature adults), but Reith's strictures ensured that first they had to endure performances of operas, symphonies, concerti and other forms of 'serious' musical enlightenment. There were programmes aimed at children, and at adults, but nothing before the 1950s that might appeal specifically to those aged between (say) 12 and 25. Morals had to be carefully safeguarded, forcing the banning of all material likely to corrupt, shock or even mildly disturb the tiniest portion of the public. All references to commercial products were banned; so too songs (such as 'Love For Sale') which hinted even vaguely at the existence of sexual relations. For a while, Reith even refused to allow the titles of songs to be mentioned when acts were performing, in case that might be interpreted as a form of advertising. In later years, equally arbitrary restrictions were briefly imposed: a rationing on the proportion of American compositions, for example; a cull of vocal records, which were taken to be a distraction for the audience; and, consistently into the 1960s, an outright ban on any popular song that dared to take its melodic inspiration from a classical theme.* This act of artistic

---

* The Swedish Music Academy warned in 1961 that it was illegal to release pop interpretations of melodies by Edvard Grieg. Offending items were marked in the Swedish radio archives with a death's head stamp, to ensure that they weren't broadcast.

outrage was held to be offensive to all persons of taste. At any moment of potential conflict, the highbrow was always favoured over the populist. And, of course, no popular music at all could be aired on Sunday evenings.

Regardless of these barriers, the BBC did create and maintain stars every bit as enduring as those fostered by the American networks. As in the US, the 1920s and early 1930s were the era of the dance band. Few of the American outfits ever performed in the UK, especially after disputes between the respective musicians' unions halted the transatlantic trade in everything but variety entertainers between the early 1930s and the mid-1950s. So Britain nurtured its own talent; much in thrall to the American originals, it was true, but also boasting distinctively local attractions.

While many members of the leading American bands harboured secret ambitions to play jazz, which could be satisfied with a discreet four-bar solo between the choruses of a popular melody, jazz might not have been discovered at all had the quest been left entirely to the British dance bands. Fads and gimmicks took months or even years to cross the Atlantic. Tunes travelled more quickly, especially if aided by theatrical revues or (from 1930 onwards) films. But there was still a distinct lag between the two cultures, which could mean that – in a slightly later era – the boom in American swing bands would not be echoed in Britain for the best part of a decade. Many British vocalists sang as if they were wearing the dinner jackets and black ties demanded of the BBC's newsreaders and announcers. But whether or not they betrayed any hint of jazzy arrangements and 'hot' playing, the British bands supported a culture that enveloped the most aristocratic and lowly in the land in an orgy of dancing.

Only the richest and best-connected personages on the social scene could expect to hear the Savoy hotel bands in their natural habitat. The nation's top bands played hotels and nightclubs in London's West End, because the financial and reputational rewards were so obvious. But beyond the Monseigneur and the Café de Paris, vast crowds were drawn to dance halls, where they were admitted for a few pennies that wouldn't have bought them a soft drink at the Savoy, while in small towns and villages couples shut their eyes and whirled the foxtrot or the waltz to the sound of a radio or gramophone, imagining themselves 'up West' in the company of the Prince of Wales and his chums. As jazz historian Catherine Parsonage explained, 'The dance hall was the only form of entertainment that could rival the cinema and public house [and which] gave women the opportunity to go out and enjoy themselves.' The licence allowed to women during the First World War, then gradually withdrawn in the first years of peace, was seized back, never to be relinquished.

Magazines such as *Radio Pictorial* (but not the BBC's more reserved *Radio Times*) spotlighted the personal lives of Britain's most prominent bandleaders, without ever the hint of scandal. Not that the genre was short on personalities. By far the most popular London band was led by Jack Hylton, the biggest-selling British artist before the Beatles. He knew the value of self-promotion, flying several members of his band around Blackpool Tower at the height of the summer season in 1927, and dropping leaflets on holidaymakers below to publicise his latest release, 'Me and Jane in a Plane'. Hylton gauged the changing times by studying the sheet music for all the latest American hits, and then applying what he called mysteriously 'the British touch' for his native audience. With a repertoire that extended from Gilbert and Sullivan's musical comedies and light classics to songs from London's hottest revues, he set out to appeal to all possible tastes without veering too dangerously close to the 'nerve-torturing riot' of jazz.

Billy Cotton (still the host of a TV variety show in the 1960s) built his reputation on his mastery of all the latest dances, and was a particular favourite of the ubiquitous Prince of Wales. While Cotton could barely disguise his anger when His Royal Highness insisted on taking over the drums, all London's leaders knew that the royal imprimatur was a guarantee of success. The suave and sophisticated Ambrose (son of an East End rag-and-bone man) encouraged the young royals to attend his performances at Ciro's or the Café de Paris. If you weren't a royal, then Ambrose was less welcoming: while his band was a hotbed of musical talent, and his name a watchword for smooth entertainment, the leader was prone to lambasting his public on the slightest provocation. As his fellow bandleader Ted Heath recalled, 'a person felt honoured if Ambrose deigned to reply to him; to be insulted by him was the accolade of social success'.

With the royals, of course, deference took precedence over self-expression. As bandleader Jack Payne explained, 'Royal interest can obviously be of untold value to a band, but woe betide any pushy young person who is foolish enough to presume. The Prince of Wales has sometimes asked me to play certain tunes – when "Two Little Worlds" was popular, he would sometimes like to have it played seven or eight times in an evening – but because he might do one the honour to come up and speak to one, it does not give one the right to ask him what he thinks will win the Derby.'

Embarrassing the prince was also an appalling faux pas: Geraldo, who made his reputation as the leader of the Gaucho Tango Orchestra at the Savoy, and offered what the British assumed was an authentic blend of South American rhythms, had to reveal himself as an East Ender called Gerald when HRH spoke to him in Spanish at the 1933 Royal Command Performance. Such subterfuge was common: Bertini was actually Bert Gutsell; Alfredo, with his band of gypsies, was Alfred Gill; Chaquito was Johnny Gregory; and Waldini was known to his mum as Wally Bishop.

For a genuine taste of the exotic, dancers could relish the sound of the bandleader who billed himself initially as Leonelli Gandino, but enjoyed more success between 1926 and his death in 1980 as Annunzio Mantovani, from Venice. His flair for publicity put Jack Hylton to shame. He claimed to own a 200-year-old instrument, which he christened 'the Violin of Death' because it had been 'cursed with evil power'. To reinforce his reputation as the Alice Cooper or Ozzy Osbourne of the 1930s, he recounted how he had been hired at great expense to play at a private supper party. So private was the engagement, indeed, that only his host was present, demanding to hear a series of classical melodies. When Mantovani appealed for a break after an hour or two, his patron is said to have flourished a knife, and shouted 'Continue! There is a singing bird within you, and if the bird dies, I must stab it!' As Mantovani told the story, he might have been playing to this day had neighbours not burst in to rescue him. All of this was hardly in keeping with the light orchestral repertoire that was his reliable stock-in-trade, but it sold records and dance-hall tickets.

Magazine readers of the era relished the exploits of Harry Roy,* who devoted several years to courting a princess from Sarawak in Borneo, whom he had met at a Mayfair party. Their long-distance affair delighted the public, especially when he proposed by mail, prompting 'Princess Pearl' to make the perilous eight-day journey to London by flying boat to accept. They were subsequently seen together in the 1936 musical film, *Everything is Rhythm*. Harry Roy enhanced his fame by riding an elephant down London's Oxford Street to publicise an appearance at the Palladium.

---

* Roy's patron, Felix Mendelssohn, proved to be equally adept at influencing the public, falsely claiming to be a relative of the nineteenth-century Romantic composer. He formed the Hawaiian Serenaders, boasting that they hailed from the South Seas, with the aim of converting the UK to the delights of the steel guitar and the hula dance, although most of his musicians had a strangely British appearance.

In all the dramas surrounding the British bands of the 1920s and 30s, however, there was nothing to match the fate of Bert Ralton. His Havana Band (no more Cuban than Geraldo was Argentinian) secured a lucrative booking in South Africa over Christmas 1926, after which Ralton went on safari. While hunting game in the bush, he stepped backwards against a rifle held by one of his companions. It discharged, causing a fatal leg wound. As he lay bleeding on the ground, Ralton is said to have asked for his ukulele and sung repeated choruses of Irving Berlin's ballad 'Always' until he fell unconscious.

It is tempting to imagine that in the same situation, Jack Payne would have reserved his last moments of consciousness for cursing everyone around him. Between 1928 and 1932, he was the irascible leader of the BBC Dance Orchestra, which was in effect the national dance band. His outfit was invited to perform over the air so regularly that they amassed 650 hours of live broadcasts in 1931 alone. Payne believed that there was virtually no audience for jazz (a prejudice in which he was supported by both record sales and opinion polls in the UK), that 'Many a tune has gone to its grave through being too complicated', and that the infallible judge of a new song was an errand boy: if he whistled it, it was a hit. Despite enjoying an audience which was predominantly female, Payne had little time for women: it was 'pointless' for them to sing in front of a band, he declared, while he claimed to 'loathe and abominate those sickly letters which some women send me'. The culprits were apparently 'foolish flappers and silly spinsters'.

Perhaps because of his unpredictable temperament, Payne was replaced in 1932 as Britain's most influential musical personality by his polar opposite: the bespectacled, nervous, modest Henry Hall. Whereas Payne would probably have spanked any children within arm's reach, Hall realised that they might be listening to the radio, and ensured that he added suitable material to his broadcast repertoire, such as the perennial 'Teddy Bears' Picnic'. When the BBC broke with Reithian tradition by allowing him to introduce his own numbers, his unassuming charm and gentle voice enchanted the public. He became something of a national idol, celebrated (as indeed Payne had been) by a hastily assembled feature film, *Music Hath Charms*. The sense of familiarity which he inspired in his listeners was evidenced by a letter sent to him from Aberdeen: 'Dear Mr Hall, Will you please get your band to play louder, as my batteries are run down.'

All of these bandleaders, and dozens more, mirrored their American counterparts by maintaining a fiendish schedule of live performance, radio broadcasts, and recording. Jack Hylton, for example, accumulated his 7 million disc sales between 1923 and 1930 by making literally hundreds of records during that period – although none of them came remotely close to challenging the 750,000 sales of the Savoy Orpheans' 1926 coupling of 'Valencia' and 'The Student Prince'.* While many of the American bands commanded a loyal British following, the reverse was rarely true: Hylton and Hall made a passing impression on the US market, but it was the record rather than the band that appealed.

Such was not the case with Ray Noble, who like Harry Lauder in the vaudeville era, and the Beatles three decades hence, carried a distinctively British sound across the Atlantic and persuaded sceptical Americans that they had something to learn from the old country. He was, said the magazine *American Music Lover* in 1935, the 'Jazz-King of England', although the title was scarcely accurate; indeed, Noël Coward congratulated Noble on creating a dance sound that did not rely on ragtime and jazz. Cambridge-educated, Noble was recruited by HMV in London as both a classical pianist and dance-band arranger, the former skill assumed to assist the latter. By his late 20s, he was functioning not only as a bandleader, songwriter and studio arranger, but also as the company's recording manager, overseeing music from grand opera to low comedy. He led the company's house band, the New Mayfair Dance Orchestra, some of whose members were (according to the publicity department) polo players who regularly turned up for recording sessions in jodhpurs. Not that Noble required such PR gimmicks. As an American profile noted, while most bands based their success on 'the constant use of certain mannerisms of orchestration and rhythm' or 'the more or less potent physical allure of the leader', Noble's secret was 'a guiding musical intelligence of an exceptionally high order ... Here, at last, was a dance band which one might be certain of being able to listen to without insulting one's intelligence.'

Every aspect of Noble's work attracted praise, from the sonic clarity of his recordings (only possible in Britain, American reviewers insisted) to the sophistication of his arrangements – the subtle strokes of tone and colour with which he could enrich the most hackneyed of material. Amongst

---

* The most popular record in Britain during the inter-war period is believed to have been 'Hear My Prayer' by the Temple Church Choir, with more than 800,000 copies sold. William MacEwan's 'The Old Rugged Cross' (1929) also outsold all but a handful of 'pop' releases during this era.

his generation of British arrangers, only the maverick Reginald Foresythe could match his delicate use of a dance band: emotions were described and released with gentlemanly control, in keeping with his near-aristocratic image. (He played up to his 'posh' origins with a dry version of Irving Berlin's 'Slummin' on Park Avenue', castigating his neighbours' vowel sounds in appalled tones.) The buried eroticism of genteel romance was often apparent in his songs, three of which – 'Goodnight Sweetheart', 'Love is the Sweetest Thing' and 'The Very Thought of You' – have passed into the 'standards' repertoire.

High among the Noble band's attractions in the 1930s were the vocal talents of Al Bowlly, remembered today as Britain's only viable rival to the American crooners. He was born in East Africa, and then apprenticed in South Africa, India and finally Germany before reaching London, and working with several of the era's finest bands. To modern ears, Bowlly's style can sound both stiff, like a Victorian balladeer, and as flexible as Sinatra, with an easy physicality which enhanced his sex appeal. Noble and Bowlly intended to take America by storm in 1934, but were prevented by union rules from importing their entire British band – the equivalent, perhaps, of Lennon and McCartney being forced to recruit American backup for *The Ed Sullivan Show* in 1964. Instead, Noble assembled a union-approved outfit which never quite matched the dexterity of his British crew, though it did provide the young trombonist Glenn Miller with a rapid education in arranging and band-leading.

Beyond the bands, Britain's most successful export was one of the last great stars to emerge from the music halls: singer, actress and comedian Gracie Fields. Like Al Jolson, she began her career as a pre-teen 'stooge' for an older performer, planted in the audience so she could 'spontaneously' deliver the chorus of Lily Turner's songs. 'This worked well', her biographer recounted, 'until an irate theatregoer took her for a heckler and hit her with her umbrella.' Given star billing at the age of 13, Fields built a lasting career out of her self-deprecating Lancashire humour, command of sentimental balladry, and apparent ability to synthesise the emotions of ordinary working folk. The British public relished her often saucy comic songs, especially when – as in the opening monologue of 'In the Woodshed She Said She Would' – she pretended to find them disgraceful. It was a rare talent who could sell novelties such as 'Let's All Go Posh' and 'What Can You Give a Nudist on His Birthday?', and then reduce an audience to tears with a mournful tale of lost love. 'Poor Gracie,' her record company lamented in a promotion for a song entitled 'He Forgot to Come Back Home', 'tearful and lonely, destined to be the plaything of fate – and wicked men. Take her, neglected and forgotten, to your heart . . . and she'll give you half-a-crown's worth of honest glee every time you put the record on. Which will be very, very often.' This pleasure-through-pain rhetoric resembled the way in which blues records were being sold in America. An authentic taste of Gracie's 'everywoman' appeal was provided by a set of three 78 rpm discs made before an audience at the Holborn Empire in October 1933, one of the earliest 'live' recordings.

On her initial trip to the US, Fields was billed as 'The Funniest Woman in the World', to the bafflement of those who could not decode her Lancashire accent. She recalled an embarrassing encounter with George Gershwin, who was the designated host for a New York show-business party in her honour: 'There were lots of film stars there, and he was playing some of his own music on the piano. So I thought, "I'll just show off and sing it with him." I started to sing the song with him, and I suddenly got nervous in the middle and forgot every word. He was quite interested in me at the beginning, but when I forgot the words he looked at me with disgust. I felt proper daft!'

If Gracie Fields traded on her fans' feeling that they might encounter someone just like her in the corner shop, the radio also intro-duced them to music that sounded strangely, even dangerously, alien. While the BBC's entertainment was carefully moderated to reflect Britain at its most reserved, * more diverse fare was offered by the Continental stations which could easily be picked up by a short-wave set. Based in Luxembourg, Normandy, Paris, the Côte d'Azur and dozens of equally exotic locations, their programmes were sponsored, just as they were in America, by the manufacturers of such strange products as Zam-Buk (a herbal balm) and Bile Beans, an all-purpose pick-me-up which promised: 'If you want to hear how young you're looking, begin by taking nightly doses of Bile Beans.'

While much of their output sounded sufficiently mild to appease BBC executives ('Sea Shanties', 'Songs with a Guitar', 'Some Old-Fashioned

---

* In 1939, the BBC tried to straitjacket its bandleaders, by issuing them with a list of thirty-two songs, from which they had to select at least 40% of their output. This anticipated the Top 40 playlists of future decades, but proved so unpopular with musicians and public alike that it was dropped after a month.

Dances'), other programmes were more daring. Radio Paris offered the Murphy Minstrels with 'A Real Nigger Minstrel Show'; Radio Normandy sampled the sounds of the steppes with 'Balalaika Songs'; and Radio Luxembourg's 'Plantation Love Songs' series promised that the listener would 'Hear the nightingale singing down the old tobacco road and the Baccy Pickers over in their shanties', with no American slavery-era cliché left untouched.

The unchallenged king of esoteric broadcasting in the Europe of the mid-1930s was Carson Robison. Oxydol detergent presented his weekly show, declaring: 'There's romance in the far, far West.' Robison was the self-declared 'Hillbilly King', the aural equivalent to the cowboy heroes of the early talking pictures. 'I spoke the language of the country folk, who snapped 'em up and played my records every Sunday night (their night off) as regularly as they read the Bible', he explained to his English fans. 'Then city folk got the hillbilly craze.' It was a craze rooted in the ideals of the distant past, and brought to life by the most modern of inventions: the radio transmitter.

⚡

'I'd lower the volume on the radio and put my ear right up against it. The music I heard became the best thing in my life. Daddy didn't like that. "You're wasting your time, listening to them old records on the radio," he'd say. "That ain't real, you know. Those people ain't really there. That's just a guy sitting there playing records. Why'd you listen to that fake stuff?"'

Johnny Cash

CHAPTER 6

BLUES IN THE NIGHT

'Hill Billies are the most incorrigibly lazy mortals it is possible to meet ... The greatest difficulty is to keep them quiet while recording. There is much scraping of boots, and usually after the third verse the artist wishes to clear his throat, with commendable thoroughness, and spit very audibly. Many waxes are spoilt also by the "artist" refusing to stop when the end of the record is reached.'

Cyril Ricketts, folklorist, 1931

Record companies originally called them 'Old Familiar Tunes', unable until the Second World War to find a valid description for the music of white rural America. 'Hillbilly' was one label that stuck, though (like the N-word in hip hop) it was an insulting term applied to country folk by outsiders and only adopted by performers with a mixture of defiant pride and (here the rap comparison fades) self-deprecation. The song-collector John A. Lomax named his 1910 anthology *Cowboy Songs and Other Frontier Ballads*; Cecil Sharp's research in Kentucky and Tennessee yielded *English Folksongs from the Southern Appalachians*. Both those strands contributed to the multifaceted genre that became known (but only after 1945) as country music, or country and western, or even 'folk'. But by the time the folklorists reached the American South, the 'purity' that they hoped to discover in the region's music had already been tainted by countless other influences, black and white, popular and traditional. After radio reached the mountains, prairies and swamps of rural America, 'hillbilly' singers (and their African-American equivalents) would be just as likely to entertain their friends and neighbours with show tunes and vaudeville novelties as with anything that could be traced back to their forefathers.

Similar problems had been experienced by Cecil Sharp and his peers when exploring the folk heritage of Britain. They had chosen not to document or preserve any song with a commercial root, opting for the supposed purity of 'traditional' material. (Moreover, many collectors bowdlerised lyrics that were bawdy or likely to offend polite ears.) There was a certain doomed majesty to the process, as the poet and collector Alfred Williams conceded in 1923: 'The songs themselves, as far as singing goes, are practically defunct. There is no need to revive them. To do so, in fact, would be impossible. It is also desirable. We live in a new age, almost in a new world . . . Let us, then, be content to say that folk-song is dead.' But Williams insisted that the old songs should be saved, 'not for their artistic or strictly literary value, but in order to have records of that which amused, cheered, consoled and so profoundly affected the lives of the people of an age that has for ever passed away'. There was a sense of *noblesse oblige* within this impulse: of educated men preserving the culture of those too ignorant to perform the service themselves. Most American collectors adopted a somewhat less puritanical and patriarchal attitude towards the material they gathered.

To avoid the denigrating connotations of the H-word, performers from the rural South would accentuate the heroic qualities of cowboys and mountaineers, traditions which were rooted in a kind of fact and which could be cleaned up and polished for national and (later) international consumption. Tempting though it is to imagine that the pioneers of the blues and country were inspired only by an excess of emotion, both traditions quickly extended beyond local entertainment into a form of career structure. Rural musicians, toting a banjo, fiddle or guitar, would travel from community to community, with commerce on their mind, as country-music historian Charles Wolfe explained: 'Many of the songs were printed on small cards about the size of a postcard (still called "ballet cards" by old-timers), usually signed by the composer or singer; rural minstrels wandered through the mountains singing at rural courthouses and making some money by selling their ballet cards for a penny or a nickel each.'

In 1923, radio station WBAP in Fort Worth broadcast ninety minutes of old-time dance music by fiddler Captain M. J. Bonner, eliciting more telegrams and calls of appreciation than any previous presentation. Thus began the tradition of the radio barn dance, reaching an early pinnacle with the launch of the *Grand Ole Opry* from WSM in Nashville two years later. These shows were self-consciously 'old-timey' from the start: their appeal was to the entire family, especially those old enough to imagine that they remembered when mountain music and cowboy ballads were heard at every fireside. The advent of radio sparked a passion for old-time fiddlers – boosted, ironically, by that pioneer of mass-production engineering, Henry Ford, who reckoned that rural fiddle tunes could calm the immorality of the iniquitous modern age. The star fiddlers, as determined by nationwide contests, were showcased on the *Opry*, initially alongside brass bands and vaudeville stars, until primitive market research determined that the audience preferred their music to sound as if it came from their own kind.

There was a field of opportunity in the old-time milieu for anyone brazen enough to reap it – for Vernon Dalhart, in particular, with his mid-1920s rural ballads describing train wrecks, or prisoners' laments. The first of these, 'The Prisoner's Song' (1924), is estimated to have sold more than 6 million copies.

The tradition was inaugurated when folklorist Ralph Peer journeyed to Atlanta in 1923 to record Fiddlin' John Carson's 'The Little Old Log

Cabin in the Lane'. The song had been familiar for decades; modern technology's freshest inventions were being used to deliver comfortable nostalgia. Radio (and, in time, electrical recording techniques) might have been invented to display the fireside intimacy of such performances, and the second half of the decade produced such unlikely star performers as Gid Tanner & the Skillet Lickers, a prototype string band, whose 'John Henry' seemed to have been cut amidst a moonshine orgy; and Uncle Dave Macon, the self-proclaimed 'King of the Hillbillies', who travelled the South in a horse and cart when everyone else was using a Model T Ford. His cart carried an advertising slogan: 'Uncle Dave Macon, Slowing Down But Still Moving. Old Time Religion, Old Reliable Way, My Gasoline Consists of Corn, Oats, Whip and Hay.'

Radio exposure ensured that Uncle Dave would never be short of his 'gasoline'. Such determined primitivism was clearly a trademark of rural authenticity for the 'hillbilly' audience: why else would Vernon Dalhart record a series of disaster ballads (floods, train wrecks, the death of Rudolph Valentino) with a deliberately out-of-tune guitar? Ralph Peer criss-crossed the South in search of talent to tap into Dalhart's huge audience, and in Bristol, Tennessee he uncovered two of the most influential American acts of the century. The Carter Family was a trio made up of husband, wife and wife's sister (who was conveniently married to A. P. Carter's brother). The sister was 'Mother' Maybelle Carter, widely credited with inventing a style of country guitar picking that is still prevalent today. Her brother-in-law, A. P., was, like John Lomax and Cecil Sharp, a song-collector. He was also a canny entrepreneur, who mined the collective memories of the towns and villages that the Carter Family visited, uncovering 'traditional' melodies and lyrics which he updated for a modern audience – carefully claiming the composing credits and royalties for himself. Soon he was being sent such material through the mail, a mix of age-old oral tradition and modern efforts in the same vein, all of which was incorporated into the Carter Family songbook. The trio's backwoods harmony singing, naïve but unaffected, has survived virtually unchanged into modern Americana, a genre that pays passionate homage to the Carters' memory.

Ralph Peer's other 1927 discovery was too idiosyncratic to be imitated so widely. Jimmie Rodgers (alias 'The Singing Brakeman') was, in the opinion of 1930s–40s country star Alton Delmore, 'simply the greatest. There has never been one man in the whole history of entertainment that packed the wallop he did by himself. There have been good singers, good players and performers that have made great hits with the public and made millions of dollars. But there has never been one man with a single instrument that could sing and play like he could.' Had Rodgers not been felled by tuberculosis in 1933, aged just 35, he might have carried his fearless blend of hillbilly sentimentality, cowboy swagger, blues emotion and (his trademark) Alpine yodelling into the mainstream of rock 'n' roll and beyond, as the white equivalent of a Muddy Waters or John Lee Hooker. But in a six-year recording career, his procession of 'Blue Yodel' songs conjured up the image of the lonesome troubadour, patrolling the prairies with his guitar and dawg for company. (He had no first-hand experience as a cowboy, but he had indeed been ridin' the rails and hoppin' the freights since his early teens.) Rodgers provided a template for the singing cowboys who populated the 1930s, on record or on screen, and for those – such as Bing Crosby – who imitated them so profitably. The cowboy tradition strayed into the mainstream of popular music with Billy Hill's 1933 song, 'The Last Round-Up', the first in a long tradition of western-themed hits which would stretch into the early 1960s.

By recording with Louis Armstrong, and casually sweeping the blues into his music, Jimmie Rodgers blurred the lines between white and black entertainment. He was not alone: the Allen Brothers duo were recorded on location by a Columbia engineer in 1927. He sent their discs to New York, where executives noted that both songs were blues tunes, and promoted the Allens amongst the label's black performers. But the Allens were white, and threatened to sue Columbia for the damage to their reputation. Despite the racial tension and segregation still scarring the US, however, many musicians kept their ears and minds entirely open and free of prejudice. The radio barn dances (notably the *Opry*) were consumed avidly in black and white homes across the South, and such notable contributors to African-American music as Louis Armstrong, Ray Charles and Chuck Berry soaked up as much of the hillbilly tradition as they could.

Yet music made by rural performers of their own race was carefully ghettoised, to prevent black styles and ideas veering in the opposite direction. When Ralph Peer began to record black artists such as Ed Andrews, he was forced to tread warily in the marketplace: 'We were afraid to advertise Negro records, so I listed them as "Race" records.' Even when, in 1930, the blues trio the Mississippi Sheiks blatantly imitated Jimmie Rodgers's style with 'Yodeling Fiddling Blues', their music had no chance of reaching Rodgers's white audience. But this segregation allowed the blues, as it grew from a style into a culture, to spark emotional and physical responses that would have been considered taboo in a more integrated milieu.

> Blind Lemon [Jefferson] and Lonnie [Johnson] hit me hardest,
> I believe, because their voices were so distinct, natural and
> believable. I heard them talking to me.
>   B. B. King

> It's funny how collectors want to know about records. In those days
> [we] just made them and forgot all about it. If we had known the
> interest that those things would arouse today, we would have paid
> more attention.
>   Victoria Spivey

Gertrude Pridgett – known as 'Ma' Rainey after her marriage to William 'Pa' Rainey in 1904 – could command a crowd. 'She wouldn't have to sing any words', poet Sterling Brown told blues scholar Paul Oliver. 'She would moan, and the audience would moan with her ... Ma really *knew* these people.' She'd learned to gauge their temperature at 14, when she first took the stage at an Atlanta music hall. At 19, she was one of the Rabbit's Foot Minstrels who worked a tent show across the South, eventually recruiting the young Bessie Smith to join the company. By 1914, Ma and Pa were an after-hours attraction with a travelling circus: something for the adults to enjoy once the kids had been sent home, when the self-styled 'Assassinators of the Blues' could play out sexual passion and romantic despair for folks who identified with every word.

By the time she recorded 'See See Rider Blues' in 1924, Ma Rainey was 38 – a performer with every inch of her body: flamboyant, charismatic, theatrical, unchained. She invested the song with such desolation that it barely moved at all: voice and instruments, Louis Armstrong's cornet and Don Redman's clarinet, merged into a seamless groan of anguish, a vision of despair that, like the best of the silent films, could convey the story of a lifetime via only one of the senses.

The greatest of the so-called classic blues singers were great actors, as Rainey must have been. They dressed to dazzle, sang to kill or thrill. With few exceptions, the material they sang was generic – albeit from a genre so compelling that many of its songs have survived undiminished for almost a century. Performers could, and did, swap verses from one number to another; repeat lines that tore out an audience's heart; claim ownership (until the copyright lawyers were alerted) of scenarios and phrases that were the shared currency of a generation. What counted was the moan; the catch and flutter; the full-throated roar or half-choked sigh; all the tricks and idiosyncrasies of phrasing which separated Ma Rainey and Bessie Smith from the dozens of other women who were out to seize their thrones in the 1920s.

Blues aficionados often lament Bessie Smith's decision in the late 1920s, when she was struggling with alcoholism and her voice was fraying, to coarsen her appeal with the double entendre of 'You've Got to Give Me Some' and 'I'm Wild About That Thing'. Subsequent critics might have preferred more subtlety, but in the 1920s, only the blues made it possible to admit that sex existed, and make a shameless declaration of how it felt to fuck, and want to be fucked.

It was not only women who laid themselves bare this way. The jocular 'Shake That Thing' by Papa Charlie Jackson from 1925 masqueraded as a dance tune, but Papa's gal must have been a private dancer. More explicit still was 'It's Tight Like That' by Georgia Tom and Tampa Red from 1928, an unashamedly rude set of nursery-rhyme lyrics which could only allow for one interpretation. At a time when the pinnacle of pop eroticism was Ukulele Ike crooning 'I Can't Give You Anything But Love', the blues skipped dinner and the walk in the park and raced straight to the bedroom.

When folklorists and record company scouts set out to discover the 'authentic' black music of the American South in the 1920s, much of what they unearthed was soaked in everyday passion. One of the most successful early field recordings was made in Atlanta in 1927, when Columbia Records documented Peg Leg Howell's 'Beaver Slide Rag' – a rambunctious fiddle and guitar instrumental interrupted by barely decipherable shouts about what animals did in the stall. Impossible to categorise today, pitched as it is somewhere between blues, folk and country, 'Beaver Slide Rag' sold more than 10,000 copies to people who recognised it instantly as their music. Figures such as this persuaded record companies big and small that they should delve beyond the female veterans of tent shows and the vaudeville stage, in search of more varied fare – anything to part black Americans in the country and the city from their dollars and cents.

Each male performer of the late 1920s had his own idiosyncratic route to what passed for fame – $5 advance from a big city record label, and (in the case of an unmistakable hit) enough cash to buy a car. In late 1925,

Paramount Records were alerted by a Dallas store owner to a blind guitarist who played regularly down the street. His name was Lemon Jefferson, but when Paramount took him to Chicago and heard his selection of down-home gospel songs, sung to the accompaniment of his solitary guitar, they renamed him Deacon L. J. Bates. The Deacon then made way for Blind Lemon Jefferson to become the (literally) inimitable father of a new tradition: the blues soloist. B. B. King talked of him in the same way Sterling Brown remembered Ma Rainey: as someone whose plaintive moan expressed the hidden feelings of everyone who heard him. 'I believed everything he sang', King recalled. 'Blind Lemon sang for sinners.'

Jefferson's moaning sounded positively polite alongside the raucous howl of another sightless Texan singer, Blind Willie Johnson. Columbia Records promoted him as 'The new sensation in the singing of sacred songs – and what guitar accompaniment!' He used the neck of a broken bottle to slide across his guitar strings, which let out an eerie, keening counterpoint to his tortured voice. Johnson offered no easy road to salvation: 'I was sick and I couldn't get well', he cried on his first release, which was supported by a song entitled 'Jesus Make Up My Dying Bed'. On the terrifying 'Dark Was the Night – Cold Was the Ground', he stumbled out into a darkness that only a blind man could feel, transcending the lasciviousness of blues or the hope of a second coming with a ghostly, lupine howl of despair.

At the opposite end of the emotional spectrum was Lonnie Johnson, a blues crooner who emerged as the victor of an eight-week singing contest in St Louis, and became one of the best-selling black performers of the century. Future generations revered his guitar playing, which was rich in vibrato, with a fluency matched only by the premier jazz instrumentalists. His contemporaries were sold on his voice, a comforting purr which coated even the bleakest of scenarios in fireside warmth. For the African-American audience of the late 1920s, a hint of urban sophistication trumped the echoes of the cotton fields every time. Hence the success, during his brief professional lifetime, of pianist Leroy Carr: with guitarist Scrapper Blackwell, he recorded the 1928 hit 'How Long, How Long Blues', phrasing as smoothly as Lonnie Johnson. This was the blues that black America most wanted to hear during the era of the Harlem Renaissance: it represented the promise of a less turbulent future, not the scars of a traumatic past.

What made the culture of the city so appealing? For the many thousands of black Southerners who came north to Chicago and Detroit in the early decades of the twentieth century, the city offered the hope of rebirth: financial security, escape from back-breaking labour, and refuge from the lingering shadows of the South's slave tradition. Not that labour was much softer in the north, where factory floors replaced the sun-scorched fields of the Southern states. Nor was the promised land free of prejudice; or, indeed, of violence, as the prolonged race riots in many cities, notably Chicago, demonstrated with fatal consequences between 1915 and 1919. In such an uncertain climate, black people clung to what they knew was true: the Father, the Son, the Holy Ghost, heaven and hell.

While the blues singers offered uncertain redemption, there was more encouragement from their evangelical peers – men such as Blind Joe Taggart, whose blues guitar licks were cleansed by his assurance that those who bought his records could 'Take Your Burden to the Lord', and Reverend E. W. Claydon, who put a bottle neck to sacred use on 'The Gospel Train is Coming'. Gospel quartets (the so-called 'jubilee' singers) brought the sanctity of the church to the phonograph, with harmonies that would eventually reach secular ground via the vocal group boom of the 1940s and 50s. But by far the most popular African-American records of the era confronted their audiences rather than comforting them.

Between 1925 and 1930, much of the newly settled black population of the north chose to fill its brief hours of leisure with the sound of preachers in full hellfire cry. Reverend J. C. Burnett declaimed on the subject of the 'Downfall of Nebuchadnezzer', while his congregation hummed in soulful warning. There was a 'Black Diamond Train to Hell', according to Reverend A. W. Nix, who shouted and groaned like the rawest bluesman from the Mississippi Delta. 'Death's Black Train is Coming', said Reverend J. M. Gates, transforming his lament for the fate of his flock into a passionate gospel chorus. As gospel historian Viv Broughton noted, these records illustrated 'the prevailing atmosphere that encompassed all the extremes of show-business melodrama and religious ecstasy'; and they previewed the ambiguous careers of the tele-evangelists to come.

For those who chose to avoid the preacher's call, there was both sweet and sour fruit. With the death slab revealed in Louis Armstrong's funereal 'St James Infirmary', the mortality of flesh was laid plain. Not that life was any more welcoming: Ethel Waters, stepping gracefully along the border between jazz and the blues, exposed the weight of adult experience on the rhetorical 'Am I Blue?' That was merely the prelude to the much darker colouring of '(What Have I Done to Be So) Black and Blue', a vivid portrait of her race's suffering. With typical insouciance, Louis Armstrong chose to laugh in the face of such truth-telling: he sang all around the melody of 'Black and Blue', as if dismissing the burden it carried, and then let his cornet carry the voice of freedom, as it climaxed with a sustained high note which would become first a trademark, and then a gimmick, in the years ahead.

The most carefree vision of the future, however, came from an Alabama piano player named Clarence 'Pine Top' Smith, who had followed the trail up to Chicago. Late in 1928, he recorded 'Pine Top's Boogie-Woogie', an early celebration of the eight-to-the-bar piano style which, complete with the left hand walking up and down the scale, would become one of the steadfast foundations of rock 'n' roll in the 1940s and 50s. Not content with signposting the destiny of young America, Pine Top stamped his egotism across the tune, firing out dance instructions like a jaundiced drill sergeant: 'When I say "Hold yourself", everybody get ready to stop . . . Boogie-woogie – that's what I'm talking about!' He was Jerry Lee Lewis, glossing every piano solo with self-congratulation; Ray Charles, calling his crowd to 'shake that thing' and 'mess around'; even Ian Hunter of Mott the Hoople, targeting 'you in the glasses' amongst all the young dudes. But he was destined to die in his natural habitat, just three months later, victim of a nightclub shooting. A shock of even greater magnitude awaited America before the year was out.

> The day of the popular record as a big money maker is past.
> *Phonograph Monthly Review* magazine, New York, August 1931

> The public has lost its thrill in record-buying. There is little enthusiasm, and the hope of a return to the previous high figures is still remote.
> *Music Seller* magazine, London, October 1931

'I thought I was building a dream', sang Bing Crosby in 1932, in a timely borrowing from a Broadway show named *Americana*. 'Why should I be standing in line, just waiting for bread?' He was excoriated for delivering anti-capitalist propaganda, but the song in question, 'Brother, Can You Spare a Dime?', provided a rare insight from the creators of American popular music into the prevailing mood of their nation. Al Jolson redressed the political balance by portraying a 'happy hobo' with 'Hallelujah! I'm a

Bum'. But as ever, Louis Armstrong had a more ambiguous response to Armageddon. His 1933 hit 'Hobo You Can't Ride This Train' was playful, exuberant, swinging as if all the carriages were swaying from side to side – and pointed, too, in its exclusion of those without a penny to their name from a train that might just as well have been bound for glory.

The Wall Street Crash of October 1929 wiped almost 40% off the value of American stocks in less than a month. As *Variety* magazine, the daily showbiz newspaper, declared: 'Wall Street Lays an Egg'. The Great Depression, as the financial crisis that afflicted the entire Western world was known, left many millions unemployed, plunged their families into poverty, erased the optimism of a generation, and arguably set Europe on a collision course with the illusory salvation of fascism. It was certainly not the only slump within living memory: the depression of 1893–7 had thrown a quarter of American men out of work. The reason why the 1929 crash passed into mythology as well as history was the abruptness of its arrival, just as America's financial community was boasting that the nation was about to enter a decade of unparalleled prosperity.

In such a crisis, music can offer consolation. Despite the popularity of 'Brother, Can You Spare a Dime?', there was little appetite for grim social realism. But several of the most compelling songs of 1930–1 betrayed America's rickety state of self-confidence. While Harry Richman invested 'On the Sunny Side of the Street' with a young man's carefree zeal, the public preferred Ted Lewis's reading of the lyric as an old man's regret for pleasures that could never return. In such a climate, dignity and decorum had to be sacrificed. Ruth Etting revealed the despair of the overworked dance teacher in 'Ten Cents a Dance', where 'trumpets are breaking my eardrums'. (The lyric by Lorenz Hart included an almost modernist rhyme of '*hero*' and '*queer ro*mance'.) Several months of dire necessity later, Libby Holman – her voice jaded with exhaustion and self-disgust – was offering 'Love For Sale', albeit 'love that's only slightly soiled'.

'There was a kind of desperate urgency that took over all of us in the early 1930s', recalled singer-songwriter Hoagy Carmichael. 'Everyone who could tried to shut out personal loss [and] the depression, and carry on as if the era were to last a thousand years.' As cultural historian Evan Eisenberg recounted, 'poor and rich alike felt shattered, splintered, isolated. What they found in radio, I think, was the solace of solidarity and of predictable, structured time.' More prosaically, radio required a modest initial outlay, and then continued to provide entertainment, week after week, for the price only of batteries or electrical current. Record companies had already viewed radio as a threat to their business when stocks were riding high; now, during capitalism's most profound slump, radio appeared to be smothering their industry in its adolescent prime.

Two days after the crash, Thomas Edison pulled the plug on his own faltering record business, ceasing manufacture of discs, cylinders and the equipment with which to play them. Instead, he concentrated his production lines on radio. Corporations slashed almost thoughtlessly at their rosters, erasing entire divisions which promised to be unprofitable, regardless of individual sales figures. In an industry controlled by whites, black music was a predictable victim: only the most prominent performers, such as Duke Ellington and Louis Armstrong, retained their contracts. Popular singers and sweet dance bands survived; jazz was marginalised. Wall Street's excesses effectively killed the 'classic blues' tradition overnight: when Bessie Smith was asked to record again, in 1936, it was because producer John Hammond felt nostalgic for the pleasure she had brought him a decade earlier. Highbrow classical selections were also dropped in favour of light orchestral pieces and mock-serious arrangements of popular tunes. In 1927, more than 100 million records had been sold in the United States. By 1932, the collective figure had fallen to somewhere between 6 million and 10 million (embarrassment prevented some companies from revealing the depth of their commercial failure).

The more pessimistic analysts of the music business examined the decline in ticket sales for theatrical productions (although the newfangled 'talking picture' bucked the trend), the slashing of profits from sheet music, and the catastrophic collapse of the record market; and predicted that in future their industry would exist merely to service radio. Even that medium briefly seemed to be in jeopardy, as advertising revenues plummeted, and many smaller stations went into liquidation. In such a dark climate, however, radio was a familiar, comforting presence. Many of the biggest names in show business transferred their attentions from the variety theatres to the radio networks, where a single broadcast exposed them to more people than a year of vaudeville or concert performances. The likes of Bing Crosby and Rudy Vallee were now radio stars first, with the movies a close second, and records trailing far behind. There were exceptions to the prevailing gloom: the specialist trades in so-called 'hillbilly' and 'race' recordings weathered the hurricane with more courage than their mainstream 'popular' counterparts. The rest struggled: dance bands set out on ever more treacherous tours of far-flung small towns that they would never have deigned to visit five years earlier, sometimes performing for free in the hope of creating a loyal audience for the better days to come.

Many of the leading record companies in Britain and America amalgamated or changed hands. The Victor label in New York warned its artists that they would only be allowed one 'take' of each song they recorded, to save on studio bills. The same company also led a frenzied death-dance of technological innovation, in the apparent conviction that a change in record size or speed might revive a business that was being enervated by poverty. In the winter of 1931–2, Victor made the prophetic but tragically ill-timed decision to launch a new series of extended-length records, which would play at 33 rpm rather than the industry standard of 78 rpm. The new format would allow symphonies (Beethoven's Fifth was the initial release) to be contained within a single two-sided disc, rather than comprising four or five 78s in an 'album', as in the past. Besides full-length classical works, the longer-playing record – as yet untitled – could collect together all the songs from the score of the new Fred and Adele Astaire musical, *The Band Wagon*. Twenty years later, original cast recordings and anthologies of music from film soundtracks would help to guarantee the success of 33rpm reproduction. In 1931, when few potential buyers could afford the discs, let alone the machines on which to play them, no manner of creative thinking could give the new format life.

If length didn't work, then brevity might, or so Victor hoped. When the Woolworth's chain of stores issued its own brand of eight-inch discs featuring dance tunes, Victor copied the idea, and slashed their price to a dime, making it impossible for anyone else to undercut them – or, indeed, for Victor's scheme to be commercially viable. In Britain, a company named Homophone effectively invented another popular format of the 1950s, the extended play (EP) disc, featuring four songs for the price of two: another bright but doomed initiative. All the while, the established companies were losing profits to the Durium label, which was marketing ultra-cheap, single-sided recordings of current Broadway favourites. They were sold at news-stands rather than in music stores, and briefly commandeered the market, until the major labels persuaded the public that they should pay a little more to hear authentic Broadway stars instead of Durium's bargain-basement nobodies. To accentuate the charisma of their famous performers, labels such as Columbia indulged in gimmicks such as manufacturing records in bright colours, rather than a greyish-black, or engraving them with realistic autographs of the performers in the grooves. In the early 1930s, however, there was an easier way to manufacture stars: by ensuring that they were represented in the medium that was rivalling radio as the Western world's most intoxicating form of entertainment, the talking picture.

> The talking films are going to be a real nuisance. We are going to be deluged with a particularly unattractive form of American sentiment because, with few exceptions, the talkies make their appeal through sentiment and not through wit and humour.
> *Gramophone* magazine, July 1929

At home, and in the synagogue, he is Jakie Rabinowitz: a cantor's son, groomed as his father's successor, to place his voice at the service of Adonai. At night, on the vaudeville stage, he is Jack Robin: serving up sentimental ballads and ragtime for the Gentiles. 'The songs of Israel are tearing at my heart', he declares, 'the call of the ages – the cry of my race.' But the theatre has its own siren call, and for most of the action he is pulled between the secular and the spiritual. When his father arrives home unexpectedly to find him serenading his mother with a jazzed-up rendition of Irving Berlin's 'Blue Skies', full of vim and voo-dee-o-doh, he refuses to acknowledge his son. Jakie opts to live as Jack, until he hears that his father is on his deathbed, and the synagogue has no cantor. Can he still sing the 'Kol Nidre' that will send his father to his rest with a satisfied mind?

This was a movie, so of course he could; faithful to his race, respectful to his family, Jakie can become Jack once more with his mother's blessing, for which she is serenaded with the Oedipal love song, 'My Mammy'. Yet Jack is cursed with a compulsion which proves more telling than the mark of Cain. To become who he is at heart, he must pretend to be what he is not, and don the stage make-up which delights his mother, but will damn his act for posterity.

The movie is *The Jazz Singer* (1927), the first full-length feature in history to include synchronised dialogue; and Jakie and Jack are two of the faces of Al Jolson. We see him adopt another face during the movie: the burnt-cork make-up, exaggerated white smile and curly black wig of the 'blackface' performer.

Like Jolson himself, *The Jazz Singer* was both intensely modern, and a throwback to a minstrel tradition that was already in decline. Sixteen years after his first appearance on Broadway, there was still nobody with Jolson's charisma or panache; nobody who could match the way he threw his arms wide as he sang to encompass the world, and punched home the key syllables of every line. Critics found the film's drama meretricious and banal; but the public lapped up every word (and gesture, during the lengthy silent-film sequences between songs). Jolson's career scaled new heights, and Hollywood reacted predictably by shepherding him through a series of hasty follow-ups, among them *The Singing Fool*, *Say It With Songs*, *Mammy* (with a final reel in Technicolor, no less) and *Hallelujah I'm a Bum*, by which time audiences were reacting to Jolson's trademark cry of 'Wait a minute, you ain't heard nothin' yet' with a jaded 'Actually, I think we have'. But *The Jazz Singer* offered a propulsive boost to his popularity, ensuring that his career would survive the onslaught of the Great Depression.

The tale of Jakie and Jack was far from being the earliest merging of music and film. During the silent era, pianists would improvise an emotionally appropriate soundtrack to what they and the audience were watching, or small bands would perform specially written scores. In many picture houses, the management installed one of the mighty theatre organs that are so redolent of the pre-talkie age: with multiple keyboards and even more multiple 'stops', they acted as a manual precursor to the synthesiser, allowing one man to represent the entire palette and scale of the orchestra. As early as 1894, music publishers concocted what were, in effect, promotional films for their latest offerings. A succession of slides would be arranged to accompany a song, delivered either by a live performer or a phonograph.

The popularity of the silent film, and the increasing vogue for recorded sound, convinced many entrepreneurs and inventors that there must be a viable method of combining the two. In the winter of 1894–5, inventors Thomas Edison and William Dickson combined a Kinetograph camera and an Edison phonograph to produce a sixteen-second synchronisation of sound and vision, Dickson playing an operatic theme on a violin while two men danced uneasily alongside him. In 1909, several leading Broadway stars were filmed while singing their best-known songs, and this footage was screened in a Brooklyn vaudeville theatre while gramophone records of the same songs were played simultaneously. The audience was unimpressed by this early experiment in lip-syncing, because the discs produced insufficient volume to reach beyond the front rows of the stalls. Sonic shortcomings also doomed another Edison venture, the Cinephonograph, which was used in 1913 to capture *Nursery Favorites*, an eight-minute operetta.

Not until 1923 did the physicist and inventor Lee de Forest succeed in using strips of film to document not only visuals but an appropriate soundtrack: a process he dubbed Phonofilm. Around 200 short films of vaudeville and (in Britain) music-hall stars were made and exhibited until the end of the decade, early offerings including *A Few Minutes With Eddie Cantor* (chronicling his collection of mother-in-law jokes), duets by ragtime pianist Eubie Blake and singer Noble Sissle, and a delightful routine by Mark Griver and his Scottish Revellers, whose riotous mix of jazz and comedy included a surreal medley of 'Rule Britannia' and 'Ain't She Sweet'. Business intrigue and battles of ego doomed de Forest's venture to failure, although his invention was effectively borrowed by Walt Disney for pioneering animations such as *Steamboat Willie* (1928), during which Mickey and Minnie Mouse 'performed' the traditional tune 'Turkey in the Straw' on a variety of helpless cartoon animals.

Meanwhile, Warner Brothers were investing in a rival system named Vitaphone, which depended heavily on 'live' recording while filming was in process. Inevitably the microphones sometimes mislaid the voices of the performers, and picked up the whirring of the cameras instead. This revolutionary (according to Warners) innovation was showcased with a gala premiere in New York on 6 August 1926. Guests were treated to a succession of classical performances, interrupted only by a showcase for the multi-instrumentalist Roy Smeck ('The Wizard of the String'), showing off his talents on Hawaiian guitar, banjo, ukulele and harmonica. Two months later, a second Vitaphone presentation featured lighter fare. Its highlight was *A Plantation Act*, a short film featuring Al Jolson in rags and blackface delivering two of his hits plus his latest recording, 'When the Red Red Robin'. Here, encapsulated, was all the Jolson charisma. It might be grotesque, from this distance, racially demeaning, awash with fake sincerity, yet it was still utterly compelling – a testament to the ability of show business to build and sustain illusions beyond sober analysis.

As the *Daily Mirror* noted when *The Jazz Singer* opened in London, and Jolson made his first appearance at the Piccadilly Theatre, 'He has a knack of establishing a feeling of intimacy.' Jolson had been wary of performing for the British public, in case his reputation should be dented by a moment of fallibility. Better, as many of his peers concurred, to capture perfection on screen, and let it tour the world in his place. 'It was made obvious', said another London newspaper, 'that we are on the eve of a revolution in cinematography and that the talking picture will introduce an entirely new type of entertainment that will sound the death knell of the sort of thing to which we are at present accustomed.'

This was entertainment literally larger than life, and for a year or two the spectacle conquered all qualms about the content. In Jolson's wake, a generation of vaudeville stars rushed to duplicate his success. The required ingredients, *The Jazz Singer* seemed to suggest, were a proven entertainer, songs for them to perform, and a luscious coating of sentimentality, preferably related to the deep love between a parent and a child. Film historian Richard Barrios relates that these projects were known sarcastically in the trade as 'mammy pictures', and there were dozens of them, featuring singers such as Maurice Chevalier and Sophie Tucker, whose stage experience enabled them to transcend the limitations of the medium. Less reliable was the songwriting, which – in an eerie preview of Elvis Presley's lame ducks of the 1960s – prioritised quantity over quality.

Regardless of their banality, film songs provided the leading entertainers with a promotional vehicle of unchallenged vitality and reach. Blues icon Bessie Smith and hillbilly pioneer Jimmie Rodgers made short films in 1929 (*St Louis Blues* and *The Singing Brakeman* respectively), which assumed enormous historical value as the only surviving footage of either performer. Without film, too, we would have no evidence of the prodigious and precocious talent of 7-year-old Sammy Davis Jr. In the wonderful 1933 short *Rufus Jones for President*, he is elected US president, with Ethel Waters as the maternal First Lady. By the end of the 1920s, 90% of the best-selling records in America were taken from films, and movie songs also dominated the sales of sheet music. 'Each Talkie', as a critic wrote in 1930, 'has one big theme song; many have four.' But the novelty value of the talking picture was soon exhausted, and audiences began to tire of musical films.

No wonder that a professional observer of the British film market, lamenting the death of the silent era, described 1929 as 'the most upsetting year in the motion picture industry', and groaned that '1930 marked its continuation'. One of his colleagues explained how 'Picturegoers made it quite clear that they objected very strongly to the substitution of screen music for the human orchestra, and many of the biggest cinemas paid respect to the wishes of their patrons by bringing back the orchestra.' There was a concerted campaign to have the reckless experiment with sound and film reversed, and to revive the altogether more artistic silent medium – in which actors were arranged on screen for aesthetic reasons, rather than because they needed to stand next to a microphone hidden in a bunch of flowers. But there were no such qualms about the arrival of the 'talkie' in India, where the first sound film was released in 1931. The following year, the musical *Indrasabha* squeezed no fewer than seventy songs into its 211-minute running time. Movies and musicals were synonymous in India for the next twenty-five years, a period during which only two commercial films abandoned the convention that a story should always be told via song.

American cinema had ridden out the first wave of financial uncertainty after Wall Street's 1929 cataclysm with aplomb, but within a couple of years it seemed to be joining the record business in suffering from the relentless advance of radio. Several extravagant productions were shut down in mid-shoot, among them an epic entitled *The March of Time*. One of its dance routines, a prison-cell sequence featuring the Dodge Twins performing 'Lock Step', clearly remained in MGM's collective memory, as its set design and gimmicks were revived twenty-seven years later in the Elvis Presley vehicle, *Jailhouse Rock*.

By 1934, however, amidst the optimistic climate signalled by Franklin D. Roosevelt's New Deal, the movie musical was back in business. The revitalised American economy was not the only spur to this rebirth, nor perhaps even the most important. Hollywood producers benefited from the fact that the American popular song was enjoying a period of rare riches, focused not on the cinema screen, or the vaudeville stage, but in an arena which the movies had briefly threatened to make redundant: the Broadway musical comedy.

> Dance music is in the thraldom of the musical comedy song; a worse thraldom it is difficult to imagine, not so much because it is alien, but chiefly on account of the miserable degradation of the words of the so-called 'lyrics'.
> *Gramophone* magazine, January 1926

> I just read a magazine article in which he explains the secret of a real song hit. He says when a boy and girl are dancing together and they hear a perfect lyric, the boy wonders why he didn't think of that line, and the girl believes the line was written exclusively for her.
> Dance-band singer Carmen Lombardo on lyricist Gus Kahn

In May 1932, Broadway welcomed the return of a musical that had already enjoyed an eighteen-month run on the 'Great White Way' between Christmas 1927 and summer 1929. 'Musical comedies do not act that way', *Time* magazine reported. 'They make what money they can while they are new, then fade into limbo forgotten except perhaps for a stray tune. But four years ago, even before the first curtain went up, Broadway sensed that Jerome Kern's *Show Boat* was different.' When the curtain did rise, it presented a world far removed from the traditions of musical comedy: a line of black men loading a boat with cotton, singing 'Niggers all work on the Mississippi/Niggers all work while the white folks play.'

Kern was the composer, and Oscar Hammerstein II the lyricist, of a musical comedy that brought new levels of sophistication to a jaded genre. The standard item of the 1920s was either a trivial romance, an anthology of songs and routines held together by the flimsiest of plots, or a revival of Gilbert and Sullivan or Victor Herbert (who penned forty full-length operetta scores between 1894 and 1924). Even Kern's earlier work, for all the comic genius of P. G. Wodehouse's lyrics, had not transcended those limitations. But *Show Boat* was based on a critically acclaimed novel by Edna Ferber, which ensured a compelling narrative, and the songs consolidated or propelled the action. Moreover, as the *Time* reporter noted, 'Its prelude establishes the play's mood, introduces definite themes, just as Wagner introduced themes in his preludes to develop them later on. The people in *Show Boat* have characteristic motifs just as Wotan and Siegfried have theirs in the *Ring* operas.'

Kern and Hammerstein's creation launched the era of the 'book musical': a golden age of internally coherent, eminently revivable productions. They also helped to refine the film musical: while Broadway hits did not always translate comfortably to the screen (in the 1930s, at least), they set standards of excellence which film-makers found other ways to match during that decade, particularly when Fred Astaire and Ginger Rogers were available (together or separately) to invigorate *42nd Street*, *Flying Down to Rio* or *The Gay Divorcee*.

With such writers as Kern and Hammerstein, Richard Rodgers and Lorenz Hart, George Gershwin and his brother Ira, and the extraordinarily gifted composer/lyricist Cole Porter all in their prime, this was, as Gary Giddins has reflected, 'an explosion of melody and harmony to rival the recently faded glory days of Italian opera'. Alec Wilder, a songwriter in the same tradition, described its graces: 'More sophistication, more complex melody writing, much more involved harmonic patterns, shifting song form, greater elegance, and infinitely superior theatre song writing.' The key word is 'theatre': for Wilder, Broadway represented the pinnacle of American song before the Second World War; second in rank was the Hollywood musical; finally, lagging in disgrace, 'pop music', by which Wilder meant the novelty tunes and sentimental ballads with no deeper intent than filling the dance floor.

If one accepts Wilder's criteria, 'sophistication' and the rest, it is difficult to disagree. The auteurs of this era, from Jerome Kern to Noël Coward, assumed an adult audience that was educated, literate, alive to the potential of social satire, not yet dead to the possibility of romance. The doyen of what theatre critic Mark Steyn called 'the Park Avenue smart set' was Cole Porter, a rare master of both words and music in an era when most songwriters hunted in pairs. His work has been described as 'a unique blend of the passionate and witty'; the wit apparent in his internal rhymes and wordplay, his casual references to (for example) Chopin and Georges Sand, and (in the same song, 'Let's Not Talk About Love', from 1941's *Let's Face It*) such tongue-twisting, uber-eloquent lines as 'Let's curse the asininity of trivial consanguinity.' And the passion? As a semi-concealed homosexual, Porter knew all about desire and how it could be expressed or suppressed: witness the tense beauty of such songs as 'Ev'ry Time We Say Goodbye' and 'What is This Thing Called Love?'.

Britain's nearest equivalent to Porter was Noël Coward: novelist, playwright, actor, director, cabaret performer and, certainly not least, a songwriter whose passion and wit were coated in a distinctively British layer of irony. Unlike Porter, however, Coward never really transcended his surroundings; his songs and plays exist only in their milieu, while the charm and bite of Porter's writing has proved to be universal.

So too the work of composer Richard Rodgers, whose career in the theatre came in two acts, each with its lyricist partner: Lorenz Hart until his death in 1943; then Oscar Hammerstein II, fresh from collaborating with Jerome Kern. Rodgers and Hart, said Alec Wilder, 'produced what is argu-ably the most brilliant collaborative work of the American musical comedy'. In just one show, 1937's *Babes in Arms*, they introduced five future standards: 'My Funny Valentine', 'Where or When', 'The Lady is a Tramp', 'I Wish I Were in Love Again' and 'Johnny One-Note'. There were many more: 'Blue Moon', 'Little Girl Blue', 'Bewitched, Bothered and Bewildered' – all adding to a catalogue that has survived attention from a bizarre array of singers, from Fred Astaire to Elvis Costello, Ella Fitzgerald to Janis Joplin.

After Lorenz Hart succumbed to alcoholism, Rodgers and

Hammerstein established arguably the most successful team in the history of the musical. They were responsible for five shows which – the least of their achievements, perhaps – dominated the album market in Britain and America before the Beatles: *Oklahoma!*, *Carousel*, *South Pacific*, *The King and I* and *The Sound of Music*. Where Hart was brittle and debonair, Hammerstein was corny and sincere; and Rodgers adjusted his melodic lines to adapt. Again, a list suggests (but merely skims) their legacy: 'Happy Talk', 'Hello Young Lovers', 'Some Enchanted Evening', 'You'll Never Walk Alone', plus the perennial score for *The Sound of Music*, which seems to have been passed through the blood to each successive generation since its Broadway premiere in 1959. There was an easiness about Rodgers and Hammerstein's work which revealed that – personal tastes aside – they were working in a country that had been stripped of its formality by jazz, the crooners, radio, hillbilly and the blues: all the contemporary influences that were changing the way people spoke, felt and moved.

Other writers who worked in Broadway and Hollywood between the wars were active participants in the Jazz Age. Gus Kahn, working with Walter Donaldson and then bandleader Isham Jones, contributed enduring marvels to the century's repertoire: 'Makin' Whoopee', 'My Baby Just Cares For Me', 'I'll See You in My Dreams', 'It Had to Be You' and many more, rich in colloquial dialogue but never banal. Likewise, as a melodist, Harold Arlen, often teamed with lyricist Johnny Mercer, from whom came such timeless gems as 'Stormy Weather', 'Over the Rainbow', 'One For My Baby (and One For the Road)', 'Come Rain or Come Shine', 'Blues in the Night'; as relaxed and yet compelling a set of tunes as any American has ever assembled. And above and beyond them all, there was George Gershwin, his most common helpmate his brother Ira: creators of such astonishing musicals, with films usually to follow, as *Lady Be Good*, *Funny Face*, *Girl Crazy* and of course *Porgy and Bess*.*

If there was one performer equal to all of these shades and moods, it was Fred Astaire. He was not only the most brilliant dancer ever to grace a Hollywood sound stage; he was also, albeit with a clipped, almost stunted voice, an equally fluent, intuitive singer. As Irving Berlin (himself a master of the stage and film musical) recalled, 'He's as good as any of them – as good as Jolson or Crosby or Sinatra . . . not necessarily because of his voice, but by his conception of projecting a song.'

---

* It is often forgotten that the Gershwins' original four-hour production was a comparative flop in 1935; it only reached a wider audience after George's death, in much-truncated form.

Without ever pledging himself to the cause, Fred Astaire danced and sang like a jazzman. Jazz was also the lifeblood of a composer who never wrote a full-length score, but who contributed some of the most enduring songs of the standards repertoire. Hoagy Carmichael was a piano-pumping student in 1918 when he performed before a fraternity audience. 'I had never played with drums before,' he remembered, 'and had no conception of the surging emotion that I felt in my head. It was like a machine, a perfect machine that automatically placed my fingers on keys that I had never played before.' Like many of his kind, he fell under the spell of Bix Beiderbecke – except that this was no long-distance passion but a close friendship, ended only by the cornetist's death in 1931. Beiderbecke's playing was the inspiration for one of the most popular melodies in history, 'Star Dust', which Carmichael first recorded himself in 1927.* It proved to be an endlessly malleable vehicle for everyone from Bing Crosby (who approached it with a degree of care that was almost religious) to Louis Armstrong, for whom it was both a plaything (typically, he ignored the memorable melody of the opening lines) and an expressway to a level of spontaneity that is the very essence of jazz.

There was nothing else quite like 'Star Dust' in Carmichael's oeuvre (although 'Georgia On My Mind' ran it close). But his songs were permeated with the music of black America, imbued with his irrepressible humour, and filled with self-confidence. Like the young Bing Crosby, he epitomised a kind of hipness that white America had never glimpsed before, and which made it inevitable that he would wind up collaborating with a third member of the species, Johnny Mercer. Individually, Carmichael and Mercer made a series of records in the 1930s and 40s that have all the carefree assurance of Sinatra in his prime. They're witty and poignant at turns, occupying some strange place on the musical spectrum halfway between Bing and Jerry Lee Lewis. Indeed, it's possible to track the Carmichael spirit all the way to the Grateful Dead and the Band, while Willie Nelson (who adopted 'Star Dust' as his own) is arguably the logical inheritor of his style.

Carmichael made suitably relaxed cameo appearances in a dozen movies, notably *To Have and Have Not* (where the teenage Andy Williams was asked to provide ghosted vocals for the barely older Lauren Bacall). Anticipating Chuck Berry's 'Roll Over Beethoven', he and Mercer also

---

* In October 1931, jazz critic Edgar Jackson of the *Gramophone* informed his readers that 'Star Dust' was actually a reference to cocaine; just as the children's song 'Puff the Magic Dragon' was later believed to encourage the use of marijuana.

concocted 'The Old Music Master', a charming creation myth for 'swing, boogie-woogie and jive', which imagined 'a little coloured boy' teaching a nineteenth-century classical maestro the secrets of the 'happy cat hit parade'. And that was precisely the venue for the music that swept this golden era of American composition aside, with a relentless outpouring of riff and rhythm which issued a single stern command: swing!

CHAPTER 7

BUGLE-CALL RAG

'Not 25% of lowbrows care a hoot for the strictly American hotted rhythm which is only a blaring succession of trumpet or sax screeches.'

Letter to *Radio Pictorial* magazine, 1935

'Swing is the voice of youth striving to be heard. Swing is the tempo of our time. Swing is real. Swing is alive … The older folk may be more conservative and truly shocked at swing, but they should realise that our fast-moving world makes swing acceptable.'

Letter from a female fan to the *New York Times*, 1939

4

'Swing cannot be defined', declared the American jazz magazine *Metronome* after its practitioners were unable to explain the exact nature of their art. Others valiantly continued the quest. The critic Enzo Archetti said that 'swing' was simply a new title for 'Hot Jazz – the real jazz, not the insipid and weak-kneed tunes and rhythms which are blared from every radio station in the country'. Another writer, Ralph Yaar, declared that swing was evident when 'the sound comes forth with accents which are so spaced out as to cause a rhythmic exhilaration in the mind of the listener'. Fats Waller described swing as 'two-thirds rhythm and one-third soul', which was eminently quotable, but ultimately meaningless.

Nor could swing's detractors offer a more coherent account of the music. 'It is akin to the wriggling of a child with an overcharged tummy', offered Compton Mackenzie. Another opponent was less metaphorical, dismissing the new sound as 'a combination of exhibitionism and the negro influence' – both of which, excusing the dated terminology for a second, were elements of the new style, but hardly a comprehensive account. Then there were the alarmists, who won headlines by equating swing music with 'musical Hitlerism', 'orchestrated sex', 'an epidemic' arising from a 'mass contagion' which required parents to quarantine their children, and various permutations of the words 'savage', 'noise' and 'jungle'.

Analysis of the thousands of 'swing' records made between 1935 and 1945 would betray a decisive shift in the way that arrangers approached their task. Early jazz sides had depended upon either a democratic inter-play of instruments (with varying degrees of spontaneity), or the favouring – albeit only perhaps for a single chorus – of one instrument above the ensemble. But the jazz and dance-band records of the swing era often separated their ever-growing orchestras into discrete sections: the brass, the reeds and the percussive instruments. Each of these would provide a separate function: would move or riff en masse; would offer counterpoint or harmony to the other sections; would keep the palette amused and the feet, always, moving. At its most direct (or banal), all three sections in a swing band would combine to slam home a riff with the impact of an express train rocketing through a country station. For its listeners, swing was either a crude demolition of all the subtlety of jazz, or the first musical form that screamed 'That's me! I'm alive!' to sensation-hungry teenagers who were finding their financial feet and securing their cultural independence.

In 1936, the American jazz writer Peter Hugh Reed set out to challenge the enemies of swing. His particular target was Compton Mackenzie, whom he quoted thus: 'Jazz is a surrender, paradoxically a tired surrender, of the mind to the body.' For Reed, swing was jazz, and he was prepared to state what made the music so compelling: 'I surrender unconditionally "my mind to my body". And why should I not do this? After all, why should we not succumb in part or upon occasion to our fundamental animal and primitive heritage, which lies back of the thin veneer of civilised life?'

Reed was conceding one of the fundamental arguments against swing, jazz and a dozen equally convulsive genres to come. Civilisation, so the guardians of morality claimed, was under threat from the animal, the physical, the erotic, the emotional. The defenders of jazz highlighted its aesthetic appeal, its complex harmonies, its modernity, its life-affirming spontaneity, anything that would remove it from the primitive and impulsive. Reed refused to play the civilisation game: for him, jazz was a physical medium, and he was not ashamed of his physical response.

The most instinctive reaction to the rhythm of swing was to dance: not with the regimented patterns of the waltz or the foxtrot, but with movements as unrestrained as the music. The godfather of swing dancing was the Lindy Hop, which originated in Harlem almost a decade before the swing boom. From its eight-to-the-bar rhythm (which made it the perfect partner for boogie-woogie piano) to its flamboyant acrobatics, the Lindy Hop was faster, wilder and more daring than any ballroom dance. It had no rules beyond the desire to express how the music sounded, and how it made you feel. But once it was captured on film – for example, in the Marx Brothers' 1937 movie *A Day at the Races*, demonstrated by Whitey's (all black) Lindy Hoppers – it became something to be imitated and mastered, rather than experienced in the moment. Black kids who saw their white peers struggling to match their moves dismissed them as 'jitterbugs' – squirming insects, in other words. The name stuck, and was flung constantly at teenagers by adults. Eventually every variant on the Lindy Hop, from the collegiate shag to the truck, the Suzy-Q to the dipso doodle, was subsumed into the single word 'jive', which was still being used to describe what adolescents did on the dance floor until the twist became a cultural obsession in the early 1960s.

Whatever its title, Helen Ward (singer with the Benny Goodman band) 'thought it was great, because it was expressing the spirit the guys had in them up on the bandstand . . . the gals began wearing saddle shoes and the socks and the very full skirts, which was the necessary gear to do all those gyrations . . . it was very exciting to me'. And also to the dancers, the jitterbuggers or (a self-imposed term) 'alligators': so excited did 25,000 of them become during an all-day swing festival at Randall's Island, New York in May 1938, that (reported the *Daily Express*) 'thousands broke from the two-dollar area, smashed up seats, and shouted and danced their way to the reserve seats . . . In this most frenzied of America's musical carnivals, housewives, office girls and businessmen, intoxicated by the blare of the 25 bands, leaped into the air yelling "Floy, floy", "Give it, cats", "Killer Diller", like mad people.'

Even the outbreak of war couldn't calm the delirium. In 1942, a swing session and jitterbug contest was staged in a Washington, DC stadium. 'When the bands started to send,' *Billboard* magazine reported, 'all hell broke loose. The audience jumped all over the place, piling out in the aisles and milling around the bandstand. Those in the upper tier of the stadium complained that they couldn't hear the rhythm and tossed a few pop bottles. Those that missed were returned . . . Final score: 13 arrests, 10 injuries, three broken gates, hundreds of tattered zoot suits, and 30,000 hepcats returning to their jukeboxes.' Moralists began to pine for the innocent days of ragtime and the foxtrot.

The unwitting catalyst for this confusion was a ferociously talented, emotionally closeted white bandleader named Benny Goodman. Bespectacled, besuited and clean-cut, Goodman might have been a bank manager had he not been leading an orchestra described by the *San Francisco Chronicle* as bedlam: 'Gene Krupa riding his hi-hat like a dervish. Harry James puffing out his cheeks till surely they must burst, the rhythm always burning and churning and driving you out of your mind, and then, just when you thought nothing could get hotter, Benny's clarinet rising like a burnished bird out of the tightly controlled maelstrom and soaring to the heavens, outscreaming even the crowd.'

Like Hoagy Carmichael, Goodman lapped up jazz in his teens; he was only 16 when he was invited to join one of the hottest white bands in America, led by Ben Pollack. In 1934, at 25, he secured a residency for his own band in midtown Manhattan. As Goodman's biographer explained, their audience was baffled by the ferocity of their sound: 'The music was too loud for them. They couldn't figure out how to dance to it . . . the customers just milled around the bandstand or sat at the tables,

stomping their feet.' There they might have remained, had the band not
been recruited by the McCann Erickson advertising agency to take part
in a networked Saturday night NBC radio show: *Let's Dance*. They were
booked to represent the 'hep' extreme of contemporary dancing taste,
alongside a unit offering Latin rhythms and another for close-dancers
and smoochers. The National Biscuit Company, which sponsored the
show, was appalled by what Goodman was playing, but sales of Ritz
biscuits soared, so the band kept their jobs. When the show was forced
off the air by a technicians' strike in summer 1935, however, the Goodman
outfit was booked into the prestigious Roosevelt Grill in New York,
where diners forced napkins into their ears to escape the din. Goodman's
orchestra were given their cards on opening night.

Out on the West Coast, they swung at full volume, and the dancers
stayed off the floor – until Goodman pulled out a batch of dated arrangements and forced his boys to pretend that they were a 'sweet' band at heart.
But one night in Oakland, he recalled, 'there was such a yelling and stomping
and carrying on in that hall I thought a riot had broken out. When I went
into my solo, the noise was even louder. Finally the truth got through to me:
we were causing the riot.' The Palomar ballroom in LA reacted the same
way: 'After travelling 3,000 miles, we finally found people who were up on
what we were trying to do.' Once more, dancing had ceased, but only
because everyone was crushed against the stage, hypnotised by the band.

As the furore of swing spread, the audience for Goodman's band
grew younger: from courting couples in their early 20s, to students and
then, by March 1937 when they reached the Paramount in Times Square,
to teenagers. Like many film theatres, the Paramount combined a movie
with a musical attraction, alternating throughout the day; a band could play
five shows between early morning and evening close, before heading to a
late-night club for one final blast. The Goodman orchestra arrived for a
soundcheck at 7 a.m., to discover hundreds of children already queuing for
admission, determined to cut school. By the first show at 10.30 a.m., the
kids were primed to explode, responding to the repeated crescendos of the
music with a roar that was, said *Variety* magazine, 'tradition-shattering in
its spontaneity, its unanimity, its sincerity, its volume, in the childlike
violence of its manifestations'. Most upsetting for the management was
that the fans danced in the aisles. The jitterbug was denounced as a teenage
hooligan, too young to appreciate the finer points of harmony and rhythm,
desperate only to swing.

In January 1938, swing achieved a measure of respectability when Goodman's orchestra were booked at Carnegie Hall. The show was picketed by supporters of the Spanish rebel leader General Franco, protesting that Goodman must be a Communist because he had recently played a fundraising benefit for the republican Spanish government. But the only disruption inside came from, as *Melody Maker* reported, 'those near-maniacs who act like they have St Vitus' Dance or ants in their pants . . . their stupid habit of whistling and clapping vociferously each time one of the boys took a hot chorus very soon became objectionable'. One jazz aficionado could eventually take no more, and screamed, 'Shut up you punks!' at the miscreants.

For Goodman, who that week had performed Mozart's Quintet for Clarinet and Strings on radio, this adulation was an ambiguous blessing. Ten days after the Carnegie show, he was back at the Paramount, and the fans were even more frenzied than before. His long-time admirer, the critic and producer John Hammond, claimed inside knowledge of his dilemma: 'The behaviour of his audience has set the guy on edge for the last six months . . . The crowd's exhibitionism at the earlier performances had so disgusted him that he could not even bring himself to face the well-behaved patrons at the quiet supper show . . . He genuinely wants the public to appreciate the music, and he hates to see it "fooled" by tricky stunts – even though he has been largely to blame for the public's gullibility.'

Certain stage antics were guaranteed to bring down the house: squealing high notes from Goodman's clarinet or the horns; ensemble riffs, repeated to the point of exhaustion; a drum solo; indeed, any solo that could possibly be designated 'hot', regardless of its musical value; and, unfailingly, the technique that the Glenn Miller band would use over and again, whereby they played softer and softer . . . and then came blasting back at full volume for a final chorus. However much Goodman despised these tricks, he couldn't avoid them, and his competitors displayed few scruples about exploiting and exhausting them all.

An early hint of that hysteria was evident on a record which would seem increasingly prophetic. Late in 1929, Louis Armstrong returned to 'St Louis Blues', which he had first recorded with Bessie Smith in 1925. Not a man to treat any text as Holy Scripture, he toyed with it like a terrier with a rag doll – playing it as a tango, then a madcap romp, growling the lyrics, accentuating random syllables, and finally hitting repeated accents just as Bill Haley & His Comets would on 'Shake, Rattle and Roll' twenty-five years later. Within its three minutes, 'St Louis Blues' held the future of swing, R&B and rock 'n' roll.

Something about that song obviously appealed to iconoclasts. The following year, Cab Calloway scatted his way through 'St Louis Blues' with surrealist abandon, W. C. Handy's song barely recognisable through the torrent of verbalised noise. While Louis Armstrong was the master of every mood, Calloway only knew one destination: party town. He billed himself as 'The King of Hi-Di-Ho'. That was one of his vocal riffs from 1931's 'Minnie the Moocher', a tour de force of jive-speak (he eventually issued several volumes of his *Language of Jive* dictionary) and vocal antics. By the end of that year, Cab was leading the hottest, fastest band in America, and no matter how shameless his material – 'Reefer Man', say, or 'Minnie the Moocher's Wedding Day' – the party never ended. It was he, not Goodman, who first celebrated the 'Jitter Bug' in song, a full eighteen months before Benny's band conquered California.

For anyone seeking novelty and energy, the early 1930s was a miraculous era. The Boswell Sisters – leader Connee, Martha and Vet – recruited some of the hottest white musicians in jazz to support their daring rearrangements of popular tunes old and new, each delivered in tight sisterly harmony. (Sisters were in vogue: the Ponce Sisters' 1932 rendition of 'Fit as a Fiddle' encapsulated the charm of this formula.) Their black vocal counterparts were the Mills Brothers, who capped their harmonies with imitations of jazz instruments. Their 1931 recording of 'Tiger Rag' (with its refrain of 'hold that tiger') showcased their almost preternatural ability to conjure up the sound of horns and upright bass with voices alone. Gene Austin steered pop closer to the boogie-woogie rhythm with his playful 'Please Don't Talk About Me'; Fred Astaire, as sure-footed before a microphone as on a ballroom floor, impersonated a German ('I love her great big bosoms') on 'I Love Louisa' and introduced Cole Porter's 'Night and Day'; Duke Ellington extended the harmonic and structural range of jazz with 'Creole Rhapsody' and 'Limehouse Blues'; and Mae West extended anything she could lay her hands on with 1933's 'A Guy What Takes His Time', arguably the rudest, most lubricious hit record to emerge from the first half of the twentieth century.

An entirely different taste of the forbidden arrived in New York from Latin America and the Caribbean. Increasing numbers of Puerto Ricans and Cubans had taken up residence in the city, and the daily newspaper *La Prensa* carried regular ads for visiting bands. In 1930, midtown

Manhattan played host to a series of Cuban outfits who expected to play only to their compadres, but Don Justo Azpiazu's orchestra from Havana, starring vocalist Antonio Machin ('the Cuban Rudy Vallee'), caught the attention of white journalists. *Billboard* magazine complained that Machin 'does two numbers, one as a peanut vendor, and a waste of good time as far as we were concerned'. But his 'Peanut Vendor' song, a familiar piece of showmanship in Cuba, became a national hit, especially once it had been purloined by jazz musicians such as Louis Armstrong and Red Nichols.

So America was formally introduced to the rumba (often 'rhumba' in English) – which was both a Cuban genre involving dance, percussion and topical lyrics; and, adapted for white tastes, another name for the Cuban dance rhythm more accurately known as the *bolero-son*. 'Peanut Vendor' fell into the latter category (even if musicologists might more exactly describe it as a *son-pregón*). This multiplicity of rhythms reflected the equally rich make-up of Cuban music, which boasted its *danzón* bands (sweet and hot, like American jazz units) playing four-section compositions and variations on European classical themes; the tango, imported from Argentina; the bolero, a romantic vocal/guitar style; and the *son*, a working-class, often satirical blend of music and dance which from 1920 onwards started to exhibit a jazz influence. All of this was concentrated into an island much smaller than Florida, which had endured regular occupation by US marines, and was now a holiday destination for rich Americans. Dance bands (white only) regularly played the Havana hotels; in return, Cuban bandleaders set up home in New York, often as illegal immigrants.

A second Cuban hit, 'Siboney', reached America in 1931, albeit sung by Alfredo Brito from the Dominican Republic: such distinctions were too fine for the US audience, and white listeners registered all music from south of its borders as 'Latin'. The most successful of all the Latin imports to America in the 1930s was Xavier Cugat, a Spanish violinist who led a band in Havana, and offered carefully Americanised versions of Cuban tunes (and vice versa). Cole Porter wrote 'Begin the Beguine' in his honour, and Cugat's tight arrangements offered an orderly pastiche of 'Latin' music which any American or European could understand. To complete the circle of influences, Chick Bullock's white American band concocted a loping rhythm on 1932's 'Underneath the Harlem Moon' which would reappear more than twenty years later in Jamaica's ska sound. In the musical melange of the 1930s, no style retained its purity for long.

Amidst this jumble of rhythms, it is not surprising that musicians did not always realise what they had found. In 1931, two of the most successful bandleaders of the swing era, Glenn Miller and Jimmy Dorsey, were learning their trade in Red Nichols's band when they recorded 'Fan It', a twelve-bar blues romp. Banal it may have been, but it was also an uncanny forerunner of both the jump blues style favoured by black musicians in the 1940s, and its direct descendant, big-band rock 'n' roll. Louis Armstrong came closest to exploring this opened vein, with 'Hobo You Can't Ride This Train', which built on a tune that was already a jazz standard, 'Tiger Rag'. (By contrast, the Boswell Sisters' 'Rock and Roll' from 1934 was neither a proto-rock tune nor an exploration of sexuality, but merely a novelty dance item.) While Red Nichols pioneered two genres, Duke Ellington christened another with 'It Don't Mean a Thing (If It Ain't Got That Swing)'. Suddenly the future was visible everywhere, from the self-referential postmodernism of Louis Armstrong's 'I Got Rhythm' to 1932's dance medleys from Broadway shows, pre-empting the likes of Stars on 45 and Jive Bunny by half a century.

Swing delayed its arrival for another year or two, as if anxious for the world to catch up. There was a flurry of riffing at the start of 1934, which must have provoked ensemble dancing across America, to the sound of Ben Pollack's 'Got the Jitters', Claude Hopkins's 'Washington Squabble' and Benny Goodman's 'Riffin' the Scotch'. The last of these featured a supremely elegant and relaxed vocal debut from the 18-year-old Billie Holiday. Chick Webb contributed an enduring swing anthem later that year with 'Stompin' at the Savoy', his soloists audibly divided between those who liked it hot and those who preferred a more tepid baptism. But it was left to Benny Goodman to pull America irreversibly into the new age with 'Bugle Call Rag' – blaring brass riffs, boogie bass runs, a solid backbeat, everything that drove the kids wild in Oakland the following year and set the jitterbuggers on their frenzied passage along the aisles of the Paramount.

Goodman may have been the pioneer (among the white bands) and populariser of swing, but hundreds of big bands operated across the United States in the late 1930s and early 1940s. The most notable, led by warring brothers Jimmy and Tommy Dorsey, Harry James, Glen Gray (fronting the Casa Loma Orchestra) and Artie Shaw, each had loyal and combative followings amongst teenagers – though polls of American students throughout the swing era regularly documented their educated taste for sweeter, more melodic fare. Meanwhile, there were black bands, led by Count Basie (briefly with Billie Holiday as featured vocalist), Chick

Webb (with the young Ella Fitzgerald in tow), Erskine Hawkins, and Duke Ellington, for whom swing was already second nature.

Some of those caught up in the hysteria of swing were dubious about its merits. Artie Shaw had emerged with a Swing String Ensemble in 1935, which as its name suggested daringly pitched his brass instruments against strings. Shaw himself played a clarinet as fluent as Goodman's, and as hot, as his 1936 hit 'There's Frost on the Moon' demonstrated. His stylistic range was incomparable: within two months in 1938 he recorded an exquisite version of 'Begin the Beguine', which has often been proposed as one of the finest American records of the century, and the eerie, lyrical 'Nightmare', as evocative a mood piece as anything in Duke Ellington's catalogue.

Shaw's problems were that he was a perfectionist (eight failed marriages, two of them to Hollywood stars Lana Turner and Ava Gardner, speak for themselves); he wanted to stretch and preferably snap fetters and boundaries, as when he recruited Billie Holiday for his band in 1938, until he was forced to respect the unofficial racial segregation of the day; and he hated to be pigeonholed. In 1940, he gave controversial interviews ('I'd think twice before advising anyone to follow in my footsteps ... popular music in America is 10% art and 90% business'), complained that the band business was a 'racket', dissolved his orchestra and retreated in a sulk to Mexico. A few weeks later, he was back.

His temper snapped again in 1945 when he was quoted as saying that jazz was 'a dying duck', that radio was terrible and fan magazines idiotic. For good measure, the fans themselves didn't know how to behave when they watched a 'star' perform, screaming hysterically for reasons that had nothing to do with music. Then, in 1949, he announced that he was fed up with jazz, swing, the audience ('morons') and anything to do with dance bands, and wanted to play 'long-hair' – period slang for classical music, orchestral conductors supposedly being so bohemian that they sometimes let their hair touch their collars.

He turned up that spring at Bop City in New York, and proceeded to play a selection of 'long-hair' pieces by composers such as Prokofiev, Debussy and Ravel. The jazz magazine *Metronome* reported the fans in the cheap seats screaming out 'Let's jump!' and 'Give us a break.' Shaw was a man 'way out of his depth, attempting to bamboozle a whole section of the populace into believing they were hearing good music. [It was] the worst musical fiasco staged in this country within the last twenty years.' Within a couple of months, he was promising to perform anything that the 'morons' wanted to hear. 'It's necessary to give an audience some familiar points of reference before you can expect it go along on new things', he admitted humbly. But then he rolled out the Ravel again, the dancing stopped, and one fan at Boston's Symphony Ballroom called out across the hall: 'Artie, you *stink*.' In 1954, he laid down his clarinet and never performed in public again, although he lived for another half-century.

Shaw might have been impossible to live with and to manage, but his skill as a musician was as sizeable as his insight into the business of fame. He peppered his autobiography, *The Trouble With Cinderella*, with sardonic references to 'succe$$'. To swing aficionado Fred Hall, he gave a memorable apologia, in which he captured the dilemma of being an artist in a commercial industry: 'What happens is you make 300 arrangements and you arrive at one, say "Begin the Beguine", and you like it; it's good enough, you like the tune, you like the arrangement, it worked and the audience liked it, so everybody's happy. But all of a sudden, you try to go past that. And you *can't* go past it. In a sense it's as though the audience is insisting you put on a straitjacket: "Don't grow anymore." It would be like putting a pregnant woman in something where she couldn't grow. I happen to have a need to continue to grow. This is a curse I have, an overwhelming compulsion to keep developing. Well, if someone says to you, "You can't develop; we want *that*, over and over", you can go crazy.'

No such fears afflicted Glenn Miller, who – despite Benny Goodman's stature – has passed into the collective memory as the king of the swing era and the big bands. His mysterious death in 1944 (or presumed death, to be exact) cemented his legend. His friend and biographer George T. Simon wrote that Miller 'was honest enough to recognise and admit his limits as a jazz trombonist', and certainly his reputation amongst jazz aficionados is tarnished, to say the least. Simon remembered that Miller 'definitely decided that he wasn't going anywhere by trying to outswing the Goodmans and the Shaws and the Dorseys. A basically sweet band with a unique identifiable sound, but which still could play the swing the kids wanted, would, he was convinced, stand a much better chance.'

His gimmick, the sound that made his band instantly recognisable, was the way he used a clarinet as lead instrument, doubled an octave below by a saxophone, while the remaining saxes contributed their own three-part close harmony. It was heard via coast-to-coast radio hook-ups in the summer of 1939 from the Glen Island Casino outside New York, a popular rendez-vous for wealthy college kids who relished the acoustics of the ballroom, and the vista of Long Island. Miller adopted 'Moonlight Serenade' as his theme, before his band swung gently but firmly for the remainder of the evening.

While other bands yearned for complexity to show off their technique, Miller favoured the simplicity of 'Little Brown Jug' or his most famous number, 'In the Mood'. The latter was a hybrid, its hallmark riff borrowed from Wingy Manone's 1930 side 'Tar Paper Stomp' (and reappearing at half-speed the following year in Fletcher Henderson's 'Hot and Anxious'). Composer Joe Garland retrieved the motif and presented an embellished version to Artie Shaw, who turned it down because it was too long for a single 78 rpm record. Miller solved that problem by cutting and simplifying, until all that was left was the riff, played loud, played soft, then softer, and finally with orgasmic volume and release. He performed similar magic with Erskine Hawkins's 'Tuxedo Junction', before achieving the biggest sales of any American record since Gene Austin's 'My Blue Heaven' with his million-selling 1941 hit, 'Chattanooga Choo Choo',* for which he was presented with the first ever gold record award. Predictably, Artie Shaw was not enamoured of the Miller sound: 'That band was like the beginning of the end. It was a mechanised version of what they called jazz music. I still can't stand to listen to it.' But no fewer than twenty-three of Miller's records topped the American best-sellers listings between 1939 and 1943, occupying the No. 1 position for 105 weeks in total – chart domination never matched before or since.

> When the historians of 2037 come to write of this chromium-plated, streamlined age, they'll have to devote a lot of space to dance music. It can't be ignored. We children of this radio era dance to it, eat to it, bath to it, drink to it, listen to it, sing, whistle and hum to it, even talk with it as a background.
> *Radio Pictorial* magazine, January 1937

Decca's studios in New York City were a long, rectangular room. At the far end was a large picture of an Indian maiden, standing up and holding her hand in the air, as if signalling that she had a question. In the 'dialogue balloon', she's asking, 'Where's the

---

* Bandleader Woody Herman, whose outfit could really swing, took pleasure in satirising Miller's success with a song about playing records backwards, 'Ooch Ooch A Goon Attach'.

melody?' . . . At Decca, you played and sang the melody, and
never mind a whole lot of improvising, or you didn't record for
Decca again.
    Maxine Andrews of the Andrews Sisters

His first sight of Chick Webb's swing band at the Savoy Ballroom in
Harlem drove the British jazz writer Leonard Hibbs into a frenzy of
excitement. 'Dancing, for the boys and girls in Harlem, is the very essence
of living', he wrote on his return. 'Unlike the average dancer in this country,
who walks the foxtrot to almost every number, these happy people improvise their dancing and translate their happiness into inspired rhythmic
movement . . . By dance, I mean really move in rhythm with the music,
sway with the rise and fall of the music. Relax and swing. Let yourself go!'
    Many did not care to plunge into 'that little world of red-hot
rhythm'. Anyone who was too old, or didn't dance, or preferred a wider
palette, resented the dominance of the swing bands. For all their airplay,
and despite Glenn Miller's success, their sales did not always match their
publicity, and only aficionados relished the hotter and more liberated
forms of jazz music. In future, *Variety* magazine suggested at the end of
the 1930s, 'records will have to let the fans know what they are playing and
keep within recognition distance of the melody as originally conceived'.
    That was the manifesto in Britain, where swing (beyond the in-
evitable Glenn Miller releases) was slow to take off – so slow, in fact, that
it was only after the Second World War that bands such as Ted Heath's
could build flourishing careers. For aficionados of the British bands, this
was a golden age, free of the excesses of swing, as the historian Peter Cliffe
explained: 'The more established British bandleaders continued to delight
their followers in ballrooms, hotels, nightclubs and restaurants, at the
theatre and, for the majority as the Depression tightened its grip, over the
air and on gramophone records. There were no startling musical events,
and few sensational hits; just a cavalcade of pleasant songs, stylishly
arranged and melodiously performed.'* The word 'pleasant' would damn

---

* As a snapshot of the chasm between British and American tastes, *Gramophone* magazine
reviewed competing interpretations of a new song in 1932. US torch singer Ruth Etting
performed 'with all the American's lack of reticence'. How much more delightful was 'the clear,
soulless voice' of the British contender, Anona Winn (actually Australian). This was probably
the last occasion on which 'soulless' was applied to a performance as a compliment.

this era for posterity. Yet for those who wished for nothing more than to be entertainingly diverted from a world hell-bent on a second global conflagration, the dependability of the British dance bands was a virtue rather than a sin. As Edgar Jackson explained, 'The dance record-buying public can be divided into two classes – those who buy for the performer and those who buy for the tune. The former are mainly fans who like clever and very up-to-date rhythmic stuff; the latter are more interested in instrumental melody which they can recognise easily, learn, and hum in their baths.'

BBC bandleader Jack Payne might have complained that 'Dancing is under a temporary cloud ... it has undoubtedly lost something of its fascination.' But innovation was at hand: in the 1930s, Britain was swept by a passion for the cinema organ, and there was a constant supply of records by performers such as Reginald Dixon, the Wurlitzer organist at the Tower Ballroom in Blackpool, who even dared to tackle the jazz anthem 'Tiger Rag'. Dance bands could not encompass so costly an instrument, but they found a viable substitute: the accordion (piano-accordion, to give its proper title; squeeze-box to its admirers; accordeon, in deference to the Continentals, in 1930s magazines). Its sound was both gently exotic – evoking visions of gypsies in colourful headscarves, or the *bal musette* bars of Paris – and reliably restrained. Besides the Street Singer and his 'ghosted' accordion, acts such as Billy Reid's London Piano-Accordeon Band and Carlos Santanna's Accordeon Band began to supplant conventional dance outfits. Many observers reckoned that a line-up of three or four accordions in front of a rhythm section could provide more depth and variety than the yawningly familiar horns and reeds. A magazine entitled the *Accordion Times* enjoyed wide circulation, only perishing in the late 1940s when it was relaunched as the (later *New*) *Musical Express*. By the end of the 1930s, movie stars were boasting that they had mastered the instrument, as it boosted their romantic appeal – not least because of its links to Paris, the city of lovers, where the accordion was a regular feature of hit records until the mid-1950s.

Anyone for whom the accordion was not diverting enough could always amuse themselves with the electrified guitar (a real novelty, this) of Len Fillis on his instrumental 'Dipsomania'; the controversial music hall song, 'The Pig Got Up and Slowly Walked Away', which was banned from BBC airplay for reasons that nobody could quite fathom; or even a recording of the circus from London's Olympia, spotlighting a group of sea lions performing 'God Save the King' on trumpets.

Amidst these diversions, there was a determined effort to recreate a more innocent age. The mid-1930s saw a revival of classic music-hall songs, which – as bandleaders faced with a pugilistic audience discovered – could calm shattered nerves. The BBC gave airtime to Les Allen and Kitty Masters, whose act involved impressions of showbiz figures, and old-time ballads – 'the sort of numbers', *Radio Pictorial* explained, 'that make the elder members of the audience feel furtively for each other's hands, and cause the younger members of the audience to experience a strange, peaceful thrill which is uncommon in this blasé age'. Bringing all his showbiz experience to bear, Les Allen declared confidently that 'Audiences resent "bounce" in an act', in which case swing was certainly beyond the pale.

For adults who wanted a more subtle form of nostalgia, Britain in the 1930s was a haven for that elusive style known as 'light music': more sophisticated than the written-to-order Tin Pan Alley song, more accessible than serious, 'long-hair' compositions, more sedate than jazz. Its historian, Geoffrey Self, averred that it 'should divert rather than disturb; entertain rather than disquiet'. But light music was more than what the French called *musique-papier* (wallpaper music): it had its own method of stirring the emotions. The novelist J. B. Priestley caught its appeal: 'Because, unlike serious music, light music lacks musical content, it acts as a series of vials, often charmingly shaped and coloured, for the distillations of memory. The first few bars of it remove the stopper; we find ourselves reliving, not remembering, but magically recapturing, some exact moments of our past.' At its most vivid – in the work of Eric Coates, or later Ronald Binge (who wrote BBC radio's beautiful close-down theme, 'Sailing By') – light music could evoke at first hearing an imaginary nostalgia, in which sadness and joy were carefully balanced; a gorgeous comfort leavened with loss, as wistful as the fleeting memories of a dream. Coates was the light-music master of the age, whose work endured via radio themes such as 'By the Sleepy Lagoon' (*Desert Island Discs*) and 'Knightsbridge' from his *London Suite* (*In Town Tonight*). The latter was so popular in the 1930s that it was taken up by dance bands, to the horror of a *Daily Mirror* reviewer: 'In my view the melody is too good to be "murdered"; it is real music, not a foxtrot.'

There were few such defenders for the vast proportion of songs emerging from the publishers' factories in New York and London. 'It was quite apparent that too many popular songs were being published', a historian noted from the lofty perspective of 1948. 'Even the bally-hoo of radio's *Hit Parade* could not hide the poverty and shabbiness of much of the material ground out by Tin Pan Alley.' It was dominated by unrealistic portrayals of young love, using scenarios and rhymes that had long since lost their flavour. 'We have heard all these words in a thousand different disguises, coupled with the most trashy and slobbery sentimentality,' *Radio Pictorial* complained in 1937, 'and sung by crooners until a kind of nausea has been reached.'

Such material kept the wheels of the music industry turning briskly, however, especially when stoked by such networked radio shows as America's *Make Believe Ballroom* (showcasing dance bands) and *Your Hit Parade*. The latter began in 1935, and soon adopted a familiar countdown format leading up to the announcement of the week's most popular song. Its playlist was, in theory, determined by checking which twelve or fifteen songs had been broadcast most often across the land in the previous seven days, but the format was wide open to corruption and what became known as 'payola' – the payment of bribes to hosts or producers in return for airplay. It was no longer enough for a publisher to command a stable of talented writers: their skills were secondary to those of the 'pluggers', whose job it was to create hits, by legal means or foul. So dubious did the business of determining America's favourite songs become that *Variety* magazine suspended its 'best-sellers' listing in 1938, fearful that many of the 'sales' it was reporting existed only on paper. None of this prevented the title of *Your Hit Parade* from becoming a catchphrase, or the show from providing early exposure for Frank Sinatra and Doris Day.

Sceptics were convinced that radio would eventually run out of songs, because it quickly sapped even the most popular tunes of their freshness. 'Our songs don't live anymore', said Irving Berlin who, as America's leading songwriter of the century, was entitled to be concerned. 'They fail to become part of us. In the old days Al Jolson sang the same song for years until it meant something – when records were played until they cracked. Today, Paul Whiteman plays a hit song once or twice or a Hollywood hero sings them once in the films, and the radio runs them ragged for a couple of weeks – then they're dead.'

Novelty was everything in this market, surprise and wit a bonus. The unexpected hit of 1936 was 'The Music Goes Round & Round' – meta-pop, if you like, which spent three minutes discussing how a tune travelled from trumpet mouthpiece to horn. 'The Broken Record' extended this postmodern approach, mimicking a needle stuck on a disc: some versions, such as Wingy Manone's, ended with the offending item flying out of the window; others, like Guy Lombardo's, found the band slowing gradually to a halt like an exhausted gramophone. There were idiosyncrasies of timing to conjure with, such as the bar-long pauses that must have terrified any radio announcer playing Tommy Dorsey's 'Posin'; exotic instrumentation, as on Raymond Scott's 'Twilight in Turkey' from 1937; or language, on Slim & Slam's guide to Harlem jive talk, 'The Flat Foot Floogee'; even good old-fashioned innuendo, either gentle ('Sweet Violets' by the Sweet Violet Boys) or more blatant (Tampa Red's 1936 blues, 'Let's Get Drunk & Truck', accepted somehow as nothing more risqué than an invitation to dance).

Perhaps the most surprising trend of the late 1930s was triggered by a song written for a Yiddish musical comedy in 1933. Five years later, 'Bei Mir Bist Du Schoen' became an international hit for the Andrews Sisters, another trio in the Boswells' mould. It encouraged a boom in 'international' songs, borrowed from America's immigrant communities. There was already a market for ethnic music amongst the first generation of settlers, their children preferring to assimilate themselves into America's mainstream. Now the two strands became one stream, as a host of diverse Central and Eastern European traditions and dance rhythms were awarded the catch-all description of 'polka'. The catalyst was Will Glahé's 'Beer Barrel Polka', accordion to the fore, which was rapidly seized upon by the Andrews Sisters. Its popularity was attributed not to radio, which had done its best to ignore the craze, but 'coin-operated phonographs' – or jukeboxes – which allowed consumers to programme their own entertainment.

> Take the family out for dinner – where they have Wurlitzer Music. Your friends will be there with their families. All of you, young and old, will have fun talking, laughing and listening to tunes as stimulating as your first fresh breath of spring.
> Advert for Wurlitzer jukeboxes, c.1947

At a Wurlitzer sales convention, one of the company's executives revealed the secret of their market-leading jukeboxes. In front of a hall packed with eager sales staff, he opened up the front of their most popular model – to reveal a scantily clad young woman inside.

Commercial boxes operated more conventionally, using state-of-the-art mechanical and electrical engineering. Wurlitzer came late to the jukebox industry, though the company could be traced back to a mid-seventeenth-century family musical instrument business in Saxony. The family name became synonymous with the cinema organ ('the mighty Wurlitzer') in 1910. But the invention of the talking picture drained the cinema market dry, and so the company joined forces with a pioneering jukebox manufacturer, Homer Capehart, in 1933.

Capehart and his competitors had followed different routes to the same destination. Seeburg made their name with coin-operated pianos, before developing the all-in-one Orchestrion, which mimicked the sound of an entire band with one pneumatically driven instrument. When Brunswick launched the all-electric phonograph for domestic use in 1926, Seeburg and Capehart investigated the possibilities of using similar technology to create record players which would hold multiple discs, and offer customers a choice of titles at the drop of a coin. After Wurlitzer bought Capehart out, they and Seeburg were joined in the race by AMI, Rock-Ola and Mills – flooding America with their machines through the mid-1930s until every conceivable outlet had been serviced.

The jukebox industry was so successful that it seemed to have put itself out of business. But in the great tradition of consumer capitalism, Wurlitzer introduced premature obsolescence into their sales patter, constantly updating and refining their boxes. To ensure return sales, they offered to remove outdated machines free of charge. In a competitive market, bars, restaurants and clubs felt the need to modernise their equipment annually – especially once they discovered that patrons were selecting their venues for drinking and dining on the quality of their jukeboxes.

City bars would often rent the machines for the weekend, on the assurance that the manufacturer would refresh them with the latest jazz, blues or hillbilly tunes, depending on the location. The jukebox offered a choice of music far wider and earthier than any American radio station. In time, though, as the jukebox migrated from bars of ill repute into upmarket establishments, the musical menu varied. Wurlitzer's marketing campaigns hailed the choice of 'sweet numbers, jazz classics, hillbilly hits, waltzes, foxtrots [and] polkas' on offer, and promised: 'You'll go home humming their haunting melodies, higher in spirit, happier at heart for having spent a pleasant musical interlude by spending only a few small coins.'

Before the Second World War, the jukebox was a peculiarly

American innovation. 'Phonograph kiosks' had been installed in several major British railway stations, but they were a short-lived gimmick. The jukebox was launched in Britain in 1932, but didn't catch on. A second marketing campaign followed in 1935; again the response was nugatory. When war broke out, there were fewer than a hundred functioning boxes across the British Isles, while in America, a population four times larger was being serviced by more than 200,000 machines. Anyone in Britain who wished to seek out the best of American jazz, blues and country music had to enlist in what amounted to a secret society, and go underground.

> We demand that this habit of associating *our* music with the primitive and barbarous negro *derivation* shall cease forthwith, in justice to the fact that we have outgrown such comparisons.
> *Melody Maker* editorial, 1926

It was a subject of some embarrassment to British lovers of jazz that the music owed its existence to African-Americans. In the 1920s, this prejudice was justified on purely aesthetic grounds, as Albert McCarthy explained: 'The sophisticated music of the white New Yorkers was considered the epitome of jazz, and when the classic Louis Armstrong Hot Five and Seven recordings first appeared in Britain they were dismissed as crude, while blues in their purest form were virtually unknown and would have been met with incomprehension.' Armstrong's first appearance in Britain in 1932 was met with vile insults from the press, who described him as the 'ugliest man' ever to appear on a London stage, an 'untrained gorilla'. The usually liberal-minded *Pearson's Magazine* warned: 'Negroes Invade Our Theatres'. Only a minority of aficionados acknowledged that both black and white performers had contributed to jazz. Their enthusiasm persuaded the Parlophone company to issue a limited number of hot-jazz items to the British public, in its 'New Style Rhythm Series'. Despite its early racism, *Melody Maker* provided a rallying point for Britain's scattered jazz fans. It was through the newspaper's pages that a Hot Rhythm Club (officially named Rhythm Club No. 1, in the accurate expectation of many more to follow) was established in June 1933, its first gathering held in London's Regent Street. Jim Godbolt, who played key roles in British jazz history between the

1940s and his death in 2013, joined Rhythm Club 161 at the Station Hotel in Sidcup. There 'the club – maximum attendance of nine – met and listened to records played on a portable turntable plugged into the electric light socket . . . Our sessions were solemn affairs. Jazz was a serious matter that called for avid listening and profound comment. We would take it in turns to give "recitals" followed by fierce and asinine debates . . . We were an underground movement. There was a pristine spirit of romance, the adventure of discovering new musical joys on record, and these were rare enough, as the record companies issued only one new jazz record a month.' Across the country, these isolated assemblies gathered and swapped information (and misinformation), creating godheads of their favoured instrumentalists.

Such obsessions were anathema to those who hankered after a more resolutely English form of entertainment. Among the most vocal proponents of this doctrine were Oswald Mosley's blackshirt-clad British Union of Fascists. 'The fight to build the Greater Britain is giving rise to a new national music', claimed the paper *Fascist Week* in 1934. The entertainment they favoured included the Blackshirt Military Band, and communal singing of such anthems as 'Come All Young England', 'Mosley!' and 'Britain Awake!' (exclamation marks testified to the urgency of their crusade). Fascist commentators found it simple to apportion blame for Britain's appallingly decadent modern culture: it was, said Dr Leigh Vaughan-Henry, all the fault of 'the Negroid-Jewish strata which is undermining American life'. Captain Cuthbert Reavely recommended the BUF's String Quartet to his fellow fascists, as an escape from 'Jew-boys wailing jazz and gold-toothed niggers disseminating the "culture" of the jungle and the swamp'. The BBC was apparently engaged in a plot to convince the public that only Jews could play dance music: 'The Jew and the alien generally ruin the music with the aid of the British subscribers – with their ten shillings a year [radio licence fee] – to hear Jew jazz bands.' To prove that ethnically pure jazz was achievable, the fascist paper *Action* advertised an 'Aryan Dance Band', who guaranteed to play 'Jazz without Jews'. But the same journal also covered the latest films, and a few weeks later their reviewer blatantly evaded the party line: 'Louis Armstrong, the famous coloured trumpeter, puts in a welcome appearance [in *Pennies from Heaven*, 1937]. We should see more of him; he acts as well as he plays.'

Such treachery would not have been allowed among fascists in mainland Europe. In Germany, as the paper *Blackshirt* boasted, 'there is no jazz. Hitler has strenuously discountenanced it. He sees no national ascent through the crooner's adenoids. More, he realised, being, like his fellow dictator [Mussolini, in Italy], a keen music lover, that jazz is the expression of neurasthenia, debilitating to the youth exposed to its down-grade influence.' Hitler's propaganda supremo, Joseph Goebbels, had ridiculed 'America's contribution to the music of the world' as 'jazzed-up Nigger music'.

That contribution had been pervasive in Germany since the early years of the century, when the first strains of ragtime reached the Berlin cabarets. Germany's defeat in the Great War sparked economic chaos, death to convention and censorship, and an obsession with the apparently liberated culture of America. Jazz took Berlin by storm, as it had Paris and London. But whereas Paris adopted it and London imitated it, Berlin assimilated it into the explosion of modernism and the bohemian which reached from concert halls to nightclubs. 'The Negroes are here', proclaimed the poet Yvan Goll in 1926. 'All of Europe is dancing to their banjo. It cannot help itself. Some say it is the rhythm of Sodom and Gomorrah. Why should it not be from Paradise?'

That ambiguity was reflected in *Jonny spielt auf*, or *Jonny Strikes Up* (*the Band*), a 1927 jazz-inspired opera by Ernst Krenek – based on a 1920 cabaret tune about a seductive American violinist. The opera extended that theme, as the African-American Jonny brushed aside the music of classical Europe with his hypnotic, barbaric jazz rhythms. The academic Alan Lareau explained: 'The nightmare image of the Black taking over Germany, seducing white women and destroying the national culture, had a special topicality and political resonance in the early 1920s, for French colonial troops from North Africa had been sent to occupy the Rhineland following the war. This occupation, seen as a rape of German soil and industry, was popularly referred to as *die schwarze Schmach*, "the black disgrace".' No wonder that the infiltration of jazz into German culture provoked reactions every bit as alarmist as anything heard in Britain or the United States. In Vienna, meanwhile, a performance of *Jonny spielt auf* was greeted with stink bombs and sneezing powder by 'race-conscious Austrian students'.

When Austrian-born Adolf Hitler assumed the chancellorship of Germany in January 1933, he resolved to preserve the nation's culture from foreign influence. In his textbook for his obsessive pursuit of power, *Mein Kampf*, he had lamented Germany's 'collapse in its political, cultural, ethical and moral aspect', under artistic influences that 'could be regarded as entirely foreign and unknown', which had caused 'a spiritual degeneration that had reached the point of destroying the spirit'. He was alluding to Jewish culture, not black America, but in his world view both races were equally subhuman. Jazz was not only American, but it came from an inferior race, and was transformed into songs which emanated from another (via the supposed Jewish domination of Tin Pan Alley). The genre was denounced alongside other pernicious examples of modernist culture in the fields of art, classical music, literature and architecture. The Nazis staged an exhibition of 'Degenerate Art' in 1937, and another of 'Degenerate Music' the following year – the catalogue for which displayed the image of Jonny, from Ernst Krenek's opera. Hitler's regime had already banned broadcasts of jazz music in 1935, widened the restrictions to include all recordings by Jewish or black musicians in 1937, and even abolished the trade of musical criticism. With compositions by Jews also prohibited by 1938, the German public was denied access to the work of Irving Berlin and George Gershwin, either on record or on film.*

Despite those strictures, jazz musicians and dance bands continued to play and perform in Nazi Germany as long as they did not openly challenge the new laws. Certain musical motifs were overtly 'jazz-like', and therefore forbidden – the drum solo, for example, or anything that provoked an outburst of jitterbugging. But there remained a wide audience for American jazz tunes, often with their titles translated into German to suggest that they were authentic products of the Third Reich. Some jazz clubs in Berlin were also allowed to operate openly, with the aim of encouraging foreign visitors to believe that Nazi Germany was not a repressive society.

As the European situation deteriorated, British bands continued to accept lucrative invitations to tour Germany. Jack Hylton's outfit had paid regular visits to Europe during the 1930s; Hylton was even awarded

---

* Other totalitarian regimes were not as strict. In 1933, Alexander Tsfasman was forced to bring his band before the Moscow Workers Theatre Club to decide whether his Soviet equivalent to Paul Whiteman's arrangements was suitable for working-class ears. His orchestra passed their political audition with such ease that they were required to play an encore. As a contrast: dance bands in post-Second World War Hungary were instructed to perform a smattering of American material during each performance, so that Communist Party officials could note the names of those rebels who didn't immediately leave the dance floor when these dangerously decadent pieces began.

the *Légion d'honneur* in 1932 for services to French music. In 1937 and 1938, the band broke box-office records in Berlin. 'These days nearly everyone here is doing the Lambeth Walk', a German reporter noted of a song and dance that Hylton had helped to popularise. Another British bandleader, Jack Jackson, was offered the phenomenal salary of £1,500 per week in 1938 if he would relocate to Berlin, take control of Germany's output of light music, and record anthems for the Hitler Youth movement. 'I was offered a guarantee of diplomatic immunity for myself and the band', he told a British magazine. 'Although the band then included two "star" instrumentalists who are Jews, this was not to be a stumbling block.' Fortunately, the future BBC disc jockey declined the invitation.

Concerned about the plight of Jewish refugees from Nazism, many branches of the British entertainment industry offered a day's profits from their work in January 1939 to a charitable fund. Two weeks later, Henry Hall – who had recently left his post as the BBC's official bandleader – led his orchestra on a four-week visit to Berlin. 'They will play at a State Ball attended by high German state officials,' the magazine *Radio Pictorial* said proudly, 'and provided they're not called upon to give the salute in the middle of a number, everything should go with a swing. Luckily for the project, there are no Jewish members in the outfit.' To ensure that there would be no embarrassment, Hall dropped all songs by Jewish composers from his band's repertoire for the duration of the visit. 'Naturally, I don't want to spoil good relations by behaving in a way that would offend in Berlin', he said. 'What I am doing is merely a matter of common sense.' 'I don't blame him for that, as some papers have', a friendly magazine journalist wrote. 'He's got to earn his living like the rest of us.' Their engagement at the Scala was a sell-out, and Hall's band received a rapturous reception. Anti-fascist campaigners were outraged by Hall's behaviour, while *Melody Maker* said merely that 'nobody could possibly challenge his patriotism'. Less than three weeks after Hall's band returned to Britain, the German Army invaded Czechoslovakia, and British musicians no longer had to battle with their consciences about the ethics of performing under a fascist dictatorship.

WHITE CHRISTMAS

Words and Music by IRVING BERLIN

FROM THE PARAMOUNT PICTURE
IRVING BERLIN'S

"HOLIDAY INN"

FEATURING
BING CROSBY AND FRED ASTAIRE WITH

MARJORIE REYNOLDS, VIRGINIA DALE, WALTER ABEL and LOUISE BEAVERS

A MARK SANDRICH PRODUCTION

BE CAREFUL, IT'S MY HEART   1/- net
WHITE CHRISTMAS   .   .   .   .   1/- net
SONG OF FREEDOM   .   .   .   .   1/- net

THE VICTORIA MUSIC PUBLISHING COMPANY LTD.

52 MADDOX STREET, LONDON, W.1

IRVING BERLIN INC., NEW YORK

2346

Authorized for sale only in the British Empire (except Canada, Newfoundland, Australia and New Zealand)
MADE IN ENGLAND

CHAPTER 8

Millions Like Us

'In a few years, radio will be more powerful than print for purposes of propaganda. Therefore the organization of the radio has always been and always will be one of my most important tasks.'

Joseph Goebbels, March 1937

'I want to take people out of the war.'

Gracie Fields, October 1939

On 17 September 1939, the British aircraft carrier HMS *Courageous* was torpedoed off the coast of Ireland, and 519 of her crew were lost. Adrift in the sea, the survivors sang music-hall tunes such as 'Daisy, Daisy' to keep their spirits up.

Britain's shared heritage of popular music was vital to wartime morale. In Frank Launder and Sydney Gilliat's patriotic 1943 film *Millions Like Us*, Celia (played by Patricia Roe) is working in an aircraft factory. When her husband is killed, Celia forces herself to attend a concert in the factory canteen. Music-hall star Bertha Willmott sings 'Just Like the Ivy (I'll Cling to You)' from 1903 and then the equally venerable Vesta Victoria vehicle, 'Waiting at the Church'. Watching her today, you'd expect Celia to find this sentimentality unbearable; but instead she is unable to resist the communal celebration of national identity. As the film ends, she is caught up in the singalong of 'My Wife Won't Let Me' – just another of the 'millions like us', determined to see it through and win the war.

After Britain declared war on Germany, on 3 September 1939, the public seemed far more resolute than its national mouthpiece, the British Broadcasting Corporation. *Gramophone* editor Compton Mackenzie reviewed the first fortnight of schedule changes, with popular programmes cancelled and the BBC's airtime drastically reduced, and lamented 'the most pitiful exhibition of complacent amateurishness to be heard in the whole of this planet during the first weeks of war'. With most popular music exiled from the airwaves for the winter of the so-called 'Phoney War' (1939–40), how could morale be sustained?

The entertainment industry rallied to the flag. As the nation's favourite singer, Gracie Fields's contribution was vital. Although she was still convalescing after surgery for cervical cancer, she kept up a fierce schedule of patriotic duties, from radio concerts to a live recording of *Gracie with the Troops*. (Her audience of soldiers recorded their own sing-song of First World War favourites, entitled *Flanders Memories*.) On Christmas Day 1939, Fields performed at a secret location 'somewhere in France' as part of another live broadcast. But three months later, she married an Italian-born film director, Monty Banks (né Mario Bianchi). When she realised that he was liable to be interned by the British government as an alien, Fields took her husband to Canada and then California, provoking criticism that she was abandoning her homeland at its hour of need. As if to fill the gap, the much-loved balladeer of the pre-jazz era, John McCormack, emerged from retirement to raise funds for the Red Cross.

While HMV trumpeted his return, Decca Records were eager to be seen as even more patriotic. 'As in 1914, so in 1939', they declared in an advertisement, 'Decca Keeps The Flag Flying With Entertainment for the Troops and the Home.' A flurry of suitably war-themed records was released, including Annette Mills's composition 'Adolf'; Gracie Fields's 'Old Soldiers Never Die'; revivals of anthems from the Great War; a medley of soldiers' songs from Jack Hylton's band; and comedian Tommy Handley's inspired coupling of 'Who Is That Man (Who Looks Like Charlie Chaplin)' and 'The Night We Met in a Blackout'. Cabaret star Ronald Frankau penned a droll supper-club novelty entitled 'Heil Hitler! Ja! Ja! Ja!', which made the great dictator sound like a harmless fool. ('There are plenty more better verses,' he mumbled at the end of the record, 'but I'm not allowed to sing them.') Arthur Askey reworked the popular song 'Run Rabbit Run' as 'Run Adolf Run', delighting King George VI so much that the monarch asked for the revised lyrics to be sent forthwith to Buckingham Palace. The popularity of such songs placed an enormous strain upon the stockpile of raw materials. As sales soared amidst the decline of BBC airplay, record companies agreed to ration the number of records that could be issued, and by 1942 there was a noticeable scarcity of discs in the shops.

The most enduring song of the war's early weeks was 'We'll Meet Again'. As the academic Christina Baade wrote, 'The song combined the first person plural, which had been so popular in more jingoistic numbers, with romantic longing and an insistent faith in the couple's eventual reunion. It was also unabashedly sentimental, a mood that bewildered critics who called for more bracing wartime fare.' Soldiers were often ambivalent about the song, one of them asking the BBC to refrain from playing material which reminded them that they would shortly be bidding farewell to their loved ones. The song became indissolubly linked to a young band singer, of whom the *Daily Express* trumpeted: 'There's a new star ... She is quite unsophisticated. But Vera Lynn sings sentimental songs that sell more records each month than Bing Crosby, the Mills Brothers, the Andrews Sisters or any of that formidable gang of trans-atlantic songsters.' As a final compliment, the *Express* added: 'She sings high in her nose, and she never wavers from a note. In this age, when crooning is the rage, such simple balladry is startling.' When Lynn was added to the cast of BBC radio's *Sincerely Yours*, another newspaper declared: 'Vera brings joy and comfort to thousands in the Forces and those they love. She is establishing herself as Everybody's Friend. Keep the good work going, Vera.' She was so popular with the troops that the BBC forbade any comedian from imitating her on air. Indeed, disliking Vera Lynn – and there were plenty who did, on musical grounds alone – was considered nearly as unpatriotic as hanging the swastika from a window. Behind the doors of BBC committee rooms, however, as Christina Baade has discovered, there was disquiet that (in the words of the head of the Empire Entertainments Unit) 'The type of songs being written and sung by [Lynn] has a drugging effect on troops, but drugs are bad for one. It will have the opposite effect to making any of them "fighting mad" and rather turn them to "wishing it could all be over and done with".'

Realising that the armed forces might require stiffer stuff, the BBC launched forces programming, containing 'hot' jazz numbers which were rarely aired to the public at home. (This prompted complaints that the regular morning service was sometimes followed by indecorous swing tunes.) Forces broadcasts also demolished one of the great taboos of BBC programming: for the first time, dance music was allowed to invade the previously sacred schedule of a Sunday evening. When civilisation survived this sacrilege, the British homeland was given the same licence, and Mantovani's orchestra occupied a space that would once have been devoted to classical music.

In the summer of 1940, the BBC responded to the agony of the Dunkirk evacuation by launching a new form of programming: two half-hour slots, mid-morning and mid-afternoon, entitled *Music While You Work*, which were intended to double the output of those in munitions and aircraft factories. Their contents were lively but not too engaging. The American polka tune 'Deep in the Heart of Texas' was barred from inclusion, despite its enormous popularity, because it inspired workers to drop their tools and clap along.

Musicians in dance bands occupied an ambiguous position during the war years. Many were called up, and formed service bands, such as the Skyrockets, the Blue Rockets and the Squadronaires, whose swing music was hotter than anything from Britain's more renowned orchestras. Those who remained behind were charged with raising morale, but often maligned as unpatriotic because they weren't fighting. 'Swingsters Want Exemption

From Military Service', claimed the *Evening Standard* in 1940, while the *Daily Express* countered with 'Many Dance Band Boys Dodge the Army'. Neither story was based on fact; nor was the rumour that the popular American-born pianist Charlie Kunz was using his BBC broadcasts to send coded messages to the Nazis via his keyboard. Another even more outlandish story was accurate: bandleader Arthur Lally, then in his late 30s, demanded that the War Office allow him to fly a plane over Germany so that he could personally drop a bomb on Hitler at his mountain retreat. When this offer was politely refused, and doctors suggested that he might consider more restful pursuits, Lally was so outraged that he committed suicide.

Musicians shared the hazards faced by the civilian population. The American bandleader Carroll Gibbons had been resident in the UK since 1929, and often broadcast from the Savoy hotel during the Blitz of 1940. During one performance, a German bomb knocked Gibbons and his musicians off the bandstand, and Noël Coward had to man the piano to keep the transmission afloat. The country's most revered swing band, an all-black West Indian unit led by Ken 'Snakehips' Johnson, was performing during a March 1941 air raid at the Café de Paris in London. A bomb hit the club, killing Johnson and his sax player, and at least thirty members of the audience. Four months later, Britain's most popular crooner, Al Bowlly, was killed during another raid as he slept in his London flat. His final recording was Irving Berlin's hopeful valediction to Hitler, 'When That Man is Dead and Gone'.

A more subtle challenge was faced by Victor Silvester, once the world champion foxtrot and waltz dancer, co-writer of the definitive guide to *Modern Ballroom Dancing* and, by 1935, bandleader. He abhorred the tendency of other orchestras to alter the given tempo of a tune, protesting that it made dancing impossible. Instead, he guaranteed 'strict time' musicianship: melodic, silky with strings, and rhythmically unwavering. He was the obvious choice to lead a wartime programme entitled *Dancing Club*, in which he read out the required steps for each number, then paused for several seconds while his audience wrote them down. He discovered that the Brooklyn-born propagandist William Joyce, known to everyone as Lord Haw-Haw, was intercepting the BBC's signal from Berlin, and filling these silences with anti-British rhetoric.

Other efforts by Germany's propaganda ministry were equally cunning. Between 1940 and 1943, the Nazi regime financed the recording and broadcast of dance-band records intended to dent British resolve. They were credited to Charlie and His Orchestra, the leader being a crooner named Karl Schwedler. Charlie's strategy was simple: he performed ostensibly straight renditions of popular songs, but revised the lyrics to add a crudely satirical message. Like Lord Haw-Haw, Charlie masqueraded as a British aristocrat. 'Here is Winston Churchill's latest tearjerker', he would announce gleefully, before singing 'The Germans are driving me crazy.' On 'Makin' Whoopee', he impersonated the Jewish-American crooner Eddie Cantor, with barbed couplets such as 'Another war, another profit, Another Jewish business trick.' (Charlie's lyrics did not rhyme or scan quite as meticulously as the originals.) There is no evidence that these German short-wave broadcasts had any propaganda value. But bizarrely, an era in which American music was officially *verboten* in Germany proved to be a golden age for the country's jazz: 'The fact that Nazi Germany should become the swing band centre of Europe is the supreme irony of dance band history', historian Albert McCarthy noted.

There was a similar flowering of jazz in France under German occupation and Vichy government. Clubs and dance halls closed briefly when the Nazis arrived in Paris, then adjusted themselves to the new regime. Aficionados of swing called themselves *zazous*, a name inspired by Cab Calloway. Their anthem was 'Je Suis Swing' by Johnny Hess, effectively a declaration of defiance to fascism. The *zazous* defied official bans on late-night jazz, and the German authorities appear to have ignored these breaches of discipline, feeling that it was better for young Frenchmen to be jitterbugging than plotting with the French Resistance. (Many did both.) When Vichy propaganda told the French people, '*C'est l'heure de travail*' ('It's time to go to work'), the vocalist Georgius recorded a provocative song entitled 'Mon Heure de Swing'. French radio announcers took heart from this cultural rebellion, and began to broadcast a diet of American jazz records, carefully giving all the titles in French to obscure their origins (and the fact that many were written by Jewish composers). Jazz became a symbol of freedom, as the historian Matthew Jordan wrote: 'The Allied troops entered Paris on August 25, 1944, and the celebration began. Once again [as after the Great War of 1914–18], jazz was the collective soundtrack for the liberation of France.'

For the established stars of French music hall and cabaret who remained throughout the occupation, plotting an ethical course was perilous. If they refused to perform for their compatriots, they risked being branded as disloyal. If they took part in entertainment that was officially sanctioned by the invaders, or sang for German officers, they might be classed as traitors. Jewish musicians and singers fled, if they could; others had to submit the texts of every song they performed to the German authorities, or be barred from public appearances. The best-known French entertainer of the era was Maurice Chevalier, a Hollywood star since the birth of the talkies. He was a national hero in France, but his decision to appear on radio programmes during the occupation, and to perform for German officers, caused him to be classified as a collaborator after the liberation. He was refused permission to fulfil a theatrical engagement in London in March 1945, because he was considered not 'likely to contribute to the British war effort'. A decade later, he had been forgiven by most, and toured the world with a cabaret act which included a love song in German, which he delivered in a screaming pastiche of the Führer's familiar voice.

Perhaps the cruellest use of popular music in wartime Europe occurred at the Czech garrison town of Terezín (Theresienstadt to the German occupiers), which became a holding camp for Jews who were being sent to Auschwitz. In 1944, it was the location for a German propaganda film intended for international consumption, called *The Führer Gives a Town to the Jews*. The camp was painted and filled with props for the movie-making, to ensure it resembled a functioning urban community. Happy young Jews were pictured at work there, entertained by a swing band called the Ghetto Swingers. Once the film was completed, the participants were sent to Auschwitz, where they formed what musical units they could to ease the agony of their fellow prisoners. Most of the Ghetto Swingers perished there, while cabaret star Kurt Gerron, who was forced by the Germans to direct the film, was marched to the gas chamber by guards who insisted that he sing one of the melodies from *The Threepenny Opera* for which he was most famous.

Men in America's armed forces abroad indicate a clear preference for taking their music hot. At the rate he's going, Johnny Doughboy will do an even greater job of spreading the gospel of the Dixieland beat than was done in the first World War, when the entire European continent was made jazz-conscious.

Billboard magazine, October 1942

> One name band leader experienced a tough two or three minutes
> the other evening while singing 'This is Worth Fighting For'. At the
> end of the tagline, one of the dancers loudly demanded, 'Well, why
> don't you get into a uniform and fight, then?'
> *Billboard* magazine, August 1942

Little more than twenty-four hours after the Japanese attack on the Pearl Harbor naval base in December 1941, which resulted in the deaths of more than 2,000 people, the American government formally declared war on the Empire of Japan. No sooner was the announcement made than comedians Bud Abbott and Lou Costello, stars of the military comedy *Buck Privates*, were whisked into a Hollywood recording studio. They recorded a spectacularly ill-timed vaudeville routine with an orchestra and vocal quartet entitled 'Laugh Laugh Laugh', the chorus of which announced: 'Things have been worse before.'

This was not destined to become the most enduring American song of the Second World War. Indeed, as composer Hoagy Carmichael noted in 1942, 'I think everyone in the music world is conscious of the lack of an outstanding popular song in the present war. For some reason or other, nothing written so far has clicked. I believe it's because the tunes haven't gotten underneath the surface enough. Their treatment of the war has been too superficial. America is in a situation today that calls for a tune with real depth of sentiment. I think people are past the stage where they're impressed by songs that indulge merely in flag-waving or boasting of our national might.'

That was not the prevailing assumption as war began, and music publishers reported being 'bombarded with variations of the "Beat the Axis" and "Smash the Japs" type tunes', as professional songwriters competed to display their patriotism. Early entries included 'Let's Remember Pearl Harbor', 'Slap the Jap Right Off the Map', 'The Sun Will Be Setting for the Land of the Rising Sun' and 'When Those Little Yellow Bellies Meet the Cohens and the Kellys'. The most successful songs in this vein were 'You're a Sap Mr Jap', recorded by Carl Hoff's orchestra; 'Goodbye Mama (I'm Off to Yokohama)', a swing tune by Teddy Powell; and drummer/bandleader Gene Krupa's 'Keep 'Em Flying', which began with growling saxophones imitating the planes of the USAAF.

The sentimental ballad 'The White Cliffs of Dover' – an American song, despite its title – dominated the airwaves in the weeks after Pearl

Harbor, reflecting the public need for reassurance. 'Miss You' (Dinah Shore) and 'I'll Pray For You' (the Andrews Sisters) mined a seam familiar from the previous catastrophe, of girls waiting loyally for their boys to return from the front line. Peggy Lee, with the Goodman band, revived Vera Lynn's 'We'll Meet Again'. 'Don't Sit Under the Apple Tree (With Anyone Else But Me)' by Glenn Miller highlighted the fear that these girlfriends might not be as faithful as they promised.

The folk singer Carson Robison picked up sales throughout the early months of the war with a succession of sarcastic 'tributes' to the enemy leaders, such as 'Mussolini's Letter to Hitler'. Musical madcap Spike Jones fashioned a satirical attack on Hitler, 'Der Fuehrer's Face', which became the theme of a Walt Disney cartoon (*Donald Duck in Nutziland*). But as America's war entered its first full year, three songs became instant standards. 'This Is Worth Fighting For' portrayed America as a land of swaying cornfields and country cabins, where rosy-cheeked kids waited with their apron-clad mothers for daddy to come home. 'There's a Star-Spangled Banner Waving Somewhere' tied the hillbilly market to the war effort, Elton Britt's rendition outselling every other offering in that genre for the next two years. Most successful of all was 'Praise the Lord and Pass the Ammunition', available in various competing versions by choirs and quartets. It was based on the quite possibly apocryphal tale of a sermon given by a navy chaplain during the Pearl Harbor attack. Combining military zeal with religion, it tapped simultaneously into two sources of American pride, and it prompted many rivals, the most enduring of which was 'Comin' In on a Wing and a Prayer'.

By April 1942, there was talk that a forthcoming Hollywood musical, *Holiday Inn*, would contain a Bing Crosby ballad guaranteed to seize the country's heart. By September, 'White Christmas' was on course to become the best-selling single of all time, securing the first of its more than 50 million sales over the next seven decades. Lushly orchestrated, the hum of a chorale adding to its atmosphere of wistful reverence, the disc's immediate success owed something to its wartime context: the narrator was dreaming of a white Christmas because he was destined to spend it in a humid Far East jungle. But patriotism and romance were not enough in themselves to inspire such an instinctive response from the public: the hook was the low, rumbling purr of Bing Crosby's voice, as warming as the healthiest of Yuletide log fires. A year later, Bing offered another seasonal message. 'I'll Be Home for Christmas', he crooned, and more than a million disc-buyers chose to believe, against all the military evidence, that it might be true for them and their particular boy. 'The American GI is getting the war songs he wants,' reckoned Irving Berlin, 'something sentimental about home and love.' *Billboard* magazine agreed that 'our war songs have no reality to lads who are learning how to annihilate Fascists', and concluded that GIs were choosing 'to get their belts from the solid stuff' – swing, in other words.

Aware that music would perform a vital service in maintaining morale, the US government attempted to co-ordinate the entertainment industry. The military had already founded the USO (United Service Organizations) to arrange concerts for the troops at which top names from Hollywood and New York's nightclubs performed free of charge. Once war was declared, the OWI (Office of War Information) issued complex instructions to songwriters and publishers about the material that would aid the war effort. There should be no lyrics about the horror of war, and soldiers should only be described as dying in circumstances that would provide a heroic example for their comrades. Families and loved ones should be portrayed as patient, loyal and fully committed to the American cause. There should be no doubts expressed about America's part in the war, and no hint of troubles at home, in the form of strikes or food shortages. Songs must convey the message that America was going to win the war, but only with a determined effort from every participant. Lyrics that hymned the praises of airmen or sailors rather than soldiers should not be published. Most importantly, lyricists had to affirm American superiority without suggesting that the enemy was stupid or inferior: the worst enemy during wartime was complacency. Songwriters struggled to remain creative whilst stepping through this potential minefield. In addition, restrictions were imposed on songs already in circulation. Anything that sounded German or Italian was banned from jukeboxes, and US citizens with roots in those countries consoled themselves with polkas and traditional folksongs.

Vital raw materials were now reserved for military purposes: petrol was rationed for artists and audiences alike, which had an immediate impact on live performances (although leading bands were allowed an extra ration because of their importance to national morale). Record-buyers were encouraged to bring back old discs to be melted down before they could buy new ones. Phonographs gradually vanished from the shops; so too did harmonicas, the finest specimens of which had previously been imported from Germany and Japan.

It was at this parlous moment in American history, when the fate of its European allies seemed uncertain, and huge numbers of its young men were facing death overseas, that the American Federation of Musicians (AFM) chose to go on strike. Their leader was James Caesar Petrillo, a union boss worthy of a James Cagney film noir, who represented his members with ironclad conviction. His case was simple: American musicians were losing money to jukeboxes and radio. Unless they were paid royalties every time their work was broadcast or aired in a bar, they would withdraw their labour from the record companies. 'After August 1st [1942],' he announced, 'we will make records for home consumption, but we won't make them for jukeboxes. We will make them for the armed forces of the United States and its Allies, but not for commercial and sustaining radio programs.' As it would be impossible to control where discs would be sent, this was in effect a total ban on any recording by union members; and only union members were allowed to make records. There was one exception: musicians could record V-Disks, which were then carried on USAAF planes to troops around the world.* The *New York Times* complained that Petrillo's ban was the equivalent of banning phone calls, because they put cabbies out of business: 'The net result will be simply that the public will hear less music.'

That was certainly not true at first. The US record companies took advantage of the advance notice that Petrillo had given them, and scheduled round-the-clock recording sessions for their top artists right up to the deadline. As a result, they were able to continue releasing material by the likes of Bing Crosby and the Andrews Sisters for another year. With the public desperate for entertainment to distract them from the war, there was a brief boom in sales. Beyond that, the back catalogue could always be exploited. There was also a loophole: vocalists who did not play an instrument were not required to join the AFM, and could record with the backing of a vocal quartet or choir. There were elaborate schemes to bypass the ban by using instrumental tracks which had been pre-recorded outside the country; or by sending American musicians to work in British studios; or by teaching foreign artists how to sing in English using phonetic scripts; or

---

* British troops did not receive these V-Disk shipments, but POWs in German camps were sent Decca Portable Gramophones, and a batch of about thirty records. One prisoner wrote from Stalag XXB to *Gramophone* magazine in 1942: 'A fit subject for a Bateman cartoon is the POW who wanted to listen to Bach. I personally have been told, in no uncertain terms, just where to go when attempting it. The war cry is "Give us Bing."'

(most effectively) by employing anonymous artists and musicians at back-street studios to record new songs, which were then marketed as 'imports' from Mexico.

The strike held for a full year before Decca Records caved in; and another before their two biggest competitors, Columbia and Victor, could no longer bear to see Decca prospering at their expense. The record companies survived the dispute in better shape than they might have expected, thanks to the public's willingness to buy almost anything that was issued. Perhaps the biggest losers were the songwriters and publishers, who for several years were denied the opportunity to have their latest songs plugged on record.*

For the American record-buying public, the strike was less worrying than the simple lack of discs in the stores. When 1943 dawned in Philadelphia, the city's record shops were empty. By spring, the magazine *American Music Lover* noted that releases were 'scraping the bottom of the barrel' and that new dance tunes were virtually extinct. Only in November 1944, when the AFM strike was settled, did record companies have access to raw materials, songs and artists, ready for a frenzy of recording as prolonged as that which had preceded the ban.†

> From the standpoint of appearance, [Frank Sinatra] could use a few extra pounds.
>   *Billboard* magazine, July 1942

> To a mere male, there is no sign of the alleged hypnotic power [of Sinatra], but only a rather pleasant and very softly modulated crooner.
>   *Gramophone* magazine, June 1944

---

* When Dooley Wilson sang 'As Time Goes By' in the film *Casablanca* (1942), he was unable to exploit his brief moment of fame by releasing a record. Instead, the public had to choose between 11-year-old recordings by Jacques Renard and Rudy Vallee, both of which made the best-sellers lists.

† Not that this was the last industrial action by musicians in the 1940s. No sooner had the war ended than the AFM barred any US radio station from broadcasting programmes made overseas, ending a long-held reciprocal agreement with the BBC. Then the British Musicians' Union refused to co-operate with the BBC without extra payments; and in 1948 the AFM launched another, less protracted, recording strike.

Unlike those in Britain and Europe, the vast majority of American citizens could enjoy a wartime life of almost surreal calm. Bandleaders took the temperature of America, and found it lukewarm. A poll of college students discovered that 'the harum-scarum jitterbugging is definitely a thing of the past', with 'smooth' music much preferred. 'Dance music lost most of its swing and sting during the past year', reported *Billboard* magazine at the end of 1942. The conclusion: 'The middle-aged [musicians] left are playing it sweet, which seems to please the middle-aged customers who are buying it.' In Manhattan lounges, all the talk was of cocktail combos and speciality acts: Snub Mosley, 'The Man with the Funny Little Horn'; Marshal Martz and his Three-Manual Electronic Organ, 'the only one of its kind in the world'; Joe (RubberFace) Franks, 'that Funny Man with that Funny Band'; not to forget 'Liberace: Concert Pianist; Synchronisations with Recordings of Noted Pianists & World Famous Symphony Orchestras', duetting with his classical record collection at the Park Lane in Buffalo, New York.

Beyond the metropolis, there was a craze for cowboys and anything that reeked of the country. Bob Wills and His Texas Playboys were selling a hillbilly dance concoction (retrospectively dubbed western swing) which combined polka, folk, boogie-woogie, blues and unashamed Texas honky-tonk country. Honky-tonk provided the soundtrack of adult courtship across the Southern states, its songs filled with adultery, lust and alcohol – themes also to be found, in very different geographical surroundings, in the *ranchera* of Mexico (its closest cousin), *rebetika* of Greece, the *canciones* of Mexico, the fados of Portugal or the tangos of Argentina. You could dance to this music, fuelled by its electric lead guitar or amplified pedal steel, or cry to it; its scenarios were scarred by adultery, disappointment and self-delusion. Like the classic blues of Bessie Smith, honky-tonk expressed the actual or imagined fears of its audience: hence the appeal of a song such as Ted Daffan's 'Born To Lose', one of the biggest hits of the war in any musical genre. 'There are indications that a flood of country-type tunes may be recorded by name maestri in the pop fields', *Billboard* announced in April 1942, as acts such as Bing Crosby raced to tackle 'You Are My Sunshine' and 'Deep in the Heart of Texas'. Twenty stars from the *Grand Ole Opry* radio show were squeezed on to a row of buses, and sent across America to play at military bases, hospitals and airfields. Even Manhattan fell for cowboy chic, when singing westerners such as Roy Rogers and the Sons of the Pioneers headlined a giant rodeo show at Madison Square Garden.

Children would have relished the rope-twirling and lassoing, but even in Texas honky-tonk was not intended to win adolescent hearts. With most of the swing bands broken up or opting to sugar-coat their style, the freshly discovered teenage market required its own diversions. For girls, it arrived in the frail, scar-necked frame of 26-year-old Frank Sinatra. Harry James's band was one of the country's finest, and Sinatra just one of his vocal troupe, the Music Makers. But from his first show, young girls started screaming at him, and a cult developed, to the chagrin of male audience members. 'The minute Sinatra started singing,' said reporter James Bacon, 'every girl left her partner on the dance floor and crowded around the microphone on the bandstand. He was so skinny the microphone almost obscured him.'

In 1940, Sinatra was poached by the even more powerful Tommy Dorsey band, whose leader recalled: 'I used to stand there on the bandstand so amazed I'd almost forget to take my solos. You could almost feel the excitement coming up out of the crowds when the kid stood up to sing. Remember, he was no matinee idol. He was a skinny kid with big ears. And yet what he did to women was something awful.' You can get a taste of it on the 1940 Dorsey/Sinatra hit 'I'll Never Smile Again', as Sinatra slides out of the chorale and into the audience's ear, just as he'd insinuated his way into their dreams. In spring 1942, he cut his first solo disc, 'Night and Day', which *Billboard* promised would be 'a cinch to make the girls, especially, give up all their nickels'. Once again, he conjured up a mood that teetered on the border of sleep and wake, whispering and cooing with an apparently guileless sensuality.

Dorsey and Sinatra broke box-office records at the Paramount in New York, and then Sinatra told his leader that he wanted to go solo. 'I hope you fall on your ass', Dorsey replied. For a few painful weeks, it seemed Dorsey might get his wish. Then in December 1942, back at the Paramount in fourth-billing behind comedians and the Goodman band, the phenomenon the press dubbed 'Swoonatra' began. Biographer James Kaplan retold the story through the eyes of publicist George Evans: 'The place was absolutely packed with hysterical teenage girls . . . The air in the great auditorium was vibrating, both with earsplitting screams . . . and with the heat and musk of female lust . . . The publicist's ears picked out one sound above the din: a low moan, emanating from a lanky, black-haired girl . . . It was a sound he had heard before – only in very different, much more private circumstances.'

This was the Sinatra secret: evoking desires that the youngest of his fans might not have even realised they possessed; and hypnotising them into behaving in ways that they would have been too shy to mimic in private, even with their husbands or boyfriends. Realising that this was the stuff of financial dreams, George Evans set out to ensure that it would not be a solitary outburst of hysteria. He hired girls to attend each Paramount show: if nobody else was screaming, it was their job to trigger the surge of emotion. Meanwhile, he tutored Sinatra in how to elicit that response. This did not entail crude theatrics or overt sexuality, which would have killed his career in the early 1940s, but delicate hand movements, such as the way he clutched the microphone like a baby reaching for its mother's breast. Evans dubbed Sinatra 'The Voice' and the nickname stuck, just as his voice sometimes caught in his throat accidentally as the moment swept him away. Sinatra was soon trained to perform that trick on demand. With subtle variations on his natural style, and without cheapening his act or his music, he became, par excellence, the teenage singing idol of the century. He wasn't the first young man to elicit screams when he sang (Rudy Vallee probably deserves that honour), and was far from the last; but everyone in his wake did so in the knowledge that Sinatra was a pioneer. 'The scenes at the Paramount, and later at broadcasting studios,' wrote Arnold Shaw, 'were the nearest thing to mass hypnosis the country had seen until then, with girls moaning ecstatically, shrieking uncontrollably, waving personal underthings at him, and just crying his name in sheer rapture.'

Two years later, the Paramount played host to the 'Columbus Day Riot' – a school holiday coinciding with Sinatra's return to the theatre that had made him famous. Girls queued all night for the morning show, and then wouldn't leave their seats, ensuring that thousands of thwarted fans were marooned outside. When someone (paid by a newspaper, he admitted later) pelted Sinatra with eggs, the fans attempted to lynch the culprit, screaming out, 'Catch him! Kill him! Cut him up like a rug!' They were 12–16 years old, mostly, on the cusp of innocence and sexual knowledge, and in Sinatra they found – well, a father figure, according to one journalist, or a child needing to be mothered, so psychologists said. But as one teenage fan recalled thirty years after her infatuation: 'Whatever he stirred beneath our barely budding breasts, it wasn't motherly. And the boys knew that, and that was why none of them liked him.' She remembered how 'We loved to swoon ... we would gather behind locked bedroom doors, in rooms where rosebud wallpaper was plastered over with pictures of The

Voice, to practice swooning. We would take off our saddle shoes, put on his record, and stand around groaning for a while. Then the song would end and we would all fall down on the floor.' The fans were not victims but willing accomplices in this loss of inhibition.

Girls, it was universally agreed, wanted romantic ballads, and Sinatra and his peers did their best to satisfy them. But what of teenage boys, too old for model planes and too young for the forces? There was a growing fear that while their elder brothers were offering their lives, those left behind were slipping out of control. The *Pittsburgh Press* newspaper complained about 'the behavior of children – and some not so young – in theatres, laughing and hooting during quiet, serious movie sequences and shouting and jitterbugging, under the influence of popular music or similar stimulants'. The near-riot during the 1942 swing festival in Washington, DC added racial overtones to the disquiet. In Cleveland, there were reports that 'juvenile hoodlums' were ruining dances and concerts. 'They take particular delight in heckling big-name bands ... with their stentorian wise-cracking, catcalls and whistles ... Once these entertainment gang- sters leave their seats, having had their fill of bratful play, their annoying tactics do not end. Marring walls, tearing up washroom fixtures and other acts of vandalism follow. Ushers and managers are threatened with bodily injury. Patrons in lobbies are insulted.' In Detroit, meanwhile, the 'angle appears to be that the youths, earning top money as young defence plant workers when they would normally be in school in other times, are spending their spare time and earnings in riotous show-off stuff'.

Beyond the testosterone-fuelled antics, there was a looming sense that these teenagers constituted a movement, with its own uniform: a riotous counterpoint to the equally fearsome discipline of Germany's Hitler Youth. It comprised, as historian Luis Alvarez recounted, a 'signature broad-brimmed hat, drape pants that ballooned out at the knee and were closely tapered at the ankle, oversized jacket and, on occasion, gold or silver watch chain hanging from the pocket. Young women also crafted their own zoot style by wearing short skirts, heavy make-up and the same fingertip- length coats as their male counterparts.'

This garb was known as a 'zoot suit' – a phrase, like the French *zazous*, borrowed from the jive slang of Cab Calloway. To the authorities, it signified violence and nonconformism; a break in America's seamless resistance to the fascism of Germany and the fanatical militarism of Japan. (Communist countries soon had their equivalents: the *stiliagi*, or style-chasers, in Russia; the *jampecek*, or dudes, in Hungary; and the *bikiniarze*, who took their name from Bikini Atoll, in Poland.) There was an attempt to brand all of those who wore the zoot suit as being black or Latino, although it was just as popular with working-class white youths and (on the West Coast) those of Asian origin.* And the music that the zoot-suited rebels championed was jazz, swing and the style still described by the industry as 'race' or 'sepia' music, but which would soon become known as rhythm and blues.

A decade before Norman Mailer identified 'The White Negro' – a white hipster who adopts black style as a statement of defiance and alien-ation – the prototype of the species existed on America's coasts and in its major inland cities. Nightlife was still effectively segregated in wartime, but at jazz clubs such as the Savoy Ballroom in Harlem, increasing numbers of zoot-clad white teens were sharing the dance floor with their black coun-terparts – and without the violence that pessimists might have anticipated. The Savoy was soon shut down by New York police, officially because the dubious morals of the ballroom's female clientele were infecting innocent sailors with venereal disease; but it is more likely that the city's intervention was prompted by the alarming sight of black and white kids dancing together.

Life at war was less segregated by race than at home, and many white soldiers discovered that their black buddies were enjoying music that packed the same visceral punch as swing, but with more swagger and less noise. Contemporary white music, for example, had nothing as sly, saucy and gently swinging as the music of Fats Waller, or the jive-talking Slim & Slam. Boogie-woogie piano was at the heart of black music in the early 1940s, and it quickly fed into white pop, enabling the Andrews Sisters ('Beat Me, Daddy, Eight to the Bar') and Will Bradley ('Down the Road Apiece') to exploit its rolling momentum, though they failed to match the ease of the originals.

'Negro band leaders have held their own through the years because they presented a brand of music whites could not easily duplicate', opined *Billboard* in January 1943. The magazine had recently launched a weekly 'Harlem Hit Parade', listing the ten best-selling records in a small selection of stores in this predominantly African-American district of New York. The

---

* The fashion spread around the world: in the Afghan capital, Kabul, young men wore zoot suits while their girlfriends remained veiled.

early charts featured a medley of styles: boogie-woogie, gospel, the placid harmonies of the Four Ink Spots, some swing (black and white), even a Paul Whiteman dance-band ballad which reached a black audience because of its poised vocal by Billie Holiday. Bing Crosby's 'White Christmas' also figured, to prove that sentimentality knew no racial boundaries.*

But there were some records that could never have been played on mainstream radio in the war, or at any dance where white adults might chance to hear them. Bonnie Davis played the erotic teaser on 'Don't Stop Now'. Louis Jordan, part country bumpkin, part lyrical genius, channelled all the wit and panache of his race into 'What's the Use of Getting Sober When You Gonna Get Drunk Again', anticipating the approach that would prove so successful for the Coasters fifteen years later. Most outrageous of all was Tampa Red's plea to his woman, 'Let Me Play With Your Poodle', in which any canine references were purely accidental. (Three years earlier, Fats Waller's equally juicy aside on 'Hold Tight' – 'I want some seafood, Mama' – had passed the nation's censors by.)

Since the summer of 1939, the music of black America had burst its banks in every imaginable direction, sending out waves that would reach around the world. In jazz, Art Tatum ('Tea For Two') and Coleman Hawkins ('Body and Soul') tossed away melody with an abandon that Louis Armstrong would have envied, exploring the distant harmonic potential of tunes that were already a familiar playground for their peers. Duke Ellington fine-tuned the swing genre ('Take the "A" Train') having sketched the blueprint for the film noir jazz of the 1950s ('Ko-Ko'). Billie Holiday tantalised and disturbed in equal measure with 'Strange Fruit', the portrait of a society in which lynching was acceptable. It was greeted by the *New York Post* as the unofficial national anthem for America's 'exploited' black population, and dismissed by one of her most vehement supporters, critic John Hammond, as 'artistically the worst thing that has ever happened'. She redeemed herself in Hammond's eyes via her deliciously restrained reading of 'God Bless the Child', which offered the sting of fine whisky against the sugary soda of Tin Pan Alley's output.

From today's perspective, it's difficult not to categorise the music of this era – to set up an artificial divide between jazz and blues, for instance, and then shepherd artists into genres that were only identified in

---

* The scenario was reversed when *Billboard* began to document the best-selling 'Folk' records, and discovered that rural whites had a secret passion for Nat King Cole and Louis Jordan.

retrospect. For its contemporary audience, this music was simply there to enjoy: a banquet of riches encompassing big bands, boogie-woogie piano romps, stately blues ballads, scratchy guitar blues from the Deep South, rowdy dance tunes and steel-guitar instrumentals. The 'top favourite of hep Harlemites' in 1942 was the band of Jimmie Lunceford, which apparently swung harder than any other band on the circuit (not that their records reveal it today). The self-professed 'World's Biggest Little Entertaining Band' was fronted by Louis Jordan: 'They clown! They sing! They swing!', their management boasted. With 1943's 'Five Guys Named Moe', they matched their advertising, setting up a jumping rhythm and topping it with a babble of scat and jive-talk that Cab Calloway would have been proud to own.

The blues ballad of the 1940s could be anguished or merely slow; sad, sentimental or at times no more than bland. But its simplicity stripped away the prettification that permeated Tin Pan Alley romance. It could also encompass bawdiness (Jimmy Rushing's jibe at his woman's 'big fat rusty dusty' on Count Basie's 'Rusty Dusty Blues') and sophisticated wit. The latter was an early trademark of Nat King Cole, a jazz pianist and vocalist whose voice was so mellifluous that most of his audience missed the hip humour of his songs.

It was Cole's dream to lead a big band, but commercial necessity led him to create the King Cole Trio, utilising the unusual (for the time) instrumentation of piano, guitar and bass, and demonstrating that you didn't need volume to swing. This was the music of a man who didn't seem to sweat or worry, a man so cool that he could breeze through any situation and steal any heart. With songs such as 'That Ain't Right' and 'Straighten Up and Fly Right', Cole created music that was both unashamedly black, full of street smarts and hipster slang, and also sufficiently mellow to ensure that nobody would move away from the jukebox. Just about the only white man who could compete with him was the lyricist and co-owner of Capitol Records, Johnny Mercer, whose 'GI Jive' was both a crude impression of the voice of black America and a loving tribute to its spontaneity.

If Nat King Cole's radicalism was subtle, other black performers signalled the path to the future with rockets and flares. Lionel Hampton recorded the instrumental that would become his anthem, 'Flying Home', in 1940, and then revised it in 1942, with saxman Illinois Jacquet honking away at a single note like a bloodhound shaking a rabbit. Lucky Millinder wanted a 'Big Fat Mama' in 1941, and organised a contest in Philadelphia to find the biggest woman in town. He cut half a dozen sides that year which squeezed all the momentum of swing into the tight formula of the twelve-bar blues, and then let it explode across the grooves. The titles spoke for themselves: 'Ride, Red Ride', 'Shout, Sister, Shout', 'Apollo Jump' and, most prophetically, 'Rock! Daniel'. That key word was in the air: *Billboard* reviewed a show by the Original Carolina Cotton Pickers, and reported that their repertoire offered 'wild swing in its raw stage' and was 'loaded with original rock and stomp opuses'.

In uncanny anticipation of what would happen a decade later with Bill Haley and Elvis Presley, it was the white bandleader Tommy Dorsey who compressed all this energy into a twelve-bar instrumental which seemed to sample the future – with a title that also seemed to come from a decade ahead: 'Well, Git It!' Here were most of the ingredients that would set boppers and jivers in motion: cacophonous drum rolls, horns squealing for attention, a propulsive rhythm and riffs that nobody could miss. It wasn't subtle, or even original; but it opened up a road that could have led Dorsey to rock 'n' roll immortality. Instead, he remembered his core audience. His grim fate was to wind up persuading adults whose first flash of passion had long passed to get back on the dance floor and pretend that they still felt the same about their now all-too-familiar spouse. For Dorsey, 'Well, Git It!' was both a novelty and a final fling of his distant youth (he was 36 when it was released). It would be left to the black originators to round up all those symbols, the 'jump', 'shout' and 'rock', and translate them into a fresh language for American youth.

↯

'Many musicians are expressing alarm at the large number
of their colleagues who are "on the needle", and there is
considerable fear of a big blow-up soon.'

Melody Maker magazine, July 1946

CHAPTER 9

Let's Get Straight

'[FBI agents] have really been on the warpath the last few months, with emphasis on nabbing musicians for holding tea or even looking at it or smelling it. The FBI has its eye firmly fixed on 52nd Street in seeking offenders.'

Metronome magazine, August 1945

4

The link between narcotics and jazz had been forged in the 1920s. In Chicago, the clubs on the South Side resounded to the sound of King Oliver and Louis Armstrong, while the audience selected their poison from a menu of bootleg alcohol and marijuana (alias 'gage' or later 'tea'). In London, the West Indian drummer Edgar Manning played in a West End jazz band, when not dealing dope (marijuana again, though cocaine was also freely available). 'It is significant', noted historian Catherine Parsonage, 'that the image of jazz as presented in contemporary [1920s] songs is so consistent with the conventionally understood effects of drugs: addiction, swaying, hypnosis, craziness, abandon, excessive emotion, sexual desire and escapism. In addition, there were clear links between jazz and intoxicating substances due to the freedom of women to both take drugs and dance to jazz; activities which became symbolic of their post-war independence.' The classical composer Constant Lambert, an early convert to jazz, pointedly described the music as 'a drug for the devitalised', supplying emotional content for those steeped in repression. A psychiatrist from Johns Hopkins University went further, declaring in 1942 that jazz music had medicinal value in dealing with psychological problems, although its efficacy in dealing with physical illness had yet to be demonstrated.*

For musicians, so *Time* magazine reported in 1943, marijuana 'seems no more harmful than alcohol' and 'is less habit-forming than tobacco, alcohol or opium'. It even facilitated the playing of jazz: 'It is no secret that some of the finest flights of American syncopation, like some of the finest products of the symbolist poets, owe much of their expressiveness to the use of a drug. The association of marijuana with hot jazz is no accident. The drug's power to slow the sense of time gives an improviser the illusion that he has all the time in the world in which to conceive his next phrases. And the drug also seems to heighten the hearing – so that, for instance, strange chord formations seem easier to analyse under marijuana.'

---

* It was easy to find a conflicting opinion. The dean of the Eastman School of Music in Rochester, New York declared that dissonance in music was bound to lead to emotional problems: 'I hesitate to think of what the effect of music upon the next generation will be if the present school of "hot jazz" continues to develop unabated. It should provide an increasing number of patients for [psychiatric] hospitals.'

Alcoholics, *Time* concluded, frequently died young, lost in delirium tremens – and any jazz fan could recall the tragic legend of Bix Beiderbecke, who drank himself to death at 28. But 'vipers [marijuana users] frequently live on to enjoy old age'.

Despite this recommendation, US police departments and the owners of clubs in 'Swing Alley', Manhattan's 52nd Street, were unable to treat marijuana so lightly. Swing drummer Gene Krupa, fresh from boosting the US Air Force with patriotic songs, was sentenced to one to six years in San Quentin in 1943. His crimes were possession of two marijuana cigarettes, and recruiting a 'minor' to transport his drugs. (He eventually served just three months, and resumed his career untarnished.) Two years later, there were police raids all down 52nd Street, after reports that such clubs as the Three Deuces and the Spotlite were harbouring known 'tea' dealers. So regular was police harassment that the manager of the Spotlite eventually figured it would be less trouble to reopen as a strip joint.

More problematic was the prevalence of heroin use amongst jazz bands. Members of the big swing bands not only had to endure the showman's perpetual curse, of unwinding after hours of solid adrenaline; but they were also burdened with travel schedules that made sleep impossible and ensured only the artificially sustained could survive. Nobody claimed that 'junk' improved the music; indeed, the worst offenders were prone to 'nodding off' mid-set.

When saxophonist Lester Young faced a court martial on drug offences at the end of the war, he was asked if he had come across any other jazz musicians who were using heroin. 'Yes, all the ones I know', he replied. By the summer of 1947, there were regular 'busts' of jazzmen, and observers worried that it was only a matter of time before the scene claimed its first major casualty. Jazz critic Barry Ulanov demolished *Time* magazine's argument: 'One of the unmistakeable deficiencies of jazz and jazzmen is lack of intellectual discipline, poor musical education and equipment. Lacking the discipline and equipment to express the more complicated ideas ranging confusingly through their brains, they look for some way out, some expression for the impulse to large feeling and complex formulation. Hence the grain of happy escape and the leaf of easy dreams . . . Marijuana does not enhance musical performance in any direct physical way . . . Too often, because marijuana is not the magic potion its devotees expect it to be, tea-smokers go on to really nerve-breaking drugs, such as heroin . . . Under the effects of heroin, all moral restraint goes.'

As a witness for the prosecution, Ulanov produced saxophonist Charlie Parker, one of the pioneers of the 'strange chord formations' that *Time* had mentioned. At a July 1946 recording session, Parker arrived under the influence of heroin, topped up by a quart of whisky. He completed the cocktail by swallowing six phenobarbital tablets, blew some erratic, edge-of-the-world solos, and stumbled back to his hotel. There he used the public phone while stark naked, not once but twice, and was locked in his room by the manager. Then smoke began to ooze beneath his door: Parker had set his mattress ablaze, and collapsed. He regained consciousness in time for a brawl with firemen and police officers, still naked, before he was coshed to the ground, subdued and escorted to jail. Doctors ruled that he was clinically insane, and so he was transferred to an asylum, where he kicked his habit and was released in February 1947. He immediately resumed his heroin use.

He was still using when he gave Ulanov what he wanted: 'I don't know how I made it through those years', he admitted. 'I became bitter, hard, cold.' Most of all, he regretted the impact his addiction might have on impressionable fans. His manifesto for the future was simple: 'Let's get *straight* and produce some music!' In March 1955, he died at the age of 34; examining his body, the coroner assumed that he must be 60 years old.

His tragedy was mirrored by that of Billie Holiday, who was raped as a child, raised in a brothel and a workhouse, and fronting name orchestras when she was just eighteen. Her first husband was a dope dealer, who encouraged her to become a junkie. She endured a series of 'cures', busts and court cases, which hooked her fans into the soap opera of her life. There followed a series of relationships with narcotics abusers, each of whom assumed he should be her manager. To cure her heroin addition, she became an alcoholic. 'We try to live a hundred days in one day, and we try to please so many people', she told a TV talk-show host. In the late 1950s, she steered the ravaged shreds of her voice on an exquisite path across a set of standards (the album released as *Lady In Satin*), and then spent two months in hospital, scoring junk all the while, until expiring from heart failure at the age of 44.

As a human melodrama, Holiday's career was rivalled only by the perpetually troubled cabaret star Judy Garland, who reached 47 before suffering an accidental overdose of barbiturates; by China's most successful singer of the pre-Mao era, Zhou Xuan, who died aged 38 in 1957, after several nervous breakdowns; and by the remarkable French artiste, Edith Piaf.

Raised in a brothel, a parent herself at 17, Piaf was plucked from the seed-iest bars in Paris by club-owner Louis Leplée at the age of 20. (Her 1957 hit 'C'est à Hambourg' reflected her familiarity with the life of a prosti-tute.) The following year, she was implicated in his murder, but escaped without charge. For the rest of her life, she floated from one male saviour to the next, many of whom met untimely ends. Like Billie Holiday, she channelled a lifetime of poverty and peril into her music. Her performances were soul-baring and heart-wrenching; her material, frequently self-written, starkly emotional. Many of her songs were built around short, almost abrasive musical motifs, as if mirroring her angular, skeletal frame, yet filled with defiance, like 'Non, je ne regrette rien'. In her final years, she could no longer choose whether to kill herself with alcohol or pills. She played out her tragedy in charismatic appearances at the Paris Olympia: a recording of a 1960 performance remains as compelling a study of human frailty and pride as any music from the twentieth century.

Such lives failed to dispel the glamour of addiction. 'Any musician who says he is playing better either on tea, the needle or when he is juiced is a plain, straight liar', Charlie Parker declared in 1949. 'In the days when I was on the stuff, I may have thought I was playing better, but listening to some of the records now, I know I wasn't.' His actions spoke more vividly, and drugs became so closely entwined with the image of jazz – dope as an expression of bohemianism, dope as a way of handling the savage pain of the genuine artist – that through the 1950s and beyond, a habit was as glorious a way of proving oneself a jazzman as technical virtuosity or harmonic invention.

Mistakes – that's all rebop is. Man, you've gotta be a technician to know when to make 'em.
    Louis Armstrong, 1947

I don't think the public wants bop . . . it gets mighty boring . . . The public wants something it can whistle, sing and hum – something to dance to.
    Al Hibbler, singer with Duke Ellington's band, 1949

The jazz magazine *Metronome*, anticipating the imminent US victory over Japan in the summer of 1945, opined: 'The advances bands have made during six years of war are so great that musicians who have been in the services for any part of that period will have to study hard and earnestly to come abreast of them. Harmonically jazz is not at all as it was in 1939; its colours are different, its resources are so much broader, that comparison with the music of that blissful era is ridiculous.' The editor concluded: 'This is the beginning of maturity for America's greatest art. Jazzmen who are still in their musical infancy, childhood or adolescence will be left behind, as the art squares its shoulders, settles its stomach, alerts its brain, and accepts its adult responsibilities.'

So jazz was now an 'art', not a form of entertainment; it carried a moral requirement to mature; it could no longer be a plaything, as it carried 'adult responsibilities'. With those words, one of America's most influential voices of jazz cast off the music's mainstream appeal, and aligned it with the avant-garde – as a modernist voice to join cubist painting, surrealism, the stream of consciousness in fiction, the twelve-tone scale in classical music. It was late to the party, compared to the plastic and literary arts, but alive, at least, in a fearless terrain where all that mattered was to push further and harder and faster without concern for a destination.

When *Metronome* was promoting 'the advances bands have made', it was not referring to music that 99% of America could possibly have heard. This voyage into the jazz unknown had taken place on 52nd Street and in Harlem, at late-night jam sessions, and occasionally on experimental recording dates. There was no hint of it on radio, or on the jukebox, or wherever dancers still gathered. Anyone who followed the jazz magazines would have known that something had changed – there was constant talk of 'bop', and 'rebop', and 'bebop', too – but the aural evidence had been obscured by the AFM strike, which left the two most important years in the development of the new sound undocumented.

Even in peacetime, a few singles aside, 'bop' happened just out of earshot. It wasn't evident on jukeboxes or radio stations; nor was it played in most jazz clubs, at least until the early 1950s (by which time its main proponents had moved on). So the 'bop' movement was both one of the most dramatic revolutions in twentieth-century American popular music; yet also a purely academic debate which took place in the pages of the jazz press.

At rare moments in music history, there has been such a shift in grammar and language that it is almost impossible for an outsider to understand what has happened. Here are some pertinent quotes about the theory behind the move towards chromatic harmony from Donald Maggins's 2005 excellent biography of bop's prime mover, Dizzy Gillespie:

'In chromaticism, chords can be built on all twelve of the notes, not just seven. This greatly expanded the improviser's resource and made his or her task considerably more complex.'

'The path into the chromatic universe was discovered by moving up into the second octave . . . There one found the "higher intervals" – the ninth, eleventh and the thirteenth – of the chord.'

'The crucial interval for Dizzy [etc.] – the key that unlocked the door to chromaticism – was the eleventh, which, to avoid dissonance, was sharpened.'

'The beboppers discovered that: Any major scale built on a note a flatted fifth away from another contains all five of the chromatic notes missing from the first scale and vice versa; and, Using the scales in partnership makes fully harmonic the five notes that were non-harmonic in the diatonic system.'

'In other words, using the flatted fifth to find two scalar routes to the same resolution enables the improviser to build chords on all twelve notes of the octave instead of just seven. The improviser now had a full rainbow of musical colours to work with instead of just the basic hues.'

That is both a brilliant summary of bop theory, and a signal that this was not a style for the untutored. Performing in a dance band and, hence, a jazz band usually required the ability to read music as well as play it; each band had its 'book' of arrangements which were unique to its own repertoire, even if the basic melodies were shared by every other orchestra on the circuit. The difference between bop and previous changes in jazz music was that only those who understood the theory could fully appreciate its magnitude. The musically ignorant, who comprised the vast majority of bop's potential audience, might relish the new colours that bop brought to the palette, but not grasp exactly what made them so spectacular.

The 'adult responsibilities' demanded by that *Metronome* editorial did not equate with adult respectability, the aim of earlier attempts to alter the face of popular music. By teaming jazz with classical music, Paul Whiteman, George Gershwin, Igor Stravinsky and Artie Shaw had all hoped to persuade the doyens of the art establishment that jazz was worthy of their consideration. With bop, however, nobody cared about any kind of establishment, or any audience. Dizzy Gillespie and his co-conspirators were exploring the limits of the music: creating new rules, not attempting to squeeze inside the old ones.

Ray Charles, who became a professional musician in the late 1940s, felt that bop sold the jazz public short: 'The one thing which bothered me about some jazz players I met around that time was their strange attitude. They'd say to a crowd, "This is my music. If you like it, cool. If not, fuck it!" I thought that was wrong. People give you their bread and are entitled to some kind of musical return on their dollar. I don't mean you got to give them exactly what they want. But you do have to keep them in mind.' To which Dizzy Gillespie could have replied (as he said in 1990): 'With gusto I dissected individual chords, turned them inside-out, upside-down. I gradually began to realise that the harmony in our popular music was pretty limited . . . and I started to think that I could create something much richer than that.'

While Charlie Parker has garnered the legend – he took drugs, he died young, and he played the saxophone, which is a sexier instrument (bigger, deeper, earthier) than the trumpet – his friend and sometime collaborator Dizzy Gillespie was bop's key protagonist. It was he who provided the first recorded evidence of chromatic playing (or at least the first to be *consciously* that way) on Lionel Hampton's 1939 side 'Hot Mallets'. Parker extended the technique in 1940, as he medleyed 'Honeysuckle Rose' and 'Body and Soul', but only for private consumption. It was Gillespie who fashioned the initial bop anthem, 'Salt Peanuts', in 1941 (although it wasn't recorded until 1945), and who delivered the first bop solo on a commercial disc, 'Jersey Bounce' by Les Hite's orchestra. He also wrote and arranged Woody Herman's May 1942 tour de force, 'Down Under', on which the entire band had bop in mind.

Dizzy and Bird played alongside each other in the 1944 big band fronted by the soon-to-be-famous baritone crooner Billy Eckstine, predictably alarming his fans with their exotic harmonies. By contrast, Donald Maggins reported the reaction of jazz drummer Thad Jones, who was with the army in Guam when he heard the Gillespie/Parker collaboration 'Shaw 'Nuff' on forces radio: 'We went out of our minds! . . . It was something we were probably trying to articulate ourselves and just didn't know how. And Dizzy and Bird came along and did it. They spoke our minds.' Somewhere in the gulf between a style that alienated its public, and an invention that fulfilled the wildest dreams of a musical generation, bop inaugurated the most creative, progressive period in the history of jazz: one which twisted and divided and reinvented the music to the point where it was no longer a single genre but a dozen, many of them unrecognisable to those who had worshipped the ODJB or Louis Armstrong. There would be commercially successful jazz records after bop, but jazz would no longer be the premier vehicle for popular music, as it had been between 1918 and 1945. That task would fall upon styles and musicians representing opposite extremes of tone, volume and ethos, but sharing one vital quality: the art of appealing instantaneously to their audience.

> The increasing specialisation which has taken 'jazz' out of the ballroom and almost on to the concert platform has presumably meant that fewer music lovers now buy ordinary dance records, and that in turn probably accounts for the increasing space given to the vocal.
> *Gramophone* magazine, January 1947

> First it was symphonies, concerti and tone poems which were raided for themes on which to build swoony love songs or dripping, sentimental ballads. Now it's songs and concert or salon pieces . . . To me, these indicate an admission by popular music writers that the creative wells are running dry.
> *American Music Lover* magazine, January 1947

After the rush of victory, there was an assumption that the British entertainment business would resume where it had laid down its instruments in 1939. The public, bandleader Joe Loss declared, needed 'bright and melodious music in perfect tempo'. To his horror, some of Britain's leading outfits attempted in a single bound to catch up on a decade of musical development in America. The nation's first home-grown bebop record was probably Harry Hayes's 'Scuttlebutt', and even amongst jazz fans, there was little market for so shocking an innovation. But Britain was finally ready for the swing explosion that had hit America a decade earlier. Isolated pockets of the UK population had been introduced to the big bands at their most intense either via wartime concerts, or American Forces Network radio. The traditionally minded critics described 'modernistic swing' as 'a choking creeper that is poisoning the body of jazz . . . It is not jazz – not even bad jazz – and it must be smashed up and killed if jazz is to live.' But from 1945 onwards, there were swing nights at the Adelphi Theatre in London with Jack Hylton's band, and also at the Palladium, with Ted Heath.

'Each fortnight,' the *Daily Mirror* blared, '[Heath's] powerhouse band lets off steam to an alternately rapt and rowdy audience of 3,000', reprising the reception given to Benny Goodman in 1935. 'I was quite uncompromising in my determination to play a very modern form of dance-music', Heath declared in his autobiography, by which he meant the style epitomised by the Glenn Miller Orchestra with its 'beautifully disciplined precision and power'. The BBC were dubious, and dropped him from their dance music schedule in 1947 because, they said, middle-aged listeners found the band's music 'incomprehensible'. The manager of the Palladium, Val Parnell, was equally perturbed: 'He'd heard about swing fans', Heath recalled. 'They were, he felt, more than a little on the rowdy side and given to jitterbugging and other noisy and even destructive forms of exhib-itionism.' After what they had endured during the war, young Britons could perhaps have been excused their response to the most thrilling music ever heard here − a wall of noise, brass to the fore, each section of the band standing up in unison for its chorus in the spotlight, the entire orchestra operating like a supercharged, thrillingly dangerous machine.

There were other attractions to a band such as Heath's. 'While swing fans are in the majority,' the *Daily Mirror* explained, 'many girls go to hear Paul Carpenter. Paul, once a Canadian war correspondent, is Britain's Frank Sinatra. A flutter of Paul's eyelids will launch a thousand sighs, and girls fight for his autograph more fiercely than for nylons.' Carpenter soon left to concentrate on an acting career, and his place was taken by a shy young man named Richard Bryce. Heath renamed him Dickie Valentine, which appealed to the band's increasingly passionate female following, and sentimental, guileless songs such as 'All the Time and Everywhere' ensured that he was rewarded with, as a pop annual of the period put it, 'one of the biggest fan followings of any British singer among the country's teen-agers'. Heath's singers were not the only local rivals to Sinatra: such long-forgotten names as Benny Lee, Denny Dennis and Steve Conway captured female hearts in the post-war years.

Romance had to be taken where it could be found in the mid-1940s. Britain might have won the war, but peace carried a ruinous cost: unemployment, inflation, shortage of fuel for cars and heating, power cuts, rationing of food and clothing, and an infrastructure that had been bombed, disrupted and drained of cash. By the end of 1946, the musicians' paper *Melody Maker* was predicting: 'We face a slump in general theatre and dance-hall business, which is entirely due to economics.'

The situation for American dance bands was equally parlous. The Benny Goodman Orchestra, which before the war could sell out any theatre in the land, could now only pull a hundred people to a 1,000-capacity New York venue. Some of the biggest names in the business were winding up their bands, or cutting them down to supper-club size: among them Harry James, Woody Herman and Tommy Dorsey. In the 1920s, vocalists had been a minor attraction in a band's armoury; in the 1930s, they were featured more heavily but still subjugated their personalities to their bandleader. The enduring success of Bing Crosby, and then Frank Sinatra's dramatic break with the Dorsey orchestra in 1942, encouraged other performers to go it alone: among them Perry Como, his voice so silky that it made Bing sound abrasive, Jo Stafford and Dinah Shore. Gone were the days when a singer would have to wait ninety seconds or longer for their cameo appearance on a dance-band disc: orchestras that had once been distinctive and experimental were now reduced to providing syrupy instrumental support for the personality vocalist of the moment.

In a telling switch of emphasis, the once-youthful sirens and crooners of the pre-war era were now sounding like mature adults addressing their own kind. With Sinatra, it was evident when he greeted the end of the AFM strike in 1944 with a swinging rendition of 'Saturday Night is the Loneliest Night of the Week', which anticipated his triumphs with Nelson Riddle arrangements a decade ahead. Doris Day, as versatile a singer as Sinatra but with Bing Crosby's velvet tone, delivered 'Sentimental Journey' with the dignity of someone who knew that for many of her audience, a loved one's journey might already have reached a premature close. Then there were earthier adult pleasures, signposted with joy by Betty Hutton's sex-charged 'Stuff Like That There', and with pain on Billie Holiday's 'Lover Man', which on feel alone deserves to be considered the first 'soul' record. Even those old enough to be grandparents had a representative, as Al Jolson returned to the best-sellers lists in 1947 with the Italianate 'The Anniversary Song', and an affectionate revival of 'Alexander's Ragtime Band' with Bing Crosby.

Of all these figures, Sinatra seemed best able to explore a world that was short on innocence after the ordeal of war, and the discovery of unimaginable horrors in German camps. He it was who dared to explore the limits of democracy in a society still riven by racial prejudice, in the film, and the song, 'The House I Live In'; to envisage not just the prime of adulthood but the certainty that it would pass, in 'September Song'; and to confront the vocal and emotional rigour of the 'Soliloquy' from the Broadway show *Carousel*.* Like *Oklahoma!* (1943), *Carousel* (1945) was written by the team of Richard Rodgers and Oscar Hammerstein II. Both soundtracks were issued as 'albums' – first as a book of 78 rpm singles, and later on long-playing discs – inaugurating an era in which almost every adult record collection was dominated by stage shows (and, subsequently, their film equivalents). Beyond the stage and movie musical, however, the popular song was in steep decline, as naked commercialism triumphed in post-war America's search for rapid economic expansion.

> The popular songs of the day, they've become so decadent, they're bloodless . . . I've been looking for wonderful pieces of music in the popular vein – what they call Tin Pan Alley songs. You *cannot* find any . . . The songwriter in most cases finds he has to prostitute his talents if he wants to make a buck.
> Frank Sinatra, 1948

> Right now, everyone is aware of the fact that popular music is going through one of the most depressing, retrogressive, uninspired and totally uncreative stages in its glittering history . . . Singers can also help. The stagnation is in part our fault. If we'd refuse to do the lousy material being handed to us by the publishers (and I'm as guilty as anyone of accepting and recording at least a few pieces of junk), then the world would be a better place in which to sing.
> Mel Torme, 1950

The Salt Lake City disc jockey Al 'Jazzbo' Collins was so disgusted by the success of Art Mooney's 1948 pop hit 'I'm Looking Over a Four-Leaf Clover' that he devoted his two-hour jazz show to playing it, over and over again, 'in gleeful anticipation that his hip fans would howl in protest'. Instead, he fielded dozens of phone calls congratulating him 'for playing something good, for a change', and sales of the song soared the following

---

* At nearly 30, he was perfectly poised to act as the narrator of an expectant father's confusion. As a singer, however, he perfected the song in the 1960s, and his late 40s, on the album *The Concert Sinatra*.

day. 'I never knew they were so square', said Collins of his audience. But he gained so much publicity that when he moved to New York, he repeated the stunt with the Chordettes' 'Mr Sandman'.

Mooney's hit answered the question Jack Kapp had posed in the Decca studios before the war: 'Where's the melody?' Brass, woodwinds, strings and what sounded like the entire membership of a big city glee club offered the melody and nothing but the melody: no syncopation, harmony or variation, merely the simplest and most memorable of tunes, with corny lyrics to match. Mooney was not alone: three months earlier, the biggest record in America had been Francis Craig's 'Near You', another tavern singalong which opened with a honky-tonk 'tack' piano, redolent of the Old West (or at least its Hollywood equivalent).

The country had been thrown headlong into one of the strangest eras in its musical history: a time when nothing counted more than novelty, unless it was the most basic form of nostalgia. Benny Goodman was reduced to declaring 'Give Me Those Good Old Days', with the vocal combo the Sportsmen requesting a return trip to 'the golden past . . . when the boys played the melody'. Another singing group, the Pied Pipers, dredged the lake of banality to its bottom for 'Ok'l Baby Dok'l' and T. Texas Tyler introduced the world to the convoluted metaphor that was 'Deck of Cards'. Eventually, even the likes of Frank Sinatra would be dragged into the mire. He was forced by his producer, Mitch Miller, to record 'Mama Will Bark', a novelty duet with TV glamour girl Dagmar, on which the one-time teen idol was required to bay like a hound. 'I guess it sold,' Sinatra conceded, 'but the only good it did me was with the dogs.'

This, some jaundiced jazz writers complained, was the world that bebop had built: one in which an entire generation (or more, as these records sold to young* and old alike) had turned its back on the genre's need for constant reinvention in preference for safer pleasures. This was a moment for nostalgia and simplicity, the two qualities not always coinciding. No sooner had swing been declared dead in America than it was back. Disc jockey Martin Block had hosted his *Make Believe Ballroom* radio show throughout the swing boom, and now he rejuvenated it in New York, prompting similar showcases across the country. Soon there were biographical movies about

---

* As *Down Beat* magazine noted in July 1949, 'An important facet in the polka trend is that its principal support comes not from elderly people nostalgic for the old country, but from youngsters who would normally be expected to be infesting bop dens.'

Glenn Miller (played by James Stewart) and Benny Goodman (Steve Allen in the lead role). The acetate discs of Goodman's Carnegie Hall concert from 1938 were unearthed and spruced up for release. Returning to this music twelve years later, *Metronome* decided, 'marks a kind of infantile regression which is more important psychologically than musically'. Meanwhile, as Glenn Miller wasn't available to cash in on his posthumous fame, other men competed to carry his torch. The Miller estate initially gave his former sideman, Tex Beneke, the right to lead the orchestra after Glenn's death, but withdrew permission in 1950, because he was shifting away from the original arrangements. So Beneke formed his own band in Miller's image, as did other leaders keen to exhibit their willingness to stay in the past, such as Ralph Flanagan, Jerry Gray and Ray Anthony. After the biopic, the estate allowed another Miller alumnus, Ray McKinley, to resurrect the band.

Earlier eras were also considered ripe for renewal. In the early 1920s, musicians such as Zez Confrey had reacted to the emergence of jazz by reigniting the flame of ragtime – albeit, as the genre's historians complained, 'a pseudo-ragtime "novelty" mode designed to show off virtuoso style, at the expense of ragtime's basic drive, form and consistency. This branch of ragtime developed into the empty pyrotechnics of the cock-tail pianist, a style based on cascades of arpeggios' (and perhaps encapsu-lated best by the florid playing of Liberace).

Twenty years later, Lu Watters' Yerba Buena Jazz Band were formed in San Francisco, billing themselves as a ragtime revival band, to the delight of magazines which regarded swing and the early stirrings of bebop as perversions of the true jazz spirit. (The same city would soon become the home of the folk revival, with musicians scuffling for jobs at 'banjo bars'.) Not that Scott Joplin would have recognised their music as his own: although much of their repertoire comprised pieces with the word 'Rag' in their title, their sound was closer to that of the Original Dixieland Jazz Band. But their much publicised antics enabled genuine ragtime pianists to record once again, although it was only with the success of Marvin Hamlisch's movie soundtrack for *The Sting* that ragtime was played as its early twentieth-century composers would have wished. His perfor-mance of Joplin's 'The Entertainer' ensured that a man who had died in 1917 became the composer of the best-selling US single of 1974.

A less accurate retread of Joplin marked the commercial peak of the passion for what was called 'Dixieland' music, which effectively meant wrapping the most melodious elements of the New Orleans jazz scene *c.*1920 in cotton wool, and presenting them as a circus act. Original protagonists from that era were welcomed as conquering heroes, as long as they didn't think about updating their style, while college audiences relished bands such as the Firehouse Five Plus Two, tooting away in their red firemen's uniforms, and Doc Rando and His Pills, clad in white coats with stethoscopes draped around their necks. Pee Wee Hunt's orchestra proved to be the most successful of these throwbacks, his 1948 revival of Joplin's 'Twelfth Street Rag' topping the American chart.

In Britain, this craze had started in 1943, with George Webb's Dixielanders – playing not for laughs but in deadly earnest, as befitted men who believed that they were keeping a cultural artefact alive. 'Their repertoire was the tunes of the New Orleans pioneers,' their sometime manager Jim Godbolt recounted, 'the style a combination of solo and collective improvisation in the fashion of their models. Quite astonishing, then, was the seeming authenticity of their music . . . They were utterly dedicated to absorbing the soul and essence of early jazz, notwithstanding their technical limitations. In our eager acceptance of these sturdy pioneers' principles, we overlooked their faulty technique.' The Dixielanders were pioneers indeed, their commitment to the past triggering the trad-jazz boom of the 1950s and 60s, in which uniforms every bit as garish as the Americans' would flourish.

The penchant for vintage jazz styles was matched by another revival, which provided enormous reassurance for any American with European blood. After its brief flowering in the late 1930s, it was time for the nation to take the polka to its breast. As early as June 1946, 8,000 fans filled the City Auditorium in Milwaukee for a contest to discover the country's premier exponent of the art. The winner was Frankie Yankovic, the accordion-toting son of Slovene immigrants, who once said that 'I like to think of myself as the blue-collar worker's musician.' For this was working man's (and woman's) music, entirely free of snobbery and elitism. It invited everyone to enjoy its simple pleasures, a philosophy which enabled another accordion-playing polka king, Lawrence Welk, to entertain audiences for almost sixty years with his 'Champagne Music', and to front a popular US TV show for twenty-seven years. Television talent show host Arthur Godfrey also cashed in: first with 'Too Fat Polka', a quasi-inebriated attack on an overweight woman; and then 'Slap 'Er Down Again, Paw', a comic defence of child-beating. Even the Andrews Sisters, who had explored every fad from boogie-woogie to the rumba over the previous decade, were inveigled into playing along, with 'Toolie Oolie Doolie (Yodel Polka)'. Needless to say, these songs did not require a master's degree in chromatic harmonies to understand.

The polka craze was not strictly limited to polkas: it encompassed waltzes, ballads and even revamped hillbilly tunes – anything that would encourage a tribe of immigrant Americans to remember a Europe which in many cases they had not even seen. Not that the polka passion ended there: Yankovic enjoyed lengthy seasons in Hollywood and Las Vegas, playing to the same audiences who might also have relished more overtly American entertainers, such as Judy Garland or Bing Crosby. Ultimately, the polka was doomed as popular culture by the rapidly changing market of the 1950s: as its historian, Victor Greene, noted, 'the American elite in the 1950s and 1960s regarded polka and like music as part of the mediocre, distasteful culture of beer-drinking, half-literate, white working-class clods'.

For many sophisticates, the tastes of another frequently lampooned section of society, the rural working class, were equally appalling. As early as January 1945, the jazz magazine *Metronome* was promising that 'Cowboy and hillbilly music are fast fading from the LA scene.' But four years later, its rival *Down Beat* was forced to admit, through clenched teeth, that 'the mountain music and oaters' odes [alliteration and condescension hand in hand] are just about pushing popular tunes, jazz, swing, bebop and everything else right out of the picture'. Four years further along the range, *Down Beat* lowered itself to print a regular hillbilly column, 'Sashayin' Around'. It assumed that anyone reading it would require prose to match the music: Tennessee Ernie Ford, fans were told, loved 'that old-fashion home cooking . . . I reckon he's just as plain as you and me and the next-door neighbor. Bein' a top western star doesn't keep you from having a notion you like black-eyed peas, grits, gravy and fried catfish.'

In the British magazine *Gramophone*, Oliver King concocted a line of attack that, suitably amended, would be flung by parents at teenage fans of Elvis Presley, the Beatles and their successors: 'I often wonder how cowboys ridin' the range manage to play an electric guitar. Do they have horses fitted with dynamos, or do they plug the guitar into a cactus?' ('What would happen if there were a power cut?' was the sardonic response of many elders to the sight of rock groups on television.) A more effective form of satire was used by Jo Stafford – who must, secretly, have loved this music – when she adopted the widest of hillbilly twangs, and the pseudonym 'Cinderella G. Stump', for a rendering of 'Tim-Tayshun'.

Ironically, it was exactly temptation, and the other sins and snares haunting adult life, that formed the raw material of hillbilly music. Whereas the emotional range of the late 1940s pop song did not extend beyond 'He loves me; he loves me not', the fledgling country-music genre could handle everything from adultery to alcoholism without losing its wits (or its morals, because a hillbilly temptation always yielded retribution). This was music with consequences, not simply dreams or (in the rhythm and blues field) erotic fantasies. It lacked musical sophistication, but then so did the blues; it was frequently sung off-key (especially when Ernest Tubb, one of the stars of the honky-tonk sound, was at the microphone) or with instruments that were jarringly out of tune. Yet it was rarely banal in the sense of avoiding reality: its imagery was paper-thin, but its scenarios were as deep as life itself. As singer/guitarist Merle Travis reflected, 'country music has been twisted, braided and finally welded together until it's a piece of music that's Americana. It's Hollywood and Tin Pan Alley and hillbilly blended together in the diamond ... I believe our fans are made out of a little better timber than others. The barn stands longer.' One of the great clichés of the country market, which held true until the 1990s, was already in evidence. Its audience was incapable of disloyalty. If an artist remained true to the music, and didn't try to disguise his or her origins, then the fans would keep faith. It was a style, and an audience, that was guileless and without novelty: unassuming, solid and fiercely slow to change.

By 1951, when Hank Williams was in his prime as a songwriter (and cunning magpie of other people's songs), when Eddy Arnold was walking the narrow line between hillbilly and crooning, when Tennessee Ernie Ford was milking America's mythology for all it was worth, and Ernest Tubb was still wailing just out of tune, country had become the bedrock of US popular music. Jazz was no longer providing suitable material for pop singers to steal, and much of the blues repertoire was too risqué or overtly black to be tackled by anyone who was targeting middle America. So singers such as Tony Bennett, Perry Como and Frankie Laine were turning their hand to the dependable simplicities of the country market. Rather than protesting that their work had been stolen, the original creators of such songs as 'Cold, Cold Heart' and 'Don't Let the Stars Get in Your Eyes' considered the pop covers a compliment and a way of reaching listeners who would never have discovered the unrefined hillbilly source. Meanwhile, Patti Page's cover of Pee Wee King's 'Tennessee Waltz' became America's best-selling record – Bing Crosby's Christmas tunes aside – in almost twenty years.

With 'Tennessee Waltz' and 'Cold, Cold Heart', the newly dubbed country and western music was still selling Tin Pan Alley's vision of American life: its success or failure dependent on the yin or yang of a romantic affair. But one country song from the early 1950s offered a more difficult choice. With 'It Wasn't God Who Made Honky Tonk Angels', Kitty Wells took a hillbilly standard, 'The Wild Side of Life', and reversed its scenario and its moral. In the original, a man dolefully scolded his wife for her promiscuity. In Wells's re-reading of the text, the husband was the barfly, picking up women on a whim. 'Too many times men think they're still single', she sang, nailing the double standard in a single line. There had been strong women before on record: sexual, proud, larger than life to the point of being unreal (unless you believed in the mythology of Mae West). But this was something else – a woman strong enough to speak the truth, but not sure whether she could carry its burden. None of the wholesome pop singers who sang 'Tennessee Waltz' went anywhere near Kitty Wells's song. It would take the likes of Aretha Franklin and Joni Mitchell to make universal entertainment out of a woman's view of marital discord.

⚡

'The public is confused about bop now. They think everything they hear is bop – even an old-fashioned swing sax solo … So many of the kids think that all you have to do to get hip to bop is to act weird – grow a goatee and wear a beret and those heavy horn-rims.'

Nat 'King' Cole

CHAPTER 10

MUSIC FOR GRACIOUS LIVING

'To succeed in America, I gave the Americans a
Latin music that had nothing authentic about it.'

Xavier Cugat

It was less a goatee than a tuft, like a Hitler moustache transposed beneath Dizzy Gillespie's bottom lip. But the beret and horn-rimmed spectacles were real enough, and together they constituted a persona which was caricatured in the papers and copied by his fans, male and female. In France, they fought over him, bop *zazous* and swing *zazous* coming to blows over a set of jazz harmonies. In America, they bought his records, especially when – in a 1945 collaboration with Charlie Parker – he could squeeze bop solos into a rhythmic novelty called 'Salt Peanuts' (itself based on a piano phrase Dizzy had borrowed from a Count Basie record).

Time magazine informed adult America that bop had its own motto ('Be hip, be sharp, be bop!') and language, in which the people who wanted to turn jazz back into Dixieland were 'moldy figs'. It also provided a definition: 'hot jazz overheated, with overdone lyrics full of bawdiness, references to narcotics and doubletalk'. They were actually referring to the jive-filled R&B records of Slim Gaillard, but the link was sufficient for a Los Angeles radio station to ban bop because it incited juvenile delinquency.

Within nine months of throwing out their 'Salt Peanuts', Gillespie and Parker had drifted apart. Dizzy appeared in a low-budget performance movie, *Jivin' in Bebop*, and then set out with a big band. Charlie Parker, who had declared that bop wasn't a descendant of jazz but an entirely new species, criticised Gillespie's conservatism: 'A big band slows anybody down because you don't get a chance to play enough. Diz has an awful lot of ideas when he wants to, but if he stays with the big band he'll forget everything he ever played. He isn't repeating notes yet, but he is repeating patterns.' Gillespie replied: 'Bop is part of jazz, and jazz music is to dance to. The trouble with bop as it is played today is that people can't dance to it.'

Consciously or otherwise, Gillespie was in the throes of a musical discovery that would alter the course of American popular music; but it wasn't bop. It was his intention, he said, to combine bop not only with Broadway standards, but also with the rhythms of Cuba, 'which will make it truly a music of the Americas'. Whereas the harmonies of bop passed pop by (until they were incorporated, suitably refined, into the jazz-tinged movie and TV soundtracks of the 1950s, the first of which was Alex North's score for *A Streetcar Named Desire*), Gillespie's Afro-Cuban jazz concoction would help to smooth the path for that Caribbean island to claim a disproportionate influence over the American mainstream. During 1947, Dizzy slipped the Cuban percussionist and composer Chano Pozo into his big band. At a Carnegie Hall show in September, and two fertile recording sessions around Christmas, the two men concocted a heavily percussive blend of their native styles. On the two-part piece 'Cubana Be; Cubana Bop', Chano's chattering congas and eerie chanting gradually seized control of the music, like a riposte to the frequent American invasions of his homeland. The pinnacle of their collaboration was 'Manteca', a 1948 jukebox favourite anticipating the Latin groove of the early 1970s funk scene, with hand-drum breakdowns ripe for hip-hop sampling. But then Chano Pozo was dead: he had beaten up his dope dealer for selling him substandard marijuana, and the man returned two days later with a pistol to hunt him down. Regardless, Cuban percussion remained in the jazz armoury, and from there it slipped into everything from rock to easy listening in the years ahead.

In time, other Cuban echoes would also be heard across America. In the singing of the island's 1930s icons, Miguelito Valdés and Arsenio Rodríguez, it is possible to hear the sultriness of Billy Eckstine or the Elvis Presley of the early 1960s. For America, 'Latin' equalled 'romance'; just as Britain found its symbol of love in Paris (and France invoked the names of cities in Italy, Portugal and Spain to achieve the same effect). But Cuba also offered a more physical presence in its hypnotic rhythms, which would leave their mark everywhere from mid-1950s mambo novelties to the syncopated basslines of James Brown's band a decade later. The Cuban band led by Tito Puente in the late 1940s were heavy on timbales and vibes, with rhythms that would recur throughout the early work of Stephen Stills, and the most popular Latin-rock band, Santana.

In 1951, Gabriel García Márquez, yet to conceive the fictional art of magical realism, was a journalist in Colombia, looking out across the Caribbean towards Cuba. It was from that vantage point that he passed judgement on a Cuban style which had recently swept on to American dance floors, by shedding the bop elements of Dizzy Gillespie's Afro-Cuban experiment and focusing entirely on the groove. 'Possibly the mambo is an outrage', Márquez wrote. 'But everybody who sacrifices five cents in the jukebox is, in fact, sufficiently outraged to hope it says something to him that resembles what he wants. And possibly also, the mambo is a danceable outrage . . . America is shouting itself hoarse with healthy admiration, while maestro Pérez Prado mixes slices of trumpets, chopped-up saxophones, drum salsa [sauce] and pieces of well-seasoned piano.'

The man born Dámaso Pérez Prado (his stage name was actually his surname) not only popularised the mambo in America and beyond: he taught the fundamental lesson of Cuban music, which was that the body had to be moved in a different way to anything seen in English-speaking nations before. 'It frightens inhibited people,' Perez Prado said, 'but whips up the blood of those who really love life.' With the mambo, everything was centred on the hips, which didn't thrust like a piledriver, as a novice lover might, but undulated, slid, swayed, circled like someone for whom sex and sensuality were the same thing, tantalising and arousing with their passionate rhythm. Admittedly, the mambo couldn't always evoke those feelings when it was borrowed by the likes of Rosemary Clooney ('Mambo Italiano') and Perry Como ('Papa Loves Mambo'). Pérez Prado's greatest American success came when he cooled his mambo into something resembling a cha-cha-cha for 'Cherry Pink and Apple Blossom White', in which only an occasional groan – as if a boxer had been punched in the solar plexus – retained any physicality. The hook for that record was the humorous slurring of his lead trumpet, a pale facsimile of the massed horns of his earlier hits, such as 'Mambo No. 5' and 'Que Rico el Mambo'.

Although he came from Spain rather than Cuba, Xavier Cugat – last sighted in this narrative in 1935, submitting Cole Porter's 'Begin the Beguine' to the rumba rhythm – proved to be the island's most enduringly popular representative in the United States. It is perhaps fitting that his biggest US hit was entitled, misleadingly, 'Brazil', bringing a little indeterminate south-of-the-border exoticism to the wartime landscape of 1943.

Five years later, the same tune reappeared on radio: this time credited to a guitarist named Les Paul. He was not just a virtuoso and, as time would tell, one of the most important innovators of the electric guitar,* but also a showman. With Mary Ford, who would soon become his second wife, he dressed in a blue work shirt and hilariously multicoloured socks, the epitome of a graceless hillbilly. The couple sat down while he played and she sang, and frequently interrupted their songs like

---

* As *Metronome* magazine reported in 1953, when Les Paul was unveiling a new solid-body electric guitar, he 'doesn't look upon it as merely a straight guitar with amplification, but instead as an entirely new and different instrument in appearance as well as performance', a prophetic remark if ever there was one.

real rubes, to pass on a rib-cracking joke or wave to someone in the front row. It was calculated crowd-pleasing, and somehow it kept audiences at both jazz and country and western clubs satisfied. 'The people you're playing for,' Paul insisted, 'they work all day, they don't go to music schools and study harmony. They pay their dough, they come in, they listen. If they don't understand what you're doing, they walk out. What are you supposed to do, tie 'em with a rope while you explain you're playing great music?'

Those antics slandered what he was ready to sell. With 'Brazil', Paul discovered a way of layering one electric guitar part over another, and again, until there were no fewer than six fighting for space – a baffling array of sound effects, tonal variations, percussive clicks, hot country picking, jazz fingerings, even some primitive ancestors of the power chord; some of these performances speeded up, some slowed down, by a manipulation of time that defied the imagination. That was Les Paul the solo artist: with his wife, he concocted records that carried multiple versions of her voice issuing simultaneously from the grooves, and label credits reading: 'Vocal trio – Mary Ford'. He was not the first to determine a way of combining separate elements on to a single recording, soon using as many as twenty-four different components, while professional studios struggled to cope with more than three; but he was the first to perfect the technique, and sell it to the public. It was the dawn of a new era, in which the gramophone record would no longer be a documentary, capturing a particular performance for posterity, but a glorious fiction, a manipulation of man and machine that extended the revolution launched by the birth of electrical recording in 1925.

Some took offence at the blatant artificiality of the new recording techniques: overdubbing was cheating the listener, they declared. One could no longer trust that even a symphony orchestra were capable of performing in real life as they did on disc. The practice of 'fading out' a performance, which became prevalent in the overdubbing era, was deplored as being lazy and uncreative. The American evangelist, Bill Gothard, 'believed that, any time a song faded out instead of resolving itself naturally, it promoted ongoing anarchy'. There were misgivings, often justified, that the early experiments in multi-dubbed one-man-band recording – as attempted first in America by Sidney Bechet, and later in Britain by Victor Feldman, Humphrey Lyttleton and Steve Race – failed on aesthetic grounds, not least because the addition of each extra recording 'track' seemed to muddy the sound.

Always quick to condemn innovation as a threat, the American

Federation of Musicians did its best to impede technological progress by instructing its members not to take part in any recording session which involved overdubbing. The AFM was especially alarmed by the process whereby an orchestra would prepare a backing track without a singer being present: producers assumed that the singer was more likely to make mistakes than the seasoned session pros, and therefore the record companies would not have to pay musicians their union scale while a budding Sinatra or Garland repeatedly flubbed their top note.* Eventually the union realised that the improvement in recording quality allowed by overdubbing would be good for everyone in the business, and the ban was lifted. As Columbia producer Mitch Miller noted in 1952, 'No science has progressed as far as electronics has in the last ten years. I think that anybody who doesn't take advantage of these advances is an idiot.'

> That **** television! Business is pretty good in some places. But in a **** television area, we're dead before we start. As soon as we enter a town and I see those **** antenna things, I holler murder. People go in debt to buy a **** TV set, and nobody has any dough left. So they stay home.
> Tommy Dorsey, 1951

> There will be a place for music in television – all kinds of music – when television producers recognise the fact that they have a completely new medium to work with and stop trying to use it to revive forms of entertainment that went out of style twenty-five years ago.
> Stan Kenton, 1951

One of the forgotten heroes of twentieth-century music, Raymond Scott was a composer and arranger who announced himself in the late 1930s with such unconventional sides as 'Dinner Music for a Pack of Hungry Cannibals'. He toyed with the rules of rhythm and harmony, juxtaposed previously unimaginable combinations of instruments, pioneered research

---

* One side effect of this policy was the 1949 release of *Songs Without Words*, which featured Paul Weston's orchestra presenting completed tunes by some of the finest writers in the business, including Ray Noble and Johnny Mercer, but no lyrics. Customers were encouraged to buy the discs and write their own words.

into electronic sound, and wrote scores so packed with innovation and surprise that their only possible destinations were the hundreds of film animations (Bugs Bunny and the like) for which they eventually provided a soundtrack. Scott's surreal innovations were only matched by the experimental compositions of Louis and Bebe Barron, created by fiddling with electronic circuits, which were heard on the soundtrack for the 1956 science-fiction movie, *Forbidden Planet*.

Scott was not a man who recognised limits, and in 1949, after nearly a decade away from commercial recording, he revealed the results of his experiments with the studio, the orchestra and the technical processes whereby music was brought to the public. His new compositions – which sound today like classical–jazz amalgams waiting for cartoons to accompany them – included 'Ectoplasm', 'Snake Woman' and 'Dedicatory Piece to the Crew and Passengers of the First Experimental Rocket Express to the Moon'. But he was unwilling to pass them to a record company, he explained, because the merest collision with commerce would rob them of their artistic merit. Instead, he proposed that he should convey his music to his listeners via thought transference. In the future, so *Down Beat* magazine reported, 'perhaps the composer will sit on the concert stage and merely think his conception of his work. His thought waves will be picked up by mechanical equipment, and transferred to the minds of his hearers.'

Scott was undoubtedly a visionary – he insisted on closed-circuit TVs being installed at a Detroit club in 1950, so that everyone in the place could see him – but his music was destined to remain mired in physical technology, never rising to the purely psychological realm. Yet his spirit of adventure was typical of the years after the Second World War, when the innovation that had been focused upon military needs could now fuel a consumer boom – and, almost by accident, spark vast improvements in the choice and quality of entertainment available to moderately wealthy citizens of the Western world.

Britain's economy, like those of the nations it had helped to defeat, was in ruins. There were numerous hiccups in its recovery, such as the fuel crisis of early 1947 which led to the BBC's television service being discontinued, radio broadcasts being curtailed, newspapers failing to appear and cinemas closing. Yet from this denuded nation, suffering under the harshest European winter in living memory, came an innovation in sound which was widely acclaimed as the most significant development since the birth of electrical recording. This was Decca Records' 'ffrr' (full frequency range recording) system, first employed for classical music, and still in use when Decca signed the Rolling Stones in 1963. The recording techniques available before the war could only handle frequencies up to 6 kHz; most gramophones could only reproduce up to 4.5 kHz; and yet the average adult could hear sounds up to 16 kHz or beyond. The range of many musical instruments also extended beyond the 6 kHz limit, with the effect that some recorded sounds had been impossible to distinguish from each other: the tenor saxophone, for example, resembled the cello, and an alto sax could be confused with a clarinet. The 'ffrr' system delivered, for the first time, an accurate representation of music's sonic landscape.

There were two drawbacks to the 'ffrr' revolution: it could only be appreciated if you bought a new gramophone; and it was still subject to the aural flaws of the 78 rpm shellac record, with its background hiss and easily scratched surface. One possible solution was a switch from disc to tape, which was already being used in many recording studios. In September 1947, the Radiolympia exhibition in London introduced the British public to the EMI Broadcast Tape Recorder and the GEC Tape Recorder – as yet only available for professional use, but with the promise that they would soon be appearing in every household. Meanwhile, America's two largest recording companies were working simultaneously on competing formats to replace the brittle 78. 'The talk of the record industry these days is Columbia Records' revolutionary new Microgroove record,' *Melody Maker* announced in July 1948, 'which plays 27 minutes on one 10-inch double-faced record, and 45 minutes on a 12-incher. This new platter may eventually revolutionise the entire recording industry.' By the use of Vinylite instead of shellac, surface noise would effectively be eradicated. Symphonic works could be contained on a single disc; jazz artists could extend their improvisation beyond the four-minute barrier imposed by the 78; there could be themed collections of popular songs. The US company Philco announced that for $30, listeners could purchase a device to enable their existing equipment to play the new discs at 33 rpm.

Meanwhile, RCA Victor had secretly staked its future on a miniature alternative to the 78: again made from Vinylite, but this time just seven inches across, and playing at 45 rpm. They announced in March 1949 that this would be 'the first integrated program of records and player planning in the 70-year history of the business', as the 'unbreakable' records were accompanied by a choice of two new record decks. RCA proposed seven series of releases, each colour-coded for instant identification: classical (with the old Red Seal logo, and a retail price twice that of popular recordings); semi-classical; pop; children's; western; international; and folk. (RCA clearly did not recognise a need to distinguish between different varieties of 'pop', a description so broad that it stretched from Bing Crosby to bebop.) This duel between the long-playing record and what would be known, by the early 1950s, as 'the single' was viewed as reckless by many observers: *Gramophone* magazine deplored the two companies' 'buccaneering adventures which neither they nor the individual can afford'. As an American journal noted, 'The well-equipped record collector of the future will have to furnish his living room with at least three machines. A single machine with various speeds will be inadequate, since the manufacturers are getting an added kick out of confusing the issue. Not only will platters be made to play at different speeds, but the centre holes also will be of varying sizes.'

There were a few months of direct competition, with RCA Victor's 45s by Perry Como and Vaughn Monroe pitted against Columbia's big-band long-playing discs (or LPs) by Woody Herman and Gene Krupa. In Britain, initial reaction to the seven-inch 'midget disc' was disapproving, as it was felt to be too small to handle easily. Black record-buyers in the States, who were on average poorer than their white equivalents, were also slow to adapt to the new formats. RCA did their best to promote the single by issuing 45 rpm editions exclusively for several weeks, before the corresponding 78 was available. But by the start of 1950, record companies in the US had reached a tentative concord: rather than choosing between formats, they would provide material for all of them. As one industry pundit noted, however, 'It seems unquestionable now that the future of the record business is two-speed: 33 for longer works, 45 for single records.' And so it eventually proved. Although the 78 rpm record survived in Britain until 1960, and in territories such as India throughout most of the subsequent decade, it was destined for extinction as soon as the 45 grabbed a share of the market.* Seeburg was the first manufacturer of jukeboxes to switch formats, and by the mid-1950s all the leading companies were offering machines which contained a hundred or more 45s – ensuring that

---

* There was a brief experiment in the late 1950s with extra-long LPs, which played at 16 rpm, and could hold twice as much material as a 33 rpm disc – approximately the same as a compact disc twenty-five years later. This format made no commercial headway, but into the late 1960s it was standard practice for turntables to offer a choice of four speeds: 16 rpm, 33, 45 and 78.

the jukebox would become a potent symbol of teenage pleasure during the white rock 'n' roll explosion.

While the 45 was effectively a straight replacement for the 78, albeit with enhanced sound quality, the panoramic scope of the LP offered both opportunity and a challenge. The record companies were never averse to making money from nothing, and many early LPs were simply collections of previously released 78s, repackaged as a 'gift' to the artist's fans. As the public was already acclimatised to the ten-inch record, most companies opted to use the same size for their LPs; they feared that consumers might reject a larger format, which might not fit their existing storage space. (Warehouses faced the same problem, as did retail outlets.) When they decided in the early 1950s to explore the extended landscape of the twelve-inch disc, they embarked on another round of creative marketing, by adding a handful of additional tracks to their existing ten-inch albums and presenting them as new product.

For composers such as Duke Ellington and Alec Wilder, who were already composing on a scale more epic than the four-minute 78 would allow, the LP was an overdue opportunity to indulge their suites and song cycles. Lowering the tone a little, record companies were also quick to see a potential market amongst those who were keen to dance, at a record hop or with the rugs folded away in their own sitting rooms. Convinced (as was the entire industry, until it was too late) that a revival for the dance bands of the 1930s and 40s was only a moment away, the major labels prepared series of themed albums. Each was devoted to an individual band, under a generic title such as *Design for Dancing*. These records conformed to the familiar pattern of a three-minute performance and then a pause before the next song began. Columbia offered an alternative with its quartet of *Your Dance Date* LPs: these were programmed for non-stop dancing, 'with four numbers tied together by piano, celeste and chimes interludes', pioneering an approach that would provide a lengthy career for German bandleader James Last from the late 1960s onwards.

Capitol went further, commissioning Paul Weston to craft his own sequence: *Music for Easy Listening* being followed by *Music for Dreaming*, *Music for Memories*, *Music for the Fireside* and *Music for Reflection*. Not to be outdone, bandleader Skip Martin added to the series with *Music for Tap Dancing* (full instructions included). Weston responded with *Moods for Candlelight* and *Moods for Starlight* . . . and almost accidentally, an entirely new musical genre – mood music – had been born. From Columbia came a series of *Quiet Music* LPs, providing 'easy listening for your relaxation'; from Coral, a collection of songs for all weathers from Les Brown's orchestra; from RCA Victor, the *Moods in Music* (for *Dining, Daydreaming, Relaxation*, even ultimately *Music for Faith and Inner Calm*, which anticipated the New Age phenomenon of the 1980s). As British producer and mood-music composer Norrie Paramor explained, 'it's meant to entertain without being obtrusive, to put you in an easy frame of mind. In other words, perhaps it is music to be heard but not necessarily to be listened to.' After decades of music that demanded the listener's attention, or even (like bop) risked alienating it, here was something genuinely different: music that did not offer anything, but which took away the distractions and dilemmas of everyday life. In the successful middle-class home of what author William H. Whyte (in 1956) called *The Organization Man*, the well-oiled cog in a smoothly functioning society, mood music kept the machine running in optimum order.

At its most grandiose, this (absence of) style could be promoted as *Music for Gracious Living*, as in a series of LPs by Peter Barclay's orchestra; at its most self-effacing, it could be quite unashamedly reduced to *Background Music*, a four-album series from Capitol in 1953. You could take your pick from *Light and Lively*; *Show Tunes*; *Bright and Bouncy* (but presumably not so bouncy that it might be noticed); and *Songs We Remember* (but do not necessarily want to be aware of hearing). Western society had not yet become addicted to chemical sedatives: while companies such as Hoffmann-La Roche were perfecting their pills, mood music attempted to provide the same service.

Before Librium and Valium, America and (more slowly) Britain fell under the sway of another form of tranquilliser: television. Its domination of the American home was sudden and rapid: only 2% of US households had a set in 1948, but by 1956 the figure was above 70%. More than any other factor, television shifted the location of entertainment from the dance hall or the cinema to the family home. Receipts for live music events, with or without dancing, fell rapidly during that period, the only exception being those aimed at teenagers. Their heroes were rarely seen on TV (especially during the rock 'n' roll era) and the increased access to cars amongst US teens in the 1950s enabled them to make both a cultural and a physical escape from the benign tyranny of their parents.

Like mood music, television provided a backdrop to the dramas of family life. Some shows demanded attention; others, to misquote Norrie

Paramor, were there to be seen but not noticed. In either case, the ubiqui-tous set provided a form of competition to the record player that was different from the radio, which did at least depend on raw material from Tin Pan Alley and the record companies. Television's attitude to music was very different. Until the show *American Bandstand* became a national attraction in the late 1950s, there was no room in the US TV schedule for records to be played.* This was a medium which demanded live (or at least the pretence of live) performance. The strongest cards in its pack were variety shows, in effect an updated version of the old vaudeville and music-hall traditions, featuring comedy, singing, dancing and maybe dogs leaping through hoops of fire or jugglers sending crockery spiralling into the air. Only the least abrasive musicians could fit into such a format: no space there for a bop jam session, or even a Duke Ellington suite. Families wanted shows that were safe, predictable and acceptable to all, and TV gathered up anyone with a recognisable name who might fit the bill. The most capti-vating and least grating performers were awarded networked shows. The likes of Perry Como, Dinah Shore and Mario Lanza became familiar names in America far beyond the audience for their records. In Britain, their role was occupied by the George Mitchell Minstrels, 'blacking up' every week in *The Black and White Minstrel Show*.† To ensure that they would not alienate adults by presenting material which was too obscure or too oriented towards teenagers, these stars were encouraged to deliver songs which had already proven their mettle – especially if they came from long-running Broadway shows or hit Hollywood musicals. The result was an American songbook of what were soon known as 'standards', sometimes selected for their quality (and nobody could question the aesthetic value of Cole Porter or Rodgers and Hart), but more often for their familiarity alone. The same selection of songs was handed from one performer to the next, revived on television and (increasingly) on album, year after year, and thereby consolidated its permanent status in the national memory. To this day, television keeps many of these songs alive, as theme tunes or adver-tising jingles.

---

* One exception: a 1954 TV murder mystery, *Studio One*, required a disc jockey to play snippets of 'Let Me Go Lover', by the unknown singer Joan Weber. Within two weeks, the single had sold 500,000 copies.
† As late as 1973, singer-composer Neil Sedaka was still adopting 'blackface' as part of his stage show.

Musicians who would once have toured the country with a band now remained in the TV studio as part of a resident orchestra. Initial experiments with presenting music on television in the late 1940s quickly revealed that viewers felt uncomfortable if there was no reaction at the end of each song, so live audiences were brought in for some shows, and 'canned' applause used elsewhere. On the rare occasions when a jazz band was requested to appear, certain guidelines had to be heeded, as *Down Beat* magazine warned: 'One of the rules peculiar to a TV music show is a strict taboo on slow numbers. Everything must have jump and verve, and if a ballad is allowed, it has to be a rhythm ballad with which liberties can be taken. Novelty tunes are more successful, and no number must last longer than 2:45, with the exception of the finale. For television, a band must have totally different arrangements than for ordinary dance dates. For one thing, there must be plenty of sections [e.g. saxophones, trumpets, etc.] playing, since the cameras have to keep changing pace to maintain audience interest.'

Ultimately, the two acts to attract most enthusiasm from US audiences in the 1950s were not jazz stars or even crooners, but performers who were carefully removed from the music that had been driving young America wild since 1935. One was Liberace, the unctuously sincere, extravagantly tasteless pianist, who used his classical training to froth up every piece of material with excess arpeggios, trills and flourishes. 'The secret of his success is his knack for reducing music to small, easily swallowed capsules', a critic wrote. 'Liberace makes his fans feel that he is helping them to enjoy "good" music, treating them to a cultural and uplifting experience ... [He is] pioneering in a field in which the great bulk of listener-watchers are not sensitive to musical values.' Here was a new genre entirely: music for people who didn't really like music.

His companion in vapid musical entertainment on 1950s US TV was Lawrence Welk and his 'Champagne Music': 'a carefully devitalised style of dance music', the same critic adjudged, while admitting that at least Welk wasn't pretentious. With his gentle rhythms, seamless style and ever-smiling young dancers, Welk set the tone for variety TV shows worldwide into the 1970s and beyond – in Britain, that endless parade of song-and-dance, stage-school troupes, from the Tiller Girls to the Young Generation, who delivered the veneer of youthful happiness for audiences whose own youth had been lost to war or the Great Depression.

If the Liberace and Welk vehicles were equivalent to the personality radio shows of the 1930s, how could television conjure up an alternative to radio's staple diet of gramophone records? One of the stars created by radio, Rudy Vallee, believed he had engineered the answer. In 1949, he formed Vallee Video in the old-time movie capital of Culver City, California, to produce '16 mm telepix' designed to accompany an individual song – with either a live or a mimed performance. He envisaged these being shown alongside feature films, and then on TV. Another company, Telescriptions Inc., went further, producing several hundred three-minute films during the early 1950s, in which artists from Nat King Cole to R&B star Amos Milburn performed their hits. These were screened across America, both as fillers between scheduled shows, and as thirty-minute packages. Similar films, known as Scopitones, were made in the late 1950s and 60s, although (like the MTV videos to come) these featured lip-synced performances on stage sets.* Each new venture in combining music with television edged closer towards a core audience of teenagers, who had otherwise been ignored by programming targeted either at adults or children. The sociologist David Riesman had noted that for teens, the contents of their record collections helped to establish their position within their peer group: 'the teenagers showed great anxiety about having the "right" preferences', he said. The record industry had identified the existence of this market, but had no idea how to satisfy it. In a 1948 advertisement, the British label HMV offered a selection of records 'For the Teen-Ager', which included Perry Como, Duke Ellington, Artie Shaw and Fats Waller – any of whom a teenager could feasibly have enjoyed, but none of whom had set out specifically to attract a teen audience. Yet the style which would bind teenagers to popular music for life already existed: it just hadn't been brought to their attention.

> [Teenagers] are still swooning to mellow music, but this year they sigh and 'oooh' at the pulsating tones of Frankie Laine or the heart-rending throbs of Mel Torme. Their old yearning for Frankie Sinatra has faded into nostalgia. 'Poor Frankie,' said a girl in Chicago. 'He's old now and has three kids.'
> *Life* magazine, December 1948

---

* One of the few surviving Scopitone machines can be found in Jack White's Third Man Records store in Nashville.

It all started with Vaughn Monroe's 'Riders in the Sky'. Remember?
Forest murmurs . . . Cowboys added to angels . . . Before long, all
manner of fauns and satyrs began to clutter up the backgrounds of
vocal records. Vaughn started it; Mitch Miller took it from there. He
laid on the wild animal and woolly plant life so thick you couldn't
hear Frankie Laine for the hollering and the whooping.
    Metronome magazine, July 1950

'Arrangements and interpretations have become so big that they're
bigger than the music', complained producer and bandleader Paul
Weston in 1950. 'You've got to snap whips and crack bones to get attention now. Playing and singing a song is nothing.' The fetish of sound
effects, one of the unforeseen products of multitrack recording, had
become so prevalent that the most talented songwriters couldn't compete
with the gimmicks. 'I don't think anything has been written in the last
few years that has a chance of becoming a standard,' Weston added,
'nothing that can compare with the wonderful tunes that were being
turned out in the 30s.'

Weston was perhaps overlooking the Nat King Cole hit 'Nature
Boy', one of the more individual compositions of the immediate post-war
period. But even there, the selling point was less the jazz hipster's almost
static performance than the way that the arrangement jumped, sprite-like,
around him. This was an era for novelties, for sonic tricks, and for records
on which the crack of a rider's whip – as on Frankie Laine's 'Mule Train' –
counted for as much as a memorable chorus. (Typically, the AFM set out
to investigate all the cover versions of 'Mule Train', to ensure that on each
of them the whip had been handled by a union member.) Yet Laine's early
hit singles had already won him a following that was both younger and
more passionate than those of his rivals. It stretched beyond the English-
speaking world into territories such as Argentina; evidence of a steady and
unstoppable drift in international tastes from local talent to a homogenised
form of American pop, in keeping with the United States' apparently irresistible strategic power.

After a decade as a minor jazz singer, Laine had broken out in
1947 with the blues ballad 'That's My Desire' – not a paragon of melody or
lyrics, but a blank canvas for what *Metronome* called his 'shameless emoting',
his vocal slurs and rasps and affectations, borrowed from black band singers
rather than Bing Crosby or Rudy Vallee. With its simple orchestration, this

was a record that sold nothing weightier than Laine's presence: an almost physical intervention into the listener's life, with a lack of subtlety which made it perfect teenage fare. He continued with a mixture of ballads and mock-western story-songs that were corny beyond belief, but which were unashamedly *his* – a quality that no cover, regardless of its pedigree, could match. The critics were appalled (*Gramophone* said he had 'no voice') but the fans packed out the halls in which he played, and responded to his unfussy charisma with near-hysteria. Nor was Laine alone in eliciting this reaction: white girls screamed for the veteran band singer Tony Martin in New York; black girls for Duke Ellington's vocalist, Al Hibbler, in Oakland. Newspaper columnists decried the stupidity of the teenagers' reactions, without realising that they were based on a mixture of calculation (it was safe to let go in the company of those equally afflicted) and instinctive frenzy, beneath which was the word nobody dared to mention in the late 1940s: sex.

While Laine, Martin and Hibbler were all old enough to have fathered their fans, the biggest teen idol of the early 1950s was just young enough to serve as a fantasy lover. Moreover, Johnnie Ray was needy (with a severe hearing deficiency which required him to wear an aid offstage) and every bit as hysterical as his followers. His gimmick was apparent on the 1951 single which coupled 'Cry' with 'The Little White Cloud That Cried': 24-year-old Ray was so emotional that he could not help but weep. 'I just felt like God picked me up in his arms and said, "Johnnie Ray, I love you", and then he kissed me', he announced on stage, before another bout of sobbing racked his body. Fans didn't know whether to mother him or ravage him. 'One mournful note from Johnnie', a concert-goer reported, 'and the audience shrieked in animal ecstasy.'

Adding to his unique appeal, his voice was pitched so high that listeners approaching him blind assumed that he was a woman (and many thought him black, too). For anyone attuned to the leading popular singers of the moment, such as Perry Como and Doris Day, Ray sounded sloppy and uncontrolled. But that was what sold him so effectively: an eruption from the stifling conformity of post-war America, with its white-bread fear of Communism and its emotionally restrictive Christianity. His act was both contrived and utterly instinctive, while the confusion of his persona – was he a wounded baby or a surging lothario? – reflected his own hidden turmoil, briefly revealed when he was arrested for soliciting a policeman in the men's room of a Detroit theatre. No wonder Johnnie Ray cried so easily, flung himself around as he sang, winced and contorted his face as if meeting the blows of an invisible foe. Like his pubescent fans, he was in the midst of a torment that he could not explain.

British audiences were more reticent than their American counterparts: they were not quite ready to tear each other to pieces in the race for one of Johnnie's discarded cigarette butts, as had happened outside the Paramount in New York. But on his frequent visits to the London Palladium in the early 1950s, he elicited screams which had rarely been equalled inside a West End theatre. 'You can see what the girls like,' sniffed a reviewer from the *Daily Express*, 'he looks amiable, even lovable, and is idiotically sincere. But he is a side-show freak rather than an entertainer.' He was one of the artists Frank Sinatra had in mind when he complained, 'Man, it's worse than ever. These trick songs are coming out of my ear.' Maybe Sinatra was simply jealous, as the screaming spread. When Frankie Laine followed Ray into the Palladium, it was reported that in the cheap seats (the boxes and the balcony), 'they were Frankie's own – screaming, screeching, squealing, squawking, wailing, weeping, bawling', until the thesaurus was exhausted. Many of the fans were wearing home-made sweaters into which they had knitted Laine's name. 'I'm worried over the effects of such singing of such songs on such youngsters', the journalist concluded.

Worse was to follow. At the end of 1953, Clyde McPhatter (himself one of the many 'scream-age' idols) led his R&B vocal group, the Drifters, through an overtly lascivious – indeed, downright sexual – song entitled 'Such a Night'. Then Johnnie Ray tackled the same material. To demonstrate exactly how wild his night had been, he let out a succession of coos and moans that didn't so much hint at sexual ecstasy as broadcast it. His orchestrations were still rooted in the variety tradition, but his voice signalled something very different: a recognition of teenage sexuality.*

* At a London Palladium show issued as a best-selling album in 1954, Ray repeated the final section of the song again and again, as if to make sure that all of his fans would be fulfilled. In Elvis Presley's hands seven years later, the same song became positively multi-orgasmic, the [male] Jordanaires answering his every groan.

'Never have there been as many dirty blues records on sale as today … No effort is made to conceal them … Usually these words, of innocent connotation to the naïve, deliver the listener directly to a bedroom and roughly describe sex activity. By cunning inflections and constant usage, such words as "rocking", "roll", "bit", "rider", "grind" and "grass" have become standard dirty-record vocabulary.'

Jet magazine, January 1952

CHAPTER 11

Real Rock Drive

'The music business in this country is sick, despite the fact that people want music as never before. It is sick for the same reason that American art as a whole is sick and stagnant – too much standardisation. Too many people are afraid to admit that their preferences in music – and many other things, from automobiles to washing machines and even the way they eat and drink – might be different from the preferences of the guy next door.'

Stan Kenton, 1951

Post-war America was terrified of Communism, and the belief that it was making insidious inroads into the nation's everyday life. The AFM – happy to withdraw its labour while the US was at war – rallied to the flag in peacetime. It issued strident statements of loyalty to democracy 'in the struggle for worldwide domination by Communism'. The Soviet government responded with criticisms of America's popular music, which 'hypnotises one with the dead cold mechanics of its rhythm and the poverty of its melody . . . which poisons the artistic taste of our youth and helps plant an ugly example of bourgeois modernistic dance forms'. (Meanwhile, an Associated Press reporter in Moscow discovered a keen cabal of jazz fans at the heart of the Russian Empire: 'They even know about rebop.') The Communist takeover of China in 1949 illustrated vividly what America feared. 'The Communist authorities look upon dancing as frivolous and unnecessary', a jazz magazine noted, adding that the former cabaret centre of Shanghai was now entirely free of foreign entertainment attractions.

Everyone in the American music business agreed that its wares represented the best of their nation: its freedom, its democracy, its openness to competition and consumerism. But there was a common assumption that the beacon of US popular music was jazz, and that jazz had entered a steep decline which owed nothing to Communist interference. 'Jazz is dead,' said pianist Teddy Wilson, 'you can't make people listen to it anymore.' Nat King Cole concurred: 'Jazz is pretty dead commercially.' 'Something new in music is needed,' concluded George Hoefer in *Down Beat*, 'something akin to the excitement aroused by discovering an Armstrong, a Bix, the Ellington cohesion of sound, the electric shock of the rhythmic power of Basie', and so he went on, each name from the past reinforcing the poverty of the present.

For a wider audience, the record business provided vocal personalities who might become teen idols, or who could provide mellifluous wallpaper for adult homes; or big bands with their horns muted and drums brushed rather than beaten. The decade between 1945 and 1955 spawned some of the most perfectly produced popular music of all time, especially at the studio in Hollywood's Capitol Records Tower, where sonic clarity and instrumental precision became trademarks of impeccable quality. Mario Lanza* imported operatic drama into pop as a statement of manhood, echoed by the likes of Al Martino and his British equivalent, David Whitfield. Dean Martin toyed with sensuality beneath his mock-Italian mannerisms. Doris Day emerged as the most strident and confident female voice yet heard on record, whether she was sassing her way through 'The Deadwood Stage' or declaring her 'Secret Love'. Still, there was an air of safety and sobriety about this entertainment which made it acceptable for all the family, and thereby removed it from a sense of ownership by any generation or racial group.

Yet there was a radical change afoot in America, beneath the gaze of its majority white population. As historian Russell Sanjek recounted, during the decade after 1942 'the income of the average black family tripled, while that of a white family had doubled. In New York, the city with the sixth-largest black population, one-third of the residents of its leading black ghetto – Harlem – left to settle in other parts of the city, and high-priced staples and luxury items were purchased by blacks in greater quantities than by any comparable population group in the city.' There was still racial segregation, and the economic trends didn't redress the financial imbalance between whites and blacks in America. Twenty-five years after giving the world jazz, however, the black community was ready to make another weighty cultural contribution to the nation.

Jazz had spread rapidly from black musicians to white, from the clubs of New Orleans to the plush hotels of Manhattan and London. What's surprising in retrospect about the musical revolution of the late 1940s is that despite national media which could transmit the latest novelties from coast to coast, white America simply did not notice what was happening in its midst. As jazz faded from prominence, black America produced a substitute which would literally change the world. But not yet: rock 'n' roll music would exist for almost a decade before its impact was registered outside the African-American community. Only then would it emerge, as if newly born, in the mainstream of popular culture: slightly stale, yet ripe for exploitation.

After Dizzy Gillespie's 'Salt Peanuts' and his flurry of Afro-Cuban experiments with Chano Pozo, bop exiled itself from a mass audience, black or white. As rock historian James Miller explained, 'the hot new style was

---

* His career faltered when it was revealed that – having lost his voice after excessive dieting – he had mimed to records when performing 'live' on CBS-TV's *Shower of Stars* show.

jump, a simplified and super-heated version of old-fashioned swing, often boogie-woogie-based, usually played by a small combo of piano, bass and drums, with saxophone and trumpet'. In 1949, the US music paper *Billboard* changed the categorisation of its black record sales chart from 'Race' to 'Rhythm and Blues', reflecting the roots of the new music, and its key element: rhythm.

The precursors of jump were bands such as Count Basie's and Lionel Hampton's; the boogie-woogie piano players; the jive-talking hepcats, Slim & Slam and Cab Calloway; and the blues. As Susan Whitall wrote, 'The blues were not yet constricted by subgenre classifications such as Chicago blues, or electric guitar rock infused with blues, or folk-blues sung by geezers in denim overalls. In the 1940s and 50s, people said "the blues" when talking about rhythm & blues, jump blues – anything with a pulse. In the black community, people would dress up in their best clothes and go out to dance in the evenings, it was a vital part of life.'

Like their white counterparts, the black big bands – all but the most prestigious, such as the Basie orchestra (and even he disbanded for a year after the war) – fell victim to economic pressures in the 1940s. Widespread use of the electric guitar, and its accompanying amplification, ensured that a small band could make as much noise as a big one, and persuade just as many people to dance, while remaining cheaper to run and to hire. As the war ended, juke-boxes in African-American bars were playing dozens of records that swung and moved, but with minimal orchestration. Sister Rosetta Tharpe, rebounding between the spiritual and the secular, rattled her electric guitar and sang with gospel fervour on the prophetic 'Strange Things Happening Every Day'. Arthur 'Big Boy' Crudup came out of Mississippi with a Delta growl and a simple plea: 'Rock Me Momma'. Private Cecil Gant ('I'm Tired') and Joe Liggins ('The Honeydripper') rolled out the blues over bare-bones piano, Gant purring sensuously, Liggins too cool to emote.

The key song of summer 1945 was 'Caldonia', with its errant heroine and shouted refrain: 'What makes your big head so hard?' The original ('Caldonia Boogie') was by pianist Louis Jordan, pumping his left hand in a frenzy; white bandleader Woody Herman arranged it as a sprint; the black trumpeter Erskine Hawkins had his band slow it down a little, to let its blues come out. In their different ways, all three renditions lived up to the phrase coined by *Billboard* to describe Hawkins's effort: 'right rhythmic rock and roll'.

By the end of the year, Helen Humes was skipping across the

nonsense syllables of 'Ba-Baba-Leba' ('it's what the hep cats say') with an ease and swagger that defined the word 'cool', while Bill Doggett's Octet maintained an almost erotic restraint behind her. Illinois Jacquet's band hammered a simple twelve-bar riff while Wynonie 'Mr Blues' Harris bellowed 'Wynonie's Blues' like a gospel preacher. 'Look out Illinois Jacquet!' he shouted as if a train was coming, to introduce his leader's solo. ('How long can you play that kind of music when a hundred or more gibbering idiots gang up around the bandstand and keep shouting, "Go, go, go, go!"?', asked an incredulous British jazz journalist after witnessing Jacquet in action.) And they kept coming, for the next two years: Roy Milton, T-Bone Walker, Joe Turner, Louis Jordan again (inventing Chuck Berry's signature 'Johnny B. Goode' riff on his piano introduction to the 1946 hit 'Ain't That Just Like a Woman'),* and always Wynonie Harris, hottest of them all. 'She shakes like jelly, and jelly don't shake itself', he roared on the lubricious 'Lollipop Mama', the forerunner of a thousand rock 'n' roll trash-talking metaphors to come.

As if creating rock 'n' roll weren't enough, this mercurial era of rhythm and blues translated the sound of the Southern cotton fields into urban electricity, with Arthur Crudup soon outpaced and overpowered by the Chess Records stable in Chicago. Muddy Waters's sharecropper vocal sent the tape-deck needles soaring into the danger zone as he drawled and snarled 'I Feel Like Going Home' over bottleneck guitar that cut like a switchblade. 'This was the first Rock & Roll band', claimed Chess historian Rich Cohen, which might have riled Louis Jordan. But there was no disputing the rest of his account: 'It was the loudest music anyone ever heard. It had the drive of an engine, the hum of a diesel on an inky black night – music that makes you feel like staying out late, driving too fast, drinking more than is advisable, starting a fight.' And as one of the anthems of the 1950s would say, baby, that is rock 'n' roll.

You needed more? There was country blues from Lowell Fulson and Brownie McGhee; Delta rhythms from the original Sonny Boy Williamson and John Lee Hooker; the roots of Chuck Berry's proto-rock guitar sound, on records from T-Bone Walker and Pee Wee Crayton; and,

---

* You could also make a case for Louis Jordan prefiguring the art of the rapper with late 1947's 'Look Out'. And check out the ska rhythm on Jordan's 'Salt Pork, West Virginia'. It would almost be possible to build the musical history of the next three decades out of his 1940s catalogue alone.

for a change of pace, to prove that not everyone needed to rock all night, the ethereal harmonies of vocal groups such as the Ravens and the Orioles, as silky as Muddy Waters was raw. For a final glimpse of the future, the jukebox of December 1948 offered Charlie Parker's 'Barbados': a touch of Latin, a calypso lilt, modal lines, and Miles Davis on trumpet – modern jazz, so fluid that it sent bop sliding down with a spoonful of the sweetest sugar.

Records only hinted at what was going on in bars and clubs, on what was known as 'the chitlin circuit', as this description of T-Bone Walker demonstrates: 'As the show reached its climax, T-Bone pushed his guitar above his head, still playing, extending his arms, building to the song's crescendo. As he inched the guitar down behind his head, he spread his feet and slid his slender legs further apart, still playing, the room's ecstasy building. Now the guitar strings ran parallel to T-Bone's shoulder blades, he popped a last pyrotechnic note, and as he landed the splits, the floor around him was covered with cash and feminine undergarments.'

And we were still in the 1940s: awaiting the golden years of Chess and Atlantic R&B to come, the discovery of Ray Charles and B. B. King, Fats Domino and Smiley Lewis sending the gumbo of New Orleans around the world, Lloyd Price and Johnny Ace turning R&B into the stuff of teen fantasy – and, yes, the 1951 session at which Sam Phillips of Sun Records recorded Jackie Brenston's band with Ike Turner as they romped through 'Rocket 88', and cut what has been acclaimed as the first ever rock 'n' roll record. Except that, as we know, rock 'n' roll was actually invented, and named, six years earlier.

Economists have long predicted that the flood of new babies born during the recent war would one day make themselves felt as a greatly inflated teen-age market. Now the record business is feeling the effects of the high World War II birth rate, as these youngsters, just now moving into teen-age brackets, are helping to swell the teen-age influence on the single record market.
Billboard magazine, January 1956

Rhythm and blues may turn out to be the most healthy thing the music business has had in years. For one thing, it has made the kids

dance. True, it's a pretty elementary sort of dancing, but it's better than standing there, gazing at the band. And if they listen to enough R&B long enough, the elemental rhythm and vocal won't be enough for them. They're going to want music, too.
Down Beat magazine, March 1955

In the summer of 1954, *Billboard* reviewed *Teen-Age Dance Session*, an album by Dan Terry & his Orchestra: perfect, the review suggested, for teenagers who wanted to roll back the rug. What music did Terry suppose would send the teens on to the dance floor? Eight orchestral instrumentals which, as *Billboard* noted, were 'a deliberate attempt to simulate the music of the 30s and early 40s': in other words, exactly the same music that had thrilled their parents.

In January 1956, the magazine noted with an air of slight bemusement that the baby boom of the Second World War was creating a new generation with needs of its own. Just this month, it remarked, no fewer than five songs had been released which directly referenced this audience: 'Teen-Age Prayer', 'Teen-Age Heart', 'Teen-Ager', 'Teen-Age Meeting' and 'Nina, the Queen of the Teeners'. Even the archaic hyphen in 'teen-age' hinted at the novelty of the whole affair: those aged between 13 and 19 were of 'teen age', not yet a recognisable social grouping of 'teenagers'. They were cutting their wisdom teeth on music which their parents could scarcely have imagined.

The audience for blues and R&B was almost entirely black (although reissues of earlier blues recordings appealed to white jazz fans like those who attended the pre-war rhythm clubs in Britain). There were few white-owned radio stations where managers were prepared to waste their valuable airtime on a minority audience. It required mavericks to buck the trend: people such as Dewey Phillips, a hyper-charged ball of verbal energy who broadcast a dedicated R&B show from WHBQ in Memphis. It was, as Peter Guralnick wrote, one of several similar enterprises 'springing up in one form or another all across the South: black music on a white radio station for a strong Negro audience and a growing, if for the most part unacknowledged, core of young white listeners with a growing, if for the most part unexamined, buying power'.

Phillips had no ambitions beyond Memphis, though he deserves his place in history for encouraging his unrelated namesake Sam to launch Sun Records in 1950, and being the first man to broadcast and interview

Elvis Presley four years later. Both Dewey Phillips and Presley would die at the age of 42 – just a year younger than a Cleveland disc jockey named Alan Freed, who latched on to the audience for R&B a little later than Phillips, and commandeered it with an entrepreneurial zeal which had international repercussions. In the summer of 1951, he began to broadcast a nightly late-night (11.15 p.m.–1 a.m.) show of 'Blues, Rhythm, Jazz' on WJW in Cleveland, which was advertised with the somewhat baffling couplet: 'He spins 'em keed, He's Hep, that Freed!'

The show was called *The Moon Dog House*, and Freed's use of the word 'Moondog' would eventually attract a court case from the blind street musician and composer of that name. Freed denied ever calling himself 'Moondog', but the tag was emphasised when he launched a series of events in Cleveland. The first, hyped as 'The Most Terrible Ball of All', was the Moondog Coronation Ball – held, ambitiously, at the 10,000-capacity Cleveland Arena. It featured a bill of black R&B musicians, headlined by Paul Williams, creator of 'The Hucklebuck', a 1949 dance novelty. Some 25,000 people forced their way in, and the show was abandoned. On air the next day, Freed broke down, aware at last of the power of what he had unleashed.

Subsequent Freed presentations, all using the Moondog brand, were better organised, although the rush for admission often sparked violent confrontations. As photographs of the Cleveland gathering illustrate, his audience in 1952 was almost entirely black. Within two years, however, whites were buying between a third and a fifth of the tickets, although the musicians – Muddy Waters and the Clovers in New Jersey, for example, or Roy Hamilton, the Drifters and Big Maybelle back in Cleveland – were almost exclusively African-American. 'The kids want that music with a beat to dance to', *Billboard* reported. 'Alan Freed has found what they want.'

As Ray Charles recalled, 'White singers were picking up on black songs on a much more widespread basis . . . it meant that White America was getting hipper.' White teenagers were now mouthing black American slang: 'having a ball', 'cool', 'bug', 'drag', 'funky', 'split' and the rest. No wonder that in 1958, nearly a decade before the enactment of President Johnson's civil-rights legislation, commentator Paul Ackerman was able to claim: 'In one aspect of America's cultural life, integration has already taken place.' Not that this was apparent in the Deep South – in Birmingham, Alabama, for example, where in 1956 singer Nat King Cole agreed to play before a racially segregated, entirely white audience. His first song passed off without incident. Then the curtain behind him was raised, to reveal that this black man was performing with the all-white band led by Englishman Ted Heath. 'There was an immediate reaction', Heath recalled. 'A man leapt clean over the floodlights up on to the stage and hurled himself on Nat King Cole. Nat floundered away from the vicious attack, falling headlong over the piano stool behind him, to land in a heap at the feet of the brass section. A whole gang then rushed the stage, but were foiled by the police, who had been standing by in the wings. They charged on stage with batons flailing. Below the footlights, there was a seething mass of fighting men and screaming women, and the skirmish looked like developing into a full-scale riot.' Heath reacted as only an Englishman could, leading his band into the familiar strains of 'God Save the Queen', whereupon, even 5,000 miles away from Buckingham Palace, most of the audience rose respectfully to their feet, and calm ensued. (It was perhaps reports of this fracas that caused a Nat King Cole concert in Newcastle, England a few weeks later to be cancelled: 'Jazz audiences are too rowdy and destructive', the manager explained.)

If the sight of black and white musicians on stage together could arouse such fury, it is easy to imagine how alarmed the more conservative sections of American society became when white kids began to fraternise with their black counterparts at Alan Freed's Moondog Balls. 'Teenagers are instigating the current trend towards R&B and are largely responsible for keeping its sales mounting', a trade magazine noted in April 1954. 'The teenage tide has swept down the old barriers which kept this music restricted to a segment of the population.' Rhythm and blues was 'no longer the stepchild of the record business', an analyst noted; another adding, 'Jukebox operators are reporting requests for orders for R&B tunes from pop locations which previously detested the low-down, noisy but exciting numbers ... The majority of the locations which are calling for R&B tunes are teen-age spots, transient places and late-closing taverns. The strictly neighbourhood or family-type location still prefers its music on the pop side.' Black music was a secret pleasure for white kids, not to be shared with parents or teachers. It marked them out as rebels, transgressors, participants in a ritual from which they were supposed to be excluded.

No coincidence: when it became known that whites were listening to R&B, concern rose about the lyrical content of blues songs; especially their blatant sexuality. In Memphis, which was a cauldron of both racial intolerance and R&B, the mayor's office had already ordered police to search out and destroy copies of three offensive black records. (The mere titles of 'Move Your Hand, Baby' and 'Take Your Hand Off of It' were suggestive; only a few seconds' exposure to Amos Milburn's 'Operation Blues' were required before it became obvious that Milburn's doctor was using an unorthodox needle to insert his medicine.) The Dominoes' 1951 hit 'Sixty-Minute Man' was an obvious target; less so Willie Mabon's 'I Don't Know' (countered by his wife Beatrice's 'Why I Didn't Know'), which was singled out for its line 'sprinkle goofy dust round your bed', supposedly an invitation for kids to practise witchcraft.

'The R&B field has been doing this sort of thing all along', one radio host said in 1954. 'It only came into prominence when the pop kids started buying R&B discs . . . In most cases, the pop kids are buying the R&B discs because of the beat, rather than the lyrics.' His peers were not convinced. One federation of American disc jockeys in 1954 issued a 'thumbs down on "way out" dialect, obvious double entendre and "liquor" songs where drink is suggested as the cure for all ills'. Another insisted that it 'is not against blues records as such, but it is against a record in which "rock", "roll" or "ride" doesn't deal with the rhythmical meter of the tune'. The problem was that it was hard to tell whether, for example, the teenage protagonists of the Flairs' 1953 single 'She Wants to Rock' had in mind a gentle sway on a rocking chair, a romp on the dance floor, or a few minutes' animalistic coupling.

The antics of Alan Freed did little to clarify the issue. His radio persona was racially ambiguous (black teens who attended his early Moondog Balls were apparently amazed to discover he was white), adrenaline-charged and fluent in hipster slang. He tossed around the key signifiers of the music in random order, promising listeners 'your favourite blues and rhythm records', addressing them as 'all you moondoggers' or 'all you rock 'n' rollers'. By late 1953 (and possibly earlier, though recordings don't survive to prove the point) Freed was twinning two sexually loaded words into a single badge of identity: his blues and rhythm records were also, in his vocabulary, rock 'n' roll. By this, he meant anything he played on the show, which could rage like a hurricane or lilt as romantically as a black Bing Crosby. If it was African-American music, it was rock 'n' roll. After he was legally required to abandon the 'Moondog' name in late 1954, he simply retitled his programme *Alan Freed's Rock 'n' Roll Show*, which is how the sound of black America reached its now increasingly white audience via radio station 1010 WINS in New York through 1955 and 1956.

For defenders and opponents alike, then, rock 'n' roll was simply a synonym for R&B, as targeted at a teen audience. '[Freed] feels that this term better serves his long-range goal of getting the country's kids back to the dance floors', said *Down Beat* magazine in February 1955. But as Freed set that equation in play, record companies – perhaps keen to obscure any sexual connotations – preferred to talk about something they called 'cat music'. Once again, its origins were tangled. When a US Army private in Korea wrote in 1951 that 'we intend to teach the POWs here how to become a "Cat" in ten easy lessons', he was planning to introduce his Communist enemy to jazz, and specifically bebop. By 1954, however, 'cat music' was being employed by teenagers in the Southern USA as a euphemism for R&B: it was, simply, music for hep cats like them. As parents remained ignorant about the implications of the phrase, MGM Records could inaugurate a 'Cat Music' series of R&B singles, many of them performed by black men who until very recently had been making their livings from jazz. (One of these releases, by the Cat Men, was a reworking of a Debussy melody, unlikely to set any adolescent libido aflame.)

Echoes of this unashamedly direct sound could be glimpsed in the otherwise snow-white landscape of mainstream popular music in the early 1950s. Repeated piano triplets supported rhythmic ballads; boogie-woogie motifs underpinned defiantly unswinging dance tunes (Kay Starr's 'Come-A-Long-A-Love' from 1952 offering a vivid example). The over-blown mock-religious sentiments of Frankie Laine's 1953 hit 'I Believe' (which spent several months atop the British hit parade) could be traced back to the gospel-schooled passion of black balladeers; so too the extended, fluttering notes offered by everyone from Johnnie Ray to Dean Martin, which were gently suggestive of sexual anticipation. There were honking saxophones, basses throbbing four to the bar, even a pronounced backbeat on Bonnie Lou's 'Tennessee Wig Walk' (1953). The Crew Cuts' 'Sh-Boom' from 1954 has been labelled by chart historian Joel Whitburn as America's 'first #1 rock and roll song', even though it was nothing more incendiary than a barbershop vocal quartet crooning nonsense syllables. In its original form, as sung by black group the Chords (on the Cat label, naturally), it was altogether more propulsive – less a romantic singalong, a parent might have felt, than an invitation to steal hubcaps.

It was the Chords rather than the Crew Cuts* who inspired the musical satirist Stan Freberg to create his own version of 'Sh-Boom' – the first of a series of parodies which harpooned America's changing music trends through the mid-1950s. 'Now, this is a rhythm and blues number,' Freberg's barely articulate lead singer pronounced, 'you gotta be careful, or someone is liable to understand what you're singing about.' With its unrelenting bass thump, snarling saxophone and frantic guitar solo, Freberg's 'Sh-Boom' ironically became the first R&B, rock 'n' roll or indeed cat-music entry in the British hit parade.

It was not, however, the first record to become an anthem for the young Britons known originally as 'mashers', then as 'creepers' and eventually as 'Teddy boys' (and girls). 'Mashers' were, in the late nineteenth century, effete ladykillers. By 1954, the term had acquired an air of violence. 'Creepers', by comparison, was drawn directly from 'The Creep': a vaguely smouldering instrumental penned by saxophonist and bandleader Ken Mackintosh. It was accompanied by a simple dance step, the popularity of which cynical journalists ascribed to the prevalence of 'youngsters who couldn't cope with the usual ballroom dancing steps'. As for 'Teddy boys', that description arose from the youngsters' revival of Edwardian fashions: narrow-sleeved jackets, turned-up cuffs, velvet trims, drainpipe trousers. 'When Edwardian-style coats came out,' recalled Teddy boy John Fox, 'Flash! You could go out there and you could make it with the birds. If you had a car, say a Ford Consul or a Cresta, you could pull any bird you wanted. And you used to go on the dance floor and say, "Lend us your bones, doll." For a jive, see. We used to go down to the Palais on a Saturday night and we'd sit in the corner and just watch them all, and everybody was having a ball.'

Teddy boys were a working-class phenomenon. As sociologist Stanley Cohen explained, they were 'the first group [of teenagers] whose style was self-created, although they were reacting not so much against "adults" but the little that was offered in the fifties: the café, the desolate town, the pop culture of the dance halls, Locarnos and Meccas aimed at the over-20s'. At their most menacing, the 'Teds' rampaged through town centres smashing

---

* Aware that jazz had altered beyond recognition since 1917, *Down Beat* magazine launched a competition in the early 1950s for readers to name the music's modern incarnation. The winner? 'Crewcut'; the polar opposite, one must suppose, to the stuffy 'long-hairs' of the classical world. Needless to say, nobody ever referred to 'crewcut music'.

windows, brandishing switchblade knives – and had the rhythms of rock 'n' roll coursing through their veins. After the sinuous appeal of 'The Creep', and the comic novelty of Stan Freberg, more red-blooded stimulation was suddenly available at the end of 1954, in the unlikely and unexpected shape of a white rock 'n' roll group: Bill Haley & His Comets.

> It's all jazz, of course. Just a question of beats to the bar. It's the simplest form of music: a bit of Dixieland, four-bar rhythm and jazz.
>   Bill Haley

> Viewed as a social phenomenon, the current craze for rock and roll material is one of the most terrifying things to have happened to popular music . . . the rock and roll technique, instrumentally and vocally, is the antithesis of all that jazz has been striving for over the years – in other words, good taste and musical integrity.
>   *Melody Maker*, May 1956

Even before 'Rock Around the Clock' and 'Shake, Rattle and Roll' carried the gospel of rock 'n' roll around the world, Bill Haley's songs were filled with hints of salvation. 'It's the Real Rock Drive and they play it in a real gone way'; 'man, that music's gone'; 'a band with a solid beat'; 'that music fractures me'; 'we're gonna ROCK!'

With the Four Aces of Western Swing, the Saddlemen, and finally the Comets, Bill Haley had played country dance halls and bars where the patrons wanted to fill their brief hours of leisure with dancing, drinking and sexual conquest. Like the blues, the hillbilly music of the late 1940s was overrun with boogie-woogie, from the Delmore Brothers' 'Freight Train Boogie' to Arthur Smith's 'Guitar Boogie'. In the city or the backwoods, people with country roots accepted the boogie beat as easily as the two-step and the waltz. On his early records, Bill Haley offered up a stew of all those rhythms, and was not beyond adding some Latin spice to the pot. 'I was doing country and western on a little radio station,' he recalled in 1974, 'and before my programme there was a show called *Judge's Rhythm Court* which was just negro blues . . . Because I'd be listening in the studio to the programme, I used to sing some of the blues tunes to country and western. I could see no reason why a country and western group couldn't be doing that sort of music – even though it was very segregated. I started doing those kinds of songs in clubs, and they were accepted tremendously. I knew right away what I had, because nobody else had it and people were going crazy.'

Haley capitalised on his discovery in June 1951, when he went further than any white musicians had ever been, at least in a recording studio. Within five weeks of Jackie Brenston's 'Rocket 88' bursting on to the *Billboard* Rhythm and Blues chart, Bill Haley and his Saddlemen had tackled this prototype blend of automotive passion and (black) rock 'n' roll – losing the song's erotic edge, it's true, but retaining enough propulsion to suggest that they didn't regard it as a novelty. A month later, Haley concocted his own recipe for rock 'n' roll: the 'Green Tree Boogie', with a slap-bass solo and stop-start breaks to heighten the tension. By April 1952, his Saddlemen were delving deeper into the black rock 'n' roll canon, reviving Johnny Preston's three-year-old regional hit 'Rock the Joint', juvenile-delinquent imagery and all. Danny Cedrone contributed a finger-shredding guitar solo, which with its repeated climaxes and staccato notes supplied the raw sexuality missing from Haley's recalcitrant vocals.

These illicit journeys across the border came to a head in early 1953, when Haley's renamed Comets tackled 'Crazy Man, Crazy'. 'Go, go, go, everybody', screamed the chorus; to ram it home, producer Dave Miller hired a vocal combo to sound like teenage hoodlums. When that still wasn't rowdy enough, he and his staff joined in. (On the flipside, another Haley composition, 'What'cha Gonna Do', opened with the 'one for the money' routine which Carl Perkins would borrow for his 1956 rock anthem, 'Blue Suede Shoes'.) This was a national hit, considered so ethnic that (as so many black R&B songs would be over the next few years) it was immediately 'covered' by a more established white act for mainstream consumption. The fact that Haley's original outsold Ralph Marterie's sterling reconstruction proved that public tastes were changing more rapidly than the industry could imagine.* But Haley's record company were careful not to alarm anyone. The Comets were promoted not as a rock 'n' roll band, but as 'The greatest Dance Band ever on wax', as if they had Paul Whiteman or Glenn Miller in their sights.

With 'Rock A-Beatin' Boogie', Haley introduced white America

---

* The earliest British release of a white rock 'n' roll song was a cover of 'Crazy Man, Crazy' by that veteran of Ted Heath's band, Lita Roza. It's worth hearing today as a demonstration that it is impossible for a record to swing if it's sung by someone with her arms clamped rigidly to her sides.

to the wagon cry 'rock, rock, rock . . . roll, roll, roll', and maybe that's where Alan Freed found the slogan for his crusade. By the end of 1953, the Comets were an R&B band, in the same way that the Original Dixieland Jazz Band had stated their claim to jazz: they loved the music, and they couldn't disguise the thrill of being allowed to perform it.

By the late spring of 1954, Bill Haley & His Comets were signed to a major national label, with a producer (Milt Gabler) who admitted of his protégé: 'He didn't have a good voice, but he had a feel for what he was doing.' Faced with converting a novelty rock 'n' roll tune into something that would trump Haley's recent sides and still sell, Gabler insisted that the Comets needed some instrumental hooks, and hummed a few to the band: 'I just used all the tired old riffs I'd known all my life from R&B records.' On the label of 'Rock Around the Clock', Decca described the song like any other dance-band tune: 'FOXTROT. Vocal chorus by Bill Haley.' A studio drummer doubled the backbeat on the snare drum, and Gabler asked Danny Cedrone to reprise his exhibitionist guitar solo from 'Rock the Joint'. But the record was, by Decca's standards, a flop. Two months later, the Comets tackled a proven hit, in the frankly obscene (and definitively sexist) black rock 'n' roll of Joe Turner's 'Shake, Rattle and Roll'. Haley dropped the most blatantly erotic verse – though not the 'one-eyed cat' lines which registered white pop's first overt reference to a penis – and doubled the backbeat. Suddenly the Comets were national stars.

What added notoriety to their fame was *Blackboard Jungle*, a movie in which jiving teens equated to juvenile delinquents. The director, Richard Brooks, elected to run Haley's 'Rock Around the Clock' over the opening credits, at full volume. 'When *Blackboard Jungle* opened,' Milt Gabler recalled, 'and you heard the slap of the bass and the drums and the bite of that guitar, it just knocked the kids right out of their chairs.' As James Miller described, 'for most people it was the loudest music they had ever heard . . . A crude but effective symbolism was put into play: the louder the sound, the more strongly it would connote power, aggression, violence.' 'It's the vilest picture I've seen in 26 years', said the Memphis city censor, Lloyd Binford. 'The teenagers start off bad. I thought they would reform and we would have to pass it, but they were just as bad in the end.' The film set box-office records, and sent 'Rock Around the Clock' towards a total of more than 20 million sales around the world. So stimulating was the song that it even sparked disorder at the Ivy League college of Princeton. 'Lively strains of the disk first emanated from one of the student dormitories', it was reported. 'Other phonographs joined in, making a mad medley which led to chanting and stamping by the staid Princetonians. About midnight they gathered on the campus, set fire to a can of trash, and paraded through the streets until an assistant dean dampened their hilarity by pointing out the advantages of a more sedate mode of life.'

In Britain, everything happened more slowly, but reached the same conclusion. On its original release, 'Rock Around the Clock' was described by the magazine *Jazz Journal* as 'two jump blues sides by a relatively unknown coloured group in the style of Louis Jordan, and obviously slanted at the R&B market . . . The band plays in modern Harlem swing style.' Then jazz aficionados discovered that Haley and his group were white. In the *Daily Mirror*, Patrick Doncaster said that 'Bill Haley and his Comets are rated by the experts as not really the real thing when it comes to Rhythm and Blues. But they rock and roll the sales into millions.' In 1956, when 'Rock Around the Clock' became the title song of Haley's first film, the Comets sent Teddy boys and other errant teens wild in Britain's cinemas, jiving in the aisles and taking razor blades to their seats. The problem, said the *Daily Express*, was the 'primitive, hotted-up jazz music by Bill Haley's Comets', which had even led fans to sing and dance through the streets of Twickenham. As the film travelled north, so did the hysteria, to the point that the teenage John Lennon was disappointed when nobody in Liverpool tore up the seats. He should have been in Manchester, where members of the audience turned the cinema's fire hoses on each other and on the manager, before spilling out on to the street singing Haley refrains.

There followed a month of the media-induced furore at which Britain has always been expert. Numerous cities banned screenings of *Rock Around the Clock*, while Queen Elizabeth II (herself now 30 years old) asked for a print of the film to be sent to Buckingham Palace. Her younger sister Princess Margaret demanded that the Royal Marines Band, serenading her on the royal yacht *Britannia*, should improvise a version of Haley's theme song. His music was also played to six chimpanzees at a Liverpool circus: 'They just looked around and scratched.'* Newspaper columnist Eve Perrick reasoned that if rock 'n' roll caused the same problems as alcohol, its sale should likewise be restricted. The Bishop of Woolwich called for Haley's

---

* In Pittsburgh, a gentleman named Joe Bruno vowed to live in a tree until rock 'n' roll had died out: 'If we are going back to the days of chimps and apes, I might as well get in on the top floor and live like one.' He proved to be a songwriter, frustrated because rock 'n' roll was selling and his songs weren't.

movie to be withdrawn. The BBC broadcast a TV show in which Victorian songs were rearranged with a rock 'n' roll beat. At the height of the Suez crisis, the Conservative MP Major Tufton Beamish said in the House of Commons: 'The Opposition, in my opinion, should be thoroughly ashamed of its "rock 'n' roll" behaviour.' A reader's letter to the *New Musical Express* demanded to know: 'Why is it that a rhythm-crazed maniac can pick up an electric guitar and play tripe, which is now given the name rock 'n' roll?' The secretary of the Musicians' Union, Harry Francis, commented: 'The British public doesn't want rock 'n' roll – only a few silly kids do.' And they were under malign influence, it seemed: at the Pentecostal Church in Nottingham, the pastor asked two teenagers to jive during a service while the organist played a 'rocked-up' version of the hymn 'Lion of Judah'. This was offered as demonstrable proof that 'Rock 'n' roll is a revival of devil dancing, the same sort of thing that is done in black-magic ritual.'

Fans who were arrested for antisocial offences or criminal damage after viewing Bill Haley's film had a different explanation. 'That rhythm is terrific', said Tony Scullion. 'We didn't try to keep in our seats. I don't think I could have done, anyway. When they got to "See You Later Alligator", I just signalled the boys and we went out in the aisles. After that, I didn't hear much of the music. We were jiving and stomping – even when they cut the film. Friday night it's going to be just the same story all over again. I don't care – it's worth it for that rhythm.' Another fan, Kenneth Gear, added: 'This music is different from anything I ever heard before. There's nobody sends me like Bill Haley – except for Elvis Presley. There must have been four or five hundred of us in the street. I've never felt so excited in my life. This rhythm is exciting and lively. It makes me feel as though nothing else mattered.' This was transcendence: the power of music to carry people out of the everyday into a realm where consequences were irrelevant, and everything existed in the moment.

Britain was not alone in its uproar. In America, too, the term 'rock 'n' roll' could ignite trouble without provocation. But there, unlike Britain a year later, this music was still considered to be black in origin. When *Variety* magazine described it as 'the most destructive force in the country ... a lewd, lascivious and larcenous influence on youth', they were making not just a musical and social point, but a racial one, albeit in disguise. This was all part of what *Down Beat* magazine called 'a high-pressure crusade against R&B'. Rock 'n' roll dances were banned in Connecticut in April 1955. 'Teen-agers virtually work themselves into a frenzy to the beat of the fast swing music', a police chief explained. 'The Big Beat has arrived', Alan

Freed responded. Psychiatrists duelled over the origin of the rock 'n' roll riots. One said that they were 'symptomatic of something wrong with the kids' home environment, rather than due to any evil in rock & roll'. Another called rock 'n' roll 'a communicable disease . . . cannibalistic and tribalistic . . . it appeals to the adolescent insecurity and drives teenagers to do outlandish things'. He would have felt at home with the North Alabama Citzens' Council, which had led the assault on Nat King Cole in Birmingham (and would shortly change its name to the Ku Klux Klan of the Confederacy). It described rock 'n' roll as being part of a plot initiated by the National Association for the Advancement of Colored People (NAACP) 'to undermine the morals of the youth of our nation' by 'pulling the white man down to the level of the Negro'. This music was 'sexualistic, unmoralistic, and the best way to bring young people of both races together'.

That was exactly what was happening to rock 'n' roll music itself. It had become sufficiently broad, and multiracial, for Alan Freed to book the white pop singer Tony Bennett as headliner for his August 1955 *Rock & Roll* show in Brooklyn (although Bennett was unable to appear, and a black singer took his place). A few weeks later, the first cash-in movie was released, entitled *Rock 'n' Roll Revue*. It was a cheaply shot compilation of studio performances by an entirely black cast of R&B and jazz performers, ranging from Joe Turner to Nat King Cole, and Ruth Brown to Duke Ellington. A very similar cast was promised for the hasty follow-up, *Rhythm and Blues Revue*. If the two descriptions appeared to be interchangeable, then clarification was on hand in February 1956, when a pundit noted that rock had an air of respectability about it which R&B couldn't muster: why else would there be a Rock 'n' Roll Ice revue in New York? 'There's even a rock and roll type of cigarette commercial', he concluded. 'This one plugs Pall Mall cigarettes with a beat which bespeaks the sponsor's understanding of the idiom.' By June, an industry observer noted that 'the real, full-time R&B record companies have displayed an inclination to go back to R&B-type material. Can this mean that rock and roll, the adulterated product, is being surrendered to the country and pop performers?'

As early as January 1955, disc jockeys in the country and western market were complaining that their artists were expending too much effort on trying to appeal to R&B fans. 'Suddenly [in 1954] we were deluged with records by country music artists that were not country music,' said Randy Blake, 'gosh-awful, brazen attempts, at something these artists can't do and never will be able to do.' They were acting out of desperation, and the will to survive. A year later, the hillbilly singer Carl Perkins saw his debut hit, 'Blue Suede Shoes', rise to the top of the American charts in three sales categories: Pop, Country and Western, and Rhythm and Blues. As *Billboard* noted: 'The continued merging of the country & western, pop and rhythm & blues fields into one big "mongrel music" category is more evident than ever.' Country singer Bill Haley had ignited this flame; then a young man ten years his junior threw gasoline on the fire.

FOR ROCKIN' REPLAYS

A BRAND NEW SINGLE BY

GENE VINCENT
AND HIS BLUE CAPS
YES I LOVE YOU, BABY
ROCKY ROAD BLUES

Capitol RECORD NO. 4010

JULY 7, 1958

HOT ROD GANG

ROCK N ROLL DANCE · GENE VINCENT

COURTESY OF BOB CLARKE

Faron poses with his good friend, Gene Vincent, who also records for Capitol.
COUNTRY-SONG ROUNDUP

60

CHAPTER 12

Bad Motorcycle

'Take a dash of Johnnie Ray and a sprinkling of Billy Daniels, and what have you got? Elvis Presley, whom American teenagers are calling the King of Western Bop.'

Daily Mirror, March 1956

'If what I play is Rock'n'Roll, then it's a lot different from what other groups using the same name are playing. I'm confused, frankly. What I've tried to do is combine rhythm and blues, country and western, popular and Dixieland into one form, keeping a little of the flavour of all four.'

Bill Haley, January 1957

When 19-year-old Elvis Presley issued his first single for Sun Records in August 1954, the label's office manager Marion Keisker admitted: 'The odd thing about it is that both sides seem to be equally popular on popular, race and folk record programmes. This boy has something that seems to appeal to everybody.' The national Country and Western charts were the first to carry his name, followed nearly a year later by the Pop and Rhythm and Blues listings. His entry on the country best-sellers chart in 1955 was not a honky-tonk two-step or hillbilly ballad, but a cover of a black R&B tune on which Presley stuttered and hiccupped like one of the dancing frogs that his future manager Colonel Tom Parker used to tout as an exhibit around the country fairs.

Presley wasn't the first young white man to be heralded for crossing into the R&B bracket: a few weeks before his initial Sun session, a 19-year-old named Pat Boone had seen his own debut, 'Loving You Madly', covered for the pop market by Alan Dale, because Boone's version was thought by disc jockeys to be only suitable for R&B stations. (Sixty years on, any blues influences on Boone's single are difficult to trace, though his slightly later 'Tra La La' fits the bill.) But Presley's Sun release combined a country tune (a hopped-up version of Bill Monroe's bluegrass hit, 'Blue Moon of Kentucky') with a cover of Arthur Crudup's late 1946 blues song, 'That's All Right'. The Monroe side broke first, but it was the Crudup cover that inspired Memphis teenagers to greet each other with Elvis's scat vocal riff – just as jazz fans had done with Louis Armstrong's 'Heebie Jeebies' twenty-five years earlier. 'His style is both country and R&B, and he can appeal to pop', said *Billboard* prophetically in November 1954.

Bill Haley's Comets moved like vaudeville troupers, echoing stage tricks they'd learned from swing bands – the saxophonist lying on the floor during solos, Haley and his guitarist nearly colliding in their gawky enthu-siasm – while Haley was pudgy, balding and no one's idea of a teen idol. Presley, by comparison, was lean, quiffed, and jerked himself around the stage like a backstreet stripper. Haley may have made his British fans feel as if nothing else mattered, but when Presley performed in front of girls in 1954 and 1955, there was only one agenda – sex, right now, hard, fast and dirty. No singer had ever gyrated his hips and pumped his groin like that in public before. If a black man had done the same in front of a mid-1950s white audience, he'd have been lynched. As far as many adults were concerned, Presley deserved a similar fate.

Rhythm and blues, rock 'n' roll – they already held the triple threat of noise, violence and (in the parlance of the times) Negro origins. With Elvis Presley, the trio became a quartet, and the fourth member was the most dangerous of all. Sexual desire had been implicit in the relationship between performers, black and white, and their audiences as far back as Rudy Vallee – and certainly when Sinatra was at the Paramount in 1942, even if it was disguised as an innocent romantic infatuation. The hints of sexual innuendo on 1930s jazz and blues records had become lurid declarations of lust by the 1940s and 50s. White parents wouldn't have trusted their daughters with the likes of Louis Jordan or Wynonie Harris, certainly; but such an encounter existed only in the depths of their nightmares. Now here was a boy – from the wrong side of the tracks, to judge by his clothes and his deep-country voice – who might conceivably have rolled up outside their house, in a Cadillac convertible, to steal their innocent teenage virgin for a date and then delivered her home besmirched, violated, ruined (but with a secret smile on her face).*

Nor was Presley alone. Between 1955 and 1957, a succession of ever more alien beings appeared on national TV networks and in main-stream Hollywood films, each one representing his own moral and musical assault on traditional values. First there was Bo Diddley, black and cropped and bespectacled and almost as rectangular as his guitar, thrashing out a rhythm that sounded like a voodoo ceremony. His version of its origins was suitably obscure: 'I'd say it was a mixed-up rhythm: blues, and Latin American, and some hillbilly, a little spiritual, a little African, and a little West Indian calypso . . . and if I wanna start yodelling in the middle of it, I can do that too.' He appeared during a rare R&B segment on Ed Sullivan's top-rated TV variety show, where the producer instructed him to perform a cover of the sedate country hit 'Sixteen Tons', set up cue cards by the cameras so he couldn't get it wrong, and instead watched in horror as Bo delivered his own theme tune. 'Man, maybe that was "Sixteen Tons" on those cards,' Diddley said afterwards, 'but all I saw was "Bo Diddley".'

---

* What these parents wouldn't have realised was that Presley's heartfelt ambition before his rise to fame was to join a gospel quartet. Not that even they were immune to suggestions of im-morality: his favourites were the Statesmen, whose bass singer, 'Big Chief' Wetherington, wiggled and shook himself in a frankly profane manner while delivering songs of salvation.

Chuck Berry was an ex-convict (future convict, too, as the subject of a long procession of spurious police busts in the late 1950s), as old as Haley, with a sly grin on his face which betokened evil intentions, and a line in lyric-writing which mixed beat poetry with schoolyard slang. He held his guitar like a phallus, tossed off solos as if he was shelling peanuts, and hit all of young America's obsessions head-on – cars, consumerism, romance, teachers, parents, every kind of monkey business. Then – and we are still in 1955 – adult America had to face a semi-crippled black man sporting pancake face-paint, with a pompadour almost as tall as his body, and an unstoppable predilection for screaming and hollering what sounded, even to teenagers, like gibberish. But what gibberish: Little Richard was speaking in tongues to the congregation of rock 'n' roll, his nonsense syllables and scenarios piling up into an alternative prayer book for the satanic hordes – tutti frutti all rootie, good golly miss molly, long tall sally she knows how to ball, ooo my soul, a-wop-bop-a-loo-bop-a-lop-bam-boom. 'How can I reject it, when I can't even understand it?', said a censor for NBC-TV, on hearing Little Richard's 'Long Tall Sally' for the first time. A reviewer in the *New Musical Express* was equally overcome: 'His antics and appearance reminded me of an animated golliwog – and I don't mean that in any way disparagingly.'*

These men had gathered up all the imprecations and implications of the original black rock 'n' roll, blended them into a hot gumbo, added some teenage spice (lust of adolescent girl, swagger of pubescent boy) and then aimed them at anyone who would listen. It's doubtful that any of them imagined at the outset that their audience (or at least a sizeable portion of it) would be white; or, more pertinently, that it would be whites rather than their own race who would keep their music and their careers alive, greeting them as authentic folk heroes long after their appeal to the African-American R&B audience had dissipated.

Once Elvis Presley had left Sun Records, with its limited span across the South, and signed to RCA, with its national clout, he was ready to trump Haley and all the black princes of rock 'n' roll. Journalists compared

---

* Little Richard provided the theme song for the brilliant rock 'n' roll movie satire *The Girl Can't Help It* in 1956. Princess Margaret went incognito with friends to a screening at the Carlton Cinema in London's Haymarket. 'Her enthusiasm was so keen', Fleet Street reported joyously, 'that a quarter of the way through the film she took off her shoes and waved her stockinged feet in the air.' The British public must have been relieved to learn that her cousin, 19-year-old Princess Alexandra, 'has stood well aloof from the more eccentric parties being given by the "rock 'n' roll set"'.

him to Johnnie Ray ('with cowboy boots') until it was clear that his popularity and potency outstripped all his predecessors. 'Heartbreak Hotel' was the record that gift-wrapped his sexuality for a global audience. Swathed in echo, it slowed his natural exuberance to an eerie crawl, which was both more threatening – and more erotic – than the frenetic rockers which followed. It suggested nothing less than a slow grind in a back alley; his young fans may not have been able to imagine the scenario, but they could imagine how it would feel.* A paper in Minneapolis called him a 'young bump and grind artist', and noted that his fans didn't seem to care that when they were screaming for him, they couldn't hear him sing. 'If the future is important [for him]', a disc jockey commented, 'Elvis will have to drop the "hootchy-kootchy" gyrations, or end up as "Pelvis" Presley in circus sideshows and burlesque.' After he performed in Jacksonville, Florida, preachers held special services, as if to exorcise the town, while concerned teenagers prayed that his soul would overcome his 'spiritual degeneracy'. 'If he did that in the street', said an Oakland policeman after a Presley show, 'we'd arrest him.'

Not all white rock 'n' rollers were so threatening. A New York psychologist attempted to find an erotic message in Carl Perkins's breakthrough hit: 'I think that there is some sexual component in this, that the blue suede shoes represent something that has not been tried yet by the adolescent.' But Perkins's backwoods style and prematurely adult demeanour (by late 1956 he already carried the burden of the alcoholism that would blight his life for the next decade) diminished his threat to the status quo. Much more alarming was the leather-clad, clearly troubled Gene Vincent, a survivor of the Korean War and a life-threatening motorcycle crash. On his tension-fuelled hit, 'Be-Bop-A-Lula', Vincent (said the *Daily Mirror*) 'sounds as if his mouth is stuffed with lettuce', though the pent-up violence and ill-disguised sexual rapaciousness of his music suggested he'd been fed on raw steak. Most devilish of all the rock 'n' rollers (to this day) was Jerry Lee Lewis, who'd been thrown out of Bible college for setting hymns to a boogie-woogie beat, had been married three times but only divorced once, had a bride who was several years below the age of consent in many countries and most American states, wore a grin of preternatural

* As proof that it was not the song, the tempo or the echo that sold the record, but Presley's animal magnetism, compare his recording with the cover by the man who became known as 'the Japanese Elvis Presley', Kazuya Kosaka.

self-satisfaction, and didn't so much suggest sexual conquest as slap it on top of his piano and then wiggle it in the face of his audience.

All these acts were available to American audiences on package tours or at Alan Freed spectaculars. In 1955, almost all the acts on rock 'n' roll shows were black. Through 1956, an occasional white act infiltrated the R&B vocal groups, crooners and rhythm specialists, but most of Presley's peers followed his course through country and western packages or on variety bills. By 1957, some rock bills were entirely white; others included a token black man or two, usually Chuck Berry or Fats Domino, but were now being headlined by one of the white pretenders who were emerging from every label and city in America. As a music expert from a Russian cultural magazine commented, the nation was now awash with 'a vulgar, unmelodic cacophony of sounds accompanied by crazy, chaotic drum playing. The soloist merely yells disconnected sounds into the microphone.'

Similar reactions were reported from adults who strayed across the US radio dial and tuned in to one of the frequencies offering the nation's hottest new format: the Top 40. Around 1949, radio station KOWH in Omaha, Nebraska had been one of the first outlets to impose playlists on its presenters. The aim was maximum listenership: by avoiding records which weren't already popular, KOWH lowered the risk that someone might be confronted by an unfamiliar tune, and go elsewhere for their entertainment. In 1955, the station changed hands, and the new owners fine-tuned its philosophy. All day, every day, with few exceptions, KOWH would play nothing but the Top 40 records in Omaha, as determined by a mixture of local sales and persuasive marketing from record company pluggers. Within a year, their innovation was being imitated across North America. The contents of the Top 40 might vary from city to city,* but the formula remained unchanged. Record producer Mitch Miller complained that pop radio had sold out to 'bobby-soxers and babysitters', but the ratings spoke more persuasively. For every adult who turned the dial in disgust, two teenagers tuned in, happy to know that they would hear nothing but the hottest, hippest records of the moment. As one commentator reflected, stations were now 'at the mercy of the taste of the populace';

---

* St Louis was often furthest removed from national tastes. When Bob Dylan's 'Like a Rolling Stone' was No. 1 on the East and West coasts in 1965, it didn't make the St Louis Top 40. By contrast, Bob Kuban's 'The Cheater' reached the summit of the city's chart in 1966, a full month before it appeared on the national Hot 100 listing.

a dictatorship of the commercial, which removed maverick, taste-forming DJs such as Alan Freed and Dewey Phillips from the equation. Rock 'n' roll had found its perfect radio format – at the expense of the men who had first brought it to national attention.

> I don't like [Presley's] work and neither will, I feel, the vast majority of our listening public.
> British bandleader Jack Payne, 1956

> It is deplorable. It is tribal. And it is from America. It follows ragtime, blues, jazz, hot cha-cha and the boogie-woogie, which surely originated in the jungle. We sometimes wonder whether this is the Negro's revenge.
> The *Daily Mail* reviews rock 'n' roll, September 1956

In 1960, one of Decca's representatives in London let slip a trade secret: 'We certainly do our best to discourage our top American artists from singing in public over here. What happens is this: while British singers build up their prestige on the stage, the Americans start so big – they have been built up into such fabulous characters – that when they come over here and appear in the flesh it's a big disillusion. The fans see they're only human beings after all.'

American rock 'n' rollers, black and white, were indeed an almost mythical species in the Britain of 1956. Their fans had no opportunity to see the likes of Bill Haley or Bo Diddley in person; nor were they witness to the controversial early television appearances by Elvis Presley. Their conception of rock 'n' roll was based on records, publicity hype, and the staged cameo performances visible in films such as *Rock Around the Clock* and Presley's debut, *Love Me Tender*. But on Boxing Day that year, American idol Pat Boone arrived in the UK. He had been the second rock 'n' roller, after Haley, to reach the British charts, though his cover of Fats Domino's 'Ain't That a Shame' (unlike his earlier US hit with 'Two Hearts') had offered only a vague facsimile of the original, as if glimpsed through frosted glass. It was Boone's misfortune to be required to tackle two of Little Richard's most chaotic anthems, and his 'Long Tall Sally' suggested that his notion of fun extended no further than snoozing in a rocking chair. 'It just sounded so raw', he recalled, 'that it was like asking me to jump into the middle of a

Zulu dance.' Boone was, by contrast, an expert balladeer, more controlled than Crosby, more relaxed than Bennett or Sinatra, and he has been unfairly pilloried for his crimes against rock 'n' roll when he was merely attempting to translate raw exuberance into genteel family entertainment.

In Britain, he took the stage in 'a light sports jacket and dark grey pants', his white shoes the only diversion from his college-boy persona. But his repertoire, however restrained his delivery, was pure rock, borrowing from Haley and Presley as well as his own catalogue, as if he realised that he was being asked to fulfil a nation's need for their presence as well as his. He mimicked none of Presley's movements, however, allowing himself nothing more dramatic than a wave of his right arm (though only from the elbow). 'You don't have to do all that gyrating around', he explained. 'The kids will scream anyway.' The *New Musical Express* declared that 'His boyish freshness is a tremendous asset, and healthy advertisement for rock 'n' roll', although many fans would have preferred something less salubrious.

They expected to get their chance when Bill Haley & His Comets arrived on these shores in February 1957. The *Daily Mirror* elected to cover his tour with the gravitas reserved for a royal visit, journalist Noel Whitcomb flying to New York so he could accompany Haley to Southampton by ocean liner. (Whitcomb's expert knowledge was revealed as he recounted 'the day when Bill accidentally plonked his guitar instead of plunking – and that compulsive backbeat of rock and roll was born'.) A train was hired to carry Haley, a British rock band and several hundred fans up to Waterloo, where the *Mirror* pronounced his tumultuous arrival 'Fantabulous', and the competing *Daily Express* focused on 'faces turned upwards, crumpled in fear by now, the ecstasy gone . . . faces bewildered like faces in the panic scenes of Russian films; children tossed like jetsam in the swaying human tide'.

A similar dichotomy was evident the following day. In the *Mirror*, Patrick Doncaster sounded transfigured: 'They clowned, they fooled, they gagged. The first burst of rock music blasted the place. Amplifiers on the stage emphasised each throbbing note. It hit you, bounced off the roof, and hit you again . . . It was a mood that had never hit a British stage before.' If that was the stuff of every rock 'n' roll fan's fantasies, the *Express* heard only 'weak wisecracks and scatterbrained gimmicks'. Then 'the curtain came down to a storm of boos', because the Comets had been on stage for only thirty minutes. Haley shared their frustration, and revealed that he 'would like to do a two-hour rock 'n' roll show – but it would just be physically impossible'. Only supreme physical fitness allowed him to play for as long as half an hour, based on a diet of 'eight hours' sleep each night AND good food AND a clean life'. Another reviewer offered the kindly note that 'Bill looks and sounds exactly like the homespun fellow whom his fans have pictured in their minds', while his performance was 'as wholesome and forthright as a Billy Cotton Band Show'. This was not the spirit that had inspired seat-slashing and public revelry the previous year. Neither did the one-man percussive bedrock of the Comets resemble the reinforced thrust of their records. The reality of rock 'n' roll – not for the last time – did not resemble its fantasy.

When Haley brought his updated version of swing to the British charts in 1955, our own bandleaders and singing personalities dutifully followed this latest American novelty, just as they had mimicked all its predecessors. None of them was aiming at teenagers; all of them provided a dance beat, with a hint of swing but no swagger, no rasp, no threat of violence or sexual promise. To prove the point: take your pick from Jack Parnell's band smothering 'Shake, Rattle and Roll'; Don Lusher, with Ted Heath's band, struggling through 'Rock and Roll' like a duck wading through treacle; and, most surreal of all, the Big Ben Accordion Band squeezing and fingering like demons on a medley headed by 'Rock Around the Clock'. (They may make you want to slash your sofa, but not in excitement.)

The village nature of the UK recording industry, which was centred around the publishing offices of London's Denmark Street, the impresarios of Soho and a handful of major record companies based in the capital, ensured a uniform and anodyne product. When Britain created its own rock 'n' roll star, he had to trick his way past the doormen to gain admission, and was quickly swallowed up in show business. This was Thomas Hicks, a teenage merchant seaman from London's East End, who claims in his autobiography to have heard Buddy Holly sing 'Peggy Sue' in Texas more than a year before the song was written. But the man who became Tommy Steele can be allowed some tall stories, for the process whereby he became a star was both archetypal and gloriously ridiculous.

In Soho, he first met two professional songwriters (one of whom, Lionel Bart, would soon transform the British musical stage as the composer of *Oliver!*) and then a Fleet Street photographer, John Kennedy, who offered to act as his manager. Together, they concocted Hicks's stage name, and a suitable pastiche of Bill Haley, 'Rock with the Caveman'. Kennedy procured him headlines ('"He's Great, Great, Great!" Says the Duke of Kent'), hired prostitutes to pose as aristocratic daughters besotted with this cockney discovery, and announced him as Britain's home-grown Elvis Presley. 'Does Tommy Steele expect to gain more popularity by appearing with untidy hair?', asked the *New Musical Express* reprovingly in November 1956. That month, he appeared on the country's only popular-music TV show, *Off the Record*, and launched a national tour at the Sunderland Empire – supported by such acts as Reg 'Unknown to Millions' Thompson and Thunderclap Jones, the Wild Welshman of the Keyboard. Amidst such company, he was bound to impress, and several thousand well-primed teenage girls dutifully screamed and rushed the stage if Steele so much as moved a muscle.

By comparison with the officially sanctioned entertainment of the day, Tommy Steele was as savage as his critics declared all rock 'n'roll to be. In a letter to the BBC's *Radio Times* magazine that December, an exasperated viewer wrote: 'How any sane person, young or not so young, can find pleasure in cavorting and jerking about in a raucous cacophony of jungle noises, in a manner which proves conclusively that the usual decent inhibitions have been swamped by sensual and emotional strain, passes my comprehension.'*

But the majority of Steele's fans were not, as with other adoles-cents' idols, in their teens, but aged between 5 and 12. Children had already spotted the scallywag exuberance that would translate Steele into a star of film comedies and West End musicals. Touring South Africa in 1958, he was greeted as a threat to social order, but the audience response was so restrained that the police who'd been primed to quell riots were reduced to watching the show. By 1959, Steele was concentrating on comic songs, and securing a lengthy career, rather than the brief moment of notoriety allowed to most of his rivals.

They each needed their own John Kennedy, and most of them found a businessman named Larry Parnes, who created a star out of Billy Fury. The latter was a shy ornithologist, with a weak heart but a talent equally adaptable to switchblade rock 'n' roll and emotion-racked balladry, who was described in the national press as 'a sex symbol of deformed contortions and suggestive songs the minute he walks on stage'. Parnes's

---

* Another correspondent watched teenage girls dancing on the 1957 pop show *6.5 Special*, and wrote: 'I feel thoroughly disgusted to think that the powers that be give time to exhibitions such as these. I cannot imagine that any decent-minded girl would permit herself to be pulled around in such a way.'

interest in his male clients preceded him: rock 'n' roll hopefuls were said to have shared a secret ditty which climaxed, 'Larry fucks our arses/and we become stars'. Except that they didn't, not all, unless their vision of stardom amounted to a one-disc recording contract and a forced rechristening. Their manager insisted that they should jettison such unimpressive monikers as Reg Smith and John Askew to become Marty Wilde and Johnny Gentle. (Parnes's arch rival, Reg Calvert, claimed to have boys named Ricky Fever and Eddie Sex on his books by the end of the decade.) Almost regardless of their talent, they were duly signed by a major record company, and became the recipient of screams from teenage fans. 'We all do it', a 16-year-old named Beryl explained. 'It's something inside of you. We're so pleased at seeing our favourite that we have to let ourselves go. It's an expression of liking him. We're his fans. And he knows we're there.'

The acme of British rock 'n' roll in the late 1950s was a television show entitled *Oh Boy!* which, for the first time, allowed the public to experience this phenomenon in all its animalistic glory. 'Artificiality is death to good television', declared its producer, Jack Good, who as a drama graduate understood the power of image and movement. He insisted that all the acts should perform live: 'If conditions are right, and the performer feels good, you may create something that perhaps isn't on the disc – the magic thrill of an inspired impulse.' Marty Wilde was booked as the show's star, until Good saw an 18-year-old signing to EMI: a factory hand who had been born in India, and then reborn to show business as Cliff Richard. As showbiz writer Peter Leslie explained, 'the new star looked more like the hero of a picaresque 19th-century romance than a purveyor of pelvic gyrations on a 20th-century stage'. Good stripped away Cliff's Elvis-like sideburns and guitar, and encouraged him to writhe and smoulder (provoking one of the great British headlines of all time: 'Must we fling this filth at our pop kids?'). 'Rock 'n' roll has to be sung with the face and the body', Cliff explained. 'I like to fix my eyes on them, to get them going.'

He posed for publicity photographs with a cross around his neck and a rabbit mascot, claimed that he loved Elvis Presley so much that he dreamed about him, and when quizzed about the juvenile content of rock 'n' roll music, he protested that 'older people like it too'. How old? 'Sixteen.' (He also said that he hated the name 'rock 'n' roll': 'Call it rhythm and blues.') Like a handful of his peers (notably Fury and Wilde), he could boast a genuinely convincing rock 'n' roll voice, a naïve understanding of the music, and a charisma which was heightened by the tension between his slightly babyish features and his contortions on stage. But in Britain there was no strategy for an entertainer which did not lead inexorably to pantomime, *Sunday Night at the London Palladium* and film musicals. Even the nation's belated acceptance of the jukebox, which in a 1957 court case was said to have 'a rather fatal fascination for the young 18-to-19-year-old', did not signal that a viable commercial career could be erected around their preferences alone. By November 1959, the *Daily Mirror* was asking: 'Is Cliff Richard, the Golden Boy of British Beat, turning "square"? This young master of the rhythmic twitch, the hooded eyelid and the snarling smile has released an LP (*Cliff Sings*) on which only half the numbers are rock. The others are nostalgic "oldies" like "Embraceable You".' Yet this still-teenage rock 'n' roller was not the industry pawn that observers assumed him to be. Given the options of retiring gracefully into obscurity, or steering himself towards a lifetime as a song-and-dance-man, Cliff Richard invented a third course: becoming the only original 1950s rock 'n' roller in Britain or America who was able to remain a viable pop star until the end of the century, by mastering the stylistic changes that were within his grasp and skilfully evading those (such as heavy metal and punk) that did not suit him. More so even than Elvis Presley, he was the first man to demonstrate that teenage pop stardom could escape its momentary hyperbolic bubble and become an enduring career. His fame stretched to almost every nation on the planet, and for many years he was more popular than Presley in Europe, Australia, New Zealand and South Africa. Only the United States, where his hits were sporadic and almost random, failed to be seduced by his gentle brand of rebellion.

The only conceivable rival to Cliff Richard's eclecticism was Johnny Hallyday, just 17 years old when he first reached the French charts with 'Souvenirs, souvenirs' in 1960. France had proved to be defiantly immune to rock 'n' roll during the late 1950s, opting instead for the personality vocals of 23-year-old Dalida.* When US rock hits were translated into French – as when the Coasters' 'Three Cool Cats' became 'Nouvelle Vague'

---

* Young women with no surname were in vogue across Europe: Germany's hottest teen stars of the late 1950s included Conny (15 at the time of her first hit), 12-year-old Gabriele and 9-year-old Brigitte, dubbed 'Die Kleine' like 'Little' Stevie Wonder. France boasted Sheila; Spain had Gelu; Italy's favourite was Mina; and Denmark offered Gitte. But the most potent female star of the era was allowed two names: Rita Pavone, from Italy, the local equivalent to America's Brenda Lee.

for Richard Anthony, and Sacha Distel took on Lloyd Price's 'Personality' – their rebellious swagger was replaced by nightclub charm. Hallyday was the first Frenchman to sound as if he was singing rock 'n' roll by choice. His success heralded the handover of French pop from young adults to teenagers, and from original *chansons* to a shameless reliance on American archetypes. Eddy Mitchell led Les Chaussettes Noires (the Black Socks), whose debut hit 'Tu parles trop' seemed to prefigure the arrival of the Beatles; Dick Rivers was just 15 when he fronted Les Chats Sauvages (the Wild Cats). Neither of them could match Hallyday's raw energy on 'Si tu me téléphones', 'Dis-moi oui' and 'Elle est terrible' from 1962. (He claimed that he sustained his frenetic pace on stage by only drinking milk.) It's commonplace for British commentators to mock French rock 'n' roll, but these sides were easily the equal of anything produced on the opposite side of La Manche. *

> The idea of English people singing Negro blues strikes me as so ridiculous that I cannot take records such as this one at all seriously. [It's] almost blasphemous. All concerned should hang their heads in shame.
>   *Jazz Monthly* reviews Lonnie Donegan, December 1955

> Rock 'n' roll is out of date – old-fashioned as aspidistras. Skiffle music is the coming craze. I'll take a bet on that . . . They're turning London's expresso bars into modern versions of the old-time music-hall.
>   Noel Whitcomb, *Daily Mirror*, September 1956

The most incendiary rock 'n' roll record to come out of Britain in the 1950s – the closest equivalent to the wildest music emanating from Sam Phillips's Sun Studios in Memphis – was an Appalachian folk song from the nineteenth century, performed by a jazz guitarist and former soldier born in Scotland and then raised in the East End of London. Nothing else taped in London came closer to capturing the essential spirit of rockabilly, the newly coined term for country-based rock 'n' roll, than 'Cumberland Gap'

---

* In 1961, France had suffered its own rock 'n' roll riots. 'Fans ripped out over 2,000 seats,' one reporter noted as Vince Taylor played the Palais des Sports, 'wrenched water pipes from the wall and fought among themselves.'

by Lonnie Donegan. Yet its creator claimed to hate rock 'n' roll, and distanced himself throughout his life from the teenage rebellion that it represented. It's one of the ironies of musical history that a man who considered himself part of an elite not only became an all-round entertainer, a one-man inheritor of the music-hall tradition; but also did more to popularise the guitar and encourage teenagers to play rock 'n' roll than anyone else of his era.

Donegan tied his flag to the mast of jazz; then, when he was cast overboard, he claimed the standard of another genre, and refashioned it in his own image. The style he commandeered was skiffle, a name taken from a 1920s American blues party record entitled 'Hometown Skiffle' (not released in Britain until late 1949). A skiffle, according to a surprisingly early reference in the *Daily Mirror*, 'is the Chicago Rent Party, which thrived during the hard times of American prohibition . . . an all-night session of Blues and Boogie-Woogie, pianists, guitarists and blues singers'. That certainly captures the spirit of 'Hometown Skiffle', but when Britain's skiffle bands emerged amidst the undergrowth of the traditional jazz revival launched by George Webb's Dixielanders, there was no piano – merely guitar, banjo and percussion. And the music was not strictly urban blues but a much broader assembly of African-American folklore, much of which had passed through the white hands of singers such as Woody Guthrie and Pete Seeger before it came to British attention.

Anthony Donegan was so besotted with the 1920s blues guitarist Lonnie Johnson that he stole his hero's name as his own. But the prime musical inspiration for skiffle was a man who had died in 1949: Huddie Ledbetter, known better as 'Lead Belly'. He was serving a sentence for murder in a Louisiana prison when he was discovered in 1934 by folklorists John and Alan Lomax, who were on a quest to track down the original folk music of black America before it was lost to posterity.* Ledbetter was pointed out to them as the best singer in Angola Prison, and the Lomaxes assumed that he might broaden their knowledge by a song or two. Instead, he reeled off dozens of tunes in a bewildering variety of styles – some immediately classifiable as blues, others as ragtime, others claimed by Lead Belly

---

* Other folklorists spent the decade documenting the 'authentic' local music of the African continent, discovering to their chagrin that where a community had been exposed to a wind-up gramophone, native singers were as likely to offer them a Jimmie Rodgers tune or an operatic aria as anything that had been passed down from their forefathers.

as his own creations. John Lomax petitioned the governor to have the prisoner released as a benefit to the wider cultural community. He then arranged for a *March of Time* newsreel to be filmed, offering a mythologised version of Ledbetter's return to polite society and his meek obedience to his new master. Saviour and prodigy eventually fell out – Lomax describing the musician in 1944 as 'a triple murderer, a drunkard, a congenital liar and a super double super hypocrite' – and while the folklorists went on to make an equally significant 'discovery', in the form of blues singer Muddy Waters, Ledbetter amassed a formidable recording catalogue, encompassing everything from children's songs to field hollers from the slave era.

Perhaps Lead Belly was the perfect icon for a genre that claimed the authenticity of traditional folk music, but relied upon more than an element of showbiz hoopla (and Lonnie Donegan's ravenous egotism). It is certainly striking that skiffle musicians found an exotic thrill in Americana which was not matched by any curiosity about Britain's folk roots. For the early 1950s was the era when collectors and singers across the British Isles began to revolt against the colonialism of American culture, and pursue more local traditions. Some acted with political motives, keen to preserve the submerged culture of the working class in an age when historians were finally beginning to realise that they could dig beneath the familiar tales of kings and prime ministers; others were simply appalled by the banality of commercial music. They unearthed the surviving singers of traditional songs, and revived the process of documenting Britain's folk heritage in print, on record – and on radio.

In the early 1950s, the BBC broadcast a series by Francis Collinson and Francis Dillon entitled *The Postman Brings Me Songs*, devoted to ballads which had been submitted to their weekly *Country Magazine* show about rural affairs. But the key figure in the BBC's almost unwitting revival of British folk was A. L. 'Bert' Lloyd: singer, folklorist and Communist. He prepared a series of radio documentaries in the late 1930s, which ostensibly chronicled the traditional songs associated with specific professions; although, for example, his programme *The Voice of the Seaman*, based on his experience on a whaling ship, carefully glossed over the fact that most of his shipmates had preferred to sing Tin Pan Alley hits rather than age-old ballads. After the war, he enlisted folksinger Ewan MacColl (real name James Miller; an experienced radio actor) in his crusade to shape the nation's perception of its musical history. MacColl poured his enthusiasm into a pioneering series of 'radio ballads': programmes which examined themes of working-class life, from love to work, the city to the sea, travellers to fighting men. Broadcast between 1957 and 1964, they offered a version of traditional music far removed from the genteel ballads gathered at the start of the century, and even further distant from the revamped Americana that had been dominating the skiffle clubs. Yet they, and the work of other folklorists, left their mark. From the late 1950s onwards, a network of folk (as distinct from skiffle) clubs was established across Britain – the root of a genteel tradition that stretches to this day.

There is little evidence that Lonnie Donegan ever paid much attention to the unearthing of Britain's folk heritage, scholarly or political. Nor did he seem to stand out from his colleagues in Chris Barber's Jazz Band in 1954. He only took centre stage as an intermission novelty, wherein Barber, Donegan and their pals would change instruments, romp through some American folklore, and then return to the serious business of reviving 1920s jazz. When Barber's band recorded their first LP in July 1954, a week after Elvis Presley's initial session at Sun Records, two of the eight songs were credited to the Lonnie Donegan Skiffle Group. These weren't the first commercial skiffle recordings in the UK – Ken Colyer's group, to which Barber and Donegan had once belonged, beat them by a month – but they were the first to be released. 'Isn't it time to call a halt to the sloppy use of the term "skiffle" before it changes its meaning altogether?', complained jazzman Humphrey Lyttleton when the LP was released in 1955. 'Country folk songs and urban rent party music are not the same thing!' The *Gramophone* magazine added snidely: 'Lonnie Donegan still sounds rather too much like a hog-caller from up-country.'

The album was forgotten by the time that London's first skiffle and blues club opened in September 1955. The Round House in Wardour Street formalised a scene that was already operating (literally) below stairs in 1954 and 1955, as amateur guitarists, inspired by Barber's and Colyer's bands, gathered in cafés and coffee-house basements to swap earnest renditions of tunes by Lead Belly and Woody Guthrie. As *Jazz Journal* noted in November 1955, 'skiffle music has now become an industry in itself'. A month later, the Barber/Donegan LP was broken up into singles, as an attempt to recoup some money from the project. Donegan's 'Rock Island Line', a propulsive American folk tune collected by the Lomaxes at an Arkansas prison in 1934 (and subsequently claimed by both Lead Belly and Donegan as their own), was played as a Christmas novelty by two British disc jockeys, and then startled everyone by becoming a pop hit in the New Year – as Peter Leslie reported, 'without benefit of plugging, publicity or ballyhoo'.

This horrified the jazz purists: *Jazz Journal* jibed that Donegan 'sounds like a number of intoxicated hillbillies returning from some over-lengthy orgy'. But for British teenagers who, at that point, had heard nothing more fiery than 'Rock Around the Clock', 'Rock Island Line' sounded both impossibly alien, and also eminently reproducible with only the minimum of instrumental knowledge. Sales of acoustic guitars soared during 1956, mothers' washboards were 'borrowed' for their percussive effect, and schoolboys learned how to manufacture an upright bass from an old tea chest and some string. Bizarrely, 'Rock Island Line' also caught on in the United States, thereby becoming the first instance of a British act selling black American music to a white American audience. (Stan Freberg, ever awake to good comedy material, immediately recorded a hilarious satire of Donegan's performance.) There was no skiffle boom in the States, but in Britain, the music not only took off, but was widely viewed by the media as a healthy alternative to the sick hooliganism of the rock 'n' roll brigade. Donegan seized the moment by dismissing rock 'n' roll as a 'swindle', although a fan retorted that the great rock 'n' roll swindler was actually Donegan himself, as his career would never have flourished had Bill Haley not broken the stranglehold of the post-war balladeers.

'At worst, [skiffle] becomes an amateur rock-and-roll', noted John Hasted in the British Communist Party paper *World News*. 'At its best, it could lead to a new style of national people's song, with a truly popular basis.' Hasted added, with an unknowingly prophetic ear: 'British singers can seldom make a success of singing like Negroes. It is not easy to achieve a convincing accent.' Similar statements were aired during the British R&B boom of 1963–5. Another jazz critic considered that skiffle might spawn 'Britain's future Billie Holiday or Jimmy Rushing', on the assump-tion that once the adolescent infatuations with rock 'n' roll and skiffle had passed, big bands would inevitably rekindle the splendour of the late 1930s. Instead, Donegan's success prompted an outbreak of teenage music-making unprecedented in the nation's history. Thirty-four groups took part in the National Skiffle Contest of 1957, held in Bury St Edmunds, some even daring to wield electric instruments. The same week, a skiffle group formed by a 16-year-old boy named John Lennon performed at a church fete in Liverpool – where a converted warehouse named the Cavern was now hosting four nights a week of traditional jazz, plus two lunchtime jam sessions, in which skifflers were able to participate. So widespread was the phenomenon that the novelist Valerie Hastings wrote a children's book entitled *Jo and the Skiffle Group*; the Salvation Army formed its own band to play spiritual material folk-style; comedian Peter Sellers issued a skiffle demolition of the music-hall favourite 'Any Old Iron'; and readers of the weekly magazine *Woman* were offered bank-holiday advice on how to prepare for 'your outdoor skiffle party'.

Tens of thousands felt the urge to take part. At a time when guitar tuition books were designed either for the classically inclined, or for those wishing to play complex jazz chords, there was a space in the market for those who preferred to emulate Donegan, Steele or Presley. In the spring of 1958, Bert Weedon was given a Guitar Corner spot on the ITV television show *Children's Hour*. His first appearance is said to have prompted 3,000 letters. 'I am teaching them rock and skiffle, to accompany themselves', Weedon explained. He capitalised on this enthusiasm with the encouragingly titled instruction manual, *Play in a Day: Bert Weedon's Guitar Guide to Modern Guitar Playing*. This offered hints on how to tackle skiffle, rock 'n' roll and jazz, with a chart of common guitar chords, and suggestions on how to play a solo.*

When teenagers began to form their own rock 'n' roll combos, they were mirroring what had already happened in the United States, where both money and instruments were more accessible to those who had not yet reached adulthood. Many young men posed for the first time in front of a bedroom mirror, guitar or (failing that) tennis racket in hand, imagining the screams as they inherited Elvis Presley's audience. If his rich, playful, endlessly flexible voice was strictly *sui generis*, Jerry Lee Lewis's piano pumping inimitable and Little Richard's hollering simply impractical to imitate, then other rock 'n' roll stars appeared to offer a more accessible target. The Everly Brothers demanded only a rudimentary knowledge of chords, and the ability of two boys to harmonise their voices with a brotherly bond. Buddy Holly was even more within reach, or so it seemed: anyone could attempt his mannered, hiccupping vocal

---

*Those who found Weedon's *Guide* beyond them could opt for the Dial-A-Chord, a plastic device which required no more musical skill than the ability to flick a plastic wheel. Historians might like to compare *Play in a Day* with Thomas Morley's *Plaine and Easie Introduction to Practicall Musicke* (1597), which was also published in response to the enthusiasm for amateur music-making, although the instrument of choice in the late sixteenth century was the lute, not the guitar.

tone, while his self-penned songs employed the minimum of basic guitar chords, and (deceptively) simple wordplay.

'After 1955, the amateurs took over', said the songwriter Alec Wilder, lamenting the passing of the era in which Cole Porter, Rodgers and Hart and their peers had lifted popular song to unaccustomed heights of sophistication.* His judgement was equally applicable to the process of recording in the rock 'n' roll era, when the emotional impact of a record was more important than its sonic clarity. The two qualities were not mutually exclusive, but 1956–8 marked a rare moment in the technical history of popular music, when the notion of progress went into reverse. The industry's goal had always been to produce cleaner and more distinct sound, with electrical recording replacing acoustic, 'ffrr' widening the frequencies available to the engineer, and multitrack tape allowing musicians and producers to paint with sound. Suddenly, teenagers were buying records on which it was not clear that the musicians knew how to play their instruments (the 1958 instrumental 'Green Mosquitos' by the Tune Rockers), and where noise that was either chaotic or compressed into an indistinct sludge was an acceptable basis for a hit song. There was a burst of records in the early months of 1958 – 'At the Hop' by Danny & the Juniors, 'I Wonder Why' by Dion & the Belmonts, 'Jennie Lee' by Jan & Arnie, 'Do You Wanna Dance' by Bobby Freeman, 'Endless Sleep' by Jody Reynolds – which suggested that adolescents had seized control of an adult industry. Simultaneously, guitar instrumentals as savage as Link Wray's 'Rumble' and as cavernous as Duane Eddy's 'Movin' & Groovin'' (on which, unusually, Eddy himself did not actually perform) helped to create an ethos of rock 'n' roll that went beyond words and actions into the realm of merely *being* – being rougher, louder and more defiant than anyone else.

This was the birthplace of garage rock, of punk, of every genre in which feel transcended perfection, and swagger trumped technique – the irony being that it was their very fallibility which made these records so perfect. Rock 'n' roll fans could relish Scotty Moore's lost-in-a-maze guitar solo on 'Too Much',[†] or the Silhouettes' speed-freak incoherence on 'Get a

---

* *Time* magazine suggested that 'a decade of simple-minded children's records has conditioned today's teen-agers to their infatuation with equally simple-minded rock 'n' roll'.

† The explosion of noise which opens his second guitar solo on Elvis Presley's 'Hound Dog' is perhaps the definitive expression of rock 'n' roll. Moore admitted that he was never able to reproduce it.

Job', or Eddie Cochran's sly pronunciation of 'peanuts' as 'penis' on 'Drive-in Show'.

Yet the summer of 1958, when many of these strange records were still on the American charts, was also when many pundits declared that rock 'n' roll had passed its peak; had lost its excitement; was, effectively, dead. Even Alan Freed, the populariser of rock 'n' roll, was careful to avoid using the phrase on the air. The key word now was 'beat' – the Big Beat, for Freed; 'beat music' for TV producers in Britain; soon enough, 'teen-beat', a description which named the music's audience and its prime characteristic, whilst shedding the pejorative sexual verbs and the hooliganism which supposedly went with them. It marked the beginning of an era in which Tin Pan Alley tried to regain control of the music business, and pop became more varied and more bizarre than ever before.

> If you gave the public what it wanted, you could smuggle in all sorts of extras – good tunes, good lyrics, good musicianship – even bits of real jazz; but it was the beat that sold the music.
> Ernest Borneman, *Melody Maker*, January 1959

> If popular music is truly the mirror of the people, then rock 'n' roll is truly a people's music – for this is the kind of stuff that anybody can sing . . . we are treated to an orgy of gut-spilling, whimpering and sobbing, which is more embarrassing than soul-stirring. Couple this with the hypnotic beat, and utter lack of vocal ability, and it can add up to a pretty shattering experience.
> Edward Joblonski, *American Record Guide*, April 1959

When Elvis Presley was summoned by the US Army in 1958, he left a vacant crown. Little Richard might have seized it, but he was on what the press called 'an evangelical kick', though that didn't prevent him launching his own range of perfume. (First scent? Princess Cheri.*) There were confused reports from Australia that Richard had retired from rock 'n' roll. 'If you want to live for the Lord, you can't rock 'n' roll too', he told reporters in Sydney. 'God doesn't like it.' His saxophonist had teased him that he was

---

* There was also a range of Elvis Presley lipsticks on sale, with a choice of colours: Cruel Red, Tender Pink and of course Hound Dog Orange.

only paying lip service to his faith, so Richard had flung his precious jewellery into Sydney Harbour. He would be returning to Los Angeles to be baptised into the Seventh Day Adventist Church and 'prepare for the end of the world'. Then he claimed that he had changed his mind, thrown by the launch of the Russian satellite *Sputnik*. Or, in the next breath, *Sputnik* had triggered an apocalyptic dream where 'the world was burning up and the sky was melting with heat'. Back in America, he began to cancel dates, and was dropped from radio playlists. He went out on the road as a gospel-singing evangelist – and drew only a few dozen people to the sizeable Atlanta City Auditorium. Richard wasn't perturbed: he cut his hair, because the Bible told him to, and warned his fans that 'rock 'n' roll glorifies Satan'.

In this belief, he was strangely in harmony with Presley's most obvious successor: Jerry Lee Lewis. Raised in a Southern Baptist church, he was torn between hedonism and a mortal fear of hellfire. His music pumped a young man's bravado into the traditions of gospel, country and boogie-woogie, with sexuality oozing out of every bar. 'Whole Lotta Shakin' Goin' On', a hit across every imaginable US market from blues to hillbilly, even provided instructions for foreplay and orgasm, prompting an inevitable sequel, 'Breathless'. But Lewis's momentum was halted when he took his 13-year-old 'child bride' to England. He was forced to abandon his tour following a media campaign to have him deported. When he arrived home, he sorted the issue to his own satisfaction in one quip: 'She'll be 14 in July. But she's ALL woman.' The photographs of his barely pubescent bride screamed otherwise.*

Scandal seemed to attract itself to rock 'n' rollers. Screaming Jay Hawkins (creator of the immortal 'Constipation Blues') pleaded guilty to 'statutory rape' of a 15-year-old girl, and possession of illegal drugs. Billy Guy of the Coasters was also convicted of underage sex, the girl this time being 16. The male members of the Platters were discovered in a hotel room with three naked call girls (and a fourth in a slip). Chuck Berry was first arrested as a robbery suspect (a case of mistaken identity); then for having a concealed weapon; for 'weaving his pink Cadillac on a St Louis highway'; and for attempting to date an underage white girl at a high-school fraternity dance. Finally, in 1960, he was jailed for having allegedly escorted a 14-year-old girl

---

* The cockney comedian Tommy Trinder capitalised on the furore when he opened a church fete in Southend a few days after Lewis had left the country. 'Sorry we couldn't get Jerry Lee Lewis to open the fete,' he wisecracked, 'but unfortunately his wife is teething.'

over state lines for immoral purposes. There were deaths, of course, too: Buddy Holly, Ritchie Valens and the Big Bopper in a plane crash; Eddie Cochran in a car accident whilst on tour in Britain.

British rock 'n' roll scandals were, on the whole, more restrained. Young rocker Terry Dene was involved in a tempestuous relationship with another singer, Edna Savage. Their ferocious arguments led to his being arrested twice for vandalism. When he joined the army for his national service, his minders assumed that his reputation would be enhanced, as Elvis's had been, but within days of his conscription, he was revealed to be suffering 'an emotional crisis' and was placed in a military hospital. His crisis became a nervous breakdown, so he was swiftly demobbed – only to discover that his bride no longer wished to be associated with him, and neither did most of his fans. He survived to find Christianity a decade later, and pen a mournfully titled autobiography: *I Thought Terry Dene Was Dead*.

Having ousted Marty Wilde from the starring role in TV's *Oh Boy!*, Cliff Richard endured nothing more damaging than assault with rotten eggs and tomatoes during a 1959 performance at the Lyceum Ballroom. 'Boys out for an evening with their girls get jealous', he explained. Eggs were a fashionable weapon in the late 1950s: they were aimed at Shirley Bassey during a 1958 performance at the Chiswick Empire, shortly after she had been accused in the press of 'faking' a kidnapping. Just 21, she had already been scolded for recording indecent material, and then involved in an unsavoury incident at the Cumberland Hotel in London, where she was staying with a 35-year-old man. One of her ex-lovers arrived at her suite with a gun, assaulted her companion, and then held Bassey hostage for three hours, firing occasional shots into the furniture. She was eventually rescued by police, but during subsequent court hearings her ex maliciously alleged that she had 'got rid of' four children from four different men. She was forced to admit that she had given birth to an illegitimate daughter when she was 17, who was being raised by her sister. But whereas a rock 'n' roller's career could be ruined by notoriety like this, Bassey continued untarnished, topping the British singles chart in 1959, winning popularity polls, and enjoying a *succès d'estime* at a New York cabaret club in 1961. Britain was unwilling to lose its sassiest and most sultry stage performer, at a time when most of the country's stars were pale imitations of American originals. Skiffle and Tommy Steele aside, British acts virtually vanished from the charts during 1956 and 1957, the only convincing moments coming from singers reared in the variety tradition, such as

Frankie Vaughan and Alma Cogan. Hence the jolt to the teenage nervous system provided by Cliff Richard's debut, 'Move It'. Spare, hip and as smooth as a snooker ball racing across the green baize, it was the first (and arguably last, until the arrival of Johnny Kidd & the Pirates in 1959) British rock 'n' roll record to capture the rebellious spirit of the Americans.

This was an era when Britain waited to see what was selling in the US, and then attempted to copy it before the original release could take off. But the variety of music coming out of America was bewildering, and singers often found themselves in a London studio struggling to imagine what songs such as 'My Boy Flattop' and 'Green Door' might possibly symbolise. At least they were dealing with their own language. Performers elsewhere in the world could sense the visceral impact of rock 'n' roll; the challenge was to adapt it to the culture from which they came. It helped if they were performers for whom English was not entirely foreign. Vince Taylor could take France's rock 'n' roll scene by storm because he was British-born and American-raised; Mickey Curtis, both of whose parents were Anglo-Japanese, could head the *rockabiri* craze in Tokyo. White South Africans preferred to borrow their idols from the US and UK; their black counterparts, left unexposed to the rock 'n' roll of African-Americans by the nation's racially determined radio playlists, considered that the likes of Bill Haley and Elvis Presley had nothing to say to them.

Rock 'n' roll also penetrated the Communist bloc in Eastern Europe, carried by the Voice of America radio network, and hence by word of mouth. Indeed, the military presence of Elvis Presley in Germany between 1958 and 1960 briefly encouraged the US government to think that rock might be a potent cultural weapon against Marxism. In response, successive waves of liberalisation and repression, ultimately emanating from the Kremlin, sent confusing signals to citizens behind the Iron Curtain. Western influences might be discreetly ignored by the authorities one year, and barred the next. Below the surface of Communist culture, young people maintained a semi-concealed network of musicians, fans and venues. Russian gangs operated a flourishing underworld trade in American rock 'n' roll recordings, often 'pressed' on postcards or X-ray plates which had been smuggled out of state hospitals. These 'records of a criminally hooligan trend' were swiftly declared illegal. The authorities in Moscow complained that dance bands were smuggling rock into their repertoire by pretending to mock it. In Czechoslovakia, Jiří Suchý (a less threatening version of Bill Haley) performed translations of US hits at clubs off

Wenceslas Square. In East Germany, the authorities sanctioned the creation of a dance called the *lipsi* ('a mixed-up rumba', said *Time* magazine),
to discourage teenagers from jiving to rock 'n' roll. 'Dancers bending at the
knee were pulled up by their hair', according to historian Timothy Ryback:
'People caught dancing apart were beaten up and thrown out of the bar.' It
took a public demonstration of the twist by Communist Party leader Walter
Ulbricht in 1962 for the censorship of Western dances to be withdrawn –
although not in the Soviet Union, where the party continued to promote
officially approved dance steps such as the *moskvichka*, the *terrikon* and the
infiz. (Only government officials chose to employ them.)

All American music of the era was regarded indiscriminately by
the Communist regimes as 'jazz' or 'rock 'n' roll'. But the USA was big
enough to encompass a dozen different trends simultaneously – some
emerging organically from within, others imposed by Tin Pan Alley and
the publishers' enclave of the Brill Building.* A persistent motif throughout
the mid-1950s was American folklore, from 'The Ballad of Davy Crockett'
in 1955 (a TV theme which inspired a rich trade in Davy Crockett hats and
dolls) to 'The Battle of New Orleans' and 'Tom Dooley'. The latter, by the
Kingston Trio, helped to maintain a commercial revival in folk music which
would survive into the mid-1960s, until it was smothered by more vivid
contemporary material from writers such as Bob Dylan and Tom Paxton.†
The Kingston Trio were pursued by such imitators as the Brothers Four
and the Limeliters, while Joan Baez and Odetta adopted a more reverent
attitude towards traditional material. With America perceiving itself under
constant threat at home and abroad, ballads about its past – mythical or
otherwise – provided a reassuring sense of continuity.

Another menace, the persistence of rock 'n' roll, prompted the
music business to act in concert. Decisions about popular taste could not be
left to the vagaries of public opinion. A British pundit broke the news in
February 1957: 'Experts say the latest craze – despite Bill Haley – will last
at most another year. The preparations are already being made to start off

---

* The Brill Building is at 1619 Broadway, Manhattan; in fact, many of the era's hit songwriters,
such as Carole King and Gerry Goffin, were housed across the street at the Aldon office in
1650 Broadway.
† This fad had its equivalent in West Germany, where the first LP to sell 100,000 copies was a
collection of sailors' ballads by the mellow-voiced pop star Freddy Quinn. He had earlier tried
to masquerade as a Mexican in a vain attempt to secure stardom in the US.

the new trend. In Britain, it will be "sweet" music: smooth, tranquil, something to dance cheek to cheek to. In America, the decision has been made to try West Indian Calypso beat . . . Already [vaudeville veteran] Sophie Tucker is presenting herself as "the Calypso Mamma", and new records by Harry Belafonte will be given a big push.' As an American trade paper confirmed, 'all of a sudden the business is interested in songs with a calypso beat', especially those facets of the business which were orchestrating the trend. Soon Harry Belafonte LPs, as yet unissued in Britain, were being sold under the counter in London stores. It was, said a London newspaper, 'Calypsomania'.

Twenty years had passed since the earliest attempts to market calypso to audiences in Britain and America; and nearly forty since the style had first been recorded in Trinidad. But its origins could be traced beyond the Caribbean to the West African tradition of *kaiso*, a word of encouragement shouted by slaves who communicated in song while they laboured. In the twentieth century, it was carnival music in Trinidad, improvised in the streets or delivered by professional singers in large tents. Like rap, it depended on verbal dexterity rather than musical originality; it carried political unrest, subversive humour, bawdiness and proud nationalism into places conventional media could never reach. By 1939, Trinidad was staging national calypso contests. Several of the prime contenders for the prize, such as Lord Beginner and Lord Kitchener, joined the flow of West Indians to Britain on the *Windrush* in 1948. Beginner delighted newsmen at the dockside by apparently ad-libbing 'London is the Place for Me', although he had written it before the trip. Thereafter calypso found its way into British culture via unexpected routes – translated into skiffle, when Johnny Duncan recorded the 1950 Trinidadian hit 'Last Train to San Fernando'; cross-fertilised with jazz, as Britain's small cabal of bop musicians found employment on such records as 'Kitch's Bebop Calypso'; even adopted by British satirists, when comedian Lance Percival delivered a calypso commentary on recent events in BBC TV's *That Was the Week That Was*. (In Paris, meanwhile, a calypso variant had been introduced by Henri Salvador, from French Guiana, who was later persuaded to write some of the earliest French rock 'n' roll songs – a sin for which he never forgave himself.)

In Hollywood, there had been a spate of rock 'n' roll exploitation films, almost all of which (*The Girl Can't Help It* aside) revolved round a single plot, and offered the same moral: those rock 'n' roll kids aren't as bad as they seem. Calypso was next, with movies such as *Calypso Heat Wave*, *Calypso Joe* and *Bop Girl Goes Calypso*. The last of these starred 'Route 66' songwriter Bobby Troup as a psychology professor researching 'Mass Hysteria, and What Makes It Tick'. To demonstrate his thesis, he persuades a female 'bop' singer (rock 'n' roll, not jazz) to convert to the calypso craze. 'Here we go again', wrote Barry Ulanov in *Down Beat* magazine. 'Another fad, another fashion . . . carefully organised spontaneity . . . the next precisely plotted wave of popular music . . . yesterday's rock 'n' roll hollerers become today's banana hoofers . . . It's extraordinary that year after year, decade after decade, the beautifully polished machinery of manufactured spontaneous combustion can be set in motion in our popular culture without any protest.' Ulanov concluded: 'If a whole country can be such a pushover for a song and dance, what does that suggest about that same nation's political susceptibilities?'

Even Harry Belafonte, the putative leader of the calypso wave, was sceptical: 'Calypso is going to become a caricature of itself once the fast-buck guys hop on the bandwagon.' Already a noted performer in several Hollywood 'issue' movies, the half-Jamaican, half-Martiniquan club singer explored what would now be called 'world music'. 'Elvis was interpreting one kind of black music – rhythm and blues', he wrote in his autobiography, 'while I found my inspiration in black folk songs, spirituals and calypso, and also in African music.' His 1956 LP *Calypso* spent seven months at the top of the American charts, and included two songs that became instant pop standards: 'Jamaica Farewell' and 'Day-O' (alias the 'Banana Boat Song'). Belafonte vetoed the record company's original artwork: 'The first mock-ups I saw had me with a big bunch of bananas superimposed on my head. I looked like Carmen Miranda in drag, only in bare feet, with a big toothy grin, as if I were saying, "Come to dee islands!"' His subsequent releases touched upon a variety of American and Caribbean folk traditions, leading one British critic to describe him as 'the greatest musical sensation of the century'. Belafonte would offer Bob Dylan early exposure in the recording studio, and become an enduring symbol of the civil-rights struggle.

Those singers who did not follow Belafonte into calypso attempted to turn rock 'n' roll rhythms to their own devices, often to engaging effect, as with Guy Mitchell's 'Crazy With Love' and Andy Williams's 'Baby Doll'. Williams also tried (at 29) to masquerade as a teenage pop idol, though he was undercut by 26-year-old film star Tab Hunter with the lighter-than-air country tune 'Young Love'. The authentic article arrived in February 1957 in the shape of 17-year-old Tommy Sands, the first in a long succession of clean-cut, unthreatening young Americans who could muster a jog-trot if required but were more comfortable with a romantic ballad. His successors ranged from *Rebel Without a Cause* actor Sal Mineo, who simply couldn't sing, to Ricky Nelson, whose cover of Fats Domino's 'I'm Walkin'' revealed an intuitive feel for rock 'n' roll which would ensure him a lengthy career. As if to acknowledge these younger contenders, Elvis Presley softened his style to match them, restraining both his sexuality and his guitarists on 'All Shook Up'. When he returned with the razor-edged 'Jailhouse Rock', it sounded positively menacing alongside the jauntiness of Frankie Avalon and Paul Anka.

In a singles market now focused on teenagers and their younger siblings, little shots of adrenaline were available in every imaginable flavour. During 1958, nobody knew what would sell, and novelty was all, much of it apparently pulled straight from the pages of *Mad* magazine – speeded-up vocals on 'Witch Doctor' and 'Purple People Eater' (and a Joe South song in which the two monsters met); horror rock ('Dinner With Drac'); street-corner hoodlum harmonies ('At the Hop'); biker fantasies ('Bad Motorcycle'); Latin instrumentals ('Tequila'); rock 'n' roll phone calls ('Chantilly Lace') and parental lectures ('Yakety Yak'); rock 'n' roll mythology ('Johnny B. Goode', 'All American Boy'); raw sexuality ('Fever', 'I Got Stung'); and guidebooks for teenage etiquette in which sex was definitely taboo (the ultra-conservative 'Teen Commandments', No. 4 insisting: 'At the first moment, turn away from unclean thinking'). The Everly Brothers charted the turmoil of teen romance, from the trembling seduction of 'All I Have to Do is Dream' to the curfew-busting 'Wake Up Little Susie'. The Chordettes even brokered the first stirrings of feminism, on 'A Girl's Work is Never Done'. And amidst all this teenage mayhem, there was 42-year-old Frank Sinatra, like a dad who had forgotten he was hosting his daughter's party and had invited the boys around for a hand of poker.

There were two men who could have pulled off that embarrassment with style, because even in their 20s they were plotting how to translate teen appeal into a career. Bobby Darin started out as a novelty rock 'n' roller, one of the host who annoyed Jerry Lee Lewis so much: 'All they played was them Bobbys – Bobby Vee, Bobby Vinton, Bobby Rydell, Bobby Darin. If your name was Bobby, you were in with a sporting chance.' (Not making illegal wedding vows with your 13-year-old cousin helped, of course.) He seemed no more substantial than Fabian, a 15-year-old who – like the hero of Stan Freberg's 'The Old Payola Roll Blues' – was signed for his looks and scored several hits without being able to sing a note. *Time* magazine called Fabian 'the tuneless terror'. But, as Atlantic Records boss Ahmet Ertegun recalled, Bobby Darin 'was a person with great ambition and endless vision. He could see no limit to his potential. He wanted to be a bit of everything. He wanted to be a rock and roller, he wanted to be a pop singer in the mode of Sinatra and Dean Martin, he wanted to be a folk singer.' From 'Splish Splash' and 'Plain Jane' he switched to 'Mack the Knife', swinging as hard as Sinatra – and taking the teenagers with him. 'Nearly everything I do is part of a master plan to make me the most important entertainer in the world', he revealed. He moved swiftly from rock 'n' roll package tours to wearing a tuxedo in Las Vegas, where Jerry Lewis told him: 'Do you realise you're alone in your generation? Sammy, Dean and I are all ten years ahead of you. Unless you destroy yourself, no one else can touch you.' He suggested a future in which swing and standards might be the final destination for every first-rank rock 'n' roller; and had Elvis Presley followed suit, and spent the 1960s with the Cole Porter songbook rather than his inane film soundtracks, Darin might have seemed like a pioneer rather than a maverick.

In Britain, the nearest equivalent to Darin was Anthony Newley – less convincing as an Elvis or a Sinatra, but (like Darin) a first-rate actor with (unlike Darin) a touch of comic genius, a schooling in music hall and the ability to write West End musicals and enduring standards. His early records oozed personality and cockney humour, satirising the very medium he was exploiting. By 1962 he was arguably the world's most versatile pop performer, with the potential to reassemble the all-ages audience of his youth, which had been shattered into distinct adult and teenage fragments. But in a field increasingly dominated by the mercurial demands of the young, that was a dream even Elvis Presley and Frank Sinatra couldn't hope to fulfil.

CHAPTER 13

SOUL FOOD

'It is recognised as one of the most poetic traits of the Negro's character that he reveres his river as he does his God ... There is no doubt that Negro music, of whatever kind, is often so intriguing . . . because they always believe so profoundly in the merit of it, and put their whole soul into it.'

Gramophone magazine, 1932

'90% of the popular stars today, including myself, have no voice, but they have soul, that appeal that will touch the average guy.'

Nat 'King' Cole, 1954

On 17 October 1961, more than 30,000 Algerians and other North Africans gathered in Paris to protest against a police curfew which had been imposed upon their ethnic grouping. The demonstration was part of the National Liberation Front's campaign to free Algeria from French colonial rule. The French authorities responded with a ferocity which ensured that this would be remembered as one of the grimmest days in the nation's modern history. 10,000 people were arrested and detained before they could join the march; as many again were dispersed by riot police. But several thousand marched through central Paris by the River Seine – to be met with baton charges and live ammunition. As many as 200 Algerians are believed to have died that day, of bullet wounds or drowning, after being forced into the river.

Approximately 6,000 prisoners were held in the Palais des Sports arena, where many were randomly taken to the dressing rooms to be beaten and tortured with electric batons. But after three days, prisoners and interrogators had to move elsewhere, so that Ray Charles could begin a week of appearances in the venue. Charles was, according to his record company, a genius, with an uncanny ability to channel the emotions of his audience into his music. 'The same match that burns you burns me', he explained. 'The things I write and sing about concern the average Joe and his general problems.' It's not clear whether he ever learned what atrocities had occurred in his concert hall; or whether the febrile atmosphere captured on a live album that week was coloured by the echoes of brutality and anguish. There were protests by students after several of his shows – not because police had murdered and tortured peaceful demonstrators, but because Ray Charles had dared to insert ballads into a repertoire which they had hoped would contain nothing but rock 'n' roll.

Ray Charles was widely seen as the international representative of a musical movement which had assumed ideological proportions: a cultural shift that combined rhythm and blues music with the crusade for equality and civil rights. 'There is in the music a new racial pride,' said the African-American magazine *Ebony* in 1961, 'a celebration of ties to Africa and a defiant embrace of the honky-tonk, the house-rent party and people who say "dis here" and "dat here" – an embrace, in short, of all that middle-class

America condemns. Martin Luther King Jr is in the new music too, and Little Rock', where troops had been required to assist nine black students as they enrolled at the city's Central High School in 1957. The name of this politically charged, culturally radical music? Soul.

As early as 1928, an article in *Gramophone* magazine declared that, at its best, jazz music 'has soul'. More than twenty-five years later, the word came easily to Ray Charles's lips: 'I try to bring out my soul so that people can understand what I am. I want people to feel my soul.' In his autobiography, he put that feeling into context: 'I became myself. I opened up the floodgates, let myself do things I hadn't done before, created sounds which, people told me afterward, had never been created before . . . I started taking gospel lines and turning them into regular songs.'

And that was where the controversy started. To the blues critic, and subsequent British R&B pioneer, Alexis Korner, the juxtaposition of an almost religious passion and Charles's own emotional outpourings was 'almost blasphemous' and 'vaguely horrifying', indicative of 'a lack of taste'. But there had been shared DNA between spiritual and secular black music since the early 1930s, when Georgia Tom, co-creator of the lascivious blues record 'It's Tight Like That', became Thomas A. Dorsey, originator of modern gospel music. After the death of his wife in childbirth, Dorsey was moved to write 'Precious Lord, Take My Hand', which gospel historian Viv Broughton called 'a masterpiece of gospel hymnody – part spiritual uplift, part blues melancholy'.

Soon afterwards, Dorsey met a young woman named Mahalia Jackson, whose career he would oversee for the next decade. She made a solitary record in the 1930s, singing with a freedom found nowhere in the blues tradition. Resuming her recording career in 1946, she cut 'Move On Up a Little Higher', a righteous gospel performance which contained almost everything that Aretha Franklin would ever need to learn. Within a decade, she had become an international celebrity, her salvation open to all. 'She lost the black market to a horrifying degree', record producer John Hammond sneered. 'I'd say that by her death she was playing to a 75% white audience, maybe as high as 90%.'

Inherent to the black gospel tradition is the trading of lines between preacher and congregation, the call-and-response, a regimented structure which is the living likeness of spontaneity. Like Sister Rosetta Tharpe, whose tightrope walk between blues and gospel in the 1940s and 50s saw her don a rough-toned electric guitar and commit her marriage ceremony to vinyl, Ray Charles saw no difficulty in applying the trademarks of gospel to the blues, and vice versa (although he claimed to have turned down lucrative offers to make entirely spiritual records). He went a stage beyond: subtly reworking the words of familiar gospel tunes to carry them into the secular world, so that 'This Little Light of Mine' became 'This Little Girl of Mine'. By 1959, when 'What'd I Say' acted as a melting pot for R&B, rock 'n' roll, blues and gospel, he was openly expressing the groans and grunts of sexual intercourse. 'I sing with all the feeling that I can put into it, so that I can feel it myself', he explained. Only later was it revealed that he insisted on squiring a long succession of his (always) female backing vocalists, adding an erotic frisson to his music. Mahalia Jackson probably had him in mind when she noted: 'Some of these record companies are trying to make gospel singing a competitor of rock 'n' roll . . . Gospel singing doesn't need artificial, unnecessary, phony sounds.' Or, as Thomas Dorsey, complained in 1961: 'I turn on the radio and I can't tell the gospel singers from the rock 'n' rollers.' Ray Charles would probably have taken that as a compliment.

If gospel and Ray Charles were the progenitors of soul, the movement soon became as much a political as a musical force. 'Soul' entered jazz, as a description for the music of artists such as Oscar Brown and Cannonball Adderley, who were combining a hip contemporary sensibility with a willingness to revive memories of an even darker age – the work-songs, chants and desperate spirituals of the slave era. For decades, black Americans had measured their success in terms of assimilation: the more they adopted the manners of the white bourgeoisie, the closer their race had progressed towards civilisation. (Carl Van Vechten explored the ramifications of this impulse in his novel *Nigger Heaven*.) After the Second World War, the African-American community sought out its own culture. Novelists such as Ralph Ellison and Richard Wright dared to explore the otherness of the black American. Local acts of revolt against racism and segregation fired the national civil-rights movement. And many urban blacks brazenly adopted customs that they had once tried to conceal in their hope of being accepted by white America. Their language changed: as *Ebony* magazine noted in 1961, 'The real Negro folk idiom becomes chic' – the word 'funky', for example, passing from being taboo to being shouted aloud. Likewise 'soul food', the down-home cooking which would have been despised by polite society, but which stood for home, solidarity, comfort and belonging: 'collard greens and ham hocks, chitterlings, pig ears and pig feet'. Soul equalled community; soul equalled blackness; soul was a race unafraid to revel in its own culture. And soul was soon borrowed by white critics to describe their own, when under the influence of 'Negro' music. In 1962, not only did Elvis Presley have soul, according to a jazz magazine, but the Italian-American singer Timi Yuro borrowed the word for an album title.

For Aretha Franklin, the daughter of a preacher man, 'soul' was how her father sang and declaimed from the pulpit. To Thomas Dorsey, 'soul' was an adjective that should be reserved for one form of music: African-American gospel singing. The soul was for Christ, the heart for politics and romance, so the secular brand should be known as 'heart music'. It didn't catch on. A more considered objection came from the writer Horton Floyd, in a polemic he titled 'I'm Sick of Soul'. Why, he asked, was the Negro race eulogising a quality inspired by its experience of slavery and segregation? 'By isolating what they believe to be a superior Negro characteristic, they are merely giving credence to the racists' dogma', he argued: all racial superiority was wrong, whether it was white slave-owner over black slave, or black 'soul' over white 'soul-less'. The questions could spiral from there: did everything black automatically have soul? If soul came from oppression and defiance, what would happen when the black community was free from racism? Were the Black Muslims justified in preaching black supremacy? In the words of a hit by black singer Ben E. King, 'What is Soul?'

By 1963, it was clear: 'soul' was the name for contemporary black music, while any white singer who could convincingly echo the passion and rhythm of a Ray Charles or an Aretha Franklin was said to be singing 'blue-eyed soul'. The blues tradition, traced back to W. C. Handy and proudly carried forward by three generations as the emotional expression of black America, was now an embarrassment, reeking of slavery and the acceptance of inferiority (which showed how little people understood the rugged defiance that was at its heart). B. B. King recalled that 'I was hurt, really hurt, because many times in the past I was friendless, especially around young people ... [they] didn't appreciate me. There were many nights when I went back to my room and cried.'

In later years, soul (like blues) would be re-categorised, sorted into neat and restrictive genres, from Northern soul to uptown soul, deep soul and pop soul. It would also cast its reach backwards, to claim the singers who dominated the Rhythm and Blues charts after the initial burst of black rock 'n' roll in the 1940s. These were men such as Bobby Bland, Clyde McPhatter and Little Willie John, who in their very different ways expressed the sexual thrills and torments of everyday black life. Willie John was the most potent (and now least remembered) of them all: a consummate and consummating ladies' man, whose stage was customarily littered with underwear and room keys. He dominated an audience with a swagger that would later be copied by James Brown, then by Tina Turner, ultimately by the young Michael Jackson. He sang with utter self-assurance, his voice able to cruise all around the melody and then come back to claim it when it counted (a quality which Stevie Wonder compared with jazzmen such as Miles Davis and John Coltrane).

Ultimately, Little Willie John wanted to be Frank Sinatra, just as Nat King Cole did: to win the respect of an audience in Vegas or on Broadway, not to be scuffling on the so-called chitlin circuit. Cole made it; John fell into romantic and psychological turmoil, which would result in his being sent to jail for murder. But although he too might tackle a Broadway hit, James Brown never set his sights on cabaret. His aim was to be the hardest-working man in show business, with the tightest band and the most compelling act in the world. In the decade before he discovered the complex rhythmic patterns of funk, he concentrated on delivering a shattering emotional experience with each record and every performance.* That process began with his first release, 'Please, Please, Please', on which, as his baffled white label boss accurately exclaimed, 'He's just singing the same damn word over and over!' And if the feeling of soul was there, one word was more than enough.

> The entire R&B market today is dominated by three factors: vocal groups who seem to have issued to one another a challenge boasting, 'We can sing out-of-tuner than you can'; tortured, tortuous ballad singers, who would lose all their appeal if they were fitted with spines; [and] instrumentalists who made names for themselves on personal appearances by playing a solo and simultaneously removing their jacket, pants, shirt and teeth while suspended from a chandelier.
> Leonard Feather, *Down Beat*, May 1955

---

* James Brown was an original, but an original with influences. Years before he learned to draw out the finale of his live shows into a portrayal of apparent hysteria, Billy Ward and the Dominoes had 'the entire crew breaking down and sobbing for a full five minutes' as they sang 'Have Mercy Baby'.

The groups are all getting to sound like each other. Those crazy falsettos and bass voices alternating in a tune sound all the same in most of the groups. And you know, man, they're full of those high-school romance thoughts like, 'Why did you leave me' and 'The stars above shine down' and all that baloney. After a while, the stuff gets on your nerves.

Savoy Records boss Herman Lubinsky, 1958

Suits were obligatory; ties long or bowed; hair processed or cropped; voices arranged from bass (comedic, sexual) to falsetto (anguished, vulnerable) via tenor (romantic) and baritone (sensual). Their antecedents were the Mills Brothers with their vocalised jazz instruments, and the Ink Spots' impossibly angelic chorus. For a dozen years after the Second World War, the vocal group was a repository of emotions which veered between the extremes of sentimentality and eroticism. Only then, when all the permutations of carnality and romance had been exhausted, did white kids join the game, to provide the bridge between the wild-man tradition of rock 'n' roll and the collectivism of the 1960s rock groups.

The 5 Red Caps laid out the boundaries with two singles in 1944: the almost a cappella 'I Learned a Lesson', slow and saintly; followed by 'Boogie Woogie Ball', which was playtime for a street-corner posse. In 1946, the Delta Rhythm Boys accidentally provided a title for this often-overlooked chapter of R&B history, their background singers crooning 'doo doo doo-wop' behind the jocular bass lead of 'Just A-Sittin' and A-Rockin''. But it was the Ravens with 'Write Me a Letter' the following year who made the case for doo-wop vocal groups to be classified as rhythm and blues – and as men, not teenage boys. For almost a year, they ruled unchallenged, until the Orioles offered the ethereal 'It's Too Soon to Know'. By the early 1950s, as one bird group begat another, a menagerie was uncaged, which was chiming with Larks, Swallows, Robins and Crests. But the church-or-street, good-or-bad division remained, with the same unit often switching back and forth on each release.

The Orioles evoked the high church, with the 1953 reverence of 'Crying in the Chapel' followed by 'In the Mission of St Augustine'. The alternative was a blues two-step which swaggered with street smarts and blues mentality, usually dripping with wry humour and self-deprecation: the catalogue of the Clovers, for example, which led inevitably to the three-minute musical cartoons of the Robins and finally the Coasters.

By 1951, there was a group who could straddle both extremes, and touch places where the others would not dare to go. With 'Do Something for Me', the Dominoes (led by Billy Ward) featured a lead voice that soared as it fluttered, lost in the ambiguous ecstasy of its emotions. Though Ward took the credit and the money, that singer was Clyde McPhatter, who reached his peak of passion on 'These Foolish Things', which sounded as if it had been recorded during an attack of delirium. Not surprisingly, as *Jet* magazine reported, 'Teenagers used to go into hysterics' when he performed. But the same group could intersperse McPhatter's sentimental agony with a song as carnal as 'Sixty Minute Man', in which the bass man boasted of his impressive sexual endurance. When it was finally released in Britain five years later, *Jazz Journal* said that 'this ugly record' was 'not recommended for the private turntable . . . we plunge into the sediment of the music business . . . If this record can be likened to any one thing, it must be indecent exposure.' It topped the American Rhythm and Blues chart for more than three months. When McPhatter joined the Drifters in 1953, tired of Ward's inequitable financial arrangements, the Dominoes secured a new lead vocalist whose flamboyance could handle everything from fiery sexuality to teenage infatuation: Jackie Wilson.*

The sexuality of 'Sixty Minute Man' led to the notorious 'Annie' records by Hank Ballard & the Midnighters in 1954, in which Annie first gave Hank a good working-over, then (in a scenario worthy of a country record) fell pregnant, leaving Hank to tackle 'Annie's Aunt Fannie'. He interrupted the sequence only to praise another girl's 'Sexy Ways'. Choirboy harmonies wouldn't have suited scenarios this lascivious, and the Midnighters were able to capitalise on an abrupt shift of style amongst black vocal groups in 1953: from ballads and blues to romping rock 'n' roll. Suddenly the white boys were listening as well – to the Clovers, for sure, as their 'Good Lovin'' was the skeleton for Elvis Presley's 'Too Much', while a chunk of 'Lovey Dovey' was reproduced twenty years later on Steve Miller's 'The Joker'. But the trend that inspired white kids to gather on street corners and imitate what they'd heard on the jukebox was the combination of rock rhythm and a barrage of nonsensical syllables – parodied, inevitably,

---

* So compulsive was the fever he aroused amongst his fans that in February 1961 one of them shot Wilson outside his Manhattan apartment. 'I didn't want to hurt him,' she cried, as he was taken to Roosevelt Hospital, 'I am all mixed up.' He would not be the last pop star admitted to Roosevelt having been shot by a supposed admirer.

by Stan Freberg. His target was the Chords' 1954 hit 'Sh-Boom', which set a hookline from the nineteenth-century children's song 'Row, Row, Row Your Boat' ('life is but a dream') against a track that anticipated the Jamaican ska sound, and then freed the background singers to conjure up as many vocal sounds as they could without uttering a recognisable word. From that glorious moment, it was a short step to 'Ling, Ting, Tong' (the Charms), 'Chop Chop Boom' (the Dandeliers) – and, indeed, Gene Vincent's anthem of incoherent lust, 'Be-Bop-A-Lula', and years later, the Crystals' proof that words sometimes aren't enough, 'Da Doo Ron Ron'.

There were numerous white attempts at this doo-wop glossolalia, although most of them concentrated on the syllables at the expense of the beat, and the groups looked and sounded like barbershop quartets; or, perhaps, college glee clubs, a category into which you could squeeze the jazz harmonies of the Four Freshmen (a key influence on the Beach Boys) and the jog-trotting harmlessness of the Four Lads' 'Standing on the Corner'. Only in late 1957 did white America launch its own doo-wop tradition, with the banality of the Royal Teens' 'Short Shorts', leading to the gum-chewing, leather-clad machismo of Danny & the Juniors and (the apex of this short-lived movement) Dion & the Belmonts.

While the young men crooned, rocked and boasted about their sexual conquests, their female counterparts were more restrained. The exceptions were Shirley Gunter & the Queens, who inaugurated the decade-long tradition of the black 'girl group' with 1954's hard-rocking 'Oop Shoop'. Three years passed before the Bobbettes and the Chantels picked up the torch, with records ('Mr Lee' and 'He's Gone' respectively) accentuating their youthfulness; ensuring that romance, rather than ravishment, would be their eternal destiny. This mirrored the fate of the countless combinations of young white women who had followed the jazz-inspired Boswell Sisters and the boogie-woogie-loving Andrews Sisters – a trail towards complete sexlessness which culminated in the almost eerily pure outings of the Chordettes ('Mr Sandman' and 'Born to Be With You', for instance).

Only their best prom dresses would suffice for these girl groups, black and white. As such they offered little temptation to the Jewish writing and producing partnership of Jerry Leiber and Mike Stoller, who opted to declare their love for rhythm and blues by producing delicious mini-movies which sold equally well to whites and blacks. The most colourful of these were reserved for the Coasters, who sounded like a bunch of hoodlums who'd opted for careers in stand-up comedy. The roles they were given – every line and audible grimace pre-rehearsed – created stereotypes of both black men and teenagers, but were assembled with such love and craft that it is hard to view them as demeaning.

It was Leiber and Stoller, too, who tipped rhythm and blues into a new era of sophistication, as they married the soul of Ray Charles with a Brazilian beat and a swirling string section on 1958's 'There Goes My Baby' by the Drifters.* They remade the pop single as a dramatic vignette: a compressed bundle of emotion and action, which could explode to fill the listener's imagination. What they achieved with subtlety, their protégé Phil Spector would soon pursue with cathartic excess: a 'scorched earth' philosophy against the expertly placed landmines with which Leiber and Stoller dotted their aural landscapes. In his (white) hands, black music became a personal statement rather than a badge of racial identity.

For Ray Charles, whose progress through the 1950s involved urban realism and sexuality, strings represented not just prestige (Sinatra and Sammy Davis had strings too) but freedom. 'Us rhythm and blues musicians had had a label slapped on us', he recalled. 'Strings were out.' By the end of the 1950s, he was recording both carnal incantations and time-honoured Broadway songs – the first with yelps of sexual ecstasy, the second with an orchestra Sinatra would have relished. From there, demolishing barriers as he went, he set out to bridge the racial divide, and cut albums of country songs. 'After all,' he explained, 'the *Grand Ole Opry* had been performing inside my head since I was a kid in the country.' It would take another two decades, and the passing of civil-rights legislation, for Ray Charles to feature on country radio; but in 1962 he succeeded in crossing the other way, persuading R&B (and pop) record buyers to sample the best of Nashville's songs. 'I Can't Stop Loving You' topped both charts for weeks. 'I wasn't aware of any bold act on my part or any big breakthrough', he said, while conceding that his country style 'made the black stations, simply 'cause they had no choice; the record was too important to be ignored'.

---

* One of the most startling arrangements of the 1950s, 'There Goes My Baby' was not the first R&B hit to feature strings. It was preceded by several Platters singles and also, depending on how you draw your genre boundaries, Nat King Cole's 'Nature Boy', while the Orioles and the Cardinals also employed strings on several releases that didn't chart. But it was arguably the first pop record to use strings as an additional, almost distracting element of the production, rather than as an extension of the mood already created by the song.

This revolution took its toll. In the early 1960s, Ray Charles became one of an entire generation of R&B stars – each one a distinctly individual voice – to be wiped out or sidelined by accident or self-harm. Thanks to Don McLean's 'American Pie', the plane crash that killed Buddy Holly is remembered as 'the day the music died'. For aficionados of black music, there was no day of infamy, merely a procession of disasters. It began with the fatal car crash of Jesse Belvin in 1960; then the shooting of Jackie Wilson, the drug overdose of Dinah Washington, the arrest of Little Willie John, the heroin addiction that crippled Ray Charles's career, the slaying of gospel star turned pop idol Sam Cooke, and finally the succumbing of Nat King Cole – a man who claimed that he chain-smoked cigarettes to ensure his voice retained its appealing huskiness – to lung cancer. In their place arose a new generation of black stars, who didn't trace their roots back to jazz and blues, but to the vocal groups of the late 1950s, the gospel soul of Ray Charles, and the constant quest for new dance novelties which reached an insane peak with the twist.

> Just pretend you're wiping your bottom with a towel as you get out of the shower and putting out a cigarette with both feet.
> Chubby Checker, 1960

> The World's Wackiest Dance Comes to Britain – the wackiest, gayest dance since the Charleston.
> *Daily Mirror*, October 1961

As late as the 1950s, many publications reviewed new pop releases using a single criterion: the appropriate dance step for each song. Until jiving and jitterbugging snapped propriety's tight fetters, almost every tune was described as a 'foxtrot' (unless, of course, it was a waltz), and most casual dancers applied foxtrotting steps to everything they heard on the dance floor. The foxtrot was considered respectable, as it involved heterosexual couples maintaining physical contact without expressing sexuality. But dances in which the body was moved with total freedom were morally suspect. Hence the panic aroused by the Charleston and its successors, which was revived by the epidemic of jiving that greeted swing, R&B and rock 'n' roll, and kept aflame by the purposeful swaying and grinding of the bop, the teenage dance sensation between 1956 and 1958.

As the bop lost its momentum, Hank Ballard & the Midnighters offered America a new, unrelenting rhythm. It subjected the hucklebuck (a brief dance craze from 1948–9) to a streamlined makeover. Their instructional record, 'The Twist', charted only briefly in 1959, but maintained its popularity in Philadelphia, where TV impresario Dick Clark suggested that it deserved a revival. The song fell into the lap of Chubby Checker, a 19-year-old black kid. He would eventually find himself amidst the kind of media storm that would become an everyday occurrence in the Internet age, but had not been witnessed before in popular music. Not that this was immediately apparent: the Twist appeared to be nothing more than another dance craze, as it quickly killed off the Madison and the hully gully, though for a while the shimmy stood its ground. Every American teenager knew about it; every industry pundit assumed it would only last for a season.

But Chubby Checker had canny handlers, and they presented him and the twist with a stay of execution. In 1961, he released 'Let's Twist Again', to remind its audience of what 'we did last summer'. Its success returned 'The Twist' to the top of the American charts, and suddenly the whole country appeared to lose its senses, and its inhibitions. Albums were retitled to cash in on the twist mania, and soon there were twelve twist hits in the Hot 100, five of them in the Top 20. What had triggered this madness? Simply a publicity campaign for the Peppermint Lounge, a bikers' bar in midtown Manhattan with its own twist band. Within a couple of weeks, New York's cognoscenti were sporting their pearls or leather jackets at the Peppermint, where English aristocracy mingled with pop artists, authors and even the reclusive actress Greta Garbo.

By November 1961, the twist was being demonstrated on British television and in a top London ballroom. In Paris, it had 'become a sort of national malady, infecting everyone from three-year-olds in rompers to middle-aged sophisticates at Maxim's'. In South Africa, where rock 'n' roll had been viewed by the majority population as a strictly white affair, the twist was welcomed as the authentic voice of black America. *Melody Maker* reckoned that in 1962, the twist would quite possibly 'sweep big bands back into popularity'. 'It is expected that in the skiing centres of Europe this year, it will be non-U not to know the twist', one report claimed. You could buy twist slacks and twist shoes, but still hospitals reported a plethora of slipped discs from those twisting without due preparation. Moralists warned that the twist was 'synthetic sex turned into a sick spectator sport', the kind of publicity that only big money could buy. Even the Communist countries of Eastern Europe were not immune, as Jiří Suchý and Jiří Šlitr concocted the cacophonous 'Semafor twist'. As the Romanian state newspaper reflected mournfully, 'How can we feel happy about the crazy jitterbugs and modern dances of today that make our young people look like victims of palsy?'

Liverpool, it was said early in 1962, was proving equally resistant to the twist, although one of the city's leading rock groups, Howie Casey & the Seniors, cashed in with their own variation, the 'double twist'. They also came south to Ilford in Essex, where they played six nights a week in the Twist at the Top skyscraper room – but only for a month, after which the twist had lost its novelty. The death knell was probably the moment when 46-year-old Frank Sinatra, no teenager's idea of a dreamy dance-hall date in 1962, belatedly jumped aboard the slowing bandwagon, declaring that 'Everybody's Twisting'. Almost immediately, they weren't.

Back in Liverpool, meanwhile, a rock group called the Beatles had adopted the Isley Brothers' 'Twist and Shout' as their own, unembarrassed to keep the memory of pop's first great publicity hype alive. The twist had proved that with blanket exposure, every age group and social class could be seduced into slumming in the world of pop. The Beatles would soon demonstrate the potential power of that strategy, on a global scale.

Record companies create scores and scores of synthetic phonographic personalities every year . . . concocted from varying portions of human voice, and electronic manipulation . . . The sounds that are heard from their records may bear only a passing resemblance to those that were crooned into the microphone.
  Hi Fi/Stereo Review, August 1962

As it stands today, there's virtually no difference between rock and roll, pop, and R&B. The music has completely overlapped.
  Leonard Chess, Chess Records, 1962

Written at the end of a tumultuous, brain-scrambling decade, the first book-length surveys of rock 'n' roll, published around 1969, propounded myths that stand to this day; and deserve to be questioned. At the most banal level, it is simply not true, for instance, that it was the assassination of John F. Kennedy that prevented Phil Spector's legendary Christmas album from being a hit. (Elvis Presley's *Fun in Acapulco* was issued on the same day, and sold more than a million copies.) The killing did halt the record trade for about a week, but when it resumed, there were healthy sales for dozens of seasonal records – but not Spector's, which was the victim of financial disputes with his distributor, not a nation's sorrow. (No country that could send the Kingsmen's gloriously incoherent 'Louie Louie' to No. 2 in the singles chart immediately after the murder of its president could have been entirely overcome by grief.)

With a wider perspective, America in the early 1960s has often been portrayed as a musical desert, waiting for the Beatles and their British allies to spring it to life. In fact, any level-headed study of the era suggests otherwise. It's arguable, in fact, that the terrain was fertilised more richly before the arrival of the Beatles than it was after the so-called British Invasion uprooted flowers and weeds indiscriminately. Nor is it accurate to say that it took British bands to help Americans rediscover their own black music. Quite the opposite: the US charts in 1963 were full of remarkable music which you could call R&B, or soul, or pop. As Berry Gordy of Motown Records noted wryly of 'Do You Love Me', the Contours' No. 3 smash from 1962, 'It was recorded R&B, but by the time it reached the half-million mark, it was considered pop. And if we hadn't recorded it with a Negro artist, it would have been considered rock and roll.' What happened between 1960 and 1963 was that rock 'n' roll returned to its African-American roots; was reclassified as rhythm and blues; and then flowered for more than a decade to come as soul.

It is tempting merely to provide a list of life-affirming, thrilling records, from Barrett Strong's 'Money' to Chuck Berry's 'Let it Rock' to James Brown's 'Think' to Wanda Jackson's 'Let's Have a Party' to the Miracles' 'Shop Around' to Cleveland Crochet's 'Sugar Bee' – and we're still in 1960. Rock 'n' roll was dead? Teen-beat was offering productions of such quality – Roy Orbison, Brenda Lee, Gene Pitney, Ricky Nelson's 'Summertime', which incidentally is where the riff for Deep Purple's 'Black Night' originates – that it is a shame to categorise it with such a demeaning title. And the next three years still had the Beach Boys to come; Phil Spector; the golden era of Goffin/King, Mann/Weil, Greenwich/Barry and all those remarkable writing partnerships at 1650 Broadway; Burt Bacharach and Hal David; the Four Seasons; plus more soul, more girl groups, white and black; Aretha Franklin, Bobby Bland, Sam Cooke, Marvin Gaye, Mary Wells; a dozen bizarre, hysterical dance crazes, with rock 'n' roll gems to match; Latin soul, from Ray Barretto and Joe Cuba – the soundtrack, much of this, for the nascent British mod movement. Then there were hit singles from jazz artists (Dave Brubeck, Mel Torme), British groups (the Tornados, the Caravelles), Australian country singers (Frank Ifield), even a Singing Nun (whose sales certainly did benefit from JFK's death).

There were also strange signposts to the future, visible only in retrospect. The instrumental sound behind the Beach Boys' early hits came from the Viscounts' 'Wabash Blues' (and the vocal sound was influenced, arguably, by Gene Vincent's 'Git It'). Roy Orbison's 'Only the Lonely' and Dorsey Burnette's 'Hey Little One' presaged pop as melodrama, and careers ahead for Gene Pitney and P. J. Proby. (Not to overlook Connie Francis and 'Malaguena': flamenco as teen soap opera.) 'Spanish Harlem' by Ben E. King must have triggered Burt Bacharach's penchant for sinuous, switchback melodies which only the most dextrous of singers could master. Paul Revere & the Raiders echoed the beatnik movement with the title (but not the music) of 'Like, Long Hair'. 'Underwater' by the Frogmen (with frog noises to identify them) inaugurated the surf instrumental sound. Little Caesar and the Romans introduced instant rock 'n' roll nostalgia with 'Those Oldies But Goodies' – in late spring 1961, no less, when only goldfish would have forgotten what had happened just a few months earlier. 'It Will Stand', the Showmen chirruped prophetically.

Teen America was exposed to hardcore R&B, from the likes of Freddie King, Slim Harpo, B. B. King, Jimmy Reed, John Lee Hooker – no apparent need there for the Rolling Stones to offer a history lesson. Gary 'US' Bonds created the rock 'n' roll sound of John Lennon's dreams with 'Quarter to Three', like a garage band glimpsed briefly through dense fog, while all Lennon's guitar needs were supplied by Bobby Parker's propulsive 'Watch Your Step'. Teen movie starlet Ann-Margret's 'I Just Don't Understand' was soaked in fuzz guitar from the aptly named Billy Strange, and was soon followed by the Ventures' even more raw 'The 2,000 lb Bee'. Solomon Burke and Ray Charles combined country and soul as if they were first cousins; likewise Latin and soul, on the Impressions' 'Gypsy Woman'.

Still looking forward: the Everly Brothers hit upon the jinglejangle guitar sound of folk rock three years early, with the ironically titled 'That's Old Fashioned', then anticipated the soon-to-come Beatles with 'How Can I Meet Her?'. Session drummer Bobby Gregg worked up a credible funk precursor with 'Potato Peeler', echoed by Booker T & the

MGs. Spector's production of 'Zip-A-Dee-Doo-Dah', slowed to half speed before the vocals were added, was a gothic vision of pop as a Satanic plaything; and in that context, Rolf Harris's 'Sun Arise' was eerie, anticipating the cosmic drone that would fuel the sitar-inspired records of the mid-1960s.

Strange anticipations everywhere: the tune of Neil Young's 'Pocahontas' on Carole King's 'He's a Bad Boy'; the pre-teen vivacity of the Osmonds and Jackson 5 on 'Killer Joe' by the Rocky Fellers, a Filipino boy band; Jackie DeShannon's 'Needles and Pins' merging Spector, folk, soul, rock 'n' roll and teen-beat into one all-American noise; protest songs from Joan Baez and Peter, Paul & Mary, before most people even knew that US troops were in Vietnam; and feminism, thank goodness, in the teen commentary of the girl groups, and the unashamed message of Leslie Gore's 'You Don't Own Me' (written by two men).

Everything climaxed in the autumn of 1963, with Phil Spector and the Beach Boys' leader, Brian Wilson, competing to compress more and more emotion and sound and rock 'n' roll attitude and apocalyptic vision and ceaseless ambition into every record – resulting in the Ronettes' 'Be My Baby' from Spector and, more bathetically, 'Be True to Your School' from the Beach Boys. And then, in January 1964, fifteen months later than in Britain, the Beatles: after which nothing was ever the same again.

ϟ

'Most of our best numbers were in what I call the tempo of the heartbeat. Music to me is sex – it's all tied up somehow, and the rhythm of sex is the heartbeat. I usually try to avoid scoring a song with a climax at the end. Better to build about two-thirds of the way through, and then fade to a surprise end. More subtle. I don't really like to finish by blowing and beating in top gear.'

Nelson Riddle

CHAPTER 14

MUSIC FOR MODERNS

'Bad rock and roll is through. You see a record like "Who's Sorry Now" by Connie Francis and you know that the kids are buying something better than they used to be.'

Record company boss Lou Krefetz, June 1958

Never was the 'music is sex' equation illustrated more vividly than on 'I've Got You Under My Skin', recorded by Frank Sinatra – Cole Porter song, Nelson Riddle arrangement – in January 1956. Sinatra rode the spiralling mid-section towards one climax, achieved by arguably the most thrilling brass crescendo ever captured on record, and then roused himself for a second climb. As Frank slipped cosily into afterglow, Riddle sprang his last surprise: a key change in the final chord of the arrangement, as refreshing as a quick shower, hinting that the 40-year-old Sinatra was ready to do it all again.

'I've Got You Under My Skin' was one of the highlights of *Songs for Swingin' Lovers!*, a landmark 1956 album made in the same week that Elvis Presley first explored the echoing corridors of 'Heartbreak Hotel'. Two artistic breakthroughs, signalling in precisely opposite directions: one bringing shameless sensuality to the teenage pop market; the other announcing the record album as a work of art. *Songs for Swingin' Lovers!* is frequently tagged as 'the first concept album', although there wasn't a concept beyond the unifying, sparkling brilliance of Nelson Riddle's scores. Riddle had earlier arranged Sinatra's *Songs for Young Lovers* LP, while previous Sinatra LPs had been devoted to the work of a single arranger and conductor. As early as 1939, Lee Wiley had anticipated Ella Fitzgerald's *Songbook* series by issuing entire (78 rpm) albums by one songwriter. (Thematically, there is a case for proposing country Jean Shepard's *Songs of a Love Affair*, also from 1956, as being more conceptually coherent than *Songs for Swingin' Lovers!*.)

The album – originally consisting of several ten-inch shellac discs, contained within a single binding – had been a marketing tool for Sinatra since *The Voice of Frank Sinatra* (1946). *Sing and Dance With Frank Sinatra* (1950) was his first self-contained album, not comprised of earlier recordings, although by then Sinatra's popularity was trailing behind rivals such as Frankie Laine and Perry Como. His networked CBS-TV series flopped; and his producer, Mitch Miller, was encouraging him to cut novelty songs. That's why the Sinatra catalogue includes such dandies as 'Tennessee Newsboy' (with Speedy West making his steel guitar cluck like a chicken), 'The Hucklebuck' (slow-motion 'dad' dancing), and 'Castle Rock' (proving that Sinatra was making rock 'n' roll records, albeit terrible ones, three years before Elvis Presley; in July 1951, to be exact).

Then, in the familiar Sinatra legend, he leapt from Miller's Columbia empire to the more receptive Capitol label, won an Oscar for his role as Maggio in *From Here to Eternity*, and set out for vocal immortality. He was still making hit singles as late as 1980 ('Theme From New York, New York'), some of which reached people untouched by his albums: 'Strangers in the Night' and his father/daughter duet, 'Somethin' Stupid' from the mid-1960s, for instance, and 'My Way' from 1969 (which stands alongside Sammy Davis's contemporary 'I've Gotta Be Me' as a defiant generational anthem for the over-40s). But the best of Sinatra from the Capitol and Reprise years was in his LPs: frequently themed, sometimes on rather flimsy foundations, but often making an artistic statement. Those ranged from the mid-life laments of *Only the Lonely* and *No One Cares* to the song cycles of later years, *Watertown* and *Trilogy*. His albums were packaged and publicised as instalments in the life of a great artist and an emblematic human being – a lover, a father, a winner, a loser, an American ageing alongside the rest of what Tom Brokaw called 'The Greatest Generation'.

Sinatra was part of their shared soundtrack, but far from the entirety of it. He and his peers represented old values which were threatened by teenage culture; adult pleasures, too, whether they were adultery, alcohol and the roulette wheel, or in Sinatra's case hobnobbing with the mob. From their artwork to their rich orchestrations, they symbolised sophistication: hard-won, well-earned, part of the post-war settlement between America and its middle class. With the swing and swagger of Sammy Davis Jr's dance steps, the teasing sensuality of Dean Martin's voice and the carefree ease of Sinatra's phrasing, adulthood had never seemed so desirable or so hip.

It was inevitable that the most durable and malleable of the teenage stars would share the same goals – after all, Sinatra had been the subject of adolescent screams himself. So Elvis Presley was eased, after his return from the army, into pop confections such as 'It's Now or Never' and 'Surrender', on which he sublimated the reckless sexuality of his earlier rock hits into adult flirtatiousness. His biggest 1960s hits were borrowed from the Italians, for whom operatic drama and epic romance were second nature. Bobby Darin modelled himself on Sinatra; even teens such as Bobby Rydell and Paul Anka were persuaded to record cabaret favourites. In 1960, Presley appeared alongside Sinatra on a TV special, while Darin and Anka recorded live albums at the Copa nightclub in New York (and Anka subsequently penned the English lyric for 'My Way', of course).

But it was the older generation, veterans of the dance-band era, who established the market for albums. LP records were priced as luxury items for adults (even more so, the equipment on which to play them). During the late 1950s and early 1960s, the likes of Tony Bennett, Sammy Davis Jr, Dean Martin, Nat King Cole, Ella Fitzgerald, Doris Day, Johnny Mathis and dozens more enjoyed lucrative sales with records that often drew from the same limited pool of 'standards' and recent Hollywood movie themes. What they were selling, ultimately, was their vocal personality, and the guarantee of quality entertainment: quality implying dependable and familiar, as well as aesthetically pleasing. If you were investing in an album, you expected a laminated, full-colour sleeve; tasteful art direction; liner notes to reinforce the virtue of your choice; and music to create a mood, and sustain it.

Other artists than Frank Sinatra offered a soundtrack for a lifetime, evolving alongside their audience in ways at which he would have baulked. In France, the *chansons* of Gilbert Bécaud, Jacques Brel and the notoriously risqué Georges Brassens offered sophistication with a hint of the gutter, preparing the path for the even more outspoken Serge Gainsbourg. The scenario of Brassens's 1952 hit 'Le Gorille' – a giant ape extravagantly well endowed for sexual congress – would have been unimaginable fare in any English-speaking culture before the 1970s. *Time* magazine recounted that his repertoire covered 'the brutalities of war, the vagaries of love, the folly of politics, and the hardships of being a gravedigger or a streetwalker': the stuff of literature, not the romantic ballad.

Petula Clark's world was more respectable. She had been a child prodigy in wartime Britain, a pop starlet in the early 1950s, a songwriter, a star in her adopted homeland (by marriage) of France, and finally, in the 1960s, the UK's closest equivalent to a Sinatra or Bennett, who could channel their sometimes bitter experience into the way they phrased a line. Her equivalent in Japan was Misora Habari, whose forty-year career spanned everything from swing to boogie-woogie, tango to twist, cabaret sophistication to bubblegum pop. Like Clark, her catalogue provided a one-woman history of pop's surreal progress from the Jazz Age to the Swinging Sixties.

Even more central to the album market were the collections of songs, themes and incidental music from Broadway shows and Hollywood musicals. ('It looks as if the minds of those who commission LPs can only think in terms of tinselly pastiches of the so-called Roaring Twenties, or of Broadway show-tunes, or albums designed to exploit every percussion instrument', *Gramophone* complained in 1962.) In the 1950s, only Elvis Presley's *Christmas Album* (itself a common gimmick for the adult market) out-sold the cast LP from *My Fair Lady*, featuring Julie Andrews and Rex Harrison. The film soundtrack for Rodgers and Hammerstein's *Oklahoma!* set rural nostalgia to music reminiscent of an operetta: quality, indeed. Most popular of all was *South Pacific*, as cast album and then movie soundtrack, from a drama involving – scandalously – inter-racial romance, although the liaisons between an American serviceman and an island girl, and an American nurse and a Frenchman, were carefully designed not to rile the Ku Klux Klan. This was Rodgers and Hammerstein again, with such enduring songs as 'Some Enchanted Evening' and 'Nothing Like a Dame'. Yet the cultural reach of the Hollywood musical paled alongside the all-conquering force of its equivalent in India. There, almost all films were musicals, and the handful of 'playback singers' who provided the vocals for the actors on screen were stars as potent as any Sinatra or Presley. (And much more prolific: in a career stretching from 1948 to 1984, Lata Mangeshkar recorded approximately 30,000 songs for cinematic use.) The instrumental arrangements of India's so-called 'Golden Era', from 1950 into the mid-1960s, were as extravagant as the emotional dramas that they decorated.

The 1950s was also the decade of mood music, easy listening, what the French composer Erik Satie called 'furniture music'. (He once held a recital at which he demanded that the audience talk while he performed, and was outraged when they insisted on listening.) The vast majority of popular albums during this decade fell into one of these categories. The finest auteurs attracted sales and loyalty worthy of any pop star. Mantovani, for example, used Decca's 'ffrr' sound enhancements to create a cascading string sound, which was debuted on the 1951 hit single 'Charmaine', and then dominated more than fifty chart albums over the next twenty years. So luscious was the orchestration on his 1958 LP *Film Encores* that its effect was positively unnerving, as if aliens were using violins as methods of mass hypnosis. Ray Conniff was just as popular: his trick was to identify hooks, or patterns, beneath the obvious pull of the melody, and accentuate them. His breakthrough album was *S'Wonderful* from 1957, demonstrating the wordless chorale (four men, four women) that was his trademark. *Concert in Rhythm* applied the same almost seamless blend of voices and instruments to familiar classical themes. His only unsuccessful venture was

Dance the Bop, a pseudo-rock album which was too … not abrasive, perhaps, but *present*, too obtrusive to work as background music. Conniff's singers set the pattern for easy-listening music to come. As the chronicler of 'elevator music', Joseph Lanza, wrote: 'Shadow choruses were so common by the late 1950s and early 1960s that few instrumental artists prospered without featuring them on at least one album, and hardly any pop singer could decline to enlist their powerful background magic. The singing style went completely counter to the sweat-passion of jazz, soul, rock and folk. When not voicing wordless choruses, these singers practiced subdued lyricising with a willingness to be as self-effacing as the quiet, dreamy fiddles sharing their space.' Commercial king of the chorale was Mitch Miller, whose Gang – twenty-eight men, harmonising on old, familiar tunes – gained enormous success with their *Sing Along With Mitch* albums between 1958 and 1962.

This was an art of exquisite touches, and consummate marketing. Once established, the brand of the 101 Strings, the Living Strings or the Mystic Moods Orchestra could prosper for decades, living proof of the power of what Vance Packard, in his 1957 exposé of the advertising industry, called *The Hidden Persuaders*. Classical pianists Ferrante & Teicher doubled as experimentalists for the gorgeous, almost obese romanticism of their keyboard, chorale and orchestra concoctions. 'They devised a series of "original gadgets" to extend the tonal range of the pianos', historian Joseph Murrells described. 'They used strips of sandpaper, cardboard wedges, etc., in their pianos applied to the strings for weird effects to resemble drums, xylophone, castanets, gongs and harpsichord, reaching into the pianos to pluck, strum and pound on the strings in novelty numbers.' Scientific invention and musical proficiency combined to create aural stimulation – but not too much of it. As *Reader's Digest* magazine noted of the Muzak service in 1946, 'brain workers find that it lessens tension and keeps everyone in a happier frame of mind' (although a minority of passengers in Washington, DC protested vehemently in 1948 when authorities extended Muzak to the city's buses). To ensure that the service would never take its listeners by surprise, Muzak's engineers would 'squeeze down the dynamic range to a maximum of 25 decibels (compared to 50 on normal LPs)'.

Those who bought easy-listening records – or wallowed in their radio equivalent, the so-called 'good music' shows – were not buying into the jazz or rock ethic of constant reinvention and progression; not, at least, in terms of musical progress. For this was an era of dramatic changes in the process of sound reproduction. Bizarre though it might seem to anyone raised in the era of surround-sound cinemas and stereo headphones, recorded music was an entirely monaural affair before the late 1950s: one speaker, one channel of sound. Then, a revolution: two speakers, two separate sources of music: the stereophonic era had arrived.

> The light shines in the eyes of every recording musician, the least important man in the band is now on an equal level with the soloist, *his performance can be heard*. He plays with a fresh spirit. The bandleader knows that the whole world can now hear the band as he's always heard it – standing in the middle of it. This is something we all dreamed about and never thought would happen. This will be looked back on as the golden age of sound.
> Bandleader Ted Heath, 1959

> Each manufacturer has invented some damned silly name by which its recordings are more sonic than others.
> *American Record Guide* magazine, September 1962

In the final weeks of 1959, more than 2,000 people filled Portsmouth Guildhall for a demonstration of the new stereo sound. Composer and arranger Stanley Black was in attendance, as the audience studied everything from his film scores to excerpts from Wagner's operas, all blaring out in this artificially separated format. Almost thirty years after EMI had first patented a system of stereo sound recording, it was finally being made available to the public (a year later in cash-starved Britain than in America).

Each record label coined its own hyperbolic language to describe its stereo releases: the Full Dimensional Stereo of Capitol, for instance, the 360 Degree Sound of Columbia, Visual Sound Stereo from Liberty, Stereosonics, Living Presence and the rest. Decca trumped them all with Phase 4 Stereo, and its saga of engineers marching towards sonic perfection. Phase 1, apparently, replicated the experience of being in a concert hall; Phase 2 allowed tricks that were soon known in the industry as 'ping-pong music', whereby sounds skipped from one side of the room to the other; Phase 3 involved 'moving' sound; and in Phase 4, the culmination of mankind's millennia on Earth, there were 'new scoring concepts incorporating true musicalese of separation and movement'. It was, Decca concluded, the equivalent of leaping from two to three dimensions. (Fortunately for the addled brains of its consumers, Decca never reached Phase 5.)

Initially viewed as a gimmick, stereo was soon appreciated on aesthetic grounds. 'The more spacious the music and the larger the orchestra,' said British bandleader Cyril Stapleton, 'the greater the thrill.' To illuminate the fact, countless stereo demonstration albums were recorded, between 1958 and 1970. Percy Faith was one of the first arrangers to glimpse the potential of being able to alter the sound picture with sudden or slow movements of instruments (though one American reviewer dismissed this style as 'music to test your speakers'). Capitol Records exposed their thinking with their *Staged for Stereo* series, boasting: 'It is obvious that the audio engineer has become an important creative force in the presentation of musical ideas.' This prompted a sniffy response from the *American Record Guide*: 'The music is being made to fit the medium; the medium is not being used to serve the music.' The doyen of this style was Enoch Light, dismissed as 'the King of the Bouncing Ball' by the media.

The phrase 'high fidelity' (hi-fi for short) had been popularised in 1954 to describe the sound offered by 33 rpm LPs; and it became short-hand for the constant developments in phonographic sound. This was a lucrative industry: sales in the US increased by 500% between 1952 and 1955. 'Dedicated audio fans', one report noted, 'insist on buying components separately . . . the price can go as high as $2,500.' It was soon a cliché, albeit one with a certain wry accuracy, that some consumers were more interested in the fidelity of their sound than the content of their records; the opposite end of the spectrum being occupied by those who used antique or damaged equipment to indulge their passion for music. (Hi-fi enthusiasts, it should be noted, were said to be almost always male, often middle-aged, usually single, and with a 'compulsive personality'. In some cases, a clinical psychiatrist claimed, their record collection represented a 'symbolic harem'.)* The record industry always viewed the classical market

---

* A dealer wrote to *Gramophone* magazine in 1925: 'In most instances when a lady is calling with her husband to purchase a machine, her interest is in the instrument as "an article of furniture" only. Its capabilities as a musical instrument are really of little interest to her. I find that the great majority of them simply do not understand *tone* at all, although they frequently *pretend* that they do . . . They will keep talking incessantly when the most perfect records are being played, and one can see that they really do not understand the music at all and do not wish to.'

as being the target audience for its sonic innovations. But the ability to paint more expansive pictures in sound inspired artists of varied ambitions.

No act received more intense and widespread acclamation from the critics in the early hi-fi age than the Sauter-Finegan Orchestra. Formed by two of the top swing arrangers, Sauter-Finegan set out to occupy the previously unnoticed gap between dance music and light music. Their gimmick (every band needed one) was their experimental use of as many unorthodox instruments as their orchestra could muster hands and mouths. Their repertoire mixed original material with reworked classical themes and revamped pop standards, achieving a peak of ambition with the extended suite 'Pictures from Sauter-Finegan Land' and the luscious instrumental 'Sleepy Village', of which the Beach Boys' Brian Wilson would have been proud. One critic described them as 'the first band whose existence has been made possible by the widespread use of high-fidelity equipment'. 'We sound awful on a jukebox', Eddie Sauter admitted. They toured with a 'special rheostat control panel' with which their two arrangers could mix and remix their orchestra's sound *in situ*. But their organisation proved too expensive to keep on the road, and instead the two men were reduced to creating jingles for advertising agencies.

Sauter-Finegan were never a jazz band – they abhorred improvisation on stage – but their willingness to cross artistic borders was shared by the most controversial bandleader of the post-war era: Stan Kenton. His orchestra debuted in New York in 1942, and was immediately criticised for its over-serious tone. Voted the Best Band of 1946, it was described – in what was intended as a compliment – as inducing 'a kind of musically manic state in a land of music lovers whose tastes are as wild and as varied as the violently opposite reactions of any manic-depressive can be'. In late 1948, Kenton followed Artie Shaw's example by quitting the business rather than trying to satisfy an audience he viewed as innately conservative. This was a representative reaction from a British jazz fan: 'If playing flat simultaneously in five different keys ... if collecting a large group of presumably accomplished musicians only to set them to work doing sound effects for a paranoid nightmare, if all these things add up to anything remotely deserving the title progressive jazz, then I'm a Carpathian mountain goat.'

A year later Kenton was back, daring his listeners to brave a tour entitled *Innovations in Modern Music*. (British bandleader Vic Lewis borrowed a sheaf of Kenton arrangements and billed them as 'music for moderns'.) Some found his new sound explosively inspired; others showed their displeasure by sitting on the edge of the dance floor until he agreed to dust down his wartime swing arrangements. Meanwhile, his records became increasingly modernist: he moved beyond the conscious polytonality of Darius Milhaud's compositions into areas where Schönberg might have feared to tread, notably with the *City of Light* and *This Modern World* suites written and arranged by Bob Graettinger. Their structure, it was revealed, was planned using 'mathematic computations, colour charts and graphs'. *Jazz Journal* responded with a 'progressive' joke: 'During a long intermission, a waiter dropped a tray of dishes, and three couples got up to dance.' There was no further that jazz could go whilst masquerading as a form of popular music: free jazz would prove to be an aurally and intellectually stimulating arena in the late 1950s and throughout the 1960s, but only for a cult audience.

There's always an uncomfortable feeling when I listen to modern jazz. The American people have created modern jazz out of a world of nervousness, confusion – and when I listen to modern jazz, I too become very confused, emotionally, and I want to get away from it.
　　Eartha Kitt, 1954

If this is what jazz is going to sound like in a few years' time, then I hope I won't still be listening to new records.
　　Jazz Journal review of Ornette Coleman, August 1962

'I saw such men as Miles Davis and Lee Konitz playing to the furniture', revealed a *Melody Maker* correspondent after a tour of New York's barren jazz clubs in autumn 1956. In 1950, Teddy Wilson proclaimed that 'jazz is dead'. For Stan Kenton, the realisation that 'jazz is finished' came in 1964. Yet this was an era of jazz landmarks: the 'birth of the cool', the West Coast sound, *Kind of Blue*, free jazz; Miles Davis collaborated with Gil Evans, and with John Coltrane; Gunther Schuller imagined music that would be neither jazz nor classical but a 'third stream' pitched midway between those poles; the Modern Jazz Quartet refashioned jazz as chamber music; Ornette Coleman, Archie Shepp and many more explored the liberation of pure self-expression. Yet in retrospect what is stunning about all this music is its comparative unpopularity. Even *Kind of Blue*, the most famous jazz album of all time, could not muster enough sales to feature amongst the Top 50 LPs in America: its renown was accumulated slowly, almost by word of mouth, and many could not initially grasp the beauty of what Davis and Evans had created. The riches of this era, and those that followed, seeped with agonising slowness into the collective consciousness.

There was one medium in which modern jazz was not just tolerated but almost demanded, however. Just as the public was prepared to accept modernist classical motifs when they were tied to the madcap antics of a Tom and Jerry cartoon, jazz became an increasingly familiar adjunct to Hollywood thrillers from the 1950s onwards – signifying urban angst, tension, a bohemian milieu and the threat of violence. Film soundtracks began to attract maverick talents from diverse backgrounds: Italian pop arranger Ennio Morricone, former Dizzy Gillespie sideman Lalo Schifrin and, most successfully of all, jazzman turned British rock 'n' roller John Barry. He supplied scores for no fewer than eleven James Bond vehicles, his collaboration with Shirley Bassey on the theme for *Goldfinger* inaugurating the tradition whereby contemporary pop stars would routinely deliver a movie's keynote address. This was the future of jazz, it seemed: increasingly ostracised as a commercial medium in its own right, but considered almost essential as an atmospheric cinematic accessory. Rock, by comparison, began to occupy the cultural stage which jazz had once considered its own.

There were hit jazz albums after the late 1950s: reissues or re-recordings by the swing bands of the 1930s; Ella Fitzgerald's *Songbook* collections of standards, and her duets with Louis Armstrong; an occasional Kenton or Ellington; revivals of Dixieland; orchestral sets by Erroll Garner or George Shearing, which offered mood music with the faintest of jazz trimmings; and, out of nowhere, live recordings by Ahmad Jamal's mellow trio, which sold on the basis of his original tune 'Poinciana' and the familiarity of songs such as 'Cheek to Cheek' and 'Secret Love'. But only two jazz formulae really connected with the American public; and each of them demonstrated that what people wanted from jazz was not the 'complete freedom of expression' sought by Ornette Coleman, but a diverting, though not disturbing, sense of timing.

One was the combination of jazz soloists and Latin rhythms; the other, the work of Dave Brubeck, whose popularity and playing infuriated the critics. 'It would seem that jazz is not his natural form of expression,' wrote Joe Goldberg, 'as if a man who knew 500 words of French were to attempt a novel in that language.' Those who believed that jazz was fundamentally an African-American art form resented the colour of his skin, while the fact that his quartet included a black bassist caused some venues to cancel his bookings. There was almost universal agreement that the Brubeck quartet didn't – indeed, couldn't – swing. But this critically derided group achieved a run of ten successive Top 30 albums in the US; became virtually the only American jazz act of the era to make a commercial impression in Britain and Europe; and also achieved the biggest jazz hit since the swing era, with 'Take Five'.

It came from *Time Out*, which (like its successor, *Time Further Out*) was an almost mechanical exploration of time signatures. Experts believed that the public would only respond to songs in 4/4 and 3/4 (waltz) time; but 'Take Five' was in 5/4 and another single, 'Unsquare Dance', in 7/4. Brubeck's rhythms were tied to accessible melodies, allowing the audience to congratulate itself on its daring leap of taste without being subjected to atonality or dissonance. His quartet also carefully groomed the college market.

The taste of American students was not always predictable (unlike in Britain, where undergraduates were divided between classical-music buffs and aficionados of traditional jazz). A fertile audience for 'hot' jazz during the 1920s and 30s, college kids opted for smoother rhythms during the 1940s. In 1950, the author Studs Terkel took a roadshow entitled *I Come for to Sing* around US campuses, introducing impressionable students to the blues stylings of Big Bill Broonzy. Echoes of that intervention persisted, until the folk revival of the late 1950s saw the clean-cut Kingston Trio, the Journeymen and the Chad Mitchell Trio become role models for the college crowd. Yet in 1957, a wide-ranging survey across US educational establishments found that the most popular musical act was not a trio of harmony-singing folkies, or Brubeck, or Broonzy, or even Elvis Presley, but Mantovani. There was a high proportion of students amongst the audience at the Newport Jazz Festival, but their goal was cheap booze and easy sex, rather than jazz, and they were regularly accused of inciting drunken disturbances.

While students enjoyed the fringe benefits of jazz, many of their parents relished easy-listening records which claimed to swing, but never did more than sway. These were tightly orchestrated and mellifluous collections by jazz musicians who never strayed away from their scores; Al Hirt, for example, whose fluent, ever-smooth trumpet playing hinted at jazz just as a Tom and Jerry cartoon might hint at surrealism. Those with vivid imaginations sampled albums that promised to bring the jungle, the southern seas or a desert island into the American home. Les Baxter, a former jazz arranger, first adventured into these uncharted lands as the producer of Yma Sumac, the girl with the 'wonder voice', which supposedly spanned four octaves. A soprano folk singer from Peru, she was promoted as being an Incan princess, though her vocal performances were sufficiently exotic not to need further hyperbole. Baxter followed with his own 'jungle' albums, such as *Ritual of the Savage*, which mixed jazz scoring with vaguely ethnic ornamentation. But the most effective, and successful, exponent of sound-effect jazz was Martin Denny, whose two albums of *Exotica* from 1959 were laden with animal noises and instrumental subtleties, any of which might have been drawn from the soundtracks of vintage Tarzan movies.

Within three years, however, American music was visited by exotic rhythms which could be traced to an exact location, and a precise moment in cultural history. For the Brazilian authorities, music had long been a tool of international propaganda. Now the nation launched a new rhythm upon the world, with a dangerously bohemian ethos. The bossa nova was not just an innovation in jazz, but a way of moving which was both easeful and yet laden with a strange tension.

As far as the record business is concerned, it's a great, big bossa-filled world we live in.
Billboard magazine, October 1962

The whole thing is pretty much a bore . . . So the samba now swings. This proves what? That modern jazz people can blow long, tedious solos in front of a swinging samba beat. Wonderful! Practically without exception, all bossa nova records sound alike.
American Record Guide, March 1963

Carnegie Hall, New York, 21 November 1962: the venue which had once played host to Paul Whiteman and Benny Goodman opened its doors to an event billed 'Bossa Nova (New Brazilian Jazz)'. So effective was the publicity that more than 1,000 people were turned away at the door. Yet the show, co-ordinated by jazz critic Leonard Feather, was a disaster: 'sloppy and non-professional', with microphones ill-placed on stage, performers apparently unused to connecting with an audience, and a sound balance that rendered much of the music inaudible. Only one act survived with its reputation intact: the combo led by saxophonist Stan Getz and guitarist Charlie Byrd, who were also the hottest commercial attraction on a bill divided between Brazilian visitors and the American jazzmen they had entranced. Their instrumental version of Antonio Carlos Jobim's tune, 'Desafinado' was already one of the best-selling singles in America; their album, *Jazz Samba*, became the first instrumental jazz LP to top the US charts.

'Desafinado' translated as 'Off-Key', with lyrics – by Newton Mendonça, though unheard on Getz's rendition – which parodied a frequent criticism of the bossa nova style. A cunning marriage of words and music, 'Desafinado' offered such a demanding melody line that vocalists had to cling to their technique for dear life.

Jobim was among the native Brazilians who arrived for the Carnegie Hall concert, and stayed in New York. Another was João Gilberto, who had originally performed 'Desafinado' in Brazil with an intimacy that was both sensuous and yet symbolically held in check. For bossa nova was not just a rhythm, or (as it rapidly became) an exotic gimmick for the global music industry, but a generational statement, a philosophy of life and thereby, in a country which was stumbling from corruption to dictatorship, a stark refusal by the young to sustain the culture of their parents.

If Anglo-American popular music had reached a pinnacle of musical and lyrical sophistication during the 1930s – which would (so traditionalists said) never be matched again, or perhaps only be surpassed in the late 1960s – Brazil's was a culture in which poetry was always expected from its wordsmiths and melodists. Their influences were diverse: the maxixe, for example, which reached Europe around the time of the First World War, threw the Argentinian tango, the Cuban habanera, the European polka and the Brazilian lundu into a melting pot, to emerge with a dance that required men and women to press their bodies together in ecstasy.

From the maxixe emerged the samba, Brazil's most durable export of the twentieth century: percussive, joyful, idiosyncratic, and designed to shift the body from side to side with seductive informality. Samba represented an idealised Brazil: smiling, effervescent, irresistible, perpetually in motion. The arranger and composer Pixinguinha carried the samba to Europe in the 1920s, describing his music as jazz to ensure he garnered an audience. Yet the most effective ambassador of Brazilian music before the

Second World War was also the most controversial. Carmen Miranda became a star in Hollywood and on Broadway by offering a caricature of South American ethnicity: her head topped by what looked like a basket of fruit, her clothes scanty, her songs (for Brazilian taste) too Americanised. She answered this criticism with a bitterly humorous song, 'Disseram que voltei Americanizada' ('They said I came back all American'). As Caetano Veloso explained, 'Carmen Miranda was first a cause of a mixture of pride and shame ... the opposite of our craving for good taste and national identity.'

The samba was not a straitjacket: it could encompass ballads, dance tunes, lyrics that were romantic or wry or satirical. There were subgenres of samba: *samba-canção* from Rio, the music of urban sophisticates; *samba exaltação*, paeans of praise to Brazil and its culture; *samba de morro*, the sound of the hills rather than the city, as traditional in its claim to unpretentious virtues as was country music in America. Ary Barroso wrote the samba with the longest reach: 'Aquarela do Brasil' ('Water colour [portrait] of Brazil') was used by Walt Disney in the movie *Saludos Amigos*, where a talking parrot taught Donald Duck how to dance Brazilian-style.

The bossa nova arose out of the cultural ferment that greeted the democratic government of Juscelino Kubitschek in 1956. Brazil belatedly dived into modernism, compressing fifty years of European artistic development into five. Its arts seized upon the new: first Cinema Nova; then, inevitably, the bossa nova (an untranslatable phrase denoting that this was a new rhythm with an ethos to match). The style could be dissected to reveal jazz chords, the cool elegance of *samba-canção* and unexpected harmonies; or accepted as the sound of a youthful generation which wanted to reflect its Brazilian identity and its utopian dreams. Gradually, the key figures fell into each other's company: composer Antonio Carlos Jobim; poet Vinicius de Moraes; guitarist and singer João Gilberto, from whom came the single 'Chega de saudade', which drew the barbs about a style that was off-key and almost insultingly lazy. After 'Desafinado', bossa nova historian Ruy Castro explained, 'a common obsession united young men: to free themselves from the accordion and take up the guitar which, incidentally, would make them much more popular with girls'.

João Gilberto, said Miles Davis, 'would sound good reading a newspaper'. Like Sinatra, his phrasing was as precise and certain as a surgeon, maintaining perfect composure even as his guitar and his voice obeyed different rhythmic commands. His music gradually infiltrated the

USA. Lena Horne was the first to tackle a bossa nova tune; Sarah Vaughan and Nat King Cole also paid close attention. But it was Charlie Byrd who brought a copy of Gilberto's debut LP home to play for Stan Getz, with the result that Americans assumed that bossa nova was a school of jazz, a rhythm rather than a youthful revolution. During 1961 and 1962, several American acts devoted entire albums to the sound of Brazil, with varying degrees of integrity. Flute player Herbie Mann was the first to record in Brazil; Paul Winter and Cannonball Adderley followed. But these 'authentic' excursions were swamped by more exploitative ventures. Records such as Elvis Presley's 'Bossa Nova Baby' and Eydie Gorme's 'Blame It on the Bossa Nova' were as authentic as Carmen Miranda's headgear, and merely convinced the casual listener that bossa was an ethnic novelty. No commercially minded jazzman or bandleader could resist cashing in; nor could advertising agencies, who tied the bossa nova tag to everything from restaurants to clothing lines. By 1963, the business decided that the bossa nova was stale, and plans for bossa movies (*Don't Knock the Bossa Nova*, to follow *Don't Knock the Rock* and *Don't Knock the Twist*) were abandoned.

That March, Stan Getz and João Gilberto recorded an album of duets, augmented on two songs by João's German wife Astrud. 'Garota de Ipanema' was a sinuous ode to an anonymous girl whom its composers had seen passing a café day after day. Several Brazilian artists had already cut it: the *Getz/Gilberto* album rendition was five minutes long, Astrud's un-tutored vocal (off-key, indeed, and off-tempo too) a mere afterthought. But the track was edited to create a single ('The Girl from Ipanema') which sold in its millions, and enabled *Getz/Gilberto* to stay in the charts for almost two years. From this marriage of Brazil, America and Germany came one of the defining records of the 1960s. And then Brazil's democracy was overthrown by an American-backed military coup, and bossa nova, with its vision of a society liberated in body and soul, lost its birthright amidst the chaos and social repression that followed.

This political turmoil passed Frank Sinatra by, and his belated bossa nova moment came in 1967, when he made an album of duets with Antonio Carlos Jobim – an exquisite collection, on which the 51-year-old maestro of swing discovered a new way to sing, a fresh rhythm to command, and a vocabulary to replace the one he had been wasting on such fripperies as 'Winchester Cathedral' and 'Downtown' (a song he hated so much that he mocked it as he sang). It was his last major stylistic invention, and it marked the end of an American quest: an attempt to create sophisticated and experimental popular music for an adult audience whose children had already ruled that form of sophistication obsolete.

'When we play at the Cavern, the girls often queue all night to get in – it's very flattering. I wouldn't queue all night for anybody. It's as much as I can do to wait for a bus.'

Ringo Starr, 1963

CHAPTER 15

REVOLUTION IN REVERSE

'The Beatle People care about clothes without being obsessed by them ... They're sold on rhythm-and-blues, modern jazz and a touch of Beethoven. They frequent coke-and-coffee jazz clubs, where they dance a sort of Mashed Potato/Twist ... Of average intelligence, reasonably educated, they have views on everything, live for the present and will try anything once ... The Beatle Trend is friendly, unselfconscious, amusing and prepared to be amused. They like fast cars, living it up, painting, poetry-writing and new-wave films.'

Honey magazine, June 1963

4

Like a besotted adolescent, the UK's entertainment industry was pathetically grateful for any attention from its more mature American counterpart. If a leading US performer deigned to record a British song, it sparked headlines in the pop papers. When Frank Sinatra agreed to visit London and tape an entire LP of material written by British composers, it was as if the nation had been acknowledged by a global monarch. (Sinatra thought so little of *Great Songs from Great Britain* that it was not issued in America for thirty years.)

British chart success in America, no matter how meagre, attracted similar attention. So there was enormous excitement when New York was subject to a barrage of British pop talent which was, said *Billboard* magazine, 'taking on the character of a mass migration'. It was October 1962, when a Liverpool beat group had just released its first single, and the British performers about to 'invade' America were jazzman Acker Bilk, country singer Frank Ifield (raised in Australia) and Indian-born teen idol Cliff Richard.

Almost a year later, in August 1963, TV variety host Ed Sullivan came to Britain (a newsworthy event in itself) to sample the best of the country's young talent; he filmed performances by Richard, Ifield, the Dallas Boys, and Kenny Ball. Richard and Ifield then made return trips to Sullivan's Manhattan studio. It was the most concentrated British assault ever on the heart of America's pop industry, aided by the surprise prominence in the Hot 100 of the Caravelles' retro-styled singalong 'You Don't Have to Be a Baby to Cry', which reached No. 3 just before Christmas.

Elsewhere in New York, there was pandemonium during a pop concert at Carnegie Hall, when an evening of Italian performers, starring teen-beat group Peppino & His Rockers, 'wound up in a riot of screaming fans that had to be quelled by officials'. Ed Sullivan played host to the man *Newsweek* called 'The King' and *Life* magazine said was 'a thumping teenage idol who is part evangelist, part Pied Piper and all success': surf guitarist Dick Dale. In California, a bill of folksingers, led by Peter, Paul & Mary, broke box-office records at the Hollywood Bowl. Meanwhile, a talented young group was set for international success: the Osmond Brothers, promoted weekly on *The Andy Williams Show*, and preparing to introduce their newest recruit, 5-year-old Donny. Williams and the

Osmonds won numerous standing ovations at a Chicago concert the day after JFK's assassination. 'If we've just succeeded in giving you a couple hours' pleasure in this otherwise terrible weekend, it was all worthwhile', Williams told the crowd. Perhaps expressing the national mood, cabaret singer Eartha Kitt issued a new single two weeks after the tragedy: 'I Had a Hard Day Last Night'.

While *Billboard*, America's music-trade journal, was chronicling the surprising revival of rock 'n' roll that season (it made a 'Very Lively Corpse'), it began to note the success of British groups unknown to its readers. 'From Liverpool? You're a Hit!', it trumpeted in June 1963. The prime movers were the group it insisted on calling Gerri & the Pacemakers, the year's hottest new act in Australia, and (with equal disregard for detail) 'the Beetles'. By November, both acts had been booked to follow Cliff Richard and Frank Ifield on *The Ed Sullivan Show*. And then, without any warning, *Billboard* provided strange Christmas cheer for Britain: 'Beatlemania seems to have taken off in the United States', it announced. This was three weeks before the proposed release date of Capitol Records' first Beatles single, 'I Want to Hold Your Hand', when hardly any American citizens had been exposed to their music. *Billboard's* explanation was that 'the publicity ruckus stirred so far is of major proportions'. Their record company had already decided that the Beatles were going to become American stars, or they would bankrupt them-selves trying. They arranged lavish advertising spreads and a campaign suggesting that Hollywood star Janet Leigh, of *Psycho* fame, would adopt the Beatles' trademark haircut. (Leigh preferred not to play along, and her place was taken by 'starlet Gail Stevens', who after being spotlighted in a Beatles fan magazine was rarely seen again.)

Although the *New York Times* declared that America was unlikely to fall for the 'dated stuff' being offered by the Beatles, 'I Want to Hold Your Hand' quickly reached No. 1. By late spring 1964, the group occupied the top five places on the US singles chart. 'Great Britain hasn't been so influential in American affairs since 1775', the first year of the Revolution, wrote columnist Jack Maher. Even adults were cueing up Beatles records on jukeboxes, so they could try to understand why their children were so excited. Soundtrack composer Henry Mancini predicted that the Beatles 'would never last. How can they? How can anyone sustain the sort of mete-oric rise that shot them to stardom?' American reviewer Edward Jablonski claimed that the group had 'left no lasting impress upon our culture . . . Their style is an English parody (although possibly not so intended) of our popular country style, plus a dash of the blues . . . they seem to be pleasant enough chaps. That they cannot sing or as much as carry one good note is immaterial.' The Beatles' most bemused critic, however, was R&B singer Ben E. King. 'These boys, however good they may be, are playing the same music the Drifters and half a dozen other American groups were producing six or seven years ago', he noted with a slight air of grievance. This was a revolution in reverse; a bold step towards the past.

In 1961, when the Beatles had not yet met their manager, Brian Epstein, or recruited drummer Ringo Starr, the disc jockey at Liverpool's Cavern Club, Bob Wooler, had already examined the group's stunning local popularity. They were, he said, 'the biggest thing to have hit the Liverpool rock 'n' roll set-up in years . . . because they resurrected original-style rock 'n' roll music . . . To those people on the verge of quitting teendom – those who had experienced during their most impressionable years the impact of rhythm 'n' blues music (raw rock 'n' roll) – this was an experience, a process of regaining and reliving a style of sounds and associated feelings identifiable with their era . . . Here was the excitement – both physical and aural – that symbolised the rebellion of youth in the ennuied mid-1950s.' Wooler concluded: 'I don't think anything like them will happen again.'

There were countless rock 'n' roll bands – teen-beat groups, in the modern parlance – keeping the faith across Britain in the early 1960s. What enabled the Beatles and the other Merseybeat groups to gain such momentum was the island culture of Liverpool. Though London determined the mood of the nation, Liverpool had declared silent independence, maintaining its own heroes and obsessions. Other cities strived to attract London's attention, but in Liverpool, fame on Merseyside was enough. London's teenagers regarded themselves as a national elite, and saw no kudos in resurrecting an exhausted fad. So while Liverpool's musicians stoked the damp embers of rock 'n' roll, throwing the latest American soul and girl-group hits into the fire, London's young bands pursued something more self-consciously elitist: US R&B and jazz – music which marked out its followers as modernists, not traditionalists.

Out goes the Rock, in comes Trad.
Melody Maker, January 1961

Uniforms – Has Trad Gone Mad?
Melody Maker, August 1961

Like the Dixieland revivalists who vowed to expel bebop from American jazz in the late 1940s, the doyens of Britain's traditional jazz movement wanted to retrieve a golden age, and comfort themselves in its glow. The 'trad' boom of the early 1960s coincided with a culture-wide nostalgia for a romanticised version of the 1920s: all flappers and gangsters, bobs and bowlers. In the hands of Kenny Ball's Jazzmen and the Temperance Seven, trad was family entertainment, as harmless as the greasepaint and canes of *The Black and White Minstrels* or the car chases and gunplay of TV's *The Roaring 20's*.

Yet trad was born in deadly earnest, as observer Jim Godbolt noted, by people 'obsessed with the concept of instrumental purity'. It traced its British heritage back to George Webb's Dixielanders in 1943, eschewed the evil saxophone, and prided itself on its intimate knowledge of obscure recordings by a select pantheon of 1920s instrumentalists. Godbolt astutely recognised that this was 'the first ever example of a musical culture to be absorbed from gramophone records'. Attaining its musical peak in the early 1950s, with bands led by Chris Barber and Ken Colyer, and accidentally spawning the skiffle craze, trad attracted a loyal audience of students, dancers and drinkers. Their arch-enemies were those who followed the credo of 'modern' jazz, and this bitter rivalry ensured that by the early 1960s, British festivals could boast pitched battles among their attractions – each side blaming the other for besmirching the good name of jazz. (These incidents paled alongside the virtual ransacking of the Olympia theatre in Paris in 1955, by teenage 'trad' fans of jazz saxophonist Sidney Bechet.)

The *Daily Mirror* helpfully provided a guide to the warring parties. 'Trad fans are usually younger than Mods', it revealed in March 1963, by which time trad had already been ousted from the best-sellers charts. 'They may be school-children, students – or sometimes an earnest 40-year-old with a beard. Mod enthusiasts are usually in their 20s and do a job of some kind. Trads mostly look on Mods as a lot of slickly dressed phoneys pretending to get intellectual pleasure where none exists. Mods mostly consider Trads to be a lot of kids who like dressing up and don't recognise a cheap, commercial sound when they hear one.'

Until 1960, there had been virtually no territory over which to squabble. Aside from cartoonish music-hall revivals by the likes of Billy Cotton's orchestra and the Big Ben Banjo Band, British jazz made little commercial impression in the 1950s. The exceptions were Johnny Dankworth's satirical 'Experiments with Mice', on which he parodied America's leading modernist bands, and Chris Barber's 1959 instrumental 'Petite Fleur' (on which Barber did not actually perform). Then, as the likes of Emile Ford and Joe Brown – and, in America, the Everly Brothers and Clarence Henry – translated the hits of the 1920s into teen-beat style, the public indulged a brief passion for clarinet solos, which trad bandleader Acker Bilk was ideally placed to satisfy. As Humphrey Lyttleton reflected when it was all over, 'The worst thing that happened to jazz was when it suddenly invaded the pop field. It was like a rabbit invading a python.'

At least the rabbit was well dressed. Acker Bilk was subjected to perhaps the most sophisticated marketing campaign yet employed by any pop performer. His publicist, Peter Leslie, suggested that he wear a bowler hat and a striped waistcoat, an unmistakeable visual identity. The clarinettist was billed as 'Mr Acker Bilk', clad in a variety of period costumes for his *The Seven Ages of Acker* LP, and gifted with such contemporary advertising slogans as 'There IS no substitute for Bilk' and 'An Acker a Day Keeps the Bopper Away'. Leslie described his fans as being under the shadow of the atomic bomb: 'since Today is so bloody awful, ergo anything to do with Yesterday must of necessity be better'. Ironically, Bilk's most lucrative record, 'Stranger on the Shore', a lusciously intimate setting of clarinet against strings, had nothing to do with jazz and was a conscious effort to echo the US easy-listening success of the 101 Strings. It was selected as the theme for a children's TV series, and surpassed Dave Brubeck's 'Take Five' as the world's best-selling 'jazz' record of the era. It also assured Bilk of a lifelong audience for his stage shows, where he ranged from 'pure' trad to something verging dangerously close to rhythm and blues.

Inevitably, there was a movie, *It's Trad Dad* (filled with cameos from pop stars); a TV series called *The Trad Fad*; a pastiche from a BBC disc jockey, Brian Matthew, entitled 'Trad Mad'; a trad-themed episode of the TV comedy *Hugh and I*; and a virtual monopoly of the British Jazz LP chart by Messrs Bilk, Barber and Ball (interrupted only by Brubeck). Trad even conquered Europe, with the million-selling 'Schlafe mein Prinzchen' by Papa Bue's Viking Jazz Band.

At its moment of commercial triumph, trad was ambushed by a younger, rowdier rival. As late as November 1962, pundits predicted that the New Year would be dominated by jazz. Within a matter of weeks, trad had vanished from the UK charts, leaving scarcely a trace beyond the

packed houses who loyally attended Bilk, Barber and Ball performances for
the next fifty years. Otherwise, the clubs which had once comprised the
trad circuit were now bastions of beat music – or, in Newcastle, Birmingham
and especially London, something altogether rougher and, to its devotees,
decidedly more 'authentic'.

> The music which is currently drawing the biggest crowds
> in London clubs these days is plain, unadulterated
> rhythm-and-blues.
>   *Melody Maker*, November 1962
>
> All the loud, death-dealing groups are going to ruin the entire
> movement unless audiences become more discriminating.
>   *R'nB Scene* magazine, September 1964

In March 1962, Mississippi-born bluesman Howlin' Wolf, his voice as
jagged as a broken beer bottle, his songs steeped in sexuality and voodoo,
was booked to appear in front of the Staffordshire Society of Jazz Music,
before taking his place at the Hammersmith Palais International Jazz Band
Ball. Illness prevented him from flying to England, and his place was taken
by Scottish folksingers Robin Hall and Jimmie MacGregor, creators of the
novelty song 'Football Crazy'.

Wolf's brand of music was virtually unknown in Britain, where a
band led by Alexis Korner and Cyril Davies, who called themselves Blues
Incorporated, could bill themselves at London's Marquee as 'Britain's only
Rhythm & Blues Group'. Pop star Mike Sarne was one of those who questioned the very notion of British blues: 'It's very dangerous to play in other
people's playgrounds . . . I could find 300 Negro kids in Harlem who could
sing the blues with reason and a thousand times better than anyone here.
So why do they try in this country?'

By September 1962, despite Sarne's warning, R&B clubs were
opening all over London. Georgie Fame offered a blend of modern jazz
and blues at Rik Gunnell's All-Nighter at the Flamingo; Blues By Six
were at Studio 51; the Rolling Stones at the Woodstock Hotel in Cheam;
the Manfred Manne Mike Hug (*sic*) Quartet mixed jazz and blues at the
Greenford Hotel; while Dave Hunt's R&B Band, about to recruit a
guitarist named Ray Davies, were at the Chinese Twist Club (motto:

'Chop Chop, Velly Velly Good'). Blues Incorporated continued to set the pace: 800 'fervent fans' packed out their Marquee appearances, where the band recorded a live album, delivering music 'to twist to, to jive to, jump to, swing with and get with', or so *Melody Maker* declared. (The paper also asked: is Blues Incorporated the loudest band in Britain?)

'I'm a purist', said the group's co-leader Cyril Davies, preparing for a struggle with those who wanted to meld R&B with mainstream pop. 'I don't like to see the music messed about. It would be great to use acoustic instruments. I'd much prefer string bass and ordinary guitar. But what can you do in a fair-sized club?' There was an additional pressure, soon faced by every blues band in the country: the lemming-like flood of musicians and fans alike towards the teen-beat and rock 'n' roll hybrid of the Beatles. *Melody Maker* noted with disapproval in June 1963 that 'One of the more established and more respectable R&B groups has suddenly turned up in Beatles haircuts and dark sweaters, and recorded a roll-along Chuck Berry number named "Come On".' The culprits were the Rolling Stones. Pop balladeer Craig Douglas pronounced their single 'very very ordinary. Can't hear a word they are saying . . . definitely not a hit'. But at the Station Hotel in Richmond, they were attracting a crowd which 'in its fervour was like a revivalist meeting in America's Deep South'. They were, said the ever-watchful *Melody Maker*, 'five young men who see themselves as pioneers of authentic beat music on the dangerous fringe of pop and R&B'.

The notion of authenticity shadowed the entire British R&B scene (eventually being parodied by the Bonzo Dog Band, with their musical question: 'Can Blue Men Sing the Whites?'). Though most British buffs paid lip service to any American veteran who could be linked to the blues, the flourishing outfits ignored the successful jump blues and proto-rock 'n' roll stars of the late 1940s in favour of 'real' blues from the South, via the Chess studios in Chicago. Even at Chess, the roster was divided between artists who targeted youth (Chuck Berry and Bo Diddley) and those whose age and eerie atmospherics required a more mature and world-weary audience (Muddy Waters and Howlin' Wolf). Bands such as the Rolling Stones, who stuffed their repertoire with the rock stylings of Berry and Diddley, were disparaged by those with more 'pure' tastes.

The ultimate badge of authenticity amongst white bluesmen, however, was reserved for those who adhered to the cult of a singer who had died some twenty-five years earlier. 'At first the music repelled me,' Eric Clapton recalled of his indoctrination, 'it was so intense, and there was no attempt being made by this man to sugar-coat what he was trying to say, or play. It was hardcore, more than anything I had ever heard. After a few listenings, I realised that, on some level, I had found the master, and that following this man's example would be my life's work.'

Clapton's master, who echoed through the young Englishman's work from the Yardbirds through John Mayall's Bluesbreakers to Cream and into a new century, was Robert Johnson: delivered posthumous and pure to Clapton, and a generation of wide-eyed aficionados, as (in the title of a 1962 LP) *King of the Delta Blues Singers*. This anthology of his 1936–7 recordings, none of which had matched the sales of Blind Lemon Jefferson or Skip James, let alone Leroy Carr or Lonnie Johnson, left its mark on everyone from Bob Dylan to Keith Richards. Packaged with academic care, it described Johnson's uncanny art and life in mythological terms: 'He seemed constantly trapped . . . He was tormented by phantoms, and weird, threatening monsters . . . Robert Johnson appeared and disappeared, in much the same fashion as a sheet of newspaper twisting and twirling down a dark and windy midnight street.' Unphotographed (as it seemed at the time), vague even in the memories of those who knew him, gripped by existential dread ('Hellhound on My Trail') and insuperable obstacles ('Stones in My Passway'), Johnson was accepted without question as the godhead of blues lore. Only more recently have scholars such as Elijah Wald unpicked the myths to reveal a more human Johnson: one who, like all his peers, stole lines from the repertoire of those around him; who made his living from pop hits and even polkas amidst his blues; who, despite the cinematic splendour of the scene, never sold his soul at a crossroads or walked hand in hand with Satan. As a historical document, however, the Johnson album was and is remarkable. It demonstrates his carefree attitude towards time-keeping (bequeathing his legacy of the eleven-and-a-half-bar blues to John Lee Hooker and then Bob Dylan); his early mastery of the boogie rhythm; the repeated guitar riff he used to stamp his identity on the blues; his command of several diffuse blues traditions, as if he'd been raised in them all; and the way in which, on his first Columbia disc, 'Terraplane Blues', he sounded as if he were sketching out parts for an electric band, when he probably never heard (or imagined) an electric guitar in his lifetime.

It's intriguing to imagine how Johnson would be viewed had he lived long enough to tour Europe like Big Bill Broonzy, or indeed Muddy Waters, who supposedly scandalised British blues fans in 1958 by touring with an electric band, and disappointed them on his return in 1963 by playing acoustic. (Recordings from the first visit dispel this myth, incidentally.) Johnson's absence allowed Eric Clapton to seize upon the image of 'one man and his guitar versus the world . . . one guy who was completely alone and had no options, no alternatives other than just to sing and play to ease his pains': a vision of the ideal bluesman which had more to do with Clapton's psychological needs than with what a blues singer actually represented in his own milieu.

Schooled in such fact and legend, a generation of white blues musicians, critics and prophets felt qualified to judge the worth and authenticity of the music being made in Britain. 'All over London clubs are springing up with claim to feature R&B and many new groups are being formed to make R&B noises', wrote *Jazzbeat* editor Pat Richards in 1964. 'That does not mean the sound they make *is* R&B.' Whereas Blues Incorporated were, by his reckoning, 'legitimate and honest', the work of their copyists 'is often dishonest, shallow and worthless'.

One man's dishonesty was another's authenticity. As Eric Clapton admitted later, 'I was very pompous towards white blues groups . . . my ego made me regard it as being all right in my case, but not in anybody else's.' Some believed that you could only play the blues if you were black; some if you were white but suffering; some if you were white, and had devoted yourself to forensic study of black artists and their records, 'tempering enthusiasm with a degree of critical appreciation of the music', as journalist Roger Eagle insisted. While purists abhorred the Rolling Stones, some R&B fanzines preferring not even to mention their names, they deserved credit for persuading the networked American pop programme *Shindig!* to showcase Howlin' Wolf; for promoting John Lee Hooker to the point that he could score British hit singles; and for topping the UK charts with arguably their least commercial single, a cover of Willie Dixon's 'Little Red Rooster' soaked in bottleneck guitar and animal sexuality. A few months earlier, another British blues band, the Animals, had achieved the same feat with 'House of the Rising Sun', a tense and guttural traditional ballad about life in a brothel.

Some of their peers remained unconvinced: Brian O'Hara, of the Merseybeat band the Fourmost, dismissed American blues as 'bad guitar playing, bad singing and bad lyrics'. But while his career foundered, blues was briefly the lingua franca of British pop. Then it passed: its mystique shattered by overfamiliarity, the mission of the blues evangelists achieved and lost in that same instant. Just as had happened in America, the Delta and country blues were superseded by urban R&B and soul. The blues became a cult once more, its disciples the likes of Clapton, Tony McPhee and Peter Green. In their hands, blues became a British phenomenon, with its own pantheon of divinities, each sporting an electric guitar. Their heroes, the 'authentic' American prophets of the blues, were swept aside by these new messiahs, whose destiny was to obscure the music they loved as they transmitted it around the world.

> Can anyone explain why modern jazz lovers must play their records full blast? My husband seems to have an acute attack of this disease which he shares with his jazz-loving friends.
> Letter to *Melody Maker*, February 1963

> Donald Zec's [article] made the Beatles appear to be a lot of thick-headed Rockers, but all their fans know them to be Mods.
> Letter to *Daily Mirror*, September 1963

At 15, future underground poet and teen pop star Marc Bolan was profiled by *Town* magazine as one of the 'young men who live for clothes and pleasure'. More than either, Bolan (known then as Mark Feld) wanted to personify the present day: to be more contemporary, more alive, more perfectly styled for this moment than anyone else. It was an exhausting regime, *Town* suggested, and one doomed to end in failure. Easier, indeed, to follow trad-jazz fans or blues purists or aficionados of mid-1950s rock 'n' roll, by selecting a golden age from the past and dedicating oneself to its survival. That would never satisfy Bolan's generation of impeccably tailored young men: they had to be eternally modern,* and so the only possible word to describe them was 'modernist', or in an age where every split second counted, 'mod'.

'Modernist' had no connection with the aesthetic notion of modernism, the deconstruction of traditional artistic forms by the likes of Picasso, Joyce and Schönberg. It was, however, linked with 'modern' jazz, drawing on both its sense of 'the cool', and its stylish imagery and typography. Miles Davis was a modernists' icon, although his credo of continuous reinvention ensured that anyone who wanted to frame his image at any

---

* The so-called 'mod revival' which began around 1979 was the antithesis: a static cult devoted to being eternally like their predecessors in 1964.

particular moment would soon feel betrayed or bewildered. But the original mods loved or affected a love of modern jazz, alongside Italian suits and scooters, and French cigarettes.

To become a national movement, mod required a more accessible soundtrack, and as contemporary jazz overlapped with American soul in the early 1960s, mods found new role models. They came from Motown, Atlantic and Stax, from Detroit, New York, Memphis and Los Angeles, even from London, where all these sounds (plus the ethnic exoticism of Jamaican ska, or 'bluebeat') could be heard at clubs such as the Flamingo. In residence there in 1964 were the Blue Flames, led by Georgie Fame – the one man in London capable of blending jazz, blues, soul, ska and even African highlife into a coherent sound. As the modernists' soundtrack altered, so did their identity, until by summer 1964 *Jazz Monthly* reported that 'the well-scrubbed youths with their ashen-faced and eye-shadowed partners have given way to a sartorially less conformist crowd that is at least 50% non-white'. At the end of the year, Georgie Fame released the exuberant 'Yeh Yeh': a Latin soul instrumental by a Cuban jazzman, augmented with lyrics by a black American beatnik, which topped the British charts to suggest that this was after all a mod country in a mod world.

This cultural supremacy had not been won easily. 'Youngsters beat up seaside town: 97 Leather Jacket Arrests', announced the *Daily Express* after an explosion of violence on Easter Saturday 1964, which spread from Clacton to Margate, and even involved weekend trippers waiting for the ferry home from Ostend. By the Whitsun bank holiday in May, there were skirmishes all along the south coast, with Brighton a focal point for vandalism and grievous bodily harm. The participants identified themselves as the warring tribes of mods, clad for motor-scooter-riding in baggy parkas, and rockers, the leather-clad hooligans of the *Express* story, whose machines were more potent than their opponents' imported Vespas and Lambrettas.

The first documented scuffles between the young men the press would dub 'Scooter Groups' and 'Wild Ones' (the latter after a Marlon Brando biker movie, which had not yet been screened in the UK) took place a year earlier, in the unlikely surroundings of the London Stock Exchange. In spring 1963, rival gangs of messengers engaged in petty acts of violence when they weren't conveying vital bulletins about share prices. That May, the two tribes fought on the dance floor of the Lyceum Ballroom in London. By late summer, 'The War of the Rockers and Mods' erupted into street battles in Basildon town centre. For the media, this was more glamorous than gang warfare: the rivalry between mods and rockers seemed to offer a rationale for violence that was fuelled as much by testosterone and social inferiority as tribal affiliation.

'Purple hearts and beat music' were widely accused of exacerbating these incidents. 'Every time something like this happens, they blame the music', Stones guitarist Brian Jones complained. 'Beat music does not build up tension. It allows young people to let off steam.' For sociologist Stanley Cohen, the disputes were triggered by a minute distinction of social class: 'The typical Rocker was an unskilled manual worker, the typical Mod a semi-skilled manual worker.' Cohen also declared that 'Music was much more important for the Mods than the Rockers – and also than for the Teds, who had not grown up as a generation through the whole Rock explosion.' As a corrective: an anonymous mod interviewed in 1964 noted that 'Rockers buy more records. Mods knock theirs off at parties.' Cohen's view of Teddy boys – packs of whom continued to prowl through Britain's streets well into the 1970s – may have been misguided. Teds' loyalty to the rock 'n' roll stars of the late 1950s expressed itself whenever Bill Haley or Jerry Lee Lewis came to Britain, Haley's increasingly tame sound invariably provoking riots, almost as a badge of honour. But rockers' aggression was fuelled by the power of their bikes, the borrowed machismo of their leather jackets, and (ironically, given the subsequent prevalence of gay biker porn) a sense of machismo that was offended by the close attention paid by mods to their appearance.

Early reports claimed the Beatles as the exemplars of mod. Asked if he was a mod or a rocker, Ringo Starr quipped that he was a 'mocker'. (Journalists also claimed to have identified 'mids', who for financial reasons could not perfect the image required by either tribe. As ever, there was a silent majority of young people, perhaps amounting to more than 90% of the total teenage population, for whom the mod vs rocker debate was irrelevant.) With their collarless suits, Cuban-heeled boots, exquisitely shiny hair and obvious passion for American soul, the Beatles certainly seemed to qualify as mods; yet vintage photographs identified all four of the group as ex-Teddy boys, even if none of them seemed sturdy enough to handle a 500 cc bike.

In any case, the Beatles were too popular with adults and young children by the end of 1963 to act as heroes for a self-confessed league of elitists, and so mod adulation was transferred to the Rolling Stones, then to the Who and the Small Faces, each sacrificing some of their lustre when they achieved widespread popularity. (Hence the devotion shown by mods to the undeservedly ignored mid-1960s London band, the Action.) So rapid was the shift in collective taste through 1964 that even journalists contributing to magazines specifically aimed at mods could commit such faux pas as claiming that Cilla Black and Cliff Richard were mod icons, or that rocker idol Bill Haley was becoming the movement's standard-bearer in summer 1964.

A constant in mod affections that year was the style dubbed blue-beat, after a record company launched in London at the start of the decade. Its aim was to distribute Jamaican R&B and rock 'n' roll (or 'Jamaican boogie') to Caribbean emigrants who had settled in Britain. That community adopted bluebeat as their own, staging bluebeat balls in London and Birmingham. The phrase remained intact as the music changed, with what its Jamaican creators called 'ska' taking precedence in the early 1960s. For white British listeners, ska's off-kilter rhythm proved disconcerting, and prompted some strange speculation. The pseudonymous 'Terry', writing for *Boyfriend* magazine's 1965 annual, approached the sound of Jamaica as if it were a dangerous dog: 'Ah yes, Blue Beat. I wasn't really sure about that at first. I couldn't get used to the vocal being in a different key to the backing – sounded all wrong. But when some of the British groups started to play Blue Beat, it really started to swing. I suppose the original Blue Beat sounds great played on the sun-kissed beaches of Trinidad' – which it probably did, even if it was recorded more than 1,000 miles away in Kingston.*

Mods quickly adopted bluebeat as an addition to the 'one-new-dance-a-week' cult, alongside the likes of the slope, the shake and the nitty gritty. Bluebeat clubs opened across the country, slowly conquering Britain from south to north. The style was briefly propelled to mass popularity by the sales of 'My Boy Lollipop', an imitation by 17-year-old Millie Small of a 1950s R&B tune, and a No. 2 hit in Britain and America. Effervescent and joyous as it was, 'My Boy Lollipop' was regarded as a novelty by most white listeners. Rather than spreading the gospel of ska, it effectively quashed the music at birth, and for the next few years only Jamaicans (and mods) remained loyal to its rhythmic vivacity. Many Caribbean immigrants opted to attend London soul clubs in the mid-1960s after persistent outbreaks of violence at such ska venues as the Ram Jam, the 007 and the Ska Bar.

---

* In the same book, young girls were helpfully advised to learn the waltz, the foxtrot and the cha-cha, as they would be guaranteed to need them when they grew up and started attending formal ballroom dances.

The furore over the mods and the rockers faded during 1965, although the English summer bank holidays continued to entice scooter crocodiles to Brighton in search of tribal solidarity and perhaps some therapeutic violence. By June 1965, being modern appeared so old-fashioned that Pete Townshend of the Who, regarded as a mouthpiece for the movement, could declare: 'We think the Mod thing is dying. We don't plan to go down with it, which is why we've become individualists.' For the next decade, indeed, mod seemed to surface only in Townshend's frequent interviews about the philosophy of the Who, acting as a touchstone for his own lost youth and his idealistic conception of rock's potential. In 1968, he saw it as 'an army, a powerful aggressive army of teenagers with transport', within which 'You could be a bank clerk, man, it was acceptable.' Two years later, he had assimilated himself back into the pack, claiming of mods that 'We made the establishment uptight, we made the rockers uptight, we made our parents uptight and our employers uptight.' By 1973, he had fashioned the Who's *Quadrophenia* double album as an exploration of what mod had meant to him (and, by his logical extension, the whole of British youth). But as he recalled, back in 1965, 'kids would reach the age of 22 and lose all interest in music because they had to concentrate on the factory'; so the mod impulse of the early 1960s was destined to die – a victim of pop's apparently inevitable struggle to speak to adults with the same intensity it offered to the young.

Interlude: The Screamagers

Q: I am 15 and madly in love with a pop star. I know if I could meet him he would fall in love with me.
A: My dear, hundreds of girls your age imagine they are in love with a film or pop star. Don't brood about this star, he probably gets hundreds of letters like yours every day.
   Problem-page enquiry, *Honey* magazine, March 1963

I've never seen a mob mind working so beautifully. Note how they're all writhing in unison. Their screams are like the noise of excited goats. Most of the audiences are young, and are maturing sexually with no outlet for their emotional urges. Music has broken down their inhibitory checks . . . played in this atmosphere it is just

as powerful in its effect on the nervous system as whisky.
Sociologist's verdict on the audience at a swing concert by
Benny Goodman, 1938

The other day I turned on a Frank Sinatra program and I noted the
shrill whistling sound, created supposedly by a bunch of girls
cheering. I thought: how easy it would be for certain-minded
manufacturers to create another Hitler here in America through the
influence of mass hysteria! They intend to get a Hitler in, by first
planting in the minds of the people that men like Frank Sinatra are
OK, therefore this future Hitler will be OK.
Letter to the FBI, 1943

I keep wondering if it's really me they are screaming at. I keep
wondering who is behind me that is causing all the excitement. I say
to myself, 'Elvis, this is you that is doing it.' And then I think it *can't*
be me. I don't like them pulling my clothes and writing on my
cheeks in lipstick and wanting me to kiss them. I don't see any
sense for them to dance rock 'n' roll on the hood of my car or drive
a knife into the upholstery. But some of them do it and look at me
with the queerest look in their eyes while they're doing it. That part
kind of frightens me.
Elvis Presley, 1956

They made it clear they had come along to hear themselves scream.
In Manchester, they only want to hear themselves.
Cliff Richard, 1963

[P. J. Proby] seems to exploit sex, unaware that many of the girls
screaming in the stalls are only just in their teens.
The Sun, 1965

You come out of a council flat, and you've been struggling to
make it with the bird in the pub who works behind the bar.
Suddenly you're in a theatre with four or five thousand birds
screaming at you, to take your choice of.
Adam Faith, 1973

Peter and Marty were almost pushed off stage; girls fainted in the traditional fashion, floodlights and coppers' helmets were knocked over – and you could hardly hear the New Seekers singing for the fans' frenzied screaming.
  Music Week, 1973

Don't you think, in this day and age, when we have so much trouble and terrorism and blowing-ups and things like that, that the kids *do* want to be entertained and be happy and go along to a concert where they can scream, wet their knickers and have a great time? Isn't that what music's *really* about?
  Bay City Rollers manager Tam Paton, 1974

After a while I realised there was no music being made. The instrument was 20,000 screaming females – pure unadulterated noise. It didn't matter what I did up there.
  David Cassidy, 1976

You get some really wild old women at James Last concerts. They go mad . . . nearly as bad as the Beatles. There's all these old grannies screaming for him.
  Security man for James Last, 1988

With the advent of the Beatles and their peers, pop reached unimagined heights of audience hysteria. An admirer from their pre-fame days in Liverpool was shocked to witness a Beatles performance in 1963, at which every note of their music was buried beneath the screams of young girls. Why didn't they listen to their idols? she asked. 'We came to *see* the Beatles', a fan replied. 'We can *hear* them on records. Anyway, we might be disappointed if we heard them in real life.'

'The raucous sound', reported *Time* magazine before the group arrived in America, 'makes a Beatles performance slightly orgiastic.' That was an understatement. Such was the level of excitement at their concerts that the seating was soaked in urine and other bodily fluids. Sociologists noted that witnessing a pop group provoked orgasms amongst girls too young to understand what they were feeling. In the *New Statesman*, Dr David Holbrook confirmed that it was 'painfully clear that the Beatles are a masturbation fantasy, such as a girl presumably has during the onanistic act – the genial smiling young male images, the music like a buzzing of the blood in the head, the rhythm, the cries, the shouted names, the climaxes.'

The same political journal printed a prurient letter from a teacher at a boys' secondary school. 'Since Beatlemania became the craze,' he wrote, 'I have detected a somewhat disturbing change in a few of my 13-year-old boys. I was recently shocked to find that two of my most promising boys, both of whom sported Beatle mops, had taken to walking together hand in hand.' He added: 'During a recent "wet day", when pupils were confined to the classroom over the lunch break, I came into my room to find a dozen boys congressed round transistor radios, with a terrifying blankness on their faces, moving their pelvises rhythmically in time with each other. When they noticed me, the same furtive, shameful glances as I have some-times noticed in the school lavatories were turned towards me.'

The observer may have imposed his own agenda upon the boys in these stories, just as political commentator Paul Johnson revealed his prejudice when he described Beatles fans as 'the least fortunate of their generation, the dull, the idle, the failures'. The audience on TV's *Thank Your Lucky Stars* pop show, meanwhile, aroused an even more vitriolic response from the 35-year-old Johnson: 'What a bottomless chasm of vacuity they reveal! The huge faces bloated with cheap confectionery and smeared with chain store make-up, the open, sagging mouths and glazed eyes, the hands mindlessly drumming in time to the music, the broken stiletto heels, the shoddy, stereotyped "with-it" clothes . . . How pathetic and listless they seemed: young girls, hardly any more than sixteen, dressed as adults and already lined up as fodder for exploitation.' This was not so much sociology as middle-aged panic disguised as contempt.

As Brian Jones of the Rolling Stones noted, 'We seem to rouse some sort of personal anxiety in people. They think we are getting away with things they never could. It's a sort of frustration.' For a generation that had endured war, the expending of emotional energy on such apparently undeserving targets as the Beatles and the Stones seemed both appalling and indecent. Husband-and-wife social commentators Grace and Fred Hechinger saw rock 'n' roll as 'an indication of the adult failure to offer a better focus for the adolescents' creative interests'. More deplorable still, the Hechingers proclaimed, was the trend towards 'creeping adult adolescence': the willing-ness of adults to share the same banal pleasures as their children, rather than encouraging their kids towards more substantial artistic experiences.

The three-way relationship between performer, fan and parent could be complex. Fifteen-year-old Anne Hungerford of San Diego had been trying to convert her parents to the Beatles in 1964, when she learned that the unmarried members of the group had taken their girlfriends away on holiday, without chaperons. 'I feel I've been betrayed', she admitted. 'We convinced the older people that the Beatles were really nice, clean-cut young men. Then they go travelling around the world like that with girls, and you feel like the whole world has come down on your head. After all, how can you be loyal to boys who do things like that, even if they are the Beatles?' But overt adult acceptance might damn an act in the eyes of their teenage followers: sociologist Peter Laurie noted rather prematurely in 1965, 'Now only the socially inept teenager reveres the Beatles. The establishment has absorbed them.' The Rolling Stones, by contrast, were assured of parental disapproval: 'If the Rolling Stones need to seem almost obscene [to achieve this], they will. They know they are not and the kids know it is only an act; the only people taken in are the grown-ups.' As if to prove that the Stones' fans saw sweet boys beneath their boorish masks, girls well below the age of consent wrote romantic love letters to the group: 'You are Mr Wonderful, Mick, gorgeous, and I want to marry you. I have blonde hair (which is going brown). I am growing it long. I have grey eyes and I'm nearly 14. If you wait another year we can go to Southern Ireland and get married.'

While fans viewed their idols as potential sexual or romantic partners, psychologists pondered over the significance of the long hair worn by the Beatles and their successors. Did this give the group a glow of femininity which made them less threatening to pubescent or prepubescent girls? Did their flowing locks allow their male fans to view them with the same mixture of lust and longing that they would have harboured for young women? Were the hirsute groups expressing their own latent homosexuality? Or, in contrast, so confident a grasp of their own heterosexuality that they could afford to disguise it behind the veneer of androgyny? Were both musicians and fans locked into a mutual display of narcissism, concealing a vacuum of self-doubt? Such intriguing debates preoccupied academics for years to come, as if teenagers and their idols were aliens beyond our ken.

Although nobody reported the fact, pop stars such as the Beatles could take their pick from a procession of willing fans, to the point that they became disgusted by the simplicity of their conquests. By 1966, indeed, the Beatles had become so exhausted by the constant adulation, the relentless horror of grasping hands and shrieking voices, the imprisonment in hotel rooms and airport lounges, the music drowned by noise and delivered without a modicum of care – so bored, in short – that they opted never to tour again. The trappings of Beatlemania seemed irrelevant and anachronistic when the music and its lyrical content had altered so profoundly and so quickly. The new pop demanded to be heard; now it needed an audience who were prepared to listen.

> Everybody concerned has got to learn that to saturate the disc world with hundreds of tunes sounding the same is to court disaster.
> Record producer Joe Meek, 1963

> On one point, the record makers are unanimous. By Christmas, the public will have tired of background sounds created by three guitars and a drumbeat.
> *Daily Mirror*, September 1963

Had their producer George Martin not backed down, the Beatles' second single would have been a song by Mitch Murray, 'How Do You Do It'. Instead, the song was inherited by their Liverpool friends Gerry & the Pacemakers, and topped the British charts. So did a second Murray song, 'I Like It', while a third, 'I'm Telling You Now', was an American No. 1 for Manchester's Freddie & the Dreamers. Murray was therefore ideally placed to publish a pamphlet entitled *How to Write a Hit Song*. Like Charles Harris half a century earlier, his advice exposed the limitations of the style that had made him famous.

　　'I normally try to start a song with a catchy title', he declared, preferably located at both the beginning and end of each verse. 'Each song is, or should be, a story, and the story should be told in simple and direct stages from the very beginning to the death.' He posited a promising pop scenario: 'boy meets girl, boy loses girl, boy wins girl back again'. The conclusion had to be happy, or at least hopeful: 'It is very rarely, these days, that a miserable song will sell.' His final instruction put paid to any notions of originality or novelty. 'If you really study your market,' he told his readers, 'you will get to know what particular tempo and beat-style is in vogue at the present time. Use this beat, because, simply, this is what is selling.' And would presumably always do so.

Murray's book inspired at least one highly successful songwriter: Gordon Sumner, alias Sting, who read it when he was 13. But the advice reinforced the stereotype that every beat-group hit sounded the same. Instrumentation might vary: Gerry & the Pacemakers boasted a keyboard player instead of a second guitarist; other Liverpool bands used a saxophone. But there was an instantly recognisable and generic 'beat-group sound', based on the Everly Brothers and Buddy Holly, popularised by the Beatles, and so dominant for the remainder of 1963 that between 30% and 50% of the songs in the Top 30 would squeeze within its narrow boundaries. In retrospect, you can find stirrings of this sound in pre-Beatles British pop – the smooth teen-beat of Cliff Richard's 'Please Don't Tease', Shane Fenton's 'I'm a Moody Guy' and Joe Brown's 'A Picture of You'. The Beatles' debut, 'Love Me Do', with its maudlin, soul-inspired harmonies, stood out from the forced breeziness of its contemporaries. But 'Please Please Me' in January 1963 was the real birth of the new: more driven than any previous British pop record, with John Lennon's almost frighteningly intense vocal supported by an instantly fresh harmonic blend. Most of all, the Beatles sounded like a gang: forceful, persuasive and sexually potent. That sense of self-belief stoked the otherwise banal 'She Loves You', and was redoubled on 'I Want to Hold Your Hand', where the lyrics promised tame romance, while the rhythmic thrust of the music delivered something altogether more phallic.* By the summer of 1964, when the Beatles were capable of filling an album with their own compositions, their sound had become plumper yet more streamlined, Lennon's voice more cynical (his vocals between 1964 and 1966 seemed to carry their own subtitles, which read: 'If you think I believe a word of this romantic nonsense, you must be an idiot'). Thereafter, they were ready to fulfil the prediction of the *Daily Mirror*'s Judith Simons, who astutely suggested in autumn 1963 that 'when they have passed through their present phase of just-beyond-the-amateur, the potentially brilliant team of songwriters, John Lennon and Paul McCartney, will come up with some modern folk music of lasting worth'. And that was precisely what they did, once the definition of folk had been broadened sufficiently by their American friend Bob Dylan.

---

* When Gerry Marsden sang 'I like the way you tickle my chin' on Mitch Murray's 'I Like It', it was hard to imagine that the tickling stopped there. The Liverpool bands had, after all, paid their dues in the red-light district of Hamburg.

On their first album, recorded in February 1963, the Beatles had already explored, in simplistic fashion, the notion of solipsism and/or daydreaming, in 'There's a Place'. (The Beach Boys' Brian Wilson would revisit the same scenario in a slightly more disturbing way, with 'In My Room'.) Yet even when their lyrics offered nothing more outré than combinations of personal pronouns and the word 'love', the Beatles almost always sounded committed to what they were singing. Cliff Richard's 'Summer Holiday' was sung without any hint of involvement, so that fans could sketch in their own fantasies. The Beatles left the listener no choice but to succumb to their power.

Their sound was now being reproduced not only by optimistic amateurs, but also by existing stars such as Johnny Kidd & the Pirates, Adam Faith & the Roulettes – even Cliff Richard & the Shadows, who had vowed to remain above the fray. Few dared to buck the trend. Arguably the bravest pop decision of 1963 was Gerry & the Pacemakers' choice of Rodgers and Hammerstein's ballad from the musical *Carousel*, 'You'll Never Walk Alone', as a single: orchestrated, epic, their third No. 1 hit. 'I knew it would happen', crowed the UK trade paper *Record Retailer*. 'After all the whoa-whoa-whoa's and yay-yay-yers, all the frantic guitars misplayed, and see-you-at-the-Palais type songs, we're turning slowly back to the oldies.' But that was as forlorn a hope as the constant refrain that the big-band days were about to return. When even the Salvation Army was promoting its own beat group (the Joystrings), the battle was already lost.

Many of the beat groups, from the Beatles downwards, were prepared to accept that they might need to broaden their audience by mixing ballads and even an occasional Broadway standard into their repertoire. It was a way of safeguarding their future, in a business which appeared to offer no enduring career prospects beyond light entertainment: pantomime, seaside variety shows, comedy films, eventually (sporting a bow tie and ruffed shirt) cabaret. Every previous British act had been guided down that path: the Beatles weren't joking when they assumed they would only have two, or three, or at most five years at the top.

At least Lennon and McCartney had the option of making a career as professional songwriters, and perhaps even composing a West End musical. 'They are the only two with enough talent to do something new', their Liverpool friend Bob Wooler said. 'I don't think any of these r-and-b groups' – he was including the Beatles – 'will produce a song about Liverpool; they would find it embarrassing. They don't see anything romantic here.' Paul McCartney revealed in 1964 that they had begun to sketch out a musical based on their home town, but abandoned the project when Lionel Bart beat them to it, with *Maggie May*.

McCartney's throwaway remark hinted at a different Beatles, led by a student of English literature and a former art student, who had befriended a bunch of 'exis' (existentialists) in Hamburg. During 1964, newly settled in London, the two songwriting Beatles were inundated with social invitations by members of the British establishment, eager to view the latest additions to the human zoo. Lennon and McCartney gravitated naturally towards those who were young, and could widen their horizons: photographers such as Robert Freeman and Bob Whittaker, film-maker Dick Lester (who directed their pop-art feature films *A Hard Day's Night* and *Help!*), publisher Tom Maschler, beat poets, hip comedians, bedsitter novelists, fringe actors and directors, journalists and television pundits. Lennon published books of his semi-satirical, semi-nonsensical, semi-surreal writings and drawings. McCartney (especially after he began a relationship with actress Jane Asher) explored theatrical first nights and Soho art exhibitions.

This was new territory for pop, which threatened to undermine the certainties of the British class system. It involved the Beatles (and later the leaders of the Who and the Kinks) stepping out of the classic working-class pop milieu, into an arty middle-class environment which, by 1964, also boasted teenage chanteuse Marianne Faithfull and Peter & Gordon (Peter being Jane Asher's elder brother, and a vital link between McCartney and the fledgling British underground). As if to balance the Beatles' invasion of London society, well-bred middle-class stars such as Mick Jagger began to fake a backstreet drawl to enhance their credibility as working-class heroes. Generations of social etiquette were overturned in a matter of months.

4

LOVE the "BEATLES"
LOVE the "BEATLES"
LOVE the "BEATLES"
LOVE the "BEATLES"
I'M A BEATLE FAN In Case of an Emergency CALL PAUL
I'M A BEATLE FAN In Case of an Emergency CALL PAUL
I LOVE PAUL
I'M A BEATLE FAN In Case of an Emergency CALL PAUL
I LOVE RINGO
I LOVE GEORGE
I'M A BEATLE FAN In Case of an Emergency CALL RINGO
I LOVE RINGO
I LOVE JOHN
I'm a OFFICIAL BEATLES FAN
I LOVE JOHN
I LOVE The "DAVE CLARK" "FIVE"
GIVE ME A LITTLE KISS!
I'm a OFFICIAL BEATLES FAN
I LOVE The "DAVE CLARK" "FIVE"
I AM THE GREATEST
I LIKE SEX
I'M A PSYCHIATRIST LAY DOWN
I'M A VIRGIN
I'M A VIRGIN
KISS ME I'M IRISH
KISS ME I'M IRISH
OFFICIAL FALSIE
I AM AN ALCOHOLIC In Case of an Emergency BUY ME A

CHAPTER 16

SORRY
PARENTS

'Dylan reduces the idiosyncratic styles of certain Negro blues singers to a level of grotesque (even if unintentional) parody, gasping and blurting his way through some remarkably fine songs and missing the point every time.'

Gramophone review of Bob Dylan, September 1962

'So the Beatles like Bob Dylan. Great news, for it shows taste. However, I pray they don't record any of his material. I dread to think of Dylan's commentaries beat-ified and prettied-up with harmonised voices.'

Letter to *Melody Maker*, December 1964

⚡

When John F. Kennedy was assassinated, the best-selling album in America was *In the Wind*, by a folk trio named Peter, Paul & Mary. It featured sleeve notes by the man who had written the trio's No. 2 hit single, 'Blowin' in the Wind' (described as 'a sailor's lament' in one contemporary review). 22-year-old Bob Dylan was, *Billboard* magazine noted, 'the ultimate influence in the current movement' because of his 'absolute commitment to what he believes in'; he had 'brought on an intensity in the folk world bordering on worship'. He had also written a song commercial enough to top the US Middle-Road Singles chart.

So lucrative was folk in the months before America succumbed to the Beatles that 'hootenanny' became a popular radio format, mixing live performances with records such as 'Walk Right In' by the Rooftop Singers, and the already inevitable 'Blowin' in the Wind'. 'Hootenanny' denoted a gathering of folk performers in a spirit of collectivism. But *Hootenanny* was also a scene-dividing ABC-TV show, which required singer Pete Seeger to sign a 'loyalty oath affidavit' before he could perform. (He refused, and was blacklisted from US TV for the next two years.)

Almost anything could be classified as folk, as long as it didn't feature electric instruments: glee-club choirs, nightclub singers, barber-shop quartets, even a group called the Topsiders, who strummed rock 'n' roll hits such as 'Heartbreak Hotel' and 'Ain't That a Shame'. But increasingly folk was being associated with protest,* which in Dylan's work alone could stretch from the vague ('Blowin' in the Wind') to the viciously pointed ('Let Me Die in My Footsteps'). At a time when the Beatles (with 'She Loves You') were being accused by a friend (the BBC's Brian Matthew) for having carried their lyrical simplicity 'to the idiotic', Bob Dylan's finger-pointing, coruscating, elemental songs threatened to capsize the romantic banality of the pop industry. As Paul & Mary's colleague, Peter Yarrow, said: 'The vast teenage population has become fed up with the pseudo – the rocking, the surfing, and everything. We

---

* 'This particular decade has not, as yet, progressed very far,' one songwriter said, 'and what with the prevalent "ill will to all men", nuclear fission, and the industrious piling up of weapons of annihilation, it may not even get beyond the half-way mark.' This gloom-struck rebel was none other than 64-year-old Noël Coward.

give them meat, a message in a song, and find that young people are getting keen on intelligent songs.'

Yarrow's judgement was premature. The audience for the folk boom in 1962–3 paled alongside others which were masterfully exploited by the record industry. The eternal sunshine of southern California provided the backdrop for the boom in surfing. Its catalyst was *Gidget*, a teen novel translated into a Hollywood movie in 1959, starring Bobby Darin's future wife, Sandra Dee. A cult sport once centred around Hawaii was served up as a universal teen culture. The guitarist Dick Dale – himself a practised surfer – began a residency at the Rendezvous Ballroom in Balboa, where he fixed the sound of instrumental surf music for posterity: cavernous reverb, staccato picking, a thick and incisive tone, and a rock 'n' roll rhythm section. 'Let's Go Trippin'' established his brand, before the Beach Boys' debut single, 'Surfin'', a throwback to the garage rock 'n' roll of 1959, staked a lyrical claim to wave-catching, woodies and hanging ten.

The Beach Boys weren't the first American vocal group to exploit the vogue: an outfit called the Surfers had issued a 1959 album of harmonised Hawaiian songs. Nor did they create the first sports-themed LP with 1962's *Surfin' Safari*, as folksinger Bob Gibson had already released a set of novelty tunes entitled *Ski Party*. But the Beach Boys seemed to inhabit surf culture with a naïve enthusiasm that immediately chimed with their peers. So naïve were they, in fact, that leader Brian Wilson imagined they would be able to rewrite the lyrics for Chuck Berry's 'Sweet Little Sixteen' as 'Surfin' USA' without legal retribution. (Again, someone else was first: the Stompers' spring 1962 hit 'Quarter to Four Stomp' was simply Gary Bonds's 'Quarter to Three' with new beach-culture words.) Within a year, Wilson and the Beach Boys were at the heart of a surf-music industry that was even enticing Lawrence Welk ('Breakwater') and Bobby Darin (in disguise, as the City Surfers).

Brian Wilson had inadvertently launched a parallel but rival trend in 1962 with '409', inspired by a Chevrolet 'Big Block' sports engine. It took nearly a year for the industry to recognise 'what looks like the next big teen-age fad – hot rod music', with Capitol Records' Voyle Gilmore claiming that 'drag racing is practically the national pastime of American teenagers'. Or perhaps it was motorbikes (chronicled by the Beach Boys in 'Little Honda') or skateboards (the subject of Jan & Dean's 'Sidewalk Surfin'', itself a rewrite of the Beach Boys' surf anthem, 'Catch a Wave').

What distinguished surf as a form of cultural tourism was its popularity in places where surfing was either unlikely (Sweden) or simply unrealistic – such as Chicago, where it was reported that teenagers were donning surf costumes, carrying around boards they would never use, and dancing 'the surf'. Where there was a dance craze, Chubby Checker was sure to follow: he rushed out the *Beach Party* LP in 1963, which climaxed with the inevitable 'Let's Surf Again'.

There was no shortage of dance phenomena for Checker to exploit in the early 1960s: the slop, the turkey trot, the stomp, the method, the Popeye, the monkey and many more. (The comedian Charlie Drake invented the tanglefoot, which he guaranteed would injure anyone who attempted it.) Gradually all these dances and teen obsessions, all these musical expressions of being young and alive in the America of 1963, collided and coalesced into a style which would comprise the US equivalent to Merseybeat: frat rock. Its name implied the involvement of college students, but anyone with a garage and an electric guitar could participate. Across America, local kids made their two-minute throws at rock immortality – rarely reaching anyone but their classmates, but sometimes exploding from some far-flung corner of the nation into the national charts.

The most notorious of these frat-rock anthems was 'Louie Louie', written and recorded in the mid-1950s by teenage R&B singer Richard Berry, and then revived in shambolic, lumbering style by the Kingsmen. Spending six weeks at No. 2 in the US chart after JFK's assassination, the song became a cause of national outrage, when the governor of Indiana announced that he had been sent the record by a traumatised high-school student, who feared it was obscene. A bunch of college kids obligingly provided a suitably raunchy transcript, supposedly taken verbatim from the Kingsmen's slurred and unintelligible recording. Even more perverted lyrics were passed from hand to hand across the country, each set claiming to reveal the ultimate taboo-busting reality of the song. Meanwhile the publishers of 'Louie Louie' offered $1,000 to anyone who could prove the song was obscene. The FBI did its best to solve the mystery, before concluding after more than a year that the exact nature of the song's lyrics was impossible to ascertain.

Surf, hot rod, frat rock and manufactured dance crazes continued to pepper the US charts in the wake of the Beatles. Indeed, three of those trends coincided sublimely in the Beach Boys' 'I Get Around', its complex harmonic blend supporting lyrics of stunning banality, while their diamond-cut 'Dance Dance Dance' in late 1964 rendered all other dance records irrelevant. At the other extreme, the Premiers' 'Farmer John' reduced frat rock to its essentials, making the Kingsmen sound baroque by comparison. Surprisingly few American bands in 1964 were capable of echoing the sound of Liverpool, the ironically named Chartbusters coming closest with 'She's the One' (peak position No. 33). For a coherent response to what was already being dubbed 'the British Invasion' of 1964, American teenagers had to wait until the final weeks of the year. The Gestures' 'Run Run Run' and the Beau Brummels' 'Laugh Laugh' grabbed the essentials of Merseybeat, and smoothed them into sophisticated fare for the world's leading consumer economy.

Then, in March 1965, the leading protagonist of the folk protest movement issued a rock 'n' roll single which merged beatnik poetry with nihilistic philosophy. Even the title of Bob Dylan's 'Subterranean Homesick Blues' sounded subversive. It utilised language that had never appeared in any pop song – words such as 'government', 'medicine' and 'No-Doz' (caffeine tablets). Its moral was simple: don't trust any form of authority except Dylan's. 'It's taken over the radio stations', declared Columbia Records. 'It's a sellout in record stores from coast to coast.' As a psychologist noted: '[Dylan], as a personality, has captured a cult and unwittingly made himself a leader. His clothes are copied by thousands, his roving way of life envied. But more important, the message in his songs (against injustice and for the dignity of man) is being embraced by a generation so often accused of indifference by parents. Sorry, parents, but your generation never produced lyrics like these.' In two minutes, Dylan had exploded all the conventions of popular music, ready to rebuild the edifice in his own mercurial image.

I reckon the Beatles have wider acceptance now. They're liked by older people. We could never hope for such acceptance.
  Mick Jagger, February 1964

[The Stones] are probably the coolest, most undemonstrative bunch who ever got together. And not even with your tongue in your cheek could you call them well dressed. Their clothes are not just casual – they positively don't care.
  Records magazine, May 1964

The success of the Beatles, said sociologist David Riesman in February 1964, was 'a form of protest against the adult world'. That month, adults were enjoying the music of Andy Williams, the Singing Nun, Henry Mancini and the original cast album for the show *Hello, Dolly!*. A week later, 'March is Mantovani Month', declared London Records, while Decca chose to revive the 1930s dance bands. Then: insanity.

America lost its mind over the Beatles, with politicians vying to be photographed in moptop wigs and celebrities besieging promoters for complimentary tickets to their New York debut. Perhaps symbolically, the week that the Beatles entered the American charts, Elvis Presley was widely reported to have been killed in a car crash. Within weeks, Presley's one-time rivals Bill Haley & His Comets had donned Beatles hairpieces and filled their stage repertoire with Lennon/McCartney songs.

The group's impact can be measured by the speed with which acts who had previously regarded the teenage market as anathema clamoured to acknowledge the Beatles' existence. Mantovani managed to hold youth at bay until 1966, when he finally succumbed to the melodic charms of Paul McCartney's 'Yesterday'; but by June 1964 Arthur Fiedler's Boston Pops Orchestra ('I Want to Hold Your Hand') and Stu Phillips's Hollyridge Strings ('All My Loving') were offering up Beatles songs as easy listening. Indeed, Phillips hastily concocted an entire album of such delights. 'To many, the tunes have never sounded so good,' *Billboard* exclaimed, 'in all their majestic string and muted brass splendour.' *The Beatles Song Book* sold in such quantities that Phillips prepared a second collection, alongside LP-length tributes to the Four Seasons, Beach Boys and Elvis Presley. Bob Leaper arranged *Big Band Beatle Songs* later in the year. The Golden Gate Strings were impressively quick to recognise the potential of *The Bob Dylan Song Book* in 1965, released while 'Subterranean Homesick Blues' was still in the charts. Joshua Rifkin and the New Renaissance Society, respectively, shepherded the Beatles and the Rolling Stones into the bygone world of the baroque; jazz guitarist Joe Pass swallowed his pride for an album entitled *The Stones Jazz*; and by 1967 there were several full-length orchestral tributes to the Monkees, and one to John Sebastian of the Lovin' Spoonful.

Such projects marked a belated attempt to recreate the one-nation audience of the past: to unify parent and child on vaguely neutral territory. Easy-listening artists were extending their commercial life by widening their repertoire beyond a predictable canon of Broadway standards; they also imagined they were preparing the teenagers of 1964 for the more sedate pleasures of adulthood. The most urgent impulse, however, was naked commercialism: this was a social phenomenon which nobody could afford to ignore. It was a vintage era for exploitation. Elvis Presley had been pop's first commodity, but the onslaught of ephemeral artefacts aimed at Beatles fans between 1963 and 1969 dwarfed every previous campaign. Once the love-crazed fan had purchased Beatles talcum powder and jewellery, Beatles pillowcases and sheets, Beatles stickers and badges, it was indeed possible that they might recklessly splash out on product as calculating as *The Chipmunks Sing the Beatles' Hits* or the pre-karaoke LP, *Sing a Song with the Beatles* (featuring 'Instrumental Background Recreations of Their Biggest Hits').

There was now a distinct teenage culture stoked by pop magazines and photo books, Top 40 radio stations blanketing the airwaves, even networked television shows on both sides of the Atlantic: *Top of the Pops* and *Shindig!, Ready, Steady, Go!* and *Hullabaloo*. Teenagers felt that they *owned* these programmes and publications, forgetting that they arrived via adult mediation. The process also worked in reverse, however, as teenage idols infiltrated adult media. The most powerful of these was, of course, television, which had extended its demographic reach (especially in the UK) since the white rock 'n' roll explosion of the mid-1950s. American audiences had been exposed to Elvis Presley, Jerry Lee Lewis and even Bo Diddley (but not Little Richard or Chuck Berry) via prime-time variety shows. British viewers witnessed Buddy Holly, Eddie Cochran and Gene Vincent on their screens. But none of those cameos could match the impact of the Beatles' appearances on *Sunday Night at the London Palladium* in October 1963, and *The Ed Sullivan Show* in February 1964. The first of those shows prompted the British press to coin the term 'Beatlemania' ('It was the last night of the Proms, and New Year's Eve in Trafalgar Square at midnight, all rolled into one'); while the second attracted what was then the biggest audience in US television history. Both were preceded by hyperbolic publicity: young people insisted their parents tune in, entailing that adults were fully exposed for the first time to the men who had kidnapped their children's minds. The mere fact that the Beatles had been invited on to such prestigious programmes smoothed their path to near-universal acceptance.

Such tactics convinced American parents and children alike that the only music worth hearing in 1964 was by British artists. First to benefit were the Dave Clark Five, whose foot-stomping, anthemic style was a throwback to the energy of the mid-1950s, packaged with contemporary finesse. The musical abilities of the group's drummer, and leader, have been questioned; but Dave Clark's skill as a businessman and publicist were incomparable. As early as March 1963, seven months before their first UK chart appearance, they won national attention when thousands of fans signed a petition demanding that the Mecca chain of ballrooms return the group to their home-town residency in Tottenham, after they had been transferred to Basildon. It was like the Beatles suddenly being exiled from the Cavern in Liverpool to the Black Cat Club in Sheffield – with the difference that Clark's quintet were regularly performing to several thousand people, not the 500 who squeezed into the Cavern basement. Once the DC5 began scoring hits, all of them featuring the thrillingly raw vocals of Mike Smith, and a percussive punch of which Phil Spector would have been proud, Clark's acumen came to the fore. He effectively managed his group, owned his publishing, oversaw the production of his records, won composer credit on almost all their songs, and secured an independent producer's deal with EMI whereby all rights to his recordings reverted to him after three years. Nobody in 1960s rock achieved such masterful control of all the mechanisms of fame. That grip extended to teenage girls: as one fan remarked of Clark, 'He's dreamy and has that little-boy look which makes me want to take him by the hand and walk him home.'

Once the Beatles and the DC5 had established a bridgehead, it was easy for other British acts to cross the Atlantic. Even groups who weren't successful at home, such as the Hullaballoos, could find a stateside audience. (Other avenues were open: the Scorpions, from Manchester, became huge stars in Holland.) America's frail grasp of British geography freed publicists to make wildly inaccurate claims, with the Beatles being credited for spreading the 'Thames beat' and London's DC5 offering 'The Mersey Sound with the Liverpool Beat'. In the era of James Bond and the Beatles, being English was suddenly very sexy, and independent producer Mickie Most capitalised with Herman's Hermits, fronted by a goofy 16-year-old singer. 'I thought Peter Noone looked very much like President Kennedy, and they'd make it big in the States because of that', Most recalled, and his instinct was unerring. Noone's cheeky-little-boy image quickly won over fans in Britain ('He's the sort of boy a girl could fall head over heels in love with, and find herself looking after') and America (where he was 'everybody's dream in the whole world'). The Hermits struck a golden vein of hit singles by reviving cockney music-hall tunes, which allowed them to show off their penchant for comedy. The same impulse saw the even more cartoon-like Freddie & the Dreamers transformed from lightweight British R&B band into pre-teen American heroes, with a level of success far beyond what they could achieve in Britain.

While Freddie Garrity was effectively the Norman Wisdom of pop, Noone and Clark extended the teen-idol syndrome that had existed since the late 1950s. When the Monkees were formed in 1966 to pose as a pop group for a US TV series, Davy Jones – like Noone, a baby-faced Mancunian of limited vocal means – was groomed to capture the hearts of young girls. This was an inexhaustible market, each new arrival sparking a renewed rush of hysteria. In 1970, for example, Bobby Sherman – who had been making records since 1964 – was suddenly reinvented as the heart-throb of every 12-year-girl in the United States, thanks to a combination of fresh-faced looks and a lead role on TV's comedy western series, *Here Come the Brides*. Whilst relishing his fame, Sherman expressed bemusement at the hysterical behaviour he was inspiring amongst girls barely out of kindergarten: 'When you see a six-year-old sitting in the front row, screaming and flashing the peace sign, it kind of scares you.' Or worse: Sherman suffered permanent hearing impairment from exposure to his shrieking fans.

Of all these acts, only the Beatles were able to sustain and even extend their audience as they progressed. The others enjoyed their year or three of intense fame, and were then thrown aside as easily as a broken toy. This even applied to the Monkees, whose intelligence and musical prowess were more substantial and subversive than their handlers had bargained for. Emerging just as the Beatles cast off their image as teen idols in preference for more adult preoccupations, the Monkees briefly made Beatlemania seem staid. The intensity of their success inspired a cartel of American businessmen to secure the rights to franchise teenage discotheques (or 'soft-drink nightclubs'), known as Monkees Clubs, across the nation. For $15,000, you could buy into a guaranteed money-machine, which would 'win you the devotion of the teenage market in your community . . . the possibilities for your growth as star-builder and successful nightclub owner are tremendous'.

Fans were sure to flock to your venue for 'an evening's live entertainment in an atmosphere that is "groovey", one where they feel "in", "together", "with it" . . . a place where they're treated right, enjoying kooky soft-drink and ice-cream concoctions'. Sadly, this scheme never extended beyond a single short-lived venue in New Jersey. Against all predictions, the Monkees themselves outlasted their spasm of TV-enhanced popularity, even surviving their self-destructive joy in satirising their own fame as it dissipated. Their 1968 movie *Head* was a masterpiece of psychedelic incoherence and ruthless self-sabotage. Together with their willingness to experiment with the Moog synthesiser and country rock, it won them retrospective acclaim, which would never be awarded to Herman's Hermits or Freddie & the Dreamers.

Other teen movies lacked the surrealism and iconoclasm of *Head*. They might be painfully idiotic (like the Dreamers' appearance in *Seaside Swingers*, or the Hermits' vehicle, *Hold On!*) or, almost by accident, capture the spirit of the age (as with the pop and pop-art pastiche of the Beatles' films, and the Dave Clark Five's *Catch Us If You Can*, with its satire on the advertising industry). The Rolling Stones would have been counted among their number, had any of their cinematic plans come to fruition. The most substantial would have involved the group starring in *Only Lovers Left Alive*, based on a 1964 fantasy novel in which teenagers were required to run the world. Later variants on the same theme, portraying the pop star as political messiah, included *Privilege* (1966) and *Wild in the Streets* (1968): perfect time capsules, but aesthetic disasters. By escaping this fate, the Rolling Stones kept their mystique intact, enabling Mick Jagger to subvert the messianic role in *Performance* (also shot in 1968).

As Brian Jones noted in early 1964, parents would change the TV channel to let their children watch the Beatles, but not the Rolling Stones. 'When they are accepted by adults, the Rolling Stones should start worrying', advised *Melody Maker*'s Ray Coleman. 'Young fans, who make up the bulk of the pop market for beat groups, could react against them if their elders condone them.' The Stones' US record company reinforced this image: 'They're great! They're outrageous! They're rebels!', before adding a note to record stores: 'They sell!' (But not immediately in America, where their first tour was near-shambolic.) Even in Britain, pundits predicted their imminent demise. Their appearance on BBC TV's *Juke Box Jury*, on which the Beatles had shone several months earlier, was dismissed as 'inarticulate', 'childish', 'incoherent' and 'a disgusting exhibition'. 'Elvis has proved he has real lasting power, but where will the Stones be in five years' time?', asked the pop paper *Disc* in 1964. A measure of compensation came from an insightful *Melody Maker* report, which concluded that although the Stones could not match the parental appeal of the Beatles, 'they have caught the imagination and minds of a huge section of Britain's fans. For the Stones have become a way of life, not just a beat group.'

What did that way of life encompass? Adult derision, teenage alienation, a refusal to conform to societal expectations, outlandish appearance – every badge worn proudly by James Dean, multiplied by five, and then exploded into new dimensions by the visceral punch of their music. If the Dave Clark Five's 'Do You Love Me' and 'Glad All Over' forced a teenager's body to move, then the Rolling Stones' 'Not Fade Away' – arguably, as of February 1964, the most aggressive hit in the history of popular music – encouraged a ritualistic shedding of inhibitions. Its sexual message was scarcely veiled, and brazenly rapacious. The erotic urges of pubescent boys were now being expressed openly, in the thrust of an electric guitar and the swaggering egotism of a voice: alternately frantic and controlled, with the artfulness of the practised tease, on the Mojos' 'Everything's Alright'; pulsating with spasms of sexual ecstasy, on the Kinks' primeval 'You Really Got Me'; ultimately, as the year ended, near-psychopathic, with Them's 'Baby Please Don't Go' and the Pretty Things' 'Don't Bring Me Down'. There was no respite in 1965, as the adolescent confusion of the Who's 'I Can't Explain' led inexorably to the Rolling Stones' taboo-shattering 'Satisfaction', which stared morality, decency and convention square in the face – and knocked them all aside. And every one of these records reached the British Top 10, aided by airplay from the so-called pirate radio stations moored precariously offshore, whose playlists were markedly more youthful and adventurous than the BBC's.

As the walls fell, the sonic weapons being employed by young musicians grew ever more inventive. The journalist Ed Ward reflected in 1968, 'Suddenly popular music was faced with an infinite number of new ways of reaching the emotions through the tension/release methods of noise and music.' The Kinks explored the limits of power and distortion; meanwhile, their leader, Ray Davies, declared his love for the musical drone he'd heard in Indian restaurants, and raced his rivals to place that noise on to vinyl. John Lennon conjured an eerie whine of guitar feedback from his amplifier to open 'I Feel Fine' (an effect idiotically explained at the time as a mistake), and Pete Townshend of the Who channelled the howl of feedback into an emotional weapon. The Yardbirds edged closer to a dislocation of the senses on 'For Your Love', after which guitarist Eric Clapton left the group. 'Why is it criminal to be successful?', he had asked rhetorically in November 1964, before deciding that he preferred to be unsuccessful and play the blues. The Beatles toyed with the conventions of pop by fading their US single 'Eight Days a Week' in, rather than out, as was the custom. And a group called the Supremes aped this experimentation with the opening seconds of 'Stop! In the Name of Love', which sounded like a robot being awakened and then exploding into life. Yet they alone deviated from the nonconformist norm: they were black, American, and had no intention of upsetting anyone's parents.

⚡

CHAPTER 17

HIGH
LIFE

'[They're] the undisputed rulers in teenage record-dom –
even hotter than the Beatles.'

   Ebony magazine on the Supremes, June 1965

'Motown is black music but not soul music. Its appeal is aimed
as much at the white audience as it is at the black one.'

   Rolling Stone magazine, December 1967

'We call it sweet music', said Diana Ross of the Supremes' sound in 1965 – presumably ignorant of the pre-war rivalry between 'sweet' and 'hot' jazz. But definitions were fluid, and confusing. The Supremes' boss, Motown Records founder Berry Gordy, claimed his artists were delivering 'The Sound of Young America', black, white, Latin, or Asian. Black stations were playing the work of white 'blue-eyed soul [brothers]', such as the Righteous Brothers, whose epic 'You've Lost That Lovin' Feelin'' epitomised the genre. One New York R&B station even added the Beatles' performance of 'Yesterday' to its playlist, 'because Paul McCartney puts a lot of soul into the song'. Black listeners were buying Bob Dylan and the Rolling Stones, while their white counterparts were snapping up Wilson Pickett, Otis Redding and the Motown stable.

Assimilation was the apparent goal of American society in 1965, the year when the Voting Rights Act – following hard on the Civil Rights Act of 1964, which ostensibly outlawed racial discrimination in America – finally enacted one of the aims of the protest movement that had swept the nation over the previous decade. It gave all black citizens the right to vote (and the right to be able to *register* to vote, this still being a subject of contention in twenty-first-century America). Assimilation was certainly high on the agenda of Berry Gordy, who had unashamedly established his web of record companies (besides Motown, there was Tamla, Gordy and soon Soul, too) as a black-owned corporation. But he was not afraid to hire white staff, or indeed an occasional white artist.

By pursuing the whole of American society, and then rolling out that strategy around the world, Gordy was hoping to reach an audience which would even extend beyond that of the Beatles. Hence his concentration on the Supremes, who achieved eleven No. 1 singles on the US pop charts in just over four years. Tellingly, only six of those eleven reached the same heights on the R&B listing, illustrating how quickly African-Americans grew suspicious of the Supremes' slick, sweetened sound. In interviews, the carefully groomed and chaperoned group consistently stressed the importance of 'glamour'. Motown insisted that all their acts study etiquette, to avoid upsetting any sector of the market.

While the mid-1960s hits by the Supremes and other Motown

acts were cut from almost identical cloth for Top 40 radio, their albums and concert schedules revealed Gordy's desire to capture an audience that was not only white, but adult. Almost all of the stable's best-selling artists recorded albums of standards (it was all Marvin Gaye ever wanted to do); they were booked into plush cabaret venues in Hollywood, New York and London; and on their frequent television appearances they leavened their teen fodder with a song from *West Side Story*, *The Sound of Music* or *Mame*. Gordy was delighted when the Supremes won a review like this in 1965: 'While the Supremes will probably keep their teen-age following for some time, there appears little question that the act will last a lot longer as staple adult fare, not too dependent on the chart position of their latest single.'

But Motown had more substantial achievements to trumpet. Gordy had created an entire roster of stars from the black community of Detroit, and encouraged, cajoled and threatened his staff, front- and back-line, to maintain more than a decade of consistent hits and constant, if subtle, innovation. He carried the quality control of the Motor City's flour-ishing automobile factories into the music business, subjecting even his most prestigious stars, and brilliant writer/producers, to the same stringent checks and restraints. Nothing escaped his attention, at least until he left Detroit to establish a new Motown empire in Hollywood. Ultimately, by using the same tight-knit group of musicians, composers, arrangers and producers for almost every record, and concentrating his attention on the 'Hitsville USA' studio complex on Detroit's West Grand Boulevard, Gordy created an instantly recognisable Motown sound – so distinctive that as early as 1965 his prime creative team, Holland/Dozier/Holland, could satirise themselves on the Four Tops' 'It's the Same Old Song'.

That creative trio was responsible for the Tops, the Supremes and a dozen other acts during their 1964–7 commercial peak. Their skill – or curse – was to force everyone into the same mould: jazz fan Marvin Gaye, teenage girl groups, the muscular male combinations of the Four Tops and the Temptations, even the doo-wop-rooted Miracles. Each lead voice regis-tered a unique personality, and when Miracles frontman Smokey Robinson, Gordy's first sidekick, was let loose in the studio, whichever act he handled suddenly found themselves gifted with seductive melodies and intricate, emotionally charged wordplay worthy of Cole Porter. But Smokey's subtle-ties were almost excess baggage within a formula so streamlined.

There was a delicious innocence to Motown's apprenticeship; a diversity of moods, too, with Brenda Holloway's 'Every Little Bit Hurts' coupling the agony of teen romance with bitter adult experience. Then Holland/Dozier/Holland stripped down the corporation to its commercial essentials, with the Supremes' 'Where Did Our Love Go' – percussive and repetitive, like the Dave Clark Five's early hits. The song repeated the same eight-bar pattern, over and over, but every bar held a hook – handclaps, stamping feet, finger-snaps – and through it all ran the pleading, little-girl-lost keen of Diana Ross's voice, her cohorts reduced to chirruping 'baby, baby' like automatons. And that was it: enough, with continuous refinement, to see the Supremes through several years of hits, and – with Levi Stubbs's guttural roar replacing Ross's lost little girl – the Four Tops too. Stubbs had gospel roots, and they showed; plus the Tops were grown men, and could handle something more world-weary and impassioned than the Supremes. But the rationale was the same: a dance beat, a chorus; ceaseless, hypnotic, irresistible.

Beyond Motown, black America was more open to diversity. In the words of Wilson Pickett's smash, it was still the 'Land of 1000 Dances'. There was a place where rhythm and blues met garage rock, and it was where Bob & Earl did the 'Harlem Shuffle', the Vibrations courted 'My Girl Sloopy', the 5 Du-Tones cried 'Shake a Tail Feather' – all black records from 1963, all immediately seized upon by white frat-rockers. After the Animals and the Moody Blues had borrowed contemporary soul hits, and the biracial instrumental unit, Booker T & the MGs, had mixed guitar distortion and R&B on 'Boot-Leg', the gulf between pop and soul had virtually disappeared. (Which is why trade paper *Billboard* abandoned its Rhythm and Blues chart for eighteen months from late 1963, believing it to be anachronistic.) While white acts purloined the best of contemporary R&B, soul stars raided the pop pantheon, easily twisting the Rolling Stones' 'Satisfaction' and the Beatles' 'Day Tripper' to their own shape.

There was one African-American doing what white copyists couldn't (although some tried): James Brown. A blues shouter and pleader in the mid-1950s, he had assembled the hardest, tightest, funkiest (in the new terminology) band in America, and a stage act that was thrillingly alive and impeccably choreographed. With 'Out of Sight' (1964), 'Papa's Got a Brand New Bag' (1965) and 'I Got You (I Feel Good)' (1965), he enacted a rhythmic revolution as profound as the invention of syncopation. His new bag entailed locked grooves, wound so tight that it was almost impossible to breathe; a skeletal frame, with the strength of a straitjacket and the sparse-ness of a bamboo cage; and space, disorderly and disconcerting, between phrases, around phrases, as the beat fell just before and just after the exact parameters of a 'Harlem Shuffle' or a 'Satisfaction'. It was like a magic trick, and it prompted movement that seemed impossible to master and then, with a shake of the hips, felt like the only rhythm that a sentient body could obey. This was funk music: an urgent future rapping at the door.

Among the first to answer the call, bizarrely, was Della Reese, a supper-club jazz singer. She borrowed 'It Was a Very Good Year' – a song first crooned by the Kingston Trio in 1961, then adopted as grizzled auto-biography by Frank Sinatra in 1965 – and took it up to Harlem, with chat-tering percussion, and a defiant vocal which suggested the best years were still to come. As indeed they were for James Brown, with 'Get it Together' in late 1967 pushing the polyrhythmic potential of his band to its edge. Over the next four years, he stripped decoration away from his music, subjugating everything to the groove.

There were other ways of extending the reach of black American music in the mid-1960s. Joe Tex (and later Isaac Hayes and Bobby Womack) brought the rap of the preacher – the preacher of love – into the heart of the music with 'Hold What You've Got'; this at a time when the only spoken voices on pop records were right-wing ideologues protesting against the sins of the young.* Shirley Ellis took the rhythm of playground games on to the dance floor, astounding the audience of TV's *Merv Griffin Show* by improvising her tongue-twisting verses. Sorrow enduring longer than joy, however, what lingered in the mid-1960s was the music known retrospectively as Southern or deep soul. Its territory was loss and heart-ache, often with a melody descending as fast as the singer's spirit. Once, the blues would have sufficed to contain that darkness; B. B. King's 'How Blue Can You Get' in 1963 was a last gasp of that tradition. But blues had become so stylised (as would deep soul itself) that it was difficult for it to convey anything beyond nostalgia. With the desolate landscape of 'I've Been Lovin' You Too Long' from 1965, Otis Redding retrieved the essence of the mid-1950s blues ballad and filled it with tense, brittle despair. Its knack of suspension – keeping time and destiny at a standstill – was repeated by Percy Sledge on 'When a Man Loves a Woman', and then turned on its head by Aretha Franklin in 1967, whose 'I Never Loved a Man (The Way I Love You)' offered the strongest female voice heard on record since the golden age of classic blues.

* Tex may have been inspired by Clarence Ashe's 1964 side 'Trouble I've Had', a lengthy blues narration about bad luck and hard times.

Three months later, she remodelled Otis Redding's 'Respect' as a proud demand for her dues – as a woman, naturally, but inescapably as an African-American too. There were urban riots in America every summer of the mid-1960s, almost always stoked by antagonism between the black community and the police. Malcolm X and Martin Luther King Jr were at odds over how to secure respect for their people; soon the Black Panther Party for Self-Determination proposed their own, more confrontational solution. Black singers refused to be silenced. Lena Horne's 'Now' (a cry for freedom set to the tune of 'Hava Negilah') was blacklisted in the weeks before JFK's assassination, and ignored afterwards. 'The lyrics are offensive', was one complaint; the song was 'too aggressive', because it demanded civil rights now, not in some fantasy land of the future; in any case, her record was 'out of the realm of entertainment'. Equally outspoken was another jazz-inspired singer, Nina Simone, to the extent that the magazine *Negro Digest* was perturbed: 'the introduction of what can only be called "militant soul music" comes as a shock . . . Fine, for civil rights – and we're all for civil rights, you bet! – but after a hard day's struggle, we like to have Nina to soothe us.' As the folk protest tradition surged into the pop mainstream during that summer of 1965, this would become a familiar call: keep music and politics apart.

There were civil-rights soul anthems which aroused less disquiet, because they were more subtle, to the point of disguise. Curtis Mayfield's songs for the Impressions, including 'Keep on Pushing' and 'People Get Ready', mentioned no crusade by name – just as Sam Cooke's final testament before his murder in late 1964, 'A Change is Gonna Come', could be interpreted as a cry of one man's heart, rather than an entire race. Stevie Wonder, just 16 years old, stepped closer than any other Motown act to the front line by recording Bob Dylan's 'Blowin' in the Wind' in 1966, at a time when both Joe Tex and Mike Williams were singing about the plight of the black soldier sent to fight in Vietnam. Every note squealed or played by James Brown screamed for black civil rights, but his most political statement that year was a gentle warning to schoolkids: 'Don't Be a Drop-Out'. This was a popular theme for black singers who wanted to prove their worth to white society, demonstrating that they could be principled without being militant. In 1968, after the assassination of Dr King, after shootings of activists and Black Panthers, after it became obvious that African-Americans were being selected for Vietnam ahead of their white contemporaries, James Brown finally came clean. 'Say It Loud (I'm Black and I'm

Proud)' was a sonic as well as a political landmark. 'We won't quit moving till we get what we deserve', he promised; and however you interpreted that phrase, he kept to his word.

> We have found that the African is pathetically incapable of defending his own culture, and indeed is largely indifferent to its fate.
> English folklorist Hugh Tracey, 1954

> I said to myself, 'I have to be very original and clear myself from shit . . . I must identify myself with Africa. Then I will have an identity.'
> Fela Anikulapo Kuti, 1966

In the early 1950s, ethnomusicologists from Britain and Europe ventured into the heart of Africa to recover its native music. Just like their predecessors in North America and rural England, they found that traditional cultures had been infiltrated and mutated by outside influences. Hugh Tracey believed the music of the Bantu-speaking tribes was 'in decay'; while Ulli Beier lamented that among the Yoruba of Nigeria, 'In January 1955, all children aged 6 will be sent to school compulsorily; and the talking drum is *not* on the new curriculum.'

Instead, much of Africa was in thrall to the electric guitar and the rhythms of Latin America and the Caribbean. One of the unforeseen consequences of colonialism was the migration of cultural influences, which carried the Cuban rumba to Africa, while bringing the highlife sound of West Africa to London's R&B clubs. The very term 'highlife' had satirical and political connotations: it was a way of claiming a sense of class for ordinary people, who could only watch from outside as government officials mingled with European visitors at state banquets and garden parties. The rhythms of the Caribbean and Africa mingled to produce a music that moved with a gentle lyricism at odds with the beat of the American continents. There were regional and national variations, each country spawning its own brand of popular music and its local heroes. But the hypnotic, repeated patterns of an electric guitar, changing chord with timekeeping that was constantly surprising to the First World ear, was distinctively African, whether it hailed from Nigeria, the Congo (Africa's pop powerhouse, because it boasted the largest concentration of recording studios) or South Africa.

Highlife itself crossed many borders, as the music of parties and dance halls. Besides Latin imports, it reflected the lilt of calypso; even, on occasions, a hint of jazz in its constant use of horns. Songs might be sung in French or English, or more often in the tongues of African tribes. Nigeria also spawned a hybrid style named juju; while South Africa produced kwela, with rhythmic similarities to the American twist. From Congo came soukous, introducing political and social commentary to the dance. As each nation secured independence during the 1950s and 60s, there would be a spark of enthusiasm for deep-rooted musical traditions, and a desire to rid their music of any Western influences. Aside from an occasional novelty hit, however, such as 1958's 'Tom Hark', none of this constant reinvention of African popular music was visible in Britain or America. Regional stars such as Jean Bosco Mwenda, Tabu Ley Rochereau, E. T. Mensah, I. K. Dairo and Edouard Masengo were unknown outside Africa. On the rare occasions when Africans travelled to the West, their audience was restricted to other emigrants from the continent; or, as when the young Fela Kuti formed a London band named the Koola Lobitos with Caribbean newcomers, the West Indian community. Only one black African succeeded in infiltrating the British beat scene: percussionist Speedy Acquaye, who spent four years with Georgie Fame's Blue Flames, playing for both white and black audiences at clubs such as the Flamingo.

The Flamingo was also a hotbed of Jamaican ska – another music which proudly displayed its working-class origins. 'Ska was typically frowned upon by the middle- and upper-class elite,' wrote David Katz, 'due to its uncouth ghetto connotations.' As bandleader and entrepreneur Byron Lee remembered, 'It was not played on the radio stations, because they wouldn't accept the quality – the guitars were out of tune, the records were hop, skip and jump.' In 1962, Lee staged a presentation called *Ska Goes Uptown* at the Glass Bucket Club in the Jamaican capital, Kingston. The same year, Lee and his Dragonaires took part in the filming of the first James Bond movie, *Dr No*. By 1964, after Millie Small's 'My Boy Lollipop' had become a global hit, she joined Lee and other ska pioneers at the World's Fair in New York. Madison Avenue advertising agencies thought that they had spotted a second bossa nova: an ethnic musical craze which could be translated into a lifestyle choice for wealthy Americans. But they misunderstood the rationale behind a genre that was rooted in Jamaican independence, black pride, and a spiritual connection with Africa.

Jamaica's status as a holiday destination for rich Americans, and its British colonial legacy, ensured that the Caribbean island maintained a network of luxury hotels and chic nightclubs. Barred from participating in this hedonism, Jamaica's black inhabitants (few of whom owned radio sets in the 1950s) depended on sound systems for their entertainment. These temples to electrical amplification could be found in the city or the country; in fixed locations or carried on the backs of trucks; anywhere a crowd might gather for music and dancing. They were owned and operated by entrepreneurs who could be showmen, gangsters – or both. In the late 1940s and early 1950s, their fodder was American R&B. Operators would compete to discover the hottest sounds from Louisiana or Texas, and then try to obscure the identity of what they'd found from their competitors. Their shows might incorporate talent contests for local teenagers; or the operator might stamp his authority on the music with the way he would talk over the records, interacting with the recorded sounds like a jazzman jamming with a band.

To ensure exclusivity, many operators began to experiment with primitive recording studios, where they could cut songs that they knew their rivals would not be able to play. Originally, these R&B sides – soon dubbed Jamaican boogie – were preserved only on acetate discs, for the solitary use of one sound system. But from 1956 onwards, when Laurel Aitken recorded the first in a long series of boogie hits, 'Roll Jordan Roll', they were made for commercial exploitation. Raucous and frequently chaotic, as if they'd been cut in a single drunken take at gunpoint, the Jamaican boogie hits added only the slightest hint of a Caribbean rhythm to the formula of New Orleans R&B. Gradually, as the island prepared for independence in 1962, it shed its reliance on the rhythms of America, and determined the pulse of its own future.

In musical terms, the change was subtle – and revolutionary. Musicians chose to accent the second and fourth beats of every bar; or rather, just behind those beats, adding the merest hint of delay to American syncopation. What emerged was a jerky, convulsive sense of timing, with dance moves to match. As described evocatively by ska performer Ezz Reco, they were reminiscent of Chubby Checker's account of the twist: 'It looks like somebody's sufferin', man. Imagine a man who has terrible tummy ache and a twitch at the same time, and he's just gotta move around to relieve the pain, and you will get the idea.' Trying to explain the beat to a British audience, a record company said ska had 'the insistent thrump of a locomotive tackling a gradient'.

Ska quickly became the common music of West Indian immigrants in Britain, but having shed its imperial rulers, Jamaica no longer needed British approval. Instead, many of its poorest inhabitants chose to identify with Africa. The focus of their adoration was Ras Tafari, alias Haile Selassie, emperor of Ethiopia – identified as a divinity, they believed, in the teachings of the Jamaican-born, pan-African orator and activist, Marcus Garvey. Rastafarian influence was first displayed in ska on the Folkes Brothers' 1960 hit 'Oh Carolina', through the unashamedly African burru drumming of Count Ossie – a style retrieved from slave tradition as an emblem of black solidarity. But the Jamaican folk style of mento (known locally as 'country music') had already produced its back-to-Africa anthems, notably Lord Lebby's 'Ethiopia' from 1955.

Thereafter, politics, religion and the ska tradition were rarely separated – not that most ska records touched overtly on such issues; they merely arose from the same social climate. In the early 1960s, Derrick Morgan's 'Forward March', the Maytals' 'Six or Seven Books', and 'Judge Not' by the teenage Bob Marley all evoked spiritual yearning and social upheaval, violent or otherwise. This was an era when ghetto discontent crossed with gang violence in the Kingston suburbs, as country boys who had been lured to the capital by the optimism of the independence crusade found only poverty awaiting them. 'Consequently', as Don Letts recounted, these so-called rude boys 'became outsiders and turned to crime to survive, whether on their own or with their street gangs'. Marley's group, the Wailers, were the first to confront this trend in song, commanding the rudies to 'Simmer Down' in a 1964 hit. For the remainder of the decade, Jamaican popular music was both enthralled by the gangsters, and anxious to find salvation without a gun.

Perhaps subdued by the weight of these problems, perhaps merely responding to the smothering heat of a freak summer, musicians and dancers slowed and refined the ska rhythm in the mid-1960s, into a style known as rocksteady. This emphasised the third beat of every bar with the 'one-drop' of a bass drum – creating a sound that allowed artists to be more soulful, more reflective; more sensuous, too, compared to the spasmodic sexuality of ska. It was a music which begged for harmony, as the sweet-soul groups of America (notably the Impressions) were reflected by the Maytals, the Wailers, the Paragons, the Melodians and their peers. Yet at the same time, it increasingly carried a message of civil rights also borrowed from America, preparing for the late 1960s transformation into the faster and often more militant groove of reggae.

While Jamaica established its musical identity with ska, rocksteady and reggae, many black African musicians chose to retain their allegiance to American R&B. Afrobeat was the name given to the blend of highlife, soul and funk which dominated the West African club scene in the latter half of the 1960s, thanks to pioneers such as Geraldo Pino from Sierra Leone. Fela Kuti from Nigeria mirrored Pino's example, until he experienced a musical revelation on a trip to Ghana: African musicians needed to make African music. But it was only when he visited New York in 1969, and was introduced to the writings of Malcolm X, that he felt able to step outside of the American tradition. 'I said to myself, "How do Africans sing songs?"', he recalled. 'They sing with chants.' He channelled this awareness into the creation of 'My Lady Frustration', its James Brown structure overlaid with a defiantly African feel: 'The whole club started jumping and everybody started dancing. I knew then I'd found the thing.' Like Jimmy Cliff and Bob Marley in Jamaica, he had hit upon a combination of dance music, cultural pride and political protest: music that would function on every level, reaching the head, the spirit and the body with different messages without ever losing touch with the eternal groove.

> We can make any location into a Discotheque in just three hours.
>   Seeburg advert, February 1965

> [LSD] is turning discos into freakish and often nightmarish places of entertainment . . . The music is a complex of sounds, all seemingly magnified a hundred times and building up to a climax which some people find brain-shattering.
>   *Rave* magazine on Hollywood discos, June 1966

When Smokey Robinson and the Miracles hymned 'a brand new place I've found' as the hottest dance venue in town, it was no accident that their anthem was called 'Going to a Go-Go'. That suffix – 'a Go-Go' – was first attached to a dance club in 1947, when Paul Pacine opened the Whisky à Gogo (which translates as 'Whisky galore!', borrowed from Compton Mackenzie's novel) in Paris. It was an attempt to milk the success of another venue, established under Nazi occupation in 1941 with the prophetic name of La Discothèque (or 'the record collection'). It played host to *zazous*, entertaining them in a secluded basement with the forbidden treasures of American swing.

There were similar clubs across France after the war, many bearing the 'a Gogo' name, most famously in the Riviera resort of Juan-les-Pins. As other entrepreneurs imitated Pacine's formula, he persuaded a Parisian scene-maker and chanteuse to front a club known as Chez Régine – which was frequented both by gamine actresses and ageing existentialists,* and became the Parisian home of the twist. By 1960, establishments that we would recognise today as discotheques were established in the world's major cities. Indeed, that year, a French emigrant opened an elite nightspot in New York entitled, simply, Le Club; with a door policy and prices designed to attract only Manhattan's smartest set. The nod to French sophistication seemed obligatory: London's first such venue, in Wardour Street, was called La Discotheque. But it was the 'à Gogo' (or, outside France, 'a-Go-Go') brand that spread most quickly, to Chicago, with its Bistro-a-Go-Go and Buccaneer-a-Go-Go, Hollywood's Sunset Strip, and thence around the world.

The French connection added a certain mystique to the formula of playing records while people consumed alcohol and danced. In 1965, jukebox manufacturers Seeburg set out to franchise the French discotheque across America, offering to supply an 'Instant Dance Club' package, complete with decorative wall panels. The music would be supplied by 'New Rec-O-Dance Albums' containing 'the most danceable tunes ever . . . to give the illusion of a live name band playing on the dance floor'. Some of these records featured anonymous covers of recent hits – by the Beatles, for example – alongside written-by-numbers dance material. Others, reflecting the expected age of the patrons, concentrated on familiar swing tunes, such as 'Moonlight Serenade' and 'Little Brown Jug'. Each record provided seven or eight minutes of continuous music per side. Professional bandleaders were quick to copy this approach, with *The Peter Duchin Discotheque Dance Party* LP from January 1965 setting adult hits such as 'Hello, Dolly!' to 'popular modern dances'.

One of Seeburg's chief rivals, Roure, countered the Instant Dance Club by hiring Killer Joe Piro, Atlantic recording artist and dance teacher to one of President Johnson's daughters, as their discotheque guru. 'Frug, Watusi, Mule – Suddenly Easy', promised his advertisements. 'Give Killer Joe Piro an evening, and he'll make you a Discotheque Dance Sensation!'

---

*There were unexpected liaisons between the two categories. For example, the writer Jean-Paul Sartre penned songs for the actress and chanteuse Juliette Greco.

Just as pre-war records had been classified by their dance step, so dancers were now informed that the Miracles' 'Going to a Go-Go' demanded the jerk and the Beatles' 'We Can Work it Out' the slop. The record business continued to turn out new dance crazes by the week. Chubby Checker mimicked Freddie Garrity's madcap stage movements with 'Do the Freddie', prompting Freddie & the Dreamers to reply with a song of the same name, which topped the US charts: this was the age of 'Freddie Beat', Americans were assured. Brazil was anxious to export its latest invention, the jequibau. In Europe, the dance sensation was the letkiss, alias the jenka, to which half a dozen countries laid claim. Stig Anderson of Polar Music in Sweden (better known in the 1970s as the manager of Abba) said that only his artists' records could provide the genuine jenka–letkiss sound, which was strikingly similar to the polka. France, ever willing to assert its individuality, responded with its own derivation, the monkiss. In West Germany, the prevailing dance of 1964 was still the twist. Here the government was so concerned about vandalism on the country's railway service that it experimented with running 'twist trains' for young people, with a section of each coach prepared as a dance floor, and twist music piped through the carriages. Mexico invented a dance called the go-go, and visiting rock 'n' rollers Bill Haley & His Comets were persuaded to concoct an album to file alongside their earlier Mexican twist records. An American band called the Warlocks tried without success to promote the temper tantrum: 'Stamp your feet, and claw the air, temper tantrum, anywhere', went the instructions, as if catering for all those who were overwhelmed by the rapid turnover in dance steps.

On the Sunset Strip, spiritual home of Los Angeles teenagers, California's hottest new bands inspired fans to frug or slop. The hippest joint on the Strip was Ciro's, where (as Byrds press agent Derek Taylor declared) 'There were queues up and down Sunset Strip of desperate teenagers, clamouring to get in. The dance floor was a madhouse. A hard core of Byrds followers – wayward painters, disinherited sons and heirs, bearded sculptors, misty-eyed nymphs and assorted oddballs – suddenly taught Hollywood to dance again.' *Billboard* magazine noted approvingly that 'The Byrds' sound combines falsetto voicings with blaring guitar chords and a rock bottom drum beat, all applicable for dancing'; while Bob Dylan's 'Like a Rolling Stone' was also, it claimed, 'aimed at the teen market with dance beat to boot'. The Lovin' Spoonful, a New York band, were soon rivalling the Byrds on the Strip, prompting industry insiders such as Phil

Spector to boogaloo and jerk. Concerned that they might be missing out on a commercial bonanza, MGM Records ordered their rock band Sam the Sham & the Pharaohs to take dancing lessons, warning England's Animals and Herman's Hermits that they would be next in line.

There were now dance halls on both American coasts which offered a steady diet of rock: the Happiness, the Cheetah, Ondine's and Murray the K's Place in New York; the Avalon and the Fillmore in San Francisco; more, soon, in every major city of the land. Some acts were so famous that they could fill theatres, arenas or even, after the Beatles appeared at New York's Shea Stadium in 1965, giant sports venues; the rest performed solely for dancers. Drugs were in the air, literally in the case of marijuana; and on small tabs of blotting paper, which could deliver a dose of a powerful hallucinogenic known as LSD. As the nascent hippie movement took flight, veteran beatniks and rock bands cohered in the West Coast's nightclubs and ballrooms, while the music expanded to mirror the enhanced psychological state of the audience. From two-minute R&B covers, the San Francisco bands were suddenly stretching 'Turn on Your Love Light' or 'Dancin' in the Street' out to ten, twelve minutes or more. This was a happening, indeed, the birth of an alternative culture, labelled with a word which came to encapsulate the acidic, liberated, chaotic vibe of the late 1960s: psychedelia.

↯

JEFFERSON AIRPLANE GRATEFUL DEAD
FRI 12 AUG · SAT 13 AUG
FILLMORE AUDITORIUM

TICKETS

GRATEFUL DEAD Photo by Herb Greene

SAN FRANCISCO: City Lights Bookstore; The Psychedelic Shop; Bally Lo (Union Square); The Town Squire (1318 Polk); Mnasidika (1510 Haight) BERKELEY: Campus Records; Discount Records; Shakespeare & Co. MILL VALLEY: The Mod Hatter SAUSALITO: The Tides Bookstore; Rexall Pharmacy.

CHAPTER 18

Freak out People

'Honesty, candour, frankness. Say what you mean and no
double-talk. These were the styles of living born of the pop
revolution. An end to evasion, fake attitudes, hypocrisy.'

Rave magazine, June 1965

'I was a freshman. It was so overwhelming that nobody went
to class. We were just roaming around, talking about this song.
I didn't know what Dylan was talking about in the song. But it
didn't matter. It just made you feel like you weren't alone –
that someone was speaking your language.'

Patti Smith on her first exposure to Bob Dylan's
'Like a Rolling Stone'

Although the Beatles' music grew more sophisticated during 1964, their lyrical approach barely altered. They offered, as a reviewer of their *A Hard Day's Night* album complained, 'a complete banality of sentiment. Throughout this set of lyrics, a two-syllable word is a rarity and any reference to real life is completely excluded.' As another critic adjudged the entire pop *oeuvre* of 1964, 'They all start with strumming guitars, and they all end with a fade-out. In between, people sing about love.'

Popular music did not have to be that way. Issued alongside *A Hard Day's Night* was an album by Bob Dylan, the title of which, *The Times They Are A-Changin'*, signalled his willingness to delve beneath the vicissitudes of teenage romance. It confronted racism, injustice, poverty, patriotism and hypocrisy, employing both political rhetoric and flamboyant lyricism to widen the vocabulary of the popular song. The pop paper *Disc* was entranced: Dylan, it proclaimed in July 1964, 'could be the biggest thing yet in show biz'.

The Beatles were admirers of Dylan and his work. 'I like his whole attitude,' George Harrison explained in January 1965, 'the way he dresses, the way he doesn't give a damn. The way he sings discords and plays discords.' John Lennon admitted that the title song for their movie was originally intended to sound like Dylan (by which he meant it was performed with acoustic guitars and harmonica), 'but we Beatle-ified it'.

One fan declared that 'The average pop-minded teenager hasn't the patience to listen to or understand Dylan. Dylan has no beat or party appeal, and he is best appreciated in solitude.' Yet in March, as the title song of *The Times They Are A-Changin'* was issued as a UK single, tickets for his British concerts quickly sold out. By May, that single had been joined in the charts by the taboo-busting 'Subterranean Homesick Blues', and four of his LPs: the bard of folk solipsism and, so it seemed, radical activism was now a genuine pop star. So popular was Dylan's material with other artists that his American record label launched an advertising campaign to insist: 'No One Sings Dylan Like Dylan'. All of those parents who compared Dylan's voice to (for example) 'a dying sheep' would not have disagreed.

The songwriter was now moving so quickly that his record company could not keep pace. No sooner had they released his *Bringing It*

All Back Home LP, with its imagistic ballads and rock 'n' roll instrumentation, than he was ready to surpass 'Subterranean Homesick Blues' with
arguably the most influential record in rock history: 'Like a Rolling Stone'.
'A six-minute single? Why not!', Columbia crowed, 'When you have six
minutes of Bob Dylan.' Yet the song's duration – it was the longest single
since the 'symphonic jazz' suites of the 1920s – was the least of its innovations. There was the sound, a mesh of instruments slightly at odds with
each other, boasting the consistency of molasses. The performance began
with the whip-crack of a snare drum which immediately snagged the
listener's attention. Then the vocal: intolerably weary yet driven with a
strange (chemical) life; simultaneously hectoring and exuberant, defeated
and urgent. And the words: well, they were enigmatic, surreal, designed to
scuff up a cloud of confusion, but there were hooks to grab hold of – references to school, and a chorus that called out to every alienated adolescent,
everyone who understood more than their parents, everyone who wanted
nothing more than to imagine themselves a Rolling Stone. Six minutes?
Why not, when it felt like the baptism of a new world?

In a review that was notable for reflecting every adult's reaction to
this generation-dividing cacophony, *Melody Maker*'s Bob Dawburn
managed one (almost) accurate statement: '"Like A Rolling Stone" will
offend the folk purists with its strings and electric guitars.' The strings were
a product of his imagination – testament to the sense of dislocation that
the song inspired. But with this record (if not the Chuck Berry-influenced
'Subterranean Homesick Blues') Dylan had indeed chosen to shock anyone
who believed that virtue and honesty could only be delivered by the rattle
of an acoustic guitar. As a result, he would be booed at that summer's
Newport Folk Festival, at sundry stops on an American tour, and then
systematically on a 1966 visit to the UK which was virtually a civil war
between rock and folk fans.

Few in popular music were ready to accompany him on this
journey. If his lyrics owed more to Allen Ginsberg and the decadent French
poets of the nineteenth century than to any precursor in pop, his sound was
indebted to the spontaneity of his musicians; and, before them, to the
inspiration of his peers. Dylan had relished the spring-water harmonies
and melodic verve of the Beatles; the Rolling Stones' ragged updating of
Chicago blues; and especially the Animals' achievement in borrowing
'House of the Rising Sun' from his own first album, and translating it into
liberating rock 'n' roll. Everything about Dylan screamed freedom, from

the chaotic howl and purr of his vocal delivery to the boundless vocabulary he commanded – which in time would persuade his less inspired peers that they too could toss together random images and call it art.

At the Troubadour in Hollywood, Dylan had played 'folk twist music' with a thirteen-piece band named the Men. Then he had met five young musicians named the Byrds, and heard their reinvention of his song 'Mr Tambourine Man' – stripped of three of its four verses, set to a Beatlesque beat, and crowned with soaring vocal harmonies and a twelve-string guitar which had the seductive charm of the Pied Piper's flute. It portrayed a zeitgeist which was only just emerging, but which the Byrds would help to perfect. The Byrds' music was acclaimed as folk rock, and a genre emerged to match the definition, as groups of young guitarists raided the Dylan catalogue in search of other hidden pop gems.

Alongside 'Like a Rolling Stone' in the charts of August 1965 was the Lovin' Spoonful's 'Do You Believe in Magic' – a spiritual song of joy for a generation who had grown up on rock 'n' roll, 'the magic that can set you free'. This was a step beyond 'Those Oldies But Goodies' and other paeans to the recent past: beyond nostalgia, moving into the realms of transcendence, it chimed perfectly with the inchoate quest for freedom shared by the audience songwriter John Sebastian was addressing. One of them was Paul Williams, a 17-year-old college student in Pennsylvania, whose passion for what he still called 'rock 'n' roll' was so intense – and, he felt, so ill-served by America's pop media – that he founded *Crawdaddy!*, 'a magazine of rock'n'roll criticism'. His desire was communication across a community of listeners, a community which as yet had no name or focus. In an early issue, he located his ideal audience: 'anyone with an interest in discussing the most exciting and alive music in the world today, music that is alive not because of its heavy beat but because of its fantastic inventive-ness, its ability to assimilate widely different styles of music, its freshness and awareness of a world other forms of music seem ready to desert'. Williams didn't create that audience, but he provided its first point of contact, at a time when Bob Dylan, the Beatles, the Rolling Stones and the Byrds, among many others, were beginning to explore themes utterly beyond the control of the music industry. In that instant, rock culture was born, confirming what a generation had already known instinctively but never put into words: listening to this music marked them out from those who didn't or wouldn't hear, and united them with everyone who shared the same nonconformist values.

Let South Africa run its own policies, that's my opinion.
Cliff Richard, 1965

Stars and celebrities should not try to set any level in morals. Who
are we to say what is right and what is wrong?
Mick Jagger, 1965

In the months after Nelson Mandela was sent to Robben Island in 1964, the politically naïve world of British pop tried to establish its moral principles. Until recently a member of the British Commonwealth, South Africa was a familiar venue for the UK's entertainment stars. Cliff Richard & the Shadows had made a triumphant visit there in 1961, the year after the Sharpeville massacre. They played to white audiences in the cities, and added two shows in the black townships. 'I have to say that the native servants seemed to be treated very well in the homes I visited', Cliff said on his return.

Two years later, the Trinidadian pianist Winifred Atwell was booked to appear in South Africa, but was persuaded by the Musicians' Union to abandon her trip. In 1964, trumpeter Eddie Calvert announced that he was unwilling to tour while the apartheid regime endured. The Beatles cancelled their tentative plans to perform in both South Africa and Israel, without explanation.* So the South African government entered into subterfuge, offering contracts to Adam Faith and Dusty Springfield which promised that they would perform to multiracial audiences. They arrived, to discover that only whites were allowed inside the concert halls. Faith returned home immediately, and was condemned for staging a publicity stunt. Springfield, who had once said 'I wish I'd been born coloured', arranged her own, unsegregated event, and was expelled from South Africa. Back in Britain, Peter & Gordon star Peter Asher accused her of making life more difficult for black South Africans. 'I don't really see that playing before segregated audiences means that you support segregation', he added.†

Individual gestures aside, there was no platform within British entertainment for a political stance. The BBC refused to broadcast Manfred

---

* John Lennon was criticised by black cultural commentators in 1965, after he told *Time* magazine: 'We can sing more coloured than the Africans.'
† In 1970, soul singer Percy Sledge toured South Africa. His show in Cape Town was ruled to be an event for non-whites only, so his white fans had to adopt blackface or masquerade as Muslims to gain admittance.

Mann's cover of Bob Dylan's 'With God on Our Side' in February 1965 because 'the song might offend people'. (It also banned the Earthlings' novelty song 'Landing of the Daleks', because the tune included a message to Doctor Who in Morse code: 'SOS, SOS – THE DALEKS HAVE LANDED'. This might, the BBC feared, alarm nervous listeners.) But the merging of rock 'n' roll and folk in 1965 allowed pop to become a debating chamber for social and political issues which ranged from the banal to the apocalyptic. Every nation seemed to have its Bob Dylan: Antoine in France; Nacho Mendez in Mexico; Raimon in Spain; Claude Dubois in Canada – all young, angry, politically committed, controversial.

Hair – its length and cleanliness, or otherwise – was a cause célèbre for the young pop star of the 1960s. The Beatles were lampooned and then loved for their moptops. The Rolling Stones' immaculately shiny locks were frequently described as 'filthy' in the press. An American teen magazine gasped in wonder at Jimi Hendrix's 'African bushman hairdo'. All of them helped to extend the boundaries for children and teenagers, very slowly acclimatising parents, teachers and bosses to the recognition that long hair did not automatically signify dirt, disobedience or delinquency. A couple named Sonny and Cher – effectively the first hippie pop stars, although no one recognised them as such – cornered the market for hirsute bravado in 1965. They claimed their rights to long hair on their worldwide No. 1 duet, 'I Got You Babe', and on Sonny's self-pitying solo single, 'Laugh at Me'. So perfectly did their blend of teen-beat and folk rock catch the moment that they registered six simultaneous hits on the American chart. So convincing was Sonny's adolescent alienation that it was sobering to remember he was already 30 years old.

'A song's lyrical content could become as respected as the dominating beat', one journalist noted with an air of bemusement in June 1965, to which Paul McCartney replied: 'Protest songs make me concentrate too much on the lyric, which I don't like.' But the equation of summer 1965 was, as *Billboard* magazine noted, 'Rock + Folk + Protest = An Erupting New Sound', which was 'selling big'. The first beat-group venture into protest was so subtle that it passed almost unnoticed: in 1964, the Searchers added strings and gentle electric backing to Malvina Reynolds's vision of a world after nuclear apocalypse, 'What Have They Done to the Rain?' (The Searchers' other records of that period, especially 'Needles and Pins' and 'When You Walk in the Room', paved the musical path for the folk-rock explosion of the Byrds.) Thereafter, pop played its protest cards more flamboyantly.

For an industry unused to youth speaking its mind, there was no difference between the pacifist anthems of a Joan Baez, the moral ambiguities posed by Bob Dylan, and the all-purpose nihilism of Barry McGuire's 'Eve of Destruction', a 1965 hit which was as poetic as a dictionary and was inevitably barred by the BBC as being 'not suitable for light entertainment'. McGuire was the target of an American military clampdown on records that might prove 'inimical to military morale', and were therefore lifted from forces' playlists and banned from sale in army stores. 'It is absurd to expect that we should encourage a situation whereby US soldiers handle nuclear weapons as part of their military duties,' a spokesman said, 'then spend their off-duty time listening to music telling them nuclear weapons are wicked.'

'Eve of Destruction' did not specifically mention the conflict in Vietnam, but as the mid-1960s progressed, a protest movement against American involvement in South East Asia became apparent across the Western world. It drew the cultural fault line of the decade, and not only in nations committed to the conflict. By 1970, rock was awash in anthems decrying the war, the single crusade that could command support from every element of the counter-culture. Yet in 1965, as America's troop deployments quickened, it was those standing behind government policy who held the stage. Country music, the voice of the white South, and traditionally a conservative bastion, provided a receptive market for songs supporting the troops. 'Vietnam Blues' described a veteran's incredulity as he returned from the front line to find his fellow countrymen demonstrating in favour of the Viet Cong who had been trying to take his life. It was written by a former soldier, Kris Kristofferson, later a stalwart of radical causes. By 1966, there were almost a hundred similar records on the market.

The most successful was a country song by Staff Sergeant Barry Sadler, in praise of the special forces of the United States Army. Sadler was already recognisable as the soldier pictured on the cover of Robin Moore's best-selling book *The Green Berets*. 'The Ballad of the Green Berets' added martial drums to a veteran's pride and became the biggest US hit of 1966, aided by RCA's most lavish publicity campaign since the launch of *South Pacific*. Within a month, Sadler's single and album (the latter including such songs as 'Saigon', 'Trooper's Lament' and 'Salute to the Nurses') were at the top of the Pop, Country, and Easy Listening charts. A German translation sung by Austrian troubadour Freddy Quinn was a huge hit in

West Germany, but banned in the East, though that didn't prevent it spreading by word of mouth behind the Iron Curtain.

The rock culture coalesced around more local concerns. A curfew on Sunset Strip inspired clashes between demonstrators and police, and a strangely ambiguous protest from the Buffalo Springfield, 'For What It's Worth'. Fifteen-year-old Janis Ian wrote 'Society's Child' about a relationship that crossed taboo racial boundaries. Less than a year into their career, the Monkees targeted their fans' parents on 'Pleasant Valley Sunday', a caricature of bourgeois complacency. America was edging closer to the social satire that had surfaced in Britain in 1965, when Ray Davies positioned himself between Dylan and Noël Coward as he lampooned 'A Well Respected Man' and the 'Dedicated Follower of Fashion'. He maintained an ironic stance towards the acceptance of pop, and pop stars, by the aristocracy and by the luminaries of what was known in 1966 as Swinging London. This media-hyped caricature of Britain's booming pop and fashion scenes suggested that the entire nation, rather than just a square mile of its capital, was spilling over with the equivalent of the 1920s Bright Young Things (or, as Ray Davies called them, 'the Carnebetian Army', after London's boutique-crammed Carnaby Street). For the remainder of the decade, Davies continued to explore tensions in the English class system, via songs of almost unbearably poignant lyricism which remained defiantly out of step with his peers.

The most intense pop furore of the mid-1960s was aroused when John Lennon commented on the decline of interest in Christianity amongst the young. His words were printed in the US teen magazine *Datebook*, which highlighted the line: 'We're more popular than Jesus now.' In an uncanny preview of the 'viral' madness of the Internet age, this statement raced across the country and was widely interpreted as being blasphemous. *Datebook*'s editor, Art Unger, attempted to defuse the controversy by suggesting: 'I believe it is good for American teenagers to read a point of view with which they have very little contact.' But an organised boycott amongst religious conservatives led to anti-Beatle demonstrations, well-publicised (but actually negligible) bonfires of the group's records and fan magazines, and sporadic radio boycotts of their music. It was a haunting moment for Lennon, who for the first time since he achieved stardom was forced to face the consequences of his actions. But the airplay bans, which began in Alabama, had little effect upon the sales of their latest single, which itself suggested that the group, and the audience, had changed. In what might almost have been a calculated attempt to broaden their appeal, the record combined 'Yellow Submarine', a children's song with a chorus that could easily be rewritten to fit any crusade, and 'Eleanor Rigby', a baroque ballad set to a string quartet. At once childlike and starkly adult, the new Beatles seemed to have nothing to say to teenagers, who could be forgiven for their bewilderment as their idols appeared, quite deliberately, to take leave of their senses.

> Everyone needs kicks . . . Drugs don't harm you. I *know*. I take them.
> Pete Townshend, 1966

> Most of the kids I know about who really sing hard rock . . . most of them are hooked on drugs, and that's a big price to pay to sound colored.
> Nina Simone, 1969

Like the rest of the pop press, the girls' paper *Honey* struggled to translate the changing face of pop culture into language appropriate for its vulnerable, school-age readership. 'Psychedelia! Wot's that? It's the new kind of music', it announced in February 1967. 'When you hear it, you're meant to "Freak Out" and that means have a spontaneous reaction, only we aren't quite sure what. Still, "Freak Out" parties are held, but we can't say exactly what happens because it all depends how the "Freak Out People" react to Psychedelic music.' Another paper, EMI's *Record Mail*, edged gingerly towards the truth: 'It involves an effect produced on the audience by the sounds of psychotic music and by unusual lighting effects intended to reproduce hallucinations experienced by scientists while under certain drugs.'

That was still deliberately misleading. It was not only scientists who were experimenting with 'certain drugs', but the people who were making, and buying, hit records; perhaps even the elder siblings of *Honey's* readers. Cannabis and marijuana had been available in Britain and America for many decades (the notorious 'jazz cigarette'), and had been used by musicians black and white since the 1920s. But now the almost noisome sweetness of cannabis smoke was everywhere while, more alarmingly, the 'psychotic' music of EMI's definition was being influenced by a hallucinogenic named LSD. This had spread from the American West Coast to

Europe in 1965, and was being consumed by many of music's most creative figures. (Heroin was widely believed to be favoured only by jazz artists, while cocaine only entered the public consciousness in the 1970s.) Within weeks of *Honey*'s article, 'psychedelic' had been adopted as a blanket description for any popular music that stepped beyond the parameters of 1964–5 – and, by 1967, that covered a multitude of artists, ranging from LSD-crazed madcaps to staid light orchestras searching for a vestige of contemporary appeal.

There was, the public were told, another strand to this psyche-delic mystery: the influence of the East. The drone that had so attracted Ray Davies had entered British pop in 1965 in the Kinks' 'See My Friends'; likewise the classical Indian instrument, the sitar, which was exposed on a series of songs by the Yardbirds, Beatles and Rolling Stones. 'Soon there'll be sounds that people have never dreamed of,' predicted Barry McGuire in 1965, 'the integration of Eastern and Western music. The Eastern scales and quarter-tones will integrate well with rock 'n' roll music. The Byrds, Beatles and others are already doing it.' George Harrison adopted Ravi Shankar as his guru, with the result that the rather appalled sitar maestro found himself performing to festival crowds of stoned hippies who could not distinguish between his tuning-up and his complex compositions.

The most striking reflection of Shankar's music in Western pop was also the single most profound step towards the psychedelic world. The Byrds' 'Eight Miles High', first recorded in late 1965, marked a startling advance from the gentle folk rock of their early records. Aside from the keyword 'high' (which Bob Dylan mistakenly believed he had already heard on the Beatles' 'I Want to Hold Your Hand'), its lyrics provided meta-phorical snapshots of the band's recent trip to Britain. But so compelling was the instrumentation – Jim McGuinn's lead guitar consciously channel-ling the spirits of Shankar and jazz saxophonist John Coltrane, David Crosby's staccato chords cutting across the rhythm like an urgent bulletin from the future – that it was possible to intuit the most narcotic of mean-ings into the entire package. (McGuinn still claims that the title was simply a reference to air travel, with no drug connotations.) Yet the Byrds' invita-tion to frolic in the new world was beaten into the marketplace by 'Kicks', Paul Revere & the Raiders' warning about the perils of taking a chemical 'magic carpet ride'. Thereafter there were drugs everywhere: playfully implicit on Bob Dylan's 'Rainy Day Women #12 & 35', heightening the multidimensionality of the Byrds' '5D', and blatantly referenced on the Rolling Stones' 'Mother's Little Helper' – although that song's narcotics were sedatives designed to ease adults through a troubled world (and were portrayed negatively) rather than hallucinogenic or hypnotic. Eventually LSD would provoke the Animals' Eric Burdon into renouncing 'all the good times that I wasted having good times' ('Good Times'): 'when I was drinking', he lamented, 'I could have been thinking'. Marijuana and cannabis would become as common among the young as was alcohol with their parents, especially in America. Only a self-styled elite initially sampled LSD, but when Paul McCartney admitted his own experiments, he aroused a flurry of criticism (less virulent, however, than when John Lennon had compared the Beatles with Jesus). The extent of rock's heroin use only became apparent at the end of the decade, when it claimed casualties such as Jimi Hendrix, Janis Joplin and Jim Morrison (although its exact role in all three deaths remains open to question). The publicity attached to all these drugs (and more) would attract the attention of the police, and lead from the mid-1960s onwards to the arrest – and occasionally imprisonment – of many musicians.

Equating drugs with psychedelia was simplistic and restrictive, however. What the psychedelic experience approached – and, for some people, drugs could hasten – was a state of deeper and more truthful perception; an openness to possibility; a rejection of fear, and authority; a surrender to freedom, to pleasure, to understanding, to love. All of these elements were crucial to the state of mind known (in shorthand) as 'the Sixties': the hippie ethos, visible on the streets of San Francisco, at gatherings in Golden Gate Park or at the first rock festivals, and across the cities and communes of the world. Vintage newsreels suggest that a state of universal oneness existed amongst young people during this halcyon age, although only a tiny minority of teenagers and post-teens took an active part in the surreal, bead-laden, trip-taking, flower-wearing hippie experience. But the soundtrack of that lifestyle was available to all.

Not that it was any more unified than its audience. There were certain artists, such as the Beatles and the Doors, whose music reached right across the youth spectrum in the late 1960s. But they were the exceptions. Some music evoked the institution of 'Hippie', with its rejection of adulthood and the bourgeois lifestyle (although most of its members were actually from bourgeois backgrounds). There was music that favoured ornamentation, cultural sampling, a leaning towards art – pop art, or collage, or a throwback to the baroque. Another strand prioritised the anxiety and repression of adolescence: turbulent, angry, nonconformist. And another placed politics above the psychedelic experience, believing that there could be no freedom for the individual without liberation for the oppressed: the Vietnamese, black Americans, eventually even women and homosexuals, although neither of those categories was uppermost in the concerns of the average rock star of the 1960s.

Few artists of note restricted themselves to any of these imaginary genres, especially when they were exploring the epic landscape of the long-playing record, which finally began to outsell the 45 rpm single as the 1960s neared their end. Increasingly, artists who concentrated on making albums began to devalue the single, although some of those who mastered the extended form continued to indulge the audience for the miniature (the Beatles, the Who and Jimi Hendrix, to choose but three). By 1969, however, almost every pop performer could be categorised as an albums or singles act, and by then the audience was dividing along similar lines. Singles were intended for those who either couldn't afford albums, or were looking for a quick hit of pop exuberance rather than a cultural education. Albums, meanwhile, were either aimed at adults from the pre-rock era, and were therefore an irrelevance to rock culture; or they were for the cognoscenti, the elite, the informed, alive and turned-on. Their cultural influence depended as much on their packaging as their music, not least because distinctive artwork could enable the enlightened owners to tote copies of *Blonde on Blonde*, *The Doors*, *Cheap Thrills* or *Let it Bleed* as proof of their hipness and intelligence, claiming the rebellious glamour of their idols as their own.

There's nothing going on [in the pop scene]. It will go on the same for years.
John Lennon, October 1965

As far as the Beatles are concerned, we can't just stop where we are, or there's nothing left to do. We can go on trying to make popular records and it can all get dead dull if we're not trying to expand at all and move on to other things.
Paul McCartney, April 1966

Two philosophies collided within the Beatles in the mid-1960s, almost without their protagonists being aware of what was happening. For John Lennon, rock 'n' roll had reached an acme of perfection in its initial burst of simplicity. As he said in 1970, 'I like rock 'n' roll, man – I don't like much else. That's the music that inspired me to play music. There's nothing conceptually better than rock 'n' roll. No group, be it Beatles, Dylan or Stones, has ever improved on [Jerry Lee Lewis's] "Whole Lotta Shakin'" for my money.' He added, significantly: 'Maybe I'm like our parents. That's my period. I dig it and I'll never leave it.'

Paul McCartney never denied the importance of rock 'n' roll in his life: like the other Beatles, he found comfort in the Little Richard and Elvis Presley songs they'd loved when they were 16. But unlike Lennon, he recognised that there was more, and that music he didn't yet know might unlock creative impulses that he could never have accessed by himself. So while Lennon sat in his suburban mansion fiddling with worthless electronic gadgets, McCartney embarked on a voyage of self-education, immersing himself in musical forms that the Beatles had always disregarded – the entire gamut of classical music, from plainsong to the avant-garde; electronic sound; jazz; the standards that his father loved. Lennon stood for the purity of rock, McCartney for ceaseless expansion. Ultimately, it was Lennon's impulse that would triumph, ensuring that he would be regarded by many as the archetypal rock star. But it was McCartney's ethos that was dominant during the second half of the 1960s, and sparked much of the music – from the Beatles and many others – that is remembered with such affection today.

The same dichotomy was expressed in emotional terms. Particularly after he met Yoko Ono, John Lennon prioritised (in his writing, if not his personal life) starkness, honesty and pain. The purpose of music was to heighten the intensity of the message, not to obscure it. For McCartney, music itself was the emotional conduit and words were there as decoration or elaboration. Moreover, he saw the process of making music as being, essentially, joyful – so the dominant emotions provoked by his music were positive. Once again, Lennon won the long-term battle: the prevailing themes of rock after the early 1970s were often anger, pain and self-pity; there was ample room for depression and pessimism in the canons of metal, punk, goth and grunge. But there would always be a demand for McCartney-style optimism from those who didn't inhabit the culture of rock. And for most of the 1960s, McCartney's ethos seemed unassailable, until the darkness took hold amidst political disappointment, spiritual despair and narcotic overload after 1969.

So the period between 1965 and 1968 was a rare – indeed, possibly unique – moment in the history of American and British popular music. It was a time when exploration and discovery were everything; when all border controls were lifted; when soft drugs, modern technology and hippie rhetoric combined to make pop musicians in their 20s feel that they could create the music of the spheres – or, as Phil Spector had once put it, 'little symphonies for the kids'.*

Ironically, Spector was an early casualty of the Era of Endless Dreams: too controlling, too wedded to the single gargantuan sound that was his trademark. He was tied, also, to the single rather than the album, which was a form he never understood. The true pop genius of the mid-1960s needed to be master of both, although their commercial imperatives could be starkly at odds. Some of the most notorious pop battles of the 1960s were conducted between idealistic musicians and the businessmen who had to finance their increasingly crazy ideas. That was simply one of the reasons why the most emblematic artist of this era was the Beach Boys' singer, composer, arranger and producer, Brian Wilson. He was besieged by negativity from his father, cousin and record company, all telling him to forget musical experimentation and maintain the teen-beat formula that had made them rich. He was also subjecting his frail psyche to an alarming regimen of unsupervised hallucinogenic drugs, while sustaining a creative burden which within the Beatles, for example, would have been shared by Lennon, McCartney, and record producer George Martin. With the Beach Boys' 1966 album *Pet Sounds* – teenage pop's first viable rival to the thematic records of Jean Shepard and Frank Sinatra – Wilson retained just enough of the group's natural effervescence to sustain their commercial appeal amidst his stunningly complex and baroque instrumental arrangements.† Their single 'Good Vibrations', constructed over six months of sessions at several California studios, succeeded on sheer daring alone in unifying a dozen different melodic fragments. But – like Stan Kenton's

---

* As an example of how far the music of 1966–7 could range, and still count as 'pop', compare Herman's Hermits' 'East-West' with the performance of the same name by the Paul Butterfield Blues Band.

† Another pop myth to question: Capitol Records did not sabotage the release of *Pet Sounds*, as the group came to believe. It was promoted just as heavily as any of their previous releases.

1944 single, 'Artistry in Rhythm' – 1967's 'Heroes and Villains' was a neck-lace of unlike jewels: each stone dazzling, their collective purpose unclear. The unfinished *Smile* album in which both singles would have played a key part was both an epic artistic quest and an almost deliberate step away from commercial responsibility. Had it been completed in 1967, rather than enjoying a surreal shadow-life as a myth, then its fate would likely have mirrored the album that attracted the most gushing reviews and the sparsest sales of any front-line product of the era: Van Dyke Parks's mannered, gem-like and utterly uncommercial album, *Song Cycle*.

Foremost among the artists who could sustain economic success, pop legitimacy and rock credibility in 1967 were the Beatles. Their first single that year demonstrated the extent of their musical progress, and the split in their creative partnership. Paul McCartney's 'Penny Lane' turned their shared Liverpool heritage into hippie legend; 'Strawberry Fields Forever' expressed John Lennon's complex psychological conundrums. If the former was pop art, creating multifaceted substance out of the everyday, the latter was art pop, self-consciously excluding the mass audience. 'Strawberry Fields Forever' was a stunning exhibition of pop's daredevilry and technological prowess, a milestone in Lennon's life of compulsive self-expression, and a breathtaking record. But it was not designed to engage its audience – unlike, for example, the *Sgt. Pepper* album, which opened with a direct message to the Beatles' fans: 'We'd like to take you home with us.'

Pepper was the biggest pop happening between the Beatles' first appearance on Ed Sullivan's show and the assassination of John Lennon. There are tales of people walking through San Francisco, New York, or London, hearing nothing but that album blasting from every open window. And if they are exaggerated, then it barely matters. Examined coldly today, much of the album seems threadbare and spiritually empty: a triumph of costume over content. At the time, its variegated sheen, stylistic diversity, melodic verve and spirit-of-Swinging-London packaging added up to An Event.

It symbolised an era – a year or so – when everything was epic (everything, that is, apart from Bob Dylan's *John Wesley Harding* album: Dylan hated *Pepper*'s pretensions). There was nothing that couldn't be enhanced by an orchestra, sound effects, backwards tapes, Indian instru-ments, abrupt shifts of key and time signature, distortion, noise, random conversation, throwbacks to the past, glimpses of the future. Not only did pop embrace postmodernism almost whole, chewing up its own history and spitting it out with LSD-inspired genius, but it carried the public along. Psychedelia (or a pop impression of it, short on drugs but long on orchestral budgets) was now the mainstream. To choose records almost at random: in the final months of 1967, the Who's 'I Can See For Miles', Sagittarius's 'My World Fell Down', the Buckinghams' 'Susan', the 5th Dimension's 'Carpet Man', the Rascals' 'It's Wonderful', Simon Dupree's 'Kites', the Bee Gees' 'World', the Hollies' 'King Midas in Reverse' and Keith West's 'Sam' all attempted to cram a lifetime of ideas, inventions and madness into one four-minute single, and achieved at least some degree of commercial recognition for doing so. Of these, 'Sam' was the most revelatory: it was the second excerpt from Mark Wirtz's *Teenage Opera*, an attempt to out-*Pepper Pepper* which, like the Beach Boys' *Smile*, was the musical equivalent of one of Orson Welles's grand conceptions of a film that could never be finished.

Many of these records carried rich and glorious banks of voices, and epitomised the outer limits of a style named only in retrospect: sunshine (or summer) pop. These were songs that captured all the delicious, foolish optimism of the era, and expressed it through God's gift of vocal harmony, wedded to celebratory melodies. The roots of this technicolour spasm of pop effulgence – aired around Britain by the newly opened national pop network, BBC Radio 1 – can be traced back to the Beach Boys, the Beatles, the commercial folk revival, even the easy-listening sounds of Ray Conniff and the French octet, the Swingle Singers. But its primary exponents, the Mamas & the Papas (all ex-folkies), were also hippies at heart, and their hit 'California Dreamin'' marked the first tentative step of the West Coast counter-culture into the mainstream.

Major sections of major US cities . . . have been literally occupied by a new breed of humanity characterised by boys who dress like girls and girls who dress like boys . . . they have come to listen to a complicated staccato of amplified sounds, played by artless adolescents who go by names that rarely belie their appearance.
University of California assistant dean Donald R. Hopkins, 1967

What we may be witnessing is the creation of a new, as yet unlabelled, form of music, as America around the turn of the century saw the development of jazz.
Harvey Pekar, *Down Beat*, 1968

The apotheosis of hippie was the Human Be-In at San Francisco's Golden Gate Park in January 1967. It was a 'Gathering of the Tribes': perhaps the last occasion when all the competing passions of the counter-culture could be indulged and accepted in the same congregation without factionalism or dissension. This was also a farewell to 'Hippie' as a lifestyle existing outside commercialism. By the summer of 1967, when Scott McKenzie's 'San Francisco' was topping sales charts around the world, the city's Haight-Ashbury district had become a zoo for tourists and drug casualties.

In musical terms, the Be-In spirit survived until the Monterey Pop Festival in June 1967. 'It was not the performances on stage which made the greatest impression on most of the veteran observers', one writer noted. 'It was the festival concept itself, and the total capturing of the very best in today's younger generation and those willing to accept its philosophies as an alternative to extinction.' The performers at Monterey ranged from Ravi Shankar to the Mamas & the Papas; from the Byrds to the virtually unknown (in the US) Jimi Hendrix.* Rock bands sampled elements of folk, soul, jazz, Latin and Indian sounds, chronicling drug trips and expansions of consciousness, and offering political harangues. Jimi Hendrix set fire to his instrument; 'his modal-tuned chicken-choke handling of the guitar doesn't indicate a strong talent, either', it seemed. And various San Francisco bands, from the strangely commercial (Jefferson Airplane) to the deter-minedly experimental (Grateful Dead) demonstrated why – in the words of the Doors' Jim Morrison – 'the West [Coast] is the best'.

If the baroque pop coming from Los Angeles, New York and London expanded conventional ideas of how a popular song should be arranged, the psychedelic rock of San Francisco – soon echoing around the global community – exploded the very nature of song itself. The West Coast bands retained their dance-hall ancestry as they set out on extended excursions into spontaneity. Their music mimicked, intentionally or other-wise, the vanishing sense of time experienced during an LSD trip, which is why a reviewer of the Grateful Dead at Monterey who wasn't indulging himself with acid could criticise their 'slipshod, lazy way to play music'. At their most courageous and/or self-indulgent, bands would set off into the

---

* The bill also included the Latin soul-influenced 19-year-old genius (I do not use the word lightly) Laura Nyro. Her set passed into rock history as an ill-judged disaster. The mesmerising footage of her 'Poverty Train' suggests otherwise.

unknown with no notion of a destination,* fuelled by the equally goal-free ambience of their crowd. As Eric Clapton, whose mid-1960s band Cream soon graduated from blues to equally lengthy excursions into the void, recalled in his autobiography: '[The audience] were listening, and that encouraged us to go places we'd never been before. We started doing extended solos, and were soon playing fewer and fewer songs but for much longer. We'd go off in our own directions, but sometimes we would hit these coincidental points in the music when we would all arrive at the same conclusion, be it a riff or a chord or just an idea, and we would jam on it for a little while and then go back into our own thing. I had never experienced anything like it.'

Clapton believed it was the intoxicating light shows of the era that transported the audience into a state of unity with the musicians. For Jim Morrison of the Doors, a band comprised of film and drama students, music, lights, theatre, drugs and a sense of community could transform the rock avatars into shamans – or transcendent actors from the ancient Greek theatre, liaising between mankind and the gods. Morrison wove teenage sexuality into his strange brew, eventually becoming so aroused by his power over an audience that he could only express it by revealing his penis onstage. But the most compelling, dangerous and ultimately tragic figure of this era was Jimi Hendrix. He'd escaped the drudgery of playing a supporting role to touring R&B stars, and travelled to London, where he was greeted as the 'Negro Bob Dylan'. Because he was black, he was initially marketed as 'Destined to become 67's Foremost Soul Exponent!' It took several months for his US label to comprehend that an African-American might appeal to the white rock audience. The stage theatrics he'd learned on the road thrilled his audiences, but devalued his music, as he was the first to realise. Yet fans felt cheated of the full Jimi Hendrix experience if he did not perform his hit singles, play his guitar behind his head and then ritually destroy it.

During 1967–8, Hendrix challenged and destroyed all preconceptions about the sonic limits of the guitar, creating a precise art form out of the chaos of amplifier feedback. His playing defied genre boundaries: he

---

* I once asked keyboardist Bruce Hornsby, who'd been guesting with a later incarnation of the Grateful Dead, how the band communicated with each other on stage. Were there agreed signals to announce a transition from one song to the next? Hornsby smiled, and said: 'If there *are* any signals, they've never told me what they are.'

simultaneously played rhythm and lead, rock, R&B, jazz, a wall of noise from which he could conjure moments of beauty or terror. His three albums, *Are You Experienced*, *Axis: Bold as Love* and *Electric Ladyland*, represented an almost unimaginably lavish fusion of commercial pop and experimental rock ... and then his magic dissipated into self-doubt, traitorous business manoeuvres and an anguished decline.

Hendrix enacted the hyperbole of one of the first rock historians, Arnold Shaw, who wrote ecstatically: 'We are in the midst of an electrical explosion of sound. Magnetic tape and electronics have made the 1960s an era of echo chambers, variable speeds and aleatory (chance) and programmed (computer) composition. New procedures include manipulation of texture as a developmental technique, "wall-of-sound" density and total enveloping sound. Philosophical as well as esthetic concepts underlie these developments: a concern with sensory overload as a means of liberating the self, expanding consciousness and rediscovering the world.' He added: 'We are in an era of meaningful lyrics, protesting, probing and poetic. But we are also in a period when sound itself, as in jazz but in a more complex way, frequently is theme and content. If the folk orientation of rock emphasises *meaning*, the psychedelic stresses tone color, texture, density and volume.'

The quest for perception and self-expression ran alongside the exploration of sound and musical form; indeed, the two were as one in the most ambitious music of the psychedelic era, as if musicians had suddenly been granted the fifth dimension referenced in the Byrds' song. No wonder that Apple Computer founder Steve Jobs said that 'It was like living at a time when Beethoven and Mozart were alive.' Yet in retrospect, Arnold Shaw's conclusion – published in 1969, just as its idealistic vision began to dissipate – is as sad as the swiftly fading memory of an ecstatic dream. 'At the moment,' he wrote, 'it appears that we are on the edge of a synthesis in which composers will create, not pop, not rock, not folk, not art, but music that will embody the best qualities of each – the involvement of folk, the exuberance of dance and the dimensions of art music.' Instead: ashes and dust.

One nation alone fulfilled Shaw's dream. The sequence of mid-1960s military coups which robbed bossa nova of its cultural base in Brazil triggered confusion among young musicians, at the moment when pop was undergoing its swiftest period of metamorphosis in Britain and America. The Jovem Guarda, or Young Guard, movement led by Roberto Carlos chose to place Brazil within that Anglo-American axis, as if the studio for ABC-TV's *Shindig!* had been transplanted to Rio de Janeiro. It greeted the summers of acid and student demonstrations with the teen-beat that had been the North American sound of 1963–4. Their musical rivals were both conservative, lamenting the use of electric instruments in Brazilian music, and progressive, in the quest for a return to democracy and their wish to expose military atrocities. They were grouped under the title of MPB (Musica Popula Brasiliera), offering misleadingly gentle acoustic music with a political bite – epitomised by Edu Lobo's 'Boranda', with its jazz-tinged vocal harmonies, and Geraldo Vandré's almost ethereal protest tune, 'Caminhando'.

For a generation of young performers who cohered in São Paulo after 1965, neither the MPB nor the Jovem Guarda was quite equal to the times. Gilberto Gil and Caetano Veloso, both in their early 20s, envisaged a music that could not only combine both approaches, but was also open to artistic influences of every kind – French new-wave cinema, experimental art, avant-garde poetry. They inaugurated a wide-ranging arts movement named Tropicália, or Tropicalismo, which took its name from an art installation by Hélio Oiticica. Gil and Veloso had already challenged the MPB establishment by reflecting the inspiration of contemporary rock. Now they masterminded an album entitled *Tropicália*, to raise the flag of nonconformism, joined by the psychedelic rock band Os Mutantes, Tom Zé and Gal Costa. Attempting to perform this material in public proved to be a confrontational act, as one report explained: 'The crowd eyes the long-haired, strangely dressed, foreign-looking Os Mutantes with suspicion. Backing Caetano Veloso on "E proibido proibir" ["It is forbidden to forbid"], the band launches into an amplified barrage of distorted noise that immediately elicits a hostile response from the audience, which begins to boo, and hurl tomatoes, grapes and wads of paper at the performers. Os Mutantes increases the distorted guitar attack in a defiant mocking of the spectators.'

While Os Mutantes concentrated on an oblique restating of late 1960s acid rock, Veloso and Gil – both of whom were jailed by the dictatorship, and then forced into exile – refused to be confined even by the symbols of freedom. Over the last forty-five years, they have ranged across almost every imaginable approach to song, to dance, to poetry; Gil the more physical in his approach to music, Veloso the more cerebral, both exploring simultaneously the popular and the experimental in ways which have won them the status of prophets in their homeland (and resulted in Gil being appointed the Brazilian Minister of Culture from 2003 to 2008). Like their contemporaries – Zé, Costa, Jorge Ben, Milton Nascimento, Maria Bethânia – they have kept alive a vision of music that can be both populist and driven by a firm aesthetic vision; both traditional, in its references back to the samba and bossa nova, and radical; uncompromising and yet subtle. Only the limited understanding of the Portuguese language outside its homelands has prevented them from being recognised as the true inheritors of the 1960s revolution in popular songwriting and record-making – guardians of the magical synthesis which Arnold Shaw had envisaged in 1969.

> If rock 'n' roll, with its heavy beats and nerve-tugging twangs and rhythmic grunts, ever invades the brain, the future indeed seems perilous.
> *Ebony* magazine, November 1965

> Apparently the Communists fear that beat music may be used as camouflage for anti-Communist demonstrations and resistance. The East German press has mounted a campaign claiming that young East Germans have gone from listening to beat groups to forming gangs which attack people in the street . . . *Neues Deutschland*, the Communist Party daily newspaper, argues that Ringo, John, Paul and George, in fact, are agents of the 'British imperialist secret service'.
> *Billboard* magazine, December 1965

Mick Jagger may not, as legend has it, have goose-stepped across the stage and offered the crowd a Nazi salute. But the Rolling Stones' guitarist, Brian Jones, did pay homage to Hitler as the group walked towards the stage of the Waldbühne, an open-air Berlin arena built at the dictator's request for the 1936 Olympics.* Even without a public gesture of contempt, their

---

* Jones later posed for a publicity photograph in a Nazi uniform, crushing a doll beneath one of his jackboots. 'The sense of it is that there is no sense in it at all', he explained gleefully.

September 1965 appearance in West Berlin was a riotous affair. Hundreds of fans clashed violently with police, cars were overturned, and trains vandalised.

Across the Wall, the Stones' impact was likened to that of 'a new Führer', the most vicious insult in the state armoury. The East German administration employed these disturbances to clamp down on a convulsive R&B band named the Butlers, who had built a substantial following during a brief period of artistic liberalism. Leipzig's city authorities forced the group to disband, and then trained water cannons on fans who gathered to protest the decision. The official East German record company ceased all distribution of pop recordings from the West, and performances by local musicians were monitored to prevent delinquency.

Had the Stones realised the consequences of their Berlin performance, they would probably have been elated to discover that both capitalist and Communist officials were equally concerned about the band's cultural power. The deafening volume of the mid-1960s rock bands, and their unrestrained theatrics, made violence seem like a natural constituent of the performance.* As the Who's Pete Townshend revealed, 'When I bash my guitar to pieces, I feel like I'm light and floating.' This transcendence threatened the status quo just as much as the mind expansion of illegal drugs.

By 1967, the Rolling Stones were evoking more complaints about their drug connections and sexual morality than for any propensity to violence. In their place, a young British group named the Move took firemen's axes to puppets and stage scenery. They were refused permission to dismember an effigy of the Devil during a church service in Birmingham Cathedral, to be televised by the BBC. Other British bands that year explored the potential of noise as a means of social control, or liberation. Early performances by Pink Floyd at the UFO club in London combined 'ear-splitting vibrations' and 'liquid light that takes your breath away', even before they had begun to assemble a repertoire of songs that dealt with sexual ambiguity and madness. (Pink Floyd's 'Arnold Layne' also

---

* The Who were the first rock group to admit the danger of loud music in confined spaces. 'It's beginning to affect our eardrums', Pete Townshend said in early 1966, while Roger Daltrey added: 'You'd be surprised how many people in groups get trouble with their hearing.' By 1967, doctors in the US were warning that music in nightclubs was 'very likely causing temporary or even permanent hearing loss'.

accompanied a London striptease artist who performed an 'LSD' routine while being bombarded with strobe-lighting effects.) American rock venues were equally charged with sound, light and confusion. Phil Spector – no stranger himself to sonic overload – described the sensory assault at the Winterland Ballroom in San Francisco as 'unbelievable' and 'suggested that all visitors to America be driven directly from the airport to the nearest psychedelic rock ballroom'. In response, chains of US radio stations launched a concerted campaign to ban any disc that reflected the moral ambiguity, latent violence and political subversion which they felt comprised the ethos of modern pop. No record would be played, they insisted, unless it was accompanied by 'a VALID and ACTUAL lyric sheet for both sides'. They concluded: 'Lyrics, song titles, offensive vocal sounds and even names of the performing groups have moved from the clever and creative to the crude and suggestive.'*

Crudeness and suggestiveness could come in many forms. 'Dirty Water' by the Standells, once a lightweight dance combo transformed by spring 1966 into a snarling garage-rock band, hymned the 'robbers and thieves' and 'frustrated women' to be found by the Charles River in Boston. 'Have you heard about the Strangler?', lead vocalist Dick Dodd (once a Mouseketeer on TV's *The Mickey Mouse Club*) shouted provocatively over the fade-out. 'I'm the man, I'm the man.' Here was the rock band as a tool of incoherent machismo, arrogant, angry, self-convinced, but essentially confused – adolescent, in other words, but 100% male. As, indeed, were all the other bands who would be retrospectively packaged into the same genre as the Standells: garage punk, it was called by the early 1970s, or simply punk rock.

That was the spirit of the stuttering narrator of the Who's 'My Generation'; of Jeff Beck's inflammatory guitar on the Yardbirds' mid-1960s records; of the whole band, surging and psychotic, on Them's 'Mystic Eyes', two minutes of flashing intensity retrieved from an epic studio improvisation. While the British garage punks were children of wartime

---

* So panic-stricken did these moral guardians become that rumours rapidly ballooned into facts. There was horror when it was suggested in early 1967 that some stations were in possession of a shocking new Beatles song called 'Suicide'. One of the ringleaders of the anti-smut campaign claimed to have seen the lyrics for the Beatles' soon-to-be-released 'A Day in the Life', including a reference to '40,000 purple hearts in one arm'. Neither the quotation nor the awareness of narcotic etiquette was accurate.

fear and austerity, fighting to escape from the grey conformism that was their generation's inheritance, their American equivalents were refugees from other kinds of emptiness: geographical isolation, meaningless consumerism, the looming threat of military service in Vietnam, ambition thwarted in the interests of mediocrity.

So it's not surprising that mock-Standells and mini-Stones, besotted with what they believed was happening in England, crawled out of every community in America, and could usually find a recording studio cheap enough to hire, and a local entrepreneur who dreamed that he might become the Brian Epstein of Idaho or Maine. This was another era, like the mid-1950s, when the amateurs seized control, and nobody in a suit understood what the kids wanted, or why. At its commercial peak, garage punk could load the US charts with such strange offerings as the Music Machine's 'Talk Talk' ('my social life's a DUD!'), the Electric Prunes' 'I Had Too Much to Dream Last Night' (a confusion of shuddering and surreal sound effects, to convey the epic pain of teenage romance) and the Magic Mushrooms' 'It's A-Happening' (nuclear apocalypse as acid trip, or vice versa). After which, inescapably, this road led once more to Jimi Hendrix.

This was the point at which conflicting urges – the confusion of adolescence, the wonder of psychedelic discovery and the consciousness of music's boundless power – collided, to provide what Donovan called (in 'Epistle to Dippy') 'elevator in the brain hotel'. Jefferson Airplane issued the command of the moment in 'White Rabbit': 'feed your head'.*

Even acts as self-consciously straight, in their off-the-peg hippie clothes, as the 5th Dimension ('Up, Up and Away') and the Supremes ('The Happening') caught the vibe. The Association, whose forte was polite harmonies and snapshots of love, offered 'Pandora's Golden Heebie Jeebies', a celebration of transcendent pantheism and sonic experiment-ation. The Beatles sent out a simplistic message to the world, 'All You Need is Love' – John Lennon delivering starry-eyed panaceas to his audience in a voice dripping with acid intensity. But for the people of 1967, the people who were living in this world, one record stopped time: Procol Harum's 'A Whiter Shade of Pale', with its blend of Bach and self-conscious 'poetry'.

---

* The Airplane's brain-food included arguably the least commercial hit record of 1967: 'Ballad of You and Me and Pooneil', in which A. A. Milne sat with Timothy Leary while feedback howled around their ears.

The Easybeats' 'Heaven and Hell' was being promoted as 'The Disco-Delic Subterranean Seismic Record Experience of the Year', but the Beatles thought that Procol Harum's single was more important than *Sgt. Pepper*: a glimpse of nirvana destined never to be repeated.

"You never heard it so good...

until you've heard RCA Stereo 8!"

Henry Mancini enjoys the sound of RCA Stereo 8 Cartridge Tapes both in the car and at home. And so will you! Either way, it's a dramatic new experience in great stereo listening that puts the world of music at your fingertips. Fabulous sound . . . easy to use . . . completely automatic . . . the world's most exciting entertainers . . . over 500 tapes to choose from—that's RCA Stereo 8 Cartridge Tape. Discover it soon!

RCA STEREO 8
CARTRIDGE TAPES
The most trusted name in sound

8-TRACK CARTRIDGE TAPE: THE **AUTOMATIC** SYSTEM AVAILABLE FOR HOME LISTENING THAT'S ALSO DETROIT-APPROVED FOR NEW CARS.

LISTEN TO "THE SANDY KOUFAX SHOW" WEEKENDS ON "MONITOR" ON NBC RADIO.

flying through the air

'We were asked not to excite audiences at concerts.
I announced a Beatles number at one show and the kids
rushed the stage. I was told I could certainly sing it, but
would I please not announce it.'

British singer Bobby Shafto on touring Romania, 1966

It was the perfect European hit: sung in Italian, by a native speaker who'd lived in Belgium since childhood; set to a Spanish dance rhythm; and a million-seller in Germany. The Europe-wide success of Rocco Granata's 'Marina' in 1959–60 emphasised that the Continent shared an international culture, which might find Greek singer Nana Mouskouri, the Italian starlet Mina, Siw Malmkvist ('The Girl from Sweden') and Danish teen idol Gitte all recording in German; or indeed, French, Italian or Spanish. Whatever their nationality and chosen tongue, their music enjoyed universal appeal across Europe – but only rarely translated to lands where English was the dominant language.

In return, Anglo-American stars accepted that they must abandon English if they wanted to conquer European hearts. With the exception of rock 'n' roll, the lyrics of which were assumed to be so nonsensical that they didn't require translation, most major US and UK hits of the 1950s and early 1960s were dubbed into at least one European language. Few artists shared the advantages of Petula Clark, whose husband and home were in France, and who had consequently mastered *français*. The rest had to struggle their way through phonetic transcriptions of their hits, without understanding the implications of what they were singing. (Via this process, David Bowie's eerie study of alienation, 'Space Oddity', emerged in Italy as a conventional tale of thwarted adolescent love.) Few, if any, English-language records were accepted in their original dialect.

Gradually, however, even France – the most independent of European cultures – succumbed to the charisma of Ray Charles, Elvis Presley and Cliff Richard. Its acceptance of the Beatles was even swifter: barely a month after Lucky Blondo ('J'ai un secret à te dire') and Claude François ('Des bises de moi pour toi') registered hits with Lennon/McCartney's 'Do You Want to Know a Secret' and 'From Me to You', the Beatles' own 'She Loves You' was on the French chart. Its success was aided by the fact that its famous chorus appeared to pay homage to the dominant local sound of the era: *yé-yé*.

The ingredients of this style were girls barely old enough to understand sex; chirruping background singers; and material that bounced with perky enthusiasm but never throbbed with passion. The effect was often banal, but it appealed to adolescents, and (for less salubrious reasons) rather older males. The princess of *yé-yé* was Sylvie Vartan, 17 years old when she played the Wendy Richard role to Frankie Jordan's Mike Sarne on the 1961 hit 'Panne d'essence'. Her solo debut, 'Quand le film est triste', was a classier affair, yet still scented with the same blend of innocence and unwitting sexuality that would make a British star out of Sandie Shaw. One man who understood precisely why *yé-yé* sold was Serge Gainsbourg, who took the even younger France Gall under his wing with fatherly care – and then gifted her a hit entitled 'Les sucettes'. Gall imagined she was singing about lollipops; the transparent innuendo of Gainsbourg's song suggested otherwise. As the decade progressed, the material he crafted for female artists such as Brigitte Bardot grew ever more risqué, and more symbolic, until he became pop's closest equivalent to Andy Warhol, a mirror for the ambiguous obsessions of a decadent society.

While *yé-yé* and Gainsbourg's sly eroticism (exemplified by 'Je t'aime . . . moi non plus') remain the dominant images of 1960s French pop in the English-speaking world, many of France's most ambitious talents of the decade – the likes of Michel Polnaroff and Jacques Dutronc – went unnoticed outside their homeland. Though they were creating a distinctively nationalist model of pop culture, the remainder of Europe was overcome by the desire to ape the tones of Liverpool and London. The craze for 'Beatle bands' even extended beyond the Iron Curtain, where Bulgaria's Bundaratsite, Czechoslovakia's Olympic (known locally as the Prague Beatles), Hungary's Illes and Poland's Czerwone Gitary (the Red Guitars) all capitalised on the absence of the authentic article. Another Polish rock singer, Czesław Niemen, satirised adult reactions to the *bitelsi* (Beatle fans), with 'Nie bądź taki bitels' ('Don't Be Such a Beatle'), which mimicked many of the Beatles' early musical trademarks.

Meanwhile, Western Europe was overrun by bands who dedicated themselves to providing local translations of contemporary Anglo-American hits, regardless of their genre. Los Mustangs from Spain launched themselves as Barcelona's version of the Shadows, and moved without hesitation through the Beatles' early catalogue to songs by the Kinks, Simon & Garfunkel and the Bee Gees. Of their contemporaries, Los Estudiantes waved the flag of surrender after they'd mastered the early Beatles sound; Los Shakers devoted themselves to tackling the entire Beatles catalogue until 1966; Los Brincos mined the summer pop seam with such enthusiasm that they were invited to record in England; and Los

Salvajes picked up where Los Estudiantes had abandoned the struggle, turning in valiant Spanish translations of 'Satisfaction' and '19th Nervous Breakdown' (alias 'La neurastenia'). The same story could be told in Italian, German and half a dozen other languages.

Yet the narrative altered in 1965, after which new bands – fired by the Rolling Stones and the Yardbirds, the Kinks and the Who, rather than the early Beatles – borrowed the techniques of British R&B and psychedelic pop. The most adventurous territory was Holland, home of 'Nederbeat', where the Jay Jays, the Golden Earrings, the Outsiders, Cuby & the Blizzards and Q65 crafted their own impressively raw brand of garage rock. While Dutch, Swedish and German bands kept pace with developments in London, their counterparts in Eastern Europe had to rely on singles smuggled across the political borders – with the result that they might be two or even three years late to react to each dazzling metamorphosis in English rock. Olympic in Prague mimicked the look of the Beatles' *Sgt. Pepper* album in 1967, but didn't respond to its aural influence until the end of the decade. Regardless of whether young musicians were in Madrid or Moscow, however, their culture now revolved around Britain and America, their own traditions trampled in the rush to imitate the Beatles or Bob Dylan.

Just as America had planted cultural flags in Britain and Europe with ragtime, jazz and the Hollywood movie, now the Anglo-American bloc invaded the Continent without the slightest show of resistance. Schools and colleges across Europe reported a dramatic rise in the numbers of students desperate to learn the English language, so that they could understand their new idols. (It helped that the early Beatles songs employed only the most basic vocabulary.) The Continent would never end its quest for local talent, but henceforth Britain and America mapped out the cultural landscape, which only the most courageous of performers would choose to evade.

Listening to it is like flying through the air.
American Record Guide review of a Herb Alpert & the Tijuana Brass LP, June 1966

I almost had my Mom and Dad thinking rock performers weren't so bad, when Cilla Black appeared on Johnny Carson's show. I

must say that even I was shocked at her appearance. Her skirt
was so short that really she didn't even need to have one on!
Letter from teenage reader to *Tiger Beat*, August 1966

The Beatles aside, the world's most popular singer in 1964–6 was Julie
Andrews, star of the movies *Mary Poppins* and *The Sound of Music*. The
soundtrack albums sold in their millions; indeed, *The Sound of Music*, which
was promoted as 'The happiest sound in all the world', was Britain's best-
selling LP of both 1965 and 1966. Appealing to people of all ages, they
were bursting with songs which anyone who was alive in their era (and
most born since then) can remember without a moment's hesitation. They
made no attempt to alter the culture, or educate the listener: their sole
purpose was entertainment. As such, they have been relegated to a footnote
in the history of popular music.

In February 1967, the Beatles' coupling of 'Penny Lane' and
'Strawberry Fields Forever' was the first of their singles in four years not to
top the British chart. It was held at bay – a landmark event, this, in our
received knowledge of the 1960s – by Engelbert Humperdinck's cover of
an American country standard, 'Release Me'. Engelbert was Gerry Dorsey,
an unsuccessful pop singer from the pre-Beatles era, reinvented as a
romantic icon for listeners of a certain age.

'Release Me' epitomised the so-called 'Nashville Sound' which
dominated country music throughout the decade, as lush strings and
chorales replaced the rural twang of a fiddle and a steel guitar. Country had
been devastated in the 1950s by the onset of rock 'n' roll. The Nashville
Sound was designed by guitarist/producer Chet Atkins as an antidote,
ensuring that artists such as Jim Reeves, Patsy Cline and Brenda Lee would
fit smoothly on to either pop or country radio. Reeves, who was killed in a
1964 plane crash, was perhaps the era's closest equivalent to the young
Bing Crosby, and his purring, mellifluous approach to a song ensured him
a vast posthumous following. Engelbert Humperdinck didn't attempt a
Southern drawl, but his audience recognised him as a kindred spirit to
Reeves, romantic and safe.

The triumph of 'Release Me' over 'Strawberry Fields Forever'
may have been iconic, in a negative sense, for anyone who identified with
the counter-culture. But it simply demonstrated that until the end of the
1960s, the singles market was not the sole prerogative of the young or
hip. At the height of the beat boom, comedian and crooner Ken Dodd

sold enormous quantities of his self-explanatory hits, 'Happiness' and 'Tears'. The Stones' 'Satisfaction' and Bob Dylan's 'Like a Rolling Stone' were competing against a trio of instrumentals from Europe, 'Zorba's Dance', 'A Walk in the Black Forest' and 'Il silenzio'. In 1966, as teenage pop's experimentalism started to alarm the unwary, the British charts were awash with ballads by Kenneth McKellar, Ken Dodd, Vince Hill and Val Doonican. The Who's saga of cross-dressing and emotional disturbance, 'I'm a Boy', was outflanked by the mock-1920s revival of the New Vaudeville Band's 'Winchester Cathedral'. Throughout 1967, the so-called Summer of Love, odes to hallucinogenic chemicals and alternative lifestyles sat alongside Petula Clark and Harry Secombe's 'This is My Song', Vince Hill's 'Edelweiss', country ballads from Tom Jones, a duet from Frank Sinatra and his daughter, and a whistling novelty entitled 'I Was Kaiser Bill's Batman'. There was also pan-generational pop, premature easy listening for the switched-on generation: the Seekers' 'Georgy Girl', Sandie Shaw's 'Puppet on a String', even Scott McKenzie's 'San Francisco'.

Many of these songs became instantaneous 'good music' standards: *The Mantovani Touch* (1968) included both 'Edelweiss' and 'Release Me', for example. But the act who contributed most heavily to this repertoire during the mid-1960s was the Beatles – or, rather, Paul McCartney, whose almost preternatural talent for melody produced an array of the most covered tunes of this, or any other, era: 'Yesterday', 'Michelle', 'And I Love Her', 'Here, There and Everywhere', 'Eleanor Rigby', 'Fool on the Hill', 'Hey Jude', 'Let It Be' and 'The Long and Winding Road'. They enabled light orchestras and crooners to feel au fait with the times, persuaded mature adults that the younger generation was not entirely barren, and ensured that Lennon and McCartney would become the highest-earning composers in history.

The Beatles' string-quartet arrangement of 'Yesterday' wasn't allowed to feature in the US Easy Listening chart, but cover versions did slip through the gates, alongside the Rolling Stones' assault on the same market, 'As Tears Go By'. The pick of the Beatles' catalogue and recent easy-listening hits also entered the jazz repertoire. As early as April 1965, a pundit declared that 'Jazz today is Cannonball Adderley playing *Fiddler on the Roof*, Duke Ellington interpreting *Mary Poppins* . . . It's also *Dizzy Goes Hollywood*, Stan Kenton playing Richard Wagner and the bossa nova . . . players have stretched their horizons to the most commercial point to keep active.'* The stretching had barely begun. As the decade continued, jazz artists regularly added rock material to their repertoires, while record company marketing departments begged that each album should include one short number which could be extracted for potential pop airplay. It was much easier for them to promote *Michelle*, a 1966 album of pop covers by saxophonist Bud Shank, than Miles Davis's contemporaneous *E.S.P.* – nobody imagining for a moment that the Miles Davis catalogue might still be selling fifty years later.

Even at the height of their mid-1960s fame, few would have predicted that the Beatles could enjoy a similar afterlife. It was the lot of teenage idols to flame briefly, and then fade into a distant glow. Sinatra was the exception, against whom all pretenders paled. Presley's popularity had endured for almost a decade until sales of his records sharply fell away. But there was one immensely popular act of the era whose appeal seemed time-less and irreversible: Herb Alpert & the Tijuana Brass. They were the best-selling albums artist in America from 1965 to 1968, surpassing the Beatles' feats on an almost weekly basis: five simultaneous LPs in the Top 20, six in the Top 40, eight in the Top 100. They were praised on the floor of the California Senate for having 'contributed immensely to international understanding and promoted cordial relations with people around the globe ... In a day when discordant sounds and irregular beats seemingly have provocation attraction, it is rewarding that a musical organisation specialises in what may be called joyous music.'

Alpert's band did not come from Tijuana, or even Mexico, and played at best a distant pastiche of mariachi music. Their 1962 hit, 'The Lonely Bull', was geographical exotica, as authentic as Frank Sinatra singing about the coffee in Brazil – and overdubbed with crowd noise in an attempt to convey the fervid excitement of the bullring. As the Beatles conquered America, Alpert (a songwriter and record company boss when not playing trumpet) temporarily lost his way by trying to court a teen audience. He returned in September 1965 with his sound streamlined and simplified, and his purpose likewise: to remove his adult listeners from the cares of everyday life by making them feel as if they were on vacation, while rooting them in the familiarity of standards and recent hits. He borrowed songs from Latin jazz ('Work Song'), Broadway ('A Taste of Honey' and

---

* John Coltrane's miraculous extemporisation around the melody of 'My Favorite Things' from *The Sound of Music* was arguably the zenith of this trend.

'Mama') and Hollywood ('Zorba the Greek' and 'Third Man Theme'), and perfected a style whereby every song sounded subtly different and yet exactly the same. Ironically, the exception – a sensuous vocal performance of Bacharach and David's 'This Guy's in Love With You' – provided his biggest hit and also broke the spell.

Alpert's music would only enjoy nostalgic appeal in subsequent decades, while Bacharach and David's represented the 1960s equivalent of a Porter or Rodgers and Hart, conferring a touch of class on anyone who approached it. Listening to Bacharach's daringly tricky melody lines, alongside David's dextrous lyrics, one could feel oneself becoming more sophisticated. That was why their catalogue was widely mistrusted by late 1960s aficionados of rock 'authenticity': too little emotion, too much calculation. Worse still, because she seemed to have betrayed her generation from within, was the Broadway, cabaret and movie success of Barbra Streisand: a year younger than Dylan, two months older than McCartney, and not remotely interested in a career like theirs. She was compared to Gertrude Lawrence and Edith Piaf, the queens of vaudeville, the doyennes of the variety stage. 'She will be around fifty years from now if good songs are still being written to be sung by good singers', a columnist predicted in 1963, when she was 21. Her entrance was startling: she burst on to the first track of her debut album, 'Cry Me a River', like a clown falling through a wall made of paper and paste, arriving (as it seemed) mid-bar in full flow. That single performance demonstrated her command of the microphone, with an awareness of how to act out a song, teasing and living out its implications at the same time, which none of her peers could have rivalled. So she was revered as a throwback to a lost era, proof that not every post-adolescent was a guitar-toting, narcotised imbecile – a sign that the 'good music' might survive its bombardment from teenagers and their sulking heroes.

Why should you put music on a great big piece of plastic which gets all fucked up and scratched and dusty, when you can get little tape cartridges which are dust-free all the time, never get scratched, are smaller, more compact, easier to stack – and all you have to do is plug them into a stereophonic set and you get much better reproduction?
Graham Nash, 1967

A lot of Madison Avenue type guys on their lunch hour are shopping – they're wearing button-down collars and they're into rock records, they're no longer buying Andy Williams, they're no longer buying Percy Faith records, or buying Frank Sinatra, they're buying rock records.

Joe Smith, general manager of Warner Brothers Records, 1971

Painting, graphics, photography: with the emergence of the rock album as a counter-cultural artefact, its cardboard packaging became more than a simple marketing device. There had long been an art and a science of cover design, a collision of advertising and self-expression. Even a simple portrait photograph could be manipulated to reinforce an image: as with the arty, half-lit faces on the *With the Beatles* sleeve; the fashionably moody figures on the Rolling Stones' first LP;* the weary, dustbowl features of Bob Dylan on *The Times They Are A-Changin'*. Scantily clad young women on mood-music albums conveyed the kind of company that the male purchaser would now be certain to attract. The anonymous white girl posed sensually on Otis Redding's *Otis Blue* LP played a dual role: she represented the transcendent power of the music, and obscured the race of its creator. While the Beatles and Rolling Stones continued to test the limits of the portrait, with the distorted faces of *Rubber Soul* and the heavily tinted shades of *Aftermath* respectively, Bob Dylan went a step further, amassing a lens-eye's span of symbolic objects on *Bringing It All Back Home*. This was a self-portrait by association, a style taken to its logical conclusion by the Beatles' *Sgt. Pepper* sleeve, crowded with icons (and immediately parodied by the Mothers of Invention). By contrast, the Beach Boys' *Pet Sounds* provided a warning of what could happen when music and image parted company: songs of high romanticism, an album cover of stark banality.

Dylan pioneered another innovation: the use of prose poems as liner notes. Previously most albums had been puffed by a tame publicist or journalist. During the mid-1960s, this congratulatory prose was gradually replaced by song lyrics (the album as poetry) or additional photographs (the album as fashion gallery). Gatefold sleeves expanded the horizon, and various pop artists utilised these new landscapes to create collages and montages, in the wake of Peter Blake's and Jann Haworth's groundbreaking

---

* There were no words other than the Decca logo on the Stones' cover, a brazen act of self-confidence.

design for *Sgt. Pepper*. These artworks could then be studied (like the lyrics) as the music played, providing a multimedia experience that would not be rivalled until the invention of the music video. Perhaps inevitably, it was also the Beatles who perfected the promotional film clip, which not only freed them from touring the world's TV studios for publicity purposes, but added another facet to the audio-visual delight that was the modern pop record.

With twelve inches by twelve to fill (more for a fold-out cover), the potential for artistic expression was immense. Record artwork from the 1960s would offer a more representative survey of the decade's artistic movements than a retrospective of canvases or sculptures. Yet the visual impact and cultural significance of these exercises in creative branding were lost when the music was transferred from vinyl to another medium. Best-selling LPs had been released on reel-to-reel tapes since the mid-1950s, initially providing the only way of securing stereo sound in the home. 'Tape has unbeatable advantages over a disk', declared *Time* magazine; 'it can record sound more faithfully, does not wear out, has no needle scratch.' Tape sales fell sharply after stereo LPs were introduced, and the industry struggled to find a format that would not require the listener to hand-wind the reel on to the machine before each play.

In the late 1950s, both RCA and 3M thought that they had invented a tape system that would reverse automatically from one spool to the other. RCA's cartridges offered acceptable sound but tended to jam; 3M's didn't jam, but weren't listenable. Then two innovations were introduced almost side by side. The first comprised a tape on a continuous loop inside a sealed cartridge: it was marketed for use in automobiles, first as four-track stereo (thirty minutes of music) and then eight-track (one hour). Eight-track players were offered as a luxury item in American saloons from 1966, and soon became standard in family and commercial vehicles. (By the 1990s, US truck stops were virtually the only place where eight-tracks could still be purchased.) Meanwhile, consumers could buy into an invention from the Dutch manufacturer, Philips: the mini-cassette (or compact cassette). Launched in Europe around 1964, it reached Britain in 1966, where it was marketed as 'so simple that anyone can use it . . . on the beach or in the car, or in stereo in the home'.

The introduction of the transistor radio a decade earlier had enabled people to carry music with them to the park or to school. Now the portable cassette player refined the process, so that you could choose the soundtrack for your trip – although it was several years before new albums would automatically be issued on cassette as well as vinyl, so home-taping was initially obligatory. You no longer had to carry an emblematic album cover under your arm to display your sophistication; you could simply let the music speak for you in the street. Neither the transistor radio nor the portable cassette discriminated about its audience, and the public airing of unwanted music could constitute noise pollution or an act of aggression towards the outside world, depending on one's proximity and view.

'Frightening', was the verdict of crooner, songwriter and teen idol Scott Walker, on the lifestyle preference of the average American adult male, *c.*1967: '[he] comes home, he sits down and puts on "background music" . . . He wants to hear something that completely relaxes him and that he doesn't have to get involved with.' Walker was equally perturbed by another dislocation between music and human emotion: the desire to evoke the psychedelic experience by means of sound effects, distortion and the howl of electronics. 'One of these days you'll go into a theatre,' he predicted, 'and there'll be just a machine on the stage and you'll forget there were ever such things as musicians or the human voice on its own . . . It's going to have a deathly influence on the newer generation, maybe up to the point where they're 27 or 30. It's eliminating the whole poetic quality of a human being.'

He was echoing the qualms of *Melody Maker* reporter Chris Roberts, who had conjectured in 1964: 'I still have a feeling that any day now might find me interviewing a tall, handsome desk of recording equipment.' Technology might have supplied Elvis Presley with a Cadillac which contained 'a TV, hi-fi, electric shoe cleaner, refrigerator, telephone extension from the front, and a special round seat for two in the rear, where Elvis entertains his girlfriends'; but it also seemed, amidst the constant innovations of the late 1960s, to be imposing an alienated, emotional distance between mankind and its music. 'Here it is at last – electronic "music"!', screamed the adverts for the 1962 single concocted by future Beatles producer George Martin, 'Time Beat' by the pseudonymous Ray Cathode. 'We have a long way to go before a computer will replace a symphony orchestra', Martin promised then; but the following year, the first edition of the Mellotron was put on sale. It utilised banks of tape heads, holding pre-recorded sounds, to evoke a galaxy of noise: some of it recognisable as an attempt to sample the tone of a flute or a trumpet, other selections more unreal. By the time that the Mellotron was audible on records by the

Beatles and the Moody Blues, it had been superseded by a synthesiser invented by Robert Moog. This was a purely electronic 'instrument', which enabled the user to manipulate the tone, speed, volume and pitch of sound. Demonstrated at the Monterey Pop Festival in 1967, it was snapped up by several leading pop musicians. Micky Dolenz employed it to provide a cacophonous, unsettling accompaniment to the Monkees' 'Daily Nightly' later that year, and it soon appeared on recordings by Simon & Garfunkel, the Byrds and the Beatles. Thereafter it was turned to more conventional (and yet more surreal) use: as a substitute for a symphony orchestra on Walter Carlos's *Switched-On Bach*, and again on his soundtrack for *A Clockwork Orange*. Popular? Classical? Nobody was quite sure. Indeed, was it even music? Once, conservative thinkers had railed against the fakery of electrically amplified instruments. Now those who played electric music were fearful of the non-human music made by machines – yesterday's revolutionaries becoming today's guardians of the flame.

'Don't underestimate the power that pop has over kids. In the next fifteen years it will change humanity. All the people in power are 50 and 60 and dying, and being replaced by people that know. The beautiful thing is that everything is going in such a positive direction. The kids are seeing truth in pop, and very few [other] places.'

Graham Nash, January 1968

CHAPTER 20

the

new

prophets

'Most rock and roll musicians are banal, amateurish and insipidly stupid when they try to explain their philosophy of life in the context of popular music ... Rock and roll may be the new music, but rock musicians are not the new prophets.'

Jon Landau, *Rolling Stone magazine*, July 1968

4

Van Morrison, according to a Bang Records advertisement from 1967, was 'so bloody real he trembles in your throat and you know that it's an infinitely minute time capsule that transcends you, whirls you to him'. In the American pop paper *Hit Parader*, meanwhile, Juan Rodriguez compared the relationship between rock stars and their fans to 'mob reaction . . . The musicians dish out the most pretentious trash, and the audience hails it as "great".' Rodriguez concluded: 'Pretentiousness is the scourge of modern pop music.'

As the Morrison puff illustrates, pretentiousness – artistic ambition, cultural reach, social significance – was inherent to rock's late 1960s appeal. Once an artist (note the noun) had transcended the trappings of fame and the desires of teenage girls, then – as Graham Nash insisted – rock could challenge authority, change social conventions, maybe even transform lives. Musicians' pronouncements on Vietnam, the atom bomb and the ethics of capitalist culture were being heeded more closely than those of society's elected rulers. Worshipped like gods, rock stars moved in a closeted, fantasy landscape where they could choose their peers: aristocrats, perhaps, or poets, artists, social climbers, models, photographers, intellectuals, fools, often all masquerading in the same skin.

Egotism was a necessary ingredient of stardom: with fame came a level of attention so gratifying that it was quite possible to believe that you were 'so bloody real' that you could 'transcend' your audience – carry the weight of those who, when they listened to your music, felt as if you had taken responsibility for their souls and lives. That belief in one's own divinity could be finely balanced by a gnawing sense that, actually, one was nothing at all. Louis Armstrong never had to live with that burden, or Bing Crosby, or George Formby; they knew who they were and what they were meant to do, and did it. But from the mid-1960s onwards, the sense of one's own significance became an obstacle for everyone who achieved success in the self-aggrandising field of rock.

Rock stars believed that they possessed the latent power to effect political and cultural change: one anthem, and the walls of the citadel would crack, like Jericho under Joshua's trumpets. In 1968–9, rock stars masqueraded as political activists (and vice versa), swallowing and regurgitating whole the rhetoric of global revolution propounded by the short-lived union of hippies, Yippies, anti-war campaigners, Black Panthers and all their fellow travellers. This was the era when the cadre of Detroit radicals known as the White Panther Party could have its own in-house rock band, the MC5, complete with anthem ('Kick Out the Jams') and manifesto ('Total assault on the culture by any means necessary, including rock and roll, dope, and fucking in the streets'). The Rolling Stones adopted a coy and ambiguous stance towards political action ('Street Fighting Man'); the Beatles could debate Trotskyist tactics ('Revolution'); Jefferson Airplane called for 'Volunteers' to man the barricades and, with David Crosby, envisioned 'Wooden Ships' on which the rock elite and their 'ladies' would escape the apocalypse if their benefit concerts for the Yippies and the Panthers didn't result in the overthrow of the established order.

The music that resulted was tumultuous and exultant, naïve and overblown. Its creators, especially in America, where the crisis (under threat of the Vietnam draft) was more intense than in Britain, continued to believe that music could speak more loudly than guns or money. Under this misconception, David Crosby could be surprised, in 1970, that 'Somehow *Sgt. Pepper* did not stop the Vietnam War. Somehow it didn't work. Somebody isn't listening.' Yet the loose quartet he formed with other egotists, mavericks, freethinkers and political idealists, Crosby, Stills, Nash & Young, came as close as any rock band to, if not changing, then at least embodying the fantasies of their vast fan base. Almost alone of their fellow rock politicians, members of the quartet continued and continue to believe in the righteous power of music, and their own role as spokesmen for a generation.*

Rock's revolutionary fervour died with the fragmentation of the grand coalition against the Vietnam War in 1970, as each organisation's priorities (women's liberation, black power, global anarchy) took precedence over their collective aim. The major rock festivals of the era, notably Woodstock in August 1969, seemed to promise that fans might provide the masses necessary for any healthy Marxist rebellion. The fact that such a

---

* It takes a certain blind certainty to deliver time-sensitive protest songs such as 'For What It's Worth' and 'Chicago' with the same fervour in the twenty-first century as in 1970: naïvety, too, one might say, were it not for the fact that these seemingly exhausted anthems can still unify their ageing audience, and remind them of the crusading zeal which they all once shared, for good or ill.

large crowd (400,000 or more) had gathered in one place, short on food and water, exposed to heat and rain, had fed themselves on narcotics of dubious quality, and discovered that they did not lynch each other but collaborated in their hippie solidarity – that felt like a political triumph. (The subsequent documentary film about the festival mythologised that triumph for the world.) Repeating the trick over a single day, in more forlorn circumstances at the Altamont Speedway, proved to be impossible. A murder took place in front of the stage, captured by a film crew working for the Rolling Stones. Fans who had primed themselves for a hippie nirvana found themselves trapped in a violent biker movie. When it was revealed that another series of killings, in Hollywood, had been enacted by a gang of putative hippies fixated on the Beatles' 1968 double album, another vein of idealism was drained.

The shadows of these events seeped back through the decade, distorting the optimism that had fired *Sgt. Pepper*, gatherings of the hippie tribes, sunshine pop and the belief that it was enough to be young and awake to remake the world. An era when anything seemed possible was smothered in darkness, which to varying degrees – introspective depression, political dejection, black despair – would shape the decade ahead. The Rolling Stones turned out to have been the era's most clear-sighted prophets, via a succession of records filled with foreboding and violence, from 'Paint It Black' through 'Sympathy for the Devil' to the eschatological terror of 'Gimme Shelter'. They would signal the tribes towards the fallow ground ahead, where – like Jesus in the wilderness – they could explore the depths of their belief and self-doubt.

It is very strange making a living out of being yourself.
James Taylor, 1971

What it boils down to is that we're all potential gods in embryo,
we're all evolving towards being gods.
Alan Osmond on the Osmonds' 1973 LP, *The Plan*

'Won't you look down upon me Jesus', called James Taylor in 'Fire and Rain', the song which perhaps better than any other epitomised the new rock austerity of the early 1970s. Its three verses, delivered in a voice of spiritual exhaustion by a 21-year-old former psychiatric patient, described a friend's suicide, Taylor's junk habit and his admission to hospital: no transcendence or euphoria there. Taylor sang with the timing of Sam Cooke and the intimacy of Bing Crosby (if, that is, the man known affectionately by then as 'the Old Groaner' had ever been a heroin addict). He had roots in folk and rock 'n' roll, and enough of a Southern drawl to suggest he was a man of the fields, though he was actually the son of a professor of medicine and an opera singer. His life had been as troubled and erratic as those of any of rock's later depressives. Yet he won an enormously loyal following, especially among young women, for whom his melancholy persona – hunched frame, hair falling across his face – made him seem like a suffering messiah.

Taylor had a dry humour that redeemed his misery, even if it was only apparent in retrospect. But his confessional air and prevailing mood of self-pity (both encapsulated in 'Hey Mister That's Me Up on the Jukebox') emphasised a theme in pop writing that reached back into the rock 'n' roll era, and would shape the decades ahead. In the late 1950s, pop's melancholy was entirely romantic, and juvenile: she doesn't love me, oh woe is me. Then college kids became pop stars, and brought the trappings of romantic poetry to the teenage playground.

Misunderstanding the lyrical sensibility of Bob Dylan, John Lennon believed he was echoing the bard when he wrote 'You've Got to Hide Your Love Away' ('Here I stand, head in hand' must be one of the least promising scenarios for any song). Paul Simon – later a lyricist as flexible and gifted as any of the Broadway maestros – called darkness 'my old friend' on 'The Sound of Silence' and hid behind his poetry books on 'I Am a Rock', an abject lesson in how to pervert what one has learned on a literature course. There were others engaged in self-pity and self-loathing in mid-1960s pop: the Shangri-La's girl group fashioned an entire career from it, chronicling grief, parent–child battles, sexual dysfunction and catatonic emotional breakdown across a series of hit singles. But they were role-playing: Queens girls living out the fantasies of their producer, Shadow Morton. The vein of self-pity, self-questioning, self-annihilation only began to overflow once rock's counter-cultural spirit had been sapped by disillusion and despair.

That was the point at which the folk tradition of the sensitive troubadour collided with a culture suddenly robbed of its optimism. As confidence in the power of collective action dissipated, and the generation of 1967 realised that it was not about to remould society in its own image, inner turmoil replaced anthemic collectivism. One of the last effective slogan songs of the 1960s was 'Give Peace a Chance', by John Lennon, with a message so vague and (in retrospect) so seeped in imminent defeat that it scarcely challenged the status quo.* Thereafter – at least until he fell into radical company in New York in 1971, and attempted to fund and inspire the revolution single-handedly – Lennon turned sharply inwards: comparing himself once more to Christ ('they're gonna crucify me') and, by the end of the decade, chronicling his agonising withdrawal from heroin addiction on a hit single. The following year, he devoted an entire album, *John Lennon/Plastic Ono Band*, to the primal therapy he'd endured that summer. The technique encouraged patients to confront their deep-seated fears and pains, stripping away their defences, layer after layer, until all that was left was the final scream of the wounded baby, dragged into this world to suffer and decay.

On the album's key song, 'God', Lennon denied a list of panaceas and crutches, from Buddha to Bob Dylan, Jesus to Elvis, ending in what was (in 1970) the most blasphemous pronouncement of them all: 'I don't believe in Beatles'. Lennon was addicted to a cycle of belief and then betrayal, which primal therapy had enabled him to see, but couldn't cure. His hall of icons would also have included the figures of his parents (lost), Brian Epstein (dead) – and Maharishi Mahesh Yogi, whose transcendental meditation teachings entranced Lennon and the other Beatles in 1967, until the guru's all-too-human failings undermined their confidence. Lennon had been the most vocal apostle of Maharishi, then his most violent detractor (and, incidentally, the only Beatle to abandon his meditation practice entirely). The Beatles' immersion in meditation brought it to global attention; their rejection of Maharishi did nothing to halt the spread of his methods around the world. Rock stars, it seemed, were more influential as evangelists than they were as Old Testament prophets.

Alongside the tribal euphoria of the counter-culture, the era's infatuation with drugs triggered an acute awareness of realms beyond the everyday, of dimensions in which even political revolution might be irrelevant. Here was another facet of the self-examination to come: the search for the immortal, the transcendent, the secrets of the cosmos.

---

* The song endured, though: at the time of writing, Nigerian parents have been marching through the streets pleading for the return of their kidnapped children, using Lennon's melody as their voice.

Inevitably, many in the counter-culture were led to established forms of religion, just as many preferred to chart the unknown alone. Eastern religions promised deliverance from the petty morality of organised Christianity: Buddhism with its pantheistic acceptance of what is; Hinduism its piety and revelation of the divine. Some were even drawn back to the spirit of the early Christians, becoming Jesus freaks, who reinterpreted the Christ of the Gospels as a prototype hippie. All roads were possible; what mattered was the journey.

Yet the journey could take many forms. In 1964, as the Beatles replaced him as Britain's premier pop act, Cliff Richard made a public declaration of commitment to Christ. Three years later, he responded to the Summer of Love with a gospel album, *Good News*, and a starring role in a feature film funded by the Billy Graham ministry. Simultaneously, Elvis Presley – once feared by Christians as an instrument of Satan – issued his own spiritual collection, *How Great Thou Art*, in answer (so his record company claimed) to requests from his fans. Radio stations across America combined to promote Presley's record that Easter. Such proclamations of faith were common among artists who wanted to appeal to conservatives in the American South, or in the African-American community (the only place where it has been consistently acceptable to rock critics for people to proclaim their Christian beliefs). One of the most successful singles of 1969 was 'Oh Happy Day', by Edwin Hawkins's gospel choir. This rousing spiritual chorus inspired George Harrison to record his own non-Christian hymn, 'My Sweet Lord', a worldwide No. 1 hit in 1970–1.

As the US record company Word Records had already proclaimed, 'The Sacred and Inspirational Market is a BIG market'. With capitalist greed coated in the veneer of sanctity, Word trumpeted the economic potential of their rich catalogue of sermons, gospel quartets, choirs and patriotic anthems. 'Here's Your Opportunity For Bigger Fall and Christmas Sales!', they boasted to retailers. '70 million people like this kind of music! Why not profit from their desires with the world's largest, broadest, most complete religious catalog … there are good profits from Sacred and Inspirational sales. Prove it at NO RISK! Check the proposition below! It contains all the elements necessary to put you into the religious market painlessly and profitably.' One could almost hear the gates to the Kingdom of Heaven swinging shut.

Presumably reckoning that this approach would not inspire impressionable teens, the United Presbyterian Church's Division of Mass

Media (American religious organisations are nothing if not prepared) set out in late 1967 to create a more subtle path to the Gospel. They presented two songwriters with a theological treatise, and asked them to convert it into pop. One of them was Dickie Goodman, who with his friend Bill Buchanan had invented a surreal form of 1950s comedy record, the 'cut-in', whereby short clips from current hit singles were used to tell a humorous story.* Goodman returned with two suitably spiritual but doctrinally vague pop songs, which were duly recorded by a group called the Astrakan Sleeve, without any ensuing rush of teenagers to Presbyterian services.

Slowly, the influence of modern pop music began to seep into the Christian churches. Evangelical groups were the most willing to welcome guitars and drums into their Communion, but eventually all but the highest of congregations would become acclimatised to seeing a rock band at the head of the service, setting the Gospel to a gentle Beatles beat. More ambitious composers elected to tackle the Christian Mass, a traditional form of worship which had inspired some of the greatest composers of the millennium. Duke Ellington and Vince Guaraldi wrote gospel suites for performance at the newly opened Grace Cathedral in San Francisco. Lalo Schifrin composed *Jazz Suite on the Mass Text* in 1967. Most striking of all these ventures was *Mass in F Minor* by the Electric Prunes, in which arranger/composer David Axelrod borrowed the name of a successful garage-punk band to create a rock setting of the liturgy. 'I've played dubs of this Mass for kids who had said that if the Mass sounded like this, they would attend church every Sunday', Axelrod claimed.

Yet the kids who were most fervent about their love of the Lord in the latter half of the 1960s were not attending a conventional church. The Jesus Movement (or Jesus People Movement) was an offshoot of the hippie counter-culture which arose, inevitably, in California, and spread rapidly around the Western world. It emphasised Christ the rebel and Christ the bringer of love; no hint here of Old Testament anger and retribution. Something of the movement's spirit was caught, ironically, in the joyous chorales of the Broadway musical *Hair*, though it treated Christianity as a fit object for satire.

The burgeoning Jesus People were served by coffee houses and concerts, and ultimately – at Explo '72, in Detroit – by a festival equivalent

---

* The most shameless of these was arguably 'The Return of Jerry Lee', intended by Jerry Lee Lewis's record company to overcome the fracas of his bigamous marriage to his underage cousin.

to the great gatherings of hippie rock. Approximately 200,000 fans assembled there to witness the power of a genre known variously as Jesus rock, Jesus music or Christian rock. Its creation could be traced back to a New York DJ named Scott Ross, who around 1967 dared to add contemporary rock and pop flavours to the Christian Broadcasting Network. There were misgivings from the elders about the possible repercussions of introducing these devilish rhythms to innocent youth. As Christian rock historian John J. Thompson noted, evangelists such as Bill Gothard 'actually preached that the syncopated 4/4 beat of rock and roll collided with the natural rhythm of the human heart and would therefore make listeners sick . . . Minor keys, loud drums and non-specific lyrics were strictly of the evil one.'

Those 1950s rock 'n' rollers who had been raised as Southern Baptists had already proved that it was possible for avowed Christians to be acclaimed as rock stars (although it helped if they were backsliders as flagrant as Jerry Lee Lewis). To avoid the taint of godliness which had afflicted the likes of Pat Boone and Cliff Richard in the 1960s, however, the Jesus People created an alternative rock culture: a web of independent labels and a circuit of venues that existed not only outside the rock mainstream, but unnoticed by its mass media.

At the core of this movement, as musician, songwriter and label boss, was the messianic figure of Larry Norman. Briefly a pop star in mid-1960s America with his band People (their name a reclaiming of humanity from the Animals, Byrds and Turtles), Norman launched his solo career in 1969 with the unashamedly religious *Upon This Rock*. It showcased him as a talent comparable to Leon Russell, albeit with a maverick streak more reminiscent of David Ackles at his most eclectic (as on 'The Last Supper'). By the early 1970s, Norman was issuing albums as coherent and contemporary as *I Wish We'd All Been Ready* and *So Long Ago the Garden*, which would have fitted on to FM radio alongside Carole King and Neil Young. Both highlighted Norman's occasionally Dylanesque writing style, heard at its most dramatic on 'Nightmare #71'.

Norman proceeded to sign many of America's most talented Christian performers, such as Randy Stonehill and the band Daniel Amos, to his Solid Rock label, eventually antagonising almost all of them with business practices that they believed were underhand. His own career was dogged by illness (he claimed to have suffered brain damage in an air crash) and controversy, although not before he had issued dozens of albums and performed in both arenas and small church halls around the world. He was effectively a superstar in a milieu that survived the dissipation of the Jesus People Movement, and which existed in invisible parallel to commercial rock. Artists such as Love Song and Randy Matthews secured vast followings without ever coming to the attention of the *Billboard* charts or *Rolling Stone* magazine.

The mainstream rock exposure that might have been theirs went instead to projects such as George Harrison's harshly moralistic (albeit inspiringly tuneful) *Living in the Material World,* and a concept album by a group of pop idols in their teens and early 20s. This was *The Plan,* inspired by the Mormon faith shared by the Osmonds. Its overtly religious design – and the ambiguous relationship between orthodox Christianity and the Church of Jesus Christ of Latter-Day Saints – scared away many of their fans, particularly in America. But in Britain, where their following was at its peak, it became their best-selling record, ensuring that hundreds of thousands of homes were treated to a series of songs about the Osmonds' desire to follow the road to exaltation. By comparison, Larry Norman's albums exploring the trials of evangelical Christianity sounded positively conventional.

A racy, rollicking, black-hippie message to the Establishment.
Ebony magazine on *Hair*, 1970

It has nothing to do with Black people.
Black activist and author Amiri Baraka on *Hair*, 1970

Rock was seeking ever more grandiose canvases for its creations. Broadway desperately required a connection with the modern world. The inevitable result was *Hair,* 'a tribal rock musical' which premiered off-Broadway in 1967 as a folk-rock piece and then graduated to the Great White Way as a hippie-rock-soul-gospel contrivance. With its drug references, outlandish costumes and climactic nude scene, *Hair* attracted an enormous audience, although not amongst the communities it pretended to portray.

While the Beatles' plans to create the first Merseybeat musical had been thwarted by Lionel Bart, other groups pursued the dream of a multi-segmented, coherent, long-form song suite: the elusive 'rock opera'. The Who's Pete Townshend, an eternal self-educator, engineered arguably its most convincing sighting with 'A Quick One While He's Away', a nine-minute tale of adultery and repentance which borrowed the Wagnerian model of repeated motifs as it playfully satirised operatic musical conventions. Not satisfied with a perfect miniature, he set out on an altogether more expansive, and less cohesive, epic: *Tommy*.* In time, this became a double album, a stage show, a gloriously grotesque Ken Russell movie (perhaps the most perfect rock film of all time, both celebrating and ridiculing the genre's messianic myths) and then a Broadway musical again. By its final incarnation, *Tommy* had been neutered, its ending changed, any cultural significance long since erased. After *Tommy*, there were rock musicals galore, and a wildly successful rock band (Queen) who leant heavily on the conceptual and aesthetic traditions of opera. But for a fully-fledged stage opera by a major figure working, at least ostensibly, in the field of rock, the world had to wait for Rufus Wainwright's Verdi-inspired *Prima Donna*, premiered in 2009.

Even if opera proved too complex or alienating a form to be translated into rock, the late 1960s introduced a generation of classically trained musicians who shared the ambition of turning rock into 'serious' music. There had been jazz suites as early as the 1920s, and Duke Ellington wrote pieces on an epic scale throughout his long career. But in 1968, rock embarked on a strand of monumental composition which would (depending on one's viewpoint) enrich or deface its catalogue over the next decade. Stan Kenton had utilised the term 'progressive jazz' to describe his own voyages into the musical unknown. By the end of the decade, the term 'progressive rock' was being bandied around the music industry. It referred initially to a new American radio format, which concentrated on playing material from outside the Top 40, especially album tracks. This had been prompted not by commercial demand but by a ruling from the Federal Communications Commission. In an effort to provide more diversified listening for the public, the FCC insisted that by January 1967 any station broadcasting to a population of more than 100,000 had to offer 'split' programming: different shows, in other words, on its AM and FM wavebands. Most radios could only pick up AM stations, and so they continued to offer the most commercial programmes (principally the Top 40 format). On FM stations such as WOR in New York and KMPX in San Francisco,

---

* Rock historians argue to this day about whether *Tommy* was a concept album or an opera, and, in either case, whether it was beaten to either or both accolades by the Pretty Things' psychedelic odyssey, *S. F. Sorrow*.

however, far-sighted programme directors allowed disc jockeys to play material that would never have been aired on the Top 40.

The first beneficiaries of 'progressive rock' radio included Big Brother & the Holding Company, Vanilla Fudge, Iron Butterfly and Ten Years After, who were (said a startled analyst) 'even becoming superstars without the aid of the Top 40 stations'. Programme directors discovered that listeners did not expect, or even desire, constant rotation of the week's hit singles. Once they had tuned into a 'progressive' station, they would stay there, the only requirement being that the music was tailored exactly to the audience: late teens and early 20s, for the most part, predominantly male, with a high proportion of students. For the first time, rock radio had the space in which to broadcast songs that stepped way beyond the three-minute limit of the Top 40.

'Progressive' stations could now broadcast entire albums or such epic compositions as Iron Butterfly's 'In-A-Gadda-Da-Vida' or Procol Harum's 'In Held Twas In I' (seventeen minutes apiece). The archetype was the Moody Blues' 1967 album, *Days of Future Passed*, a song cycle devoted to what the Beatles called 'A Day in the Life'. It moved from 'The Day Begins' to 'Night' (the latter containing the global hit single 'Nights in White Satin'). Besides zealous employment of the Mellotron, the album incorporated the tonal range of the London Festival Orchestra.

Here, then, were most of the ingredients required to produce 'progressive rock': composition on a grand scale, portentous lyrical content, orchestral instrumentation and pretensions towards 'serious' music (debate still continues as to whether the Moody Blues had, or had not, originally been commissioned to create a rock equivalent to Dvořák's *New World Symphony*). If this album was more 'symphonic' than 'operatic', its classical influences and air of self-improvement struck a chord with an educated young audience who would, a decade earlier, have shunned rock 'n' roll in favour of jazz or folk. Close behind were the likes of Pink Floyd (*Saucerful of Secrets*) and the Nice (*Ars longa vita brevis*), dedicated in their very different ways to extending the outer limits of what rock could achieve on record. In America, Frank Zappa and the Mothers of Invention blended Lenny Bruce-inspired satire, 1950s rock stylings and experimental classical music into an inimitable series of pop art collages – hooligans to the Moody Blues' choirboys.

The musician who epitomised the philosophy of the new genre was the Nice's keyboard player, Keith Emerson. It was he who paired melodies by Dave Brubeck and Bach on 1967's 'Rondo', and who oversaw the side-long title track of *Ars longa vita brevis*, again building upon a Bach motif. Emerson's classical training, combined with an apprenticeship in the mid-1960s R&B group the VIPs, placed him perfectly to exploit the most theatrical elements of both traditions. When he formed the trio Emerson, Lake & Palmer in 1970, he had nothing less than full-blooded classical composition in his sights: having rearranged Mussorgsky's *Pictures at an Exhibition* suite for rock band, he eventually felt able to attempt his own piano concerto.

By virtue of its scope and ambition, progressive rock felt like an elite brand. It offered its fan base the chance to feel superior to those who continued to rely on conventional rock songs or (worse still) the Top 40 pop charts. As such, it was immediately open to criticism from those who felt that its very seriousness robbed rock of its identity. Just as the FM/AM split had emphasised the growing divide between the rock and pop markets, now rock itself was fragmenting into subgenres. It was quite possible, in 1967, for someone who identified themselves as a rock fan to enjoy everything marketed under that banner, even allowing for their specific personal tastes. By 1970, there was little crossover between (for example) those listening to Emerson, Lake & Palmer and Crosby, Stills, Nash & Young. They represented two different aesthetics, two methods of touching and energising their audience, each resolutely convinced that its own solution rendered all alternatives superfluous.

Nor were these the only themes on offer. The late 1960s also marked a renaissance of the British blues band, building on the free-form improvisation of Cream and the Jimi Hendrix Experience. Both outfits utilised the simplest of rock instrumentation on stage – the power trio of guitar, bass, drums – but were still able to conjure up wall-bending levels of sound. Techniques of amplification had advanced to the point where the average band in a church hall was using more powerful equipment than had been available two years earlier to the Beatles in vast arenas. Volume now constituted an extra instrument: a tool of exhilaration and social manipulation, deafening and thrilling the audience in equal measure.

For a year, perhaps a little longer, all of these elements could be condensed and compressed into music that would still, just, fit on to singles as well as albums. Two epics from 1968 represented the outer limits of pop's experiments with time. 21-year-old songwriter and arranger Jimmy Webb sketched out a twenty-minute rock cantata, and then squeezed its elements into almost eight minutes of orchestral fireworks, over which actor and non-singer Richard Harris delivered a mock-poetic tale of romantic disillusionment. 'MacArthur Park' scaled new heights of pop grandiosity: simultaneously magnificent and ridiculous, it inspired the Beatles to create something equally epic. 'Hey Jude' launched the recording arm of the group's gargantuan business empire, Apple Corps, a doomed attempt to merge counter-culture values with the capitalist profit motive. If any record could have made it work, it was this one, supported as it was by John Lennon's politically wary, sonically abrasive 'Revolution'. It was Paul McCartney who wrote 'Hey Jude', a reflective love song which expanded into the most populist of choruses, repeating a simple refrain with such exhilaration that its wordless content came to seem profound, a song of joy for an entire generation. The influence of these two production fiestas was so potent that even pre-Beatles stars such as Roy Orbison ('Southbound Jericho Parkway') were tempted to try their hand at something equally grandiose. Patience with such endeavours was wearing thin, however, as rock culture took a decisive turn towards more direct emotional stimuli.

If Presley were on the next plane over here, Jerry Lee Lewis, Little Richard and Fats Domino were following on another, then we could blitzkrieg England with the old-style rock. We could make it last for five years.
  Bill Haley in London, 1968

Don't be surprised if in 1978 your kids are wearing little leather jackets, raiding your record collection in the attic and looning to Elvis!
  Rave magazine, May 1968

Spring 1968: psychedelic optimism was giving way to student unrest and street demonstrations, and Britain chose to indulge itself in a return to 1950s rock 'n' roll. Once again, there were Teddy boys jostling outside theatres; the Top 40 included Bill Haley, Buddy Holly and Eddie Cochran; and stores were flooded with reissues and repackages and remakes of those oldies but goodies from 1958. 'If you are a groover and all you've got is these ballads in the charts,' Mick Jagger said, 'I can understand you wanting to go back to rock 'n' roll, but this is just living in the past.' No sooner had the class of 1963 purged their live sets of the R&B and rock anthems on which they'd been raised than they were back, their vintage swing tossed aside in favour of power chords and distortion (the Who's 'Summertime Blues', Jeff Beck's 'All Shook Up' and 'Jailhouse Rock'). The Beatles ('Lady Madonna') and the Move ('Fire Brigade') found ways to acknowledge the past without reliving it. Soon Elvis Presley would record his first television special in eight years, slimmed and sideburned, clad in biker's black leather like Marlon Brando in *The Wild Ones*. Sha Na Na, young men who resembled greased-up JDs from a lost 1958 rock 'n' roll exploitation movie, revived doo-wop as performance art, and were received so well at underground rock venues that they ended up high on the Woodstock Festival bill.

Few of the rock fans of 1968 wanted to return to the era of Eisenhower and Macmillan, James Dean and Marilyn Monroe, but there was an apparent simplicity to that time which seemed strangely appealing amidst anti-Vietnam marches, classically inspired song suites and the shadow of economic decline. By rekindling the spirit of 1958, it seemed possible to rewrite the history of the previous decade, omitting all the distractions and missteps that had led the music astray.

It was as if the contemporary world was a conundrum, to which only the past held the key; especially if it revealed roots that were hidden by the extravagant blooms of the flower-power era. In the 1950s, the British and Irish folk traditions had been revered as a touchstone of working-class authenticity, and then subsumed into the amorphous body of blues, folk and country songs raided by the skiffle boom. Over the intervening decade, several hundred folk clubs had been founded across the UK – some rigorously traditional in their outlook, some prepared to accept contemporary songwriters (as long as they avoided electric instruments). From this scene came some of the most diverse talents of the 1960s and beyond: Donovan, Bert Jansch, Martin Carthy, and many more. Inevitably, some of them were drawn towards rock and pop. Donovan pioneered a peculiarly British brand of psychedelic whimsy, while Jansch steered a unique course between blues, jazz, folk and rock, both as a soloist and as a leading force in the folk 'supergroup', Pentangle. This was perhaps a more 'authentic' approach than that adopted by traditional singers who inherited their nation's 'pure' folk heritage from records, songbooks and BBC radio shows – artificially preserving songs which would otherwise have met a natural death. Ultimately, all of these different approaches cohered uneasily in a brief but joyous explosion of British folk rock, in which Fairport Convention,

Steeleye Span, Shirley & Dolly Collins and others sampled everything from medieval plainsong to modern American ballads, in their quest to keep the traditions of the British Isles alive.

The same tangled logic and righteous enthusiasm encouraged many American rock bands of the late 1960s to explore a vital but often overlooked strand of the nation's musical web: country and western. There were political reasons why it had been ignored. Country was linked in many minds to the South, to racism,* the taint of slavery, artistic and moral conservatism, the Klan, rednecks, Baptist preachers and demagogic politicians. Yet there was another, more attractive view of country, as the so-called white man's blues, working class and proud, clinging tight to its traditions and its heroes. This was a music of bars and fields, hard drinking and long suffering – adult music, finally, for which one did not require a symphony orchestra or a studio of synthesised sound effects. It was the home of Merle Haggard, the heroes of whose songs grappled with poverty and a restless desire to escape the confines of working life; George Jones, adrift in his permanent struggle with the bottle; and Tammy Wynette, voice of those silent women desperate to maintain their marriages without sacrificing their souls.

After four years in which pop had expanded exponentially into forms that even their creators did not entirely comprehend, there was comfort to be found in a genre and a culture that seemed not to have budged an inch. The old virtues were still the true ones in country: there were mouths to feed, children to raise and relationships to preserve. The landscape might have widened, but whether the heroes of country songs were pushing ploughs, riding trucks or even taking dictation in a big-city office, their concerns and pleasures were as reliable as the twang of a hill-billy voice.

For those rock performers who'd been raised on country music, such as Michael Nesmith of the Monkees and Chris Hillman of the Byrds, reclaiming that heritage was like revisiting their childhood home. Meanwhile, lifelong country fan Bob Dylan recorded *Blonde on Blonde*, thick with the fug of narcotics, accompanied by Nashville's top session players, who struggled to acclimatise to the metaphorical landscape of

---

* There was a tradition of 'underground' country releases by artists such as Johnny Rebel, and the Son of Mississippi, which expressed violently racist views. Rebel's 'Nigger Hatin' Me' demonstrated that a country single could be ethically contemptible and musically appealing, in the same awful moment.

'Sad-Eyed Lady of the Lowlands' and 'Visions of Johanna'. The country hierarchy had been bemused enough by the arrival of the British beat groups in 1964. Roy Acuff acknowledged 'the Beatles . . . and the Animals, bears and bugs . . . They must be alright, as millions think so. They sing country music, you know, in a different style . . . I believe their hairdos put them over, but I have to give them credit for being smart.' The following year, country fan Ringo Starr spurred the Beatles into recording Buck Owens's 'Act Naturally', which was accepted by their fans as a novelty. Returning the compliment, a bluegrass band named the Charles River Boys offered an entire album of *Beatles Country*.

Behind the extravagant distractions of 1967, a growing number of American musicians began to toy with the idea of mixing country instruments with rock ideology. After Bob Dylan delivered *John Wesley Harding* that December, its harsh biblical parables set to the leanest of Nashville accompaniments, the influx of rock tourists to the self-styled Music City became a stampede. The Byrds and Beau Brummels led the way, while several former Byrds alumni combined in 1969 as the Flying Burrito Brothers to make *The Gilded Palace of Sin*. This was arguably the most significant country-rock album of them all, a set of songs that confronted the jaded decadence of Hollywood with truth-telling eyes. Just as no respecting garage or beat band had been able to perform without a clutch of R&B covers, now the least likely country boys – the Grateful Dead, Jefferson Airplane, the Kinks, the Rolling Stones, even Frank Zappa – were playing with the Southern white man's tools, even if (like Zappa) they were twisting them for satirical purposes.

This was ambiguous ground: were the country rockers revisiting American roots or stealing the symbols of a culture without understanding them? If rock signified progress and modernism, how did it fit with a style perceived as epitomising conservatism? Most acts didn't bother to confront those questions, briefly borrowing a steel guitar and a Southern accent and then quickly leaving town. Others plunged into the stew of history – English boys Elton John and lyricist Bernie Taupin reinventing themselves as veterans of the old South on *Tumbleweed Connection*, for example. Bob Dylan didn't attempt anything that drastic; he merely made records that sounded as if he'd found his peace in Nashville, allowing his retreads of traditional folk tunes and country standards on the wryly named *Self Portrait* in 1970 to be wreathed in the deep-pile 'countrypolitan' strings and chorales that Chet Atkins had fashioned earlier in the decade.

It was Dylan's one-time backing group, dubbing themselves simply the Band, who pulled the richest treasures out of the Southern earth. On *Music From Big Pink* (1968) and the utterly unimpeachable *The Band* (1969), they drew from a melting pot of – no other word for it, the tradition begins here – Americana.* Although four of the quintet, including chief writer Robbie Robertson, were Canadian, they were able to use all the tools at their disposal – country, soul and blues, jazz and rock 'n' roll, myth and legend from the Civil War and the Old West, and a unique insight into Dylan's creative processes – to refine Southern soil into jewels of mysterious import. Artists such as Eric Clapton and George Harrison instantly recognised that the Band's music offered them an escape route from the draining overload of psychedelic rock; allowed them, in fact, to dream of a rock band that might be a union of souls rather than a battleground of egos. Yet even the Band could not sustain that fantasy beyond their second album. And there was a more troubling issue to consider. Did this desperate borrowing of another genre's values and truths signify that, like an army that has advanced too quickly, rock had lost connection with its line of supply? Was it going backwards to replenish its rations? Or simply conceding that the long march towards an idealised future was over?

$$\maltese$$

---

* Given a critic's scissors and paste, and a dictator's power, I would make alterations to almost all of my favourite albums – snipping a track here, sliding an out-take into the mix here. But I make an exception for *The Band*, the only record I've ever heard on which I would not wish to alter a single note.

'The British scene has never been quite so dead
and boring as it is now.'

Reader's letter to *Rave* magazine, July 1969

CHAPTER 21

The Devil's Interval

'There is a lack of excitement in the air, it's like the days before the Beatles.'

'Rock and roll is madness, and the method that has been imposed on it is too rational, too business-like, and too orderly, and if something doesn't break loose soon, it will kill off what energy is left ... There is a new audience that grew up on the music of the Sixties that is going to require and demand a music for the 1970s.'

Jon Landau, *Rolling Stone* magazine, December 1970

John Lennon and Yoko Ono proclaimed that the year commonly accepted as 1970 AD was actually Year One AP (After Peace). But the couple's bed-ins for peace, and poster events for peace, and Live Peace concert in Toronto, hadn't stopped the Vietnam War, any more than *Sgt. Pepper* had done. Caught between drug addiction and violent psychotherapy, Lennon began to question his purpose, and that of the Beatles. Unbeknown to the public, he had officially quit the band the previous autumn. 'The Beatles pattern is one that has to be scrapped,' he said soon afterwards, 'because if it remains the same it's a monument or a museum, and one thing this age is about is no museums. And the Beatles turned into a museum, so they have to be scrapped or deformed or changed.'

To avoid becoming a museum piece, Lennon refashioned himself as a radical newspaper, chronicling the disturbances of the times. On 27 January 1970, he wrote and recorded 'Instant Karma! (We All Shine On)', in which he questioned the value of stardom, and the relationship between musician and audience, concluding that they were one and the same. In keeping with his new aesthetic, he rush-released 'Instant Karma!' as a single: it was in the shops within ten days.

On 4 May that year, four young people were shot dead by Ohio National Guardsmen on the campus of Kent State University, during a demonstration against US military action in Cambodia. Newspaperman's son Neil Young wrote an anguished song of protest after his bandmate David Crosby showed him *Life* magazine's coverage of the tragedy. Two weeks later, Crosby, Stills, Nash & Young's 'Ohio' was released, a month to the day after the murders.

Both singles were hits: 'Ohio' focused global attention on an event that might otherwise have been forgotten; 'Instant Karma!' remains one of the most compelling rock records of all time. Urgent and outspoken, they represented the culture at its most spontaneous. Rock, it seemed, might not just provide the soundtrack for a cultural revolution, but be able to carry the weight of leadership. Yet these dreams soon dematerialised, for the truth was that by 1970, after (or despite) Kent State, the counter-culture centred on the Vietnam anti-war movement, psychedelic drugs and hippie morality was in ruins. The decay could be measured in personal terms. Within weeks of 'Ohio', Crosby, Stills, Nash & Young had sacrificed their partnership to the indulgence of their egos, while John Lennon was screaming out his mother's name on the floor of a therapist's office in Los Angeles. Ultimately, neither Lennon nor CSNY could sustain the hippie dream, or erect a viable alternative; their failure testified as much to the breadth of their ambition as to their human frailty. (It's emblematic that Lennon, the composer of 'The Ballad of John and Yoko', should struggle to keep his marriage intact for the remainder of his life, while two members of CSNY fell out of harmony over their shared lust for singer Rita Coolidge.)

There was no official declaration of defeat, and for many the fantasy lived on. Indeed, the rhetoric of rebellion grew more heated as the embers cooled, thanks to the likes of Paul Kantner and Grace Slick of Jefferson Airplane, who devoted several rousing albums to a social and political revolution that was by then a figment of their imagination. By 1972, John Lennon could build an entire album, *Some Time in New York City*, out of radical rhetoric, much of it already anachronistic by the time the album was released: not so much a news bulletin as yesterday's papers.

What remained after the death of the counter-culture? A culture, certainly; a world in which rock was central to people's lives; and, inevitably, a corporate global industry to ensure its survival. No sooner had hippie become a tag with a commercial value than these corporations – and quite shamelessly, their client-artists – began to market it. The example most often quoted, because it was the most blatant, was a late 1960s campaign by Columbia Records which resulted in such deathless advertising copy as this: 'The Rock Machine never sleeps. Day or night you can hear it. With its happening sounds. Of today . . . of tomorrow . . . The Rock Machine. Its beat is relentless. Because those at work within it are . . . The Rock Machine is restive. Enter. It's wild inside.' They were speaking the truth: the Rock Machine was restive, and needed a ready supply of fresh blood to renew its grotesque soul.

The early 1970s was an era when rock stars profited from the Rock Machine and wrestled with their consciences as they banked their cheques. Some assuaged themselves with political or charitable campaigning, such as Joan Baez and Country Joe McDonald. George Harrison staged two 1971 charity concerts to raise funds for the starving refugees of Bangladesh, his selfless endeavours tarnished by the British government's insistence on claiming tax from the resulting single, album and film. In more introspective mode, stars channelled their moral dilemmas into songs questioning the very nature of the system which had made them rich. Pete Townshend grappled with this quandary at such length that it eventually inspired two best-selling albums, *Who's Next* and *Quadrophenia*. Joni Mitchell waxed cynical about the 'star-maker machinery behind the popular song'. Ray Davies of the Kinks extracted more than one album, and a TV play, from his self-doubt. David Bowie, when still a virtual unknown, challenged the iconography of fame on his *Hunky Dory* album, and then invented his own superstar, Ziggy Stardust, to show how hollow and yet addictive the notion of rock celebrity could be.

These misgivings about the meaning of fame came from the stars themselves, rather than the public – at least until later in the decade. People wanted to believe in the majesty and transcendent power of rock 'n' roll, because it still raised them up, took them away from the tedium of the everyday, provided the rhythm of their daily lives, and filled their minds with fantasies of rebellion and stardom. Everyone benefited from keeping the counter-culture dream alive, so it lived on. Rock festivals became a regular fixture in the calendar, their grim conditions (no shelter, no water, no toilets, no food) camouflaged by the potency of the collective myth. Bands who had once performed in cinemas, theatres or student common rooms now filled arenas or even, after CSNY's 'doom tour' in 1974, vast American sports stadia. Record sales increased exponentially during the early years of the decade, and so did the proceeds from rock merchandising. No self-respecting adolescent or student bedroom was complete without posters of their stardom-wary icons on the wall.

There was an irony to this mass celebration of rock's cultural importance. Once it had been possible to organise a Gathering of the Tribes in Golden Gate Park. Now, there were few tribes left who could stand each other's company. You didn't love rock, you loved progressive rock, or hippie rock, or glam rock, or hard rock, or country rock, or folk rock – only existing superstars from the 1960s bridged those divides. Holding an iconic album sleeve under your arm no longer marked you out as a member of a secret sect, but as an adherent of a subculture. Schoolboys decorated their satchels with the biro-ed names of their favourite bands: after you'd scrawled your allegiance to 'SABBATH', 'ELP' or 'HEEP', you carried it as a badge of pride.

Yet increasingly the preoccupations of rock's aristocracy – the men (and a very occasional woman) who grew up with Elvis and launched their careers in the first half of the 1960s – were distant from those of the traditional rock 'n' roll audience: the teenagers. The early 1970s saw those stars near or past the age of 30 using rock to explore the crises of privileged adulthood. If it was hard for kids in the slums or the suburbs to empathise with rich men complaining about the vicissitudes of life in Chelsea or Laurel Canyon, it was equally alienating to be sold anthems of political disillusionment, artistic self-doubt, marital strife, and existential concern about the state of the culture. These were not the crusades that would set a thousand biros to work on school exercise-books and bags. Adolescents wanted heroes who were rebellious and carefree; only adults could afford to sympathise with the decadent and jaded.

Between 1970 and 1976, the parameters of rock lyrics broadened to engage with these comparatively complex issues of adulthood. During those years, it became ever more obvious to even the vaguely intelligent observer that something had gone badly awry with the culture that those stars represented. But individually, even at their most fallow, the rock pantheon could still offer a sense of honesty and authenticity, regardless of how far removed their lifestyle was from that of their fans. The singer-songwriter tradition epitomised by James Taylor, Carole King, CSNY and Joni Mitchell allowed for extremes of self-indulgence (beautiful self-indulgence, some of it, as on David Crosby's rich, therapeutic exhibition of vocal harmony, *If I Could Only Remember My Name*). It facilitated a style of songwriting that could easily be abused, but which could also offer a degree of humanity and insight previously only available from literature. Joni Mitchell transcended her fame via the acuity with which she examined her milieu and her psyche, stripped bare her own insecurities on *Blue* and then widened her horizons to analyse her social surroundings. Yet these were necessarily removed from the experience of her audience, who weren't accompanying Warren Beatty to A-list Hollywood parties or chopping lines of cocaine on antique tables beneath windows of stained glass. Fans had to choose which was the lesser evil: songwriters who lived in mansions but still wrote about life on the streets; or those who admitted the distance between their privilege and their listeners' mundane existence.

These were the ambiguous exemplars of confessional songwriting, laying themselves bare for an audience who knew – or thought they knew – the precise personal crises which had triggered each lyric. (This was another trademark of the early 1970s: you not only bought their music, but bought into their lives.) For a brief period in the early 1970s, a handful of records provided the emotional soundtrack for a generation: Carole King's

Tapestry, James Taylor's *Sweet Baby James* and *Mud Slide Slim*, *Crosby, Stills & Nash*, Joni Mitchell's *Ladies of the Canyon* and *Blue*, Neil Young's *After the Goldrush* and *Harvest*; from Britain, too, the work of Cat Stevens and Elton John. Of these, Taylor was the most ambiguous, his almost soporific ambience masking disquieting dreams, as he battled against his discomforting fame. He subsequently admitted that his fragmentary 1972 record, *One Man Dog*, was a deliberate attempt to undermine his stardom. Neil Young cleared a more courageous path towards the same destination, outstripping even Joni Mitchell in the eagerness with which he risked psychological and physical destruction on *Tonight's the Night* and the culture-shredding *On the Beach*. Those records coincided with the re-emergence of Bob Dylan, who had been absent in all but reputation as a creative force between 1968 and 1974. He toured America for several weeks with the Band, sparking the most frenzied demand for tickets in rock history, and then proceeded to refashion the narrative song on *Blood on the Tracks* and *Desire*.

Dylan maintained that creative intensity through late 1975 and the spring of 1976, re-entering the Greenwich Village bohemia which he had dominated more than a decade earlier. He assembled a ragbag band of gypsies, folk veterans, cynical rockers, wives and lovers (past and present), and set out on two tours which he nicknamed Rolling Thunder. Each night, he revitalised his back catalogue and breathed fire into new material, marauding through some of rock's most cherished anthems with the savagery of a hungry lion. Before he set out on the road, he watched the poet turned garage-rock singer, Patti Smith, perform the songs from *Horses*, an inspired spew of beat imagery and symbolist madness, fuelled by the spirit of mid-1960s garage rock. He also encountered the latest performer to be christened with the doom-laden publicity tag 'the new Bob Dylan': Bruce Springsteen was promoting *Born to Run*, an epic (if wildly over-romanticised) expression of the gospel of rock 'n' roll. Joni Mitchell, dragged aboard Dylan's touring bus, had completed one record of forensic cultural analysis, *The Hissing of Summer Lawns*, and was assembling the material for an equally unsparing study of her own flaws and foibles, *Hejira*. Meanwhile, reggae star Bob Marley was leading the Wailers through ecstatic celebrations of Ras Tafari and ganja, with an intensity and righteousness which was provoking comparisons with the sacred Dylan.

For these few months, the spirit of 1960s rock – the best intentions of the counter-culture, the magic that could set you free – seemed to be alive and burning with radical fire. Perhaps, after all, the music could not only fill your soul, but provide a spiritual handbook to deal with age and experience. And then, almost overnight, that brief spasm of urgency and relevance was gone, its protagonists sidetracked by marital breakdown, legal entanglements and simple self-indulgence. Thereafter, the only reliable route to that idealism, and the emotions it inspired, was through nostalgia. But with each passing year of disillusion and cynicism that followed, the mythology of the 1960s – the decade which stretched from the Beatles to Rolling Thunder – grew more intoxicating and enveloping. As the past was endlessly recycled and retold, it took on the status of a golden age, which would tower over subsequent generations like the husk of a derelict skyscraper: magnificent and yet hollow.

> It is apparent that rock has dramatically lowered the age level at which consumers enter the record market, and that market, in turn, continues to reflect the taste of younger age groups. Early rock 'n' roll was recognised as a teenage product. The audience for Monkees records is regarded as subteen. And now with these new groups, we may be dipping down to the nursery level.
> Rock historian Arnold Shaw on bubblegum pop, 1969

> My birthday is March 3rd, and I will be 11. I hope I am not too old for you.
> Fan letter to Michael Jackson (aged 12), 1971

The Jackson 5 was not the first black family from Gary, Indiana to strike out into the music business. In 1952, Frank 'Al' Jenkins formed the Jenkins Family with six of his eight children, aged from 16 to 5, and a repertoire of 'everything from bebop to sophisticated swing'. What carried the Jacksons beyond other sibling groups was the audaciously precocious talent of their (then) youngest brother. Until he hit puberty, Michael Jackson was America's most instinctive soul singer, after which he learned how to replicate what he had once done unconsciously. He was a sex symbol with an ambiguous relationship towards his own physicality: pledging as an adult never to inflict sexual imagery upon his fans, he would grab at his crotch every few seconds on stage. But the pre-teen Michael had also displayed a repertoire of sexual bumps and grinds for audiences whose average age was about 10. Perhaps understanding what that symbolised better than he did, they responded with uncontrollable screams.

The Jackson 5 were moulded by Motown boss Berry Gordy, and the creative team he tellingly named 'The Corporation', into a show-business attraction without parallel. Michael alone was compared to James Brown, Sammy Davis Jr, Mick Jagger and Tina Turner, sometimes all at once. The brothers were launched with an almost peerless run of hits which fulfilled every pop requirement: explosive excitement, spontaneity, instant rapport between audience and artist, crescendos and climaxes stuffed full of melodic hooks and topped with Michael's telltale squeals.

Their nearest rivals, the Osmonds, were white, and very clean. The sleeve notes to their first teen pop album (as against the barbershop quartet records they'd made in the 1960s) promised that 'Donny [the same age as Michael] never has a bad thought toward anyone . . . After meeting Alan, you must think twice before doing anything wrong . . . The Osmonds did not need gimmicks nor stimulants to take them to the top.' Meanwhile, David Cassidy was a singer turned actor turned singer, who had aspirations to match the Beatles or the Beach Boys, but was marooned in TV's *The Partridge Family*. Less troubled than Michael, more human than Donny (he even admitted sexual relationships and mild drug use), he completed a trio of American idols who would command young girls' hearts and pubescent urges for the first half of the 1970s.

There were many more in the same vein, mostly white (the Jacksons would probably not have been accepted from any other label but Motown, which had already proved its transracial appeal with the Supremes), mostly soloists, barely older than their putative fans. They filled the gap left by the Monkees, and before them the Beatles, although the new breed was modelled on the clean-cut, winsome young men who'd offered a safer alternative to Elvis Presley: Rick Nelson, Frankie Avalon, Paul Anka. Between the prime of the Monkees and the propulsive launch of the Jacksons, however, the record industry filled the interregnum with a new genre: bubblegum pop. As its name suggested, this music was sweet, gave up all its secrets in an instant explosion of the taste buds, and was instantly disposable. The masterminds of the genre – many of whom had been crafting pop hits for a decade – preferred to use anonymous artists as the 'stars' of their records. The most potent stable was run by the Kasenetz-Katz production company, and including such imaginary groups as the

1910 Fruitgum Company and the Ohio Express. In 1968, eight of these outfits (or session musicians masquerading under their names) filled Carnegie Hall for an evening extravaganza by the Kasenetz-Katz Singing Orchestral Circus. But the K-K crew were soon outflanked by the Archies, fictional stars of a US cartoon series, and No. 1 hitmakers with the addictively perfect bubblegum record: 'Sugar Sugar'.

Here was a blatant attempt to reach an audience which everyone knew existed – children barely old enough to attend school – but whose buying power was minimal. Very young kids reduced popular music to its essentials: a rhythm, and a chorus, regardless of whether they understood the implications of either.* A market was opening for pop nursery rhymes, pop advertising jingles for toddlers, children's TV shows in which pop would be used to educate as well as entertain. But bubblegum's audience didn't end there. If there was no barrier between the ear and the commercial appeal of the song – no political agenda or cultural baggage – then these hits could provide a social function for teenagers at discos just as they captivated the pre-teen audience for teatime cartoon shows.

British bubblegum wasn't as calculated as its American counterpart or, for a while, as simplistic. In the hands of the Foundations and the Amen Corner, Love Affair and the Equals, all hitmakers in 1968, it mixed essence of Motown with spirit of Beatles, excised the desire for progression and experimentation, and staked everything on a chorus so nagging that it would enter the ear of everyone who heard it, never to be entirely removed. (Whoever invented the term 'earworm' for an unshakeable musical motif knew what they were talking about.) The results were almost refreshingly obvious and direct: 'Baby Come Back', 'Bend Me Shape Me', 'Build Me Up Buttercup', 'Everlasting Love'. This was the purest of pop, yet still constructed with enough finesse to avoid embarrassing the composer or the purchaser.

The same could not always be said for the contrivances which filled the annual Eurovision Song Contest. The late 1960s marked the finessing of Euro-pop, which crossed the directness of bubblegum with the oom-pah rhythm of the polka and the shameless banality of German *Schlager*. To

---

* Somewhere there is a landfill site which contains reel-to-reel tape recordings of the 6-year-old author singing garbled versions of 'Hippy Hippy Shake' and 'Bits and Pieces', two early 1964 hits which hooked my imagination with pinpoint accuracy. The creators of those records had probably imagined an audience that was a decade older, and female.

bypass barriers of language, words were reduced to nonsensical syllables, as onomatopoeic as possible. Massiel's 'La, La, La' won the contest in 1968; Lulu's 'Boom Bang-A-Bang' was joint victor in 1969; and subsequent competitions featured variants on the same inexhaustible theme.

By 1971, British pop had prepared its own stew of all these elements, and an audience who felt alienated by the increasingly adult preoccupations of rock could luxuriate in the joyous simplicity (or stupidity) of 'Chirpy Chirpy Cheep Cheep', 'The Pushbike Song' and 'Funny Funny'. The last of these singles was recorded by Sweet and written/produced by Mike Chapman and Nicky Chinn, who concocted an entire series of equally immediate confections: 'Co-Co', 'Alexander Graham Bell' and (most amusingly for British kids) 'Little Willy'. But something strange was happening: Sweet's 'Little Willy' was set to a guitar riff that signalled strutting sexuality, not innocent childhood fun. 'Wig-Wam Bam' completed the transfer of power: the group cavorted on TV's *Top of the Pops* in Native American costumes, with glitter arranged artfully on their cheeks, while miming to a fusion of metallic guitars and tribal drumbeats. This was cartoonish, but not like the Archies: what was being parodied here was sex, machismo, the pretensions of rock, ultimately adulthood – all in the spirit of pop. Here was irony, commerciality, artifice, compressed into an irresistible package: one that owed nothing to the rock tradition which had led an earlier generation from Elvis to Dylan to Altamont and disillusionment.

What I've been trying to do is recapture the feeling, the energy, behind old rock music without actually doing it the same technically.
Marc Bolan, T. Rex, 1971

As annoying as watching a narcissist endlessly preening himself before a mirror . . . bogus . . . a crass package of synthetic rock and roll music.
Nick Kent, *Cream* magazine, on T. Rex's *The Slider*, 1972

'They look like builder's labourers with make-up', complained Ozzy Osbourne of Sweet in 1973, by which time the former bubblegum band had adopted an image so camp that it would have shamed a pantomime dame. They were not alone. Camp was the sexuality of the age, completing a sequence that involved the Beatles' collar-length, 'feminine' hair, the mock-homosexual stage antics of the Kinks, the Rolling Stones' publicity shots in elderly drag and the 'man's dress' which adorned the body of David Bowie on *The Man Who Sold the World*. 'Are You a Boy or Are You a Girl', asked a 1965 single by the US garage-rock band the Barbarians, quoting a standard adult response to men with long hair. Now the question was irrelevant, the only possible answer being: 'Does it matter?'

Alice Cooper was an American hard-rock band from Phoenix. Alice Cooper was also the pseudonym adopted by singer Vincent Furnier, who sported an explicitly tight catsuit and horror-movie make-up, snarled like a sardonic bulldog, and yet still managed to convince 25% of his live audience (in an American survey) that he was actually a woman. David Bowie was a married man who claimed to be gay, pretended to fellate his guitarist's instrument, and dabbled in imagery that was not so much ambiguous as polymorphous.

Leader of the pack, by being the first of his generation to wear glitter on prime-time television, was Marc Bolan, eternal peacock and musical chancer (like Bowie, he'd thrown himself at every wave from beat to R&B to psychedelia to folk), with a penchant for pseudo-mystical verse and an utterly distinctive vocal bleat – an opportunist, but also a natural star. He'd won over the British underground with his hippie mythologising as part of an acoustic duo named Tyrannosaurus Rex. For the new decade, he streamlined their name to T. Rex, and reinvented himself as a rock 'n' roller: part Sun Studios, *c*.1957; part bubblegum, *c*.1969; with a mastery of media manipulation, which made him an artful self-publicist. Bolan's lyrics couldn't deliver the cosmic insight that he claimed, but he knew how to concoct a hit single, whether it was as hypnotic as 'Ride a White Swan' or as anthemic as 'Hot Love'. He would run out of tricks to turn by 1974, but had already conquered a generation for whom he represented a first encounter with the art of magic and the magic of artifice. Sadly, he lacked the innate sensitivity to the changing times which enabled David Bowie to move effortlessly through the 1970s, remodelling himself and his work with stunning efficiency and imagination.

If Bowie and Bolan were the philosopher and cheerleader of what was soon being called glam rock, there were foot soldiers a-plenty, from the Beatles-inspired craftsmanship of Slade to the Neanderthal cacophony of Gary Glitter. As Julian Cope recalled, glam 'would ultimately provide a safe haven for all the flotsam and jetsam of the music biz' who 'rushed to the pan stick and eyeliner in order to try and resuscitate their dormant, nay dead, careers'. Glitter was formerly Paul Raven, 32 years old when he scored his first hit; Alvin Stardust had been Shane Fenton (and before that Bernard Jewry), and was 31; Mott the Hoople's Ian Hunter, once Ian Patterson, was 33 when he reached out to 'All the Young Dudes'. Many of glam's icons, then, were as old as the generation they were replacing; and, as Cope reflected, 'glam rock may have had no more message than a single "Wake up!" But it was unashamedly attempting to be top entertainment at a time when most so-called serious rock was so far up its own ass that even putting on stage clothes was considered gauche by the delicate flowers of the singer-songwriter boom.'

Eventually, everyone who still believed in the power of pop jumped aboard the glam bandwagon, from delicate flower Elton John (R&B singer turned confessional songwriter, now turned trussed-up fashion victim) to stalwarts such as Paul McCartney and Mick Jagger. David Bowie even persuaded Lou Reed, veteran of the New York art-rock band the Velvet Underground, to don panda make-up and act effete, rather than his usual boorish self. Bowie and Reed would swiftly abandon glam once its shock value had eroded. Others who were less intelligent and sure-footed found the transition from camp theatricality to rock authenticity more difficult to achieve: both Slade and Sweet struggled for years to re-establish themselves as macho rock bands when TV clips of their beglittered heyday were so fresh in the memory. Bolan was the saddest case of all, living amidst the trappings of his dissipated stardom just long enough to proclaim himself the godfather of punk, before dying in a car crash. His boast seemed farfetched in 1977, but the young pioneers of London punk were the children of glam, and there was only the shortest of musical paths between the two genres. Meanwhile, glam's clown-like fashion sense was adopted by bands who took their music far more seriously, recasting the cartoons of the early 1970s as backdrops for horror movies worthy of the Hammer studio.

There's an incredible desire on the part of the public for the heavy and very unsubtle forms of music . . . Black Sabbath I would say are unsubtle. I don't use that in a derogatory sense, but they have a very blunt and personal instrument of death and torture at their hands when they play, and that is what is appealing to a lot of people.

Ian Anderson, Jethro Tull, 1971

Heavy Metal Rock is amazingly popular. If all us smart-ass rock critics put it down so much, then who's the fool? Either the audiences are out of their minds or else we are.
Charles Shaar Murray, *NME*, 1973

It was the most cynical of marketing ploys: using the name of a defunct rock group to sell tickets for a band that no one had ever heard. The manipulators were guitarist Jimmy Page, survivor of the British blues-psych band the Yardbirds, and his manager, Peter Grant. The solution? The (New) Yardbirds, boasting Page, a session bassist, and an unknown vocalist and drummer, fulfilling the commitments of a band whose two most famous assets, Eric Clapton and Jeff Beck, had long since departed. Only when the New Yardbirds reached North America in December 1968 did they dare to assume a fresh identity: as Led Zeppelin. Their bassist John Paul Jones recalled that their impact was immediate. 'There were kids actually bashing their heads against the stage', he said – not in anger or a sense of betrayal, but in the sheer elation of experiencing music so loud and relentless that its effect was transcendent.

'They are a sort of release valve for our frustration and energy', said a fan of another British hard rock band, Black Sabbath. 'I think the volume they play at has a lot to do with their appeal for me – they work you up to a sort of pitch, which is almost an hysteria. I'd be disappointed if I come away from one of their concerts without feeling physically and mentally exhausted.' The volume emitted by Deep Purple – proud of their reputation as the world's loudest band – was so extreme that one exhilarated teenage fan was unable to hear anything for two weeks after a 1971 performance in a British town hall. 'It was worth it', he said afterwards.

Noise was only one of hard rock's attractions. Another was its attitude: unpretentious, unrelenting and powerful. This was an adolescent's fantasy of adult masculinity, clad in denim or leather: the rock star as true representative of the people. A third was community: more, perhaps, than any other genre in the history of popular music, hard rock encouraged its audience to bond. They were the true believers in a world which denied their right to pleasure, and which denigrated the thing they loved. They were the provinces against London; the Midwest against Manhattan; the working class against the privileged middle; rawness against sophistication; reality against the illusions of politics or art. None of those dividing lines was watertight. One of the great joys of belonging was that nobody was excluded. Even women were welcome, if they donned denim and broadcast their allegiance with T-shirts or ballpoint-pen tattoos.

No form of music has been so roundly lampooned by the media that were supposed to serve its audience. Led Zeppelin, for example, were 'trash with a rock beat'; they exhibited a 'very insensitive grossness' (not just an insensitive grossness, but worse than that); they were, according to Pete Townshend, a 'gross, disgusting object'. And Zeppelin were one of the more critically acceptable purveyors of the genre, applauded at least for their control of dynamics and their scything sexuality. Of the other British bands who dominated adolescent male passion in the early 1970s, Deep Purple were criticised for their pretensions (they dared to work with a symphony orchestra) and over-reliance on technique; Black Sabbath for their simplicity and lack of technique; Uriah Heep for daring to exist at all. Hard rock, unless it was employed by the Rolling Stones or the Who, in which case there was assumed to be some intelligence at play, was nothing more than stupid music played by stupid (or exploitative) musicians for the benefit of very stupid people. No wonder its fans were so loyal: they were standing alongside their heroes in the path of a verbal hurricane.

From the beginning, Black Sabbath (and their near namesakes, Black Widow) were under assault on another front: from those who took their satanic references seriously. Black Widow exploited their devilish image with 'Come to the Sabbat' ('Satan's there', the chant continued). They were no more dangerous than the Crazy World of Arthur Brown, whose leader donned a flaming headpiece and screamed 'I am the god of hellfire'. Mick Jagger could flirt with Beelzebub in the late 1960s because he was a master of pose: the Rolling Stones were so powerful an emblem of adolescent rebellion that fans almost wanted Jagger to be revealed as the Lord of Darkness, just to see the reaction of their parents. Black Sabbath, however, sounded as if they might be in touch with Satan, so despairing was Ozzy Osbourne's howl, so incisive the guitar of Tony Iommi. 'Tony came up with this riff', explained Osbourne of the song which gave the band its name. 'I moaned a tune over the top of it, and the end result was fucking awesome – the best thing we'd ever done by a mile. I've since been told that Tony's riff is based on what's known as the "Devil's interval" or the "triton". Apparently churches banned it from being used in religious music during the Middle Ages because it scared the crap out of people. The organist would start to play it and everyone would run away 'cos they thought the Devil was going to pop up from behind the altar.' Despite that,

Osbourne insisted: 'I can honestly say that we never took the black-magic stuff seriously for one second. We just liked how theatrical it was.' But as his bandmate Bill Ward revealed, 'We've even had a few witches on the phone asking us to play at their Black Masses', which was a testament to the power of their image. 'I'm scared of them', admitted a 14-year-old American fan. 'They're evil and strange. I hope they sacrifice something tonight. A human sacrifice would be good.' No wonder the band was banned from the Royal Albert Hall in 1971: 'It is our policy to avoid the risk of possible inflammatory situations', the management explained.

In the mid-1960s, when the American music trade defined rock 'n' roll as anything that teenagers enjoyed (which explains why Petula Clark's 'Downtown' was chosen as the Best Rock & Roll Recording at the Grammy Awards of 1965), the term 'hard rock' referred specifically to the music of the late 1950s. The Beach Boys were said in 1967 to have 'evolved from writing hard rock to writing songs that sound like psalms'. But the controlled exercise of noise by the likes of Pete Townshend and Jimi Hendrix, and the introduction of effects pedals and supercharged amplification, which instantly quadrupled both the volume and sonic range available to a rock band, forced a redefinition. At the core of this brand of hard rock (and its close cousin, heavy metal) was the riff. Beethoven knew its power: why else would he begin his fifth symphony with a riff even more famous than the skeleton of Led Zeppelin's 'Whole Lotta Love' or Deep Purple's 'Smoke on the Water'? So did the maestros of the swing band, Glenn Miller's 'In the Mood' being the most obvious example. Like the chorus of a pop song, the riff compressed the whole of a musical experience into a few seconds: a signal as identifiable as a television theme tune or the cry of a bird of prey. It focused and magnified a band's power, took control of the body, offered elation, catharsis, a crescendo of joy, as the head instinctively rocked forward with the beat – the headbanging of metal legend.

Hard rock didn't own the riff, as there were memorable motifs on thousands of records, from the thrilling descent at the start of the Beatles' 'Please Please Me' to its echo on Freda Payne's 'Band of Gold'. The Rolling Stones were the masters of the riff as war cry: almost all of their greatest singles boasted one, from the two-chord prototype of 'Not Fade Away' to the totemic fanfare of 'Brown Sugar'. But they were merely a conduit into the song, an *amuse-oreille* to announce its arrival. In hard rock, the riff could *be* the song.

The combination of riff, volume, distortion and dynamics – the essentials of hard rock – was virtually complete on the Troggs' 1966 hit 'Wild Thing', a successor to the Kingsmen's 'Louie Louie' as a song it was almost impossible to play badly. Blue Cheer's 1968 revival of Eddie Cochran's statement of teenage angst, 'Summertime Blues', fulfilled every requirement. It didn't swing, it was drenched in fuzztone, and with its erratic sense of rhythm, it sounded as if a school garage band had inadvertently been let loose in a professional recording studio. 'We had a place in forming that heavy-metal sound', said Blue Cheer guitarist Dick Peterson modestly. 'I'm not saying we knew what we were doing, 'cause we didn't. All we knew was we wanted more power. And if that's not a heavy-metal attitude, I don't know what is.'* Soon followed the culmination of American rock's dance with death: Steppenwolf's genre-defining 'Born to Be Wild'. Here, for the first time in song, was a phrase coined to describe the firepower of military hardware, but applied to the ferocious growl of motorcycles: 'heavy metal thunder'.

A barrage of 1968 hit singles heralded an aesthetic change: Vanilla Fudge's portentous mangling of the Supremes' 'You Keep Me Hangin' On'; Deep Purple's 'Hush'; Creedence Clearwater Revival's 'Suzie-Q', a hamfisted attempt to mimic the free-form jamming of the acid-rock bands; Iron Butterfly's near-operatic 'In-A-Gadda-Da-Vida'; perhaps, for its sonic thrust and reckless distortion alone, the Beatles' 'Revolution'.

That was a prophetic title, even if the revolution was not one the Beatles would have recognised (though they anticipated it, purely for kicks, on 'Helter Skelter'). By the end of 1969, Led Zeppelin were challenging the commercial supremacy of the Beatles, with a mangled edit of 'Whole Lotta Love' reaching into the US Top 10 while demonstrating their epic assemblage of hard-rock tricks – jet-plane guitar runs across the speakers, abrupt shifts of tone and volume, a voice teasing, pleading, wailing for sexual fulfilment, a drum solo, and a guitar solo with the jaw-shattering intensity of a dentist's drill. And right behind them, hiding in plain sight, a power trio who were about to become America's biggest rock band to date: the critically derided, defiantly unoriginal Grand Funk Railroad.

American critic Richard Robinson could smell profound change in the wind. 'We've all gotten comfortable with a new music that is growing

---

* A pause to remember one of the more unusual events from the rock underground: at London's psychedelic Middle Earth club in October 1968, Blue Cheer were supported by a symphony orchestra performing pieces by Bach, Mozart and Stravinsky.

older by the minute', he wrote in 1971. 'We've all decided that rock and roll has gone through enough changes and we should settle back and relax. I say "all of us" have decided that. What I mean is all of us except the young people who like the new bands like Grand Funk and Black Sabbath. And I'd like to suggest that unless we want to wind up talking about the good old days . . . then we'd better reopen our minds and realise that once again there's a new music happening across the land. A new music that hasn't much to do with *Sgt. Pepper*, Simon & Garfunkel or CSNY.'

Its audience was not just younger, but drawn to barbiturate pills and cheap wine, to numb the brain rather than propel it into different dimensions. 'Now progressive music has grown its own teenybops', contended Charles Shaar Murray. He added that 'Grand Funk's musical roots seem to stretch no further than 1967', making them the first rock stars not to have a direct connection to the music of the mid-1950s. 'Lowest common denominator' was about the kindest expression that *Rolling Stone* magazine could find to describe Grand Funk, pegging their audience as 'young and not especially sophisticated', while granting graciously that they 'should be allowed to enjoy [themselves] without being tarred with a lot of undeserved labels'. Yet one label was well earned: GFR created the first anthem of America's most powerful rock movement during the 1970s and 80s, the radio format known as AOR (or album-oriented rock). With 1970's 'Closer to Home', Grand Funk concocted a song that was simultaneously rock and ballad. Adorned with vocal harmonies which dimly recalled the skintight arrangements of CSNY, sweetened with strings, and bearing a message so vague that listeners could fashion their own interpretations, 'Closer to Home' had an epic quality both rousing and strangely poignant. It hinted at loss while offering fans a place to belong, where they would not be pilloried for their musical choices. And it operated on a scale that could perhaps only be appreciated in a stadium – Shea Stadium, for example, which GFR had sold out more quickly than the Beatles. 'The spirit of American punk rock certainly lives on in Grand Funk Railroad', one critic wrote, in which case their success represented the ultimate triumph of the amateur – victorious even over the culture that gave them life. As Charles Shaar Murray concluded, admitting at the age of 20 that it might be time to pass on the torch: 'Maybe anybody who cannot dig Grand Funk is too old for rock and roll.'

GFR's low standing among critics was rivalled only by Chicago, who dedicated an early album to 'the Revolution' but swiftly jettisoned their radical trimmings. By the time they issued a quadruple-album live set in 1971, their name was a synonym for soulless excess. Often described as a jazz-rock band because of their rousing brass section, they were accused by writer Bob Palmer of being a jazz band who couldn't play jazz, a horn band who couldn't play R&B. 'Their roots seem to be planted firmly in AM radio', he concluded: another band damned for their lack of connection to the appropriate elements of the past. But by condemning GFR and Chicago for their rootlessness, the critics were effectively refusing to recognise any heroes but their own. The rock bands of the new decade would create a fresh tradition, which no longer depended on the shared assumptions of their predecessors.

CHAPTER 22

PUSH-BUTTON ROCK

'I don't think we'll see another Frank Sinatra again. I don't think you'll ever see Tony Bennett again, who had a run from 1950 to 1966, or something like that, as a popular artist.'

Joe Smith, general manager of Warner Brothers Records, 1971

$\notin$

It was a fact, said the minister of the Community Baptist Church in Aromas, California, that '95% of all illegitimate children nowadays are conceived following a rock concert'. Rock 'caused crime, sexual promiscuity and destruction of the central nervous system'. Music therapist Adam Kuests, also from California, agreed. Rock, he claimed, was 'more deadly than heroin . . . Rock is not a harmless pastime but a dangerous drug on which our children are hooked.' Its consequences included hostility, fatigue, narcissism, panic, indigestion, high blood pressure and hypertension. Baptists in Aromas began to experience some of those symptoms themselves when they learned about the inherent evil of music. 'To think it could cause your child to behave like a heathen, just strip off your clothes and do the sex act with a stranger', an anguished mother exclaimed. Another said: 'My children have these records, and I just didn't *know*.'

To these warnings could be added the words of the soon-to-be-disgraced vice president of the United States, Spiro Agnew. Children were being 'brainwashed' into drug-taking, he alleged, by such pernicious songs as 'White Rabbit' (Jefferson Airplane), 'With a Little Help from My Friends' (the Beatles), 'Acid Queen' (the Who), 'Eight Miles High' (the Byrds) and 'Don't Step on the Grass, Sam' (Steppenwolf). He jolted American radio stations into action, and soon programme directors were drawing up their own lists of songs that might be suspect: 'Yellow Submarine', 'Puff the Magic Dragon', 'A Whiter Shade of Pale' and, inevitably, Brewer & Shipley's gently satirical hippie anthem, 'One Toke Over the Line'. In Britain, the BBC were no more rational. They elected to ban Mungo Jerry's harmless 'Lady Rose' single until the group's record company agreed to remove one of its additional tracks, a playful revamp of Lead Belly's folk tune, 'Take a Whiff on Me'. Meanwhile, the BBC happily played Tony Christie's murder ballad, 'I Did What I Did for Maria'. Violence was entertainment, it seemed; drugs a national threat. How long, people wondered, before radio would refuse to broadcast any song from an album which mentioned illegal drugs?

All of these impulsive acts of censure and censorship signalled the alienation felt by many adults towards a rock culture that had moved beyond entertainment, into the realms of political comment and social misconduct. The parents of 1971's teenagers had been born in the 1920s or 30s, raised during wartime and economic austerity, and often regarded hedonism and nonconformism as signs of rampant delinquency. Yet they could hardly complain that their more sedate tastes were being overlooked by the record industry. A wider range of music, past and present, was available now for sale than at any time in history.

Those who had been raised on the big bands could watch the likes of Benny Goodman (then well into his 60s) lead his orchestra through his vintage repertoire. The Glenn Miller Orchestra survived, nearly thirty years after their chief's disappearance. Paul Whiteman might have died in 1967, but there was a New Paul Whiteman Orchestra to keep his arrangements alive. The Pasadena Roof Orchestra (formed in 1969) ranged across the entire dance-band era, the jazz equivalent to the fashion for performing pre-1800 classical music on period instruments. Many of the stars of the vintage British music hall could be seen weekly on BBC TV's *The Good Old Days*, while their American equivalents were the mainstays of the chat-show circuit.

Bing Crosby was still recording, exploring at last the territory of the Beatles and Jimmy Webb. Frank Sinatra had already surveyed that terrain, retired because he knew his time had passed, and then returned when he discovered that his audience was clinging to the old songs. Basie, Ella and Ellington were still on the road – in Ellington's case, composing on an epic scale until his death in 1974. Jazz was no longer a commercial force on record unless it was allied to rock instruments, but every era of its past was ripe for revival. Meanwhile, the easy-listening market was expanding with each improvement in hi-fi reproduction. Britain's belated acceptance of stereophonic sound in 1969–70 sparked a marketing campaign hinged around the assumption that the core audience for stereo LPs was adult, and required nothing more strenuous from its listening than relaxation.

The music industry struggled to comprehend that different sectors of its clientele might require individual attention. While rock culture was being served by an array of specialist journals, from *Rolling Stone* and *Creem* to *Melody Maker* and *Sounds*, and underground newspapers, more traditional media outlets vainly attempted to cater for everyone from pre-teens to pensioners. For example, a single issue of the *New Musical Express* from December 1970 contained album reviews, side by side, of Frank Sinatra with Count Basie; Yoko Ono's fusion of rock, jazz and the avant-garde;

actor Clive Dunn, aged 48, impersonating an elderly grandfather; variety drag artiste Danny La Rue; the Temptations, Motown's kings of psychedelic soul; TV glove puppet Basil Brush; country star Waylon Jennings; pub pianist Mrs Mills; comedian Kenneth Williams; and the folk guitar wizard, Davy Graham. They were all pop: all equally entitled, in the pop universe, to the attention of journalists who would rather have been interviewing Led Zeppelin.*

An equally diverse demographic was represented at concerts by the Carpenters, a brother-and-sister duo whose records blended the sexlessness of late 1950s teen pop with harmonies borrowed from the pre-Elvis era. Rock journalist Lester Bangs speculated that 'this must have been a sort of diplomatic project in many homes: Mom and Pop would come and learn to Dig the Kids' Music'. As keyboardist Richard Carpenter noted, 'There had been no brother/sister act since Fred and Adele Astaire.' He was alarmed to discover that photographers kept asking him to embrace his sister in publicity shots, while journalists sniggered about their relationship (and, on one notorious occasion, he was accused of incest in a live radio interview). His sister Karen's voice was an enigma: pitch-perfect, an emotional blank canvas, so unwavering in its mellifluousness that it was almost eerily cold – or warm: it was hard to determine which. As the decade progressed, Karen grew thinner and more troubled, while maintaining a flawless showbiz persona. Their stage act was a bizarre collage of impulses: Karen donning a pair of false breasts for a *Grease* routine, before her brother interrupted their run of hits with Richard Addinsell's mock-classical *Warsaw Concerto* – all things to everyone except themselves, until the last.

If the Carpenters were ultimately enacting a tragedy, then the James Last Orchestra, which reached its commercial peak during this decade, offered a similar audience a foolproof guarantee of pleasure and security. Last (nicknamed 'Hansi' by his fans) was a German jazz bassist who had hit upon the concept of 'Non-Stop Dancing' as a means of applying the ethos of the pre-rock dance bands to the modern era. 'All the bands were just playing music from the 30s and 40s', he explained. 'So we started with songs from the Beatles and the Rolling Stones.' Only the tunes

---

* Within two years, *NME* had reinvented itself as the hippest of all the British rock papers, filling its pages with refugees from the ailing underground press and clichés borrowed from its American equivalents.

survived, as all the symbols of rock 'n' roll were tossed aside in favour of rich orchestrations and jaunty dance beats, accompanied by wordless chorales in which even the most tuneless aficionados could participate. So uniform yet flexible was his approach that it could encompass almost every form of music, from Jimi Hendrix to Bing Crosby – all fodder for Last's non-stop party, which would force everyone from small kids to great-grandparents on to the dance floor. Arguably the world's most popular and least cele-brated artist, Last could fill enormous halls around the world for decades to come, provoking the most conservative audiences into emotional fren-zies that they could not achieve elsewhere in their lives.

The 1970s were full of such ambiguous artists, pitched somewhere between the extremes of easy listening ('You could say I'm the Ray Conniff of the pop world', said Elton John) and hard rock. Neil Diamond carried the trappings of the rock star and the sensitive troubadour, but oversold every line as if he was desperate to reach the back row of a Broadway theatre, which was his natural milieu. In an earlier age, the musical stage might also have represented the ultimate horizon for Billy Joel, who was torn between his classical training, his passion for the immediacy of rock 'n' roll, and his unashamedly sentimental storytelling – a combination more enriching than the ingredients that made up Bruce Springsteen, but lacking in the latter's innate command of rock mythology. Elton John was the most mysterious of them all, equally at home and unsettled as a pub pianist or the focus of a stadium audience. He'd debuted as a confessional singer of someone else's words; adopted a broad Southern twang to hide his roots in the London suburbs; then abandoned reticence to become the most flam-boyant pop artist of the decade, indulging himself in brilliant pastiches of so many styles that there was no longer one he could call his own. 'I'd like to have nine pianos on stage, a cascade of pianos, and make my entrance like that', he revealed in 1973 as if he was Liberace. Seven consecutive No. 1 US albums illustrated his power as an entertainer, until his revelation in 1976 that he was 'bisexual' (and the break-up of his writing partnership with Bernie Taupin) sabotaged his career at its peak. A fan from Utah greeted his honesty with a profound sense of betrayal: 'I regret facing the fact that he is a gross perverter of the sacred . . . I pity him for his sexual illusions and perversions.'

If Elton John was ultimately too unpredictable to command an all-ages audience, the likes of Andy Williams were too safe. Despite growing his hair a daring inch or two over his collar in the early 1970s, working with rock producers, and tackling material by Paul McCartney and George Harrison, Williams would have to wait another two decades or more before being adopted as an icon of kitsch easy listening by many who had despised him in his commercial prime. (Meanwhile, Linda Ronstadt occupied the role that Andy Williams had once played in musical culture, treating familiar pop hits to makeovers which sapped their original spontaneity.) Abba would experience an even more extreme reversal of critical fortune. The Swedish band's victory in the 1974 Eurovision Song Contest marked the first occasion on which a remotely modern record had triumphed in that dumbed-down arena. But it damned them by association amongst those who would relish, for example, Wings, ELO or Blondie – Abba being too slick, too commercial, too Swedish (and therefore, it followed, emotionally empty in their English-language songwriting). Redemption had to wait until their original teenage audience inherited control of the entertainment media, at which point Abba were rehabilitated – like a Stalinist purge in reverse – into an imaginary version of 1970s culture, in which froth and frivolity replaced the shadows of terrorism and economic decline remembered by veterans of the decade.

Those who had experienced adolescence during the 1960s were now reluctantly facing maturity: too old to be convinced by Grand Funk or Bolan, too young to settle for Andy Williams or Johnny Mathis. To satisfy their needs, and exploit their increased spending power, rock developed its own form of what radio had once called 'good music'. The names might have changed – no Sinatra or Tony Bennett – but the principle was the same: extracting the ethos of a musical revolution (once it was swing, now the counter-culture) and offering it with a finesse that would once have seemed outrageously un-hip.

This was rock for adults, or those preparing to reach that status: often idealistic in its social concerns (saving the whale and the planet, now, rather than overthrowing the capitalist order), and aware that the simplistic desires of youth, for sexual fulfilment or personal power, carried burdens which might remove more freedom than they granted. Its musical surface was slick, produced with consummate technical skill by the likes of Richard Perry, Lenny Waronker or Gary Katz; or, indeed, by the artists themselves, when they had the ears of a Stevie Wonder or Joni Mitchell. Jazz, the music of informed adulthood since the birth of the cool at the end of the 1940s, was rarely far from the heart of these records; likewise a set of mannerisms borrowed from soul and the blues. Because many of these urban sophisticates had flourished in the 1960s, they knew how to construct a hit single, with the result that records with such adult themes as Carly Simon's 'You're So Vain' and Paul Simon's 'Kodachrome' found their way on to Top 40 radio. The doyens of this approach – not a style, as it was too multifaceted, or a movement, as each act had its own rationale – were Stevie Wonder, already a slightly jaded veteran in his early 20s (albeit one who had mastered every instrument he could reach, and could ease himself effortlessly from sentimental balladry to politically charged funk); and Steely Dan. Their cynicism and perfectionism grew as they quit the road and devoted months of sessions to driving the most agile musical talents of their generation through countless retakes, until they had achieved the ultimate expression of their sourpuss, icy beauty.

What divided these musicians from those who were unknowingly pioneering the way for the radio format known as Adult Contemporary – the Carpenters, Barbra Streisand, Captain & Tennille, to name but three – was that they carried with them the dead weight of the counter-culture. Either, like David Crosby and Graham Nash, they continued to fight the same battles as they had a decade before, loyal to their tarnished flags; or, like Mitchell and both Carly and Paul Simon, they wrote about the death of that idealism, and its insidious effect on their personal lives. Their focus was intense, but usually aimed inward: each child of the 'we' generation struggled to come to terms with the consequences of being 'me'. While his occasional musical partner Neil Young surveyed the inevitability with which (in his phrase) time fades away, Stephen Stills notoriously dedicated an entire series of 1970s compositions to the study of his 'changes', that most 'me generation' of concepts. But at least they acknowledged the in-evitability of change. Others preferred to sustain the past endlessly, avoiding adulthood in favour of sustaining a golden (or imaginary) past.

I realise the Beatles did fill a space in the 60s, and all the people who the Beatles meant something to have grown up. It's like with anything. You grow up with it and you get attached to it. That's one of the problems in our lives, becoming too attached to things.
George Harrison, 1974

I don't like oldies or nostalgia. I don't like rock 'n' roll anyway – original rock 'n' roll. I can't stand it. I never listen to Elvis Presley,

Jerry Lee Lewis or Carl Perkins. I can't bear all those people.
I heard them fifteen years ago, thank you very much, and I don't
want to hear them now.
  Mick Jagger, 1974

So large had the Beatles loomed over the 1960s that their existence – even
as a shadow – was an embarrassment to the culture of the early 1970s.
There was no kudos to be gained from displaying an overt influence to
their music: the likes of Badfinger and the Electric Light Orchestra were
mistrusted for their undue affection for the recent past. (Other influences
from the 1960s, such as the Velvet Underground and the MC5, were
considered more acceptable by critics.) Ex-members of the Beatles were
lampooned for caring too much about politics (Lennon), religion (Harrison)
or family life (McCartney); or, like Ringo Starr, for over-reliance on more
talented friends (especially the other Beatles).

The shadow was inescapable, however, and assumed strange
shades. In 1973, and again in 1976, entrepreneurs tried to launch young
bands called the New Beatles; the first of them even released a single, 'Push
Button Rock'. 'Legally speaking, we have registered the name,' said their
manager, 'and I assume that was permitted because the Beatles have officially disbanded.' Not that this diminished the commercial value of the
original group's catalogue, which was milked by two retrospective double
albums in 1973, and then the simultaneous reissue of all their original
singles in 1976 – with the result that they filled twenty places in the
novelty-starved British chart. Beatlefest conventions offered a distant
glimpse of Beatlemania for those too young to have experienced it in
person; likewise several theatrical shows based around their songs, culmi-
nating in a disastrous movie adaptation of *Sgt. Pepper*, starring Peter
Frampton and the Bee Gees. There was even a pornographic novel,
published in Copenhagen, entitled *Insex Mania*, which climaxed (literally)
with the Beatles indulging in a rampant orgy on the stage of the Roundhouse
theatre in London.

A BBC radio series detailing the history of the Beatles in 1972 was
followed by a thirteen-part extravaganza devoted to Bing Crosby, and
another to the entire history of popular music. By that Christmas, the rock
'n' roll-free compilation *20 All-Time Greats of the 50s* was the best-selling
LP in Britain, appealing to the 'neglected market' of buyers aged 25 to 35.
Similar collections of rock 'n' roll hits followed, and sold equally well.

Meanwhile, the UK singles chart in December 1972 was filled with reissues by Carole King, the Animals, the Drifters, the Shangri-La's, Little Eva and various Motown acts – a clear sign that the incipient glam-rock movement was only reaching a minority of potential purchasers.

The desire to return to the simpler pleasures of the 1950s kept the era's surviving rockers in work. Elvis Presley was in Las Vegas, tackling his early hits at almost double their original tempo, in a desperate attempt to recreate the savage excitement they'd once aroused. Jerry Lee Lewis deliberately aggravated his Teddy-boy following by playing country standards instead of 'Breathless' and 'Lewis Boogie'. Chuck Berry was rewarded with the biggest sales of his career for the puerile novelty record, 'My Ding-a-Ling'. (Professional moralist Mary Whitehouse alleged that the song would encourage small boys to unzip their shorts and play with their penises in public.) Fellow veteran Rick Nelson returned with 'Garden Party', a lament for his inability to escape his past. In October 1972, those two records were in the US Top 10, alongside one of Elvis Presley's last convincing rockers, 'Burning Love'. Within months, poor physical and psychological health had so drained Presley that he began to approach his songs with the manoeuvrability of a giant oil tanker. Berry, meanwhile, had exhausted his creativity as a composer and was becoming an increasingly cynical performer, while their old partner in rebel-rousing, Little Richard, was reduced to stripping on stage to salvage even the faintest echo of his 1950s outrageousness.

Yet the nostalgia could not be stemmed. The promoter Richard Nader assembled an array of 1950s doo-wop groups and discovered a formula that could fill New York's Madison Square Garden's 20,000 seats. The BBC inaugurated several weekly shows devoted to 'revived 45s', and American stations, with more air to fill, invented the all-oldie radio format. Record labels established divisions to repackage the recent past, RCA taking the laurels for excess with two four-LP box sets by Elvis, the second of which – running to a limited edition of 15,000 copies – was accompanied by a piece of cloth supposedly sliced from one of Presley's stage suits. And rock 'n' roll was lending its nostalgic sheen to film soundtracks. Martin Scorsese's 1967 debut feature, *Who's That Knocking at My Door*, had been filled with frat-rock and doo-wop classics, a technique now perfected by the same director's *Mean Streets*. The latter emerged in 1973 alongside *American Graffiti*, a pitch-perfect recreation of late 1950s teenage life; like its British equivalent, *That'll Be the Day*, it mapped out its characters' lives in two-minute slices of rock 'n' roll – once ephemeral, now classic.

Packs of ageing Teddy boys still walked the streets of British cities, arousing not fear but bewildered amusement. Their London contingent flocked to Let It Rock, a King's Road boutique owned by Malcolm McLaren and Vivienne Westwood, which was devoted to original and reproduction Ted fashions. 'Very heavy, it was', said McLaren proudly of the shop's ambience. 'No one'd dare come in the place unless they were Teds. Mick Jagger stood outside the shop for half an hour once and never came in. Ringo Starr was the only one who dared to actually come in on a Saturday.' When Let It Rock was rebranded, finding fulfilment as Sex, the Teds went elsewhere, maintaining an underground revival which by 1976 had spawned a gig circuit and such new/old bands as Shakin' Stevens & the Sunsets, Crazy Cavan and Matchbox. Original Teds derided the adolescent Plastic Teds who were trying to ape them, although every generation joined forces for a march upon the BBC demanding airtime for their music.

The charts of the 1970s were full of songs which used 'rock 'n' roll' as a shorthand expression for lost youthfulness ('Rock 'n' Roll, I Gave You the Best Years of My Life', for example). There was also a spate of rock stars celebrating their roots by revisiting the songs that had fuelled their own adolescence. The Band (*Moondog Matinee*) and John Lennon (*Rock 'n' Roll*) leaned on the 1950s; the slightly younger David Bowie revived the mid-1960s London R&B scene (*Pin Ups*). Bryan Ferry of Roxy Music, a band with roots deep in the world of fine art, ranged back to the 1930s, via Bob Dylan (*These Foolish Things* and *Another Time, Another Place*). Other veterans of the British beat boom were enticed to relive their glory days by joining a 1960s revival tour across America, which Peter Noone insisted 'isn't a nostalgic get-together'. Merseybeat veterans the Searchers defiantly devoted much of their set to a lengthy rendition of Neil Young's 'Southern Man', but soon discovered that nobody wanted to see them grow. All their audience desired was the opportunity to close their eyes slightly and imagine that it was 1964 again.

A similar effect was achieved by the so-called power-pop movement, a scattering of American bands who all preferred to believe that they could erase rock's diversions into pretentiousness and politics by pretending that it was – not 1964, perhaps, but certainly no later than 1967. The paragons of this vogue were Raspberries, who concocted brilliant pastiches of the Beach Boys, the Who and the Beatles, before cramming all their fervent passion for the past (and the pinnacle of mid-1970s studio technology) into one glorious expression of pop consciousness: 'Overnight Sensation'. Todd Rundgren began the decade as a one-man compression of 1960s melodicism, before deciding that writing perfect pop songs was too easy to be interesting. As an initial farewell to the art, he devoted half of his 1976 LP *Faithful* to exact replicas of classic hits from 1966 – an exercise that was at once stunningly impressive and utterly pointless. Yet the past wasn't that easy to shake off: in the early 1980s, Rundgren masterminded an entire album of Beatles pastiches, *Deface the Music*, and many years later found himself touring in Ringo Starr's band. His imitation Fab Four paled alongside the consciously satirical version created by Eric Idle (script) and Neil Innes (songs) in *The Rutles*: a mock-documentary film in which George Harrison conspired in the demolition of his own history. Inevitably, Innes would be dragged back to the Rutles in middle age by the public's endless need for nostalgia, his lampooning of the past inspiring the same revivalism as the Beatles themselves.

As the 1970s progressed, the past reappeared in increasingly surreal ways. There was a brief craze in British discos for the hits of the swing era: enough to carry Glenn Miller's 'In the Mood' and 'Moonlight Serenade' into the Top 20, in any case. A flurry of young bands masqueraded as doo-woppers or vintage rockers, while delivering the palest pastiches of the ferocious original article: notably Mud (soon ensconced in seaside variety, mixing rock medleys with comedy routines), the Rubettes ('Letters have poured in saying how refreshing it was to see such a bunch of smart lads on the telly') and Showaddywaddy ('We're trying to create a 1974 rock and roll image . . . it isn't as raw as 50s rock'). Young girls who'd missed out on Michael Jackson, Donny Osmond and David Cassidy focused their puppy love on British groups who dressed as if they were teenage bowling teams from Philadelphia, *c.*1961: the Bay City Rollers, Kenny and Slik amongst them.

The critics preferred their nostalgia delivered with conviction: hence the enthusiasm for the pub-rock scene which emerged from early 1970s London, and provided an apprenticeship for many of the future pioneers of punk. The most feted were undoubtedly Dr Feelgood, an Essex R&B band who were greeted with ecstatic relief (as here, by the *NME*'s Tony Tyler): 'They have no record contract. They are virtually unknown outside London. They do their own roadie-ing. They mix their own sound.

They are so bloody fantastic to watch and hear that I – and many others – would sooner spend ten minutes in the company of their bone-crunching traditional rock 'n' roll than squirm restlessly through yet another electronic prima donna tarted up with dry ice and sequins.' As guitarist Wilko Johnson explained, in the studio 'we do our music live – we set the gear up, stick microphones in front and DO it!' But what they did was quite deliberately retrospective: almost a pop-art performance, in fact, fetishising the past to emphasise the distance between then and now.

> What is actually happening is a fantastic, almost hysteric,
> acceleration in the mechanics of the star-making system. To meet
> the ever-growing speed-freak apocalyptic yearnings of the new rock
> audience for new heroes, new sensations by the hour, the industry's
> back-room boys have had to get their media manipulations down to
> the finest of arts . . . talent has less and less to do with the matter.
> Andrew Weiner, *Ink* magazine, 1971

As the Beatles had demonstrated in graphically lurid terms, the rock group of the 1960s was a collective ideal rendered unstable by the heavy-handed application of egos and cash. Like most of their contemporaries, they had evolved out of a series of random encounters between like-minded individuals, who came together in their mutual love for music. Under the intense pressures of fame – and its unequal distribution of financial rewards, songwriters substantially out-earning their colleagues – their union was subjected to a stress test. Few bands could survive untouched; most of them shed their weakest or most outspoken members, or simply disintegrated.

Rock's metamorphosis from an adolescent passion into a viable career encouraged all but the least ambitious members of leading groups to imagine that they were being held back – creatively or monetarily – by their bandmates. When Crosby, Stills & Nash formed in late 1968, all of them refugees from successful groups, they carefully chose a name that would emphasise their individual independence. From the outset, they imagined that (in the California spirit of the time) they would drift in and out of each other's company, an arts collective rather than a prison gang. Several decades later, the trio was still regrouping annually, the hippie zeal of old replaced by the cruel logic of the bank balance. 'I still ask myself why anybody would be in a band with [Stephen] Stills if they didn't have to', David Crosby noted with an absence of counter-culture harmony in 2006.

The trio's phenomenal success (with and without Neil Young) encouraged musicians and businessmen alike to believe that they had found a foolproof way of sparking creativity and making money. Rather than trusting to the traditional model of the rock band they would follow CSN(Y)'s example, and combine successful individuals from existing units. The most prominent of these so-called supergroups was ironically named Blind Faith – ironically, because only that quality could have persuaded the participants that this scheme would work. Instead, the collision of members of Cream, Traffic and Family survived for less than six months, torn apart by unrealistic audience expectations and personal differences. Not that this prevented the experiment from being repeated. For every Emerson, Lake & Palmer and Bad Company, whose union made a global impact, there were a dozen outfits such as the Souther Hillman Furay Band, KGB and Widowmaker, for whom the whole was less impressive than any of the individual parts.

If the supergroup was an elusive and often illusory concept, so was its opposite: the solo career. While the individual Beatles were both popular and charismatic enough to sustain themselves outside of the gang, and CSN(Y) had built freedom into their formula from the start, the lure of seeing one's own name in lights – or on an album cover – proved to be fatally enticing during the 1970s. At its most excessive, this tendency provoked all four members of the hard-rock band Kiss into issuing solo records on the same day. The entire quartet reached the US Top 50, testament to the power of their brand. Most such ventures were less rewarding, artistically and commercially.

This mushrooming of commercial product was reminiscent of the jazz scene in the 1950s, when musicians (especially in California) would jam, and the results would be distributed across records issued under any of the participants' names, apparently chosen at random. Like their jazz counterparts, many rock fans inspected the small print of their album covers with an antiquary's zeal, as the once anonymous supporting cast was now annotated in exhaustive detail. So desperate was the search for saleable product in the booming market of the early 1970s that session musicians renowned for subtle and discreet touches on records by their more famous peers were plucked out of the darkness and encouraged to make their own music. The flamboyant success of Leon Russell, once an unknown piano player in Hollywood studios, inevitably prompted such natural sidemen as

Nicky Hopkins and Jesse Ed Davis to be offered recording contracts. Meanwhile, other rock and R&B session men formed their own bands, such as the Section and LA Express, inevitably veering towards jazz when removed from their lucrative paymasters. This was the ultimate expression of the 'me generation', with everyone believing himself entitled to become a star. The disastrous sales of almost all these projects ensured that such excess would not be repeated in subsequent decades.

But this was an era in which even accepted stars could be disappointingly anonymous on stage, and audiences were beginning to demand something more from a rock concert than simply the opportunity to be in the same stadium as their idols. Two solutions to this conundrum arose simultaneously: the creation of more visual stars, and the transformation of rock into a form of theatre, in an effort to stoke excitement from the often mundane business of playing music in public.

> The very last thing Jagger says he wants to see is the Stones degenerating into nothing more significant than their own golden oldies revival show. Not for him the point of parody in which the band would go through the motions as an excuse to take the money and run.
> Roy Carr, *NME*, 1973

> Rock music has become the new vaudeville. Consequently the music is only a part of the overall package. Every bit as important is the visual impact.
> Music journalist Jim Smith, 1974

No sooner had stereo sound ousted its monaural ancestor from the marketplace than the avaricious hi-fi and record industries plotted another coup. Marketing campaigns warned consumers that they would soon be the cause of derision amongst their friends if they didn't replace their stereophonic equipment with its ultra-modern successor: quadrophonic. If stereo was sold as the logical format for listeners with two ears, quad sound employed another dimension, with four speakers set in the corners of a room. The listener would now be placed in the centre of the music, confronted by sensory impressions from all sides, just as in real life.

The public proved resistant to jettisoning the expensive technology they'd recently purchased to play stereo records, while many artists were equally reluctant to change. They complained about the problems of mixing their recordings for quadrophonic release, with all the musicians and engineers squeezed into the exact centre of the playback studio, trying to judge whether the four sources of sound were perfectly balanced. As the subsequent success of surround-sound in the cinema and for home-entertainment systems proved, quad was simply too modern for its time. It reached an early apotheosis not on record, however, but in the concert hall, as Pink Floyd performed their 1973 album, *The Dark Side of the Moon*. A collection of songs exploring cultural stasis, collective betrayal and personal self-doubt was transformed by judicious use of sound effects – and, on stage, stunning use of lighting as a means of both bewitching and startling the audience – into the soundtrack for a generation. Its impact was more enduring than any of its contemporaries, as the album kept selling through the punk era and beyond, to become the second most popular LP of all time. It was a triumph of impersonality from a band few record-buyers would have recognised in the street, the album's unforgettable visuals compensating for its creators' lack of individual charisma. *Dark Side* carried listeners on a journey which left them mildly disturbed, gently comforted, and aurally stimulated. This was an album which exuded intelligence and significance: both serious, and dreamily intoxicating.

With each subsequent album of the decade, Pink Floyd edged closer towards rock as audio-visual extravaganza, cloaking increasingly dark and cynical songwriting with innovative stagecraft. They were the least flamboyant musicians, and the most grandiose concept artists, in 1970s rock, reaching the inevitable climax of their passage as alienated megastars by constructing a wall between themselves and their audience – and then demolishing it in a gesture that signified not liberation, but a renewal of the cycle, which would lead inevitably to despair. As if to reinforce the surreal function of nihilistic rock as mass entertainment, *The Wall* proved to be an even more lucrative project than *The Dark Side of the Moon*.

Other artists imagined equally lavish concepts, but chose to present them in more orthodox theatrical terms – Yes performing the gargantuan song suite *Tales From Topographic Oceans* on a stage designed to resemble an ocean floor; Genesis (in the person of lead singer Peter Gabriel) acting out their concept albums like an acid-fuelled mummer; Rick Wakeman concocting mock-classical suites around historical themes, and then performing them like grand opera, even staging one album inside the Empire Pool, Wembley, as an ice gala.

Like the progressive-rock genre which gave these strange beasts their life, these stage shows (and their accompanying albums) were designed not just to entertain an audience, but to congratulate it on its intelligence. Short on visceral excitement, they targeted the cerebellum rather than the hips or the groin. *NME* reviewer Nick Kent was sceptical of Pink Floyd's lack of spontaneity and dynamics: 'one can easily envisage a Floyd concert in the future consisting of the band simply wandering on stage, setting all their tapes into action, putting their instruments on remote control and then walking off behind the amps in order to talk about football or play billiards', he wrote. 'I'd almost prefer to see them do that. At least it would be more honest.'

But what were the alternatives? Those who were bewitched by the camp theatricality of David Bowie's enactment of the glam-rock ethos watched with a certain befuddlement as he remade himself as a soul artist, touring America in front of a stage set inspired by pre-war German expressionist cinema. Few artists of the time employed such subtle gestures. Between 1969 and 1972, it had been enough for the Rolling Stones simply to appear in front of a crowd; their image as rock's ultimate miscreants did the rest. By 1975, having already given the game away with a hit entitled 'It's Only Rock 'n' Roll', they were reduced to depicting the increasingly jaded milieu of their songs with banal stage props, such as a giant inflatable penis – their mystique diminishing with every gimmick. Now in their early 30s, the Stones had lost their generational hold over the teenagers of the 1970s, who in America preferred the cartoon antics and comic-book make-up of Kiss, a melodic pop band masquerading as hard-rock daredevils. Lead singer Gene Simmons breathed fire on stage, and out in the bleachers, 12-year-old boys tried to set their seats ablaze, desperate to be part of this iconoclastic ritual.

Rock now had its own language of symbols and clichés, which could be instantly understood by any audience. The simple phrase 'rock 'n' roll', delivered from the stage ('We're gonna rock 'n' roll all night!') or bellowed from the stalls, was like a mating call between star and audience – American performances offering a variation in the cry of 'Boogie!' At their most basic, a band like Status Quo would resemble its audience from head to toe, their blue denims signifying that they might easily have traded places with anyone in the theatre. If the battle cry and dress code were in place, then the music almost didn't matter: the mere promise of 'rock 'n' roll' was enough. So hypnotic was the allure of rock stagecraft that a band like Queen could achieve man-of-the-people stature while delivering songs of almost operatic construction, recorded with more lavish care to production than any British band since the Beatles. Meanwhile, their overtly camp lead singer, Freddie Mercury, managed to obscure his homosexuality from his vast heterosexual audience for more than a decade, despite thrusting it at his fans with giddy delight.

Queen's 1975 hit 'Bohemian Rhapsody' was a four-minute collage of styles, new and old – from the Beach Boys to operetta, Paul McCartney to the Who. It completed a late flowering of the pop extravagance of 1967, with psychedelic whimsy giving way to a sense of joy that was entirely self-generated – music that was about nothing more weighty than the pleasure of its own existence. The cycle had arguably begun with Queen's 'Killer Queen', and took in (depending on one's taste) 'Philadelphia Freedom' (Elton John), 'Love Will Keep Us Together' (Captain & Tennille), 'Listen to What the Man Said' (Wings), 'Miracles' (Jefferson Starship) and two almost shockingly contemporary offerings from mid-1960s hitmakers the Four Seasons, 'Who Loves You' and 'December '63'. Here were all the once-essential ingredients of pop: melodies, counter-melodies, harmonies, and hooks, clutches of them in each song; uncomplicated aural delight rooted in a decade-old vision of pop innocence, and coated in a sheen that Paul Whiteman might have envied.

The biggest-selling artists in the world over the next two years seemed to emerge organically from that same luxurious tapestry. Both Peter Frampton and Fleetwood Mac had launched their British careers in 1967, as a teen-pop star and a blues band respectively. Ten years later, they were partners in a stunning commercial coup, whereby unchallenging, effortlessly melodic pop music colonised the American rock market. Both artists had gimmicks, if you like: Frampton's curls and 'speaking guitar' tube; Mac the media fixation with their disintegrating personal relationships. But the core of their success was the simplicity of their songs, and their emotional directness. They required no translation or indoctrination: they simply blasted out of the radio into people's memories, the way that pop had always wanted to do. Their appeal was classless, all-age, region-free: just like the Beatles, for a world which the Beatles themselves had already transformed. Leading American critic Dave Marsh was baffled by Frampton's popularity, which he said 'frustrates analysis' because (Marsh claimed) the man was 'neither an excellent melodist nor lyricist, his singing is hardly above average, his guitar work is competent and no more, his showmanship equally unexceptional'. Frampton delivered one guarantee, however: entertainment that would make a huge audience feel as one.

As rock graduated from halls to arenas, arenas to stadia, each of the multiple relationships between artists, audiences, music and the wider culture was changing. Larger spaces required more grandiose gestures to fill them; more volume; more spectacle. The sense of communion and communication across the gap between stage and seating was sacrificed: subtlety and ambiguity would be lost on the wind before they reached the front row. With the rare exception of a band such as the Grateful Dead, who managed to sustain both their community and their free-form musical structures throughout their thirty-year trip, rock artists had to choose between two career models: intimacy, spontaneity and low financial rewards; or excess, predictability and riches unimagined by their predecessors. As record companies merged to form corporations, and the illusion of rock as a tool of a counter-culture vanished, rock was reinvented as the most potent entertainment phenomenon of the age – with the music to match.

Groups have tried that laid-back experimental trip too long. We're not going to use any audience to get heavy; our music is going to get simpler. We want to be seen as a dancing band whose records get taken to parties.
Paul Stanley, Kiss, 1975

Two hundred million Americans out there don't appreciate subtleties. They want to be sledge-hammered over the head with clear issues . . . Remember, it was mass-culture that created rock 'n' roll . . . I think Shakespeare is shit! Absolute shit! 'Thee' and 'thou': the guy sounds like a faggot.
Gene Simmons, Kiss, 1977

In 1970, single-minded obsessiveness and multi-instrumental prowess combined with technological innovation to create a new formula: the one-man rock group. Emblematically, Paul McCartney, with his debut solo LP, was one of the first to experiment with playing and singing an entire album by himself (albeit with moral support and occasional vocals by his wife). Emitt Rhodes reproduced the vintage sound of the Beatles in his garage; Todd Rundgren ranged from McCartney melodicism to Zappa eccentricity on his early self-made ventures, mushrooming into the synthesiser-drenched madness of *A Wizard A True Star*, while Stevie Wonder declared effective independence from Motown's hit factory by immersing himself in a recording studio to concoct ever more dazzling confections of funk, soul and pop.

While those artists won kudos for their ambition (alongside criticism that no man alone could reproduce the collective spontaneity of a band), an equally driven musician was following the same course in Boston. Tom Scholz was a mechanical-engineering graduate from MIT whose day job involved designing products for Polaroid. At night, he would retreat to his self-constructed home studio, where he devoted years to recording and re-recording the same batch of songs – layering guitar and keyboard parts like samples in a carpet warehouse, endlessly finessing the tone of each instrument, and inventing sonic gadgets to approximate the sound he heard in his head. It was, noted critic Lester Bangs, 'a parody of the mad doctor walled off in his lab'. But from Scholz's almost compulsive labours came Boston – both a band (because even Scholz couldn't command enough machines to deliver his sound alone on stage) and a self-named record which eventually sold more than 17 million copies.

Led by the anthem-like single 'More Than a Feeling', *Boston* sounded like a triumph of market research. It was as if a computer had been fed a generation of successful rock songs, and then programmed to combine the quintessential elements into coherent packages. Scholz had achieved the same effect by accident and intuition, adding the visceral thrust of heavy guitar riffs to irresistible choruses and song structures that sounded both 'classic' and entirely fresh. This was hard rock and power pop, prog and metal, every American formula of the 1970s streamlined into one seamless package. Only those who were determined to ignore the mainstream could resist.

The fruit of endless labour and individual imagination, Boston came to epitomise a style of American music-making as basic as its unmistakable brand names: Kansas, Journey, Styx, Foreigner, Starz, Heart. This was the dawn of arena rock, of AOR, although the genre was more specific than that abbreviation suggested. It denoted music that was loud but slick; built around hard-rock riffs and pop melodies; and sealed with rabble-rousing choruses that virtually defied their audience not to punch the air with delight. The AOR bands demanded no commitment from their fans beyond enjoyment: no political agenda, no qualifications in music theory or poetic structure. If the previous generation of rock musicians had sought to represent or even lead the (counter-)culture, AOR offered itself in place of a culture, its ideal audience a generation united in its instinctive, lightning responses to brazen emotional triggers. In time, AOR would widen its palette of feelings to encompass the power ballad, a form of muscular sentimentality filled with gargantuan theatrical anguish.

In retrospect, signposts towards this new American mainstream were scattered through the early 1970s: from the Eagles' 'Witchy Woman' (swamp rock from the California beaches) and the Doobie Brothers' 'Long Train Running' (rock meets funk in a sedative cloud of smoke) to Grand Funk Railroad's 'We're an American Band' (1960s frat rock for kids too young to remember the 1960s). Kiss disguised their own melodicism behind their garish make-up and daredevil posing, although no band whose most enduring hit was a ballad as grandiose as 'Beth' could ever pose a credible threat to society. Even Lynyrd Skynyrd's Southern-rock anthem, 'Free Bird', could be purloined for the new tradition, for its ability to unify a crowd in arm-swaying, lighter-holding Pavlovian response. But the band who did most to establish the boundaries for AOR were Styx, whose massed choruses and fist-pumping riffs were designed for the expanse of a sports arena.

Those fists were permanently clenched for the next decade, as the American rock mainstream recycled the same set of attitudes: defiance, triumph, resolution, commitment, passion. Disco came and went; hip hop was born; punk exploded and turned into cliché; but in the American heartland, AOR and its hard-rock cousin continued almost undisturbed, accumulating outside influences so slowly that its audience barely noticed the change between Starz' 1977 hit 'Cherry Baby', with its roots in mid-1960s British beat, and Van Halen's 1984 venture into synth-led disco rock, 'Jump'. By then, AOR had become so permanent an institution that it could jettison virtually all of its trademarks and still trigger its arena crowds with music that they would once have despised. At its most formulaic, it produced anonymity – names such as Balance, Point Blank, Silver Condor, Spider and the Dillman Band; or it could reduce rock legends, such as Jefferson Starship, to the same state. But while it could deliver an anthem as uncomplicated and chest-beating as Journey's 1981 single 'Don't Stop Believin'', it would never die – as long as there were people who needed to be told that they could make it through the storm, keep the faith, and a hundred other clichés which would soon fuel a boom in self-help books. AOR sold its audience the most seductive of emotional diets: a sense of belonging, and endless exhilaration.

'Each dances by his or her self … [there's] volume enough to make your nose bleed … the beat, always THE BEAT, smashes its way into mass consciousness. The kids here are a mixed bunch. Some in vests and bags, some in their best suits. All, though, seem to give off positive vibes.'

Tony Cummings, *Black Music*, at Tiffany's, Newcastle-under-Lyme, 1974

CHAPTER 23

UNION OF BODIES

'Black music's basically rhythmic, it's all about Africa and dancing. I think music's gradually coming back my way again, people want to get out on the floor, forget about their problems, and let their hair down.'

James Brown, 1976

4

Exhilaration: to spin the body, fall back to the floor, leap up as if propelled by a trampoline, turn, coil, unwind, all in perfect time with the vintage four-to-the-bar metronome of musicians from 4,000 miles away. The venue was the Twisted Wheel or Tiffany's; the Golden Torch or the Night Owl; the Burlesque or the Dungeon; the Casino or the Highland Room; basement or ballroom, cellar or club room. All for the sake of pleasure, liberation, the power of volume and the perfect beat – the union of bodies carving the air in simultaneous, solitary joy.

The stimulus for this ecstasy was soul; Northern soul, named not for its North American origins (its spiritual home was Detroit) but the location of its disciples, in Manchester, Wigan, Blackpool or the Potteries. Every weekend they would be drawn together by train or by coach, for a pilgrimage into the utterly reliable territory of music which immersed you in its transcendent energy (with some pills, perhaps, to keep you on your feet till dawn).

The Twisted Wheel in Manchester was where it all began: relocated in 1965 to a coffee shop in an old warehouse, above a cellar complex which played host over the next six years to visiting American soul stars and the cream of Britain's own R&B talent, black and white. It was a haven for mods, at first, until the gospel of soul music spread and another elite was formed: one without prejudice of gender or race, linked only by its obsession with the rhythms of black America. Northern soul enjoyed an occult existence until pundits began to query why the British singles chart was filled, between 1969 and 1972, with apparently random revivals of soul sounds from the past. Some of these came from Motown's biggest stars, others from acts whose records had barely been distributed in Britain before. For this was a scene that revolved around records which weren't popular; which, in the most extreme example, of Frank Wilson's hyper-charged 'Do I Love You', had never been given a commercial release. DJs and venues competed to uncover the hottest obscurities from America's 1960s soul scene, and then cover them up in plain sight – blasting their two and a half minutes of rhythmic ecstasy to a room of pulsating dancers, while keeping the identity of their find a secret from their rivals. Their goal was to locate records as thrilling as the best-loved

Motown classics, but unknown to the masses, their obscurity sealing the deal.

Each different venue and town had its own philosophy. Some wouldn't venture beyond the 1960s, while others kept pace with the ever-changing rhythms coming out of America. Most famous of all was the Wigan Casino, which ran from 1973 to 1981, pulled in punters from across Britain, founded its own Casino Classics label, made stars of its DJs, and was ultimately exploited by such hits as 'Footsee' by Wigan's Chosen Few, and 'Skiing in the Snow' by Wigan's Ovation. Its playlists ranged from vintage Detroit backing tracks ('Double Cookin'', 'I Have Faith in You'), through blue-eyed soul by the Four Seasons and Paul Anka, to the perennial Three Before Eight (o'clock) – the weekly spins of Jimmy Radcliffe's 'Long After Tonight is All Over', Tobi Legend's 'Time Will Pass You By' and Dean Parrish's 'I'm On My Way' which brought the all-nighter to a close.

Beyond Wigan, there were all-dayers and all-nighters across the North and the Midlands, and even in London, although the capital preferred to follow the contemporary pulse of America. The scene prompted a series of drug busts around 1969–70, although it was the least violent and disruptive of milieux. This stigma was so pervasive that even five years later, venues would display signs proclaiming 'We do not play soul music'.

Not that soul music was easily compressed into a sound or a style. Besides the uptown soul beloved of the Northern loyalists, and the muscular R&B sound of the American South, African-American music had been changing as dramatically as the society from which it came. Even Motown was experimenting with 'psychedelic soul', as groups such as the Temptations reflected the turbulence of urban poverty and violence, 'Cloud Nine' and 'Ball of Confusion' evoking ghettos caught between militant black activism and the lure of heroin. Sly & the Family Stone, multiracial and poly-rhythmic, became one of the biggest bands in America by providing near-manic dance anthems alongside bulletins from a generation haunted by disillusion and despair.

The mainstream exploded in bizarrely different ways – the lengthy lover-man raps of Isaac Hayes's 'By the Time I Get to Phoenix' and 'Walk On By'; the teasing sensuality of Al Green's 'Tired of Being Alone'; the combustible eroticism of James Brown's 'Sex Machine', Curtis Mayfield's eerie contrast of 'Hell Below' with the almost forlornly optimistic 'Move

On Up'; and a spate of remarkable records which reeked of paranoia, from War's 'Slipping into Darkness' and the O'Jays' 'Back Stabbers' to the Undisputed Truth's 'Smiling Faces Sometimes', in which a handshake concealed a snake and your brother might turn out to be your most profound enemy. For the first time, black artists were freed to make albums as rich and experimental as their white peers, a liberation they channelled into work as idealistic as Marvin Gaye's *What's Going On* and as desolate as Curtis Mayfield's *Superfly*.

This was defiantly black territory, as the producer of the TV show *Soul!* insisted: 'R&B music, especially with many of its new lyrics, forms the flow for black pride. It is totally ours, and cannot be purchased or properly imitated by anyone else.' But the beats of black music were constantly changing; there was nothing beyond attitude to link Isaac Hayes's expansive, languorous landscapes with the naked, taut funk of the Isley Brothers, or, indeed, with the Latin-soul pulse of the Dramatics' 'Whatcha See is Whatcha Get'. The prevailing sounds were as harsh as life in the ghetto, and as silky smooth as bourgeois existence in the suburbs – African-American, both of them, but reflecting experiences as different as those of Bing Crosby and Elvis Presley in the 1950s. Soul was either a musical incitement for riot, or (as Ronnie White of the Miracles claimed) women's music, an invitation to fall in love with a sweet-voiced tenor like Smokey Robinson.

There was another dichotomy: funk as a vehicle for cinematic tension, epitomised by Isaac Hayes's theme for the 'blaxploitation' movie *Shaft* or the Temptations' 'Papa Was a Rolling Stone', and funk as an invitation to party. Often it was hard to tell the two approaches apart, as wah-wah guitar crackled like fire over skeletal arrangements. Funk could signal fear or elation; but by the mid-1970s, as the black liberation movement collapsed into internal warfare, and hard drugs swamped America's ghettos, there was no appetite left for music which charted the desolation of daily life. Curtis Mayfield's music illuminated the bleak path ahead: within six years, he slipped from an almost saintly optimism about the fate of black America into an era of grim realism, and then the depressingly featureless vista of his 1975 album, *There's No Place Like America Today*. This music was brutally honest, and almost unbearably drained of hope: too empty to be angry anymore. Given a choice between despair and escapism, African-American people chose to party as if all they lived for was the dance.

Moving to music, and the sensation of needing to, are vital to any understanding of what black music is about . . . So much of the American black's musical content has to be understood through the body rather than the mind.

Equally clear is the link between dancing and sex. Basically, to dance is to transmit sexual messages; it is to simulate the coital tempo . . . it remains an activity of man the animal rather than man the thinker.

Robert Gallagher, *Black Music*, January 1976

I find it mind-bending. It's a contributory factor to epilepsy. It's the biggest destructor in history to education. It's a jungle cult. It's what the Watusis do to whip up a war. What I've seen in the discos, with people jogging away, is what people do in the bush.

Chief of the Rhodesian Broadcasting Company, explaining its ban on disco music, 1979

In its eternal search for a scapegoat to blame for Britain's economic and social woes, the fascist National Front party focused its hatred on the country's non-white community. Its manifesto at the October 1974 general election repeated its customary call for 'a complete repatriation of all coloured immigrants and their descendants living here'. Cleansing the British population was not enough, however. The NF also demanded that the BBC should be barred from broadcasting 'imported negro rhythms'. As the decade progressed, the party's membership embarked on a systematic campaign of intimidation aimed at British radio stations. The switchboards were inundated with anonymous callers demanding: 'Stop playing that wog music', as NF leader Martin Webster declared that reggae was music only fit for 'monkeys and degenerates'.

Even the most insightful fascist – oxymoron – would have struggled to identify precisely what constituted music with 'imported negro rhythms'. Was it soul music, played by the Average White Band or David Bowie? Or the Rolling Stones, expressing their passion for R&B or reggae? Paul McCartney recording with R&B arranger Allen Toussaint in New Orleans? Acker Bilk and Kenny Ball, reviving the fifty-year-old jazz of the Crescent City? The challenge was to find the British popular music (let alone the American or Jamaican) that *didn't* lean to some extent on a 'negro' rhythm, imported or otherwise.

Those infectious beats had inspired almost every new dance craze since the birth of ragtime, but blackness and dance music were not synonyms. The Chakachas' 'Jungle Fever' from 1972 added Latino spice to the fatback grooves of James Brown's band, overlaid with orgasmic exclamations: sex and race, red rags to the blackshirt bull. Except that the Chakachas hailed not from Spanish Harlem or Watts, but from Belgium.

Even more disconcertingly, there were now dance rhythms which emanated not from the slippery fingers and syncopated soul of musicians, black and white, but from machines. Exhibit one: 'Son of My Father', a hit for Giorgio (Moroder) in the US, Chicory Tip in Britain – a bubblegum tune powered by synthetic handclaps and percussion, and spiralling lines from a Moog synthesiser: robotic, and ominously circular, suggesting that it might, like the cockroaches, survive the nuclear holocaust. Exhibit two: 'Popcorn' by Gershon Kingsley, commercialised by the American band Hot Pepper: the catchiest of electronic earworms, caught in a blizzard of interlocking synthesiser parts, and set to an unrelentingly frenetic computerised drumbeat. Here was a future that might have appealed to the most authoritarian of *fascisti*: the soundtrack of a *Metropolis* where all humanity was in thrall to the emotionless rattle and burble of electronic devices which they could no longer control. Except that neither exhibit was emotionless: in their constant repetition was the stuff of joy.

'Here in New York,' said record mixer Tom Moulton in 1975, 'a lot of people go to the discos to get away from the world . . . and be totally free, dancing.' No community in that city required that carefree joy, and the safety on which it depended, more than the gay crowd that flocked to clubs such as the aptly named Sanctuary. There, as early as 1971, a disc jockey named Francis Grasso was pioneering the art of creating music from machinery – a pair of record decks. 'His tour de force', wrote disco chronicler Albert Goldman, 'was playing two records simultaneously for as long as two minutes at a stretch. He would super[impose] the drum break of Chicago's "I'm a Man" over the orgasmic moans of Led Zeppelin's "Whole Lotta Love" to make a powerfully erotic mix.' The sexuality extended beyond Robert Plant's groans. Grasso manipulated his turntables with a teasing sensuality which would arouse his audience into an ecstatic frenzy, as he built the music to the verge of a crescendo, let it subside for a second, built it again, until the dancers were shrieking and roaring with an explosive, almost animal energy.

Grasso's sets weren't just a parade of the funkiest music of a funky age: he homed in on the drum-breaks and riff repetitions which would ignite the crowd's erogenous zones, reducing records to their core moments of audience response, and elongating them by slipping between decks to keep the dance in motion.

Everything was geared towards extending the moment – music that was artificially prolonged, poppers (amyl nitrite) to heighten and draw out the sexual rush, the frantic coupling of the gay clubs which existed in a place beyond time and outside society's prohibitions. There was nothing inherently 'gay' about disco music: the music was merely the conduit to exhilaration, a thrilling demolition of barriers and restraints which was only available in the dance club (or the bathhouse). Tom Moulton may have conveyed more than he intended when he explained that 'I love to see people turn on like that with music'.

Moulton was the populariser of disco, who codified the innovations of others. Witnessing for himself the impact of the cross-turntable 'instant mix', he realised that there would be commercial potential in supplying ready-made extensions of hot dance cuts for those without the skill or the equipment to mimic Grasso's dexterity. Increasing numbers of dance singles now coupled vocal and instrumental versions of the same song. Using his home studio, Moulton would literally splice together elements of the two on tape, and then supply these to other DJs. By 1975, he had taken to pressing his 'disco mixes' on twelve-inch records, rightly assuming that the humble seven-inch single wouldn't be capable of encompassing such epics. As they were only available by subscription from Moulton, and weren't on sale to the public, he did not have to worry about obtaining the approval of artists or producers. In any case, his twelve-inch mixes were so popular with dancers that they undoubtedly stimulated sales of the original records. The logical step was to give the dancing public what it wanted, and sell his mixes commercially. BT Express's 1974 hit 'Do It (Till You're Satisfied)' was one of the first – seven-inch only, still, but with the heightened bass and extended percussive breaks that fuelled his club mixes. Only two years later did another DJ, Walter Gibbons, provide what was subtly described as 'Disco blending' on a twelve-inch, nine-minute mix of Double Exposure's 'Ten Per Cent', the first LP-sized single ever to reach the shops. By then, Moulton had already provided DJs with the ultimate disco experience: an entire LP side by Gloria Gaynor (*Never Can Say Goodbye*, in 1975), arranged and mixed to provide eighteen minutes of dancing in exactly the same tempo.*

Grasso, Moulton, Gibbons: these were professional manipulators of sound, demonstrating their craft to the predominantly white clientele of dance clubs in Manhattan. A few miles away, in the cash-starved, brutally 'regenerated' streets and high-rises of the Bronx, the nightclub was an abandoned space or the basement of an apartment building, and the entertainment was a young black or Latino male with a sound system and a bundle of records. Sometimes the equipment would have been lifted from a community hall. Sometimes the DJ would divert the city's electricity into his own jerry-built amplification. Like rival sound systems in Jamaica, two aspiring sound-meisters would spar across a crowded dance floor, each trying to outdo the other with volume and bass vibrations, covering up their latest discoveries like the DJs of ska and Northern soul legend.

The most charismatic players in the Bronx of the mid-1970s were both in their late teens. Clive Campbell had grown up in Jamaica, where the disc jockey was not just a supplier of music but a battle-hardened warrior. Kevin Donovan was a Bronx native, who at 16 had already bypassed the neighbourhood gang culture by forming the Mighty Zulu Nation, a collective of street kids who saw music as the key to harmony on the streets. Donovan was known to all as Afrika Bambaataa, a name he coined after a trip to Africa. When he gathered a crowd around him, fearlessly crossing the borders of gang turfs, his purpose was to raise consciousness, spinning records and spreading unity. 'When the punk rockers first came to the Bronx River and started mixing with the black and Hispanic kids,' he recalled, 'people thought there'd be trouble. But there wasn't. It was peaceful.' Meanwhile, Campbell had rechristened himself Kool Herc, and his aim was to create a righteously funky wall of sound, which none of his competitors could match. In the foundation myth of hip-hop culture, Herc's birthplace was a party hosted by his sister Cindy in the basement of their building. The handwritten invitations boasted that this was both a 'Back to School Jam' and 'A DJ Kool Herc Party' – 25¢ admission for the

---

* Disco historian Alice Echols notes: 'singers found that their vocals were no longer the defining feature of a song, but rather just one element. "I don't sing much", was Gaynor's wounded response upon hearing Moulton's final mix of her LP. Dismayed, Gaynor asked, "What am I supposed to do when we perform the song?" To which Moulton replied, "You learn to *dance*."'

ladies, twice that for the men, running 9 p.m. to 4 a.m. on the night of 11–12 August 1973. All Herc did was play records, and keep his sister's friends on the floor; but in the history of hip hop, this event has assumed monumental significance, a banner proclaiming: It Begins Here.

Yet neither Bambaataa nor Herc had envisaged the technical innovations that would soon be achieved by their peers. Herc learned to cue up records on parallel turntables, and switch between them, but his cross-mixing wasn't an exact science, and often the beats didn't match up. Enter another immigrant from the Caribbean, Barbados-born Joseph Saddler, who dubbed himself Grandmaster Flash for his skill on the decks. His equipment allowed him to fade or switch at will across his decks, while experiment yielded another gift: 'I found a way to start the first record with my hand physically on the vinyl itself. The platter would turn but the music wouldn't play because the needle wouldn't be travelling through the groove. However, when I took my hand off the record . . . BAM! The music started right where I wanted it.'

Flash's protégé, Theodore Livingston (alias Grand Wizzard Theodore), had the eyes and hands of a brain surgeon, able to replace the needle on a vinyl record in exactly the right spot without fail – even, in a triumph of self-belief, while wearing a blindfold. But his most enduring addition to the art of the record spinner was the invention of what became known – rather misleadingly – as scratching. This did not, despite its name, involve a needle being dragged horizontally across the grooves, thereby risking permanent damage; instead, Theodore would grab the outside of the record between his fingers as it was playing, and reverse it against the motor, letting it slip forward, dragging it back, until time and music were dislocated. Precision was the key, once again: the disc had to be handled as a percussion instrument, which would finally be released in perfect tempo with the original groove. With these interventions, the purely mechanical process of playing a record gained a human component – technology in service to its guardian, sound to be manipulated and reconstituted with the same ease and bravado that a guitarist would use to shape the howl and roar of feedback.

Beyond these distortions of the 'wheels of steel', the South Bronx added an equally revolutionary element to the simple spinning of a record: the human voice. DJs had always been able to impose themselves on their audience – to convey information, or even to reel off a sequence of catch-phrases and dedications, setting their personality at centre stage. Jamaican sound systems extended that tradition into a seamless blend of sound, the operator participating in the music, responding to it, cutting across it, *being* in it. Likewise the most flamboyant and egocentric of American radio DJs, such as Cousin Brucie, or Rosko, for whom the man was the show and the records simply the entourage. As the Bronx DJs extended their reach from a back room to a city park or square, they would pepper their music with grunts and shout-outs, encouraging the dancers to get down with the rhythm, move with the flow, all the clichés which fell off the lips of anyone with a deck at their control. Soon there were others alongside them who were more fluent, and the DJ became half of a double act: the bringer of sound with the master of verbiage, one controlling the groove, the other heightening the atmosphere. The deck-master was still ostensibly the star. But gradually the MCs began to ease them aside. Soon the crowd would be focused on the man with the microphone, exhorting, shouting, teasing, hyping the magic of the music, while the guy with those hard-learned skills of turntable manipulation stood silent alongside them. 'With this seem- ingly unremarkable shift in microphone placement,' wrote Mark Katz, 'the relationship between DJs and MCs began to change. The DJ was no longer at the centre of the hip-hop universe; a golden age of the DJ was coming to an end.' But before hip hop could step out of the Bronx and become a global culture, another industry had to move over – one that was still in its moment of creation when Kool Herc soundtracked his sister's party at 1520 Sedgwick Avenue.

Such has been the impact of the discos of late that today the 'sound' has completely usurped the performer. It doesn't matter who's singing as long as that dancing beat is there.
  Roger St Pierre, *NME*, 1976

The disco sound is a sound I abhor. It's one monotone driving beat. It's as if the human race is a bunch of cattle that's got to be given a beat to move to.
  Record producer Richard Perry, 1976

'The sensation that's sweeping the nation', explained the magazine *Black Music* in December 1973, 'is "party" records ("party, party, party" must be chanted monotonously over a tight and right rhythm section) and "whistle blowing" records (where whistles are blown over a similarly funky rhythm section).' Exemplifying both trends, the writer concluded, was 'Funky Stuff' by the black Jersey City band, Kool & the Gang. Their saxophonist, Dennis Thomas, admitted a year later: 'We just got carried along on the disco thing. The truth is, most of us don't go to discos, people had to *tell* us about the whistles and stuff . . . Most of us are very quiet guys . . . Partying every night wasn't our scene. When "Funky Stuff" broke, the whole thing opened up for us. We got to a white audience who'd never *heard* of us.'

'Funky Stuff', and its more generic successor 'Jungle Boogie', arrived amidst a flurry of hit records which were bursting open the borders of black music. The Isley Brothers' 'That Lady' was a Latin-funk jam which revealed how much lead guitarist Ernie Isley had learned during Jimi Hendrix's brief apprenticeship with the band. 'For the first time in my life,' reported Vernon Gibbs at an Isleys' show in New York, 'I heard a black audience reacting enthusiastically to a *loud* guitar solo.' Earth, Wind & Fire's 'Evil' channelled the psychedelic Latin rock of Santana. 'Ecstasy' by the Ohio Players kept throwing off its centre of gravity, each new layer of sound adding to the glorious sonic confusion. Most experimental of all – and No. 1 on both the US Pop and Soul charts – was Eddie Kendricks's 'Keep On Truckin'', which was almost an autopsy of the R&B tradition, each constituent part held up for display and then thrown away as if it would no longer be required.

Black identity – or at least its musical representation – was also in flux. There was music from the ghetto, signalling out: the 'blaxploitation' soundtracks of Curtis Mayfield, or Stevie Wonder's 'Living For the City'. More voices came from the suburbs, stretching hopefully across the racial divide – the remnants of Berry Gordy's crossover dream from the 1960s. Or from the bedroom, zooming in like a voyeur's camera: the erotic tingle of Marvin Gaye's 'Let's Get It On', and the pillow talk of Barry White's 'I'm Gonna Love You Just a Little Bit More'. Or from the streets, where Latin-funk band War (in the person of Papa Dee Allen) described them-selves as 'anarchy in music' before delivering a manifesto that would be echoed in Britain later in the decade: 'We would like to think of ourselves as an extension of the people. The people look *up* to stars, but they look *us* in the eye.'

Then there were the existing stars, who – like the Rolling Stones a decade earlier – wanted to celebrate the power of black music in the white community. Elton John and David Bowie were slowly working their way towards their respective destinations of 'Philadelphia Freedom' and 'Young Americans'. The Electric Light Orchestra had abandoned their ambition to out-*Pepper* the Beatles by creating 'Showdown', which (lead vocal aside) sounded like a Florida funk record. Strangest of all, perhaps, was the example of the Osmonds, now working with an African-American soul arranger/producer, whose 'Let Me In' demonstrated how smoothly the sweet-soul sound of Philadelphia could cross from black to white. (It also, incidentally, perfected the 'boy band' balladry which would fuel teenage crushes throughout the 1990s and beyond.) Within a year, it would be possible for the sardonically named Average White Band to propel their Scottish brand of funk high on the US soul charts.

Even more alarming for the record industry than racial ambiguity was the potential for hits to be created on the dance floor. 'Soul Makossa' by Manu Dibango (from Cameroon) wasn't even on sale in America when David Mancuso began to play it at Brooklyn loft parties, arousing a demand for non-existent product. If DJs could conjure hits out of obscure African funk records, then the market was escaping the record companies' control. Like every other jolt to the status quo, the explosion of 'party' music made the business of hit-making impossibly unreliable. Out of nowhere, a maverick producer such as Bob Crewe could reinvent celebrity hairdresser Monti Rock as the flamboyantly camp Disco-Tex & the Sex-O-Lettes, whose 'Get Dancin'' both celebrated and parodied the gay culture which had triggered the dance-club scene. Partying was no longer a mere pleasure dome: it was a statement of identity, or potential identity, which could find gay men and straight women, blacks and whites, parading in near-identical displays of sexual daring.

The lord of dance-floor eroticism in 1974 was Barry White, entrepreneur, arranger, producer, songwriter, keyboardist, vocalist – and sex symbol. Dismissed in the press as 'the first disposable King of Muzak', the gargantuan White both controlled and liberated his predominantly female audience, as this description of a 1975 concert from *Black Music* illustrates: '16 to 60, Barry is hurting them where it hurts so good. One girl gasps, "Oh god, oh god", over and over again as she slides into an almost hypnotic trance . . . two middle-aged ladies have to be dragged off the front of the stage as they make desperate but futile attempts to clutch at Barry's velvet-clad trouser legs . . . Dozens of women leapt from seats and fell on their hero to touch his massive body and kiss his haloed head.' White induced 'mass trance-like euphoria of which 100 faith healers would be proud'.

Male critics might carp about his 'endless tedium', 'almost complete lack of emotional substance' and 'Uncle Tom' demeanour, but they weren't Barry White's audience. When women danced to his rhythm, they had only one destination in mind: the bedroom.

Almost every form of black music – funk, Philly soul, the swamp grooves of Florida, jazz, the calypso hybrid from Barbados known as soca, the Cuban-American collage of salsa – could be stripped down to its essentials and sent out as disco: a term that now referred both to a venue, and to the music which shook its walls. It didn't matter if (for example) the leader of KC & the Sunshine Band was a white man, or George McCrae black; MFSB a faceless bunch of session musicians; Herbie Hancock a jazz genius; or Elton John a white, secretly bisexual Englishman. They were all food for the discotheque, where the only disqualification was if your music didn't make people want to get up and boogie. Disco could be reduced to something as basic, and irresistible, as Hamilton Bohannon's 'South African Man', which anticipated the house music of a decade hence with its shapeless application of the groove and nothing but the groove.

This was not a genre which appealed to those who imagined music as anything beyond entertainment. Chuck D of Public Enemy remembered it as 'the most artificial shit I ever heard'. An editorial in the rock magazine *Rolling Stone* revived an insult from the early days of jazz, describing the 'disco mix' as 'an electronically boosted bass and dance beat that would do St Vitus proud'. The white British journalist Tony Cummings, an evangelist for black American music since 1963, complained that disco producers 'seem totally committed to making singers subservient to accompaniments and hit potential – something gauged with the primeval thrust of the pelvis'. Disco, he added, was 'music evolved to meet the artificial need of a pampered public [who] demand a computer-shaped, computer-age music which can pump the endless joy of "keep dancin'" good times'. But if the desire to dance was an 'artificial need', and 'endless joy' a sin, then what was the purpose of popular music? Black performers, it seemed, *had* to express social ills and political purpose. But what if the black audience, faced with prejudice, economic discrimination, and the fallout from the spectacular collapse of the black-power movement, might simply want the same freedom to be carefree that was a given for their white contemporaries? As Ernie Isley of the Isley Brothers insisted, 'Rock and roll in its purest form was always dancing music . . . all it means is that rock and roll is going back to what its original concept was supposed to be.' That didn't prevent the Isleys recording the violently political funk track, 'Fight the Power', in 1975; it simply didn't limit them to that mode of expression.

If there was something acutely uncomfortable about white critics setting the agenda for black musicians, what about the colonisation of what had been a black art-form by white producers, arrangers and entrepreneurs? By 1975, artists as unlikely as pre-rock vocal star Al Martino and German bandleader James Last were making disco music. Bob Dylan's protest single 'Hurricane' was described by a zealous evangelist of dance music as 'Dylan goes disco'. Producer Richard Perry, who had expressed his abhorrence for the relentless sameness of the disco beat, masterminded singer-songwriter Leo Sayer's entrance into the genre with 'You Should Be Dancing'. By the end of the decade, the craze or contagion had reached Barbra Streisand, Andy Williams, vaudeville veteran Ethel Merman, Engelbert Humperdinck, Petula Clark. Even Frank Sinatra participated, as his trademark 'Night and Day' was retooled for dance consumption, though the one-time crooner was still able to find space within the skintight arrangement to toy with his phrasing as if it was Nelson Riddle's band behind him, rather than a computerised backbeat.

Commercial necessity inspired most of these adventures; few of these artists (Streisand aside, perhaps) would have chosen to roam so far from their natural turf. But disco did not define them as it did Donna Summer, an African-American working as a studio background singer in Germany. 'Love to Love You Baby' – a title she had suggested to producers Giorgio Moroder and Pete Bellotte – was extended into a seventeen-minute erotic suite, on which Summer was required to breathe and groan as if transported with sexual delight. 'I love the music', she said when the record was a global hit, 'I just wished that I hadn't sung it.' No matter: *Ebony* magazine proudly revealed that 'Disco's greatest fans are women and gays, and both groups seek her out backstage whenever she appears in public. They tell Donna how they listen to her records while making love, and they thank her for helping them discover how, finally, to "let go"!' Yet Summer herself shared none of their ecstatic liberation; nor was she thrilled by Moroder and Bellotte's next experiment. To balance the all-too-human emotion of 'Love to Love You Baby', they concocted 'I Feel Love', set to the futuristic accompaniment of a Moog synthesiser, sending out its rhythms with robotic indifference. Once again, Summer was tasked to convey carnal pleasure, but in keeping with the sci-fi ambience of the track, her consummation sounded as if it was taking place in an icy trance, perverse but curiously alienated. This, one reviewer noted, was 'the music of the brave new world'. But for Donna Summer, her fame as an erotic icon reduced her to a 'commodity'. She tumbled into prolonged depression, and attempted suicide, before finding redemption in evangelical Christianity.

If Donna Summer's success could be interpreted as racial or sexual exploitation (even though she was, in theory, a willing accomplice), the equally rapid transformation of one-time Beatles copyists the Bee Gees found them being accused of perverting black culture for their own ends. The combination of Barry Gibb's agonised falsetto lead, and producer Arif Mardin's slick dance grooves, created a sound that was both commercial, and totally unlike their previous work. To sidestep the preconceptions of disc jockeys who regarded them as passé, the group sent out promotional copies of their 'Jive Talkin'' single with blank white labels – hiding both their name and their racial identity.

In the Bee Gees' hands, disco became the basic language of popular music. Their success coincided with a shift in perception of the discotheque's function. It was no longer an arena for subverting society's sexual mores, and breaking taboos, but a proof that one belonged inside the mainstream – or, in select circles, within the social elite. *Billboard* magazine asserted confidently at the start of 1977 that disco 'is expected to move purposefully forward in the new year to shed its dubious image of freaky phenomenon and assume the more positive mantle of a sophisticated industry . . . The man or woman behind the music must take control and ensure the absolute enjoyment of the fan who plunked down hard-earned dollars to be entertained, or the club will pass from glittering lounge to abandoned warehouse.' If that sounded like a recipe for standardisation – and there were now chains of discos across most Western countries – it was quickly followed by the opening of Studio 54 in midtown Manhattan. It was unashamedly a disco, and equally unashamedly intended as an assembly hall for celebrities. On one level, this was merely returning the discotheque to its pre-soul roots in French resorts; on another, it promoted disco music as a vehicle to attract the rich and notorious, nothing more or less. The antics of Andy and Mick and Bianca and Cher commanded regular column inches; their presence outweighed the pleasure of the dance, let alone the substance or otherwise of the music.

As Steve Rubell's nightclub on 54th Street attracted celebrities and their awestruck stalkers, those who could not even dream of admission could lose themselves in the fantasy of *Saturday Night Fever*. Released at the end of 1977, this film – soundtracked by the Bee Gees, and produced by their manager – completed disco's commercial victory and hastened its downfall.* The disco had been a place of mass hedonism; the crowd was both thrillingly involving and pleasingly anonymous. Now it attracted those who would be John Travolta, as men donned white suits in his image, and risked their fellow patrons' safety by attempting to echo his most flamboyant moves. As evidence of Travolta's instant personification of the disco experience, Alice Echols points out that 'Brazilians began to use neologistic verbs and nouns from the root "Travolta" – *travoltar* (to travolt), *travoltice* (travoltage) – to describe the condition of disco fever.'

Rock critic Stephen Holden predicted early in 1979 that this would be the year when 'disco became the biggest thing in pop since Beatlemania, and possibly since the birth of rock and roll'. The charts bore him witness; likewise the annual Grammy Awards. The disco phenomenon spread beyond North America and Western Europe to reach Japan, Africa and even Russia, where Bee Gees singles became as hot an underground currency as Beatles records had been in the 1960s. Disc jockeys now required an acute statistical and psychological grasp of what would make people dance; specialists were employed to detail the 'beats per minute' of each disco track, to ensure that the atmosphere would not be broken by something unexpectedly fast or slow.† The winter of 1978–9 was also the season when Village People – a male troupe of singer-dancers adopting blatantly stereotypical gay images – were accepted by millions who got the joke, and many millions more who preferred to believe that they were just a cop, a cowboy, a construction worker, a sailor, a biker and a Native American, who happened to enjoy dancing together. It's so ridiculous that it should be apochryphal, but the US Navy really did consider using Village People's 'In the Navy' as a recruiting anthem until the semiotics of the group's costumes were explained to its senior officers.

If John Travolta was disco's role model, the Bee Gees its pop

---

* It also inspired a sequel, *Urban Cowboy*, set in the Texas honky-tonks, which briefly made country the hippest music in America. The ensuing boom-and-bust narrative was enacted so quickly that there was barely time for Nashville's record companies to capitalise on the phenomenon.

† *Record Mirror*'s James Hamilton was the master of this art, to wit: 'Atmospheric bumpy 106-104-105-104-103-102 bpm 12 in. jazz jogger', or 'Excellent remix of the lazily swaying hypnotic old 117 bpm side-to-side kicker with added jazz sax 'n' smack.'

ambassadors and Village People its tongue-in-cheek clowns, then the genre's auteurs – intelligent, brilliant, slick, pin-point accurate – were Chic. 'Every song had to have Deep Hidden Meaning', recalled the group's creative fulcrum, Nile Rodgers. 'We went out to conquer the world – one dance-floor at a time.' As he explained it, the Chic ethos was simple and devastatingly effective: 'Back then, most R&B acts wore flamboyant clothes, but we created believable alter egos: two men in impressively labelled but subtle designer business suits, which effectively gave us the anonymity of Kiss. We put sexy girls on our album cover, which was suave like Roxy Music, and we tooled a new form of Euro-influenced R&B . . . Then we put together a corporation that would manage and develop this entity and its future enterprises, the Chic Organization Ltd.' Unbeknownst to Chic, this would be the template for success at the end of the century: military planning, backed by corporate might; expansive ambition, packaged in the form of spontaneity and fun.

Those qualities seemed, in early 1979, to be obtainable only from disco. *Billboard* magazine declared that 'veteran acts' need not chase the youth market, as 'Audiences no longer leave the music scene to the kids on turning 30 . . . Ten years ago, there was a tendency to consider pop artists over the hill as they hit 30. Now the prevailing attitude seems to be that artists aren't getting older, they're getting better.' But the 'veterans' were still afraid of being considered old, and many of those who felt that their commercial standing had slipped chose this moment to make a decisive grab for the disco market. Many critically acclaimed jazz-funk artists crossed the boundary into dance music, although in most cases the shift only involved using a more persistent backbeat and simpler chord changes. Stephen Stills, best known as a confessional songwriter and blues-rock guitarist, concocted some highly professional imitations of the Bee Gees on his 1978 album *Thoroughfare Gap*, to the disgust of his existing fan base. Even more extreme was the reaction to the Beach Boys' epic disco revamp of their twelve-year-old song 'Here Comes the Night', which was extended from two minutes to eleven, as a playful pop song became a disco symphony. Their vocal blend was magnificent, but they were booed whenever they attempted to perform the piece in public, and quickly abandoned the experiment.

A month after the Beach Boys' disco record was released, a trade magazine ran an alarmist story: 'Disco Rules, But Where Are the Big Sales?' The dance craze had persuaded some LP-only dealers to resume stocking singles, but disco was not proving itself a major factor in the album market, *Saturday Night Fever* and the Bee Gees aside. 'Imagine how bad business would be if we didn't have disco', quipped Atlantic Records' producer Jerry Wexler, but even he was forced to admit: 'It could be that disco has become our new Muzak' – ubiquitous background music that nobody would dream of buying.

'People turn to dance for an electronic shot, an energy level that rock wasn't giving them', said media analyst John Perikhal. But there was a substantial audience – male, young, white, non-metropolitan, instinctively conservative – for whom disco represented everything that they despised: dancing, of course, but also rich people, black people, liberated women and, most of all, anyone who seemed even remotely gay. Shock jocks on American radio stations, whose playlists were 100% rock, launched a guerrilla campaign in 1978–9 against disco. They would smash records on air, spin them at 78 rpm to ridicule the artists, play machine-gun effects while a dance disc was being broadcast – even, in the case of Steve Dahl from WLUP in Chicago, pronounce 'disco' with a lisp to denote how 'gay' the whole culture was. And it was Dahl who provided the climactic moment of this campaign, when he staged a Disco Demolition Night between ball games at a double-header in Comiskey Park. Seventy thousand people attended in collective loathing of everything that disco stood for. Tens of thousands of dance records were piled into a crate which was set in centre-field – and then exploded. This proved so incendiary a catharsis that there was a riot, during which the stadium was severely damaged, and the ball game had to be abandoned.

Thereafter rock fans proudly wore lapel badges stating 'Disco Sucks', while still congratulating themselves on their rebel status. The record industry began to back away from the tainted term, opting to push 'dance music' as a less pejorative substitute. While disco was still spreading to other parts of the globe – Turkey reported a sudden bout of 'Travolta fever', even though *Saturday Night Fever* had not been released there – its American homeland was turning its back on the monster it had created. By autumn 1979, even the Chic Organization was signalling a move away from dance tunes to 'heavier ballads, rock and R&B', while Village People had their eye on movies and Las Vegas.

Some dance clubs refashioned themselves for roller-skating, the assumption being that the music needn't change. Some record companies emphasised that they were abandoning 'pure' disco in favour of disco rock, disco pop and even disco reggae. There was talk of introducing melody to disco, or rock guitars, or a country twang – anything that might stick.

Then, out of the blue, a novelty arrived, from below the radar of the music business. In summer 1978, *Billboard* magazine had printed a puzzled news story about a New York record retailer who was being inundated with requests for long-out-of-catalogue disco and soul records. These came 'from young black DJs from the Bronx, who are buying the records just to play the 30 seconds or so rhythm breaks that each disk contains'. These breaks were known as B-beats, the piece explained helpfully. The impetus for this buying spree was a 'mobile DJ who is known in the Bronx as Cool [*sic*] Herc' who 'rose to popularity by playing long sets of assorted rhythm breaks strung together'. Herc told the magazine that if necessary he would speed up the breaks for better effect. 'On most records, people have to wait through a lot of strings and singing to get to the good part of the record,' he explained. 'But I give it to them all up front.'

A year later, another report focused on 'Jive Talking New York DJs Rapping Away in Black Discos', as 'a jivey rap commands as much attention these days as the hottest new disk'. No connection was made to Kool Herc: the leading figures of this scene were apparently Eddie Cheeba, DJ Hollywood, DJ Starski and Kurtis Blow. Cheeba was said to tour the city with seven female dancers and a DJ. 'People go to discos every week and they need more than music to motivate them', he explained. 'I not only play records, but I rap, and they answer me.' Fans of these 'rapping DJs' made their own recordings of their favourites in action: 'Tapes of [DJ] Hollywood's raps are considered valuable commodities by young blacks here.'

Former doo-wop entrepreneur Paul Winley learned about the B-beat phenomenon from his daughters, who were experiencing it firsthand. In 1979, he prepared a series of unauthorised compilation albums containing vintage tracks which were ripe for B-beat DJs to plunder, under the wonderfully erratic title *Super Disco Brake's*. At the same time, the disco group Fatback issued 'King Tim III (Personality Jock)', which opened like a conventional party record, whistles and computerised drums to the fore. But the vocal, by disc jockey Tim Washington from Harlem, was something new: delivered in a sing-song narrative style, almost like a nursery rhyme, cadenced to the syncopated rhythm. Its content was nothing more radical than a call to inhabit the dance floor ('to the break, everybody'), but revolutions have to begin somewhere – for this was, unmistakably, the birth of rap as a mainstream commercial genre.

Fatback's single attracted the attention of Sugar Hill Records impresario Sylvia Robinson (herself a veteran, as one half of 1950s R&B duo Mickey & Sylvia; and a pioneer of disco, as the singer of the erotic No. 1 hit from 1973, 'Pillow Talk'). She asked her son to search out some rappers. He returned with a trio of novices, and a bundle of borrowed rhymes. Robinson steered her studio band through an instrumental version of Chic's 'Good Times', and let her amateur talent loose. She named them, obviously enough, the Sugar Hill Gang, and their record 'Rapper's Delight'. The first voice at the microphone carefully explained that what they were doing was called 'rapping', before the Gang embarked on some primitive self-congratulation – a style that never seems to grow old. Some radio stations who specialised in soul music complained that the single was 'too black' – a coded reference to its supposed ghetto origins. Not that there was a gangster aesthetic at work here: Sugar Hill rapper Wonder Mike said of his 'speech music', 'Our raps may be about cars, girls, food or dancing', which was the stuff of Chuck Berry's rock 'n' roll canon. He also sabotaged the genre's notion of spontaneity at its birth: 'Don't think we make it up as we go along. It's all written, memorised and rehearsed before we go on stage.' But none of that undercut the freshness of the record, which was a huge hit on the Soul charts, entered the US Pop Top 40, and enjoyed its greatest success in Britain, where it reached No. 3. BBC disc jockey Anne Nightingale predicted that this 'new-found form of black dance music' would 'give the flagging disco sound the shot in its pick-up arm it so desperately needs'. And that, for the moment, was the pinnacle of rap's ambition; after all, a novelty only lasts for a season.

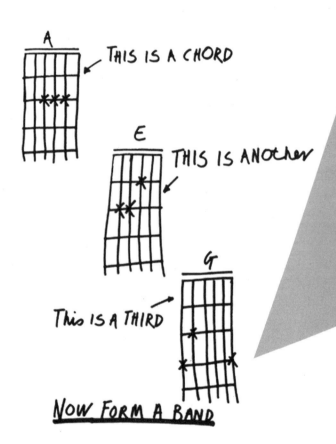

CHAPTER 24

Be DisRespectful

'Every time a 60s superstar comes up front and blows it, some egotistical little punk out in the sticks takes a listen and gets convinced that he can hack it just as good as all these biggies, and he may just be right.'

Charles Shaar Murray, *New Musical Express*, 1974

'It's a whole new generation of kids there, and the Beatles and McCartney and the Rolling Stones don't mean a thing. They're old men that are sort of parodies of rock, and kids don't want to see those guys.'

Russell Mael, Sparks, 1975

In 1972, the US satirical magazine *National Lampoon* devoted an entire issue to boredom. 'We want to tell you that what is around you EVERYWHERE, ALL THE TIME is boredom, lots of it,' its editorial pronounced, 'and we think it's about time you began to face it.'

Ennui and disillusionment were central to the culture of the 1970s. It had been, said American writer Chet Flippo in 1979, a 'decade of dullness'. A set of economic and political crises were dumped like refuse sacks across the path to the future: the oil crisis, tensions in the Middle and Far East, Western financial decline, urban terrorism, stalemate in the Cold War. For anyone who had bought into the optimism of the mid-1960s, and the rhetoric of a counter-culture, these grim realities were made more deadening by a profound sense of loss and anticlimax. It had seemed in the late 1960s that youth might be able to accelerate history and seize the reins of Western civilisation. By the early 1970s, it was as if the greyness of the 1950s had continued unchecked, imposing its moral repression and artistic conservatism on anyone who had the nerve to dream of liberation.

Dressing up, dancing or preferably the combination of the two provided a refuge. Kids could watch David Bowie on *Top of the Pops* and imagine themselves transported to an alien world of gaudy beauty and sexual ambiguity. The dance floor and the disco offered hedonism as an alternative to depression, even if one only danced to keep from crying. But for many, this was not catharsis enough.

Even rock stars imagined that their culture could only be changed with symbolic acts of violence. In their final months as a band, the Beatles fantasised that they might explode their career with a worldwide televised concert, during which they would say something so shocking – 'Fuck the Queen' was one suggestion – that all the constraints of their fame would be shattered at a stroke. Kit Lambert, the manager of the Who, imagined that (as Pete Townshend recalled) his group would perform at London's Royal Opera House, 'shit all over the stage, and storm out'. Children of the 1950s, they remembered the culture-shaking impact of Elvis Presley and Jerry Lee Lewis, and mourned their inability to rival their youthful iconoclasm.

For anyone raised on tales of 1950s and 60s rock mayhem, there were ample reasons to be disappointed by the 1970s. Glam rock or heavy metal might divert adolescents for a while, but was diversion enough? As pop culture slumbered towards the midpoint of the new decade, Britain was awash with bland boy bands masquerading as 1950s Teddy boys, while in America the new mainstream was soft pop, soft rock, soft country: James Taylor erasing his heritage of mental illness and heroin addiction, perhaps, or Loggins & Messina reviving 1950s rock tunes as aural tranquillisers. As cynical songwriter Randy Newman complained after a road trip across his radio-soaked nation, 'The big stations only play soft rock. It's all *mellow*. Now that's a hell of an ambition, to be *mellow*. It's like wanting to be senile.'

British writer Nick Kent offered a solution in 1974: 'The only way this whole rock 'n' roll mess can be salvaged and ultimately trans-formed into a feasible form again is if, as will happen, the whole schism blows itself up like some toad inhaling cigarette fumes, and sometime after the ashes have settled, a whole new breed of teenage bands will sprout up slowly who will write songs about being self-conscious and suffering from acne and having nocturnal emissions and premature ejacu-lations and all the hideous things young teenage kids really have to go through. And consequently rock music will start to have some true rele-vance again, beyond existing as some exotic musical broadsheet for other people's bloated fantasies.'

Yet Kent, for all his prophetic idealism, was equally in thrall to his fantasies. Like many rock journalists in an era when the music press was argu-ably at its most influential, he yearned for a music that would be raw, aggres-sive and fast. Writing about the American glam band the New York Dolls, he praised their ability to capture the quintessence of rock: 'total lack of self-consciousness and a commitment to full-tilt energy workouts, no matter what level of proficiency you're working at'. His *NME* colleague Charles Shaar Murray wrote about falling 'in love with rock and roll for the *right* reasons' (my emphasis): 'I mean, if you started digging rock because it provided a vital insight into the mood of the times, or because so many rock musicians today are . . . genuinely creative (you know, like Rick Wakeman or Mike Oldfield), then forget it', he insisted.

Lyricist and critic Clive James declared in 1975 that he loved rock because 'within it, you can encompass thousands of styles. It's a journalistic restriction to consider that rock 'n' roll is confined to certain ways and means.' But week after week, year after year, a critical consensus was sold to the adolescent and student readers of magazines such as the *NME* and *Creem*, until it was accepted like a catechism: the only credible form of music was (in the words of Lester Bangs) 'simple, primitive, direct, honest'. The sounds of the future had to be modelled on the most exciting sounds of the past, although most of the heroes of the 1950s and 60s had sullied their heritage by growing old and irrelevant. In place of Elvis and the Stones, then, a new galaxy of stars was installed, whose names were voiced so often by journalists and young musicians alike that they came to seem like the dominant forces of their era (1966–73).

Brightest in the firmament were the Velvet Underground and the Stooges, with the MC5 slightly in their shadow. Yet they hardly shared the same aesthetic. While the Stooges, under the leadership of Iggy Pop, had reduced rock to a blunt confrontational instrument, the Velvets, with Lou Reed in command, were graduates of the New York avant-garde art scene, fronted by a man whose desire was to transfer the techniques and narrative range of literature into rock 'n' roll. To this end, he employed three-chord rock, musique concrète, and balladry so sensitive that it made James Taylor and Joni Mitchell sound like clumsy alcoholics. Almost single-handedly, Reed had forced mid-1960s rock to stretch even further than Bob Dylan had imagined possible, to the point where it could chronicle homosexuality, sadomasochism and drug addiction in graphic detail. But his lyrical genius was less influential than his passion for garage-band rock 'n' roll; he was prone to boasting that a simple chord change from E major to A major was more profound than Nobel Prize-winning poetry.

So there was a contradiction at the heart of the new aesthetic. Iggy Pop and his 'retard bop' (Nick Kent) represented a deliberate dumbing-down of rock's capabilities: 'stupid' began to be used as a compliment. But the same journalists who abhorred the idea of rock becoming pretentious or overambitious adopted as their icon a songwriter whose efforts were steeped in pretension. Pretending to be 'dumb' was authentic and honest; wanting to use rock as a vehicle for artistic expression was 'bloated', unless you could mask your ambitions beneath naked aggression.

Pete Townshend, as astute a rock critic in the mid-1970s as he was a songwriter, hit upon the essence of rock 'n' roll when he praised the glam-rock band (and former bubblegum act) Sweet: 'I think their music does contain a lot of the tight, integrated, directed, pointed frustration of a 15- or 16-year-old.' And that was the holy grail, it seemed: music that would seize the rampant hormones of adolescent boys, and simultaneously renew that fire in the hearts of men who had long since waved their teens goodbye.

> Could this be the New Wave? . . . punky, Stones-influenced rock and roll.
>   Ed McCormack reviewing the New York Dolls, 1972

> All this talk about getting back to the streets – yeah, the streets are fine, but you won't find anything there that you don't already know.
>   Todd Rundgren, 1974

British underground theorist and Deviants singer/lyricist Mick Farren was in his early 30s when he wrote a series of self-questioning essays about the future relevance of rock 'n' roll. In 1974 he imagined the mainstream being 'challenged by a lot of wild boys from the edge whose motivation is music rather than profit . . . A lack of cash could force the music to become cheap, gaudy, vital and energetic.' Two years later, he proclaimed that 'If rock becomes safe, it's all over . . . The best, most healthy kind of rock and roll is produced by and for the same generation . . . It may be a question of taking rock back to street level and starting all over again.'

There was no handbook explaining how to achieve this cultural reversal. Among the suggestions were 'dictatorship rock . . . a neo-Nazi-type band, made up of very young Jewish boys', by American club-owner Rodney Bingenheimer; schoolgirls in fetishist underwear, envisioned by US producer Kim Fowley and personified by the Runaways; and a group that could enact the 1970 manifesto of London film-maker Malcolm McLaren: 'Be childish. Be irresponsible. Be disrespectful. Be everything this society hates.' Yet the purest approach of the era was provided by a New York quartet who offered 'a cartoon vision of rock and roll', said Charles Shaar Murray, and who were 'pocket punks, a perfect razor-edged bubblegum band'.

When the Ramones' debut album was launched in early 1976, they seemed to encapsulate the fantasy of rock as minimalist, abrupt and above all dumb. Few of their songs extended beyond two minutes and three chords; or veered far from melodies and riffs so basic that most budding musicians would have shied away in embarrassment. They played fast and relentless, while singer Joey Ramone chanted lyrics of conscious banality about teenage life.

Chris Stein of Blondie, who emerged from the same milieu, dismissed the idea that the Ramones had emerged organically in this quintessentially lowbrow state: the band was 'a preconceived idea – they worked at it a long time before they came out'. The Ramones' collective decision to adopt the same surname reinforced the notion that this was not a spontaneous flowering of basic rock 'n' roll but an exercise in performance art: Gilbert & George for teenagers, perhaps. Their producer, Craig Leon, admitted that their debut LP was 'quite layered and structured and took full advantage of the studio'. But the artifice was applied with such skill that all anyone could distinguish was the absence of art – exactly the streetwise sonic assault for which a generation of critics had been begging.

The Ramones' New York contemporaries shared their blend of rock power and artistic integrity, though not their forced stupidity. Blondie celebrated and satirised the pure American pop of the era immediately before the Beatles, although press attention focused on their archetypally glamorous lead singer, Deborah Harry. Patti Smith mixed ecstatic beat poetry with the rock spirit of 1965; her friends Television injected fresh energy and oblique lyricism into the duelling-guitar format of psychedelic bands such as Quicksilver Messenger Service; while Talking Heads oozed art-school formalism from every skeletal pore. The musician who provided a collective ethos for their efforts, and for its surreal reflection in London, was Richard Hell, the only member of this diffuse artistic movement not to become a genuine pop star. He did, however, write its anthem: '(I Belong to the) Blank Generation', which identified a cultural void and then belied it with the verbal precision of his writing. Yet Hell's title was deliberately ambiguous. Did 'Blank' denote a nihilist refusal to adopt a pose, an admission of emptiness and despair? Or was he declaring independence from the past, and allowing his generation the freedom to rewrite the history of rock from the beginning?

Ironically, the term which would ultimately define this era, in America and Britain, was rooted in the past. 'Punk rock' had been applied to America's mid-1960s garage-rock tradition since the early 1970s – a statement of pride, and also of opprobrium, as a letter to *Rolling Stone* magazine in 1973 illustrated, in its criticism of 'the punk ethic, anti-intelligence, anti-heart tide currently fashionable'. This ethic was located, the correspondent believed, in the New York Dolls, whose blend of Rolling Stones swagger and androgynous fashion sense won them critical acclaim but minimal commercial success.

The Dolls were in disarray a year later, when they first met Malcolm

McLaren, ex-art student, then tailor for London's Teddy boys, and now the proprietor (with designer Vivienne Westwood) of Sex, a shop specialising in fetish wear and confrontational fashion. McLaren offered to manage the New York band for a few chaotic months, imagining that he could mould them into an act which would embody his naïve vision of cultural anarchy. He soon realised it would be easier to force his vision upon more impressionable subjects: a bunch of musical novices in their early 20s whose ambitions didn't stretch beyond imitating Rod Stewart and the Faces. It was McLaren who made the fateful decision to combine them with John Lydon, a teenage nihilist of no apparent talent, who would soon become one of the most charismatic and nonconformist figures of the rock era.

Their manager told punk chronicler Jon Savage that he imagined the Sex Pistols (his choice of name) 'could be the Bay City Rollers . . . dour and tough and the real thing. A genuine teenage group. For me, that was anarchy in the record business.' His rhetoric would almost inevitably filter into the Pistols' songs, as they worked their way through deconstructions of 1960s pop classics towards an original repertoire. But although manager and artists shared a language, their definitions were starkly at odds. For Lydon, anarchy denoted a sullen disgust with what was on offer to him and his peers: cultural repression, unemployment, stunted prospects, harsh realities. For McLaren, it was a theoretical concept rather than a reflection of daily life: after all, as a boutique-owner he had been master of his own destiny for years. He wanted to confront the structure of society and undermine its ethical foundations. So did Lydon, but only with individual acts of dissent, rather than a philosophy of revolution. Meanwhile, his fellow Pistols wanted to be rock 'n' roll stars, yobs and party animals, and weren't fussy how they got there. This 'quartet of spiky teenage misfits from the wrong end of various London roads', as they were described in an early review, were destined for one of the briefest and most tumultuous careers in the history of popular music: a cultural explosion misinterpreted at the time, and distorted ever since.

It is very likely there will be violence at some of the gigs, because it is violent music. We don't necessarily think violence is a bad thing, because you have to destroy to create.
Malcolm McLaren, 1976

Punk rock people don't want to be pretty. They reckon they are appealing only if they seem appalling . . . They do their own horrific thing.

Daily Mirror, 1976

As their name suggested, violence was intrinsic to the Sex Pistols' manifesto, although sexuality was never on the agenda: 'Sex' was an advertisement for Malcolm McLaren's shop, rather than anything more carnal. As Jon Savage recounted, 'the Sex Pistols were programmed for confrontation. McLaren was ambitious for this group: as his instrument, they would act out his fantasies of conflict and revenge on a dying culture.' These fantasies did not involve reforming the music business, or providing a sonic template for generations of future bands to follow. It was serendipitous, rather than calculating, that McLaren's championing of a chaotic, untutored band should so perfectly answer the call of fans and critics who (like the Pistols themselves) were bored with the elitism of the rock aristocracy.

London's pub-rock movement had arisen out of the desire to return rock 'n' roll to its spiritual home in bars and basements. It encouraged a number of entrepreneurs – managers, promoters, record-stall owners – to provide an outlet for this defiantly out-of-time music by forming their own independent labels. Soon there was a recognised circuit of rock pubs and clubs, and labels such as Chiswick and Stiff to promote its luminaries, from the Count Bishops to Nick Lowe. But none of these artists could match the disturbance caused by the Sex Pistols in 1976, especially once McLaren and Westwood had incited fights in the audience at the Nashville Club that April, in front of reviewers from the pop press. McLaren's friend and rival Bernie Rhodes began to shape another band, the Clash, in a similar mould, and the music papers recognised not just an anarchistic publicity stunt but a 'new wave' of frenetic, combustible music ripe for marketing. As Mark Perry, publisher of an early punk fanzine, *Sniffin' Glue*, insisted that summer, 'This "new wave" has got to take in everything, including posters, record covers, stage presentation, the lot!' Under McLaren's guidance, the Sex Pistols were handled like a multimedia art project, providing audience and press alike with the frenzy and outrage they desired.

Aware that he required national exposure to play his spirit-of-1968 games with Britain's mainstream media, McLaren ensured that his protégés should ignore the backwaters of independent distribution, and strike at the heart of the corporate beast. The Sex Pistols were signed to EMI, and so began a sequence of disruptions and scandals which surpassed McLaren's wildest imaginings – swearing on national TV, censorship by media organisations and local councils, attacks on the Pistols and their entourage, and ultimately the implosion of the band, followed by the tawdry decline and inevitable death of bassist Sid Vicious. Even at its mid-1950s height, rock 'n' roll had never polarised opinion so starkly, or sparked such anger and disgust. No sooner had Britain's national press noticed punk's existence than they were chronicling events that still beggar belief – a 47-year-old lorry driver kicking in his television to prevent his child witnessing the Pistols, appalled rock stars in their 30s bombarding their record labels with protests when they signed these unruly punks, and claims of rowdiness and worse in company offices, airports, even on the street outside Buckingham Palace. Never had it been so simple to shock parents and other responsible adults: the punk uniform (based in part on Sex designs) turned everyone who wore it into an instant rebel. With the ripped clothes, safety pins and spiked hair came the etiquette – face twisted into a snarl, spit collected in the throat until it was almost solid, and then expelled at random targets, tribal aggression. Every antisocial act that popular music had ever been accused of encouraging was now visible on British streets; or so it seemed once the press had begun the process of demonisation.

The music itself was every bit as shocking. Amidst the pallid pop of late 1976, the Sex Pistols' 'Anarchy in the UK' exploded like a hand grenade in an elevator. Beyond the multi-overdubbed guitars and iron-foundry drumming, what endured was Lydon's voice, as menacing as a mugger's knife. There followed a year of such sonic assaults: the Clash's football terrace vocals on 'White Riot', where only the title was audible amidst the chaos; the Jam reprising the power-chord theatrics of the Who c.1965; above all others, the Sex Pistols sabotaging the much-anticipated royal jubilee with 'God Save the Queen'. Its (literal) lese-majesty was regarded by the establishment as tantamount to blasphemy, but the taint that lingered was the repeated chorus of 'No future', a generation's curse on its own inheritance.

Punk was now, regardless of Malcolm McLaren's intentions, the soundtrack of political dissent: a blaring siren call of betrayal and dissatisfaction. Veteran journalist Barry Miles cited the Clash's ability to capture 'the dormant energy of all the hours of crushing boredom of being an unemployed school-leaver, living with your parents in a council flat'.* Like ragtime and jazz, punk began to be used as an all-purpose adjective: the *Daily Mirror* headlined an editorial about youth unemployment 'Punk futures'. The *Church Times* suggested that 'There is evidence that today's "punk rock" phenomenon, with its violent language and mannerisms, has arisen directly because of unemployment among the young.' What began as a solitary gesture of opposition was cohering into a suitably anarchic political force, albeit one operating in a black-and-grey moral universe. By summer 1977, fanzine writer Danny Baker was complaining that 'Punks are the same as the government . . . If you don't believe me, try getting on stage at a punk gig and talking against the agreed pose for the night.'

Some observers saw punk's culture of uniformity – one sound, one style, one attitude – as a straitjacket. As early as February 1977, Mark Perry was writing: 'This scene, if there is a "scene" anymore, is about movement. It's about constant change, creative changes, not fashion changes.' A month later he pleaded: 'Chuck away the fucking stupid safety pins, think about people's ideas instead of their clothes.' By now, record companies were betraying the confusion with which they'd greeted each new form of popular music over the last sixty years: unable to distinguish quality from banality, they signed acts indiscriminately. 'All the new groups sound like drones', said Clash guitarist Mick Jones in spring 1977. Concerns were voiced that artists were being profiled in the music papers before they had been given time to develop a unique identity. This pattern would become the norm over the decades ahead, to the point that bands would have exhausted their novelty value before they had even made a record.

By the end of 1977, it was possible to rent a punk for £4 an hour, to enliven a London cocktail party. Young men made a living from posing for tourists' photos on the King's Road, and 'punk' became as hackneyed an image as 'hippie' in San Francisco a decade earlier. As Jon Savage wrote, 'English punk was now open to every charlatan, poseur and genius attracted by the prospects of media attention and a record contract.' 'Punk rock', said Kim Fowley that October, 'is finished'; his compatriot Greg Shaw talked about its 'built-in obsolescence'. In the aftermath of an explosion, with energy converted into destruction, all that remained were fragments. But the fragments proved to have an unexpected afterlife.

---

*The *NME*'s Phil McNeill noted cynically that the so-called 'dole-queue rock' was 'laughable': 'almost every musician in the genre is making a living, an unprecedented phenomenon'.

What I picked up most from mixing with the punks was a new way of approaching things – that whole punk DIY ethic . . . The DIY ethos was a blueprint for the working class to create their own shit despite the class system and the closed doors of the old-boy network.
  Film-maker Don Letts

There are so many new bands in England and they're all copying the Sex Pistols. It's such a joke. They might as well be copying Smokie.
  Nick Lowe, 1978

Punk? New-wave? New-wave punk? For decades, 'punk' the noun had signi-fied a hoodlum, a working-class outlaw, a biker, a rebel; 'punk' the adjective a more generalised insult (folk traditionalist Ewan MacColl described Bob Dylan's songwriting as 'punk' in 1965, for example). 'New wave' denoted a fresh approach to the business of film-making, exemplified by the *nouvelle vague*, and hence a description for any remaking of an art form, such as science-fiction writing in the 1960s or the so-called 'bedsitter' dramas of English theatre. In 1963, former Shadows drummer Tony Meehan had heralded a 'new wave' of British beat bands, such as the Rolling Stones, who were tapping into the same spirit as John Osborne and Arnold Wesker.

'Punk' and 'new wave' were used interchangeably to describe the anarchy of 1976; 'new-wave punks' distinguished the Pistols and the Clash from the 'original' punks in New York; or indeed from the 1960s garage-rock bands. Gradually, however, 'punk' and 'new wave' diverged: punk denoting explosive energy, new wave the more mannered or nostalgic forms of pop which emerged alongside it. By the end of the decade, 'new wave' was a form of denigration: a synonym for inauthenticity or shallowness. Anyone who wanted to retain the punk ethic but explore wider musical horizons was dubbed (with stunning logic) 'post-punk' – like 'new wave', so broad a cate-gory that it was effectively meaningless.

What all these adjectives shared was the power to eradicate the music that had gone before – from the British pop papers, if not from the charts. In their enthusiasm to ride this frenzied wave wherever it might take them, many journalists effectively wiped their memory clean. Regardless of their age and style, pre-punk acts were 'dinosaurs' or 'boring old farts', unless (like Lou Reed and David Bowie) they could claim some allegiance to the punk movement. (Desperate to be included, Marc Bolan claimed wildly: 'I was the originator of punk rock.') This was both an overdue piece of iconoclasm, forcing bands such as the Rolling Stones and the Who to respond (as they did with 'Shattered' and 'Who Are You?' respectively); and also a total irrelevance in the eyes of the general public, who continued to support ELO, Led Zeppelin and Genesis as if nothing had happened. It merely heightened the 'us and them' rhetoric of the times. But there were fierce debates about how to treat such borderline punks as Elvis Costello, the Jam and Tom Robinson, all of whom were suspected of leanings towards rock traditionalism, despite the righteous fury of their early releases.

In retrospect, what's apparent about the first brigade of British punk bands is that they represented less of a schism from the past than a form of rejuvenation: an electric shock applied to the exhausted carcasses of mid-1960s British pop or early 1970s glam-rock. The first punk hit in America was Plastic Bertrand's 'Ça plane pour moi', not only sung in French but a seamless blend of Bob Dylan's 'Subterranean Homesick Blues' with the sound of the Beach Boys c.1963. The Clash were already so removed from their milieu by late 1977 that their songs began to document their corporate struggles with the record business. With the Sex Pistols a spent force by spring 1978, dozens of bands emerged to imitate their sound: Sham 69, Angelic Upstarts, Ruts, UK Subs, and soon an entire wave of aggressive skinheads who were dubbed 'Oi!' by the press (perhaps the most evocative genre definition in music history). In their hands, punk was a weapon wielded with brute force: a never-changing, ever-tightening form of self-confinement which would continue for decades to wave a flag bearing the slogan: 'Punk's not dead'.

If pure punk was easy to identify, unpredictable only in its ability to attract political extremes of left and right, other musical traits which emerged between 1976 and 1978 were more malleable. The Stranglers were initially regarded as punks, despite their debt to mid-1960s American rock (never more obvious than on their cover of 'Walk On By', a pastiche of the Doors' 1967 hit 'Light My Fire'). Likewise the Jam, with their roots in the Who and the Kinks, and Elvis Costello, his passion for the same era apparent in every note of his 1978 album titled (ironically) *This Year's Model*. Eddie & the Hot Rods and the Boomtown Rats soon revealed more of an affinity with Bruce Springsteen than the Clash. Meanwhile, there was a recognisable school of 'new wave' with jerky, spiky song structures and vocals which were mannered in the tradition of David Bowie and Bryan Ferry – XTC being the most enduring example. While laddish inarticulacy and violence were perfectly acceptable punk characteristics, there was much suspicion in the press about artists who displayed any hint of intelligence or learning. The punk fanzine *Sideburns* had attempted to inspire its readership with the simplest of instructions: 'This is a chord. This is another. Now form a band.' But although two chords might be sufficient to write a punk anthem, this manifesto was never intended to be used as a weapon against anyone who dared to employ a third chord or, heaven forbid, a fourth. Musical incoherence and incompetence could spark genuine excitement or, at the very least, diverting performance art (the career of the Slits veering between the two); but as soon as punk swapped its rhetoric of liberation for the tyranny of the closed mind, all of its original impetus and significance was lost.

Fortunately, the moment when punk became a cultural prison was also, bizarrely, when it allowed a thousand metaphorical flowers to bloom. The siren of post-punk was the extraordinary Poly Styrene, who proudly wore dental braces at a time when they were an object of shame, and who launched a one-woman (and one-band, X-Ray Spex) assault on consumerist society, decades before the birth of the anti-globalisation movement. Like novelist Norman Mailer, she viewed plastic as a symbol of the inauthenticity of modern life – the irony being that she preached this gospel via the grooves of records manufactured from PVC.

Like Patti Smith before her, Poly Styrene sidestepped the two most prevalent stereotypes for a female performer in a male-dominated industry: the sensitive folksinger and the bruised and troubled blues shouter. Few of their predecessors had been able to escape these cages, and the exceptions had suffered for their refusal to compromise. Jefferson Airplane singer/composer Grace Slick maintained a stridently independent persona for more than a decade, before succumbing to alcoholism. Yoko Ono was forced to endure ridicule which frequently veered into racist contempt. Joni Mitchell's struggles to abandon her early image by exploring social satire and jazz came at the expense of commercial success. It is perhaps emblematic that both Poly Styrene and Patti Smith chose to walk away from the music business at their peak of popularity.

But the jazz-tinged, raucous defiance of X-Ray Spex did much to revive punk as an expression of freedom rather than a musical straitjacket. In her wake, Britain's final eighteen months of the 1970s were stunningly diverse, artistically courageous. It was a time when the inspiration of punk could fuel a dozen different methods of exploring and exploding pop, by merging it with Jamaican rhythms (from the ska revival to the Police's reggae/power-pop hybrid) or heavy metal (Motörhead); approaching it in the guise of a robot (Gary Numan) or a gothic princess (Siouxsie Sioux); or by living out the darkest implications of Malcolm McLaren's anarchist manifestos, as did John Lydon with the eerie, volcanic howl of 'Death Disco', his second release with Public Image Ltd. This was pop robbed of all its melodic appeal and song structure; punk stripped of its rhythm and rhetoric; music so nihilistic and forbidding that it could only have been commercial at *this* moment, from *this* man. There was no room for punk traditionalism in Lydon's disco. But this was not the denouement to punk's narrative which posterity chose to remember.

> It's the small bands that interest me most. Springing up from unfashionable, obscure towns all over the country. Dark, sleepy towns that have been ignored or just forgotten by the trendy rat-race of the pace-setting big cities. In these places, in the local clubs, pubs and discos, heavy metal is thriving.
> Mick Middles, *Sounds* magazine, 1980

> Commercial punk was a sham, part of the whole rock 'n' roll circus . . . it was basically finished by late '77 . . . I mean, they were playing a Clash record on the radio earlier on today, and it struck me that you couldn't really tell the difference between that now and the Rolling Stones. It was just rock 'n' roll at the end of the day, just music.
> Penny Rimbaud, Crass

Punk cracked open a fault line in the history of popular music. Like rock 'n' roll twenty years earlier, it polarised the mass audience between those who were offended by its raucous effrontery, and those who were prepared to acknowledge it as a timely renewal of music's innate exuberance. These two invasions of noise shared another characteristic: they represented a 'year zero' for future generations, the point at which a new culture could be said to have begun.

In both instances, the dividing line was as much tribal as musical; affiliation with the lusty invader entailed acceptance of an attitude and a look as well as a fresh approach to the mechanics of rock. Nothing illustrated the cultural significance of what seem, in retrospect, to be minor differences of style than the uneasy and frequently antagonistic relationship between punk and heavy metal. The success of Motörhead in the late 1970s clouded the issue; visually, they epitomised metal; musically, their amphetamine pace and sonic attack suggested punk (as did their early affiliation to independent record companies). Their ability to satisfy both tribes was not matched by those who emerged in their wake. While punk dominated London's rock underground in 1976–8, the British provinces spawned a melee of equally driven, loud and ferocious young bands, who unashamedly pledged themselves to the standard of heavy metal. Stylistically, there was little to separate Iron Maiden's 'Invasion' or Def Leppard's 'Getcha Rocks Off' from punk, except their creators' firm refusal to stand alongside the Sex Pistols and the Clash. Not all of their contemporaries roamed as close to the border, but the influx of youthful energy was so pronounced that *Sounds* – the first of the British weekly papers to pledge itself to punk – declared that it represented a movement, which the magazine dubbed in 1979 'the New Wave of British Heavy Metal' (or NWOBHM).

Few of the bands who were forced under this banner – Maiden, Leppard, Saxon, Girlschool, Angel Witch, Diamond Head and dozens more – recognised the existence of a 'new wave', let alone their own role in it. Heavy metal being a more inclusive and communal genre than punk, it did not employ any equivalent to the 'boring old farts' invective which was hurled at rock bands over the age of 25. But NWOBHM did act as a transfusion of fresh blood, albeit at a time when the metal mainstream was thriving, with little of the decadent decay visible elsewhere in the prepunk-rock community.

The 1970s ended with the punk movement divided between those addicted to the classic sound of 1976–7, and those (led by the Clash) attempting to maintain their ethical and tribal identity while escaping the rigidity of that formula. This crusade would lead the Clash simultaneously backwards towards the image-mongering of previous decades, and forwards into a world where a London rock band could immerse itself in the emerging culture of hip hop. Both factions were content to exist within the framework of the corporate rock business – a system which the Sex Pistols had briefly seemed capable of destroying. A handful of British bands refused to compromise so easily. Grouped under the retrospective label of anarcho-punk, the likes of Crass, Poison Girls and Conflict pledged themselves to the principles which Malcolm McLaren had employed as an art-project gesture. 'Punk is dead,' Crass declared in 1978, 'it's just another cheap product for the consumer's head.' Their ethics were not consumerist but collective; their record releases and gigs offered at little more than cost; their aim a genuine social revolution rather than celebrity. For them, punk was not a musical style which had to be maintained at all costs, but a statement of opposition to every form of collaboration with capitalist society.

This was still a positive application of punk; music being used as a tool for progress, however removed from the mainstream. In New York, an equally vehement denial of commercialism was apparent in 1978, from the bands grouped under the negative description of 'no wave'. Punk historian Nicholas Rombes described this art-graduate movement as 'music for people who hate music'; less pejoratively, as 'a disavowal – even a betrayal – of punk insofar as it rejected the populist, melodic streak that animated punk's first wave'. In its place, 'no wave' offered the atonal, the grating, the structure-free, the crushingly repetitive: a musical cul-de-sac, which almost against its own principles produced a band (Sonic Youth) who would inspire Kurt Cobain and hence the grunge explosion.

While America's East and West coasts sparked local punk conflagrations from 1977 onwards, great swathes of the United States remained unaware for several years of what had been happening in Britain. ('We got everything so late', recalled Nashville-based Jason Ringenberg, who didn't stumble across the Sex Pistols until 1981.) If there was an American new wave beyond the New York boroughs, it was a throwback to the spirit of 1964–5 – the pop song-craft of the Beatles, the attitude of the Rolling Stones, the sleek harmonies of the Byrds. While most of its protagonists settled for reviving the past, the Cars and the Knack placed themselves midway between the AOR dynamics of Boston and Journey, and the punk pop of Nick Lowe and Elvis Costello.

Ronstadt's 'Alison', Blondie, Tom Petty, the Cars' 'Good Times Roll', the Knack's 'My Sharona': however shockingly modern they sounded to the American heartland, none of them attempted to rival the earth-quaking impact of the original British punks. They redecorated rock in a slightly quirkier shade, rather than whitewashing the past from collective memory. If they wanted scorched-earth rhetoric, American kids had to locate an underground which was effectively ignored by radio and print journalism alike.

For 16-year-old Ian MacKaye in the US capital, punk rock 'seemed incredibly nihilistic' when he first read about the Sex Pistols in 1978. When he was finally exposed to the records emanating from Britain, he was 'really struck by the fact that this was completely non-commercial music . . . Punk rock introduced me to this whole underground, and in that there was this incredible array of ideas, philosophies, approaches to life – I was challenged on all these different levels.' Forming a succession of bands to ape what he had heard, he fell into a milieu of bands and venues operating beneath the radar of the rock industry. Eager to escape being co-opted into the mainstream, these acts comprised a scene which by 1981 was being described as 'hardcore' – uncompromising, relentless, viciously dissecting personal and political life with a freedom only available to those who never expected to taste commercial success.

Hardcore was all about extremes – of sound, of behaviour, of belief. Some participants followed Darby Crash, the self-annihilating vocalist of the Germs, into heroin addiction and despair. Others channelled their ferocity into an ethos which rejected all the trappings of rock stardom, especially drink and drugs. MacKaye's band the Slinkees were at the heart of this so-called 'straight edge' movement, with their formative (and unmistakably tongue-in-cheek) anthem, 'I Drink Milk'. 'We were definitely pissing off an enormous amount of people', he recalled. Becoming straight edge was no passing flirtation: it was a commitment for life. 'It really seemed like total rebellion,' explained Youth of Today vocalist Ray Cappo, 'against the typical high-school kid, the typical teenager, who would just walk around stoned and drunk with his concert jersey on, Timberland boots, going from keg party to keg party, date-raping girls.' Yet the rigour of the straight-edge philosophy embodied a conservative way of thinking which was totally at odds with punk's potential as a form of aesthetic and spiritual liberation.

Punk, then, was freedom and conservatism; experimentation and conformity; a manifesto for changing one's life, or a comfort trap which would never require one to change. It would also become, like rock 'n' roll, an all-purpose catchphrase, which stood for anything from do-it-yourself self-reliance to the most clichéd repetition of familiar musical and lyrical motifs – as hackneyed as any of the boring old farts and dinosaurs who were punk's inadvertent inspiration. By the 1990s and beyond, it would be brandished as the ultimate standard of authenticity and coolness, by everyone from depressive heavy metal fans to cute boy bands, all of them convinced that they alone were punk's truest legacy – and, in a strange way, they were.

CHAPTER 25

DANCE STANCE

'Success is nothing ... You follow the system,
and the system kill ya.'

  Bob Marley, 1976

'The poor blacks and the poor whites are in the same boat ...
[the blacks] don't want us in their culture but ... we dig them,
and we ain't scared of going into heavy black record shops.'

  Joe Strummer, the Clash, 1976

⚡

A clash of cultures was evident as early as August 1958, when gangs of working-class white men, mostly sporting the distinctive drapes and winklepickers that marked them out as Teddy boys, launched random attacks on Afro-Caribbean residents of Notting Hill in West London. Thereafter, the shadows of crime, violence and intimidation lingered over Britain's West Indian community, reinforced by scaremongering press coverage.

Yet the opposing currents were often confused and contaminated. The fighting which scarred London clubs such as the Ram Jam and the 007 in the mid-1960s was territorial rather than racial, pitting North London immigrants against their Brixton counterparts. A decade later, there was a similar division between those attempting to establish a Rasta community in the heart of Babylon, and those whose role models were the gangsters of American 'blaxploitation' movies.

When Jamaican reggae music crossed into the British pop charts in autumn 1969, five singles charting almost simultaneously, its core support outside the black community came from skinheads – their heads shaved or cropped to accentuate an air of menace which materialised in the flash of a switchblade or the crunch of a knuckleduster or 'bovver boots'. The archetypal skinhead was a white working-class male who would target Asian immigrants for brutal assaults, but who adopted West Indian rhythms as his own. A decade later, when a ska revival spawned multiracial outfits such as the Specials and the Selecter, shaven-headed disciples of British fascist parties focused their loyalty on the all-white ska band Madness. On one notorious night at the Lewisham Odeon in June 1980, skins hailed the support act, Jamaican reggae veteran Desmond Dekker, with a salute more appropriate for Adolf Hitler.

Beyond the skinhead community, the response to reggae during the punk era was equally ambiguous. At the 1976 Reading Festival, an audience drawn by the gently anarchic hippie collective Gong and former members of Captain Beefheart's experimental band – not exactly an inflammatory combination – responded to the appearance of several Jamaican artists with a shower of cans and bottles. (This debacle was one of the sparks for the formation of the Rock Against Racism collective later that year.) The punk movement regarded Rastafarian roots reggae as a kindred spirit, and audiences at British punk gigs grew accustomed to a Jamaican soundtrack, provided by such fellow travellers as Mikey Dread (who toured with the Clash) and Tapper Zukie (championed by Patti Smith). Home-grown reggae acts, often with a strident political edge (as on Steel Pulse's 'Ku Klux Klan'), were arguably a more authentic voice for Britain's streets during the late 1970s than many of the middle-class punk acts masquerading as working-class heroes. Yet as the *NME*'s Bob Woffinden noted, there was still a cultural chasm between London's Jamaican community and its white aficionados, the capital's reggae stores appearing 'dark and uninviting as the grave for any passing white boy'. In 1976, when the reggae/punk crossover was in its infancy, one of London's most renowned concert halls, the Hammersmith Odeon, placed a blanket ban on any future reggae concerts, after outbreaks of pickpocketing and petty violence at a show by Bob Marley and the Wailers.

Such incidents hardly rivalled the gangster violence and government crackdowns endemic in Kingston's shanty towns and concrete estates. This was no formulaic outburst of adolescent machismo, but a reflection of the febrile political atmosphere of the Jamaican capital from the mid-1960s onwards. Although most reggae music was rooted in love and sex, the genre's tight, electrifying rhythm was the perfect soundtrack for messages of sectarian or spiritual dissent – between rival political parties, between gangs striving for ghetto supremacy, and between police and the Rasta community. Little of this was evident when reggae broke into the British pop scene. Hits such as Desmond Dekker's 'It Miek' and 'The Israelites' were regarded as novelty dance numbers, a belief reinforced by Toots & the Maytals' 1968 release 'Do the Reggay'. Official disquiet was reserved for Max Romeo's outrageously rude 'Wet Dream', which wasn't so much suggestive as pictorial: 'lie down, gal, make me push it up'.

In the wake of London's first Caribbean Music Festival in 1969, Trojan Records, who controlled the rights to many Jamaican releases in the UK, prepared a series of budget-priced compilation albums entitled *Tighten Up*. With their frequently lascivious cover designs, they offered recalcitrant white teenagers a gentle route into Jamaican culture. By 1971, reggae was sufficiently familiar to British ears for Dave Barker and Ansel Collins to top the chart with the proud boasts of 'Double Barrel' – thereby introducing the pop audience to the art of 'toasting'.

While the producers of rock, pop and soul records were employing ever more overblown and flamboyant arrangements, Jamaica was reconstructing the very nature of recording. Sound-system disc jockeys such as King Stitt and U Roy declaimed a mixture of onomato-poeic vocal outbursts and catchphrases over instrumental tracks (often contemporary hit songs with their singers removed). Stitt's 'Fire Corner' and U Roy's 'Dynamic Fashion Way', both from 1969, exemplified the art of the toaster, their apparently spontaneous interventions offering an extra layer of syncopation over the precise, tight tracks prepared by producers Clancy Eccles and Bunny Lee respectively. These tracks would also be stripped bare of vocals to act as the B-side 'version' of a single, providing additional fodder for the dance floor.

With the reggae audience acclimatised to tracks with their most obvious (vocal) hooks removed, the stage was set for a more daring act of sonic creativity. The producer had become an increasingly engaged participant in the recording process since the invention of multi-dubbing technology, to the point where such auteurs as Phil Spector and Joe Meek could claim that their distinctive personal sound was more valuable than the songs which it ostensibly served. In Jamaica, producers such as King Tubby and Lee Perry became the creators of 'dubs' – originally a term for the acetate discs used to preview new recordings, and by extension a description of their sonic landscapes. In dub, the basic unity of a track would be subverted and shattered, as producers isolated and accentuated individual elements, such as the bass guitar and drums; applied cavernous echo delay as a form of sonic disruption; or sent instruments or vocals juddering across the speakers, emerging with tracks which were both spacey and studded with aural events. Dub manipulated and mutated the standard dimensions of recorded sound. If psychedelic rock translated the colour spectrum into ecstatic sound, dub dealt in a more menacing world that was prone to surprising shifts of gravity.

When dub was allied with the increasingly radical spirit of roots reggae, and Rasta rhetoric with toasting, reggae was transformed from a rendering of Caribbean sunshine into a searing portrayal of a society on the edge of collapse. 'The base of the music is really oppression, depres-sion, anger, deep passion', Jimmy Cliff insisted. This was the ethos which hypnotised the Clash and John Lydon, who channelled the inventiveness of dub into his early records with Public Image Ltd. But reggae culture in the 1970s was far from a monotone medium. Alongside dub and toasting,

Jamaica was bursting with vocal groups who took their spiritual and musical inspiration from 1960s soul acts such as the Impressions, just as the Wailers had done; with voices of love, such as the 'Cool Ruler', Gregory Isaacs; and with the revolutionary anthems of Rastafarianism, preaching an unsettling mixture of apocalypse and salvation.

In Bob Marley, Rasta found its prophet and broadcaster, although he became an increasingly controversial figure in his homeland. Signed to the British label Island, his band the Wailers let their 1973 album *Catch a Fire* be overdubbed by session musicians to make it more acceptable to white audiences. (For the rest of his career, Marley continued to release rough-edged tracks in Jamaica which were smoothed and sweetened for the international market.) By 1975, when the Wailers recorded a landmark live album in London, the rock community was prepared to recognise Marley as an equal to its own icons, such as Bob Dylan and Mick Jagger. Yet that was also the year when his group splintered, its other creative forces, Bunny Wailer and Peter Tosh, unwilling to accept Marley's dominance of what had once been a democracy. Marley became a global idol, whilst his recordings grew ever more distant from their Jamaican soil – his influence more apparent in African reggae than in the Caribbean.

Whether you regarded him as a hero or an apostate, Marley broadened the musical taste of millions who might otherwise have been intimidated by reggae's experiments with sound and form. The process had been accelerated by tourists such as Paul Simon and Paul McCartney, both of whom cut tracks in Jamaica. Mellifluous hits such as Ken Boothe's 'Everything I Own' slid comfortably on to Top 40 playlists, although the dub-inspired playfulness of Rupie Edwards's 'Ire Feelings' so puzzled BBC programmers in 1974 that the single was banned from daytime airplay, in case it proved to have obscene implications. Marley aside, however, reggae vanished from pop radio for the second half of the decade, until 2-Tone revived the fifteen-year-old rhythms of ska, and the Police employed dub dynamics on 'Roxanne'.

Britain's most influential reggae recording emerged in 1982 from a three-quarters white group whose androgynous (and unashamedly gay) vocalist sported chest-length braids and pancake make-up. Culture Club's 'Do You Really Want to Hurt Me' was a gentle rendering of the predominantly female and black-British style known as lovers rock, which eschewed Rastafarianism and revolutionary rhetoric in favour of charmingly naïve expressions of teenage romance. After topping the UK charts, it all but repeated the feat in America, a nation where Bob Marley never achieved a Top 50 hit, and where a Broadway musical called *Reggae* had been staged in 1980 with barely a trace of Jamaican identity. Although the US would never adapt to Jamaican beats with the same ease as Britain, reggae was now a universal language, ripe for augmentation across Africa and South America, and assimilation into the planetary melting pot of rhythms and cultures.

Yet reggae was no more static than the culture which produced it. While Britain and America clung to the Bob Marley model as a language that they could interpret and comprehend, music in Jamaica was mutating. DJs began to exert a more profound hold over the sound of Kingston, the pleasure of rhythmic innovation supplanting political or Rastafarian rhetoric. With Jamaica undergoing an economic squeeze during the first half of the 1980s, record-makers seized upon new digital technology to simplify their craft. Their purpose was apparent from the name which was applied to their music: dancehall. But there were other descriptions – digi, ragamuffin, ragga – for records which, from around 1984, replaced the rhythm sections of old with instruments run by computer chips. By then, almost every sector of the music business was witnessing the same, sometimes involuntary, revolution.

> Pretty soon a bunch of kids are going to come along and change all this and then no one'll want to know about the Rolling Stones or any of us. It'll probably be three 12-year-olds with Moog synthesisers.
> Stephen Stills, 1973

> They can get all the Moog synthesisers that they want, but nothing will take the place of the human heart.
> Johnny Cash, 1973

'As a matter of very serious principle I will never enjoy a record with synthesiser on it', announced the Smiths' vocalist Morrissey in 1984. His defiant refusal to entertain the possibility that music could be created by computerised technology was as conservative, and as ill-fated, as the judgement of those who had been equally suspicious of the electric guitar or the saxophone. A decade earlier, keyboard player Roger Powell had dismissed the qualms of those who protested that the Moog synthesiser – the first step in the revolutionary march of technology – was both unmusical and devoid of emotion. 'You can develop a physical relationship with the instrument', he insisted. 'It's just that people don't normally look at turning a knob or pushing a wheel as being an expressive way of playing an instrument.'

The invention in the late 1950s of Wurlitzer's Side Man, an electrical rhythm machine, first raised the apparently hideous possibility that men might be replaced by machines. These fears coincided with Isaac Asimov's best-selling science-fiction tales about man's ambiguous relationship with robots – reflecting the widespread dread that humans might one day become the servants of their own creations. Side Man (its very name was robotic) and its competitors were built into electric organs, the precursors of the drum machines to follow.

It was the Moog synthesiser, however, with its keyboard, modulating oscillator, tonal controls and contour generator, which transported the electronic machine into the heart of popular music. Even after the success of Walter Carlos's *Switched-On Bach* album, the Moog was primarily used as a method of augmenting music rather than creating it. But by the mid-1970s, entire rock albums were being composed and performed on the Moog. Its seemingly limitless capacity to generate diverting tones and noises lent itself to exploration on a grand scale, and the Moog was therefore welcomed by progressive-rock musicians. The launch of the Polymoog in 1977 widened the instrument's palette from single notes to chords, enabling it to be substituted for virtually any sound at a rock band's disposal.

While acts as varied as Paul McCartney and Emerson, Lake & Palmer incorporated the Moog into rock and pop, the synthesiser's capabilities were explored most radically in Germany. Its tradition of what was dubbed (by British journalists) 'krautrock' explored the limits of electronic composition, psychedelia and experimental (indeed, progressive) rock, in a merging of classical and popular techniques unmatched elsewhere in the world. Two bands broke out of the avant-garde field to attract a mainstream audience. Kraftwerk enjoyed a worldwide hit single with 'Autobahn', compressing a side-long album track into three minutes. It exposed the synthesiser as both plaything and tool of hypnosis, conjuring up the seamless eternity of a journey along one of

Germany's highways. 'We are the first German group to record in our own language, use our electronic background and create a Central European identity for ourselves', explained Ralf Hütter. Both futuristic and reminiscent of the novelty vocal group ditties of the rock 'n' roll era, 'Autobahn' was only recognised in retrospect as a key moment in the transformation of the synthesiser into a vehicle for a dance groove.

A different kind of modernity was on offer from Tangerine Dream, whose atmospheric evocations of space and time imagined a fantasy world in which American minimalist composers were providing science-fiction film soundtracks. The sixteen-minute title track of *Phaedra* (1974) was a clear influence on David Bowie's 1977 collaborations with Brian Eno, while the latter's early ventures into ambient music extended the mood of the same album's closing piece, 'Sequent C'. This was sound for a trip into inner space – for gently stoned meditation, perhaps – without any of the kaleidoscopic and potentially unsettling explosions of the senses found elsewhere in German rock.

On his *Low* and *'Heroes'* albums, Bowie explored different aspects of the 'krautrock' legacy to produce music which reflected the fragility of his own psyche, and the sonic disruption triggered by the arrival of punk. Both albums were divided between brittle deconstructions of traditional rock, and synthesiser mood music. His stature as an icon of visual style as well as sound ensured that his experiments left an impact on an entire generation of British musicians, who had grown to trust him as a guide through a turbulent decade. With *Scary Monsters (and Super Creeps)* in 1980, Bowie used his synthetic music to reconnect with fragments of his own past: as a white soul singer, a genius of image-mongering, and a master of the anthemic single.

The video made to promote Bowie's 1980 hit 'Ashes to Ashes' was filled with extras recruited from Blitz, a weekly club in London's Covent Garden. Within its walls, fashion intersected with synthesised pop and electronica, Bowie and Roxy Music acting as the venue's absent saints. (Indeed, the club grew out of the Bowie nights staged by Rusty Egan at Billy's in Soho the previous year.) 'It was very gay and there was lots of make-up', recalled DJ and label owner Stevo. 'That was the scene which engendered the New Romantics.' Dance-music historian Sheryl Garratt saw this as 'a time of experimentation: bebop, African pop, rumba, rockabilly, salsa, ska, blues. Zoot suits, cowboy hats, fifties Americana, berets and braces.' Amongst the so-called Blitz kids were the future members of many of British pop's most successful acts of the decade ahead: Culture Club, Spandau Ballet, Visage, Sigue Sigue Sputnik, Ultravox and Sade. For each of them, to varying degrees, style was as crucial and defining as music. Children of glam, survivors of punk, they eschewed the jagged aggression of the recent past, sidelining guitars in favour of the cheap, mass-produced synthesisers which had flooded the market.

The missing link between punk and the New Romantics was to be found in the experimental sonic textures of artists such as Throbbing Gristle, Chrome and Cabaret Voltaire, who – like the Velvet Underground before them – were better known for their inspiration than their own recordings. Kraftwerk's extended synth-scapes were also a profound influence; likewise David Bowie and Brian Eno's anglicised take on 'krautrock'. Three hits from 1979 – M's 'Pop Muzik', Lene Lovich's 'Lucky Number' and Buggles' 'Video Killed the Radio Star' – added an inescapable quirkiness to the New Muzik (the name of the artists behind a formative synth-pop hit, 'Living by Numbers', from the first days of 1980). The ease with which the synthesiser could be used to create a portentous wash of sound, as demonstrated by Tangerine Dream, enabled Gary Numan and Orchestral Manoeuvres in the Dark to create sinister, almost pompous pop, a trend which reached its zenith (or nadir) in the emotionless drama of Ultravox's 'Vienna'.

That was one spirit of the times, as Cold War tensions were heightened, and the British charts were suddenly filled with songs exploring the dread of nuclear apocalypse or enforced militarism. But after the paranoia of the punk years, and amidst economic gloom, young club-goers preferred to sweat away their fears. While Dexy's Midnight Runners ('Dance Stance') and Elvis Costello ('Can't Stand Up for Falling Down') self-consciously reprised mid-1960s soul, Roxy Music ('Dance Away') and David Bowie ('Fashion') provided a more contemporary approach to hedonism.

By early 1981, while rock classicists mourned the loss of John Lennon (whose final recording was a chilling rock-funk collaboration with Yoko Ono, 'Walking on Thin Ice'), the likes of Duran Duran and Spandau Ballet combined the rhythms of the dance floor with a bright, brittle pop sensibility pulled as much from Abba and Dollar as from Bowie and Roxy Music. Meanwhile, Depeche Mode's 'New Life' from summer 1981 premiered synth-pop as the new amateurism: the raucous cacophony of punk replaced by simple, one-finger synth lines, supporting bouncy pop tunes. The decadence and flamboyance of one strand and the youthful energy of the other combined in two of the biggest-selling records of the year: a revival of the 1960s soul hit 'Tainted Love' by Marc Almond, who would soon reveal himself as a sublime chronicler of emotional and sexual life on the margins; and the almost deliberately banal 'Don't You Want Me' by the Human League, one-time electronic experimentalists now offering sly vignettes of teenage trauma.

The era of synth-pop, decadent or otherwise, altered the sound, the image and the presentation of popular music. In the wake of Elvis Presley and Chuck Berry, the electric guitar had attracted an encyclopaedia of sexually potent poses and moves, lending even the weakest of performers a borrowed sense of cool and machismo (the instrument was crucial to 'cock rock', the strutting, thrusting, hard-rock style of the 1970s). Standing behind a synthesiser or another electronic keyboard was a less obvious way of displaying one's sexual prowess. As Kraftwerk were the first to realise (and to satirise), one risked being mistaken for a technician or a robot. Synths were also accused of removing emotion from music; even Soft Cell's Dave Ball admitted that 'Groups that are dominated by sequencers I find a little boring, actually.' For him, the touch of fingers on a keyboard – rather than the replaying of programmed sound – was vital: 'I play manually, rather than relying on really precise machines that lose that human sort of feel.' For Bernard Sumner, a veteran of glacial postpunk band Joy Division, and a founder of New Order, who specialised in synthetic dance rhythms, 'The important lesson to be learned from punk, which everyone gets wrong, is that it doesn't matter *how* you play, it matters *what* you play.' Technique, in this philosophy, was as irrelevant as it had been for the Sex Pistols; what counted was the emotional impact of the music, however it was procured. Yet, as Kraftwerk's Ralf Hütter insisted, 'With better machines, you will be able to do better work.'

It was perhaps essential that the era of synth-pop coincided with the rise of the music video. Equally important, as the very name of the New Romantics suggested, was the role of synth-pop in courtship rituals – as described in 'Don't You Want Me'. 'It's hypnotic as dance music', said Dave Ball. 'That's the whole essence of it. People are so limited and restricted, crammed into offices and trains. They can't move around, so they just want to shake and go wild. Dancing is what they do rather than hitting or killing somebody.' Just four years after the detonation of disco in Comiskey Park, a nightclub such as London's Camden Palace could be crammed five nights a week with office workers and teenagers displaying their peacock plumage at events billed as 'Sweat Attack' and 'Dance Your Ass Off'. Pleasure, dance and music were once more partners in delirious extravagance. Moreover, outwardly gay performers such as Boy George (Culture Club) and Marc Almond (Soft Cell) could flourish and be accepted by the British public – Boy George's endearingly gentle public persona winning him fans across the age spectrum, from those who would once have been horrified by the sexual ambivalence displayed by Mick Jagger or Marc Bolan.

There was still a conscious divide between those who welcomed the pansexual, preening extravagance of the new pop, and those who clung to the more political, abrasive textures of punk. In its aftermath, when a plethora of small labels had offered alternatives to the more regimented product of the major record companies, there was a pronounced kudos to the notion of being 'independent' in a corporate world. Echoing the pioneering adventures of American labels such as Sun, Chess, Atlantic and Motown, many of Britain's independent labels became mini-factories of pop experimentation – each of them, from Factory to Postcard, Some Bizzare to Rough Trade, boasting its own defining vision of what pop (and rock) might be. In this expanded landscape, there was room for every nuance suggested by the freewheeling invention of the post-punk bands.

Avant-garde electronica existed here alongside revivalist rock rooted in the mid-1960s, or the Velvet Underground, or in punk itself. But right across that spectrum, the early 1980s found artists of multitudinous hues accepting the inspiration of black America – soul, funk, jazz, disco, or a medley of them all. To choose one emblematic example: Orange Juice from Glasgow approached the dilemma of how to follow punk by retrieving the musical motifs of the Byrds and the Velvet Underground, and then coating them in a fey, esoteric sense of style. Within a couple of years, the band had begun to slide almost invisibly from 1960s revivalism towards a very contemporary, African-tinged form of funk, shedding few of their original devotees while achieving mainstream pop success. All roads, however recherché, seemed to lead inevitably towards the dance floor.

Equally inevitably, some found this destination intolerable. For independent purists, 'indie' music entailed guitars, rock and the tradition – from the 1960s through the Velvets to punk – which the likes of

Orange Juice had chosen to pervert. In this school, 'indie' could often entail a deliberate amateurism, with a shambling, defiantly undanceable sense of rhythm – nonconformist where punk had been iconoclastic. This approach culminated in *C86*, a mixtape promoted by the *NME* in 1986, which included such indie luminaries as Primal Scream, the Wedding Present, Stump and Bogshed. (It was originally issued on cassette, in keeping with the self-assembly ethic of the movement.)

Absent from *C86*, although they were the embodiment of the indie elite, were the Smiths – led by Johnny Marr, a guitarist who could rival the melodic inventiveness of the Byrds or Richard Thompson's work with Fairport Convention; and Morrissey, a droll and self-consciously literary lyricist, whose grasp of pop melody was somewhat more limited. He specialised in an almost adolescent self-pity exemplified by 'Heaven Knows I'm Miserable Now', and an astute grasp of English social etiquette, making him (alongside Ray Davies) the bard of embarrassment. The Smiths were both radical – Morrissey's vocabulary and wit was as ground-breaking as Lou Reed's literary depiction of New York's underbelly – and innately conservative in their refusal (or Morrissey's refusal, to be exact) to countenance the relevance of dance rhythms. Their 1986 single 'Panic' achieved notoriety via its indelible chorus line, 'Hang the DJ', which was widely taken as an attack on black music, an interpretation Morrissey did little to dispel. (The DJ had earned his death sentence by not providing an appropriate soundtrack for Morrissey's life, a peculiarly solipsistic attitude to popular music.) It was a sizeable hit, but it represented the last fanfare of a beleaguered bugler, alone on the barricades while all around him throbbed with the uncompromising rhythms of the future.

> Techno sounds like a pneumatic drill with synthesised sounds on top.
> *Daily Express*, 1994

> Most acid records have no vocals whatsoever, so it's difficult to understand how they're promoting drug use.
> *Soul Underground* magazine, 1988

Once renowned as the home of America's auto industry and the Motown Records soul empire, Detroit emitted the stench of terminal decay by the early 1980s. In a city where arson and murder were rife, and poverty endemic, young African-Americans found relief in music that emanated from elsewhere – perhaps from outer space, to judge by its alien, robotic rhythms. Like many of their peers, teenagers Derrick May, Juan Atkins and Kevin Saunderson relished sounds that bore no relation to the heritage of their own city: the computerised beats of Kraftwerk, Donna Summer's electro-disco cuts with Giorgio Moroder, the pioneering synth-pop of the Human League and Depeche Mode. The three boys formed a musical collective they named Deep Space, and embarked on individual experiments with primitive synthesisers, drum machines and tape recorders.

The first evidence of Deep Space's revolutionary impact on global music came in the form of 'Alleys of Your Mind', a 1981 single by Atkins under the name Cybotron. Its Germanic feel – as if Tangerine Dream had cut a rudimentary demo with Kraftwerk – was apparent in another release that year, 'Share Vari' by A Number of Names. Each has been claimed as the launch pad for a new genre of electronic music: Detroit techno. Over the next few years, each of the Deep Space collective toyed with similar ingredients, creating dance music gradually stripped of all unnecessary ingredients. Indeed, by 1985, when Atkins made 'No UFOs' under the name Model 500, its electronic instrumentation was almost entirely percussive, with no attempt to provide melodic hooks or enticements. Its vocals were equally inhuman, extending the featureless technique of Gary Numan or the Human League's Phil Oakey. Derrick May pushed the boundaries further away from the traditional elements of the popular song with two 1986 singles, 'Nude Photo' (synth patterns never quite gelling over a drum-machine track) and 'Strings of Life'. The latter, issued under the pseudonym Rhythim Is Rhythim, suggested that the robots were now in control of the factory, subverting any hint of melody or pitch in their sequenced frenzy. One could imagine automatons proudly unveiling this music to captured humans, to demonstrate who were the masters now.

Detroit's electro found a ready audience in Chicago's dance clubs, where local DJs and musicians were lapping up a similar mixture of British post-punk, 'krautrock' and disco. At the Warehouse in Chicago, Frankie Knuckles was pulling people on to the dance floor with his home-made amalgamations of synthesised rhythms and the emotional pressure points from Philadelphia dance hits. 'I had a razor blade, a Pioneer reel-to-reel and spools of recording tape', he recalled. Unlike his counterparts in the Bronx, Knuckles and his imitators weren't providing the raw material for rappers: their jerry-built productions were designed to be sufficient unto themselves. By the early 1980s, they were augmenting their record and tape decks with drum machines and sequencers, effectively improvising their own dance tracks which existed only in the moment that they were performed. Using a Roland TR-808 drum machine at the Playground club, Jesse Saunders recalled, 'I'd let it play along with the tracks, then I'd mix it in and out, let it run by itself, and start mixing stuff in and out.' It was like a return to the days before recorded sound; inevitably, the precedent of history ensured that Saunders would preserve his impromptu creations on vinyl.

His 1983 single 'On and On' encapsulated his approach, a barrage of percussive sounds in different registers fighting for recognition. Every element that would once have been human – handclaps, drumbeats, the feel of fingers on a keyboard or thumping a bass guitar string – was provided by machines. But like his rival and contemporary Jamie Principle, who worked with Knuckles at the Warehouse, Saunders wasn't afraid to match these electronic pulses with vocal elements reminiscent of the soul tradition, whether they were borrowed from other records using a sampler, or supplied by humans. Sampling technology also allowed producers to steal basslines and drum fills. As Sheryl Garratt explained, 'Stripped of their songs, these recycled riffs sounded alien and new, like raw, minimal messages transmitted from another world.'

While techno accentuated the machine, house music (alias the music they played at the Warehouse) blended sequenced electronica with motifs of soul. As America's club audiences were stricken by AIDS, 'The contents of the lyrics of Chicago house music were often sexually explicit', as the academic Hillegonda Rietveld noted. 'There was also a celebration of purely being alive in these hedonistic, frenzied dance gatherings.' But once established, neither house nor techno stood still. The producer Marshall Jefferson introduced a variety known as 'deep house', which heightened the soulful elements of the music, using a real string section and keyboards over the hypnotic rhythms. Jefferson also worked with DJ Pierre, who under the pseudonym of Phuture made one of the strangest and most influential dance records of the 1980s: 'Acid Trax'. Its distinctive squelching bass tone, amidst a swirl of percussive patterns, was produced by ill-treating another Roland machine, the TB-303 – a bass synthesiser and sequencer which was intended to substitute for a bass guitar, but was perverted to mess with the realities of pitch and time. In honour of this record, house records centred around the TB-303 were dubbed 'acid house' – a title which proved to be so popular in Britain that all of Chicago's house output, and much of Detroit's techno, would eventually be swept under this blanket description. Cynics dismissed house as mechanical and emotionless, but for devotees – such as Hedonism promoter Slinkey – 'it's all about feeling. You can think within it, live and breathe within very simple, very unstructured and beautiful music ... House is pure soul music.'

House arrived in Britain during a period, spanning the mid-1980s, when every corner of white pop was soaked in the influence of black music. Frankie Goes To Hollywood's production team constructed epic dance landscapes spattered with aural diversions – witty, jolting, even (on the sex instruction guide that was their debut hit, 'Relax') erotic. Dead Or Alive and Bronski Beat borrowed the hi-energy sound of gay disco; Fine Young Cannibals and Paul Young modernised the sound of 1960s Southern soul; the Style Council combined radical rhetoric with vintage Motown rhythms; Scritti Politti and Swansway focused the experimental ambition of 1967 pop on white soul, a rare gift that was imitated but not matched by Deacon Blue and Wet Wet Wet. Britain's two most enduring discoveries during this era shared this effortless command of black and white traditions, George Michael (with and without Wham!) blending Motown with sweet soul, Pet Shop Boys proving that it was possible to squeeze arch social satire and a droll expression of passion into contemporary dance tracks.

With only heavy metal (and, inevitably, the Smiths) remaining immune to this African-American electricity, the UK was prepared to have its rhythmic horizons extended. Dhar Braxton's 'Jump Back' from 1986 hid a house instrumental track beneath her semi-spoken vocal lines. Two months later, Farley 'Jackmaster' Funk's 'Love Can't Turn Around' carried the unadulterated sound of Chicago house into the British Top 10 – spasms of frantic keyboards, faux gospel chorus, layers of percussive rapture, all topped by Darryl Pandy's spectacularly effusive lead vocal. Then Steve 'Silk' Hurley's 'Jack Your Body' in January 1987 demonstrated that house wasn't just another name for soul, but a revolution of the body and the mind. This time there was no comforting R&B anthem to smooth the passage into the future: nothing obstructed the beats, played out in a variety of electronic tones and rhythms, each chorus slightly different from the last, as if house wasn't a hybrid of disco and 'krautrock' but actually a strange love child of jazz.

The British charts were already awash with remixes of vintage hits; the shops full of multiple formats of every single, each containing subtly different revamps, rearrangements and reconstructions of the same basic track. These not only boosted singles sales, as such gimmicks as picture discs and coloured vinyl had done earlier in the decade, but led embittered survivors of the pre-disco age to ask: 'Why do they need to keep remixing the same song? Couldn't they get it right the first time?'* Adventures in clubland provided the answer, each self-contained scene requiring its own tempo. Producer, songwriter and remixer Ian Levene identified the lust in Britain's clubs for dance music which could match the internal pace of brains and bodies responding to desperate sexual desire, aided by judicious use of poppers. He co-wrote and produced a dance anthem called 'High Energy', vocalised by American soul diva Evelyn Thomas. The record lent its name (suitably abridged, as time was tight, to Hi-NRG) to a style defined by its beats per minute and its message of defiant hedonism.

Poppers weren't the only stimulants on offer: from summertime clubbing in Ibiza came not only a blend of Euro-disco and house which was dubbed Balearic beat, but free access to the drug MDMA, better known as Ecstasy. It promoted a surge of serotonin which broke down social barriers, encouraged a feeling of unity with strangers, and lent itself to ecstatic dancing – requiring in turn a soundtrack of extended dance anthems building to climax after climax, the communion of the dance replacing erotic urgency as the trigger for exhilarating displays of self-abandon. As Sheryl Garratt recalled of her baptism at the Paradise Garage in New York, 'I remember how *friendly* people seemed, how joyful, only years later equating their dilating eyes with Ecstasy. I don't remember the records, or even how long I stayed. What I do remember vividly was the sound. The fact that the music didn't just hang in the air, it came inside you. It was physical. You didn't just hear it, you *felt* it.' By the time that vibe reached London, it had acquired a home-grown soundtrack: M/A/R/R/S's

---

* To quote from Wink Martindale's rhythm-free 'Deck of Cards', 'I was that soldier'. But given that I was writing about eight virtually identical mixes of Paul McCartney's lacklustre 'Press', perhaps I can be forgiven for my pig-headed myopia.

'Pump Up the Volume', Coldcut's 'Doctorin' the House', and then 'Theme From S'Express' (created by disc jockey Mark Moore), a hook-laden monster which brazenly encouraged its audience to 'enjoy this trip'. By spring 1988, that record was No. 1 in the British charts; giant warehouse parties (or raves) were spreading the ecstatic gospel across North London; and the national press slowly became aware that a sizeable proportion of the capital's teenagers were in thrall to something called 'acid house'. No matter that they were smiling and dancing, rather than rioting or fighting: this outburst of youthful expression was a menace, and needed to be stopped.

But how could you quell a storm that was thundering in every home, from every television and radio, in every high street store? As TV stations selected brief motifs from Hi-NRG, house and techno records to run beneath montages of sports highlights, or link programme trailers, and the smiley-face logo of the Ecstasy-fuelled dancing congregation was branded on to a million T-shirts, sweats and badges, the sound of the underground became a universal language – while remaining a social evil to the press. For anyone unacquainted with the multitudinous categories of dance music, there was nothing to divide acid house from the Hi-NRG sound of Britain's top pop producers during the second half of the 1980s, Stock, Aitken and Waterman. Their amalgamation of bubblegum pop and synthesised dance beats outraged musical purists, but transformed an Australian soap actress (Kylie Minogue), Anglo-Jamaican sisters from London's East End (Mel & Kim) and the drummer from a Lancashire soul band (Rick Astley) into pop stars. As Mike Stock explained, 'We worked out that the average resting heart works at 60 to 80 beats per minute, so we always made our songs twice the resting heartbeat with the intention of generating excitement and getting the feet tapping.' The climax of their colonisation of British pop was the joyous innocence – much ridiculed at the time – of the Reynolds Girls' 'I'd Rather Jack (Than Fleetwood Mac)', as emblematic a record as any generational statement in pop history: 'Golden oldies, Rolling Stones, we don't want them back', the teenagers sang, more than a decade after the Clash vainly proscribed 'No Elvis, Beatles or the Rolling Stones in 1977'.

⚡

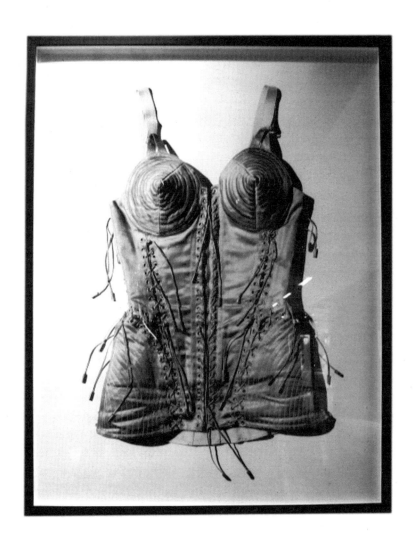

CHAPTER 26

PRESENTING THE FANTASY

'The illusion that rock and roll could change anything – I don't believe that ... I've changed. Who would ever have thought that I'd end up saying I want to be an all-round entertainer? But that's what I want to be.'

Roger Daltrey, the Who, 1984

'All these A&R people started getting the sack. Why? Because they had been trying, in their naïve way, to sell music. But it wasn't what people wanted – they'd had that. People just wanted style.'

Malcolm McLaren, 1983

$\frac{1}{2}$

The murder of John Lennon in December 1980 punctured the fantasy of a Beatles reunion. Like Elvis Presley's death three years earlier, it also offered millions of fans another chilling glimpse of their own mortality. (The fact that Lennon was shot by someone who claimed to be a fan demonstrated how dysfunctional that relationship could be.) Meanwhile, the Who had been jolted by the death of Keith Moon, after a long history of alcoholism and drug abuse. Narcotics had also come close to ending the career of the Rolling Stones, when Keith Richards was arrested for possession of heroin.

In his bid to avoid a similar fate, Bob Dylan – revered for more than a decade as a prophet who might conceivably hold the answer to life's mysteries – was seeking his own salvation. His revelation in 1979 that he had become a born-again Christian shocked many who saw him as the incarnation of their iconoclasm. But his work had long been steeped in biblical references, and many of his followers persuaded themselves that his *Slow Train Coming* album was merely a passing aberration. Those beliefs were dispelled when Dylan took the stage at the Fox-Warfield theatre in San Francisco, for a lengthy run of shows in which he performed nothing but his contemporary Christian material. 'The man must decide if he is going to be an entertainer or a preacher', said a *Billboard* reviewer. 'He took the fans' money and never gave them any of the songs they had full rights to expect to hear.' Here was a contradiction: the so-called spokesman for a radical generation was spouting not just evangelical rhetoric, but right-wing political views which could have come from the mouth of presidential candidate Ronald Reagan. Yet what could be less conservative than confronting your audience with an entire show of new material? And what of the fact that the jaded Dylan of 1978 had been replaced by a man electrified with the righteous passion of his cause? Much of his audience would have preferred him set in stone a decade earlier, offering reliable predictability.

Even when he softened his religious stance, Dylan found it no easier to fit into the rock mainstream. 'If you want to sell records, I'm told you've gotta make videos', Dylan noted in 1985, as if he had just stumbled into the new decade. 'I know they're thought of as an art form, but I don't think they are.' Twenty years earlier, documentary-maker Donn Pennebaker had shot a film clip to accompany Dylan's song 'Subterranean Homesick Blues', which had widely been acclaimed as the first music video.* Perhaps this convinced Dylan to quip 'Anyone can make a video.' But his early efforts to conform with the expectations of the video industry proved him wrong. The clip for his 1985 release 'Tight Connection' revealed a man incapable of feigning basic emotional responses in front of a camera, barely able to walk convincingly, and ill at ease even when holding a guitar.

What had transformed a man with one of rock's most arresting visual images into a bumbling, self-conscious fool? The demands of a simple abbreviation: MTV (Music Television). On 1 August 1981, it was launched via a small number of US cable networks, presenting nothing but music videos, linked by VJs (video jockeys). As outlets already existed around the world for promotional clips, especially in territories far removed from North America and Europe, many pop acts were accustomed to shooting low-budget films when they issued a new record. MTV, which erupted into a national phenomenon, and was then duplicated across the globe, turned this choice into a necessity. The network established itself as the fastest and most influential method of record promotion, tilting the balance of power within the record industry from radio to television and – more significantly, perhaps – from aural to visual.

It was quickly apparent that the television camera demanded different qualities from those that would pass muster on the concert stage. Given music of sufficient power, and that indefinable quality known as charisma, rock bands such as the Eagles (whose first collection of *Greatest Hits* remains one of the best-selling albums of all time) could fill vast arenas whilst standing stock-still on stage – an occasional grimace passing for presentation skills. Even after the advent of MTV, Bob Dylan would perform in almost total darkness, sometimes with a hoodie pulled over his head to ensure that there was no danger of being seen by the audience.

None of this worked on MTV (although in Dylan's case it might have made for more compelling viewing than his mid-1980s efforts at acting). The network returned the increasingly adult domain of rock to its original teenage audience, whose basic requirement was visual stimulation. Simple clips of artists miming to their records quickly exhausted their novelty, and so video directors were required to concoct increasingly ambitious

---

* In fact, the clip had never been intended to promote the single. It was premiered in 1967, as the opening sequence of Pennebaker's movie *Dont Look Back*.

dramas to illuminate their stars. Clips needed storyboards and visual effects, just like the movies – with the difference that directors had only three or four minutes in which to capture the aura of an artist, ensuring that subtlety was sidelined in favour of broad strokes of emotion.

Established stars had to agree to caricature, or at least compress, their three-dimensional artistry into a two-dimensional medium. For Bruce Springsteen, pulling future *Friends* actress Courteney Cox out of the audience during the 'Dancin' in the Dark' video, ten years of soul-searching about his place in American society was reduced to a cartoon: good-looking guy, muscles, gets the girl (of course). For ZZ Top, anonymous merchants of Texas boogie (bigger than the Beatles in their home state), video turned a lifetime's vocation into a snapshot – men with beards and a vintage Ford coupé, watching over the soap opera of 'Sharp Dressed Man' or 'Legs' like voyeurs. There was a simple rule of thumb for stars over 35: the less they were seen in their videos, the more effective their clips. The exceptions were those with a background in the visual arts, such as David Bowie and David Byrne (Talking Heads), whose aesthetic world view encompassed video as easily as it did music; or those like Mick Jagger, for whom movement and narcissism were second nature. For the next generation, those were the attributes which would be as valuable as the mastery of augmented guitar chords, the spirit of a poet or the voice of a raucous angel.

When we make videos, I want people to laugh at them.
  Boy George, Culture Club, 1983

Practically every video I see has the obligatory half-naked woman with a pair of high heels strutting across the camera.
  Joe Jackson, 1984

With support from MTV, British singer-songwriter Joe Jackson registered one of the biggest-selling albums of 1982, *Night and Day*. Two years later, he promoted the exuberant *Body and Soul* with a schedule so gruelling that Jackson vowed, at its conclusion, never to tour again. By then, he had already sabotaged his career as a front-line artist, taking a stand so principled – and isolated – that it left no room for manoeuvre.

On reputation alone, he had scored a 1984 US hit single without making an accompanying video. Then he published an essay in which he lambasted the video business, and by implication MTV, as 'a shallow, taste-less and formularised way of selling music'. He bemoaned the 'implicit racism of video programming', a jibe that can only have been aimed at MTV. He assaulted the industry which fuelled it: 'Desperation and greed are blowing the importance of video way out of proportion . . . artists are now being signed for their video potential rather than their musical talent.' In his most crushing comment, he spoke for many silent consumers and artists when he declared: 'Being forced to associate forever a preconceived set of images with a particular song robs the listener of the ability to use his own imagination.' This was the curse of a pop video: it took a song which might offer its audience the freedom of the universe, and forced it into a box marked 'video concept', after which the brain was hypnotised into seeing the director's images whenever the song was aired. Not that Joe Jackson was rewarded for his honesty: he never reached the Top 50 of the American singles chart again, and his album sales also went into steep decline.

Other artists positively exulted in the demands of video. The orig-inal British Invasion of American pop in 1964 had depended upon satura-tion marketing by Capitol Records, and then the innate exuberance and talent of the Beatles and their peers. Its successor, much trumpeted on both sides of the Atlantic in 1983, was effectively an accident of fate – or a gross oversight on the part of the US record industry. America had remained resolutely unmoved by British punk and new wave, and indeed the glam rock and 1950s revivalism which had preceded it. With freak exceptions (M, Sheena Easton), the only British acts to reach No. 1 on the *Billboard* Hot 100 between 1975 and 1981 were those whose appeal had become so universal that they had effectively shed their nationality: Paul McCartney, Elton John and the Bee Gees.

In summer 1982, however, America fell under the sway of an eight-month-old British hit: 'Don't You Want Me' by the Human League. It took four months for the single to climb painstakingly to the top of the chart – its slow progress mirroring the market spread of MTV across the United States. Most American record labels baulked at the shocking expense of shooting video solely for this apparently inconsequential network. As a result, the station's programmers were forced to air almost everything they were given, regardless of its content. British labels were more accustomed to creating promotional videos, and they provided MTV with an unnaturally large proportion of its infant diet. Sales of these British releases soared in markets where the network was freely available to cable subscribers. As its geographical reach expanded, so did the visibility of acts such as Culture Club, Duran Duran, Spandau Ballet, A Flock of Seagulls and Eurythmics.

Each of those groups owned a flamboyant and unmistakable visual image. Here was a version of pop which apparently owed nothing to the past, and which flaunted its sexual ambiguity and outsider chic. Britain was offering America young men with bouffant hair who seemed to spend their time cavorting with lingerie models; or whose designers had styled them like comic-book aliens, hair cut diagonally across their face or sculpted into twin peaks. The Human League's leader, Phil Oakey, admitted: 'I wear make-up because people will listen to our records more if I wear make-up, or if I've got a silly long haircut on one side. It's a gimmick.' There was a boy sporting make-up and braids like a teenage girl, with the voice to match; and a woman whose ascetic crop resembled a male prizefighter. It was impossible to imagine them in a shopping mall or a main street; only in England, exotic land of fantasy, could such diverting, distant, alluring figures exist. And even if teenage America did meet them, who knew what polymorphous lusts they might express? Alongside Boy George and Annie Lennox, Simon Le Bon and Mike Score, America's bedenimed rockers seemed as out of time as Frank Sinatra in the California of 1967.

Writing at the height of British chic, *Rolling Stone* journalist Parke Puterbaugh suggested that MTV was sparking 'good old-fashioned hysteria among teenage girls'. By comparison, 'AOR radio, the dominant 70s medium, was primarily a male preoccupation, pushing aggressive hard rock with zero sex appeal.' He concluded: 'The anaesthetic formula of corporate rock snoozers like Journey, mixed in with all the Springsteen–Seger–Petty clones, had worn out its welcome by the end of the decade.' His obituaries were premature. (Not to mention inaccurate: far from being finished, Journey were then at their commercial peak.) Rather than concede commercial territory which it had dominated since the 1960s, the American record business belatedly ingested the lessons of the MTV explosion, and retaliated with all the expertise of a military superpower.

Battle was joined on two fronts, and although Britain's stars were not entirely vanquished, the balance of power was redressed. Over the next three years, the American industry launched (or relaunched) a succession of MTV-friendly stars whose appeal stretched way beyond the network's core teenage audience. Meanwhile, it reinvented AOR, hard rock, heavy metal, all those tired genres, by coating them in acquired glamour. Rock bands no longer skulked in shady motels with cans of beer and overweight roadies; in MTV videos, they were surrounded by catwalk models, whose clothes mysteriously fell to the floor as soon as a drummer entered the room. Their power was expressed not just in guitar chords and echoed drumbeats (both of which grew exponentially bigger as the decade progressed), but in sexual and material wealth – fast cars, mansions, electronic gadgets, and the ability to procure unimaginably perverted favours from any girl who caught their eye. 'Create and preserve the image of your choice', George Harrison used to say (citing Mahatma Gandhi as the originator of the remark), and no sooner had MTV portrayed rockers as all-conquering sex gods than they miraculously acquired everything that the video director could imagine for them, and more.

In return for the wildest dreams of the male adolescent (a billion-aire's toys, porn-movie starlets and lines of cocaine that ran to a distant horizon) hard rock had to shed all its awkward ties to the past: its roots in the blues, its reliance on cacophonous guitar riffs, its lengthy instrumental solos, its preference for power over melody. The new rock was, above all else, commercial. It was studded, indeed, with hooks so obvious that even pop stars might once have found them shameless. Beyond that, as the critic Deborah Frost noted astutely, 'MTV instigated a more profound change. Where such metal pioneers as Led Zeppelin had earnest musical aims – attempting to restate the blues with a heady admixture of traditional British folk elements and Middle Eastern musical ideas – such current metal heavyweights as Quiet Riot and Mötley Crüe are really only concerned with *presenting the fantasy*. And MTV is in the fantasy business.'

Metal has broadened its audience base. Metal music is no longer the exclusive domain of male teenagers. The metal audience has become older (college-aged), younger (pre-teen) and more female.
Billboard magazine, 1985

I call it 'girl-friendly sound'. Which essentially means when you take an electric guitar you can make it squeal . . . But the tone has to be there, rich with depth, with character. So even in the super-high registers, you're not putting your hands over your ears, and the first people who will do that are women.
David Lee Roth on Van Halen

The 1984 'mockumentary' film *This is Spinal Tap* was intended as an exaggerated satire on the business of rock 'n' roll, centred around an imaginary British hard-rock band hell-bent on disaster. But, as cast member Harry Shearer explained, 'The closer we dared to get to the real thing, the closer the real thing dared to get to us. It's like reality is calling our bluff at every step along the way.'

With their kindergarten satanism and grandiose pretensions, Spinal Tap mimicked the worst of Black Sabbath and mid-1970s progressive rock. Neither influence was apparent in the bands whose excesses so amused Shearer. While Britain plunged into the New Wave of Heavy Metal, with its punky energy and horror-comic theatricality, America's metal bands reinvented the decadent glamour of the New York Dolls and Alice Cooper. To this classic rock 'n' roll stance – Keith Richards strutting on the Sunset Strip, perhaps – they added the technological overdrive of the 1980s, a penchant for coiffeured, back-combed curls apparently modelled on prizewinners from Crufts, and a disarmingly accessible melodicism. American metal was no longer a full-bore sonic assault, but a lifestyle, with pop anthems as its soundtrack.

For all its reckless, rebellious, coke-snorting, bourbon-draining, hotel-trashing, girl-exploiting reputation, the music known variously as glam metal, hair metal or even nerf metal was built to appeal to the widest possible audience. Nevertheless, it made its fans feel like a pleasure-crazed elite, whose rapacious appetite for hedonism was only constrained by those archetypal enemies of rock 'n' roll: parents and teachers. Hard rock's simultaneous capacity to encompass the extremes of sentimentality and hell-raising had been apparent in Led Zeppelin's 'Stairway to Heaven' and Lynyrd Skynyrd's 'Free Bird' – arguably the two most enduringly popular rock performances of all time. The fathers of 1980s metal, Aerosmith, Kiss and Van Halen, were equally flexible, unafraid to approach disco (Kiss's 'I Was Made for Lovin' You'; Van Halen's 'Dance the Night Away') whilst proclaiming eternal fidelity to the power chord and the all-conquering riff. While Aerosmith could be traced back to the Rolling Stones and Free, and Kiss to Tommy James & the Shondells and Slade, Van Halen were an altogether more peculiar beast. They were led by the swaggering, hell-raising David Lee Roth, whose voice was much smoother than his reputation, and by guitarist Eddie Van Halen. He was the pioneer of 'tapping': a two-hands-on-the-fretboard technique which enabled a musician to emit a cascade of notes more quickly than via the traditional division of fingers between the frets and the strings. Its effect could be noted on Van Halen's 1978 cover of the Kinks' 'You Really Got Me', the raucous fury of the original dampened by the guitarist's preference for speed over feel.

Eddie Van Halen was revered as an inspiration for 'shredding', which involved what Robert Walser (speaking of the classically inspired metal guitarist Yngwie Malmsteen) called a 'fetishisation of instrumental technique'. Here speed and dexterity were everything; musicians such as Steve Vai, Jason Becker and Vinnie Moore were acclaimed for their breath-taking command of their instruments, as if they were classical virtuosos. Whilst still employing some of the language of metal, their cerebral compositions shared none of its visceral energy or teenage fury. For anyone who cherished rock 'n'roll for its dumb insolence, the 'guitar for guitarists' school might just as well have been constructing skyscrapers out of matchsticks or mastering epic feats of juggling.

The arrival of the Australian band AC/DC – sexist, puerile, and the thrillingly obvious inheritors of the cock-rock school of the Stones, the Faces and Free – offered a traditional alternative to these newfangled apostles of instrumental expertise. Their breakthrough albums were produced by Mutt Lange, whose work on City Boy's 1978 hit '5-7-0-5' revealed his ability to make every aspect of a record seem larger than life – drums more booming, guitar chords more resounding, vocals more like an invading horde than a solitary man. Here in miniature was the sound of 1980s pop metal, epito-mised by Lange's work on Def Leppard's *Pyromania* album from 1983 – its effortlessly commercial pop melodies disguised as titanic blasts of rock 'n' roll violence.

For this was metal's secret in the 1980s: it enabled adolescent boys, with sexual insecurity lurking beneath their bravado, to feel like James Bond crossed with the Terminator; and girls to be swept up in their sway. (A sign of the times: the long-running US pop magazine *Hit Parader* was relaunched as 'The World's Heavy Metal Magazine'.) When Quiet Riot reprised Slade's 'C'mon Feel the Noize', or Twisted Sister echoed a famous Who refrain with 'We're Not Gonna Take It', all teenagers were as one – thrilled by the effect that these bands' outrageous appearance would have on their parents. But for all the epic posturing of their romantic anthems, nobody could possibly be alarmed or shocked by Bon Jovi, whose command of hard-rock dynamics was matched by the instant accessibility of their songs. Their success enabled Journey singer Steve Perry to perform 'Foolish Heart' as if his lifetime ambition had been to emulate Barry Manilow; or

David Lee Roth to shed his bad-boy image for a synth-pop retread of the Beach Boys' 'California Girls'. Image spoke louder than words – louder even than the painfully strangled, ear-piercing shriek which became another metal characteristic, exemplified by the Scorpions and Ratt. As everything grew larger and more exaggerated – hair, drum sound, video narcissism – the ground was set for a band such as Poison, who presented themselves as leather-clad outlaws but sounded no more threatening to society than the Hollies had done in 1965, or Glenn Miller in 1940.

Such paper-thin posturing left the field open for an act who could enact this outsider fantasy in real life. They arrived at the perfect moment to capitalise on MTV's new metal show, *Headbanger's Ball*, which consolidated hard rock as the most popular genre on the network. When Guns N' Roses emerged from the mid-1980s Los Angeles metal scene, a majority of the band were indulging in heroin use, and one of them was a dealer. Acolytes of both punk and metal, they were shunned by both camps, despite the fact that their sound merely sampled hard-rock signatures from the previous decade – the raunch of Aerosmith and the Rolling Stones, Van Halen's shredding virtuosity, the telltale vocal bleat of extreme metal anguish. What marked out Guns N' Roses as superstars was their ability to erase the chasm between image and reality which had undermined their predecessors. Like David Bowie, they acted as icons before they were famous, and as soon as their success matched their self-image, they immersed themselves in a regime of self-destructive zeal which rapidly became the stuff of legend (and ensured that they would never quite create music as devastating as their lifestyle). The fifteen-year gestation of their *Chinese Democracy* album began as mythology and ended as an industry joke, vocalist Axl Rose demonstrating a diva-like compulsion to sabotage his career and alienate his perennially loyal audience.

While Guns N' Roses acted out their cartoon roles as the incarnations of 1980s metal madness, another Los Angeles band stole the future from them. Eight years after their formation as effectively a NWOBHM tribute band, Metallica's 1989 single 'One', from the platinum-selling . . . *And Justice For All* album, offered music that offered no nostalgic resonances. 'One' was an epic canvas reminiscent of the conceptual reach of progressive rock, describing the agony of a military veteran trapped in his shattered body. But as a rock band, Metallica paid no homage to the Stones or Zeppelin, the Faces or Aerosmith, let alone the 1950s rock 'n' roll and electric R&B which had been their original inspiration. Where old metal swaggered, new metal lumbered, lurched, ground its opponents beneath its tank tracks – remorseless, crushing, nihilistic. In its refusal to employ syncopation or any other traits associated with African-American genres, it signalled its alienation from decades of popular music. Its roots lay in British metal, back to Black Sabbath; in punk; above all, in a generation's growing sense that it had not inherited the liberation promised by their parents' culture, but had been abandoned to fend for itself while the adult baby-boomers still gloried in their own perpetual youth.

> We came up with some fast, catchy tunes and modern, futuristic sounds, and I think we'll have at least seven hit singles off this one.
> Michael Jackson on *Thriller*, 1982

> [He] fascinated the female patrons and mystified the males . . . He wore purple tights and leopard-skin shorts.
> *Billboard* magazine on Prince, 1980

The lure of electronic sound was so compulsive – and all-pervasive – that by 1982, everyone in popular music was working with essentially the same tools: synthesisers, sequencers, syn-drums, and soon samplers as well. Musicians' interviews were now filled with references to the Yamaha DX7, the Emulator II and the Fairlight CMI, rather than the Fender Strat or the sunburst Les Paul. Tuning into Top 40 radio, everything merged into one, so that it was impossible to tell whether one was hearing Rush or Billy Joel or A Flock of Seagulls. (As an example: Phil Collins could lead Genesis through 'Abacab' in 1981, as if a tribe of robots had been let loose in the studio with the instruction to create danceable sonic mayhem; then within three years reappear as the most mellifluous of adult easy-listening artists on 'Against All Odds'.) As the technology was fine-tuned, reduced in price and simplified, not only did pop become ever more homogeneous, but every mix was crammed and cluttered with sonic diversions which were no longer noticeable amidst the percussion clatter and keyboard burble and synthesised guitar roar. Each ultra-modern sound effect was like a distress flare let off during a firework display. The only solution was to make one's effects noisier and more disruptive, crushing the song beneath the gimmicks that were supposed to enhance it.

Only the largest and most blatant gestures, the most intriguing personalities, the most daredevil images could hope to survive amidst this emotionally blinding chaos. In the mid-1980s, society had evolved into a position where it was possible for a pop star to demolish barriers of race, class and age, to conquer every form of media, from the movies to MTV, and to broadcast their one simple defining feature to the world – not in a slow succession of territorial gains, as Elvis Presley and the Beatles had done, but in one vast orgy of publicity, advertising and rabid self-belief. No wonder, then, that this era – with its rock fans now aged anything from 5 to 50 – should produce four of the biggest-selling artists of all time, their commercial peaks coinciding in two of the most lucrative years in the history of popular music.

Of the four, the most compelling was Michael Jackson, a global star since the end of 1969. He had survived the difficult transition from childhood fame to a strange form of maturity, in which he was granted the total indulgence of every child's dreams. He had outgrown two institutions, his family (the Jackson 5) and Motown Records; and aided by veteran producer/arranger Quincy Jones, he had fashioned contemporary dance music of remarkable finesse. With their 1983 album *Thriller*, Jackson and Jones surpassed not only Michael's past but the sales of every other album in history.

Of its seven hits, 'Billie Jean' was the most sublime: a masterclass in syncopation, vocal control, and a singer's ability to stamp his authority on an era with a single trick. In the mid-1950s, it was Elvis Presley's hiccupping, echoed evocation of sexual self-confidence, delivered through a snarling smile. In the 1960s, millions of teenage girls were aroused in ways they barely understood by Paul McCartney and George Harrison issuing a falsetto squeal, as they shook their moptopped heads in ecstatic union. Michael Jackson's gimmick was even more direct: a yelp which was caught in the throat, and was accompanied by an almost instinctive grab of the crotch, like a small boy attempting to mimic adult sensations. Combined with the preternatural fluency of Jackson's dance moves, it suggested a man freed from the normal rules of gravity and decency.

For 'Beat It', Jackson and Jones hired Eddie Van Halen to deliver a distinctive guitar solo. MTV had previously chosen to ignore black music, though they denied accusations of racial programming, claiming that they were simply adhering to their design as an AOR station. A combination of audience pressure and record-company threat ensured that 'Beat It' would break the supposedly non-existent colour barrier, freeing MTV to experiment with other forms of black music later in the decade – and thereby widening their audience. As a final thrust, Jackson recruited movie director John Landis to create a thirteen-minute video epic for the *Thriller* title track. In future, pop stars would be limited only by their budgets, as videos transcended their status as visual accompaniment to a song, and became larger (and longer) than the music itself – fame transcending the means of its production, and ultimately sacrificing the cultural power of pop on the altar of celebrity.

The consequences of that shift in emphasis were illustrated with an awful blend of comedy and tragedy. Having designed an album of cutting-edge black music that could be enjoyed by anyone, regardless of age or race, Jackson was unable to progress in any field apart from fame. As his music stalled into stale repetition (though Jackson's stale was still more palatable than most artists' fresh), he was consumed by his own success. He believed himself to be beyond all petty human boundaries of finance, morality and sanity, and came closer than any entertainer to illustrating the madness of unchecked wealth. At the time of his death, the self-styled King of Pop was a musical irrelevance, emaciated, drug-addicted, mutilated by plastic surgery, deeply in debt, and trapped into a future schedule of live performances which would have taxed a young man in his prime, let alone a 50-year-old who had long since abandoned the real world.

Jackson's decline into total self-gratification offered a grim warning to his fellow mid-1980s stars. For more than a decade, Prince's career suggested that it was possible to wield totalitarian control over every aspect of one's life while still growing as an artist. Perhaps the most self-willed and talented musician in the entire history of popular music, Prince could apparently master any instrument, summon up a variety of vocal personae ranging from raw masculinity to girlish femininity, write songs that were simultaneously playful and complex, and demolish every imaginable boundary – between sexual preferences, races, even genders. During the 1980s, he acted as a one-man Beatles, seemingly daring himself to take ever more risks with his music, like a blindfolded circus performer insisting on fire-eating while balanced by a single finger hundreds of feet above a pit of deadly snakes. Never shy of admitting his influences, he reconfigured them with stunning imagination, channelling the spirits of Jimi Hendrix, Smokey Robinson, Curtis Mayfield, Sly Stone, the Beatles and many more, all in their prime: ancient and modern, sexual and spiritual, bedroom and dance floor, all of pop's possible playgrounds under his total command. *Purple Rain*, an album, film and song which coupled rock authenticity and pop sentimentality, was the moment when he rivalled Michael Jackson; the 'Kiss' single and the subsequent *Sign 'O' the Times* album marked the pinnacle of his artistic ambition. If his commercial and musical decline was less Icarus-like than Jackson's, that was because he never lost his passion for music – however often he alienated his immensely loyal fan base by closing down their websites and threatening them with lawsuits.

By comparison with Jackson's compulsive celebrity and Prince's genre-free exuberance, Bruce Springsteen's ascent to global success was as workmanlike as his carefully crafted image. Like Prince, he was addicted to performing and recording; unlike him, he spent his entire career (after the joyous expansiveness of his second album) refining and reducing his options, limiting his songwriting to the minimum of guitar chords and melodic variation. With *Born in the USA*, his defiantly nostalgic brand of rock 'n' roll found its moment, not least in his homeland, where the title track became an anthem of Reaganite patriotism. It didn't matter that Springsteen expressed his own distaste for Reagan's policies at home and abroad. Audiences responded to the sound of that chorus, rather than its lyrical message, creating a roar of complacent national self-congratulation out of a song which had been designed to deflate exactly that response. D. H. Lawrence's famous dictum, 'Never trust the teller, trust the tale', had rarely seemed more pertinent.

Lawrence, of course, never had to confront a phenomenon as baffling, and compelling, as Madonna. 'Her voice is thin and not consistently successful in its search for the proper pitch', said *Rolling Stone*'s Kurt Loder in 1984, with cruel accuracy. 'Take away the ravaged tart-trappings', he added (Madonna was fond of posing in her scanties), 'and there's nothing else to talk about.' In this instance he could hardly have been more wrong: that was precisely where the enigmatic appeal of Madonna began. Her music was never groundbreaking; her voice never a distinctive expression of personality; her songwriting rarely more than functional. By comparison with Cyndi Lauper, for example, who was her most obvious counterpart in 1984, she was a non-starter. Yet despite lacking any of the qualities on which musical fame had once depended, Madonna became arguably the most important pop performer of the last thirty years.

In place of traditional artistic values, Madonna offered a rival set of coinage, which rapidly became the standard currency of global celebrity. Her assets were an instinctive command of visual style; a shameless self-confidence; and a total belief in her power as an icon. More than any previous pop performer, she transcended music: her videos counted for more than her songs, her deliberately outrageous (and playfully polymorphous) sexuality divided humanity into the bewitched and the outraged, and beyond a vague message of liberation (always centred around the bedroom) and a willingness to offend religious conservatives, she carried no deeper message than the wonder of being herself. In her early videos, an otherwise anonymous pop singer was transformed into an emblem of confrontational narcissism. She was always posing, always pushing for a reaction – pouting and flouncing, demanding to be desired. The clips for songs such as 'Borderline' and 'Holiday' nowadays resemble a collage of twenty-first-century 'selfies'. She prophesied a world in which nothing would be more important than exhibiting one's own face. The blazing image of the star was diminished into a flickering form of fake stardom which everyone could share.

I do not cling to this antiquated hippie mentality that says it's us against them. I personally do not consider Pepsi-Cola and Old Style Beer and the Health & Tennis Corporation to be the enemy. This is the age of adult rock stars.
Glenn Frey, the Eagles, 1989

I guess I used to think that rock could save you. I don't believe it can anymore . . . as you get older, you realise that it is not enough.
Bruce Springsteen, 1988

The success of MTV signalled the death knell of popular music as a purely aural medium. On the surface, it marked the return of the old-fashioned, pre-technology entertainer, who was seen as well as heard. But the effect of the pop video was to skew the balance: to favour performers who could establish a single indelible image (Billy Idol's snarl, Sting's bare torso) over those whose personality was rooted in music. With Madonna as its guide, this tendency led inexorably towards Kylie Minogue and Paula Abdul, for whom singing and self-expression counted less than dancing and pouting; then, with the inevitability of a slide into the pits of hell, towards Milli Vanilli, a Grammy-Award-winning rock-dance duo who had not uttered a single note on any of their records.

With the video threatening to replace the album as the dominant currency of the 1980s,* the entire music industry was tilted on its axis, throwing many of its denizens out of the spotlight. Even the traditionally stable arena of American country music was overturned, after the launch of the cable TV channels CMT (Country Music Television, devoted to videos) and TNN (The Nashville Network, promoting the country lifestyle) in 1983. Country had already been shaken by the swaggering iconoclasm of performers such as Willie Nelson and Waylon Jennings, who brought the fearless confidence of the rock star to an industry which preferred to sell God-fearing humility. The *Urban Cowboy* fiasco had then left Nashville's major-label offices uncertain of what they were selling, or who they were selling it to. Their initial reaction to the synthesiser-heavy MTV sound was panic, exhibited when they tried to impose a similar sound on their own artists. Then, when their audience complained that country had lost its identity, they opted to promote a collection of younger artists who revived the 'classic' sound of the 1960s and early 1970s, and who (not at all coincidentally) appeared very presentable in front of a video camera. As rock and pop clips grew artier, more narcissistic and more outrageous, country's promo videos kept to Nashville principles by opting for simple, heart-warming narratives.

The new generation of stars paid due lip service to country's pioneers, from Hank Williams to Tammy Wynette, and also let slip their debt to the icons of 1970s arena rock. Most successful of them all was Garth Brooks, whose mastery of the grand gesture ensured that he became America's best-selling artist of the 1990s in any genre. His arena shows mixed the hillbilly humility of Hank Williams with the AOR theatrics of his adolescent heroes, Styx and Kiss. Nashville was soon embarking on a series of multi-artist tribute albums which ranged from Hank to the true progenitors of the 1990s country sound, the Eagles and Lynyrd Skynyrd. (2014 brought *Nashville Outlaws: A Country Tribute to Mötley Crüe*, which seemed to demand a reprise of the 1970s Waylon Jennings hit: 'Are You Sure Hank Did It This Way?')

The young male country stars of the 1990s were lampooned by veterans as 'hat acts', for their inevitable Stetsons and cowboy boots. 'Is there anything behind the symbols of modern "country",' Johnny Cash mused, 'or are the symbols themselves the whole story? Are the hats, the boots, the

---

* 'Someday, Your Music Collection Will Look Like This', promised an advertisement for MusicVision videotapes in 1985, picturing a shelf filled with VHS and Betamax videos, alongside a handful of vinyl albums.

pickup trucks and the honky-tonking poses all that's left of a disintegrating culture?' He lamented the fact that the country audience and its heroes didn't 'know or even care about the land and the life it sustains and regulates'. But that culture survived unchanged in video clips, enriching the country music industry on a scale which it had never known before. A succession of cross-over stars – Shania Twain, LeAnn Rimes, Carrie Underwood, Taylor Swift – effectively erased the once-mighty gulf between country and pop. Meanwhile, the so-called Americana industry of the 1990s and early twenty-first century fetishised a bleached, enervated brand of traditional country music, which would have left hillbilly farmers too jaded to herd their cattle.

MTV ignored the advent of the Nashville video industry, even when Garth Brooks was outselling all the network's stars. It reacted more purposefully to competition in the rock and pop market by launching VH1, aimed at widening the video audience to include those old enough to remember the arrival of Elvis Presley. The new network featured videos by artists thought likely to appeal to the 25–49-year-old demographic, plus vintage live concerts and documentaries. There was even a show en-titled *New Visions*, encompassing mellow modern jazz and that peculiar brand of neoclassical mood music known as New Age. Exploiting the commercial potency of those former 1960s radicals who had devoted subse-quent decades to exploring their spirituality, it showcased the near-back-ground music of such anonymous stars as George Winston and William Ackerman. The manager of the Police, Miles Copeland, was one of the first in Britain to recognise that 'The New Age audience grew up on rock'n'roll, [but want something] aimed exclusively at the quiet side of their lives.' Rock and folk performers from the 1970s, including Wishbone Ash and Michael Chapman, were reoriented towards the featureless sonic landscapes of New Age – the place where the quietly claustrophobic serial music of Philip Glass met the saccharine piano variations of Richard Clayderman.

As the MTV networks exploited music's visual potential, it was inevitable that other industries would take note. The hottest NBC drama of the mid-1980s was *Miami Vice*, apparently commissioned with the simple premise: 'MTV cops'. Its stars dressed and paraded like rock stars, made their own records, and shared screen time with rockers such as the Eagles' Glenn Frey. NBC's rivals readied their own imitations, such as *Hollywood Vice* and *The Insiders*. Hollywood productions followed suit, almost every feature boasting an anthem which could advertise the film on MTV. In September 1985, America's top three singles were the themes to

St Elmo's Fire, *Hollywood Nights* and *Mad Max Beyond Thunderdome*. The cross-pollination between music and film became so intense that it was common for directors to litter their movies with unrecognisably short snippets of contemporary songs, so that a star-laden soundtrack album would coincide with the premiere.

Exposed in Hollywood smashes, let loose across entire TV channels, pop and rock were now committed to the grand gesture. As MTV boosted performers with a visual imagination and camera-friendly faces, its audience wanted to see these icons in the flesh. The cinemas, university common rooms and small dance halls of the 1960s were superseded in the 1970s by sports arenas, and in the 1980s by vast buildings better suited to staging trade fairs – even, for the most potent idols, stadia which might hold as many as 100,000 people. To ensure that those positioned a hundred metres from the stage felt involved, promoters routinely employed camera teams to reproduce the show on giant screens alongside the stage. Fans paid premium prices for what was effectively a television presentation, simply to feel the communion of participating in these vast exercises in hero-worship. Rock's traditional reliance on spontaneity and even improvisation was erased by the need for musicians to programme their sequencers and lighting rigs in advance, leaving concerts as smoothly-rehearsed as any Broadway musical.

The MTV generation, united by the medium of television and the vast camaraderie of the stadium gig, demonstrated in 1985 that it could wield more power than its politically committed late 1960s equivalent. The phenomenon of Live Aid, which involved outdoor concerts in London and Philadelphia and was broadcast live* around the globe, transformed the image of rock from a symbol of teenage rebellion into the world's most effective aid to charity. Involving many of rock's most feted celebrities, including long-awaited reunions by Led Zeppelin, CSNY and Black Sabbath, Live Aid's stature as a musical event paled alongside its financial impact. Proceeds from the concerts, the TV staging, phone donations and the heavily delayed DVD release are reliably claimed to have raised well over £100 million for famine relief in Africa.

After Live Aid, there was scarcely a charitable enterprise which did not involve a tie-in rock gig or all-star single. The Prince's Trust organisation,

---

* Although not in parts of Texas, where KAMC preferred to show the Miss Texas beauty pageant; while on ABC-TV, veteran presenter Dick Clark talked through Led Zeppelin's performance.

headed by the heir to the British throne, promoted annual concerts starring rock stars young and old – the veterans invariably clad in Armani suits and indulging in displays of self-congratulation. Noting that many of these icons had also signed up for TV beer commercials, Elvis Costello protested: 'That Michelob [beer] music has absolutely NO relationship to rock and roll music. It's *Invasion of the Body Snatchers* music. It came down and zapped Phil Collins and Eric Clapton and Steve Winwood, and left these people that look superficially the same as them, but play this kind of bland beer music.' But the classical purity of his vision of rock 'n' roll seemed woefully outdated in a decade of gestural politics and video posing.

When the surviving members of the Who regrouped for a stadium and arena tour in 1989, three of the original quartet having endured prolonged battles against alcoholism, the band agreed for several of their shows to be sponsored by beer companies. Typically, Pete Townshend felt able to bank his proceeds from this lucrative venture, whilst undermining the entire enterprise in advance: 'the name [of the Who] refers to the audience's feeling about what the band means to them. And that's got very little to do with what the band actually does these days, which is NOTHING . . . There IS no band . . . it ISN'T the Who. It's a bunch of session musicians brought together to play Who material.' The tour sold out almost immediately. As Paul Kantner of Jefferson Airplane (themselves reunited for a 1989 tour) noted with an ironic sigh, 'Woodstock is what made the music business what it is today. Promoters looked at Woodstock and thought, "Oh, if we could only put walls around this." So we ended up with stadium concerts.' Whilst veterans of the 1960s counter-culture lamented rock's decline, its audience and earnings ballooned.

Much of that expanded income came from the most dramatic change in the technology of recorded music since the invention of the long-playing album. In October 1982, Sony in Japan issued their first compact discs – shiny five-inch circles of robust plastic, encoded with digital patterns which, when exposed to the beam of a laser light, could reproduce a facsimile of recorded sound. Although there was no consumer groundswell demanding a system of music distribution that would improve upon vinyl and cassette tape, the CD appeared to offer several crucial advances over existing formats. The discs were said to be virtually indestructible; they would offer perfect sound reproduction, without any of the surface noise or scratching of vinyl, or the telltale distortion of an ageing cassette; and they would offer a playing time of anything up to seventy minutes. (In fact, the system eventually grew to hold a little over eighty minutes.*)

Initially, CD players were so expensive that they seemed like executives' toys, but as their price fell by 1984, sales began to rocket. They were still an adult purchase, so the early years of compact disc were dominated by acts who would appeal to upwardly mobile consumers aged 25 or more. The same audience was targeted by Ford, who in 1986 became the first car manufacturer to instal CD players in its new saloons. Besides aficionados of classical music, who relished the opportunity to hear an entire symphony without needing to change the disc, CDs attracted a similar audience to those US radio stations offering a format called 'classic rock' – rock, in other words, which did not depend unduly on synthesisers, and did not betray any hint of cutting-edge black music. No act benefited more from the introduction of the CD than Dire Straits, whose pristine audio clarity and sharp separation of instruments might have been designed to show off the invention. Their 1985 album *Brothers in Arms* became the best-selling compact disc of the era, fuelled by the popularity of their MTV-baiting single, 'Money for Nothing' – the video for which went into heavy rotation on the channel. Mark Knopfler's song equated commercialism with prostitution, and was sold with the dexterity and sophistication of a high-class hooker.

No current act, however, could match the commercial potency of rock's glorious heritage when it came to CD sales. Those who felt themselves excluded from the marketplace by recent developments in popular music relished the opportunity to purchase new compact-disc copies of their favourite albums. Stores reported consumers in their 30s and 40s marching to the till with fistfuls of CDs, reviving the obsession with music which had once made them feel young and alive. Glimpsing a marketing opportunity which perhaps they had not originally envisaged, record companies rushed to fill the shops with reissues and repackages of old material – usually without offering the artists any improvement on the exploitative royalty deals they had signed twenty years or more earlier. Having sold the same music again to the same audience, albeit at a vastly increased retail price, the companies then embarked on an endless succession of reissue campaigns, which would see some classic albums re-released five or six times over the next twenty-five

---

* Some vinyl albums, such as Pye's Golden Hour compilations and Todd Rundgren's *Initiation* LP, had succeeded in squeezing more than sixty minutes of music on to a twelve-inch record, but only with severe diminution of sound quality.

years, expanded with bonus tracks from the archives, long-lost photographs and lengthy prose accounts of the record's gestation. The logical next step was the box-set retrospective, a medium barely exploited in the days of vinyl. Once again, existing material could be presented in a fresh way, always with the persuasive inclusion of vintage rarities from the vaults. It is no coincidence that the rise of the compact-disc market should be accompanied by the launch of glossy publications devoted to music as a lifestyle choice, written and packaged with the same sophistication as fashion magazines. The most successful of them catered for the post-teen purchasers of CDs, guiding them through the dazzling variety of new music towards records which might remind them of what they had loved in their youth, and convincing them that rock music was still a culture, even if it involved nothing more revolutionary than the flourishing of a credit card.

Detractors railed against many aspects of the compact-disc revolution. Artists such as Neil Young (who also held out against corporate sponsorship of his consumer tours) complained that digital sound was soulless and unattractive, with none of the organic warmth of vinyl. Many consumers lamented the loss of the twelve-inch-square LP artwork, which sacrificed its visual power when reduced to 17% of its original size. One of the unchallenged advantages of the CD, its expanded capacity, also had a profound effect on the way in which music was presented to the public. The humble vinyl single – seven inches, two songs – mutated into an artefact whose temporal length was determined only by the random decision-making of the organisations who calculated the weekly pop charts. In place of the A-side and B-side, many CD singles now featured a succession of remixes of the same song, which exhausted the patience of all but the most devoted fan.

More momentous still was the effective destruction of the album as a coherent art form. When sequencing a vinyl LP, artist and producer were dealing with a medium which involved two suites of music or songs, each lasting on average twenty minutes; each with a defined beginning and end. That time span was long enough to allow for changes or flows of mood and tempo; short enough to hold an emotional or physical shape in the consumer's memory. In order to fit their work on to vinyl, musicians had to compress or edit it into its optimum form. On CD, all of these restrictions – and the need to make artistic choices – were abandoned. Every album could now last up to eighty minutes, so songs expanded (the average single now lasting five minutes, rather than three as in the 1960s) and multiplied. In theory, this benefited the consumer, offering more value for money; in practice, it turned the album into a sonic endurance test. Worse still, the album lost its familiar shape: it climaxed at the beginning, with its opening song, and then meandered until it reached its conclusion, more than an hour later. So simple was it to skip from one track to the next with the push of a button that consumers grew accustomed to omitting their least favourite songs – or merely letting the entire disc roll as background music to a dinner party or homework assignment. For those too young to remember vinyl, the CD offered simplicity of use, instant access to any song, the freedom to re-sequence any disc:* a multiplicity of advantages. But it also tarnished a medium that had been central to a generation's musical understanding of itself.

Through the second half of the 1980s, there was a series of rapid changes in the way that music was bought and consumed. The industry embarked on a deliberate policy of phasing out vinyl releases, starting with singles. Rather than switching directly to CD, as marketing departments had assumed, most casual purchasers preferred the cheaper option of cassette, tape sales outnumbering the combination of vinyl and CD by more than two to one. As vinyl singles were removed from the weekly release sheets, and young listeners were still unable to afford CD technology, cassettes became the standard way of purchasing new songs. In an attempt to boost revenue, UK labels attempted to launch the videotape single – allowing purchasers to experience their favourite clip from MTV without having to wait. It proved no more successful than any of the alternative options tossed at adult purchasers during the 1980s, in the hope that they would buy anything. There were three different formats of the laser videodisc, only one of which would also play audio CDs; the CD-video (twenty minutes of audio plus five minutes of visuals); and digital audio tape (DAT), intended to replace the cassette. DAT became a standard medium for preserving studio recordings (and unofficial concert tapes), but never prospered as a consumer format.

Having invested financially and emotionally in CD, the adult audience demanded new music which would suit their established tastes, and the medium. The heroes of the British Invasion and the Woodstock generation had struggled to adapt to technological innovation and synthe-

---

* For those with sufficient capital, a similar facility had been available for vinyl in 1977 with the ADC Accutrac 4000 ('Its father was a turntable. Its mother was a computer'); and in the 1980s with programmable cassette decks.

sised sound. Neil Young's *Trans* was the exception, deliberately confronting his audience with the necessity for change. Other artists were less sure-footed, Bob Dylan's *Empire Burlesque* and Crosby, Stills & Nash's *Live It Up* demonstrating the consequences of sacrificing integrity in a vain quest for youthful acceptance.

In their place, U2 and R.E.M. offered oblique lyrical integrity and crusading passion ('I always want an outstretched hand in music', declared U2's Bono in 1985), while younger songwriters such as Tracy Chapman, Tanita Tikaram and Edie Brickell offered familiar pleasures in fresh clothing. Paul Simon broke a United Nations boycott on working with South African musicians to produce *Graceland*, the borrowed rhythms of township jive unblocking his own muse. The Grateful Dead achieved the biggest single ('Touch of Grey', its video clip symbolically populated by skeletons) and album (*In the Dark*) of their career, to their own bemusement as much as the industry's. And in 1989, a succession of baby-boomer favourites, including Lou Reed (*New York*), Bob Dylan (*Oh Mercy*) and Neil Young (*Freedom*), appeared re-energised and focused after a decade of floundering out of time. MTV tapped into this renewed desire for 'authenticity' by launching their *Unplugged* concert series, removing performers old and new from the shelter of their synthesisers and sequencers.

Listeners to this adult-oriented music usually ignored a techno-logical innovation which altered the already complex relationship between young people, the music with which they identified, and the outside world. Utilising cassettes and then (after 1984) the CD, the Sony Walkman directed a personal choice of music from a portable player straight into the eardrum. Consumers could walk the streets, or sit slouched in the back of their parents' car, lost in a world of their own creation; and all that anyone else could hear was the rattle and hiss of excess sound escaping from the headphones. This was the technology of solipsism, allowing owners to imagine themselves the stars of their own drama – or, perhaps, isolated from a hostile environment by the songs which symbolised their existence. It was the perfect medium for music which would place itself in opposition to the adult world: the soundtrack of violent dissent, or equally aggressive self-pity, turning the angst of adolescence into a lucrative and all-pervasive industry.

⚡

'I was writing poetry, not rhymes. I would only rhyme, as a mockery, because the Sugar Hill Gang was doing it. Every kid on the block had a rhyme book. I never thought it would be rhyming as far as records went. It just seemed a fad.'

KRS-One, Boogie Down Productions, 1988

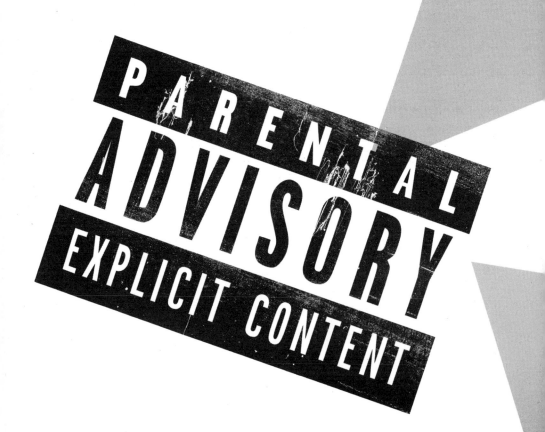

CHAPTER 27

THAT
SCREAM

'After hearing Herc, I decided to get a pair of turntables myself. Before that, I'd wanted to be a musician, a drummer. But hip hop was a new form of entertainment in the Bronx; it was more happening than playing in bands.'

Grandmixer D.ST, 1983

Exiled from New York, the Sugar Hill Gang's 1979 hit 'Rapper's Delight' was a playground novelty – first cousin, twice removed, to Shirley Ellis's tongue-twisting 'The Name Game'. If rhythmic rhyming was required, then comedians were eager to oblige, from Kenny Everett (as Sid Snot) to Alexei Sayle ('Hello, John, Got a New Motor?'), Shawn Brown ('Rappin' Duke') and Mel Brooks ('Hitler Rap'). By the end of the 1980s, even Liverpool's footballers were demonstrating their flow, with 'Anfield Rap'.

If you were anywhere outside the NYC boroughs, indeed, it was easy to believe that only white people rapped. There was Blondie, name-checking hip-hop luminaries on 'Rapture'; Tom Tom Club, reviving the girl-group innocence of 1962; the Clash's 'Magnificent Seven', Joe Strummer plodding uneasily across the beats; Adam Ant's posse channelling the Sugar Hill sound on 'Ant Rap'; soon enough, George Michael hanging tough on Wham!'s 'Young Guns' and 'Wham! Rap'. Not content with selling the punk generation leftover scraps of 1960s situationism, former Sex Pistols manager Malcolm McLaren concocted 1982's 'Buffalo Gals' with producer Trevor Horn, sampling the culture of the Bronx with the same shameless panache he'd soon focus on South Africa's township jive ('Double Dutch').

What did that Bronx culture involve? There were hints when Debbie Harry introduced the Funky 4 + 1 on *Saturday Night Live* in 1980, their youthful exuberance reminiscent of the Jackson 5 a decade earlier. But their adolescent versifying was a strip-cartoon of a multidimensional scene. It didn't reflect the rap battles between rival sound systems in parks or warehouses, MCs striving to stake their superiority over their turf; nor the artistic one-upmanship of the graffiti which adorned most buildings in the Bronx, and the city's subway trains, and was maligned as petty vandalism by civic authorities; nor the breakdancing by B-Boys and B-Girls, acting out the funky rhythms from DJs' decks with breathtaking jumps, slides, twirls and dives.* As rapper KRS-One explained in 'HipHop Knowledge', 'Rap music is something we do, but hip hop is something we live.' Rap was an element of hip-hop culture; hip hop was not just artistic expression, but

---

* The 1982 movie *Wild Style* neatly encapsulated all these elements within its naïve narrative.

a way of life which marked its juvenile adherents out from their elders and would-be superiors.

Had it never been documented on record, rap music might simply have vanished; or remained static in its virgin, pre-Sugar Hill state; or mutated in ways that we cannot imagine. Instead, it was chronicled on vinyl, exposed to influences beyond the Bronx, from Kraftwerk to Phil Collins, and grew from a neighbourhood dialect into a global language which would, by the end of the 1980s, supplant rock as the most potent articulation of youthful alienation and bravado.

In an effort to match 'Rapper's Delight', New York labels poured out songs for the same novelty audience: 'Christmas Rappin'', 'Astrology Rap', 'The Breaks'. The first and last of those were by Kurtis Blow, whose personality, skittish and arrogant, burst through his wordplay and easily memorised hooklines. With Brother D & Collective Effort's 'How We Gonna Make the Black Nation Rise?' (1980), however, rap followed soul's journey into radical rhetoric. For Brother D, rhyming and breaking were just 'wastin' time', when the point was to change the world.

That object was achieved by other recruits to Sugar Hill. DJ Grandmaster Flash pre-empted the invention of the digital sampler with his dextrous deck-switching on 'Adventures of Grandmaster Flash on the Wheels of Steel' (1981). Inevitably, he borrowed from Chic's 'Good Times', as 'Rapper's Delight' had done; but he also crossed racial boundaries by reclaiming Blondie's 'Rapture', and snipping some vital seconds from Queen's 'Another One Bites the Dust', which might have been fashioned with the sole purpose of being stripped down for hip-hop purposes. Flash also had his name on 'The Message' (1982; actually rapped by Melle Mel), which introduced British audiences to the concept of hip hop as social protest. Simultaneously, the American pop charts played host to another slant on the hip-hop revolution, Afrika Bambaataa & the Soulsonic Force's 'Planet Rock', co-produced by the decade's most powerful remixer, Arthur Baker. Funny, chaotic, confrontational, the song's universal declaration of hip hop was supported by synthetic keyboards echoing the innovations of Kraftwerk, and the soon-to-be-ubiquitous Roland 808 drum machine. Bambaataa arrived in Britain that autumn with the New York City Rap Tour, a hip-hop package comprising DJs, graffiti artists, even a set of schoolgirls showing off their skipping skills.

Along for the ride was Grandmixer D.ST, the man who transported GrandWizzard Theodore's inventive scratching technique into a commercial gimmick. It received global attention on Herbie Hancock's 1983 hit, 'Rockit', to which the contribution of Hancock himself, a pioneer of jazz-funk-rock fusion with Miles Davis, was minimal: a jingle-like keyboard riff added after D.ST and producer Bill Laswell had assembled a hypnotic electro-funk track. Other electro sides that year might have been more enduring (West Street Mob's 'Break Dance – Electric Boogie' is arguably the ultimate cross between robotics and the irresistible punch of the funky drummer), but Hancock's appearance at the 1984 Grammy Awards – complete with shop-dummy dancers, and D.ST manning his steel wheels – transformed scratching from ghetto diversion into mainstream entertainment.

It also consolidated hip hop as a synonym for partying, as breakbeats eased their way into the heart of adult-oriented soul records. The next gimmick lifted from the streets into the pop vocabulary was the human beatbox, central to the frivolity of Doug E Fresh's 1985 hit 'The Show'. The rapper, it seemed, was merely an irrelevance, as hip hop was reduced to a rhythm, a slick hand on a turntable, and a street attitude that was revitalising black music without leaving its mark.

> We don't have to go to the leather guy and get costumes made up to look like Superman, or to look like the stars of the day, cause we *are* the stars.
> DMC, Run-DMC

> Too many acts think that all there is to rap is to talk about yourself. It's killing the music.
> LL Cool J, 1987

Run-DMC, said Chuck D of Public Enemy, were 'the Beatles of hip hop'; in which case, the role of producer George Martin was shared between the co-founders of Def Jam Recordings, Russell Simmons (brother of band member Run, né Joseph Simmons) and Rick Rubin. Recalling Run-DMC's debut single, 'It's Like That', Russell said: 'No one could even imagine what the fuck it was. No melody. No harmony. No keyboards. Just a beat, some fake-sounding handclaps and these niggas from Queens yelling over the track.' Rubin, who produced the trio's 1986 breakthrough album, *Raising Hell*, boasted that 'my biggest contribution to rap was the structured-song element. Prior to that, a lot of rap songs were seven minutes long; the guy would keep rapping until he ran out of words. "It's Yours" [a 1984 Rubin production for T La Rock] separated it into verses and choruses.'

Run himself had a simpler explanation for his outfit's tight, incisive tracks: 'Back then there weren't any rap records. We'd just rap over anything with a hard beat, such as Aerosmith or James Brown, or breaks in songs like Billy Squier's "Beat Box".' And their raps connected with their local audience, who shared their taste for (in DMC's words) 'Lee Jeans, shell-toe Adidas, Pro-Keds, Pumas, Kangol hats, sweatshirts, whatever was just common at the time'. Their music was stripped down to the raw elements of hip hop: beats from their DJ, Jam Master Jay, and compelling, fresh-from-the-corner slices of everyday life from DMC and Run. This earned them ten hits with the African-American audience, before the record which carried hip-hop culture into the white heartland of America, set up a symbiotic relationship with the rock mainstream, and enabled MTV to place a rap video on heavy rotation.

The clip for 'Walk This Way' (1986) pitched Run-DMC in mock competition with hard-rock veterans Aerosmith, whose decade-old anthem the rappers had been chewing up for years. Run-DMC were persuaded by Rick Rubin to recut the song with its writers, Steve Tyler and Joe Perry, the two units battling for supremacy in front of the cameras before forgetting their enmity in their relish for the riff. With 'King of Rock' (1985), Run-DMC had already reached out to the rock audience as they rapped over the heavy-metal guitar clichés of session-man Eddie Martinez. 'Walk This Way' enveloped the rap act within Aerosmith's macho allure, no longer a threat to the status quo but merely a fresh source of energy. Within a year this union of black and white would be transposed from drama to farce as the dysfunctional remnants of the Beach Boys joined the cartoon-like Fat Boys for a child-friendly revival of the 1960s surfing favourite, 'Wipe Out'. Its video followed 'Walk This Way' on to MTV, as hip-hop clips were slotted into the network's prime-time schedule, rather than being confined to a late-night ghetto. In summer 1988, *Yo! MTV Raps* – note the surprise and pride in that title – provided the same coverage as the station's specialist shows on metal (*Headbanger's Ball*) and alternative rock (*120 Minutes*).

Run-DMC's *Raising Hell* became the first hit album in hip-hop history. To outdo its No. 3 US chart peak, Rubin and Simmons offered a white rap act who might have been constructed from a kit to convert rock

fans to rap: a former punk band named the Beastie Boys. As their subsequent career demonstrated, the trio's immersion in hip-hop culture was
total. But their *Licensed to Ill* debut album, stoked by their dorm-riot
chant 'Fight for the Right to Party', suggested that a bunch of beer-
soaked college kids had been allowed to pillage a hip-hop factory, stacking
classic rock samples across breakbeats while competing to gross out their
parents. With hard rock addicted to the bouffant curls and dry-ice posing
of MTV videos, the Beastie Boys seemed to offer the exhilarating transgression that had stoked the rise of Elvis Presley, the Rolling Stones and
the Sex Pistols: a 13-year-old's fantasy orgy with the rowdiest gang in
school.

So prominent were the trio in 1987 that their profligate use of
unauthorised samples could not be ignored. 'One of the positive things
about sampling', claimed Beastie Boys drummer Mike D, 'is that you're
incorporating a musical and cultural history into what you're doing.' This
was an early sighting of the credo which would be heard repeatedly in the
Internet age: that ignoring copyright restrictions promulgated artistic
freedom. Those whose originality was being borrowed did not agree. 'I just
got a tape from some local record company', said Don Henley of the Eagles
in 1990. 'They used part of one of our songs from the 70s and just rapped
over it. I resent that – go make up your own fucking music.' While James
Brown's long-time sideman Fred Wesley credited sampling with keeping
his music alive, the Godfather of Soul himself lambasted a generation of
black musicians who would rather steal from their idol than reward him.
KRS-One, whose Boogie Down Productions cut one of the most militant
hip-hop albums of the late 1980s, *By All Means Necessary*, seemed to suggest
that sampling was legitimate if it was white musicians who were losing out:
'No one ever brings up the human factor of sampling. Black people have
been sampled for years . . . Elvis Presley made millions "sampling" Little
Richard.' Once lawyers became involved in rap, however, unlicensed
sampling became a thing of the past, and songwriting credits on hip-hop
(and soul) albums ballooned to include all of those whose hooks or riffs had
been borrowed.

Just how creative that technique could be was illustrated in 1987.
Eric B and Rakim hung their hit 'I Know You Got Soul' around elements
of a 1971 track by James Brown's vocal auxiliary, Bobby Byrd. Eric B was
one of the first rappers to employ the devices of poetry in rap, breaking the
pattern of simple, self-contained rhymed couplets to string out extended

ideas across a series of lines, decorating his flow with internal rhymes and repeated vowel sounds. The Bomb Squad production team for the rap collective Public Enemy adopted a starkly different method, compressing what sounded like hundreds of samples – some of them a single symbolic noise, like a screech borrowed from (inevitably) James Brown's band, the JBs – across the grooves of their UK hit 'Rebel Without a Pause', and their incendiary album *It Takes a Nation of Millions to Hold Us Back*. In their hands, rap was a deadly weapon: militant, religiously severe, confrontational, purposefully designed to disorient anyone who did not share their crusade. It was Public Enemy's Chuck D who felt strong enough to say (on 'Fight the Power' from Spike Lee's *Do the Right Thing* movie) 'Elvis was a hero to most, but he never meant shit to me.' Like the Clash's similar recital from 1977, this was meant to shock and divide. When Public Enemy member Griff was quoted as saying that 'Jews are responsible for the majority of wickedness that goes on around the globe', and the collective were linked to the Nation of Islam, their reputation was scarred. Like the Beatles after John Lennon's remarks about Christ in 1966, however, their best-selling work followed on the heels of this furore.

Other hip-hop acts seemed to pose a threat to society greater than anti-Semitism, to judge from the hysterial press coverage given to rap between 1988 and 1990. NWA (alias Niggaz With Attitude) aroused political fury with their LP *Straight Outta Compton*. With its explicit anthem 'Fuck Tha Police', casual eroticism and cavalier stance towards gratuitous violence, the album confronted white America with the black men of its darkest dreams. If Public Enemy could be excused their militancy because it was accompanied by a coherent manifesto, NWA represented social and sexual terror: the unknown danger spelled out in capital letters.

Alongside NWA's distortion of the California promise there emerged a more carnal and less political threat from Florida. Miami's 2 Live Crew became the first musicians to have an album (*As Nasty as They Wanna Be*, from 1989, with its crude hit single 'Me So Horny') declared officially obscene by a state judge. Their lyrics and videos were rampantly sexist, awash with profanities, utterly lacking in irony; but it seemed no coincidence that similar lapses of taste by rock musicians had not led to court hearings. As Bruce Springsteen's producer/manager Jon Landau noted, 'Now that the focus has switched to rap music, they're trying to throw people in jail.'

> In fields and warehouses and aircraft hangers around Britain, for a
> while it felt as if we were building an alternative society of our own
> . . . [Participants] didn't fit the stereotype of joyriding, ram-
> raiding, shoplifting, drug-pushing, estate-dwelling lost youth.
> These were nice kids. The kids next door. *Their* kids. And it seemed
> as if they had all gone mad.
>   Sheryl Garratt, dance-music historian

> Football hooliganism got finished overnight. Just the strength that
> we felt with each other, just en masse . . . beautiful. It was a
> community thing.
>   Ian Brown, the Stone Roses

In 1989, when there was unprecedented dissent in Communist China, and Eastern Europe's closed minds and borders were about to be pierced, it was possible to imagine that Britain was staging a revolutionary uprising of its own – in the name of nothing more dangerous than love.

The trigger word within dance culture in 1988 had been acid, memories of 1967's psychedelia inspiring the claim that this was the second Summer of Love. In 1989, the ecstatic word was rave: another hangover from the 1960s, when it was both a pop magazine and any scene that was really happening. This time around, the ravers weren't dolly birds and office workers in mod gear, but unashamed hedonists seeking a form of spontaneous unity that could not be confined within the conventions of the music business; and hence, in its anarchic immediacy, represented a threat to the status quo.

So it was that the repetitive flurry of computerised dance beats, entirely free of angst, repression and violence, could spark police attention of an intensity not felt in Britain since 1977, the summer of punk hatred. Laws were undoubtedly being broken; empty warehouses and fields invaded by thousands of young people of all races; illegal drugs consumed, very occasionally with fatal consequences; giant convoys of pleasure-seekers circulating around the M25 motorway, waiting for the signal that would announce where tonight's rave would begin. But the only violence – the customary by-product of teenage gatherings – came when police let loose their dogs on kids who were pulsating to a rhythm that was unrelenting and transcendent. It was the product of a decade's experimentation with beats and electronics, in Chicago, Detroit and New York, on Ibiza, and in late-night clubs across London. Just as the music was a journey with no destination, so the ravers circling the capital in search of a party were engaged on a quest that might have no ending; merely a new beginning, as the countdown to the next party began.

For those unaware of these epic voyages through the darkness towards ecstasy, the music which provided their soundtrack sounded baffling. The British charts in October 1988 seemed to explode into a new, surreal dimension, twisted out of shape by records which were disorienting sonic adventures. Beneath their unwavering beats there were sharp clatters of synthesised percussion; layered above were apparently random stabs of noise, samples that might come from factory sirens or TV shows, public information films or vintage rock 'n' roll instrumentals, and war cries (of 'aciieed' or 'party') so simple that their banality started to seem profound. It was not quite, as the Pet Shop Boys promised in a contemporaneous song, 'Che Guevara and Debussy to a disco beat', but the aural assault of 'We Call It Acieed', 'Acid Man', 'Can You Party?', 'Stakker Humanoid' and the rest was almost that startling.

Under this influence, pop could not fail to react, in ways almost too strange to imagine. Fifty-six-year-old Petula Clark produced a techno version of her signature 1964 hit 'Downtown'. Forty-eight-year-old Tom Jones fell into the hands of synth-pop experimentalists the Art of Noise, and emerged with a revival of Prince's funk classic 'Kiss', which revitalised his career. Indie rock bands abandoned their fixations with the Byrds, early 1960s girl groups and the Smiths to leap into the future – none more dramatically than Pop Will Eat Itself, whose 'Can U Dig It' was a magical compression of at least half a dozen different musical cultures, a clear sign of what lay ahead. Paul Weller, once the chronicler of urban angst, a political crusader and a student of suburban English life, remodelled himself as a stylist of house music, claiming that nothing bored him more than rock music with guitars. Britain even pioneered its own distinctive vision of the junction between soul and hip hop, with Soul II Soul's 'Keep On Movin''.

It was inevitable that the rave audiences should include fledgling rock bands. 'We saw some of the spirit of Paris 1968 reflected in the acid-house movement', recalled Ian Brown of Manchester's Stone Roses. 'People were coming together and governments don't want that.' Neither did many followers of British indie, their flag defiantly reserved for bands who eschewed an overt black influence. Yet in Manchester, where the Hacienda club (owned by Factory Records) was a beacon of independence from the London corporate mainstream, and also a showcase for cutting-edge American dance rhythms, there was little opposition to this music which disposed with the instruments and symbolism of the rock tradition. 'Pop music was saved by the advent of acid house and rap because [white guitar bands] have done nothing for ten years', Brown declared.

As the decade closed, a new form of British rock came out of the international rhythms of house, and the collective culture of rave. It was unashamedly tied to dance rhythms, often (especially in the hands of the Happy Mondays) filled with exuberant wordplay, anthemic and rousing – a culture dubbed (after a Happy Mondays EP) 'Madchester'. Besides the Roses and the Mondays, there were a dozen lesser bands; exactly the kind of scene that catches the media's attention, and then burns out in a matter of months. The decline of 'baggy' culture, a term inspired by a preference for clothes that were the opposite of rock 'n' roll's traditionally figure-hugging garb, was quick and merciless, aided by the self-destructive nature of its two biggest bands. Dance culture, too, began to fragment; the all-together ethos was replaced by cults that were deliberately elitist, seeking to exclude those who didn't follow exactly the rhythmic or tonal formulae of their sect. With an increasingly fervid media ready to seize upon a new sensation or threat to social cohesion, the only way to claim ownership of a milieu was to impose ever tighter boundaries around it, and then label it as a badge of identity. Beginning with dance, with its handbag and hardbag, trance and hard trance, deep house and diva house, jungle and horrorcore, this division and division again of music into ever more exclusive categories was visible in almost every genre. The ultimate goal, perhaps, was a style which would belong to just one person: an impulse reminiscent of the desperate isolation and wilful solipsism of the tortured adolescent.

> Picture a thirteen-year-old boy sitting in the living room of his family home doing his math assignment while wearing his Walkman headphones or watching MTV . . . A pubescent child whose body throbs with orgasmic rhythms; whose feelings are made articulate in hymns to the joys of onanism or the killing of parents . . . In short, life is made into a non-stop, commercially pre-packaged masturbational fantasy.
>
> Allan Bloom, *The Closing of the American Mind*, 1993

I saw a documentary on World War Two, and somebody was saying
that a nervous breakdown is the reasonable response of a sane man
to an insane situation. I think rock and roll still has to be the sound
of the nervous breakdown. Because that scream, from Howlin' Wolf
to Nine Inch Nails, is part of it.
    Bono, 1992

If an unwavering computerised beat could arouse official condemnation for
its ability to inspire ecstatic emotional release in large crowds of young
people, how much more dangerous would it be if the same beat induced
violent self-hatred? As the West's financial system staggered into one of its
periodic spasms of panic-stricken decline at the start of the 1990s, many
American teenagers immersed themselves in the comforting nightmare of
music darker than reality.

In Los Angeles, a city beset by riots in 1992, Trent Reznor of Nine
Inch Nails purchased the house in which Charles Manson's followers had
murdered five people, including the actress Sharon Tate, twenty-three
years earlier. That year, he commissioned a video for his frenzied account
of sadomasochist domination, 'Happiness in Slavery'. The clip featured a
naked performance artist trapped in an infernal torture machine which he
has entered of his own free will, and from which he emerges only as gore
and sludge, pouring out of the machine like meat from a mincer. Reznor
was able to transform the darkest reaches of sexuality, violence and pain –
the landscape of the eternal outsider – into genuinely popular culture. Nine
Inch Nails' best-selling record was *The Downward Spiral*, described by
journalist Gavin Baddeley as 'a blizzard of suicidal self-loathing'. The same
audience relished the equally extreme sonic landscapes of Ministry, whose
music Baddeley called 'an audio horror movie of epic proportions'.

Nine Inch Nails and Ministry have each been credited as practitioners of industrial techno, although both elements of that description
have been disputed by those whose self-identity depends on strict adherence to a musical genre. However it is described, this music marries
computerised beats (usually a symbol of dancing pleasure) with the aural
assault of industrial metal. It's intended to be abrasive, vicious, torturous:
all words that could be applied with equal veracity to the central device in
Reznor's banned 1992 video. It also represented the final, vertiginous
descent of a downward spiral, indeed, transforming playful decadence into
an enactment of the agonies of hell.

The romanticism and eroticism of death fuelled the Gothic literary tradition of the eighteenth and nineteenth centuries, entranced Edgar Allan Poe in the 1840s and 50s, and was rekindled by the decadent writers and illustrators of the Victorian and Edwardian eras. Thereafter its fantasies were eclipsed by the realities of twentieth-century carnage; then reproduced as farce in the horror films of the 1950s, whence it seeped into popular music via the exaggerated scenarios of Screaming Jay Hawkins and Lord Sutch. The colour of Gothic fantasy was black, which in pop culture was also the shade of motorcycle machismo and hipster artiness. In the aftermath of punk, however, black was reunited with its trappings of lace and garish make-up, as Siouxsie Sioux and, soon afterwards, Robert Smith of the Cure led an adolescent generation into a gloriously *noir* portrayal of glamour: black lipstick, black nail varnish, black lace sleeves, spiked black hair, set off against the pale skin of imminent death. While Siouxsie & the Banshees extended their Gothicism into a near-psychedelic flirtation with exotic rhythms and cultures, Smith recognised a more primal need to retain his slightly batty air of darkness. 'If I hadn't written those songs,' he recalled, 'I would have become a fat, useless bastard. I went through a period of thinking everyone was fucked, and then I started to write these songs. I channelled all the self-destructive elements of my personality into doing something.'

Smith's whimsical, ironic lyrics and ability to conjure up pop hooks ensured the Cure an enduring career. Less predictable was that his quintessentially English band would become major stars in the United States; or that Depeche Mode, lightest and least enigmatic of Britain's early 1980s synth-pop outfits, would simultaneously be greeted in America as chroniclers of mental disintegration (to borrow the title of a Cure album), with music that was, on the surface, no more harrowing than their early hits. (*Violator* from 1990 was the first of a series of Top 10 US albums.)

Depeche Mode were certainly not considered to be part of Britain's goth movement of the 1980s, which can be traced back musically to Bauhaus's 'Bela Lugosi's Dead' from 1979 or, in more troubled mode, to the brief career of Joy Division; and visually to London clubs such as the Batcave. There the likes of Siouxsie Sioux, Nick Cave and Marc Almond painted the flamboyance of David Bowie and the New Romantics in bleaker hues. Cave (an Australian obsessed with the American South) filled his Gothic legends with ghostly visions of souls haunted and cursed by fate and blood. Britain's goth bands, such as the Sisters of Mercy, the Mission and Fields of the Nephilim, preferred to explore the boundaries of sexual identity. Like the Cure, they offered a home to anyone who felt alien from their surroundings or their psyches. Arguably no musical movement has ever been more welcoming to those who were confused about their sexual orientation or indeed the gender of the body they inhabited; or to women, so often confined as the passive consumers of male libido.

The emergence of Nine Inch Nails and Ministry diverted music towards the nihilistic excess of the Marquis de Sade, severing the Gothic tradition from its playful self-discovery. While these adult male protagonists, aggressive in their victimhood, eviscerated themselves for public entertainment, the gentler, more feminine instincts of 1980s goth re-emerged in different media and art forms. From a musical cult with a penchant for dressing up in black, the Gothic turned into an all-pervasive culture. It spread from fashion into literature, in the form of Anne Rice's vampire novels, and from there into television and film – *Buffy the Vampire Slayer, Twilight, True Blood*, all targeting that moment of adolescence when the child feels itself an outsider, full of knowledge but restlessly adrift from adulthood. Beyond the American evangelical right, adults have regarded these tales as harmless entertainment. Music still has the potency to disturb parents and politicians, however; and to provide a medium for both lacerating self-examination and cartoon outrage. This combination would turn Marilyn Manson into the most hated figure in 1990s American rock, blamed for school shootings and suicides, self-harm and drug use.

> Maintaining the punk rock ethos is more important to me than anything.
> Kurt Cobain, 1990

> I don't feel the least bit guilty for commercially exploiting a completely exhausted Rock Youth Culture, because at this point in rock history, Punk Rock is, to me, dead and gone.
> Kurt Cobain, 1992

In his 1994 suicide note, Kurt Cobain declared: 'The worst crime I can think of would be to rip people off by faking it and pretending as if I'm having 100% fun.' It is doubtful that even the most deluded of his fans was under that misconception. So entrenched was his image as a rock star on the verge of psychological disintegration that his band Nirvana contributed a self-mocking song entitled 'I Hate Myself and I Want to Die' to a 1993 compilation album.* His eventual demise, a month after a failed attempt on his own life, was as inescapable as gravity. It ensured that the most emblematic rock star of the 1990s would be a man worshipped as a victim rather than a survivor; on his own harsh terms, a failure for having committed exactly the sins against his beloved punk rock that he regarded as most heinous.

Cobain's appalling death, and his all too public descent into addiction and despair, spoke volumes for the changing role of rock in modern culture. Once a naïve symbol of optimism and liberation, it had slowly and inexorably been turned inside out by a succession of ruptures in youth culture – metal, punk, goth, now the unappealingly named grunge. (Jonathan Poneman of the Seattle indie label Sub Pop is often credited with naming this unfocused genre. 'It could have been sludge, grime, crud, any word like that', he noted later.) There was still hedonism to be found in the rock canon of the grunge era, but only from bands who were bent entirely on entertainment, rather than chronicling the dysfunctional psyches of a wounded generation of adolescents. The closest that the so-called Seattle scene came to reckless pleasure was the frenetic desolation of Mudhoney's punky thrash, 'Touch Me, I'm Sick' – a phrase that might have been coined as a grunge manifesto. Pearl Jam, despised by Cobain as corporate beasts, may have launched their career with a single called 'Alive', but its lyrics revealed a complex tale of betrayal and incest. Grunge, like the industrial techno it shadowed, was intended to validate the agonies of growing up, not relieve them.

Cobain's depression was heightened by his ambivalence about his band's rapid ascent to fame. Like the Sex Pistols before them, Nirvana were a band who preached punk-rock spontaneity and then delivered a record (*Nevermind*) of exquisite studio perfection. They inherited a tradition which the music industry had named alternative rock, and rendered that description redundant by releasing one of the best-selling American albums of all time. 'Alternative' was a blanket description for everything in US post-punk which was not explicitly designed to appeal to MTV, from the hardcore-pop hybrid of Hüsker Dü and the experimental guitar tunings of Sonic Youth, to the traditional pop structures and quiet/loud dynamic switches of Cobain's most obvious influence, the Pixies. (In fact, there was another industry definition

---

* The album was 'hosted' by MTV's animated stars Beavis and Butt-Head, stereotypically inarticulate teenagers who devoted their show to satirising the video clips that the network played, Nirvana included – a piece of self-sabotage Cobain must have enjoyed.

of 'alternative', which ranged wider still, encompassing everyone from Elvis Costello to U2.) When *Nevermind* succeeded Michael Jackson's erroneously titled *Dangerous* at the top of the American album charts, it had a symbolic resonance – even if Nirvana's reign lasted no longer than seven days.

Their brief career was the squeezed heart of the Seattle grunge scene, which existed before them in the shape of Soundgarden, Mother Love Bone and Green River, and survived to deliver chart-topping albums in the mid-1990s for both Pearl Jam and Soundgarden. Yet death cemented an image of Cobain which would – like those of Jimi Hendrix and Jim Morrison before him – become more familiar than it was in his lifetime. Those earlier icons, celebrated on T-shirts by people born after their deaths, appeared wild and seductive, alien and magnetic. Cobain's face, by comparison, passed into history with a blank, mesmerised glare: a casualty who could never be rescued. Teenagers of the twenty-first century proudly sport the Nirvana shirt with the acid house 'smiley' logo twisted by Cobain's own pen into a wobbly grimace, part amused, part disturbed. A casual doodle from 1991 was transformed into a fashion statement, alongside the Ramones, Run-DMC and even Sonic Youth T-shirts which adorned the bodies of thousands who did not know, or care, what they signified. (Miniature versions of all these designs and many more, featuring artists from Bob Dylan to the Clash, were available for those desperate to treat their babies as style accessories.)

In an era where self-harm could become the stuff of legend, the MTV-friendly hard rock of power ballads, permed hair and bubblegum refrains was perversely out of step with the times. Just as hardcore had jettisoned all the facets of punk which could be assimilated into pop, the plethora of fiercely guarded metal subdivisions which surfaced in the early 1980s were a deliberate step away from commercial appeal. Thrash metal, death metal, black metal and their offspring were designed to alienate the masses, and identify their followers as a misunderstood elite. Of these styles, thrash was the simplest to quantify: it was punk-fast, metal-heavy, relentlessly unyielding until it stopped.* Death and black metal – the latter

---

* It could stop very suddenly. The British band Napalm Death compressed the entire history of rock music into their 1.3-second-long recording 'You Suffer', though purists would note that Napalm Death were officially a grindcore band, mixing thrash with hardcore punk. Even that performance trundled by comparison with the single abrupt chord of the Electro Hippies' 'Mega Armageddon Time'. Bands in the post-punk tradition tended to go about their business more succinctly than those whose narrative began with metal.

a particular favourite among the pale white musicians of Norway, for climate-related reasons – prioritised gloom over speed, preferably while considering eviscerated corpses and bleeding wounds. Two archetypal band names: Dismember and Carcass (who should perhaps have combined forces to form the ideal death-metal supergroup).

Despite being the very stuff of cult appeal, thrash metal mutated into a major commercial force, to the extent that Metallica's 1988 album . . . *And Justice For All* sold 1.5 million copies within three months of its US release, without the benefit of radio airplay or promotional videos. Its landscape of self-harm, alienation and drug addiction – set to music which was resolutely stripped of all reference to rock's roots in black music – reflected the isolation of its white teenage audience. Over the next decade, Metallica would edge themselves towards a broader acceptance of rock's traditions, via the more direct song structures of their self-titled 1991 album and the daringly (for a thrash band) blues-tinged metal of 1996's *Load*. This would become a familiar path: Megadeth abandoned the politically cynical thrash of their mid-1980s albums to achieve their biggest success with *Countdown to Extinction* (1992), alarming long-term fans with its comparative accessibility. The Brazilian* band Sepultura, brutally monotoned in 1987, had varied their tempos by 1993's *Chaos AD*. Even Anthrax, who in the 1980s maintained a ferocious intensity leavened only by frat-boy jesting, betrayed the hints of a melodic sensibility on 1993's *Sound of White Noise* – demonstrating how influential Nirvana's success had been.

In 1994, the year Kurt Cobain committed suicide, one of America's best-selling books was Elizabeth Wurtzel's memoir of adolescent depression, *Prozac Nation*. Around 2.5 million prescriptions for the mood-altering drug were written in America during 1988; by 2002, the *New York Times* reported, the number had risen to more than 33 million. Between 5% and 10% of US teenagers were using antidepressants at any one time, many of them spending years or even decades on the drug, unable to gauge what their authentic emotional reaction to any situation might be. Many more teens suffered without medical help, either unnoticed by their parents or refusing to swallow their emotionally anaesthetising pills. One survey in

---

* The Brazilian city of Belo Horizonte became the nation's capital of death metal as many citizens took to the streets in 1983–4 to protest about the military government's refusal to allow the return of democracy. Feeling themselves powerless, young people channelled their frustration into the most violent music they could imagine.

1988 suggested that as many as one in seven American teenagers had attempted to end their own lives.

For these adolescents, the lacerating fury of bands from the thrash- and death-metal traditions might represent a connection with grim reality, more honest than the panaceas or chemically induced calmness they were being offered by their elders. Few metal albums of the 1990s were as successful, or as overwhelming, as Pantera's 1994 release, *Far Beyond Driven*. It became America's best-selling record. As *Rolling Stone* reported, 'Pantera have the ugliest fans in the world – proudly, defiantly, gloriously ugly – fans who revel in their ugliness, wear it as a badge of honour.' That ugliness could reside within, as well as on the surface; it could manifest itself in the epidemic of heroin and crack-cocaine abuse which ran through the metal and grunge communities in the early 1990s, publicly affecting such bands as Nirvana, Hole, Alice In Chains, Jane's Addiction and the Red Hot Chili Peppers (outsiders on the metal scene because of their overt use of funk rhythms). Guns N' Roses' career was stalled by the musicians' conflicting attitudes to addictive practices. Stone Temple Pilots, extending the melodic grunge tradition of Nirvana, were lent glamour by the well-publicised dramas of vocalist Scott Weiland.

To many adult eyes, the growing teenage preoccupation with tattoos and body piercings – once associated predominantly with bikers, criminals and the military – represented another expression of self-hatred. Adolescents regarded their augmented appearance as a symbol of rebellion and/or artistic self-expression: hence the prevalence of these fashion choices on the 1980s goth and hardcore scenes, and in the skateboard culture of the next decade. At the end of the century, a new wave of metal bands emerged who spoke directly to the trailer parks and council estates, the skaters and loners, their musicians sporting the same ink designs, studs and rings as their fans. Bands such as Korn and Limp Bizkit unashamedly reached out to an audience proud to be considered 'white trash' or 'trailer trash'. Childhood anguish and generational disquiet fired Korn's 1998 album *Follow the Leader*, an American No. 1 record, which in its unwavering, headbanging tempos seemed to offer a negative mirror image of contem- porary dance music – a barrage of agony replacing the ecstatic celebration.

There was another form of metal nonconformism, however, which represented a more direct threat to America's self-perception. In the music of Rage Against the Machine, on their 1992 debut and 1996's *Evil Empire*, metal and the stylistic emblems of rap music were set to serve a political agenda which hinged around a simple message: America was a haven of imperialism, corruption and authoritarianism. 'Bullet in the Head' confronted government manipulation of the media; 'People of the Sun' the nation's brutal foreign policies; and 'Bulls on Parade' the distorting power of militarism and the arms industry. Yet, isolated incidents aside, Rage Against the Machine were free to promulgate their anti-American views from the heart of the US entertainment business, via a multinational corporation. African-American performers would not always be so fortunate.

> Rap is media control. Everything else in the world about the black situation comes to you from another perspective.
>   Chuck D, Public Enemy, 1992

> I didn't want to be no R&B rapper and no motherfuckin' crossover rapper . . . That ain't me. I want my shit to be 100% gangsta shit . . . A gangsta runs his own thing. He's got his own mentality, he's his own gang, he don't listen to nobody but himself.
>   Snoop Doggy Dogg, 1993

Some 150 years before the rivalry between the Crips and the Bloods, America's first street gang – the Forty Thieves – was active in Manhattan's Lower East Side. So gangland America did not require hip hop, or the formation of the Black Panther Party, to spur it into life, although both have been blamed. Nor is gang membership a predominantly African-American trait: today Hispanic members outnumber their black counterparts approximately three to two. As urban deprivation and decay spread across inner-city America in the closing years of the last century, however, it was convenient for commentators to point at the drug addiction and casual violence, attribute it entirely to turf wars between African-American gangs, and then draw a thick black line towards the prominence of the provocatively named gangsta rap.

US Vice-President Dan Quayle declared in 1992 that an album by rapper 2Pac (Tupac Shakur, the son of Black Panther activists) 'has no place in our society'. Soul singer and producer Barry White, who might have been presumed to be a political conservative, did not agree: 'The greatest thing that ever happened to young people is rap music', he told *Vibe* magazine. 'It gives them an outlet to express their frustration – and get it out of them.' Rapper/producer/entrepreneur Puff Daddy (Sean Combs) expressed similar sentiments in more vernacular language: 'The young kids – all the real motherfuckers across the world that's young and black – they need that real shit . . . They got to hear it. Like, if records stopped being made, motherfuckers would be jumping out of windows or something. That shit is almost like a drug.'

Given the links between street gangs and narcotics, and the heavy influence of 'weed' on much 1990s hip hop, that was perhaps not the happiest of analogies, though no one could dispute its accuracy. Unfortunately, violent rivalry proved to be equally addictive. In the summer of 1996, sparring rap collectives released provocative declarations of geographical superiority: 'New York, New York' (Tha Dogg Pound) being answered by 'LA, LA' (Mobb Deep et al.) The latter was accompanied by a video in which the artists acted out the torture and killing of the Dogg Pound duo. With tensions already high between West and East Coast hip-hop outfits and their frequently more thuggish record companies, Puff Daddy called despairingly for an end to the violence.

That September, 2Pac – who often came on stage to the sound of taped gunfire – was shot as he was driven away from a Las Vegas boxing event, and died six days later. His final words, to the policeman who was first on the scene of the shooting, were symbolic: 'Fuck you.' In the wake of the tragedy, a song called 'Runnin' (Dying to Live)' was released, which featured 2Pac rapping alongside his supposed rival, the Notorious B.I.G., aka Biggie Smalls, né Chris Wallace. (Both men were actually born in Brooklyn, although Shakur was raised in Oakland, California.) Six months later, Biggie too was shot dead. Puff Daddy expressed amazement that being a rapper could get you killed: he'd always thought it was 'a way for the gangs to battle without violence'. 'It just shows you how crazy times are', he said. 'Shit is fucked up . . . they wasn't *that* gangsterish on the motherfucking records to deserve to die.'

Regardless of their gang affiliation, rappers had been battling in clubs since the style was first invented; this was a genre founded on arrogant declarations of superiority, physical, sexual and regional. One of the first entirely coherent album-length rap statements, Boogie Down Productions' *Criminal Minded* (1987), was not only self-promoting and rich with violent imagery, but it inspired a turf war with other South Bronx rap crews. (BDP member DJ Scott La Rock was shot dead less than six months after its release.) Before then, Schoolly D's 'PSK' and (more humorously, sexism aside) Ice-T's '6 in the Morning' had depicted gang violence. Ice-T, whose persona was part gangsta, part pimp, was an inspired choice to deliver the theme song for Dennis Hopper's 1988 movie *Colors*, a compelling study of street warfare in Los Angeles.

The same city (or at least its near-neighbour, Compton) spawned the rap group who would not only carry gangsta culture into the artistic and commercial mainstream, but would arguably become one of the most important musical collectives in the history of American popular music. NWA (Niggaz Wit Attitudes) was a loose assembly of Compton rappers and DJs, whose first collaboration was Eazy-E's 1987 single 'Boyz-N-the-Hood' (produced by Dr Dre; rap written by Ice Cube). With additional rapper MC Ren, NWA assembled *Straight Outta Compton*, which might have been designed to provoke outrage. 'We knew the power of language, especially profanity', Ice Cube recalled. 'We weren't that sophisticated, but we knew the power we had.' Yet the profanity merely sharpened a jagged saw, designed to slice through the frail threads connecting America's ghettos to its political establishment. The album's landscape was scattered with drug deals, unlicensed pistols, niggaz, motherfuckers, ho's (or whores): 'all about reality', as the songs boasted. 'Gangsta Gangsta' laid out the options confronting black youth on the streets, while puncturing the soul tradition of musicians offering an alternative to urban warfare ('Do I look like a motherfucking role model?'). But the killer blow was landed by 'Fuck Tha Police', confrontation explicit in every line.

As if to outstrip NWA, Ice-T formed a thrash-metal band, Body Count, and released 'Cop Killer'. 'Rap is really funny, man', he protested. 'But if you don't see that it's funny, it will scare the shit out of you.' Warner Brothers could not decipher the humour, forcing the song to be removed from the *Body Count* album, and then dropping Ice-T from their label. Sensing an opportunity, a young black man named Ronald Ray Howard, who had been arrested for murdering a policeman, pleaded that his mind had been affected by listening to rap music: NWA, of course, and also 2Pac – 'Trapped', perhaps, which depicted a shoot-out between rapper and cops.

The commercial potency of this music, to a multiracial audience, was demonstrated in 1991 when a tagging device known as Soundscan was introduced to provide a more accurate reflection of American album sales. Two genres benefited immediately from the change, at opposite ends of the musical and moral spectrum: country, and hip hop. Within a month, the second NWA album, *EFIL4ZAGGIN* (read it backwards), reached No. 1

in the US chart, having sold 1 million copies in less than two weeks. Violent and littered with expletives, of course, it also heightened the casual sexism which had been apparent on their debut. All women were ho's; all ho's deserved to be beaten or raped; therefore all women should take their punishment without complaint. The evidence for the prosecution was provided by the one-two combination of a sketch, 'To Kill a Hooker', and its musical enactment, 'One Less Bitch'.

There were other versions of rap available to the American public: rap as teenage lament, in the playful scenarios of Will Smith's hits; rap as romance, in LL Cool J's 'I Need Love' (though he was also involved in one of the first hip-hop feuds, against Kool Moe Dee); rap as mind expansion, from De La Soul and PM Dawn's hippie grooves; rap for strong women (YoYo) and young women (TLC), and young kids (Another Bad Creation); even, for a year or so, gangsta rap which came close to representing a form of feminism, with 2Pac's 'Brenda's Got a Baby' and his pro-choice, pro-mom, anti-sexist 'Keep Ya Head Up'. He followed through with 'Dear Mama', a sentiment that harked back to the days of Al Jolson, and 'So Many Tears', lamenting the casualties of the gangsta lifestyle. But at the time of 2Pac's death, *All Eyez On Me* suggested that there was more profit in stoking macho bravado than in damping it down.

Almost lost in the public debates over the ethics of hip hop – or, alternatively, rap as heinous social evil – was a sonic revolution perpetrated by NWA's Dr Dre. Apparent, in retrospect, as early as 'Boyz-N-the-Hood' in 1987, it involved synthesised bass frequencies so low and eerie that they were almost felt subliminally; beats that were slow and stoned, rather than chattering and sharp; and an air of slightly removed spaciness, starkly at odds with the uncompromising violence voiced over his grooves. In the aftermath of NWA's messy dissolution, Dre found the rapper to match his sound in Calvin Broadus, alias Snoop Doggy Dogg. He unveiled his protégé on the theme song from the 1992 movie *Deep Count*, then allowed Snoop to dominate his epic solo album, *The Chronic*. Setting aside the inevitable glorification of violence and objectification-cum-hatred of women (and those are big concessions), one could not help but be caught up in the seductively lazy, weed-heavy ambience of the single 'Nuthin' But a G-Thang': effectively an advertisement for the mental and physical pleasures of being a gangsta. Snoop Dogg impressed so many American teens that his later solo releases began to sell better to whites than to blacks.

After *The Chronic*, any sense of hip hop as the music of the underground could not be preserved. In 1993 and 1994, there was a flurry of new, compelling voices, the Notorious B.I.G., Nas and Common among them, and equally magnetic combinations of sounds from the Wu-Tang Clan, the Roots, OutKast and the Digable Planets. Then the entire industry was caught up in the beefs between 2Pac and Biggie, Death Row and Bad Boy Records, West Coast and East. After which – said Tommy Mottola, COO of Sony Records, who had a vested interest in making it so – 'Gangsta rap is over, finally, thank God. [Hip hop] is becoming more and more pop music, as opposed to being segregated.' By which he meant: there was money to be made if hip hop became a form of entertainment, rather than a chronicle of America's deepest scars and most urgent problems.

CHAPTER 28

'Touch dancing and swing music are back. It's the most exciting trend happening.'

Chicago concert promoter, 1980

'Let's face it, I'm 67, and I'm being accepted by the MTV crowd!'

Tony Bennett, 1994

4

For anyone schooled in the pop tradition of Frank Sinatra, Burt Bacharach or the Beatles, the 1990s was as confusing a landscape as Britain in 1940, with all its road signs removed or realigned to baffle an invading army. The popular song, with its recognisable structure of verses and choruses, had been smothered, subjected to a brutal post-mortem, and then sent back into the world with all its limbs awry and its organs missing. In place of melody, there were breakbeats and samples, synthesised pulses and sequenced keyboards – plenty to catch the ear, little for the proverbial milkman to sing on his rounds. Instead of romantic love and the joy of youth, contemporary music was filled to its razor-edged brim with self-loathing and despair, aggression and hatred. Vinyl was dying or dead, depending on your location; the cassette tape was being earmarked for destruction; even the video had lost its gleam, as MTV gradually sidelined its musical content in favour of comedy, game shows and a new strand of 'reality' programming which prioritised unknown members of the public over established stars.

Decrying these changes was as pointless and anachronistic as lamenting the passing of the 78, or the crushing of the dance bands by the influx of personality vocalists and rock 'n' roll. But the music industry had expanded with such rapidity that it could not afford to lose any of its audience, no matter how alienated or outdated they felt in the age of 2Pac and Nine Inch Nails.

In 1980, nostalgia for the 1950s and 60s still seemed faintly ridiculous. That year, the British songwriter Dave Montague issued a concept LP entitled *Supernova*, intended to introduce a stage musical based around eight dead rock icons, from Buddy Holly to Marc Bolan. The project was quickly as inanimate as its inspirations, but later the theatrical recreation of a rock-star life provided a foolproof route to a West End hit, as musicals such as *Buddy* and *Jersey Boys* would demonstrate.

In the same year, a desperate American manager placed an advertisement in a music trade paper, declaring bravely that 'Big bands are young again'. He raved about 'the college kids who pack concert halls to hear Big Band superstars like Count Basie, Maynard Ferguson, Buddy Rich, Woody Herman, Harry James, Ellington and the Dorseys', apparently forgetting that all but one of those bandleaders (Ferguson) was dead. No matter: the manager believed that he had unearthed 'a huge young audience who flips the radio dials and scours the record bins for brand new sounds they never heard before' – not hip hop, but 1930s swing reissues. To prove the point, he illustrated his ad with a bunch of college-age kids who could not have looked more exhilarated if they had seen all their favourite Hollywood idols walking naked down the street. Again, the sentiment was both hopelessly out of time, and premature. By the late 1980s, one of America's biggest stars was Harry Connick Jr, in his early 20s, who claimed 'I don't want to be a revivalist' while reprising the sound of the 1940s. By the mid-1990s, Tony Bennett, without a hit record to his name since 1967, was the coolest name to drop on an American campus, while cynical British journalists were suddenly promoting the joys of easy-listening albums from Bennett's prime, for their kitsch, ironic, wondrously wacky trademarks of blandness and simple melodies.

The year 1980 was also when Beatles producer George Martin, quizzed before John Lennon's death about the possibility that the group might reunite, asked contemptuously: 'What material would they do? Nobody wants to hear their old stuff anymore.' Twenty years later, a record retailer noted, 'The Beatles are still saving the industry's ass', as their greatest hits compilation *1* racked up the first of its perhaps 30 million sales – a figure which, if officially verified, would confirm it as the biggest-selling album of the twenty-first century. By 1995, the group had already concocted what Capitol Records called 'the multimedia musical event of the [twentieth] century' with their lavish *Anthology* project: a series of documentary TV programmes, three double CDs of material retrieved from the vaults and (eventually) a huge autobiography. The publicity coup was completed by one of the century's most anticlimactic media events, a long-awaited reunion of the Beatles (Lennon present only on archive tape) for two pleasant but ultimately unconvincing singles. The Beatles' attitude to money in the post-hippie, post-idealism era was instructive. When Paul McCartney toured America for the first time in more than a decade, he allowed his concerts to be sponsored by Visa. 'I don't see it as a sell-out,' he blustered, 'and anybody who does ought to go live in Russia.' Meanwhile, John Lennon's widow sanctioned the manufacture of neckwear bearing colourised versions of his doodles, and authorised reproductions of his trademark round spectacles. The Beatles even lent their corporate approval to the Franklin Mint's five-inch *Sgt. Pepper* figurines, 'meticulously hand-painted in psychedelic colors just as you remember them'.

If the Beatles could re-form, albeit only at a safe distance from their generations of fans, then no grave was deep enough to keep the nostalgia industry at bay. Elvis Presley, dead since 1977, was sent out on tour again twenty years later with his original Las Vegas band for *Elvis – The Concert*: live musicians accompanying a celluloid hero. Jim Morrison of the Doors was reawakened as a 1980s sex symbol, and then (in the person of Val Kilmer) as the star of an Oliver Stone biopic.* The Eagles returned with the most expensive tickets in show business, and an album entitled *Hell Freezes Over*, because they had once insisted that they wouldn't reunite until this happened (or their managers secured a lucrative enough deal). During the 1990s, almost every legendary band from the 1960s and 70s was reintroduced to their old repertoire and their even more elderly comrades, whether or not they were still on speaking terms. Any vestige of hipness still attached to the inspirations and pioneers for the punk movement vanished when the Velvet Underground re-formed in 1993, followed by the Sex Pistols three years later – yesterday's outrage becoming today's pantomime. Paul Weller of the Jam remained one of the few major acts to refuse the lure of a seven-figure cheque, forcing his ex-colleagues to form an ersatz replica of the group called, rather pathetically, From The Jam.

Other once-prestigious acts were forced to confront the absence of a figurehead. Bad Company, Queen and the Faces all re-formed with substitutes for their lead singers (Bad Company's Paul Rodgers complicating matters by replacing Freddie Mercury in Queen). Others, like the fictional Spinal Tap, lost members to accident, illness and overdose and carried on regardless, the Grateful Dead enduring the demise of three keyboard players before the more sizeable absence of Jerry Garcia forced them to pause – and then regroup as the Other Ones (later the Dead). Few rock legends, however, could match the convoluted history of Jefferson Airplane, who metamorphosed into Jefferson Starship in the early 1970s, then slowly shed original members and, eventually, their 'Jefferson'. As the denuded Starship, the former champions of psychedelic experimentation were reinvented as a generic AOR band, appalling anyone who remembered their past with the glib sloganising of 'We Built This City (on Rock 'n' Roll)'. After Starship finally disappeared into an intergalactic puff of

---

* *The Doors* prompted Morrison's contemporary, David Crosby, to write a bitter song, in which he declared: 'I've seen the movie, and it wasn't like that.'

irrelevance, founder member Paul Kantner relaunched Jefferson Starship on a miniature scale. He persuaded several of his fellow stalwarts to re-enlist, filling the crucial absence of lead singer Grace Slick with a succession of young women who, aurally and visually, resembled her late 1960s prime. Once again, the originals slipped away, leaving Kantner to carry his exhausted Starship, hippie ideals still aloft, around a circuit of tiny rock clubs far beneath his dignity. Meanwhile, his late 1960s compadres, such as Crosby, Stills & Nash and the surviving Dead, continued to fill arenas around the world – proof that business acumen was as important as nostalgia when it came to preserving the past.

In the fertile territory of the 1990s and beyond, there was scarcely a hit artist from the previous four decades who could not be assured of at least the vestige of a flourishing career. Those unable to draw a crowd alone were united on nostalgia tours, veterans of the 1950s to 1970s soon being outranked by packages of MTV-era stars. Those venues which were not filled with remnants of the distant past found that they could ensure a reliable income by booking tribute acts – who in less tolerant times would have been termed impersonators, and booed off stage after a couple of minutes. The most enduring of these acts are the Bootleg Beatles, whose live career (from 1980 to the present day) has lasted four times longer than that of the original Fab Four. The Abba tribute act, Bjorn Again, exploited the mid-1990s penchant for kitsch, and survived to join the Bootlegs (as their fans call them) and the Counterfeit Stones amongst the upper echelons of this surreal industry. Clubs which would once have been the breeding ground for young bands have been overrun by these much-loved imposters, while sophisticated restaurants, hotels and cabaret clubs present imitators of Tom Jones or Elvis Presley, Tina Turner or Madonna, with all the finesse that they would award an appearance by the stars themselves. There is a vast audience for whom it barely matters whether they are witnessing an authentic pop idol or a workmanlike facsimile: all they want is the chance to relive some precious pop memories.

Remakes break across the demographic spectrum. They're familiar to the parents, and they're quality records the kids haven't been exposed to.

New York radio manager, 1989

> Listening to rock radio today is like stumbling into an audio time
> warp in which the hip sounds are the Doobie Brothers' 'Listen to the
> Music', Jethro Tull's 'Bungle in the Jungle' and Lynyrd Skynyrd's
> 'Sweet Home Alabama'.
> Michael Goldberg, *Rolling Stone*, 1989

By the 1980s, many of those who had lived out their adolescent fantasies of rebellion through rock 'n' roll, beat, R&B or rock were old enough to inherit seats of power in the mass media. By the 1990s, these generations effectively controlled the Western world. Bill Clinton (saxophonist less than extraordinaire) became the first rock 'n' roll president, while former Ugly Rumours guitarist Tony Blair symbolically took his Fender Stratocaster into 10 Downing Street as prime minister. Children of the baby boomers were instructed that (a) the period from 1956 to 1977, give or take a few years, was the pinnacle of modern human history; (b) the culture of that era would never be equalled; and so (c) they had better compensate for their deprivation by lapping up the crumbs of the past before they disappeared.

This was now the culture that pop built, albeit a carefully edited version of pop, whereby drugs were fine in the past but not today; likewise political activism; likewise rock music. Oldies radio exploded from a format – a means of reaching a particularly wealthy demographic – into a global form of artistic tyranny, omnipresent and inescapable. It was as if a culture could only hold so many collective memories, and the West had chosen to fetishise the songs and sound of the 1960s for eternity. Young children grew up knowing the Beatles' songs (especially those from the *Yellow Submarine* animation movie) before they could form a sentence. Those in their teens or 20s flocked to see heritage rock acts, so they could tell their own children that they had once sat in an enormous sports hall while men in their 50s or 60s struggled in vain to sound like their 25-year-old selves. It was quite possible (speaking personally) to be enraptured by this naked exploitation of the star/fan relationship, whilst at the same time wanting to echo the words of Johnny Rotten at the final Sex Pistols concert (until, of course, the first of their five reunions): 'Ever get the feeling you've been cheated?'

The invasion of nostalgia could be traced back to the deaths of Elvis Presley and John Lennon, which the pop business commemorated in the only way it knew how: commercially. The impulse which led Presley's fans to bulk-buy his back catalogue, and Lennon's to send the nine-year-old 'Imagine' to the top of the sales charts, became a ritual: thereafter it was close to sacrilege not to mark a performer's demise with a tribute in cash. Such public tragedies sparked feverish debate about eras ending, generations passing and their relevance to the present day. But neither Presley nor Lennon would ever disappear. There was always an anniversary to celebrate and exploit, each revival widening the audience demographic for the next.

The fervour after Lennon's death prompted heavy sales for 'Stars on 45', an anonymous medley of soundalike covers of 1960s songs, dominated by Lennon/McCartney material, set to a disco beat by a Dutch producer. The theme wasn't new: there had been a brief craze for disco medleys ('Best Disco in Town', 'Uptown Festival') in 1977, and even, in Canada, an Elvis Presley tribute, 'Disco to the King'. But 'Stars on 45' triggered a manic reaction, as vast swathes of pop hits from recent decades were subjected to the same fate.* Gidea Park's 'Beach Boys Gold' was so lifelike that it won its creator, Adrian Baker, a place in the Beach Boys' touring line-up. Soon original recordings by the Hollies, the Beach Boys and the Beatles were being snipped and pasted into something that might pass for disco fare, while the vogue was extended to the big bands (Larry Elgart's 'Hooked on Swing'), music hall (Chas & Dave's 'Stars Over 45') and even classical themes (the RPO's 'Hooked on Classics').

Public acceptance of these records illustrated a strange phenomenon: at a time when contemporary pop was unmistakably modern, in tone and execution, there was an unending demand for records which sounded like the past. They ranged from straight revivals (the Pretenders' 'I Go to Sleep', complicated by lead singer Chrissie Hynde's relationship with the song's composer, Ray Davies) to open homages to bygone glories (Billy Joel pastiching the Four Seasons on 'Uptown Girl', and doo-wop on 'The Longest Time'). At a time of chattering percussion and synthetic backdrops, the blandness of Shakin' Stevens's cover of Ricky Nelson's 'It's Late' sounded positively radical. Likewise the Clash's 'Should I Stay or Should I Go', a blatant throwback to the British garage rock of 1964. So shocking was the sound of Elvis Costello crooning George Jones's Nashville hit

---

* The madness didn't end there: in subsequent decades, virtually every pop and rock anthem ever written would be subjected to an utterly uniform Hi-NRG makeover for the dance floor, from such cultural barbarians as Jackie 'O' and Micky Modelle – who has even extended his reach to Irish and Scottish folk tunes.

'Good Year For the Roses' to the British pop audience in 1981 that his accompanying LP, *Almost Blue*, was emblazoned with a warning: 'This album contains country & western music and may cause offence to narrow-minded listeners.'

Much of this revivalism induced a sense of pathos, of illusions being crushed and ideals trampled: comedy star Nigel Planer (as 'Neil') copying Traffic's once startling 'Hole in My Shoe' in the name of light entertainment, for example, or the Toy Dolls suggesting that punk was only ever a music-hall joke with 'Nellie the Elephant'. (All punks eventually returned to the music they really loved: John Lydon to progressive rock, Joe Strummer to rockabilly, Paul Weller to mod soul and late 1960s British rock, the Damned to the acid pop of Love's 'Alone Again Or'.) Planer joined the remainder of TV's *The Young Ones*, and Cliff Richard, for a single which inaugurated a new tradition: vintage pop songs being mistreated for charity. Stars who had once attempted, like Artie Shaw, to venture outside their niche in pursuit of artistic fulfilment discovered that they would only be rewarded if, like the Beach Boys with 'Kokomo', they stepped back inside their box. The Traveling Wilburys, a five-man retro supergroup formed in Bob Dylan's garage, turned this duty into a collective pleasure. Not that this was a failsafe manoeuvre: so tightly did John Fogerty adhere to his trademark sound on his 1985 comeback hit 'The Old Man Down the Road', that he was sued by his publisher for plagiarism of his own material.

When a performer was no longer available, industry and public alike attempted to find solace in his children: the Reddings (scions of Otis), Julian Lennon (schooled to sound like his father), even Lisa Marie Presley. By the 1990s, there was an entire tribe of these simultaneously entitled and cursed offspring in New York, some of whom (Rufus Wainwright, Jeff Buckley) were destined to set their fathers in the shade, while others endured careers fuelled by curiosity value alone.

As that decade began, the dominance of grunge, electronic dance music and hip hop left commercial room for any remotely contemporary American act prepared to pay homage to the baby-boomer heritage: the Black Crowes with 'She Talks to Angels', for instance, reviving memories of the Allman Brothers or the Faces; Queensryche's 'Silent Lucidity', tapping into the forgotten legacy of the Moody Blues; or R.E.M.'s 'Losing My Religion', the midpoint on an imaginary spectrum spanning Neil Young and the acoustic Led Zeppelin. The biggest arena rock acts of the

1990s, such as Hootie & the Blowfish and the Dave Matthews Band, were living replicas of 1970s traditions. In Britain, revisiting the past in the name of progress was also about to become a full-blown career option.

> There is now a formula: getting somebody to do a dance remix, getting rid of your drummer who can't play anyway, and getting some hack to put a good beat underneath. It's brought back this dull conformity. Rock music in England is terrible.
>   Mike Edwards, Jesus Jones, 1991

> Most music is lazy; it speaks in pop-speak, prodding your memory about things you've heard before.
>   Brett Anderson, Suede, 1993

The club mix of the Happy Mondays' 'Hallelujah', prepared by DJs Paul Oakenfold and Andy Weatherall in late 1989, drilled Chicago's house beats into the core of the British indie rock scene. After several years of self-enforced distance from black music, indie was once more acknowledging its ecstatic rhythms, just as the punk generation had encompassed reggae a decade earlier. Weatherall also collaborated with Primal Scream, as the Byrds' copyists of the mid-1980s re-emerged as champions of acid house – with a simultaneous desire to recreate the magisterial late 1960s sound of the Rolling Stones, as the singles from their groundbreaking *Screamadelica* album revealed.

What began as inspiration drifted into cliché, as Mike Edwards was quick to point out. His band (alongside the more anarchic Pop Will Eat Itself) had pre-empted their peers, merging punk attitude, the pile-driver impact of industrial metal and acid house into music which emphasised the sheer thrill of being alive 'Right Here, Right Now' (in the words of their 1990 hit). With 1991's 'International Bright Young Thing', Jesus Jones retrieved the inadvertently futuristic rhythm of the Beatles' 1966 tape-loop experiment, 'Tomorrow Never Knows', and fused it with utterly contemporary dance beats. My Bloody Valentine explored another rendering of the equation whereby pain would bring pleasure. Their tumultuous soundscapes found sensuality in ear-damaging waves of volume, the minor 1991 hit 'To Here Knows Where' making their sonic precursors, the Jesus & Mary Chain, sound conservative by comparison. Less confrontational versions of this technique briefly created reclusive pop stars out of bands – Lush, Ride, Curve – dubbed 'shoegazers' by the iconoclastic press, for their lack of conventional stagecraft and shy inability to engage with their audience.

Not everyone who was gathered into this self-conscious gaggle of post-adolescents shared their wilful timidity. Damon Albarn, the central figure of Blur, was a stage-school graduate who had been groomed as a slick New Romantic, before reinventing himself, with Bowie-like ebullience, as an indie disciple. He was at the forefront of what seems, in retrospect (and retrospect was the lifeblood of this era), to have been a deliberate move to relocate British indie rock to the heart of Swinging London, somewhere between 1965 and 1970. Many of his contemporaries, such as Ocean Colour Scene and Teenage Fanclub, were already channelling American folk rock from the same era. Albarn, however, led the charge towards a sound that would be unashamedly English – indeed, faux cockney – as he began to abandon his middle-class vowel sounds with the same eagerness as Mick Jagger in the mid-1960s.

An alternative route to the past was being mapped by what *Rolling Stone*, in May 1993, called 'this month's English Band of the Century': Suede. Their destination was the David Bowie of the *Ziggy Stardust* era, and their early hits ('The Drowners', 'Metal Mickey', 'Animal Nitrate') matched up to his influence. But it was Blur whose agenda triumphed, their past–present connection running from the Kinks, the Beatles and the Small Faces to the spikiness of post-punk. Between 1993 and 1996, a parade of British bands embarked on similar journeys, each with their own route: Saint Etienne's nods to the sophisticated pop of Burt Bacharach and mid-1960s France; Dodgy with their spirit-of-1967 effulgence; Supergrass with punky snapshots of the Monkees and the Small Faces. Blur inspired their own followers, including Elastica and Menswear, while Pulp's Jarvis Cocker, fifteen years into a career which had appeared to be static, was revealed as the Ray Davies *de ses jours*, an idiosyncratic social analyst with a droll sense of humour.

For many tastes, however, all this music was too considered, too cerebral, too self-conscious. Their needs were served by a Manchester band called Oasis, who embodied what journalist Sean O'Hagan dubbed 'the new lad'. Though that phrase identified a middle-class young man indulging in pleasures traditionally associated with working-class culture, such as beer, football and mindless drunken violence, it was soon embodied by the figure-heads of Oasis. Liam and Noel Gallagher were raised in Mancunian poverty, a milieu where they reckoned that only petty thieving would supply the rent. Noel Gallagher could pen melodies so accessible that they sounded immediately familiar (and sometimes dangerously familiar). Liam Gallagher sang with a defiantly Northern rasp that was nothing like John Lennon's voice, but shared his quality of being in your face with a pint of beer in hand, looking for a fight. The Gallaghers wanted to be the Beatles, and like their heroes they spawned a host of imitators: Longpigs, Heavy Stereo, Cast, Bluetones. But unlike the Beatles, who enacted constant musical revolution over seven frantic years, Oasis refused to move forward: their only development was to make their records longer and more layered, as if excess was the same as progress.

In 1995, there was a media-inspired war between Blur and Oasis – echoing, so excited commentators claimed, the rivalry between the Beatles and the Rolling Stones, although veterans of the 1960s seemed to remember that it had been perfectly possible to adore them both. Blur won that staged chart battle, Oasis commanded bigger audiences, but it was Damon Albarn and Jarvis Cocker who emerged triumphant from the so-called 'Britpop' era, while the Gallaghers slipped ever deeper into self-parody and repetition. Britpop, meanwhile, lost its lustre as quickly as the prime minister who positioned himself as its patron saint: Tony Blair proving to be no more reliable a source of British pride than the graceless, sexist drunkenness of the new lads.

The notion of being a pop star in the 90s is an anachronism, really. It's a bit like being the last of the dinosaurs.
  Damon Albarn, Blur, 1995

I think a lot of women like our music because we're not calling them names . . . We know these young women will grow up to be somebody's mother.
  Nathan Morris, Boyz II Men, 1995

It is one of the most calculating formulae in the history of popular music: you assemble four or five good-looking young men, of sufficiently diverse appearance to appeal to all female tastes, and then let them loose on the adolescent or pre-teen markets of the world. But the original boy band – the first male group whose public imagined that they knew them – emerged organically from the rock 'n' roll scene in their native Liverpool. Their success, and the wave of lookalike, soundalike beat groups who flourished in their wake, encouraged the formation of the first prefabricated example of the genre: the Monkees.

Prolific parents, such as the Osmonds or the Jacksons, could mould their offspring into a commercial proposition, sometimes at the expense of the children's psychological health. Both Michael Jackson and Donny Osmond were on stage before they were in school, the latter's more close-knit family relationship providing a stability which his more talented rival lacked.

In the black vocal group tradition, kids would gather in school classrooms or on street corners, perfecting their harmonies and dance moves, before being discovered (or exploited) by a perceptive mentor. One such was Maurice Starr, who in 1982 took control of a young black Boston quintet named New Edition – a title awarded by a former manager, to denote that they were the natural successors to the Jackson 5. As with the British family group Five Star, their early records were blatantly intended to recall the effortless exhilaration of the Jacksons. New Edition's relationship with Starr survived barely two years, but the group would eventually spin off three successful acts: trio Bell Biv DeVoe, Johnny Gill, and Bobby Brown, who before his troubled marriage to Whitney Houston had established himself as a distinctive R&B voice with such hits as 'My Prerogative'.

Having glimpsed his holy grail, a percentage of a worldwide phenomenon, Maurice Starr consciously set out to create a more commercially viable version of New Edition – comprising boys who were white. To be exact, Starr insisted that New Kids on the Block were 'white kids who are black. They have white skins but they are black. They have soul.' Initially they sounded, to nobody's great surprise, not unlike the Jackson 5, mixing classic teen pop with just enough hip-hop influence to make them hip, as least to the satisfaction of a 12-year-old fan base. They were then free to purloin pop history, their 1990 hit 'Tonight' mixing elements of ELO, the psychedelic Beatles and the Bee Gees. Their stardom endured approximately five years: any longer would have entailed their alienating their younger listeners by progressing into a more adult vein.

Suddenly boy bands were everywhere. Boyz II Men rekindled Motown's commercial fortunes with their contemporary 'jack swing' sound, and retro-styled vocal harmonies. Their 1993 single 'End of the Road', a throwback to the sweet, sultry soul groups of the early 1970s, became the longest-running No. 1 US hit since the heyday of Elvis Presley. The 13-year-old duo Kris Kross sparked a rush of pre-teen rappers, some black (Da Youngsta, Lil' Romeo), some white (the trio Immature and duo Hooliganz), some already famous (child actress Raven-Symoné from the *Cosby Show*), some nearer to nappies than maturity (4-year-old Jordy from France lamenting the misery of being treated like a baby).

By making music which was sufficiently mellifluous to appeal to a mature audience, Boyz II Men outlasted the natural lifespan of the boy band. Not so Backstreet Boys or N Sync (alias *NSYNC), for both of whom five or six years was sufficient for camaraderie and stamina to fade. Britain's Take That and Ireland's Boyzone conformed exactly to the same limitations. In Take That, however, British pop was gifted with an act who continually outgrew the expectations of their handlers. They were initially moulded to appeal to a predominantly gay male audience. Unexpectedly, they attracted a huge following amongst young girls, and in former pub pianist Gary Barlow they boasted a genuinely impressive composer of soft soul ballads. Moreover, his bandmate Robbie Williams had the irrepressible stage presence of Tommy Steele, mixed with the laddish persona of Oasis. So crushed were Take That's fans when Williams left the group in 1995 that suicide hotlines had to be set up in several countries. Having split soon after his departure, Take That not only reunited in 2006 to enormous acclaim, but rounded out their narrative arc when they were reunited with Williams in 2010.*

The only British pop acts of recent decades whose personal relationships have been studied with equal intensity by press and public alike bucked tradition by simple dint of being female: the Spice Girls, and their talent-show-based imitators, Girls Aloud. More than any previous pop stars, the Spice Girls were a media phenomenon first, a musical group second, and the compromises forced upon them by their barbed relationship with the press guaranteed that minor personal differences would be inflated into culture-shaking bust-ups. This would be the pop archetype of the future, a complex exchange of power and privilege which became increasingly unbalanced in an age when every passer-by on the street could contribute to the media via Twitter or Instagram.

---

* Williams and Barlow, whose dramatically different personalities had seemed impossible to contain within a single unit, sealed the union with a duet single, 'Shame'. Its video delivered the symbolic emotion that a Lennon/McCartney reunion might have mustered, atop a homoerotic storyline which the two men carried off with sublime aplomb.

Lost amidst the arguments between Ginger and Posh, or Scary and Ginger, and the rumours of their celebrity liaisons, was the Spice Girls' effect on pre-teen girls. They exploded into the public gaze with 'Wannabe', a boisterous, defiantly female take on the hip-hop posse – sweetened with vocal harmonies to ensure universal consumption. Not only did the group offer five startlingly different looks and personalities for young female fans to mimic, but they arrived shouting 'Girl power!' This proved to be a slogan, rather than a coherent philosophy, but for pre-adolescent girls who were being groomed to consume and ulti-mately lust after clean-cut boy bands, this hint of gender solidarity and even independence was exhilarating. What the Spice Girls suggested was that it didn't matter whether boys liked them or not: it was enough to be female, and in a gloriously rowdy gang.

The contrast with previous girl-groups was striking. The 'classic' girl group era of the late 1950s and early 1960s produced some of the most inventive and moving pop records of all time; but with few exceptions, the young women were anonymous, under strict male control, and unthreat-ening, rather than sexually rapacious. The exceptions were the Ronettes, sirens of sexuality, whose leader, Veronica Bennett, unwittingly sacrificed her independence in marrying their producer, Phil Spector. Another of Spector's groups, the Crystals, exemplified his belief that it didn't matter who sang on the records, as long as he created them. They would frequently hear 'their' new single on the radio, having not been invited to the recording session. This pattern was repeated in the 1980s, when a succession of American female groups – the Cover Girls, Pajama Party, Seduction – were assembled on the basis of appearance rather than raw talent: interchange-able sex objects first, vocalists only if strictly necessary, as session singers could compensate for their shortcomings on record.

The Spice Girls' output was less cynical than that, even if it never approached the creativity of their late 1990s contemporaries, All Saints, whose magnificent early hits successfully updated the original girl group sound for a polyrhythmic, multi-ethnic age. For all their public spats and exposés, the Spice Girls were more like cartoon characters than fully rounded humans, which is what made their 1997 movie *Spice World* so entertaining – and so unreal.

While young women are marketed for a female audience, or a male leer, but rarely for both, some of their male equivalents were able to reach teens of both sexes. Both Green Day and Blink-182 achieved success at a similar age to the Spice Girls. They emerged from the punk scenes in Northern and Southern California respectively, inevitably carrying baggage from the Nirvana-inspired grunge movement. Barely older than their fan base, they offered guides to teenage etiquette with riffs borrowed from the Clash and Buzzcocks, before diverging musically – Green Day towards a more melodic power-punk sound, and the socio-political commentary of their 2004 album *American Idiot*, Blink-182 by edging away from schoolyard anguish towards an adult sensibility (their 2011 album *Neighborhood* revealed that life wouldn't always be as simple as their early hits had promised). In Britain, the teenage band Busted retained Green Day's punk motifs, but coupled them with sexist, frothy pop tunes – the authentic voice of the cocky 14-year-old boy.

It's telling, however, that the most successful boy band of the last thirty years, One Direction, should strip away all this pubescent self-doubt and ambiguity, and return to the formula at its most simplistic. Their records typify modern pop: auto-tuned vocals, choruses so obvious that they almost come with subtitles for the audience ('wave your arms in the air . . . now it's time to get out your lighters'). But there has been a subtle shift in their emotional approach: having no doubt registered the world-wide appeal of James Blunt's ballad 'You're Beautiful', several of their songs turn the spotlight away from the stage and on to each of their yearning, lustful fans. 'What Makes You Beautiful' and 'Little Things' are aimed at young girls who will never feel so vulnerable again; who are unsure of the changes in their bodies, their emotions, their hormones, and their social role; and who are being told, by their dream lovers, that every one of them is, in her individual way, special enough to win the attention of Harry, Niall, Zayn, Louis and Liam, whichever fulfils her fantasy. Although it still places the girl in the role of supplicant rather than dominatrix, it is perhaps a healthier message to carry away from a pop infatuation than being reduced to a slut, whore or bitch.

> Miles Davis is my definition of cool. I loved to see him in the small clubs playing his solo, turn his back on the crowd, put down his horn and walk off the stage, let the band keep playing, and then come back and play a few notes at the end. I did that at a couple of shows. The audience thought I was sick or something.
>   Bob Dylan, 1985

> Playing 11,000-seater open-air theatres in Chicago with corporate
> sponsorship is not interesting. It's not interesting for people sitting
> out in the back, anyway. And it's not interesting for the band. No
> wonder people drink beer and eat popcorn all the way through
> concerts; how do you expect them to be involved from half a mile
> away?
>   Elvis Costello, 1989

At the end of a decade in which the staging of rock had developed from musical recitals into audio-visual extravaganzas capable of filling a vast sports arena, the sci-fi-inspired band Blue Oyster Cult took a momentous decision. In 1979 they announced that they would no longer be using lasers in their live shows, as they were in danger of reducing their music to a sideshow. With the honourable exception of Bob Dylan, much of whose incessant touring since 1988 has been dedicated to interrupting the sight-line of his fans, this represented probably the last occasion when a major rock act believed that less was more; sound more powerful than sound and vision.

In a dying gasp of counter-culture zeal, the rock media reacted with horror in 1984 when the Jacksons revealed that all tickets for their American reunion tour would be priced at $30. During a recession, the critics argued, the Jacksons were deliberately hiding themselves from their most loyal fans: the working-class aficionados who had worshipped Michael and his brothers since their first appearance on the *Ed Sullivan Show* fifteen years earlier, and shared the group's pride in becoming the first black family to host a networked TV variety show.

A decade later, such concerns seemed naïve. As the rock ticket breached the $100 barrier, then the £100 ceiling, and kept climbing, outrage was replaced by sullen acceptance. Customers who used a particular credit card or mobile phone were given priority booking; the best seats were crammed with corporate guests, as only corporations could afford to purchase 'Gold Circle' tickets; eventually, that humble South London R&B band from 1963, the Rolling Stones, dared to charge £375 for front-row seats to their 2012 London shows (or £950 if you also opted for the champagne reception – without the band – and three-course dinner). There was, it seemed, no price so high that some fan would not beg to pay it, no field so muddy or vast that people would not queue to fill it.

The global exposure of Live Aid, which boosted Queen and U2 into the top rank of live performers, reinforced the idea that music needed to be staged on a vast scale. Increasingly, the purpose of the live concert was not to hear the music you loved, but to say you had been there, and to share the comradeship, in sheets of rain or blistering sunshine, of tens of thousands of your peers. The shows expanded to fill the stadia, with the fireworks and lasers of yesterday supplanted by lavish scenery and special effects worthy of Cecil B. DeMille or Steven Spielberg. These presentations were inordinately expensive to stage, which in turn inflated the ticket price; and the consumer, already committed to the best part of a week's salary for admission, pledged their allegiance by buying an overpriced T-shirt or baseball cap. These were not just souvenirs, but a vital earnings stream for the stars, whose take from merchandise often exceeded their performance fees.

Amidst all this excess, popular music edged slowly back towards its roots in entertainment. Stars from the pre-MTV era could still attract consumers who expected nothing more from them than music and nostalgia – tantalising though it is to imagine the likes of Bob Dylan or CSNY breaking into a song-and-dance routine. MTV altered the expectations of its viewers: when they left the comforting glow of their TV sets and ventured into the real world, they wanted to be entertained as they were by television. So pop stars, such as Michael and Janet Jackson, Madonna, New Kids on the Block, Kylie Minogue and Paula Abdul, gave them shows which might have been designed by Busby Berkeley – flawless choreography, startling diversions of *trompe l'œil*, part circus, part carnival, pure showbiz. Cynical observers noted that some of these stars appeared to be able to cavort around the stage without missing a single note, while sounding altogether less proficient on the rare occasions they simply stood in front of a microphone and sang. It became obvious that many performers were choosing to mime to pre-recorded tapes – and equally obvious that fans didn't care. What mattered was the spectacle, and its three stages of excitement: anticipation, awareness that you were actually in the presence of a superstar, and the memory of pleasure that may, at the time, have been dampened by the weather, poor visibility, or the unwelcome company of a drunken sociopath. There was no room for foreplay in a stadium: the audience needed climaxes, one after another, each louder and longer than the last.

As theatricality became pop's dominant virtue, it is not surprising that the West End and Broadway musical theatre soared in popularity. A blood brother of the popular song until the 1950s, the stage musical was renounced by rock fans in the 1960s as a bastion of artifice and inauthenticity (especially when, as in the case of *Hair* or *Jesus Christ Superstar*, it was employing the tools and symbolism of rock). As late as 1978, there was assumed to be virtually no correlation between the audience for *Evita* and for rock concerts, even though performers such as Freddie Mercury and Meat Loaf were theatrical to their core. But Andrew Lloyd-Webber's melodies for *Evita* and its successors crossed into the pop charts, and his productions began to entice pop stars such as David Essex to venture into the theatre.

The musical itself now began to divide, with the sophisticated songs and moral ambiguities of Stephen Sondheim representing a serious, neoclassical approach to the form, while Lloyd-Webber and his peers, reversing history almost a century by reviving the convention whereby the entire narrative of a musical would be 'sung-through', opted unashamedly for populism and (in keeping with the new pop aesthetic) spectacle.

So we had actors dressed in feline costumes (*Cats*) and on skates (*Starlight Express*); or embroiled in epic tales filled with sentimentality and romance amidst historical chaos (*Les Misérables* and *Miss Saigon*). Individual songs came to matter less than the catharsis of being thrilled and moved by the totality of a production. Borders between entertainment genres were demolished: where once Hollywood had devoted itself to immortalising the hits of Broadway, now the process could be reversed, with *The Lion King* and *Billy Elliot* (both scored by Elton John) travelling from film to the stage. *Hairspray* ricocheted back and forth between the two media to the point that nobody could quite remember where it had begun. Madonna removed herself briefly from her obsession with chronicling her sexual exploits to assume the role of Evita in the movie of the show (and betray the limitations of her acting when compared to the original West End star, Elaine Paige).

These projects still represented a lengthy flirtation between pop and the musical, as did such vaudeville ventures as singalong screenings of *The Sound of Music*, or stagings of the early 1970s rock musical *The Rocky Horror Show*, where the audience was encouraged to dress up as the well-loved characters. The relationship was consummated and sealed by two theatrical projects which enveloped sizeable portions of the British public's collective pop memory: *Mamma Mia!*, a drama hinged around the Abba catalogue; and *We Will Rock You*, a sci-fi extravaganza which succeeded, where Dave Clark's 1986 effort *Time* had failed, in transferring rock's mythic power to the stage – thanks to the lavish emotional gestures and musical crescendos of Queen's array of hit singles. By transferring the songs from their place in history to the timeless, context-free scenery of the West End theatre, these productions erased any sense of pop or rock as vehicles for social change. In the end, as John Lennon had sung several decades earlier in a moment of cynical self-doubt, 'it's all showbiz'. The natural order of the entertainment business had been restored – perhaps never again to be overturned?

CHAPTER 29

THE MURDER OF MUSIC?

'I was listening to the radio and Jay-Z said the people don't wanna hear Auto-Tune no more. The biggest records of the year all had Auto-Tune – who are you to say people don't wanna hear it?'

DJ Webstar, 2009

'They're murderers of music! I stand and say it on behalf of every musician in the world and they will all agree with it … All the sexualisation of young people, all the worship of bling and money and diamonds and *Pop Idol* stuff, Simon Cowell – it all amounts to the murder of music.'

Sinead O'Connor, 2013

In October 1958, four years before it released the first Beatles single, the Parlophone record company of London proudly introduced its latest signing: Sparkie Williams. He was the winner of a BBC TV talent competition, designed to discover the most loquacious talking budgerigar in Britain. Carefully groomed by his owner, Mrs Mattie Williams, Sparkie won the judges' hearts with his rhymes and raps, as he literally sang his own praises.

The talent show has been a staple of light entertainment since the birth of vaudeville and music hall. Almost every major star of the twentieth century tested themselves in public against their peers, including Frank Sinatra, Elvis Presley, Bob Dylan, the Beatles and Jimi Hendrix. Ella Fitzgerald was merely the first icon to graduate from Amateur Night at the Apollo Theater in Harlem. Battle of the Band contests across America were a common apprenticeship for rock 'n' rollers in the 1950s and 60s (the Turtles satirising the genre on a 1968 album). The long-running ITV series *Opportunity Knocks* launched the careers of entertainers such as Mary Hopkin, Middle of the Road and the ill-fated child star Lena Zavaroni. The battle-rapping tradition offered the likes of Big Daddy Kane and Eminem the chance to spit out their rhymes, catcalls and cheers from the audience their reward. Many of the biggest acts of the past two decades also emerged from talent contests – Usher, Britney Spears, Beyoncé, Aaliyah, Christina Aguilera, Alanis Morissette, Justin Timberlake, Kelly Rowland, Destiny's Child and LeAnn Rimes, being among the many losing contestants on the US TV show *Star Search* who enjoyed substantially more success than the ostensible winners.

Their quest, and that of millions like them, encouraged the extension of the stage school and drama academy into institutes for the performing arts – or *Fame* schools, named after a 1980 Hollywood movie and a 1982 American television series. Each was located in an educational establishment where young people exhibiting a demographically satisfying array of genders, preferences and racial backgrounds gathered to pursue their dreams. (Pursuing one's dreams has been the lifeblood of popular music ever since, expressed in the bombast of AOR power ballads and the self-help clichés of singer-songwriter ditties.) Nearly thirty years after the film, the same ambition inspired Fox television's remarkably successful teen drama series, *Glee*. Set in the glee club (or, for British readers, choir) of a fictional Ohio high school, *Glee* has enabled around a dozen young actor/singers to perform, week after week, a vast repertoire of popular songs – all but a handful established hits, or staples of the musical stage. More than 200 of these – yes, 200 – entered the US Hot 100 chart between 2009 and 2013, eclipsing the achievements of every other act in musical history. The *Glee* cast recordings bring together AOR, soul, alternative rock, oldies, stage show-stoppers – some for individual voices, others delivered in choral harmony that suggests the Swingle Singers tackling the score of the rock musical *Hair*. Meanwhile, performing-arts schools have overcome the misgivings of those who felt that they were likely to train imitators rather than original talents: one such establishment alone, the BRIT School in Croydon, has already spawned the likes of Adele, Amy Winehouse, Leona Lewis, the Kooks, Imogen Heap and Rizzle Kicks.

More than sixty years after Frank Sinatra had first won *Major Bowes' Amateur Hour* with the Hoboken Four, the musical talent show appeared to have no more mileage in the post-*Fame*, pre-*Glee* era than a revival of ragtime or skiffle. Yet the New Zealand television producer Jonathan Dowling hit upon a formula, and a title (*Popstars*), which was franchised around the world. It was originally designed to uncover young women who could be assembled as belated rivals to the Spice Girls: TrueBliss in the original series, and Hear'Say and Girls Aloud in the British version. The audience could not only root for their favourites (and, as the format developed, vote for them by phone, a vast source of earnings for the TV companies); but they were also able to glimpse the audition process, allowing them to gaze like voyeurs at entrants who were tragically deluded about the extent of their own gifts. These hapless souls would once have been content to display themselves at pub pianos, or in karaoke bars, for the amusement of their drunken friends. Now their embarrassment was paraded for the TV-hungry nation.

The chief beneficiary of this sometimes barbaric entertainment was Simon Cowell, whose music-business experience involved the fashioning of singing careers for television actors (notably Robson & Jerome's run of chart-topping ballads), children's favourites (Zig & Zag, the Teletubbies) and soap-opera regulars from *Coronation Street* and *Emmerdale Farm*. He stepped away from a role in the first British *Popstars* series to concentrate on promoting the group Girl Thing, whose career foundered after two hits. He then joined forces with former Spice Girls manager Simon Fuller to create *Pop Idol*, before sidelining the show in favour of *The X Factor*. Meanwhile,

Pop Idol too was franchised overseas, and its US spin-off, *American Idol*, proved to be the networked entertainment phenomenon of the first decade of the new century, producing a succession of enduring stars, such as Carrie Underwood and Kelly Clarkson. Britain countered with One Direction, five solo hopefuls who were encouraged to become a group during the making of the 2010 series of *The X Factor*. (Ironically, One Direction finished only third in that contest, behind Matt Cardle and Rebecca Ferguson.) Whereas most of the British participants seemed to be doomed to live out their often fleeting fame within the limited parameters of Cowell's imagination, the American winners were groomed more expertly – and shared none of the 'manufactured star' stigma which afflicted their UK counterparts. The talent-show genre has since been extended by programmes such as *The Voice* and *Rising Star*, moving beyond music to cover dancing, diving and even gymnastics. But, as Cowell's biographer Tom Bower noted, 'The nature of stardom had changed. The aura, mystique and mythology which had enthralled fans for years had been ripped apart by mass exposure.'

Also damaged, perhaps beyond repair, was the notion of originality: the conviction that the most genuine performer was the one who did not sound like anybody else. Instead, all of these television contests expected their hopefuls to mimic the mannerisms and techniques of existing stars, and to reproduce the vocal tics which had come to symbolise emotional commitment.* The most pervasive role models were three of the most commercially successful singers in history: Whitney Houston, Celine Dion and Mariah Carey. Of these, the simplest, least mannered style was purveyed by Dion, a French Canadian discovered by manager René Angélil when she was 12. Dion's strengths are perfect pitch, and utter clarity of tone, which enable her to shift seamlessly from pop to torch songs to near-operatic ballads. She has become one of the world's most popular performers of all time, reaching into markets, such as China, which have previously been resistant to Western singers. Yet in the West she has frequently been criticised for the apparent lack of emotion in her voice, which (bar some tasteful vibrato) rarely slips into a forced rendering of 'soul'.

The same cannot be said for the singers moulded in the tradition of Houston or Carey. Houston has been credited, in her prime, with owning

---

* A bizarre side effect was the transformation of Leonard Cohen's subtle exploration of the thirst for sex and religion, 'Hallelujah', into a showcase for meaningless vocal pyrotechnics.

the most perfect soul voice of all time: endlessly flexible, flawless in its shifts of tone or register, equally at ease with a whisper or a scream. As with her male counterpart, Michael Bolton, however, her flaw was her inability to invest herself in her music. When Aretha Franklin sang, you could track every moment of pain or ecstasy in her life. With Houston, at least until her troubled private life began to take its toll, all the feeling seemed to start, and end, in her voice. Carey was marginally less showy, and more believable, despite the fact that her record label admitted: 'We look at her as a franchise.' But, as with Dion, there was a global market for this facsimile of passion: it's instructive that Houston's 'I Will Always Love You' and Dion's 'My Heart Will Go On' are not only each singer's most grandiose performance, but also by far their most successful. Aficionados of soul music might relish the vocal equivalent of the barest touch of the fingertip on the skin, sensuality expressed in the briefest of encounters. Countless millions prefer their gestures big and their voices bigger: a bear-hug rather than a fleeting caress.

Every successful singer has a sound; if a vocalist can't be imitated, they don't have a personality. From Crosby to Sinatra, Presley to Dylan, Michael Jackson to Madonna, popular music's icons have been copied and parodied in equal measure. But never before has a small cabal of singers, with similar range and tone, held such influence as today, when the wall-toppling vocal power and theatricality of Dion, Carey and Houston are imposed on the next generation as a *sine qua non*.

The most pervasive and damaging aspect of this almost totalitarian moulding of popular taste is the assumption that you can only express feeling with melisma – the technique of subjecting a single innocent syllable to a switchback ride. The longer the syllable is held, the more a performer carries it up and down and around and back, the more emotional and genuine the rendition is assumed to be. Gone are the Victorian days when the motto was: for each syllable, a note. Now every line of a song must be tortured this way, the melody forgotten in the desperate desire to showcase just how fluent and mobile and expressive one's voice is. A simple shrug of the shoulders in mid-phrase would convey more feeling; instead, singers are trained to replicate the false catch in the throat which began, deep in soul history, as an almost unconscious exclamation, and now conveys, in gaudy colours, the message: 'I could not be feeling this song more deeply.' And when everyone emotes at once, no one can be heard.

Yet this is also the era when almost every popular song has to be submitted to another, even more blatant adaptation of the human voice: Auto-Tune. What began as a sonic gimmick which gave Cher's 1998 global hit, 'Believe', a near-robotic atmosphere – the singer courageously burying her own unmistakable vocal signature, as if to highlight her romantic desperation – has become an all-pervasive tool, which lends every record an identical timbre. The Auto-Tune processor was envisaged as a method of pitch correction, 'bending' an errant note or line back into tune. As early as 1993, the folk singer Janis Ian was bemoaning the intervention of technological aids in the human business of making music: 'we correct pseudo-singers' pitch via synthesisers so fast that the listener never knows'. Several internationally famous acts were rumoured to owe their careers to the processor, which more recently has also been applied to live performance.*

Many performers have utilised Auto-Tune as a creative musical device, like Cher, not attempting to disguise its use. Madonna ('Music') and 3LW ('No More') were among the first to imitate her innovation. Exaggerated to the point of surrealism, it become a potent hip-hop tool on T-Pain's *Rappa Ternt Sanga* from 2005, followed by several Lil Wayne albums, and Kanye West's 2008 release, *808s and Heartbreak*. It has since been adopted as an automatic preference for any R&B-influenced pop single. This gives listening to any Top 40 station the sense that one has stumbled upon an alien culture, in which androids are attempting to rekindle memories of the long-extinct human race.

So this is the twenty-first century: vocalists are being trained to emote without emotion; or encouraged to sublimate their identity to a voice processor. Or, of course, they can rap. In addition, the melodic complexity of the popular song, at its pinnacle in the 1930s, and still apparent in the verse/chorus/middle structure of the 1950s and 60s, has been replaced by constant repetition of simple phrases – or, in the case of electronic dance music, by total deletion of melody, the old-fashioned tune giving way to rhythmic patterns, samples, and sequenced hooks.† If hip hop has elevated emotive

---

* It has long been a tradition for live albums to be overdubbed or sometimes even re-recorded in the studio, to disguise their sonic or artistic flaws. Now Auto-Tune is applied instead. For an example so blatant that it defies belief, compare any audience recording of the Beach Boys' 2012 reunion on YouTube with their utterly note-perfect performances on *Live – The 50th Anniversary Tour*. Songs such as 'Sail On Sailor' and 'Don't Back Down' suggest that the group had been replaced by automatons.

† One hesitates to imagine the feelings of a composer such as Jimmy Webb, arguably the most 'classic' and inventive practitioner of traditional values to emerge from the rock era.

speaking over singing, and pop has eliminated the potential for vocal personality, what is left? Only sonic invention, rhythm and, of course, always nostalgia. What's remarkable is that, beneath the sugar icing of global pop, mavericks of every hue have been able to manipulate these ingredients into genuinely enriching experiments in stylistic cross-pollination.

> Rock and roll is now the music of the land. Broadway, movies, TV commercials, *Miami Vice*. It's the music of America. It's certainly not the music of the alternative society.
> Concert promoter Bill Graham, 1985

> When Bono, at the Grammies, pledged to continue 'fucking up the mainstream', he didn't seem to appreciate: he *is* the mainstream, and it's as fucked up as you can get. So a few surviving grizzled old rockers totter round ever bigger stadiums with bigger lasers and bigger sound systems and the phoney rebellion seems even more fatuous . . . Rock 'n' roll is the new golf – it's something middle-aged square guys do at weekends in ridiculous clothes.
> Theatre critic Mark Steyn, 1997

In 1996, R.E.M. renewed their recording contract with Warner Brothers Records. Once the champions of independent, alternative, intelligent rock, the group were now operating inside the megalithic media conglomerate owned by Time Inc. Their deal was reported to be the most expensive in the history of the music business, its value quoted as $80 million, although the band disputed this. The aftermath was telling: R.E.M.'s sales went into steep decline.

Such disastrous business ventures were now the industry norm. Warners had already rewarded Prince, the most artistically adventurous performer of the 1980s, with a vastly improved contract in the early 1990s. He too suffered an immediate drop in record sales, and within three years was appearing in public with the word 'SLAVE' written across his face, reflecting his opinion of Warners' control over his release schedule. Numerous other artists were given equally lavish deals, just at the moment when their fortunes were slipping into reverse. Global corporations were slow to recognise that acts such as Paul McCartney and the Rolling Stones might be able to sell out stadium gigs for decades to come, at whatever ticket price they chose; but this did not mean that more than a tiny proportion of those concert-goers would be prepared to invest in their new music. McCartney's solo career has produced few more convincing albums than *Chaos and Creation in the Backyard* (2005), but its sales were barely visible alongside those of even his weakest efforts from earlier decades.

Here was a conundrum: the industry was regularly castigated in the 1980s and 90s for failing to invest in artists who might have long-term careers. But many of those who already enjoyed that status didn't sell records. Meanwhile, younger artists were robbed of the opportunity to grow into veterans. As early as 1987, Island Records boss Clive Banks lamented the short-term ethic of the music business: 'We've produced an upturned iceberg, with the image at the top and the talent out of sight at the bottom. The cost of marketing new talent now means that companies look for immediate returns. That makes it impossible for them to develop talent slowly. Instead they go for the quick kill with insubstantial singles that are heavily marketed.' The Simon Cowell business model epitomised this trend: it did not matter if the winners of his TV contests disappeared within months of their victory, as there was always another show looming in the schedule, with fresh bait for the willing public to bite.

While splashing around its multimillion-dollar deals, the record industry was searching for other media to blame for its vanishing profits. What's arresting, in retrospect, is how early that note was struck. In 1983, British music journalist Paul Rambali told *Rolling Stone* magazine: 'There was a time when music was much more pertinent to the culture. Records aren't selling as much, and people are spending more time playing video games, for instance. Generally, music doesn't play such an important part in people's lives. It's just got less to say about our lives.' With 'computer' gradually replacing 'video', exactly the same complaint could have been made at any point in the last thirty years. The more multidimensional and multifaceted the entertainment options for young people, the more modern the technology that carries them, the less appealing music becomes, unless it accompanies some other activity – voting for *The X Factor*, for instance, or stabbing one's thumbs at a Playstation controller.

In the 1960s and beyond, music had transported young people into a culture which they, and the musicians, were in the process of creating: an idealistic and even illusory culture, perhaps, but one which represented a refusal to participate in the world of their parents. Then those young people *became* their parents, and carried their cultural artefacts and heroes (now robbed of their political power) with them. Kim Thayil of the Seattle grunge band Soundgarden lacerated the arrogance of the baby-boomer generation: 'All the advertising has been directed at them since they were little kids . . . There's millions and millions of people in their 40s who think they're so fucking special. They're this ultimate white-bread, suburban, upper-middle-class group that were spoiled little fuckers as kids, 'cause they were all children of Dr Spock, and then they were stupid, stinky hippies and then they were spoiled little yuppie materialists . . . And we get *their* understanding of history. They're denying other age groups their own memories.' (In his 50s, Thayil was nevertheless touring with the reunited Soundgarden.)

Because popular music, and especially the ethos of rock culture, was so central to the baby-boomer generation, they assumed that it would always be so, just as those who grew up to the sound of the big bands imagined that there would always be Benny Goodman and Glenn Miller on the radio. For the children of the late twentieth and early twenty-first centuries, games have been as all-consuming as music was for their parents (or indeed grandparents). Belatedly acknowledging the fact, the record industry has attempted to collaborate with one of the media which has helped to make it redundant, offering exclusive soundtrack recordings, or even guest appearances by animated versions of the stars. The series of *Guitar Hero* games launched in 2005 focused on classic rock recordings, but – like TV talent shows – rewarded the ability to mimic other people, rather than display originality. (Unlike the plethora of karaoke games, *Guitar Hero* and its successors also rewarded its users for prowess at game-playing, not musical ability.)

Hip-hop artists were first and most enthusiastic in their co-operation with game manufacturers, Jermaine Dupri providing music for a best-selling American football game in 1999. 'We gotta always cross-promote, y'know?', he said. 'This could be like a stepping stone.' Cypress Hill offered beats and voice-overs to a Mafia-themed game in the same year. But their producer DJ Muggs sounded a warning. 'I started waking up every morning and playing games', he admitted. 'I had to stop fucking around. Them shits is like crack.' In the new century, music was rarely that addictive.

> Whoever put my shit on the Internet, I want to meet that
> motherfucker and beat the shit out of him . . . I think that anybody

who tries to make excuses for that shit is a fucking bitch . . . If I'm
putting my fucking heart and time into music, I expect to get
rewarded for that. I work hard, and anybody can just throw a
computer up and download my shit for free.
     Eminem, 2002

Music should be free, anyway.
     Prince, 1993

By 1997, Prince no longer existed, except in our collective memory. Four
years earlier, he had officially changed his name to an unpronounceable
squiggle, which merged the male and female gender symbols. As part of
what appeared to be a systematic campaign to sabotage the commercial
foundations of his career, he announced that in future his music would
only be sold via the Internet. Fans protested that his official website was
both impenetrable and unreliable, and that they had made credit card
payments for material which either didn't arrive, or was soon available at
much cheaper prices in conventional record stores.

     The following year, his lawyers sent out cease-and-desist orders to
numerous fans who had included his music on their websites. In 1999, he
widened his attack by trying to have both physical and web fanzines shut
down. In 2000, he resumed his Prince identity, continuing to restrict much of
his copious musical output to the Internet. In 2006, his online music store was
abruptly closed. In 2007, he allowed his new *Planet Earth* album to be given
away free, in CD form, to everyone who bought the *Mail on Sunday* newspaper. In 2010, he shut down another official website, telling the *Daily Mirror*:
'The Internet's completely over. I don't see why I should give my new music
to iTunes or anyone else . . . Anyway, all these computers and digital gadgets
are no good. They just fill your head with numbers, and that can't be good for
you.' Then in 2014, as if to prove the cyclical nature of history, Prince's lawyers
launched $1 million lawsuits against twenty-two people who had shared live
recordings of his work via their blogs and Facebook sites. 'Doing things like
this is making him lose more and more fans', one previously loyal supporter
wrote on a forum which the artist probably wanted to close down.

     Prince's ambivalent, contradictory attitude towards the industry,
his fans, and the life-altering impact of the Internet is a microcosm of a
prolonged and possibly terminal crisis within the music business. The same
word – 'digital' – which heralded an era of ballooning profitability for

record companies and artists alike now spells doom for the business model which prospered for a century. The process of transferring recorded sound on to a physical artefact, and then selling it to the public en masse, is effectively dead. Prince's dream and worst nightmare have both come true: for much of the population, much of the time, music is now a free commodity, available to anyone at the click of a mouse, a tablet or a mobile phone. As John Alderman, one of the first analysts to study the digital revolution, noted in 2001: 'Digital distribution means that music is no longer tied to an object such as a record, tape or CD, but [has] become, as it is being shared and consumed, something more ethereal. Depending on how you look at it, in the online world, music has been either stripped or liberated from its body; only its soul remains, its digital code.'

In his quasi-apocalyptic 1983 song 'Licence to Kill', Bob Dylan identified mankind's first step towards doom as being the moment that we dared to touch the surface of the moon. For the record industry, that step was the marketing of the CD. The music business had long preached against the evils of copying music illegally, but the process of transferring a vinyl or cassette recording on to tape entailed a noticeable loss of sound quality, ensuring that there would be no substitute for buying the original artefact. The digital make-up of CD sound ensured that it could be copied endlessly on to other digital media (recordable CDs, or CDRs; or digital tapes, DCCs or DATs) without any loss of sonic clarity or volume. The hundredth-generation copy should sound identical to the original source. Shortly before the introduction of the CD, the industry had launched a publicity campaign designed to tug at its consumers' consciences, with the message: 'Home taping is killing music'. Researchers discovered that the majority of home taping was actually done for the purchaser's own use – transferring a vinyl record to cassette so they could play it on a car stereo, for example. There was criticism of a crusade which treated customers like potential criminals.

CD exacerbated the problem, especially when home computers were fitted with CD drives, enabling the user to copy the contents of digital files. When CD sales were booming, as they did throughout most of the 1990s, the industry could overlook the potential consequences of unauthorised duplication. What few seem to have anticipated, despite years of warnings from in-house analysts, is that the introduction of the super-fast broadband connection to the World Wide Web would torpedo their business, the explosion occurring out of vision with a devastating after-shock.

Well into the 1990s, the Internet was regarded by most consumers as a haven for computer 'nerds'. Initial experiences with the dial-up connections which were standard until the beginning of this century did little to alter this opinion. When a song from Kate Bush's *The Red Shoes* was leaked on to the Internet before the album's release in 1993, there was annoyance but little alarm: few fans, it was believed, would be prepared to wait twenty or thirty minutes to download it on to their computers. That same year, Depeche Mode demonstrated their affiliation to modern technology by holding an interactive question-and-answer session with fans around the world. They imagined that as many as 50,000 people would be able to view and perhaps participate in the web-chat. Instead, the band's Internet server was out of action for more than an hour, and when the connection was established, fewer than 300 people managed to log in.

Depeche Mode were not alone in recognising the looming shape of the future, however. David Crosby and members of the Grateful Dead were early adopters of social media as members of Stewart Brand's online community, WELL. Bono envisaged a time when the band would place its multi-track recordings on game consoles, enabling fans to remix their music or create their own U2 videos. Todd Rundgren went a stage further, reinventing himself as TR-i. He issued a CD symbolically titled *No World Order*, with the intention that consumers should be able to reshape all the constituent parts of his songs into music of their own design. He even incorporated this principle of total democracy into his solo live shows of the early 1990s, inviting his audiences to augment his music as he performed.

Meanwhile, the industry proceeded as if the past was the perfect template for the future. Having profitably introduced the CD, it made numerous attempts between 1985 and 1995 to supersede it with a new vehicle for recorded music, which would require consumers to upgrade their equipment. After the CDV (compact disc video) failed to take off, a battle was staged between the DCC (digital compact cassette) and the MiniDisc, on the assumption that – as with the video duel between VHS and Beta – one or the other would emerge on top. Instead, the public showed no appetite for either format. Nor was there any demand for CD+, which offered additional content if it was inserted into a computer. In the years immediately before the boom in Internet access, the CD-ROM became a popular method of transporting a mass of audio-visual and textual material – encyclopaedias, for example, or multimedia ventures such as the Bob Dylan release *Highway 61 Interactive* (1995), which was part entertainment, part archive repository. But hopes that CD-ROM might become the standard carrier for music albums were quickly dashed. The only innovation which survived was the DVD, successor to the short-lived VCD (video compact disc) – itself the first attempt at a viable digital medium for films and television recordings. The DVD soon ousted the VHS tape with a speed reminiscent of the force with which vinyl had been vanquished by the CD.

The avid consumer's home might now be filled with stacks of outmoded methods of bringing music (with or without visual accompaniment) into the home. Far from offering an array of competing formats, the industry of the 1990s had only one product to offer, the CD – reminding old-timers of the period between the 1920s and the late 1940s, when the 78 rpm disc was effectively the sole medium for recorded sound.

In 1995, at the height of the music industry's doomed campaign to introduce new formats, a revolution was enacted, and power changed hands – without the rulers even noticing what had happened. That year, the Integrated Circuits arm of the German collective known as the Fraunhofer Society launched WinPlay3, an audio player which allowed computer users to play MP3s. These files compressed digital recordings so that they would occupy the minimum of space on a hard drive or floppy disc, and made it possible for music to be swapped, stolen or even sold without the necessity for a physical object to hold the sound. It was now that the flaw in the otherwise perfect design of the audio CD was revealed: it was being sold without any form of copy protection. Overnight, the MP3 shredded the century-old safeguards of copyright in musical recordings, forcing artists and/or record companies to pursue individual miscreants who had made music available online for others to download.

The launch of Napster in June 1999 increased the stakes a thousandfold. This was a peer-to-peer (P2P) operation which enabled its users to share their MP3 files with other customers. Napster's creative team claimed that they were not breaking copyright legislation, as they were not physically hosting music on their site. But that did not prevent the RIAA, the collective voice of the American record industry, from filing suit against Napster that year, or the metal band Metallica from obtaining the names of 335,000 people who had illegally (in their view) obtained their music via Napster. Metallica launched lawsuits against US colleges whose servers were hosting P2P, and threatened to extend their reach to the individuals on their list of miscreants.

Aware that something was happening that was both urgent and incomprehensible, other artists reacted in glorious confusion to the MP3 threat. Oasis, like Prince, confronted fan websites which offered even the briefest of free downloads. Meanwhile, their label, Creation Records, declared that they would make all their new singles available for free download via their website – until their parent company Sony instructed them otherwise. Tom Petty defied his record label, Warner Brothers, by posting his 1999 single 'Free Girl Now' as a free download for just two days, during which time 157,000 fans accepted his offer. The single did not reach the *Billboard* Hot 100, confirming the industry's worst fear: MP3s could eradicate record sales. Sony Music and the hip-hop label No Limit responded by selling downloads over the Internet. Meanwhile, the rappers Public Enemy removed the record label from the commercial relationship between artist and fan, by selling their new album, *There's a Poison Going On*, as a set of downloads from their own website. Here, it seemed, was the new shape of the industry. But the most radical transformation in the lives of artists, consumers and corporations was yet to come.

> With iTunes, it's not stealing anymore. It's good karma.
> Steve Jobs, 2003

> Not having a tangible item you can touch, just having it virtually – it's not the same as owning it, touching it, putting it on the turntable.
> Neil Sedaka, 2012

> It's possible the past 10 years could become the first decade of pop music to be remembered by history for its musical *technology* rather than the actual music itself.
> Eric Harvey, *Pitchfork*, 2009

The sign above the high-street store in my home town reads: 'Entertainment Exchange'. Inside, there are aisles and shelves stuffed with artefacts: DVDs, Blu-rays, games in formats that few over the age of 40 would recognise. Teenagers and young adults flick through the racks with a focused passion that I recognise from my own misspent youth in the numerous branches of the Record & Tape Exchange in West London. But one thing is missing from this updated picture: there is no music on sale in the twenty-first-century Exchange. As far as high-street retail is concerned, Music is no longer Entertainment.

Frisk their pockets, however, and those customers would almost certainly have been carrying smartphones, on which an iTunes app would give them instant access to their private stash of downloads; or a Spotify subscription might allow them to trawl through multiple millions of musical tracks dating back to the invention of recorded sound. Everything musical in the world is at their fingertips, but none of it is on their shelves. Is music central to their worlds, as it was to mine? It's certainly inescapable, piped through every café and restaurant, shopping centre and superstore; accompanying every movie and television programme; soundtracking adverts and trailers; dominating the immeasurable catalogue of YouTube videos; or trimmed to a few seconds of ringtone, a personal ID in a global web of messaging and banter.

This is the state of the music industry left by Steve Jobs, the remorseless entrepreneur who named his Apple empire after the Beatles' record company, and – after multiple legal battles – ended up owning trademarks that the Beatles had assumed were theirs. His death in October 2011 was greeted with the kind of tributes that might once have been directed at a rock star cut down in his prime. He was far from being the sole catalyst for the earthquake which has struck the entertainment landscape over the past fifteen years, but his company's impact on music was so far-reaching, and profound, that it is Jobs and his colleagues who have occupied the central place in our culture once taken by a Sinatra or a Presley, a Madonna or a Cobain.

At some point in the late twentieth or early twenty-first centuries – estimates vary – technology became sexier than the music it was invented to carry. The academic Michael Bull explained to author Leander Kahney: 'With vinyl, the aesthetic was in the cover of the record. You had the sleeve, the artwork, the liner notes. With the rise of digital, the aesthetic has left the object – the record sleeve – and now the aesthetic is in the artefact: the iPod, not the music.' That was in 2005; iPod sales began to decline in 2009, with the iPhone and its rivals picking up the slack; and by 2014 the iPod was declared extinct, eclipsed entirely by the smartphone revolution.

The link between the iPod, the iPhone and the iTunes music store – a searchable database of inestimably vast size, providing legal downloads within a couple of clicks – is Apple. The Beatles' company of that name was intended to reinvent consumer capitalism with a hippie slant. Steve Jobs's company not only succeeded where the Beatles failed (allowing for the fact that yesterday's hippies are now sometimes oligarchs), but permanently altered our outer and inner space.

iTunes was launched as a music library in 2001 with a slogan so suggestive of rock 'n' roll rhetoric that it could have been coined by Malcolm McLaren: 'Rip. Mix. Burn.' Its companion was the iPod: a tiny digital music player which became the iconic star of its era, its trademark white headphones visible on every street in the West. But the pair only flowered when Steve Jobs overcame the inertia and paranoia of the major record companies, and began to sell individual tracks via the iTunes Music Store. A million songs were sold within six days of the launch in April 2003; within three years, that figure had risen to 1 billion. During that period, iTunes not only saw off the music industry's own download stores, Pressplay and MusicNet, but also sent history roaring simultaneously forwards and into reverse. Each advancement in iPod and iTunes technology jerked the CD closer to its demise as the premier source of recorded source. That was the future: the past was evoked by Jobs's insistence that the iTunes store should be allowed to sell individual tracks, rather than complete albums. At a stroke, the purity of popular music's dominant art form for the previous three decades was destroyed. Many artists refused to allow their work to be decimated in this way, but as the industry tilted ever more violently in Apple's direction, each of them was forced to give way.

Apple's technological genius severed the link between music and artefact; it made music effortlessly transportable; and it encouraged every single user to create their own filtered world of sound. As iPod users strolled through city streets, apparently part of a community, their moods, actions and demeanours were being altered – some might say scripted – by their playlist, or the random 'shuffle' programme which transformed each device into a personalised radio station.

Other entrepreneurs offered an alternative to Apple's near totalitarian dominance of the digital music market. But when all you were buying was access to a digital file, why buy? The days when a vast LP or CD collection was a source of prestige (imaginary or otherwise) were past. Rapid advances in broadband Internet access, via mobile devices as well as static computers, ensured that purchasing (or indeed stealing) music files was no longer necessary. Indeed, both Radiohead (*In Rainbows*, 2007) and Nine Inch Nails (*The Slip*, 2008) enabled fans to download new albums without paying – although Radiohead did encourage them to contribute whatever they thought the music was worth. U2 gave their 2014 album *Songs of Innocence* to every user of iTunes for free, a novel form of corporate sponsorship for the band. (The scheme backfired when iTunes users around the world demanded that the company give them software to delete this unwanted intrusion upon their personal soundtrack.)

Even free files were soon insufficient enticement to persuade consumers that music was still something that needed to be owned. The boom in music-streaming services has enabled anyone who has down-loaded the appropriate software the chance to hear any piece of music they desire, from a choice measured in the tens of millions. The most prominent source of streaming is Spotify, accessible from computer, phone or tablet: subscribers can choose between a free service, with limitations to the amount of music you can hear, and random advertisements inserted between songs; or, for less than £10 per month, universal access, without the interruption of advertising. Dozens of competitors have been attempting to chip away at their dominance, some with a global span, others focused on specific geographical areas, such as Anghami and Ournia, both aimed at the Arab world.

Our choices in the post-artefact age don't end there. For many years, MySpace was not only the social media destination of choice for Western teenagers, but also a showcase for perhaps millions of musical performers, amateur and professional. As its users gravitated towards Facebook, music remained MySpace's primary focus: in 2014 it claimed the world's biggest digital music library, with 53 million songs and videos on offer. Or, of course, there is YouTube, a sprawling repository of video clips covering every imaginable subject and form, from the promo clips which would once have dominated the MTV playlist, to feature films and TV programmes (legally downloaded and otherwise). YouTube is also signalling another death knell to our understanding of how the entertain-ment industry functions. Much of its content is devoted to video clips made by individual users, the most successful of whom attract literally millions of viewers around the world, and are treated like superstars at YouTube showcases such as VidCon and Summer In The City. To the bafflement of music-industry pundits, today's teens and young adults have created icons out of (mostly) young men with acoustic guitars, offering pleasantly gentle covers of familiar hits, new and old: the opposite of the outrage we associate with rock, hip hop and the rest, but with a far more devastating result on the record business. Stardom is intact; but today's young consumers prefer to select their own stars, rather than meekly accepting those churned out by lumbering corporate giants.

This is how far we have come: from the days when families would give up a week's income to own a Red Seal 78 by Caruso, to open access to the entire history of recorded sound. For those of us who grew up owning a handful of records, replaying them endlessly until we had saved up enough pocket money to purchase another, today's children and teenagers seem like kids let loose in Hamleys' toy warehouse, with the freedom of taking everything home at the end of the day. But with this freedom has come a loss of perspective that can be both chilling and exhilarating. Beyond the handful of (usually) dance tunes in constant rotation on radio and in clubs, there are no signposts through the musical library of Babel. Everything exists outside history; nothing is connected; everything is equally valid (or not). The tastemakers of old, the critics and disc jockeys, have been rendered totally obsolete. But they cling on, catering to the diminishing proportion of music listeners who care about the validity of their choices. Most are happy to make their own way through the cluttered wilderness – restricted only by the fact that their choices are likely to be signalled, via one social-media connection or another, to the whole of their virtual milieu, for admiration or amusement.

There are pundits who believe that the death sentence for CDs was passed when record companies let them be given away free with magazines and newspapers. This signified that CDs were worthless; and – hey presto! – they were. But amidst the downloads and streaming and dazzling array of Internet radio options, some consumers remain faithful to their old love. In another decade, it's easy to imagine that the only viable CD releases will be expensively packaged, exhaustively curated archive collections from the vaults of Bob Dylan and his equally aged peers – until their admirers bow to senility at last, and their successors have to decide what to do with billions of utterly irrelevant, shiny, five-inch discs. Meanwhile, vinyl – condemned to death by the industry more than twenty years ago – has become the Red Seal 78 of the twenty-first century, conferring a reputation for good taste amongst its small but slowly growing coterie of admirers. Buying vinyl shows that you care – not only about the heritage of the medium, or the artwork, or the sound of vinyl itself, but about the notion of music as something to be cherished and valued.

Sound is a key issue: hasn't the history of recorded music been a constant search for clearer, bigger, brighter, more flawless, more thrilling sound? There were always diehards who mourned the loss of the 78 rpm single, in all its chunky *there*-ness, and despised the less visceral delivery of the 45 and the LP. Many felt the same when vinyl was replaced by cassette tapes, which tended to stretch and distort time and pitch; and CDs, which for all their sonic perfection had (especially in their fledgling years) a brittle, sharp, grating quality which seemed to cut into the eardrums and leave the senses in a strange state of enervation. One might dispute the result, but nobody could doubt that the aim of the CD was still a more ideal listening experience – free of surface noise, scratches, and the need to be regularly turning over the record. (Some of us still feel restless every twenty minutes, of course; the habits of one's youth are hard to shake.) But the digital age, for all its joyous ease of access, and brain-scrambling choice of pleasures, has also – so many believe – stymied the previously ceaseless quest for sound perfection.

As the first decade of the new century neared its close, increasing numbers of teenagers chose to access their music not via a CD player, or even an iPod, but from a mobile phone. They would congregate on street corners or the top decks of buses, blaring out a raucous, tinny sound almost indecipherable to adult ears as music, all of its bass sacrificed to piercing treble. This was music as a territorial marker, not an aesthetic obsession: it was a way of telling the outside world who you were, in the hope (usually fulfilled) that you would be met with sullen resentment from any adults unfortunate enough to stumble within earshot.

Via the headphones, big and small, which are essential accessories for people on the move in the twenty-first century, music's dynamic range faces a double process of compression – first by its conversion into digital files, then by the sonic failings of the equipment. The result is a pale facsimile of the sound that once issued from traditional loudspeakers.* Computers, cellphones, digital players: all of them condense the wave formation of an original recording, with its peaks of high and low, into a narrow band. If that is what you are used to (or your ears are failing with age), then you will happily accept this strangled sound. In the recent past, indeed, major record companies deliberately set out to create these aural monstrosities, during the

---

* The prevalence of headphones threatens to contribute to an epidemic of tinnitus amongst young people, already exacerbated by the crushing noise of many dance clubs and live gigs. According to a survey in 2006, 'listening at top volume [to headphones] for more than five minutes risks permanent damage'.

industry's so-called 'loudness wars'. Utilising the full dynamic range of soft and loud sound posed the danger that your song might be overshadowed by something with more consistent volume. Producers elected to make every recording appear to be equally loud. The palette of available sound was crushed into a mush of distortion, which was tiring to experience for more than a few minutes at a time. Here was music as blunt instrument; only a few steps removed from its use as an instrument of torture in twenty-first-century prison camps, where Islamic fundamentalists are exposed to cease-less hip hop or death metal at deafening volume, as part of Western culture's attempt to demonstrate its superiority even to the unbelievers.* 'These people haven't heard heavy metal', explained an American psy-ops officer to the BBC in 2007. 'They can't take it. If you play it for 24 hours, your brain and body start to slide, your train of thought slows down and your will is broken. That's when we come in and talk to them.'

This psychological torture is merely an extension of the society we have chosen for ourselves, in which popular music is almost inescapable. So the music of today – or, rather, music *in* today – is both a permanent soundtrack to our lives, and utterly disposable; a way for us to describe who we are, which we expect to access at will, but no longer believe we should pay for. That is why all complaints about musicians 'selling out' to corporate sponsorship or advertisers are so misguided: if we aren't prepared to pay artists (and writers, thank you) for their services, then how are they supposed to survive? We have arrived at the peculiar moment in history when people will queue all night in the rain to purchase a new phone; when 'cool' means carrying the latest technology, rather than an album cover bearing the faces of Jimi Hendrix or the Rolling Stones. But there is one medium in which music, and the notion of hipness, can still co-exist: one first imagined in the 1940s, which has now become a rite of passage for each fresh generation. In a world of technology designed to make solipsists of us all, music festivals turn us back, however briefly, into a community – enraptured once again, like our ancestors, by the euphoric catharsis of pleasure in which we

* Of course, those particular unbelievers – the most devout adherents of their faith – are often from societies which ban popular music entirely, as an instrument of the Devil, or the West, the two being more or less interchangeable. Ayatollah Khomeini first summoned Iran's pop stars to a revolutionary people's court in 1980, complaining that their music was 'opium'; likewise the Taliban in Afghanistan imposed a ban on all musical instruments. By 2005, all recordings or performances featuring the female voice were ruled illegal by Iranian religious courts.

can lose our identity and become as one. The most successful music of the twenty-first century has been designed to renew that feeling in each of our lives – our solitary lives, separate and yet eternally connected to our peers via the addictive ties of so-called social media.

⚡

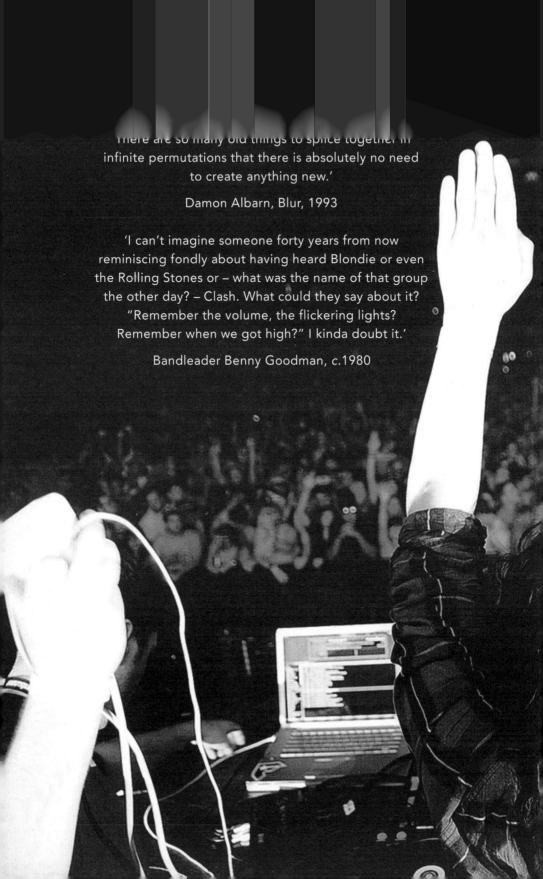

There are so many old things to splice together in infinite permutations that there is absolutely no need to create anything new.'

Damon Albarn, Blur, 1993

'I can't imagine someone forty years from now reminiscing fondly about having heard Blondie or even the Rolling Stones or – what was the name of that group the other day? – Clash. What could they say about it? "Remember the volume, the flickering lights? Remember when we got high?" I kinda doubt it.'

Bandleader Benny Goodman, c.1980

CHAPTER 30

BLURRED
LINES

Comedy, food, art, social science, reading, history, TV, spirituality – even musical genres, such as country, hip hop, folk – all share one distinction. They have been the subject of one of the most jaded neologisms of the past two decades, by being described as 'the new rock 'n' roll'. Implicit in all these comparisons is the sense that the old rock 'n' roll – the one that emerged out of the rhythm and blues scene of the mid-1940s, and became an all-conquering global culture – is dead, or dying, or irrelevant, or in some way stripped of its significance and power. Or it suggests something more insidious: that rock remains a potent idea, a concept that can rouse individuals and crowds into a state of Pavlovian excitement – but not when it is combined with rock music. As an exhibit for the prosecution, consider the potency of a brand named Rockstar, and its connotations of glamour, dominance, success. The brand in question has earned all those qualities, but Rockstar has no connection with music or musicians: it's one of the world's premier publishers and developers of games for PlayStation and Xbox. Most notably, it's the creator of *Grand Theft Auto*, a series that has revolutionised the marketing of action games. There is music in *GTA* (and cameo voice-overs from famous musicians) but it's incidental to the action: the star of Rockstar is the player, not the rock or the rock stars.*

Should we be mourning the death of rock 'n' roll? Some would say that we are nearly sixty years too late. Elvis Presley's first major hit, 'Heartbreak Hotel', was released in January 1956. By May, America's music trade papers were full of concern that rock 'n' roll was growing stale or losing its bite. By September, the *Daily Mirror* in London could suggest that 'Rock 'n' roll is out of date – old-fashioned as aspidistras.' Thereafter rock 'n' roll's demise was predicted or reported on an almost weekly basis. No wonder that defiant young songwriters penned anthems such as 'Rock and Roll is Here to Stay' and 'It Will Stand'. They emerged from an era when rock's prime movers had been conscripted or imprisoned or disgraced or even lost their lives. 'Elvis died when he went in the army', John Lennon

---

* Rockstar also invented a game called *Wild Metal Country*, which had nothing to do with either heavy metal or country music.

famously quipped, and many assumed that rock had died with him.
Aficionados of the original rock 'n' rollers thought that the Beatles had
killed their music; the Beatles thought that they were bringing it back to
life. Since then, rock has supposedly been killed by disco, punk, synthesisers, hip hop and dance music; or mortally wounded by commercialism,
corporate sponsorship, political compromise and the Internet (which has
been allotted the blame for almost every social change of the past two
decades).

Yet sixty years after rock 'n' roll became a commercial force, there
is no more reliable means of attracting vast hordes of people to stand or
camp in muddy fields at the cost of enormous personal discomfort and the
best part of a week's wages than to promote a rock festival – the bigger and
more established, the better. Demand for tickets at events such as the
annual pilgrimage to Michael Eavis's farm in Glastonbury has never been
higher, and audiences can now conceivably stretch from toddlers to their
great-grandparents without fear of ostracism or social embarrassment. As
Mick Jagger first noticed in the 1970s, rock 'n' roll 'perpetuates your
adolescence, for good or bad'. Back then, he was mildly embarrassed by
his ability, as a privileged rock star, to extend his teenage habits into adulthood, whilst most of his peers were preoccupied with career, family and
paying the bills. Now Jagger is himself a grandfather, still indulging his
18-year-old self, and his fantasy of adolescence remains a beacon to generations of concert-goers, for whom the Rolling Stones' continued existence
offers an escape from the terrifying reality of a planet bent on its own
ecological destruction.

There is a profound moment in any adult's life when they find
themselves no longer identifying with the young, but with the old – not
with the 17-year-old novice thrown on to the pitch at a moment of crisis,
but with the grizzled veteran who straps on his boots and drags his aching
knees round the park for a final hoorah. There are similar landmarks in
one's appreciation of rock 'n' roll: the first time you realise you're older than
a favourite new band; ultimately, the day when it dawns on you that your
original rock heroes are now older than your grandparents used to be when
you were a teenager. Rock once divided the generations; now it unites
them. That's why veteran rock stars are routinely employed to provide the
entertainment at events which are intended to command an all-age audience: the Superbowl, the Olympics, royal anniversaries. Their presence
does not connote any of the rebellion or subversion which their music

might originally have expressed: they are as tame and familiar as the Queen, or any of the elderly icons from our collective past.

Music has an almost unrivalled power to bypass logical thought and retrieve the past. The opening bars of (depending on one's vintage) 'Take the "A" Train' or 'Tennessee Waltz' or 'Don't Be Cruel' or 'She Loves You' or 'Whole Lotta Love' or 'White Riot' or 'Like a Virgin' or 'Wannabe' can carry us back, whole and unimpaired, to the time when we, and they, were new. That ability to rekindle our distant past is what gives popular music its unique hold on our emotions – its almost sinister power to trigger nostalgia, even if the times we remember were not as joyous as our feelings pretend.

Any music can carry this burden and unlock these sometimes false memories. But the cultural baggage of rock – its longevity and power, which are preserved by a vast industry devoted to their eternal care – marks it out from all of its predecessors in the history of popular music. Other genres and styles have held sway over a single generation, and then faded gently into cultural insignificance. Rock, in the widest sense of the term, is different: it has not only kept hold of its original followers, but swept each new generation on to (or under) the bandwagon. In the late 1930s and 40s, swing music was as dominant in the musical lives of young people as rock would be in subsequent decades. But when swing was superseded, only curious scholars of cultural history were added to its fan base, until decades later swing (like boot-scooting country music, and salsa) re-emerged as the soundtrack for dance classes. As music, swing belonged to its generation, and no other. Rock has been bequeathed to – or imposed upon – every single generation which has surfaced in its wake.

The consequences have been startling, and sometimes surreal. Rock was born as the music of youth, its lyrical content stretching no further than the pangs and passions of adolescent romance, and the rebellion of teenage hormones. Bob Dylan and his imitators added extra dimensions to rock's world, to the point where it became the vehicle for political protest and social satire, self-expression and self-questioning, confusion, turmoil and exhilaration. Throughout its history, however, rock expressed youth in preference to adulthood, even as its practitioners aged in front of their generation-spanning audiences. Those songwriters who first widened rock's horizons in the 1960s have tentatively explored the ramifications of the ageing process – their youthful optimism paled by the imminence of death or the shadow of major illness. But few of their listeners want to be serenaded with tales of reduced mobility, sexual impotence or failing mental powers. Only Leonard Cohen, by treating age as some sort of cosmic joke, has consistently managed to extend his creative range with an unflinching eye for the ravages of time. Beyond that, the middle-aged-to-elderly rock audience has to cling to a handful of messages from the edge of the grave, such as David Crosby's 'Time is the Final Currency' (from a man who has been flirting with death for decades), Tom Ovans's sobering 'Last Day on Earth' and Bob Dylan's *Time Out of Mind* album. 'Nobody's done a death album yet, or an album about death', Marvin Gaye mused in 1976. 'That's something I wouldn't mind doing.' Maybe the opportunity was missed when Frank Sinatra chose to devote his final years to a gentle reminder of past glories, instead of the searing song cycle about senility which perhaps only he had the stature to carry off.

Yet anyone witnessing rock's statesmen dealing with their advancing years has to face their own inescapable passage towards the darkness. For every act which still pretends to live outside time (the Beach Boys singing 'Be True to Your School' in their late 60s), there is another making no effort to hide the passing of youth (Bob Dylan growling like the 80-year-old bluesman he'd wanted to resemble when he was 21). Rock stars can don wigs or wear hats to conceal their hair loss, and use plastic surgery or Botox to retain their youthful appearance. But only those who have protected and mollycoddled their voices for decades can hope to persuade their fans that they are what they used to be. In middle age, singers lose their top range, then their flexibility, then their power. By the time that someone like Chuck Berry has to be helped on stage in his mid-80s, effectively unable any longer to sing or play guitar, one is left to wonder whether one is watching dignity, exploitation, or a chilling combination of the two. What we're cheering when we see men and women performing in their 70s and 80s is their survival – and, even more, our own.

Rock can't exist as an entertainment genre on those veterans alone. Yet their shadow hangs over everyone struggling to make a living within its borders. Every art form has a limited lifespan, and a moment where it will simply not allow for any further experimentation or novelty. That is the point where it has to invite fresh influence from outside, or abandon itself to self-parody and imitation. What has helped to keep the concept of rock alive, and potent, is that it is fuelled by youthful energy and dissidence. Each influx of musicians can return as new to ideas and sounds that their elders regard as clichés, simply because, for them, they *are* new. That's why a band such as 5 Seconds of Summer can reboot the apparently exhausted system of punk ebullience, as if the Clash, Nirvana and Green Day had never existed. Likewise the nu-metal explosion of the early 2000s, extending the tradition from Black Sabbath to Korn; while emo artists could offer modern teenage misfits a soundtrack, just as the Smiths and the goth tradition had done. The most static, endlessly renewed rock genre of recent decades has been the indie guitar band: a long succession of uniform outfits (two guitars, bass, drums) with identical appearance and influences have been set up by the shrinking rock press as this week's saviours of music. It doesn't matter whether their careers survive this initial exposure. All that counts is the fantasy that, week after week, rock is new and exciting, rather than repetitive and monotone. Novelty, such as it is, comes less from the music than from the lyrical perspective of a band such as Underoath, whose punk rock was fired not by juvenile delinquency, but by their righteous faith in the Christian gospel.

All this might spell death to anyone who staked their identity on the existence of rock music as a cultural force. Few take that idea seriously in 2015, when the prime – perhaps sole – purpose of rock (and pop) is to entertain. It is of no account that every review of a young artist necessarily has to spell out which particular segments of rock history they are reviving, consciously or otherwise. The vital ingredient is connection with the audience: the ability to conjure up songs that sound like anthems, which offer the opportunity to congregate in joyous union.

Imagine that you were imprisoned in the total cultural isolation of solitary confinement in 1995, and then released blinking into the daylight of 2015. As a brutal form of rehabilitation, your social workers take you to a rock festival, where many of the leading lights of the past decade are performing. Let's conceive a bill comprising Coldplay, Adele, Mumford & Sons, Ed Sheeran, Paolo Nutini, the Kings of Leon, Jake Bugg and the Arctic Monkeys. How many of those acts would leave you reeling with incomprehension, unable to grasp exactly which planet they had come from, and what they were trying to achieve? My guess is that you would be able to understand and describe them all by reference to the music you had heard before your exile – strange faces, reassuringly familiar sounds.

Elsewhere at the same festival, however, on other stages, you might find the setting and its soundtrack more disturbing or surreal. That is where you would find the acts who have pursued novelty in the shape of constant cross-fertilisation of different musical traditions, scouring the continents in search of fresh blood for rock's tired veins, and where you witness tens of thousands of people leaping about in exhilaration in front of performers whose only role is to push buttons on a machine, and wave their arms in the air.

> [The 1990s were] full of music that was sold and praised on the basis that there's something inherently thrilling about genres swapping spit down at the indie disco . . . These days, genre-blending is again just part of the landscape. Eleven years ago, Radiohead's two-footed lunge into intelligent dance music on *Kid A* had critics gasping at their boldness. Now they cross-pollinate their sound with dubstep or Afrobeat and receive a polite nod or a muffled yawn . . . From the xx through Janelle Monae to Animal Collective, almost every acclaimed act works towards forging a sound by taking cues from a mass of other styles. Hybridisation is a basic tenet of art-pop.
> Tom Ewing, *The Guardian*, 2011

Fusion was once a matter of simple arithmetic: country plus rock equals country rock; Latin plus soul equals Latin soul. These basic combinations were easy to grasp, but could offer musicians a new world of possibilities, and allow, for example, the country-rock experiments of the 1960s to fuel the fifty-year tradition now known as Americana. 'Fusion' itself was applied to the amalgamation of jazz principles with a variety of popular forms in the late 1960s and early 1970s, from psychedelic rock to progressive rock to every imaginable form of funk.

The fusion of recent decades has involved more complex equations, and a limitless array of stylistic and rhythmic variations. Some genres, such as country, metal and punk, prefer their practitioners not to stray too far off the path. But musicians such as Elvis Costello, David Byrne, Damon Albarn and Beck have based their careers on a refusal to be restrained. Meanwhile, increased migration around the globe has brought ever more diverse communities into social and artistic contact. This has encouraged endless experimentation, a constant mingling of musical genes. But it has also created a form of global pop, with the same rhythms being heard in territories that would once have owned utterly distinctive musical traditions. Almost every nation on earth seems to share the same jukebox. You could enter a bar in London, New York, Rio de Janeiro, Moscow, Hong Kong, Cape Town or Lagos and expect to hear Lady Gaga or Miley Cyrus, Pharrell or Beyoncé. Indeed, in 2012–13 it seemed as if every person on the planet was dancing to one song: 'Gangnam Style' by the South Korean pop star Psy. Via YouTube alone, there had been approximately 2.5 billion views of his video by 2014 – a number which equates to one in three of the entire global population. Its success removed any boundaries between the dance-pop that dominated the Anglo-American charts and the K-Pop and J-Pop traditions of Korea and Japan. Twenty-first-century pop could come from anywhere, and aim to please anyone.

Fifty years ago, British or American performers could only hope to conquer territories overseas if they too spoke English. To delve any further into the global community, they had to target specific audiences – French, German, Italian – with songs translated into those languages. Even the Beatles and the Rolling Stones were required to make this concession, although it was the unstoppable momentum of their success which prevented subsequent rock performers from having to follow suit. In the twenty-first century, global media corporations, and the all-access arena of the Internet, have enabled the products of America's film and music factories to be exposed and distributed almost simultaneously around the planet. The position of the United States as the wounded but still dominant financial superpower also confers on it the right to shape the entertainment of every continent. Rather than forcing its stars to reflect distant cultural traditions, America simply sells a polyrhythmic brand of danceable pop which makes sense in every culture.

Local shifts in racial demographics have contributed greatly to this redrawing of cultural identities. In Britain alone, the acceptance of reggae and its offshoots as part of our national diet is testament to the impact of West Indian immigration since the late 1940s. The influx of families from the Indian subcontinent had a less immediate effect on our popular music, until bhangra filtered out of the Sikh community in the late 1970s, acquired a persistent disco rhythm, and began to toy with Western instruments. Unlike reggae, however, bhangra developed an almost entirely independent system of record distribution and concert promotion. Only posters in shop windows or on London Tube stations would alert the non-Asian population to the existence of acts such as Heera Group UK – or to the vast ethnic audience drawn to concerts by visiting stars of so-called Bollywood cinema, whose names would not be recognised beyond those with Asian roots. In the national media, more attention was paid to artists who stepped into the Western arena, such as Sheila Chandra, Apache Indian and Fun-da-mental.

Similar trends could be documented around the world. But the most significant intervention into global popular music has come from the explosion of Latin pop in the United States and beyond. The journalist and author Robert Morales noted sceptically, if accurately, in 1999: 'Latin culture gets recycled as an American fad every decade: Ricky Ricardo, the mambo, disco, *Miami Vice*, Julio Iglesias, Menudo and the Macarena.' What distinguished the Latino influence on American culture in the late 1990s, and enabled it to survive, was the population statistic which says that those of Hispanic origin already outnumber Caucasians in the state of California, with Texas likely to follow suit. Latin culture is no longer a foreign novelty, but a major element in the American life-blood. As a result, Gloria Estefan, Ricky Martin, Marc Anthony, Jennifer Lopez and Enrique Iglesias have become stars not just amongst Spanish-speaking communities but across the whole United States – and hence around the world.

Yet the blurring of lines between Latin American and American cultures has had consequences beyond the political debate about the fate of the 10 million or more 'illegals' who have come north from Mexico to settle in the United States. On either side of the border, the Spanish-speaking community is enthralled by the *narcocorridos*, or drug ballads: a Hispanic equivalent to gangsta rap, perhaps, except that these songs chronicle and celebrate real-life outlaws, not the mostly fictional protagonists of hip hop's murder sagas. Many record stores of northern Mexico and Southern California are filled with CDs of what sounds no more dangerous than folk music, accompanied by guitars, accordions and tubas. But, as author Ioan Grillo discovered, these Mexican ballads were tales of 'prison escapes, massacres, new alliances and broken pacts' – bulletins from the front line of the drug wars. What isolated them from other forms of popular music was that, like classical pieces in the eighteenth century, they were written to commission (from murderers and smugglers, rather than noblemen and clerics). Balladeers could earn as much as $10,000–15,000 for a song which celebrated the exploits of a Mexican godfather, or the heroics of an imprisoned outlaw. The *narcocorridos* were banned from radio play on both sides of the border, but sold in enormous quantities. There were even videos to promote them, such as the all-star clip for Movimiento Alterado's

'Sanguinarios del M1' – a Tex-Mex tune in which the customary accordion was augmented by rattling percussion designed to denote gunshots.

The *narcocorridos* can be talked away as a cultural phenomenon no more injurious, ultimately, than the American tradition which connects gangsta rap to so-called blaxploitation movies, and cherishes cowboy ballads celebrating the killers of the Wild West. Transplanted across cultures, however, music can be employed for more chilling purposes. The ethnic warfare which ripped apart the African country of Rwanda in 1994 – Hutus butchering hundreds of thousands of Tutsis, plus any of their own tribe who were reluctant to join in the killing – was stoked by radio station RTLM. Its schedule was packed with material by Simon Bikindi, a Rwandan singer-songwriter whose work was not just patriotic, but sometimes incited violence. Bikindi claimed that 'Nanga Abahutu' ('I Hate That Hutu') was a song of reconciliation, but it was widely interpreted as a call to penalise those who failed to lend their support to the ethnic cleansing. He was ultimately tried and convicted as a war criminal, for his speeches rather than his songs. But the most disturbing aural evidence is provided by the surviving tapes of RTLM propaganda broadcasts. While announcers chanted slogans of tribal hatred, the station played the song which had become synonymous with this incitement to kill: 'Now That We've Found Love', a playful, benign tune by the American rap artists Heavy D & the Boyz. Gangsta rap suddenly seemed tame and parochial by comparison. But as hip hop became a global language rather than an African-American art form, such crossed wires and indistinct lines were increasingly inevitable.

> *MTV Jams* has made R&B acceptable to mainstream white America . . . white kids don't have to seek out the new R&B because it's right there in their living rooms. It is, arguably, their culture too.
> Bill Bellamy, host of *MTV Jams*, 1993

> Eminem raps like a girl, man . . . I just don't like that squeaky little voice . . . He sounds like a little wimpy girl, you know? His stuff is OK, but it's meaningless. The words are meaningless. Slim Shady? Who cares?
> Vanilla Ice, 1999

Rap history repeated itself around the world. In 1995, Kool Shen and Joey Starr were arrested for insulting police at a rally against France's right-wing party, the Front National. The pair comprise the hip-hop duo NTM, an abbreviation for a French slang expression which translates as 'fuck your mother'. Their crime was to stand on stage in Toulon and shout 'Fuck the police', which was interpreted by officers as inciting violence. For 'NTM' read 'NWA', and it could have been Compton in 1988, where California cops refused to provide security for concerts by the group responsible for 'Fuck Tha Police'.

In South Africa, where so few black citizens had access to broad-band that rap was transmitted by cellphone rather than the Internet, POC (Prophets of da City) were banned from national TV because station managers feared their music embodied 'a spirit of violence'. It was only when their video 'Understand Where I'm Coming From' received a pres-tigious award in France that the SABC withdrew its censorship. The rap collective had already received unwelcome attention from the government for an earlier recording, 'Ons Stem', which satirised the Afrikaner national anthem. Lest one imagine that South African hip hop was a bastion of righteous anti-authoritarianism, however, less progressive trends were entering the scene by the late 1990s: overtly sexist lyrics, discounting the crime of rape; and potentially lethal rivalry between crews and rappers, which stoked all-too-recent memories of the split between East and West Coast affiliations in the United States.

As the African-American writer Farai Chideya noted in 1997, 'Many African youths are looking to America to find ways to express their own hopes, fears and frustrations. American pop culture has always been global pop culture, so it's only natural that black Africans would identify with black American artists.' That pattern was repeated around the world – in Cuba, Japan, New Zealand, throughout Asia, Africa, Europe and South America. Wherever young people identified themselves as being in opposition to authority, hip hop and heavy metal provided outlets for outrage, anger and rebellion.

The African-American hip-hop community willingly accepted this global tribute to the potency of their home-grown culture: the tradi-tions of the South Bronx now spanned the globe. But white performers proved to be more difficult to assimilate. Black America had been strug-gling to hold on to its own traditions since records as white (and bland) as Paul & Paula's 'Hey Paula' had topped the *Billboard* R&B charts in 1963.

In 1969, R&B gave way to Soul; in 1982, soon after the white duo Hall & Oates had reached No. 1 on that listing, it was renamed the Black Singles Chart. That didn't exclude the likes of George Michael and Lisa Stansfield, the latter achieving three No. 1 Black hits. Hip hop remained a defiantly black culture, however, until 1990, when Vanilla Ice was dubbed the 'Elvis of rap' (a barbed compliment indeed). His performance on 'Ice Ice Baby', hinged around a sample from David Bowie's collaboration with Queen, 'Under Pressure', should perhaps have earned him the title of 'the Pat Boone of rap', but its novelty value carried it to No.1 on the US Pop charts. He was quickly followed by his Hispanic equivalent, Gerardo, with 'Rico Suave'. But there was no 1956-style takeover of this black tradition: Vanilla Ice was soon forgotten.

Hip hop may have remained black, but its audience demographic expanded through the early 1990s. By 1994, approximately half of the US Hot 100 was filled with records which bore at least some allegiance to the rap tradition. Nobody could now pretend that this was a style which appealed to black listeners alone. Inevitably white hip-hop fans wanted to participate in this culture, in a more public arena than their bedrooms. As the decade unfolded, an increasing number of white rappers began to surface: Everlast and Danny Boy, alias the House of Pain; Kid Rock; and most visible and controversial of them all, Marshall Mathers.

He emerged from a Detroit trailer park in a predominantly black neighbourhood, grew up rapping with and against black performers in local clubs, and was taken under the wing of Dr Dre. Like most of his counterparts, Mathers adopted a pseudonym, Eminem; then added a further layer of mystery and obfuscation by giving Eminem an alter ego, Slim Shady. These identities rivalled for his soul, and allowed Mathers to treat his past and private life as fuel for violently misogynistic verbal fantasies about his wife and his mother (besides gratuitous slaps in the face for his fellow celebrities and friends). If the rap form already encouraged hyperbole, Eminem simultaneously carried it into the realms of tabloid trash and experimental fiction.

No strategy could have been better designed to unsettle friends and foes alike, and leave everyone questioning his motives. One 18-year-old white fan told *Vibe* magazine: 'I love Eminem, but I don't love hip hip. He's so original. And so cute.' But like the Beastie Boys more than a decade earlier, Eminem created a door for generations of white listeners to enter the world of hip hop (and also put his money and name behind his struggling black friends). He was not alone: the boy band N Sync tackled rap music with such authenticity that Baby Gerry, from the black collective Full Force, publicly congratulated Justin Timberlake on his skills as a human beatbox.

The word now was 'crossover': no longer a sin, but – especially in a failing industry – every performer and executive's dream. Hip hop was so inescapable in contemporary music by the start of the new century that it became customary for every 'urban' (a euphemism for what the British industry calls 'Music of Black Origin') record to feature a cameo appearance by a rapper. Mariah Carey, for whom crossover was as natural as breathing, was the first major star to demonstrate the commercial potency of these collaborations, when she allowed mid-1990s singles such as 'Fantasy' and 'Honey' to be remixed with raps by the likes of Ol' Dirty Bastard and Mase. Soon hip hop grew so powerful that it was the R&B singers who guested on rap records, rather than vice versa. 'Can one artist or group hold people's attention for 3.5 minutes,' asked *Vibe* in 1995, 'or does everybody always have to be guesting in everybody else's videos?' The question was answered in the twenty-first-century, when the key words in the credits for any R&B or rap single were not the artist's name, but the identities of those listed as 'featuring' or 'with' in the small print.

Those who had staked their life on the purity of grunge in the early 1990s were appalled when superior fashion brands such as Ralph Lauren began to introduce designer plaid shirts, so that every Wall Street trader could look like Kurt Cobain at the weekend. The exploitation was only just beginning. Within a matter of months, Sears department stores launched an Urban Images line, modelled on the dress codes of the hip-hop community. Cue more outrage: except that, unlike its more hypocritical rock cousin, hip hop had never disguised its preoccupation with money and designer goods, all of which registered its escape from the ghetto and its triumph over racial stereotypes.

By 2000, brands such as Enyce and Rocawear had established themselves as major players on the fashion scene. More significant than the predominance of urban streetwear across the racial divide, and on the global stage, was the emergence of individual rappers as entrepreneurs – those two imprints having been launched by Puff Daddy and Jay-Z respectively. Whereas their rock 'n' roll counterparts had invested their riches in drugs, fast women, divorce lawyers, sports cars and, only then, real estate, the superstars of hip hop quickly established themselves as capitalists without restraint. In 2014, *The Guardian* estimated that Puff Daddy – who now prefers to be known as P. Diddy – had amassed a $700 million fortune, only a small proportion of which could be credited to his musical exploits.

Nobody exemplifies the new business dynamic in hip hop more vividly than Dr Dre. Once a Nigga With Attitude, then the pioneer of gangsta rap and bass-heavy production techniques, Andre Young is now a billionaire, thanks to the purchase by Apple of the Beats electronics corporation he formed with producer and label boss Jimmy Iovine. Dre's aim was simply to expand his urban fashion lines; Iovine suggested that there might be more money in designer headphones. Where once it was fashionable only to sport the discreet white earplugs of Apple's iPhone, Beats turned headphones into the kind of status symbol that sneakers had been twenty years before – the larger and more noticeable the better (and never mind the sound quality, which in Beats' case has often been criticised).

With its icons now among the highest-earning businessmen on the planet, it is no wonder that hip-hop culture became increasingly obsessed with wealth and its conspicuous consumption. Raps that would once have chronicled ghetto shoot-outs descended into vehicles for product placement; likewise their videos, which could not have been any more arrogant and (in every sense of the word) exclusive had they been produced by potentates and princes. Inherent to this sense of ownership – of a milieu in which a man was judged by his purchases and belongings, not his actions or words – was the belief that women, young, near-naked and bootylicious (to borrow a song title from Destiny's Child), were simply one more category of object, to be abused or disposed of with the same impunity as a horse's head in a mafia movie.

In the twenty-first century, it was easy – indeed, almost inevitable, if your body held a progressive bone – to decry the innate sexism of mainstream, macho, bling-obsessed hip hop, and to mourn the gradual triumph of that attitude in the wider urban spectrum. Nothing illustrated this trend more brazenly than the 2013 success of 'Blurred Lines', a collaboration between Robin Thicke and the ubiquitous (in 2013) Pharrell. The song, which featured a particularly inflammatory guest rap from T.I., was widely interpreted as encouraging or condoning the act of rape – the supposedly blurred lines being those that divided consent from sexual abuse. The fact that the song was released in the aftermath of the revelations of systematic, lifelong abuse of children and adolescents by the disc jockey Jimmy Savile merely heightened the controversy. The furore spread to include the gratuitous display of naked female bodies in urban and hip-hop videos; and their influence on the brazen sexualisation of women in modern society, with pernicious effects on precisely those age groups targeted by Savile and other offenders in the entertainment industry. All of these strands and concerns coincided in August 2013, when the 20-year-old former child star Miley Cyrus 'twerked' provocatively in front of a worldwide TV audience at the Video Music Awards, while Robin Thicke (inevitably) 'popped up like some kind of sex-pest Zelig', in Dorian Lynskey's words.

Here was food for a thousand sociological theses.* Aged 18, pop starlet Christina Aguilera had declared 'It's important to me to be a positive role model. Parading around in a bra and a pair of hot pants will not inspire confidence in other girls. That would just make me one more person pushing them to feel like they have to be something they're not.' Aged 21, and promoting her album *Stripped*, Aguilera offered herself to early-evening television viewers on the BBC's *Top of the Pops* as the exact antithesis of her earlier promise. Was the choice to sexualise her image entirely hers, did it come from her handlers, or was it an almost inescapable option in a society which demands that its young women offer themselves as fantasy objects of male desire?

For all the erotic deification of a talented urban singer such as Usher, however, many fans still responded with an almost stunning innocence, as if social attitudes had not changed since the era of Patti Page and Doris Day. One 15-year-old Usher fan told a journalist: 'People always ask me if he's a virgin. I don't know. They ask me if he's bisexual. I don't know. I don't care.' His virginity was obviously an ideal for this girl, raised in a religious society, but she was prepared to love him even if he had sinned. How would she react if they ever met? 'I would treat him like a regular person. I would take him shopping. I would buy him a friendship bracelet.' No blurred lines there: merely the same infatuation which young women have indulged for male pop stars since the heyday of Rudy Vallee and Bing Crosby. This was either a refreshing antidote to the sexual obsessions of modern popular music; or a sad reflection of girls' willingness to build their dreams around impossible,

---

* And here is a question for those students to debate: was the media preoccupation with sexual imagery in urban and hip-hop songs a reflection of the exploitative nature of those genres? Or was it influenced by the age-old white fear of black male sexuality?

fictional ideals; or perhaps both. One conclusion is inescapable: without teenage sexuality, there would be no teenage pop; without teenage pop, no arena in which to explore teenage sexuality. Pop has always been the antithesis of sexual repression; and often the embodiment of sexual exploitation.

> Rock has to absorb other rhythmic forms, because the underlying rhythms of music change with fashion, and people like to move differently now than they moved thirty years ago.
>   Mick Jagger, 1995

> In America now, Skrillex is the biggest thing since Nirvana. You're witnessing a whole new cultural revolution.
>   Dance-music promoter Drew Best, 2012

> Huge chunks [of the Top 40] cleave to roughly the same musical template . . . There will be a 4/4 house beat. There will be a euphoric, hands-in-the-air breakdown similar to those found on early 1990s rave tracks. There will be Auto-Tuned vocals. There will be a moment where the vocal goes 'woah-oh-woah' (or similar) in the stadium-rousing style of Coldplay . . . Representatives of genres that used to be identifiably different from each other – pop, hip hop, R&B – currently make singles that sound largely indistinguishable.
>   Alexis Petridis, *The Guardian*, 2012

In a world of instant global communication, where there is no underground beyond the so-called 'dark net', the only way to maintain elitism, the preoccupation of the adolescent and post-adolescent cult, is to label oneself. Labels explain who you are, and more importantly who you are not.

Nothing exposes an outsider (or an adult straying into youth culture) more quickly than the inability to master the language. The British grime artist Wiley satirised this fact with his 2004 single 'Wot U Call It', dedicated to everyone (which was everyone outside the grime scene) who could not define or describe his music. No sooner had scholars managed to deduce the precise chemical reaction which created grime from a blend of black cultures and rhythms, than its protagonists renamed their music.

One step ahead of the masses, they retained their mystique. Assimilated into the mainstream, they were socially dead (albeit better rewarded financially).

So it is tempting to suggest that, for anyone who is not a participant in these subcultures, or whose livelihood does not depend on being able to throw their names around with an air of confidence, it is irrelevant to attempt to chronicle the ever-mutating dance beats which have filled floors and sparked turf rivalries over the past twenty years. Their names – garage, dubstep, trap, tribal, gabba, plus the long-suffering and much-abused techno, electro, house and rave – convey the universe to their adherents; nothing to the outside world. Taken en masse, however, all of these rhythmic innovations, let loose in the digital universe for orgiastic miscegenation, have combined to immerse the modern world in the frenzy of dance. The ceaseless, ecstatic repetition of electronic, digital, computer-derived rhythms now dominates every party, whether it's in a Hoxton or SoHo warehouse or at a works' Christmas outing; filled with teenage hipsters or their embarrassingly overstimulated grandparents. There was a scene early in Paolo Sorrentino's ravishing film *La Grande Bellezza* (2013) which demonstrated this perfectly: to an insistently modern dance soundtrack, wealthy inhabitants of Rome's decadent, aristocratic milieu throw themselves into a frenzied exhibition of sensuality and physicality, careless of their age and social stature. Nobody holds back, asking for the DJ to console them with Motown or the Rolling Stones, the lambada or 'Agadoo': to a woman and man, they exist solely in the moment, and this is the moment of dance. And has been, for as many years as anyone under the age of 30 can remember.

Lost in this compression of modern culture are musical explosions so vibrant that each, individually, might have lent their name to an era: trip hop, lazy and spacious, and yet hinged around the frenetic traditions of electronica and breakbeats; ragga, its Caribbean-electro blend neatly combining the themes of the age, sexuality and technology; jungle, where electro meets rap amidst wired, clattering rhythms; grime, located in the precise quadrant of London where punk, reggae, rap and jungle coincided. Isolated against a static backdrop – like ragtime in 1900, or swing in 1935 – jungle or grime would have signalled a revolution in sound and manners. Lost in the melee of constant movement, they were both startlingly new and almost impossible to see – like the one dancer in a room of vibrating bodies who is obeying a slightly different rhythm. No sooner were they identified and described than they were gone, translated into a different subgenre or possibly even a different species. Five years later, they might return, crossed with techno or house or rave (whatever those nouns meant that week) into a style which would briefly earn its place in the ever-expanding lexicon of dance.

There was one line of movement which remained constant. That was the drift – inexorable and apparently inescapable – from black culture to multiracial mainstream. The early years of the twenty-first century were an urban era, when the defiantly black traditions of R&B and hip hop domi-nated and shaped the language and landscape of popular music. Their inno-vations were apparent in teen pop by former princesses of the Disney empire, just as they were amidst the constant rotation of rap-with-soul, soul-with-rap guest appearances. This music was built on the startling rhythmic varia-tions and sonic distractions invented by two remarkable African-American production teams: Timbaland, with various collaborators; and the Neptunes (alias NERD, or Pharrell Williams and Chad Hugo). At the time when hip hop had become nothing more radical than pop, its rage and provocation reduced to the banality of Jay-Z's 'Jigga My Nigga', Timbaland emerged with a sonic technique so spare that it sounded alien, in the most exotic interpreta-tion of that word. When he produced the 2000 hit 'Try Again' for teen soul star Aaliyah, her song was merely a distraction against synth bass riffs which invaded the ears, and constantly unnerving spurts and detonations of sound. On Jay-Z's contemporaneous 'Big Pimpin'', Timbaland painted sonic colours as if he'd migrated to Egypt; on Missy Elliott's thrillingly bizarre 'Get Ur Freak On', it was West Africa, with a tinny synth riff that resembled a one-string banjo, and layers of vocals which were both tribal and futuristic. And this single reached the Top 10 of the pop charts in Britain and America: had the mainstream ever been so experimental, so unpredictable? Neptunes were producing equally surreal effects with their manipulation of bass and percus-sion, their recording studio simply the venue for the most life-affirming joke in the history of creation. When OutKast and Kanye West joined in the fun, it was as if the psychedelia of 1966–7 was being reborn, minus its veneer of intellectual respectability.

That was too glorious an era to last, as yesterday's innovations became today's clichés, and the prime movers became distracted by their individual ambitions. As that final (to date) golden age of adventure in mainstream popular music faded away, it was time for a new generation of entrepreneurs and musicologists to translate exploration into mass enter-tainment. Remixer extraordinaire Armand Van Helden once described

Daft Punk as the Led Zeppelin of dance, popularising and formalising a seam of underground music. In their low-budget science-fiction space helmets, anonymous and unrecognisable, this French duo streamlined the sonic madness of the urban era into hypnotic computerised beats: house meets hip hop meets advanced robotics, perhaps. Layered over these deceptively simple rhythms were the sounds of technology: voices, guitars, horns, keyboards, all compressed into the wire-thin expressions of machinery seizing control of human emotions. Forty years of synthesised tomfoolery, sixty years of modern pop, were all rewired for electronic sound, to the point where they were both other-worldly and joyously familiar.

Like Daft Punk, the commercial giants of this decade – the second of this unpredictably uniform century – can command mammoth crowds with their anonymity. These have been the years of Skrillex and Calvin Harris, David Guetta and Avicii, deadmau5 and Zedd: the masters of EDM (or electronic dance music). Their talent has been, like the instruments which define their music, to synthesise generations of dance-floor innovation into seamless, ceaseless waves of manufactured exhilaration. The reward for these men (every one of them white) has been wealth of the kind which was once reserved for performers who performed, singers who sang, or musicians who played instruments. With their success, pre-recorded sound has effectively replaced live music, just as it has when pop performers mime their vocals so they can concentrate on their dance steps.

But the EDM revolution also turns us full circle, back to the irresistible effect of the syncopated rhythms of ragtime, and the epic journey that followed over the next 120 years. 'Dance music now *is* pop music', said disco producer Giorgio Moroder in 2012. Perhaps, at heart, it always has been. The world that has been soundtracked and shaped by popular music is a world of ecstasy, of rhythm, of movement – a world that ultimately is never more than two steps from the dance floor.

⚡

Picture Credits

The images at the openings of Chapters 1–16 and 20–22 are reproduced by permission of Getty Images, the pictures for Chapters 17–18 are courtesy of the Library of Congress, and the picture that opens Chapter 19 is reproduced by kind permission of Bob Gruen (www.bobgruen.com).

Every effort has been made to trace and contact all copyright holders. If there are any inadvertent omissions or errors, the publishers will be pleased to correct these at the earliest opportunity.

Acknowledgements

This project might have died at birth had it not been for the enthusiastic initial response of my editors at The Bodley Head, Will Sulkin and Jörg Hensgen. Will took well-earned retirement soon after signing his name to a contract, but Jörg valiantly saw the book through to the end. His input as a creative sounding-board, agony uncle and (not least) editor was immensely valuable and much appreciated. Many thanks also to Will's replacement at The Bodley Head, Stuart Williams, and to David Milner, Anthony Hippisley, Matt Broughton, Emmie Francis, Maria Garbutt-Lucero, Ceri Maxwell and Will Smith.

My agent for this book, Rupert Heath, helped me to fine-tune the initial proposal and the subsequent contract: thanks once again to him. As ever, Andrew Sclanders generously opened up his counter-culture archive for my perusal. His regular sales catalogues (www.beatbooks.com) have depleted my bank balance over the past 15 years but enriched my bookshelves. Many thanks also for their encouragement, support and suggestions to Colin Harper, Clinton Heylin, Johnny Rogan, Stuart Batsford, Andy Miller, Tony Nourmand, Carey Wallace, Sarah Hodgson, Alex Gawley, Max Vickers, Lily Stewart, Lou Ann Bardash, Tom Ovans, Miryam Audiffred and our neighbours, Keith and Beryl Brooks, whose reminiscences of seeing the Ted Heath band in full 1950s swing helped to kick-start this book.

Much of the research for this project was undertaken at the British Library, my home for many long days during 2012 and 2013. Thanks to the very helpful staff there, and at the University of London Library, and to the beleaguered survivors of the public library services in Ealing and Southampton. Audio research was simplified by the limitless archives of Spotify and YouTube, which enabled me (for example) to access almost every hit song and record released since 1890. This is a sign of the times: music that would once have cost me many thousands of pounds to acquire is now available for the meagre cost of a broadband connection and a streaming subscription.

The book was written at home, mostly in silence, as the days when I could concentrate while listening to music are sadly long gone. Only a few albums passed the test of placidly inspiring creativity rather than distracting it, notably *In a Silent Way* and the *Jack Johnson Sessions* (Miles Davis), *My*

Goal's Beyond (John McLaughlin) and *The Individualism of Gil Evans* – none of which was ever intended to serve as Muzak. The text was edited over long cups of coffee at Harris & Hoole in Ealing, and The Tea Party at Lee-on-the-Solent, where the staff patiently tolerated my table-blocking antics.

Our lovely daughters, Catrin and Becca, were spared most of the agony of watching this book take shape, by cleverly deciding to leave home and pursue their own exciting and very different lives. We love them more than they probably realise, and miss them while admiring their courage and independence. Freddie was a constant companion, and an inspirational one at that, as long as I obeyed her demands to be fed and let outside, so she could pursue her relentless surveillance of The Cat Next Door.

Writing a book of this scope and length has often felt like (to steal a phrase from Bob Dylan) balancing a mattress on a bottle of wine. That would never have been possible without the ceaseless love and support of my wonderful wife, Rachel Baylis – wonderfully talented, too, as a glance at her website will make clear (www.rachelbaylis.com). Constantly optimistic, positive, creative, energising and grounded, her contribution to this book has been immeasurable and invaluable. Meeting her was the luckiest moment of my life.

Finally, lifelong thanks to John Sebastian for first making me aware of 'the magic that can set you free'; and to Crosby, Stills & Nash, for more than 40 years of musical joy, accompanied by soap-opera shenanigans worthy of the Ewing family.

Source notes

Curiosities of spelling and grammar have been corrected and/or modernised where necessary to aid the twenty-first-century reader. The following abbreviations have been used to denote periodicals and newspapers: *AML – American Music Lover*; *BB – [The] Billboard*; *BM – Black Music*; *DB – Down Beat*; *DE – Daily Express*; *DM – Daily Mirror*, *G – Gramophone*; *IT – International Times*; *MM – Melody Maker*, *NME – New Musical Express*; *RP – Radio Pictorial*; *RS – Rolling Stone*.

Speaking of the Past

11 'There are towns': quoted in Sanjek, *American Popular Music*, vol. 1, p. 27.

11 'Such tunes, although whistled': *Dwight's Journal of Music*, 19 November 1853.

11 'The California beetle': *DE*, 6 September 1913.

11 '[The 79-year-old music professor]': *DM*, 15 June 1926.

11 'Jazz is born of disorder': *DM*, 13 March 1928.

11 'Music begins to atrophy': Ezra Pound, *ABC of Reading* (1934).

Chapter 1: The Voice of the Dead

13 'And the tunes that mean': Kipling, *The Seven Seas* (1895).

13 'In time we may all get': *DM*, 22 December 1903.

14 'May I ask what it is': *DM*, 7 November 1903.

14 'anything less distinguished': *DM*, 16 May 1904.

14 'the worst thing that can happen': court transcript, May 1904.

15 'Its systematic lack of harmonic': *New York Times*, 9 February 1902.

15 'a musical concert, however good': *New York Times*, 8 February 1902.

16 'You can study the great': Gramophone Company advertisement, November 1904.

16 'In your own home': Anglophone Company advertisement, November 1904.

16 'How startling it will be': Dr William F. Channing in *Popular Science Monthly*, April 1878.

16 'The Phonograph will undoubtedly': *North America Review*, 1878.

17 'In a time like ours': quoted in Eisenberg, *The Recording Angel*, p. 55.

19 'people of sensitivity': W. S. Meadmore in *G*, May 1935.

19 'not then capable of producing': ibid.

19 'You will find that the effect': *Talking Machine News*, September 1918.

19 'Attached to the wall': *Telephony*, 18 December 1909.

21 'We played that waltz all day long': *Phono Trader and Recorder*, September 1905.

21 'The young men like': *DM*, 13 September 1912.

23 'The public . . . must be very faithful': *DM*, 6 February 1904.

25 'I think the public like it': *DM*, 17 March 1904.

25 'A startled, demoralized': quoted in Behr, *Thank Heaven for Little Girls*, p. 21.

25 'writing up to three a day': this is Joseph Tabrar, reported in Self, *Light Music in Britain*, p. 37.

25 'A repertoire such as Florrie': *G*, August 1940.

26 'Only a few years ago a sheet': Harris, *How to Write a Popular Song*, p. 7.

26 'ultimate success or failure': ibid., p. 14.

27 'Avoid slang or *double entendre*': ibid., p. 15.

27 'A – The Home, or Mother': ibid., pp. 12-13.

Chapter 2:
Everybody's Doin' It Now

29 'With regard to ragtime': *DE*, 28 December 1912.

29 'The ragtime rush': *DE*, 7 March 1913.

32 'with a fast-moving program': Speath, *History of Popular Music*, pp. 88–9.

32 'suspicion that the intention': *New York Times*, 18 February 1892.

33 'The future music of this country': quoted in Abbott, *Out of Sight* p. xi.

33 'What with "coon songs"': ibid., p. 209.

33 'are a nuisance and should be abated': ibid., p. 201.

33 'Kansas City girls': ibid., p. 448

33 'a country "rag" dance': ibid.

34 'clear out of sight': *Kansas City American Citizen*, cited in ibid., p. 322.

34 'the popular music market': Schafer, *Art of Ragtime*, p. 28.

34 'Whites taunted blacks': Suisman, *Selling Sounds*, p. 38.

35 'is a term applied': *Etude*, October 1898.

35 'a libellous insult': *Negro Music Journal*, quoted in Berlin, *Ragtime* p. 42.

35 'The authors and publishers': ibid., p. 42.

37 'cannot be interpreted at sight': quoted in Schafer and Riedel, *Art of Ragtime*, p. ii.

38 'Pianola playing is *real* playing': Orchestrelle Company advertisement, November 1903.

40 'These silly dances are physically': *DE*, 21 January 1914.

41 'To imitate a grizzly bear': *DE*, 27 May 1913.

42 'The tango is a pseudo-dance': quoted in Savigliano, *Tango*, p. 116.

42 'The Dance of Moral Death': *DE*, 2 January 1914.

42 'If I catch him cutting': *DE*, 1 January 1914.

42 'nigger-dance characteristics': *DE*, 2 January 1914.

43 'only forms of the oldest dance': *DE*, 14 April 1913.

43 'inoculated with the ragtime-fever': Berlin, *Ragtime*, p. 44.

43 'virulent poison': ibid

43 'malarious epidemic': ibid

43 'syncopation gone mad': ibid

43 'can only be treated': ibid

43 'when taken to excess': ibid., p. 43.

43 'falling prey to the collective soul': ibid., p. 44.

43 'the nerves and muscles tingling': ibid., p. 46.

44 'Suddenly I discovered that my legs': ibid.

44 'Along Atlantic Coast resorts': *Edison Phonograph Monthly,* September 1911.

44 'As they would say in the States': *Phono Trader and Recorder,* April 1912.

44 'One of the Children of Ham': ibid.

45 'You don't have to stop yourself': Bergreen, *As Thousands Cheer,* p. 547.

45 'The lyric, silly though it was': ibid., pp. 68–9.

46 'Five Tunes a Day': ibid., p. 90.

46 'a Negro dresser': Freedland, *Al Jolson,* p. 40.

46 'there was the anticipation': ibid., p. 55.

46 'In the end, they placed a coat': ibid., p. 59.

47 'So nothing is to be sacred': HMV catalogue, 1912.

47 'We had our first battle yesterday': *DE,* 7 September 1914.

47 'Homely Songs Stir Nation's Heart': *DM,* 16 October 1914.

48 'Every YMCA hut': *The Voice,* July–August 1917.

49 'as happy as sandboys': *DE,* 26 February 1918.

Chapter 3: Take Me to the Land of Jazz

51 'Do you jazz-trot?': *DE,* 30 May 1918.

51 'Officers on leave complain': *DM,* 20 February 1919.

52 'The New Noise That Makes People Gay': *DE* 22, November 1918.

52 'You cannot dance the writhing': *DE,* 28 November 1918.

52 'complaining that in her craze': *DE,* 18 June 1919.

52 'expected to bring with her': *DM,* 7 February 1919.

52 'the sleek, well-dressed': *DE,* 2 February 1920.

52 'the girl who is asked everywhere': ibid.

52 'some of these girls have not': ibid.

52 'Dancing is the natural sequel': *DE,* 4 March 1919.

53 'danced night after night': *DE,* 5 March 1919.

53 'The Demoniacs': *DM,* 26 March 1919.

53 'mental opiate': *DE,* 5 March 1919.

53 'People seem to have lost themselves': *DM,* 15 March 1919.

53 'a bunch of crazy niggers': *DE,* 9 December 1919.

53 'an outlaw and a musical bandit': quoted in Carney, *Cuttin' Up,* pp. 134–5.

54 'adept at strumming jazz tunes': *DM,* 4 August 1930.

54 'of gold and silver tissue': *DE,* 25 March 1919.

54 'Just one simple, curling': *DE,* 19 June 1919.

54 'a jazz night – a mad, jolly': *DM,* 28 June 1919.

54 'Jazz was overdone during its reign': *DM,* 18 November 1919.

54 'Some of you may wonder': *DM,* 11 July 1919.

55 'has no relations at all': Henry Osbourne Osgood, *So This Is Jazz!,* ch. 2.

56 'In the year 1915': Mendl, *Appeal of Jazz* p. 43.

56 'Some say the Jass band': Victor Records catalogue, March 1917.

56 'The invention of jazz': *DB*, 1 July 1949.

58 'vaudeville's newest craze': *BB*, September 1916.

58 'The ODJB reduced': *Early Jazz*, p. 179.

59 'We won't put our stuff': quoted in Ogren, *The Jazz Revolution* p. 94.

59 'As the popularity of the dance wanes': *DE*, 28 October 1919.

60 'The year 1923 has given us': *G*, January 1924.

60 'Blues records long ago': *G*, June 1925.

60 'he found something curious': Hamilton, *In Search of the Blues*, p. 33.

61 'one of those over-and-over strains': Berrett, *Louis Armstrong*, pp. 179–80.

61 'the weirdest music I had ever heard': Handy, *Father of the Blues* (1941).

61 'My aim would be to combine': ibid.

62 'The dancers seemed electrified': ibid.

62 'The blues are such as synonymous': Murray, *Stomping the Blues*, p. 45.

63 'When singing with raucous bands': *Jazz Journal*, June 1957.

65 'I dressed her from the inside out': Schuller, *Early Jazz*, p. 367.

65 'Miss Smith walked on that stage': Stewart-Baxter, *Ma Rainey*, p. 16.

65 'the best loved of all the Race's': Columbia catalogue illustration, in ibid., p. 46.

65 'You'll feel better': OKeh catalogue illustration, in ibid., p. 92.

66 'Wanna be happy?': OKeh catalogue illustration, in ibid., p. 60.

66 'Clara Smith's tones': *Vanity Fair*, March 1926.

Chapter 4: Dance-o-Mania

69 'It would be difficult to find': *DE*, 30 October 1919.

69 'Graceful dancing is dead': *DM*, 14 May 1920.

70 'The War shattered many of our illusions': Nelson, *All About Jazz*, p. 170.

70 'What *is* a saxophone?': Mr Justice Eve, who added: 'Is it a wind or a string instrument?': *DM*, 20 January 1926.

71 'the antithesis of jazz': *DE*, 5 July 1919.

71 '*That's* music': ibid.

71 'This is the most discordant': *Encore* magazine, quoted in Godbolt, *History of Jazz in Britain*, p. 11.

71 'astonishing . . . extraordinary': *DE*, 14 August 1919.

71 'Magicians': ibid.

72 'dancing to the ragtime music': *DM*, 10 November 1916.

72 'a damn nigger': *Memory Lane*, Winter 1977/78.

72 'I am certain that although': *Memory Lane*, Spring 1978.

72 'Jazz was a novelty': Heath, *Listen to My Music*, p. 28.

74 'The first note plunges you': Columbia advertisement, February 1920.

74 'at a dance dive': quoted in Berrett, *Louis Armstrong*, p. 1.

74 'came up with the idea': Collier, *Reception of Jazz*, p. 16.

75 'Those who like his music': Kenney, *Chicago Jazz*, p. 78.

75 'Paul Whiteman was known': quoted in Cohen, *Duke Ellington's America*, p. 77.

75 'All I did was to orchestrate jazz': *Saturday Evening Post*, 27 February 1926.

76 'I intend to point out': Carney, *Cuttin' Up*, p. 125.

77 'I do not think that serious music': *Radio Times*, 3 July 1925.

77 'Jazz music is descending': *Time*, 25 February 1924.

77 'the only true American art': ibid.

77 'smoothed his harshness': *Vanity Fair*, October 1925.

79 'coldly received': *Memory Lane*, Summer 1978.

82 'The trouble with the modern girl': *DM*, 31 January 1925.

82 'We ought to consign jazz': *Time*, 17 May 1926.

83 'a nigger's shuffling step': *G*, January 1927.

83 'savages . . . still live in trees': M. Savile: *DM*, 5 October 1927.

83 'Nigger music': Dr Farrell, Exeter College: *DM*, 6 August 1927.

83 'attendant immodest dances': *DM*, 21 September 1927.

83 'We younger Negro artists': *The Nation*, 23 June 1926.

84 'The venue's exclusionary policies': Cohen, *Duke Ellington's America*, p. 54.

86 'It's impossible': Shapiro, *Hear Me Talkin' to Ya*, p. 159.

Chapter 5: Wizard of the Microphone

89 'A cheap dance record': *G*, October 1923.

89 'An innovation of this kind': *G*, May 1925.

90 'new noise': quoted in Eisenberg, *The Recording Angel*, p. 112.

90 'I do not believe any audience': ibid.

90 'Sound Photographed onto a Record!': illustration in Cliffe, *Fascinating Rhythm*, p. 83.

91 'immense loudness': *G*, May 1935.

92 'particularly partial': *MM*, March 1926.

93 'discretion won the day': *G*, September 1933.

94 'Why not learn the guitar?': *MM*, March 1926.

94 'a really confidential attitude': *G*, June 1929.

95 'The thing you have to understand': Giddins, *Pocketful of Dreams*, p. 259.

95 'the boys and girls who intersperse': *New York Times*, 24 February 1932.

95 'People sing more than they did': *Broadcasting in Everyday Life*, p. 16.

96 'Soft, foul, crooner-obsessed': *Action*, 20 August 1936.

96 'Whiners and bleaters': *New York Times*, 11 January 1932.

96 'Male crooners are quite divorced': Baade, *Victory Through Harmony*, p. 136.

96 'To exclude any form of anaemic': ibid., p. 139.

96 'Bing's singing was nothing': Giddins, *Pocketful of Dreams*, p. 203.

97 'Bing conveyed a chest-tone': ibid., p. 172

97 'Most of his predecessors': ibid.

97 'This approach made some people': Young, *Music of the Great Depression* p. 10

97 'The audience, except for the few': *New Republic*, 7 August 1929.

99 'The constant jar and rasping': Taylor, *Music Sound & Technology*, p. 299.

99 'mask the clatter of knives': Lanza, *Elevator Music*, p. 17.

100 'There was a time when dance music': Eisenberg, *The Recording Angel*, p. 64.

101 'The dance hall was the only': Parsonage, *Evolution of Jazz*, p. 40.

102 'the British touch': *G*, September 1926.

102 'nerve-torturing riot': *Radio Times*, 18 June 1926.

102 'a person felt honoured': Heath, *Listen to My Music*, p. 37.

102 'Royal interest can obviously': Payne, *This Is Jack Payne*, p. 32.

103 'the Violin of Death': *RP*, 15 January 1937.

103 'Continue! There is a singing': *RP*, 12 February 1937.

104 'Many a tune has gone': Payne, *This Is Jack Payne*, p. 83.

104 'loathe and abominate': ibid., p. 32.

104 'foolish flappers': ibid.

104 'Dear Mr Hall': *RP*, 29 November 1935.

105 'the constant use of certain mannerisms': *AML*, August 1935.

106 'This worked well': Bret, *Gracie Fields*, p. 5.

106 'Poor Gracie': HMV advertisement, late 1931.

107 'There were lots of film stars': Bret, *Gracie Fields*, p. 35.

108 'I spoke the language': *RP*, 27 November 1936.

Chapter 6:
Blues in the Night

111 'I'd lower the volume': Cash, *Cash*, p. 51.

111 'Hill Billies are the most incorrigibly lazy': *G*, December 1931.

112 'The songs themselves': quoted in Woods, *Folk Revival*, p. 14.

113 'Many of the songs were printed': Wolfe, *Tennessee Strings*, p. 8.

114 'simply the greatest': Delmore, *Truth is Stranger*, p. 98.

115 'We were afraid to advertise': Oliver, *Blues off the Record*, p. 49.

116 'Blind Lemon': McGee, *B. B. King*, p. 11.

116 'It's funny how collectors': Stewart-Baxter, *Ma Rainey*, p. 58.

116 'She wouldn't have to sing': ibid., p. 42.

118 'I believed everything he sang': McGee, *B. B. King*, p. 10.

118 'The new sensation in the singing': Columbia advertisement, 1928.

119 'the prevailing atmosphere': Broughton, *Black Gospel*, p. 37.

120 'The day of the popular record': *Phonograph Monthly Review*, August 1931.

120 'The public has lost its thrill': *The Music Seller*, October 1931.

121 'Wall Street Lays an Egg': *Variety*, 30 October 1929.

121 'There was a kind of desperate': Sudhalter, *Stardust Melody,* p. 145.

121 'poor and rich alike felt': Eisenberg *The Recording Angel,* p. 31.

124 'The talking films are going': *G,* July 1929.

126 'He has a knack of establishing': *DM,* 9 October 1928.

126 'It was made obvious': *Daily Sketch,* 14 October 1928.

127 'Each talkie has one big': *The Voice,* March 1930.

127 'the most upsetting year': Winifred Bristow: *Picture Show Annual 1931,* p. 22.

127 'Picturegoers made it quite clear': Edward Wood: ibid., p. 52.

128 'Dance music is in the thraldom': *G,* January 1926.

128 'I just read a magazine': Lombardo, *Auld Acquaintance,* p. 73.

129 'Musical comedies do not act': *Time,* 30 May 1932.

129 'Its prelude establishes': ibid.

129 'an explosion of melody': Giddins, *Pocketful of Dreams,* p. 174.

129 'More sophistication': Wilder, *American Popular Song,* p. 28.

130 'the Park Avenue smart set': Steyn, *Broadway Babies Say Goodnight,* p. 105.

130 'a unique blend of the passionate': Gottlieb, *Reading Lyrics,* p. 100.

130 'produced what is arguably': Wilder, *American Popular Song,* p. 209.

131 'He's as good as any of them': Thomas, *Fred Astaire,* p. 195.

132 'I had never played with drums': Sudhalter, *Stardust Melody,* p. 31.

Chapter 7:
Bugle Call Rag

135 'Not 25% of lowbrows': *RP,* 2 August 1935.

135 'Swing is the voice of youth': *New York Times,* 26 February 1939.

136 'Swing cannot be defined': Firestone, *Swing, Swing, Swing,* pp. 156–7.

136 'Hot Jazz – the real jazz': *AML,* November 1935.

136 'the sound comes forth': *AML,* June 1936.

136 'two-thirds rhythm': Firestone, *Swing, Swing, Swing,* pp. 156–7.

136 'It is akin to the wriggling': *G,* September 1936.

136 'a combination of exhibitionism': *AML,* September 1936.

136 'musical Hitlerism': *New York Times,* 2 November 1938.

136 'orchestrated sex': Firestone, *Swing, Swing, Swing,* p. 242.

136 'an epidemic': ibid

137 'Jazz is a surrender': *G,* September 1936

137 'I surrender unconditionally': *AML,* October 1936.

137 'thought it was great': Firestone, *Swing, Swing, Swing,* p. 197.

138 'thousands broke from the two-dollar': quoted in *Action,* 11 June 1938.

138 'When the bands started': *BB,* 1 August 1942.

138 'bedlam: Gene Krupa': *San Francisco Chronicle,* June 1986.

138 'The music was too loud': Firestone, *Swing, Swing, Swing,* p. 96.

139 'there was such a yelling': ibid., p. 148.

139 'tradition-shattering': quoted in Maggin, *Dizzy*, p. 64.

140 'those near-maniacs': *MM*, 5 February 1938.

140 'The behaviour of his audience': Firestone, *Swing, Swing, Swing*, p. 222.

142 'does two numbers': Sublette, *Cuba and Its Music*, p. 396.

144 'I'd think twice before advising': Sudhalter, *Lost Chords*, p. 587.

144 'a dying duck': *Metronome*, March 1945.

144 'Let's jump!': *Down Beat*, 20 May 1949.

144 'way out of his depth': ibid.

145 'It's necessary to give an audience': *Time*, 26 September 1949.

145 'What happens is you make': Hall, *Dialogues in Swing*, p. 149.

145 'was honest enough to recognize': Simon, *Glenn Miller*, p. 73.

145 'definitely decided': ibid., p. 119.

146 'That band was like the beginning': Hall, *Dialogues in Swing*, p. 144.

146 'When the historians of 2037': *RP*, 8 January 1937.

146 'Decca's studios in New York': Andrews, *Over Here, Over There*, p. 108.

147 'Dancing, for the boys and girls': *RP*, 5 February 1937.

147 'records will have to let the fans': Sanjek, *American Popular Music*, vol. 3, p. 137.

147 'The most established British': Cliffe, *Fascinating Rhythm*, p. 198.

147 'with all the American's lack': *G*, December 1932.

148 'This dance record-buying public': *G*, April 1933.

148 'Dancing is under a temporary': *DM*, 14 June 1933.

149 'the sort of numbers that make': *RP*, 6 November 1936.

149 'Audiences resent "bounce" in an act': ibid.

149 'should divert rather than disturb': Self, *Light Music in Britain*, p. 1.

149 'Because, unlike serious music': quoted in ibid., p. vii.

149 'murdered; it is real music': *DM*, 19 April 1934.

149 'It was quite apparent': Spaeth, *History of Popular Music*, p. 513.

150 'We have heard all these words': *RP*, 9 April 1937.

150 'Our songs don't live anymore': Bergreen, *As Thousands Cheer*, p. 328.

151 'Take the family out': illustration in Krivine, *Juke-Box Saturday Night*, p. 90

152 'sweet numbers, jazz classics': ibid., p. 91.

153 'We demand that this habit': quoted in Godbolt, *All This and 10%*, p. 19.

153 'The sophisticated music': McCarthy, *The Dance Band Era*, p. 54.

153 'ugliest man': *Daily Herald*, 18 July 1932.

153 'untrained gorilla': ibid.

153 'Negroes Invade Our Theatres': Cohen, *Duke Ellington's America*, p. 121.

154 'the club – maximum attendance': Godbolt, *All This and 10%*, p. 23.

154 'The fight to build the Greater': *Fascist Week*, 18 May 1934.

154 'the Jewish-Negroid strata': *Blackshirt*, 30 November 1934.

154 'Jew-boys wailing jazz': *Blackshirt*, 22 November 1935.

154 'The Jew and the alien': *Action*, 25 March 1939.

154 'Aryan Dance Band': *Action*, 9 January 1937.

154 'Louis Armstrong, the famous': *Action*, 27 March 1937.

155 'there is no jazz': *Blackshirt*, 7 December 1934.

155 'America's contribution': Budds, *Jazz and the Germans*, p. 157.

155 'The Negroes are here': *Die literarische Welt*, January 1926.

155 'The nightmare image': Budds, *Jazz and the Germans*, p. 43.

155 'collapse in its political': quoted in ibid., p. 155.

157 'These days nearly everyone': *G*, November 1938.

157 'I was offered a guarantee': *RP*, 26 August 1938.

157 'They will play at a State Ball': *RP*, 2 December 1938.

157 'Naturally, I don't want': *Singapore Free Press*, 19 January 1939.

157 'I don't blame him for that': *RP*, 27 January 1939.

157 'nobody could possibly challenge': *MM*, undated cutting, early 1939.

Chapter 8:
Millions Like Us

159 'In a few years, radio': *RP*, 9 April 1937.

159 'I want to take people out': Baade, *Victory through Harmony*, p. 42.

160 'The most pitiful exhibition': *G*, October 1939.

161 'The song combined the first

person': Baade, *Victory through Harmony*, p. 46.

161 'There's a new star': *DE*, 15 January 1940.

162 'Vera brings joy and comfort': *DM*, 19 November 1941.

162 'The type of songs being written': Baade, *Victory through Harmony*, p. 135.

162 'Swingsters Want Exemption': *Evening Standard*, January 1940.

163 'Many Dance Band Boys': *DE*, 26 June 1941.

164 'The fact that Nazi Germany': McCarthy, *The Dance Band Era*, p. 140.

164 'The Allied troops': Jordan, *Le Jazz*, p. 230.

165 'likely to contribute': Behr, *Thank Heaven for Little Girls*, p. 270.

165 'Men in America's armed forces': *BB*, 10 October 1942.

166 'One name band leader': *BB*, 28 November 1942.

166 'I think everyone in the music': Sudhalter, *Stardust Memory*, p. 243.

166 'bombarded with variations': *BB*, 3 January 1942.

168 'The American GI': Smith, *God Bless America*, p. 132.

169 'After August 1st': *BB*, 20 June 1942.

169 'A fit subject for a Bateman': *G*, June 1942.

169 'The net result will be simply': *BB*, 18 July 1942.

170 'scraping the bottom of the barrel': *AML*, May 1943.

170 'From the standpoint': *BB*, 25 July 1942.

170 'To a mere male': *G*, June 1944.

171 'the harum-scarum jitterbugging': *BB*, 16 May 1942.

171 'Dance music lost most': *BB*, 2 January 1943.

171 'There are indications': *BB*, 4 April 1942.

172 'The minute Sinatra started': Kaplan, *Frank*, p. 78.

172 'I used to stand there': ibid., p. 126.

172 'I hope you fall on your ass': ibid., p. 146.

172 'The place was absolutely packed': ibid., p. 155.

173 'The scenes at the Paramount': Arnold Shaw in Petkov, *Frank Sinatra Reader*, p. 20.

173 'Whatever he stirred': Martha Weinman Lear in ibid., p. 48.

173 'We loved to swoon': ibid.

174 'the behaviour of children': quoted in *BB*, 20 June 1942.

174 'juvenile hoodlums': *BB*, 28 November 1942.

174 'the angle appears to be': *BB*, 5 December 1942.

174 'signature broad-brimmed hat': Alvarez, *The Power of the Zoot*, p. 2.

175 'Negro band leaders have held': *BB*, 2 January 1943.

176 'artistically the worst thing': Margolick, *Strange Fruit*, p. 80.

177 'top favourite of hep Harlemites': *BB*, 2 January 1943.

177 'They clown! They sing!': *BB*, 26 December 1942.

178 'wild swing in its raw stage': *BB*, 18 September 1943.

Chapter 9: Let's Get Straight

181 '[FBI agents] have really been': *Metronome*, August 1945.

181 'Many musicians are expressing': *MM*, 20 July 1946.

182 'It is insignificant': Parsonage, *Evolution of Jazz*, p. 25.

181 'a drug for the devitalized': in *Music Ho!* (1966), p. 199.

182 'I hesitate to think': *Time*, 18 January 1943.

182 'seems no more harmful': *Time*, 19 July 1943.

183 'Yes, all the ones I know': Gioia, *The Imperfect Art*, p. 135.

183 'One of the unmistakeable': *Metronome*, August 1947

184 'I don't know how I made it': ibid.

184 'We try to live 100 days': on ABC-TV's *Night Beat*, 8 November 1956.

185 'Any musician who says': *DB*, 9 September 1949.

185 'Mistakes – that's all rebop is': quoted in *G*, December 1947.

185 'I don't think the public': *DB*, 28 January 1949.

185 'The advances bands have made': *Metronome*, September 1945.

187 'In chromaticism, chords can': Maggin, *Dizzy*, pp. 94–5.

188 'The one thing which bothered': Charles, *Brother Ray*, p. 100.

188 'With gusto I dissected': Maggin, *Dizzy*, pp. 39–40.

188 'We went out of our minds!': quoted in ibid., p. 171.

189 'The increasing specialisation': 'Harlequin', in *G*, January 1947.

189 'First it was symphonies': *American Record Guide*, January 1947.

189 'bright and melodious music': *MM*, 9 March 1946.

189 'modernistic swing': Brian Rust in *Pickup*, November 1946.

190 'Each fortnight': *DM*, 25 January 1947.

190 'I was quite uncompromising': Heath, *Listen to My Music*, p. 77.

190 'He'd heard about swing': ibid., p. 79.

190 'While swing fans': *DM*, 25 January 1947.

190 'one of the biggest fan followings': Rau, *Stars Off the Record*, p. 33.

190 'We face a slump': *MM*, 28 December 1946.

192 'The popular songs of the day': *Metronome*, February 1948.

192 'Right now, everyone': *Metronome*, May 1950.

192 'in gleeful anticipation': *BB*, 31 January 1948.

193 'I never knew they were': ibid.

193 'I guess it sold': *Time*, 10 May 1954.

193 'An important facet in the polka trend': *DB*, 15 July 1949.

194 'marks a kind of infantile': *Metronome*, February 1951.

194 'a pseudo-ragtime "novelty" mode': Schafer and Riedel, *Art of Ragtime* p. 105.

195 'Their repertoire was': Godbolt, *All This and 10%*, p. 20.

195 'I like to think of myself': quoted in Greene, *Passion for Polka*, p. 235.

196 'the American elite': ibid., p. 244.

196 'Cowboy and hillbilly music': *Metronome*, January 1945.

196 'the mountain music': *DB*, 3 June 1949.

196 'that old fashion home cooking': *DB*, 28 January 1953.

196 'I often wonder how cowboys': *G*, February 1952.

197 'country music has been twisted': Wren, *Johnny Cash*, p. 7.

Chapter 10: Music for Gracious Living

201 'The public is confused': *DB*, 22 April 1949.

201 'To succeed in America': Manuel, *Caribbean Currents*, p. 69.

202 'Be hip, be sharp': *Time*, 17 May 1948.

202 'hot jazz overheated': *Time*, 25 March 1946.

202 'A big band slows anybody': *DB*, 9 September 1949.

202 'Bop is part of jazz': *DB*, 7 October 1949.

202 'which will make it truly': *DB*, 11 March 1949.

203 'Possibly the mambo is an outrage': quoted in Sublette, *Cuba and Its Music*, p. 547.

204 'It frightens inhibited people': *Jet*, 21 February 1952.

204 'doesn't look upon it': *Metronome*, November 1953

205 'The people you're playing for': *DB*, 15 June 1951.

205 'believed that, any time': Thompson, *Raised by Wolves*, p. 30.

206 'No science has progressed': *Metronome*, November 1952.

206 'That **** television!': *DB*, 29 June 1951.

206 'There will be a place for music': *DB*, 20 April 1951.

207 'perhaps the composer will sit': *DB*, 26 August 1949.

208 'The talk of the record industry': *MM*, 31 July 1948.

208 'the first integrated program': Sanjek, *American Popular Music*, vol. 3, p. 234.

209 'buccaneering adventures': *G*, March 1949.

209 'The well-equipped record collector': *DB*, 11 March 1949.

209 'It seems unquestionable': Michael Levin in *DB*, 30 June 1950.

210 'with four numbers tied': *DB*, 28 July 1950.

211 'it's meant to entertain': *MM*, 12 October 1957.

213 'One of the rules peculiar': *DB*, 12 January 1951.

213 'The secret of his success': *DB*, 22 October 1952.

213 'a carefully devitalized style': ibid.

214 'the teenagers showed': quoted in Eisenberg, *The Recording Angel*, p. 19.

214 '[Teenagers] are still swooning': *Life*, 20 December 1948.

215 'It all started with Vaughn': *Metronome*, July 1950.

215 'Arrangements and interpretations': *DB*, 30 December 1949.

215 'shameless emoting': *Metronome*, September 1947.

216 'no voice': *G*, September 1948.

216 'I just felt like God': *DB*, 7 March 1952.

216 'One mournful note': *DB*, 21 May 1952.

217 'You can see what the girls like': *DE*, 24 March 1953.

217 'Man, it's worse than ever': *DB*, 25 March 1953.

217 'they were Frankie's own': *Metronome*, November 1953.

Chapter 11:
Real Rock Drive

219 'The music business in this country': *DB*, 20 April 1951.

219 'Never have there been as many': *Jet*, 3 January 1952.

220 'in the struggle for worldwide domination': *Metronome*, June 1947.

220 'hypnotizes one with the dead cold': *Metronome*, April 1948.

220 'They even know about rebop': *MM*, 25 December 1948.

220 'The Communist authorities': *DB*, 2 December 1949.

220 'Jazz is dead': *DB*, 16 June 1950.

220 'Jazz is pretty dead': *DB*, 6 October 1950.

221 'Something new in music': *DB*, 12 January 1951.

221 'the income of the average black': Sanjek, *American Popular Music*, vol. 3, p. 248.

221 'the hot new style was jump': Miller, *Almost Grown*, p. 29.

222 'The blues were not yet constricted': Whitall, *Fever*, p. 29.

222 'right rhythmic rock and roll': *BB*, 21 April 1945.

223 'How long can you play': *Jazz Journal*, March 1952.

223 'This was the first Rock & Roll': Cohen, *The Record Men*, p. 111.

223 'It was the loudest music anyone': ibid.

224 'As the show reached its climax':

Lauterbach, *The Chitlin' Circuit*, p. 131.

224 'Economists have long predicted': *BB*, 21 January 1956.

224 'Rhythm and blues may turn out': Ralph Gleason in *DB*, 9 March 1956.

225 'a deliberate attempt': *BB*, 12 June 1954.

225 'springing up in one form': Guralnick, *Last Train to Memphis*, p. 6.

226 'The kids want that music': *BB*, 15 May 1954.

226 'White singers were picking up': Charles, *Brother Ray*, p. 176.

226 'In one aspect of America's': quoted in Guralnick, *Last Train to Memphis*, pp. 39–40.

227 'There was an immediate reaction': Heath, *Listen to My Music*, p. 125.

227 'Jazz audiences are too rowdy': *Jet*, 6 May 1954.

227 'Teenagers are instigating': *Cash Box*, April 1954.

227 'no longer the stepchild': *BB*, 24 April 1954.

228 'The R&B field has been doing': *BB*, 2 October 1954.

228 'thumbs down on "way out"': *BB*, 24 April 1954.

228 'is not against blues records': *Cash Box*, February 1954.

229 '[Freed] feels that this term': *DB*, 9 February 1955.

229 'we intend to teach the POWs': *DB*, 19 October 1951.

229 'first #1 rock and roll song': Whitburn, *Pop Memories*, p. 102.

230 'youngsters who couldn't cope': *DB*, 13 January 1954.

230 'When Edwardian-style coats': *NME*, 10 April 1976.

230 'the first group [of teenagers]': Cohen, *Folk Devils*, p. 183.

231 'It's all jazz, of course': Ellis, *Big Beat Scene*, p. 36.

231 'Viewed as a social': Steve Race in *MM*, 5 May 1956.

231 'I was doing country and western': *NME*, 30 March 1974.

232 'The greatest Dance Band': *DB*, 3 June 1953.

233 'He didn't have a good voice': *RS*, 12 September 1974.

233 'When *Blackboard Jungle*': ibid.

233 'for most people it was the loudest': Miller, p. 92.

233 'It's the vilest picture': *Jet*, 14 April 1955.

233 'Lively strains of the disk': *BB*, 28 May 1955.

234 'two jump blues sides': *Jazz Journal*, October 1954.

234 'Bill Haley and his Comets': *DM*, 21 July 1955.

234 'primitive, hotted-up jazz': *DE*, 3 September 1956.

234 'They just looked around': *DE*, 13 September 1956.

234 'If we are going back': *DM*, 4 October 1956.

235 'The Opposition': *DM*, 13 September 1956.

235 'Why is it that a rhythm-crazed': *NME*, 14 September 1956.

235 'The British public doesn't want': *NME*, 17 November 1956.

235 'Rock 'n' roll is a revival': *DM*, 8 October 1956.

235 'That rhythm is terrific': *DE*, 12 September 1956.

235 'This music is different': ibid.

235 'the most destructive force': *DB*, 6 April 1955.

235 'a high pressure crusade': *DB*, 20 April 1955.

235 'Teen-agers virtually work': *Cash Box*, April 1955.

236 'symptomatic of something': *BB*, 28 April 1956.

236 'a communicable disease': *Cash Box*, April 1956.

236 'to undermine the morals': *DB*, 2 May 1956.

236 'There's even a rock and roll': *Cash Box*, February 1956.

236 'the real, full-time R&B': *BB*, 16 June 1956.

236 'Suddenly [in 1954]': *DB*, 26 January 1955.

237 'The continued merging': *Billboard*, March 1956.

Chapter 12:
Bad Motorcycle

239 'Take a dash of Johnnie': *DM*, 1 March 1956.

239 'If what I play is Rock': *NME*, 11 January 1957.

240 'The odd thing about it': *Memphis Press-Scimitar*, 28 July 1954.

240 'His style is both country': *BB*, 6 November 1954.

241 'I'd say it was a mixed-up': White, *Bo Diddley*, p. 59.

241 'Man, maybe that was': quoted in *Jazz Journal*, January 1956.

242 'How can I reject it': *Cash Box*, March 1956.

242 'His antics and appearance': *NME*, 18 January 1957.

242 'Her enthusiasm was so keen': *DE*, 15 February 1957.

242 'has stood well aloof': *DE*, 4 December 1956.

243 'with cowboy boots': *The Forty-Fiver*, May 1956.

243 'a young bump and grind': unidentified Minneapolis paper, 13 May 1956.

243 'If the future is important': *BB*, 16 June 1956.

243 'If he did that in the street': *Time*, 14 May 1956.

243 'I think that there is some': *NME*, 5 October 1956.

243 'sounds as if his mouth': *DM*, 5 July 1956.

244 'a vulgar, unmelodic': *DB*, 28 November 1956.

244 'bobby soxers and baby sitters': Fong-Torres, *Hits Just Keep On Coming*, pp. 24–5.

244 'at the mercy of the taste': Poschardt, *DJ Culture*, p. 55.

245 'I don't like [Presley's] work': quoted in Ellis, *Big Beat Scene*, p. 46.

245 'It is deplorable': *DM*, 5 September 1956.

245 'We certainly do our best': *DE*, 17 May 1960.

245 'It just sounded so raw': *RS*, 19 April 1990.

246 'a light sports jacket': *NME*, 28 December 1956.

246 'You don't have to do all that': *DE*, 5 January 1957.

246 'His boyish freshness': *NME*, 11 January 1957.

246 'the day when Bill': *DM*, 30 January 1957.

246 'Fantabulous': *DM*, 6 February 1957.

246 'faces turned upwards': *DE*, 6 February 1957.

246 'They clowned, they fooled': *DM*, 7 February 1957.

246 'weak wisecracks': *DE*, 7 February 1957.

246 'would like to do a two-hour': *DM*, 16 February 1957.

247 'Bill looks and sounds exactly': *NME*, 8 February 1957.

247 'He's Great, Great, Great!': quoted in Steele, *Bermondsey Boy*, p. 244.

248 'Does Tommy Steele expect': *NME*, 9 November 1956.

248 'How any sane person': *Radio Times*, 4 January 1957.

248 'I feel thoroughly disgusted': *Radio Times*, 22 March 1957.

248 'a sex symbol of deformed': quoted in Ellis, *Big Beat Scene*, p. 102.

249 'Larry fucks our arses': quoted in ibid., p. 27.

249 'We all do it': *DM*, 12 June 1959.

249 'Artificiality is death': *Record Mail*, August 1958.

249 'the new star looked more': Leslie, *Fab*, pp. 89–90.

249 'Rock'n'roll has to be sung': *DE*, 4 December 1958.

249 'older people like it too': *DM*, 6 April 1959.

250 'a rather fatal fascination': Krivine, *Juke-Box Saturday Night*, p. 137.

250 'Is Cliff Richard': *DM*, 30 November 1959.

251 'Fans ripped out': *MM*, 25 November 1961.

251 'The idea of English people': *Jazz Monthly*, December 1955.

251 'Rock 'n' roll is out of date': *DM*, 8 September 1956.

252 'is the Chicago Rent Party': *DM*, 9 November 1949.

253 'a triple murderer': Hamilton, *In Search of the Blues*, p. 121.

254 'Isn't it time to call a halt': *NME*, January 1955; quoted in Frame, *Restless Generation*, p. 78.

254 'Lonnie Donegan still sounds': *G*, March 1955.

254 'skiffle music has now become': *Jazz Journal*, November 1955.

255 'without benefit of plugging': Leslie, pp. 57–8.

255 'sounds like a number': *Jazz Journal*, April 1956.

255 'At worst, [skiffle] becomes': quoted in *Jazz Music* 7:6; November 1956.

255 'Britain's future Billie Holiday': *Jazz Monthly*, September 1957.

256 'your outdoor skiffle party': *Woman*, 8 August 1957.

256 'I am teaching them rock': *Record Mail*, June 1958.

257 'After 1955, the amateurs': Wilder, *American Popular Song*, p. xvi.

257 'a decade of simple-minded': *Time*, 24 December 1956.

258 'If you gave the public': *Jazz Journal*, January 1959.

258 'If popular music is truly': *American Record Guide*, April 1959.

258 'If you want to live for': *Cash Box*, October 1957.

259 'prepare for the end of the world': ibid.

259 'the world was burning up': *Cash Box*, January 1958.

259 'rock 'n' roll glorifies Satan': *Daily Mail*, 14 January 1958.

259 'She'll be 14 in July': *DM*, 29 May 1958.

259 'Sorry we couldn't get Jerry': *DE*, 2 June 1958.

260 'an emotional crisis': *DM*, 26 January 1959.

260 'Boys out for an evening': *DM*, 5 February 1959.

260 'got rid of': *DM*, 12 December 1957.

261 'records of a criminally hooligan trend': Ryback, *Rock around the Bloc*, p. 32.

262 'a mixed-up rumba': *Time*, 20 April 1959.

262 'Dancers bending at the knee': Ryback, *Rock around the Bloc*, p. 29.

262 'Experts say the latest craze': *DE*, 6 February 1957.

263 'all of a sudden the business': *NME*, 25 January 1957.

263 'Calypsomania': *DM*, 21 March 1957.

264 'Here we go again': *DB*, 2 May 1957.

264 'Calypso is going to become': *The Forty-Fiver*, March 1957.

264 'Elvis was interpreting': Belafonte, *My Song*, p. 151.

264 'The first mock-ups I saw': ibid., p. 158.

264 'the greatest musical sensation': *DE*, 14 March 1957.

265 'All they played was them Bobbys': Lewis, *Killer!*, p. 69.

266 'the tuneless terror': *Time*. 27 July 1959.

266 'Bobby was a person': Evanier, *Roman Candle*, p. 56.

266 'Nearly everything I do': *Life*, 11 January 1960.

266 'Do you realize you're alone': ibid.

Chapter 13: Soul Food

269 'It is recognized as one': *G*, October 1932.

269 '90% of the popular stars': *DB*, 27 January 1954.

270 'The same match that burns': *Ebony*, September 1960.

270 'There is in the music': *Ebony*, December 1961.

271 'has soul': *G*, December 1928.

271 'I try to bring out my soul': *DB*, 14 December 1955.

271 'I became myself': Charles, *Brother Ray*, p. 148.

271 'almost blasphemous': *Jazz Monthly*, December 1955.

271 'a masterpiece of gospel': Broughton, *Black Gospel*, p. 50.

271 'She lost the black market': ibid., p. 54

272 'I sing with all the feeling': *Ebony*, September 1960.

272 'Some of these record companies': *Jazz Journal*, May 1958.

272 'I turn on the radio': *Ebony*, December 1961.

272 'The real Negro folk idiom': ibid.

273 'heart music': *Ebony*, November 1962.

273 'By isolating what they believe': *Negro Digest*, April 1963.

273 'I was hurt, really hurt': *Ebony*, July 1979.

274 'the entire crew breaking': *Cash Box*, May 1952.

274 'He's just singing the same damn': quoted in Whitall, *Fever*, p. 76.

274 'The entire R&B market': *DB*, 4 May 1955.

275 'The groups are all getting': *Cash Box*, June 1958.

276 'Teenagers used to go': *Jet*, 13 August 1953.

276 'this ugly record': *Jazz Journal*, July 1956.

276 'I didn't want to hurt him': *MM*, 18 February 1961.

278 'Us rhythm and blues': Charles, *Brother Ray*, p. 152

278 'After all, the *Grand Ole Opry*': ibid., p. 222.

278 'I wasn't aware of any bold act': ibid., p. 223.

279 'Just pretend you're wiping': quoted in Dawson, *The Twist*, p. 34.

279 'The World's Wackiest Dance': *DM*, 27 October 1961.

280 'become a sort of national': *DE*, 30 November 1961.

280 'sweep big bands back': *MM*, 30 December 1961.

280 'It is expected that in the skiing': *MM*, 6 January 1962.

280 'synthetic sex turned': *Ebony*, February 1962.

281 'How can we feel happy': Ryback, *Rock around the Bloc*, p. 52.

281 'Record companies create scores': *Hi Fi/Stereo Review*, August 1962.

281 'As it stands today': *BB*, 5 January 1963.

282 'It was recorded R&B': ibid.

Chapter 14:
Music for Moderns

287 'Bad rock and roll is through': *Cash Box*, June 1958.

287 'Most of our best numbers': quoted in Kaplan, *Frank*, p. 706.

290 'the brutalities of war': *Time*, 13 November 1964.

290 'It looks as if the minds': *G*, June 1962.

292 'Shadow choruses were so common': Lanza, *Elevator Music*, p. 113.

292 'They devised a series': Murrells, *Book of Golden Discs*, p. 124.

292 'brain workers find that it': quoted in Lanza, *Elevator Music*, p. 47.

292 'squeeze down the dynamic range': *Time*, 30 August 1963.

293 'The light shines in the eyes': *Records Magazine*, August 1959.

293 'Each manufacturer has invented': *American Record Guide*, September 1962.

293 'new scoring concepts': *American Record Guide*, September 1961.

294 'The more spacious the music': *DE*, 4 December 1958.

294 'music to test your speakers': *American Record Guide*, December 1960.

294 'It is obvious that the audio engineer': *American Record Guide*, January 1962.

294 'The music is being made': ibid.

294 'Dedicated audio fans': *Time*, 28 February 1955.

294 'compulsive personality': *Time*, 14 January 1957.

294 'a symbolic harem': ibid.

294 'In most instances when a lady': *Gramophone*, August 1925.

295 'the first band whose existence': *High-Fidelity*, June 1954.

295 'We sound awful': ibid.

295 'special rheostat control panel': *DB*, 15 July 1953.

295 'a kind of musically manic state': *Metronome*, January 1947.

295 'If playing flat simultaneously': *DB*, 14 January 1949.

296 'mathematic computations': *Jazz Journal*, November 1954.

296 'During a long intermission': *Jazz Journal*, August 1954.

296 'There's always an uncomfortable': *DB*, 14 July 1954.

296 'If this is what jazz': *Jazz Journal*, August 1962.

296 'I saw such men as Miles Davis': *MM*, 10 November 1956.

297 'the complete freedom of expression': *MM*, 15 September 1962.

297 'It would seem that jazz': *American Record Guide*, November 1958.

299 'As far as the record business': *BB*, 27 October 1962.

299 'The whole thing is pretty much a bore': *American Record Guide*, March 1963.

299 'sloppy and non-professional': *BB*, 1 December 1962.

301 'Carmen Miranda was first': quoted in Perrone, *Brazilian Popular Music*, p. 39.

301 'a common obsession united': Castro, *Bossa Nova*, p. 147.

301 'would sound good reading': McGowan, *The Brazilian Sound*, p. 63.

Chapter 15: Revolution in Reverse

305 'The Beatle People care': *Honey*, June 1963.

305 'When we play at the Cavern': ibid.

306 'taking on the character': *BB*, 27 October 1962.

306 'wound up in a riot': *BB*, 12 October 1963.

306 'a thumping teenage idol': *BB*, 28 September 1963.

307 'If we've just succeeded': *BB*, 7 December 1963.

307 'a Very Lively Corpse': *BB*, 16 March 1963.

307 'From Liverpool?': *BB*, 29 June 1963.

307 'Beatlemania seems to have taken': *BB*, 28 December 1963.

307 'the publicity ruckus': ibid.

307 'starlet Gail Stevens': *BB*, 4 January 1964.

307 'Great Britain hasn't been so influential': *BB*, 15 February 1964.

307 'would never last': *NME*, 27 March 1964.

307 'left no lasting impress': *American Record Guide*, April 1964.

308 'These boys, however good': *MM*, 29 February 1964.

308 'the biggest thing to have hit': *Mersey Beat*, 31 August–14 September 1961.

308 'Out goes the Rock': *MM*, 7 January 1961.

309 'Uniforms – Has Trad Gone Mad?': *MM*, 26 August 1961.

309 'obsessed with the concept': Godbolt, *All That and 10%*, p. 74.

309 'the first ever example': ibid., p. 84.

309 'Trad fans are usually': *DM*, 2 March 1963.

310 'The worst thing that happened': *MM*, 1 August 1964.

310 'since Today is so bloody awful': Leslie, *Fab*, p. 117.

311 'The music which is currently': *MM*, 17 November 1962.

311 'All the loud, death-dealing': *R'NB Scene*, September 1964.

311 'It's very dangerous': *MM*, 22 September 1962

312 'fervent fans': *MM*, 17 November 1962.

312 'I'm a purist': *MM*, 5 January 1963.

312 'One of the established': *MM*, 8 June 1963.

312 'very very ordinary': *MM*, 15 June 1963.

312 'in its fervour was like': *DM*, 13 June 1963.

312 'five young men who see themselves': *MM*, 29 June 1963.

312 'At first the music repelled me': Clapton, *Autobiography*, p. 40.

313 'He seemed constantly trapped': Frank Driggs' liner notes for Columbia CL 1654.

314 'one man and his guitar': quoted in Schwartz, *How Britain Got the Blues*, p. 74.

314 'All over London clubs': *Jazzbeat*, February 1964.

314 'I was very pompous': quoted in Schwartz, *How Britain Got the Blues*, p. 142.

314 'tempering enthusiasm with a degree': *R'NB Scene*, June 1964.

314 'bad guitar playing': *MM*, 14 November 1964.

314 'Can anyone explain why': *MM*, 23 February 1963.

314 'Donald Zec's [article]': *DM*, 14 September 1963.

314 'young men who live': *Town*, September 1962.

316 'the well-scrubbed youths': *Jazz Monthly*, June 1964.

316 'Youngsters beat up seaside town': *DE*, 30 March 1964.

316 'The War of the Rockers and Mods': *DM*, 18 September 1963.

317 'Purple hearts and beat music': *MM*, 11 April 1964.

317 'Every time something like this': ibid.

314 'The typical Rocker': Cohen, *Folk Devils*, p. 35.

317 'Music was much more important': ibid., p. 186.

317 'Rockers buy more records': *Rave*, May 1964.

318 'Ah, yes, Blue Beat': *Boyfriend 65 Book* (London, Boyfriend magazine, 1964).

319 'We think the Mod thing is dying': *MM*, 5 June 1965.

319 'an army, a powerful aggressive': *RS*, 14 September 1968.

319 'We made the establishment': *Cream*, October 1971.

319 'kids would reach the age of 22': ibid.

319 'Q: I am 15 and madly in love': *Honey*, March 1963.

319 'I've never seen a mob': *DM*, 25 January 1947.

320 'The other day I turned on': Kaplan, *Frank*, p. 179.

320 'I keep wondering if it's really me': *Washington Star*, 29 October 1956.

320 'They made it clear': *MM*, 16 March 1963.

320 '[P.J. Proby] seems to exploit sex': quoted in *NME*, 2 March 1974.

320 'You come out of a council flat': *RS*, 15 March 1973.

321 'Peter and Marty': *Music Week*, 20 January 1973.

321 'Don't you think, in this day': *NME*, 2 November 1974.

321 'After a while I realized': *NME*, 21 February 1976.

321 'You get some really wild old women': *Q*, January 1988.

321 'We came to *see* the Beatles': *Mersey Beat*, 5–19 December 1963.

321 'The raucous sound': quoted in *NME*, 10 January 1964.

321 'painfully clear that the Beatles': Leslie, *tab*, p. 149.

322 'Since Beatlemania became': Laurie, *The Teenage Revolution,* p. 102.

322 'the least fortunate of their generation': Leslie, *Fab*, p. 171.

322 'What a bottomless chasm': ibid., p. 163.

322 'We seem to rouse some sort': *Rave*, April 1964.

322 'an indication of the adult failure': Hechinger, *Teen-Age Tyranny*, p. 112.

322 'creeping adult adolescence': ibid., p. 116.

323 'I feel I've been betrayed': *Teen Magazine*, October 1964.

323 'Now only the socially inept': Laurie, *The Teenage Revolution,*p. 84.

323 'If the Rolling Stones need': ibid.

323 'You are Mr Wonderful': *Rave*, December 1964

324 'Everybody concerned has got': *MM*, 31 August 1963.

324 'On one point, the record makers': *DM*, 25 September 1963.

324 'I normally try to start': Murray, *How to Write a Hit Song*, p. 4.

324 'boy meets girl': ibid.

325 'It is very rarely, these days': ibid., p. 5.

324 'If you really study your market': ibid.

324 'when they have passed through': *DM*, 25 September 1963.

326 'I knew it would happen': *Record Retailer*, 26 September 1963.

326 'They are the only two': Leslie, *Fab*, p. 136

CHAPTER 16:
Sorry, Parents

329 'Dylan reduces the idiosyncratic': Charles Fox in *G*, September 1962.

329 'So the Beatles like Bob Dylan': *MM*, 26 December 1964

330 'a sailor's lament': *BB*, 22 June 1963.

330 'the ultimate influence': *BB*, 17 August 1963.

330 'This particular decade has not': Coward, *Lyrics*, p. 361.

330 'The vast teenage population': *MM*, 5 October 1963.

331 'what looks like the next': *BB*, 23 November 1963

331 'drag racing is practically': *BB*, 12 October 1963.

333 'It's taken over the radio stations': Columbia Records advertisement, April 1965.

333 '[Dylan], as a personality': *Rave*, June 1965.

333 'I reckon the Beatles': *MM*, 8 February 1964.

333 '[The Stones] are probably the coolest': *Records Magazine*, May 1964.

334 'a form of protest': *NME*, 6 March 1964.

334 'March is Mantovani Month': London Records advertisement, March 1964.

334 'To many, the tunes have never': *BB*, 6 June 1964.

335 'It was the last night of the Proms': *MM*, 19 October 1963.

336 'He's dreamy and has that little': *Rave*, November 1964.

336 'Thames beat': *BB*, 4 January 1964.

336 'The Mersey Sound': Epic Records advertisement, January 1964.

336 'I thought Peter Noone': *RS*, 21 December 1972.

337 'He's the sort of boy': *Rave*, February 1965.

337 'everybody's dream in the whole world': *Datebook*, October 1966.

337 'When you see a six-year-old': *RS*, 1 April 1971.

337 'win you the devotion': *BB*, 25 March 1967.

338 'When they accepted by adults': *MM*, 18 April 1964.

338 'They're great!': London Records advertisement, May 1964.

338 'inarticulate . . . childish': *Disc*, 18 July 1964.

338 'Elvis has proved he has real': ibid.

339 'they have caught the imagination': *MM*, 26 September 1964.

339 'Suddenly popular music': *RS*, 10 August 1968.

340 'Why is it criminal': *MM*, 7 November 1964.

Chapter 17: Highlife

343 '[They're] the undisputed rulers': *Ebony*, June 1965.

343 'Motown is black music': *RS*, 14 December 1967.

344 'We call it sweet music': *Ebony*, June 1965.

344 'because Paul McCartney': *BB*, 9 October 1965.

345 'While the Supremes will probably': *BB*, 7 August 1965.

348 'The lyrics are offensive': *BB*, 9 November 1963.

348 'the introduction of what can': *Negro Digest*, July 1965.

349 'We have found that the African': *African Music*, Vol. 1:1.

349 'I said to myself': Moore, *Fela*, p. 75.

349 'in decay': *African Music*, vol. 1:1.

349 'In January 1955': ibid.

350 'Ska was typically frowned': Katz, *Jimmy Cliff*, p. 34.

350 'It was not played on the radio': Katz, *Solid Foundation*, p. 56.

351 'It looks like somebody's': *Record Mail*, March 1964.

351 'the insistent thrump': ibid.

352 'Consequently . . . became outsiders': Letts, *Culture Clash*, p. 35.

353 'I said to myself, "How do Africans"': Moore, p. 85.

353 'The whole club started jumping': Moore, *Fela*, p. 88.

353 'We can make any location': *BB*, 6 February 1965.

353 '[LSD] is turning discos': *Rave*, June 1966.

354 'the most danceable tunes ever': *BB*, 6 February 1965.

354 'Frug, Watusi, Mule': Roure advertisement, February 1965.

355 'There were queues up and down': *MM*, 17 July 1965.

355 'The Byrds' sound combines': *BB*, 12 June 1965.

355 'aimed at the teen market': *BB*, 17 July 1965.

Chapter 18: Freak Out People

359 'Honesty, candour, frankness': *Rave*, June 1965.

359 'I was a freshman': *RS*, 11 July 1996.

360 'a complete banality': Michael Cox in *G*, September 1964.

360 'They all start with strumming': Steve Race in *Crescendo*, September 1964.

360 'could be the biggest thing yet': *Disc*, 18 July 1964.

360 'I like his whole attitude': *MM*, 9 January 1965.

360 'but we Beatle-ified it': ibid.

360 'The average pop-minded teenager': *MM*, 23 January 1965.

361 'A six-minute single?': Columbia Records advertisement, July 1965.

361 '"Like a Rolling Stone" will offend': *MM*, 7 August 1965.

362 'folk twist music': *BB*, 15 August 1964.

362 'anyone with an interest in discussing': *Crawdaddy*, August 1966.

363 'Let South Africa run': *MM*, 30 January 1965.

363 'Stars and celebrities should': ibid.

363 'I have to say that the native': *MM*, 8 April 1961.

363 'We can sing more coloured': *Time*, 21 May 1965.

363 'I wish I'd been born coloured': *MM*, 5 January 1963.

363 'I don't really see that playing': *MM*, 16 January 1965.

364 'the song might offend people': *MM*, 20 February 1965.

364 'African bushman hairdo': *Teen Set*, August 1967.

364 'A song's lyrical content': *BB*, 12 June 1965.

364 'Protest songs make me concentrate': *MM*, 2 October 1965.

364 'Rock + Folk + Protest': *BB*, 21 August 1965.

365 'inimical to military morale': *BB*, 15 January 1966.

365 'It is absurd to expect': ibid.

366 'We're more popular than Jesus': *Datebook*, September 1966.

366 'I believe it is good': *Datebook*, October 1966.

367 'Everyone needs kicks': *Rave*, March 1966.

367 'Most of the kids I know': *Ebony*, August 1969.

367 'Psychedelia! Wot's that?': *Honey*, February 1967.

367 'It involves an effect produced': *Record Mail*, November 1966.

368 'Soon there'll be sounds': *MM*, 9 October 1965.

370 'There's nothing going on': ibid.

370 'As far as the Beatles are concerned': *Rave*, April 1966.

371 '"I like rock 'n' roll, man': *RS*, 21 January 1971.

374 'Major sections of major US cities': *Ebony*, August 1967.

374 'What we may be witnessing': *DB*, 2 May 1968.

375 'It was not the performances': *BB*, 8 July 1967.

375 'his modal-tuned, chicken-choke': ibid.

375 'slipshod, lazy way': *DB*, 10 August 1967.

376 '[The audience] were listening': Clapton, *Autobiography*, p. 99.

376 'Destined to become 67's': Reprise Records advertisement, May 1967.

377 'We are in the midst': Shaw, *The Rock Revolution*, p. 3.

377 'It was like living at a time': Isaacson, *Steve Jobs*, p. 25.

377 'At the moment, it appears': Shaw, *The Rock Revolution*, p. 195.

378 'The crowd eyes the longhaired': Perrone, *Brazilian Popular Music*, p. 107.

379 'If rock 'n' roll': *Ebony*, November 1965.

379 'Apparently the Communists': *BB*, 4 December 1965.

379 'The sense of it is that': *Rave*, January 1967.

380 'When I bash my guitar': *Rave*, March 1966.

380 'It's beginning to affect': *Rave*, February 1966.

380 'You'd be surprised how many': ibid.

380 'ear-splitting vibrations': *IT*, 13–26 March 1967.

381 'suggested that all visitors': *BB*, 8 April 1967.

381 'a VALID and ACTUAL': ibid.

381 '40,000 purple hearts': *BB*, 27 May 1967.

Chapter 19:
Flying Through the Air

385 'We were asked not to excite': *Record Mail*, March 1966.

388 'Listening to it is like flying': *American Record Guide*, June 1966.

388 'I almost had my Mom': *Tiger Beat*, August 1966.

389 'The happiest sound': *BB*, 6 March 1965.

390 'Jazz today is Cannonball': *BB*, 24 April 1965.

391 'contributed immensely': *BB*, 10 September 1966.

392 'She will be around fifty years': syndicated column, *c.*20 January 1963.

392 'Why should you put music': *IT*, 21–28 April 1967.

393 'A lot of Madison Avenue type guys': *RS*, 27 May 1971.

394 'Tape has unbeatable advantages': *Time*, 28 June 1954.

394 'so simple that anyone': *Record Mail*, September 1966.

395 'Frightening': *Rave*, March 1967.

395 'One of these days you'll go': ibid.

395 'I still have a feeling': *MM*, 8 February 1964.

395 'a TV, hi-fi, electric shoe': *MM*, 13 January 1962.

395 'Here it is at last': *Record Retailer*, 12 April 1962.

395 'We have a long way to go': *Record Mail*, May 1962.

Chapter 20:
The New Prophets

399 'Don't underestimate the power': *RS*, 20 January 1968.

399 'Most rock and roll musicians': *RS*, 20 July 1968.

400 'so bloody real': Bang Records advertisement, October 1967.

400 'mob reaction': *Hit Parader*, July 1968.

401 'Somehow *Sgt. Pepper*': *RS*, 23 July 1970.

402 'It is very strange making': *RS*, 18 February 1971.

402 'What it boils down to': *NME*, 4 August 1973.

405 'The Sacred and Inspirational': Word Records advertisement, September 1963.

406 'I've played dubs of this mass': *BB*, 9 December 1967.

407 'actually preached that the syncopated': Thompson, *Raised by Wolves*, p. 30.

408 'A racy, rollicking': *Ebony*, May 1970.

408 'It has nothing to do with Black people': ibid.

410 'even becoming superstars': *Rave*, October 1968.

412 'If Presley were on the next plane': *Hit Parader*, November 1968.

412 'Don't be surprised if in 1978': *Rave*, May 1968.

412 'If you are a groover': *RS*, 22 June 1968.

415 'the Beatles . . . and the Animals': *BB*, 9 January 1965.

Chapter 21: Devil's Interval

419 'The British scene': *Rave*, July 1969.

419 'There is a lack of excitement': *RS*, 10 December 1970.

420 'The Beatles pattern': *RS*, 7 February 1970.

421 'The Rock Machine': Columbia Records advertisement, February 1968.

425 'It is apparent that rock': Shaw, *The Rock Revolution*, p. 178.

425 'My birthday is March 3rd': *RS*, 29 April 1971.

425 'everything from be-bop': *Jet*, 10 January 1952.

426 'Donny never has a bad thought': Bill Sammett's liner notes for *Osmonds* LP MGM SE 4724 (1970).

428 'What I've been trying to do': *Sounds*, 3 April 1971.

428 'As annoying as watching': *Cream*, October 1972.

428 'They look like builder's labourers': *NME*, 11 August 1973.

429 'would ultimately provide a safe haven': Cope, *Copendium*, p. 604.

430 'glam-rock may have had no more': ibid., p. 621.

430 'There's an incredible desire': *Sounds*, 27 March 1971.

431 'Heavy Metal Rock is amazingly': *NME*, 6 October 1973.

431 'There were kids actually bashing': *NME*, 24 February 1973.

431 'They are a sort of release valve': *NME*, 14 April 1973.

432 'trash with a rock beat': *Jazz & Pop*, November 1969.

432 'very insensitive grossness': Lester Bangs in *RS*, 26 November 1970.

432 'gross, disgusting object': *RS*, 13 August 1989.

432 'Tony came up with this riff': Osbourne, *I Am Ozzy* pp. 82–3.

433 'I can honestly say': ibid., p. 99.

433 'We've even had a few witches': *Rave*, August 1970.

433 'I'm scared of them': *RS*, 28 October 1971.

433 'It is our policy to avoid': *NME*, 12 December 1970.

433 'evolved from writing hard rock': *BB*, 11 March 1967.

434 'We had a place in forming': Walser, *Running with the Devil*, p. 9.

434 'We've all gotten comfortable': *Cream*, November 1971.

435 'Now progressive music': ibid.

435 'Lowest common denominator': *RS*, 19 August 1971.

435 'The spirit of American punk-rock': *RS*, 6 January 1972.

435 'Maybe anybody who cannot dig': *Cream*, November 1971.

436 'Their roots seem to be planted': *RS*, 6 January 1972.

Chater 22:
Push Button Rock

439 'I don't think we'll see': *RS*, 27 May 1971.

440 '95% of all illegitimate': *RS*, 3 February 1972.

440 'more deadly than heroin': *NME*, 14 February 1976.

440 'To think it could cause your child': *RS*, 3 February 1972.

442 'this must have been a sort': *RS*, 4 March 1971.

442 'There had been no brother/sister': *RS*, 4 July 1974.

442 'All the bands were just playing': *NME*, 21 February 1976.

443 'You could say I'm the Ray Conniff': *RS*, 16 August 1973.

443 'I'd like to have nine pianos': ibid.

443 'I regret facing the fact': *RS*, 7 October 1976.

445 'I realize the Beatles did fill': press conference, 23 October 1974.

445 'I don't like oldies': *NME*, 10 August 1974.

446 'Legally speaking': *NME*, 20 October 1973.

446 'neglected market': *Deejay & Radio Monthly*, December 1972.

448 'Very heavy, it was': *NME*, 6 April 1974.

448 'isn't a nostalgic get-together': *RS*, 29 March 1973.

449 'Letters have poured in': *Record Mirror*, 13 July 1974.

449 'We're trying to create a 1974': *Record Mirror*, 15 June 1974.

449 'They have no record contract': *NME*, 9 February 1974.

450 'we do our music live': *RS*, 20 May 1976.

450 'What is actually happening': *Ink*, 24 July 1971.

450 'I still ask myself why': Crosby, *Since Then*, p. 121.

452 'The very last thing [Mick]': *NME*, 18 August 1973.

452 'Rock music has become': *NME*, 16 March 1973.

454 'one can easily envisage a Floyd': *NME*, 23 November 1974.

455 'frustrates analysis': *RS*, 18 November 1976.

456 'Groups have tried that laid-back': *NME*, 1 February 1975.

456 'Two hundred million Americans': *RS*, 7 April 1979.

457 'a parody of the mad doctor': *NME*, 1 January 1977.

Chapter 23:
Union of Bodies

461 'Black music's basically rhythmic': *BM*, October 1976.

461 'Each dances by his or her self': *BM*, June 1974.

464 'R&B music, especially': *Ebony*, March 1972.

465 'Moving to music, and the sensation': *BM*, January 1976.

465 'I find it mindbending': *BB*, 7 April 1979.

465 'a complete repatriation': *NME*, 5 October 1974.

466 'Here in New York': *BM*, January 1976.

466 'His tour de force': Goldman, *Disco*, p. 115.

467 'I love to see people turn on': *BM*, January 1976.

468 'singers found that their vocals': Echols, *Hot Stuff*, pp. 9–10.

468 'When the punk rockers first': *Vibe*, December 1994/January 1995.

469 'I found a way to start': Katz, *Groove Music*, p. 55.

470 'With this seemingly unremarkable': ibid., p. 70.

470 'Such has been the impact': *Record Mirror*, 10 January 1976.

470 'The disco sound is a sound': *RS*, 13 January 1973.

470 'The sensation that's sweeping': *BM*, December 1973.

471 'We just got carried along': *BM*, April 1975.

471 'For the first time in my life': *BM*, December 1974.

471 'We would like to think': *Ebony*, March 1975.

472 'the first disposable King': *RS*, 28 August 1975.

472 '16 to 60, Barry is hurting': *BM*, July 1975.

473 'endless tedium': *NME*, 16 March 1974.

473 'almost complete lack': ibid.

473 'Uncle Tom': ibid.

473 'the most artificial shit': Echols, *Hot Stuff*, p. 10.

473 'an electronically boosted bass': *RS*, 28 August 1975.

473 'seem totally committed to making': *BM*, June 1975.

473 'Rock and roll in its purest form': *RS*, 28 August 1975.

474 'Dylan goes disco': *Record Mirror*, 15 January 1976.

474 'I love the music': *RS*, 25 March 1976.

474 'Disco's greatest fans are women': *Ebony*, October 1977.

475 'the music of the brave new world': *RS*, 12 January 1978.

475 'is expected to move purposefully': *BB*, 8 January 1977.

476 'Brazilians began to use neologistic': Echols, *Hot Stuff*, p. 200.

476 'disco became the biggest thing in pop': *RS*, 19 April 1979.

476 'Atmospheric bumpy': *Record Mirror*, 24 May 1980.

476 'Excellent remix of the lazily': ibid.

477 'Every song had to have Deep': Rodgers *Le Freak*, p. 129.

477 'Back then, most R&B acts': ibid., p. 139.

477 'Audiences no longer leave': *BB*, 28 April 1979.

477 'Disco Rules, But Where': *BB*, 19 May 1979.

478 'Imagine how bad business': ibid.

478 'People turn to dance': *BB*, 27 October 1979.

478 'heavier ballads, rock and R&B': *BB*, 15 December 1979.

479 'from young black DJs': *BB*, 1 July 1978.

479 'Jive Talking New York DJs': *BB*, 5 May 1979.

480 'Our raps may be about cars': *DE*, 20 December 1979.

480 'new-found form of black dance music': ibid.

Chapter 24: Be Disrespectful

483 'Every time a 60s superstar': *NME*, 5 October 1974.

483 'It's a whole new generation': *RS*, 30 January 1975.

484 'We want to tell you that what is around': *National Lampoon*, September 1972.

484 'a decade of dullness': *RS*, 27 December 1979.

484 'shit all over the stage': *Cream*, October 1971.

485 'The big stations only play': *RS*, 17 November 1979.

485 'The only way this whole rock 'n' roll': *NME*, 16 March 1974.

485 'total lack of self-consciousness': *NME*, 25 August 1973.

485 'in love with rock and roll': *NME*, 8 November 1975.

485 'within it, you can encompass': *NME*, 26 April 1975.

486 'simple, primitive, direct, honest': in Heylin, *Penguin Book*, p. 105.

486 'retard bop': *NME*, 15 May 1976.

486 'I think their music does contain': *NME*, 27 October 1973.

487 'Could this be the New Wave?': *RS*, 26 October 1972.

487 'All this talk about getting': *NME*, 14 September 1974.

487 'challenged by a lot of wild boys': ibid.

487 'If rock becomes safe': *NME*, 19 June 1976.

487 'dictatorship rock': *NME*, 9 February 1974.

487 'Be childish. Be irresponsible': quoted in Savage, *England's Dreaming*, p. 44.

487 'a cartoon vision of rock and roll': *NME*, 8 November 1975.

488 'a preconceived idea': *RS*, 21 April 1977.

488 'quite layered and structured': Rombes, *Cultural Dictionary of Punk*, p. 223.

488 'the punk ethic, anti-intelligence': *RS*, 5 July 1973.

489 'could be the Bay City Rollers': Savage, *England's Dreaming*, p. 122.

489 'quartet of spiky teenage misfits': *NME*, 21 February 1976.

489 'It is very likely that there will': *DM*, 2 December 1976.

490 'Punk rock people': *DM*, 1 December 1976.

490 'the Sex Pistols were programmed': Savage, *England's Dreaming*, p. 150.

490 'This "new wave" has got to take in': *Sniffin' Glue*, 28 September 1976.

491 'the dormant energy': *NME*, 6 November 1976.

492 'dole queue rock': *NME*, 26 March 1977.

492 'Punk futures': *DM*, 22 June 1977.

492 'There is evidence': *Church Times*, 25 March 1977.

492 'Punks are the same as the Government': *Sniffin' Glue*, August–September 1977.

492 'This scene, if there is': *Sniffin' Glue*, February 1977.

492 'Chuck away the fucking stupid': *Sniffin' Glue*, March 1977.

492 'All the new groups': *NME*, 2 April 1977.

492 'English punk was now open': Savage, *England's Dreaming*, p. 301.

492 'Punk rock is finished': *Who Put the Bomp*, March 1978.

492 'built-in obsolescence': ibid.

493 'What I picked up most': Letts, *Culture Clash*, p. 89.

493 'There are so many new bands': *Who Put the Bomp*, January 1979.

493 'I was the originator of punk rock': *Record Mirror*, 26 June 1976.

495 'This is a chord': *Sideburns*, January 1977.

496 'It's the small bands that interest me': *Sounds*, August 1980.

496 'Commercial punk was a sham': Glasper, *The Day the Country Died*, p. 11.

498 'music for people who hate music': Rombes, *A Cultural Dictionary of Punk*, p. 167.

498 'a disavowal – even a betrayal': ibid., p. 166.

498 'We got everything so late': author interview, 1992.

498 'seemed incredibly nihilistic': Lahickey, *All Ages*, p. 96.

498 'really struck by the fact': ibid.

499 'We were definitely pissing off': ibid., p. 97.

499 'It really seemed like total rebellion': ibid., p. 20.

Chapter 25:
Dance Stance

501 'Success is nothing': *BM*, June 1976.

501 'The poor blacks': *NME*, 11 December 1976.

503 'dark and uninviting': *NME*, 7 September 1974.

504 'The base of the music': ibid.

506 'Pretty soon a bunch': *NME*, 27 October 1973.

506 'They can get all the Moog': *RS*, 1 March 1973.

506 'As a matter of very serious': *Record Mirror*, 4 February 1984.

507 'You can develop a physical': *RS*, 13 February 1975.

508 'We are the first German group': *NME*, 6 September 1975.

508 'It was very gay': Malins, *Depeche Mode*, p. 13.

508 'a time of experimentation': Garratt, *Adventures in Wonderland*, p. 72.

510 'Groups that are dominated': *Keyboard*, June 1982.

510 'I play manually': ibid.

510 'The important lesson to be learned': *Keyboard*, April 1987.

510 'With better machines': *NME*, 6 September 1975.

510 'It's hypnotic as dance': *Keyboard*, June 1982.

512 'Techno sounds like a pneumatic': *DE*, 10 March 1994.

512 'Most acid records': *Soul Underground*, December 1988.

513 'I had a razor blade': *Keyboard*, August 1997.

514 'I'd let it play along': Kirn, *Keyboard Presents*, p. 48.

514 'Stripped of their songs': Garratt, *Adventures in Wonderland*, pp. 42–3.

514 'The contents of the lyrics': Hillegonda Rietvald in Redhead, *Club Cultures Reader*, p. 110.

515 'it's all about feeling': *Soul Underground*, January 1989.

516 'I remember how *friendly*': Garratt, *Adventures in Wonderland*, p. 28.

517 'We worked out that the average': Stock, *Hit Factory*, p. 46.

Chapter 26:
Presenting the Fantasy

519 'The illusion that rock and roll': *RS*, 24 May 1984.

519 'All these A&R people': *RS*, 10 November 1983.

520 'The man must decide': *BB*, 17 November 1979.

520 'If you want to sell records': *RS*, 5 December 1985.

522 'When we make videos': *RS*, 10 November 1983.

522 'Practically every video I see': press release, summer 1984.

523 'a shallow, tasteless': ibid.

524 'I wear make-up': Malins, *Depeche Mode*, p. 33.

524 'good old-fashioned hysteria': *RS*, 10 November 1983.

525 'MTV instigated a more profound': *RS*, 27 September 1984.

525 'Metal has broadened': *BB*, 27 April 1985.

525 'I call it "girl-friendly sound"': Roth, *Crazy from the Heart*, p. 111.

526 'The closer we dared to get': *RS*, 24 May 1984.

527 'fetishization of instrumental': Walser, *Running from the Devil*, p. 94.

529 'We came up with some fast': *Ebony*, December 1982.

529 '[He] fascinated the female': *BB*, 1 March 1980.

532 'Never trust the teller': *Studies in Classic American Literature* (1923).

532 'Her voice is thin': *RS*, 20 December 1984.

533 'I do not cling': *RS*, 23 March 1989.

533 'I guess I used to think': *RS*, 5 May 1988.

534 'Someday, Your Music Collection': MusicVision advertisement, March 1985.

534 'Is there anything behind the symbols': Cash, *Cash*, pp. 12–13.

535 'The New Age audience': *Q*, June 1988.

537 'That Michelob [beer] music': *RS*, 1 June 1989.

537 'the name [of the Who]': *RS*, 13 July 1989.

537 'Woodstock is what made': *RS*, 24 August 1989.

540 'Its father was a turntable': ADC advertisement, 1977.

541 'I always want an outstretched hand': *Spin*, May 1985.

Chapter 27: That Scream

543 'After hearing Herc': *BM*, December 1983–January 1984.

543 "I was writing poetry': *Soul Underground*, June 1988.

546 'We don't have to go to the leather': Bradley, *Anthology of Rap*, p. 121.

546 'Too many acts think that all': *Soul Underground*, January 1988.

546 'the Beatles of hip hop': Weingarten, *It Takes a Nation of Millions*, p. 119.

546 'No one could even imagine': ibid., p. 123.

546 'my biggest contribution to rap': *RS*, 15 November 1990.

547 'Back then there weren't any': *Spin*, May 1985.

548 'One of the positive things': *RS*, 14 June 1990.

548 'I just got a tape': *RS*, 20 September 1990.

548 'No one ever brings up': *RS*, 14 June 1990.

549 'Jews are responsible for the majority': quoted in Myrie, *Don't Rhyme*, p. 128.

549 'Now that the focus has switched': *RS*, 9 August 1990.

550 'In fields and warehouses': Garratt, *Adventures in Wonderland*, p. 160.

550 'Football hooliganism': Spence, *The Stone Roses*, p. 125.

551 'We saw some of the spirit': Spence, p. 124.

552 'Pop music was saved by the advent': ibid.

552 'Picture a thirteen-year-old': *The Closing of the American Mind* (1993), p. 75.

553 'I saw a documentary': *RS*, 1 October 1992.

553 'a blizzard of suicidal self-loathing': Baddeley, *Goth Chic*, p. 263.

553 'an audio horror movie': ibid., p. 261.

554 'If I hadn't written those songs': Apter, *Never Enough*, p. 161.

555 'Maintaining the punk rock': quoted in Morrell, *Nirvana*, p. 83.

555 'I don't feel the least bit guilty': quoted in ibid., p. 119.

556 'It could have been sludge': quoted in ibid., p. 56.

559 'Pantera have the ugliest': *RS*, 30 June 1994.

560 'Rap is media control': *RS*. 23 January 1992.

560 'I didn't want to be no': *Vibe*, September 1993.

560 'has no place in our society': *Vibe*, February 1995.

560 'The greatest thing that ever happened': ibid.

561 'The young kids – all the real': *Vibe*, September 1993.

561 'a way for the gangs to battle': *RS*, 7 August 1997.

562 'We knew the power of language': Bradley, *Goth Chic*, pp. 127–8.

562 'Rap is really funny': *RS*, 6 August 1992.

564 'Gangsta rap is over': *Vibe* April 1998.

Chapter 28:
Audio Time Warp

567 'Touch dancing': *BB*, 8 March 1980.

567 'Let's face it': *RS*, 2 June 1994.

568 'Big bands are young again': *BB*, 8 March 1980.

569 'I don't want to be a revivalist': *RS*, 23 March 1989.

569 'What material would they do?': *BB*, 16 February 1980.

569 'The Beatles are still saving': quoted Doggett, *You Never Give Me Your Money* (2009), p. 344.

569 'I don't see it as a sell-out': *RS*, 11 January 1990.

569 'meticulously hand-painted': Franklin Mint advertisement, February 1995.

571 'Remakes break across': *RS*, 26 January 1989.

572 'Listening to rock radio': *RS*, 1 June 1989.

575 'There is now a formula': *RS*, 16 May 1993.

575 'Most music is lazy': *RS*, 27 May 1993.

577 'The notion of being a pop star': *RS*, 2 November 1995.

577 'I think a lot of women': *Vibe*, March 1995.

578 'white kids who are black': *RS*, 2 November 1995.

581 'Miles Davis is my definition': *Spin*, December 1985.

581 'Playing 11,000-seater': *RS*, 1 June 1989

Chapter 29:
The Murder of Music?

587 'I was listening to the radio': realtalkny.uproxx.com.

587 'They're murderers of music!': *The Late, Late Show* (TV), October 2013.

590 'The nature of stardom': Bower, *Sweet Revenge*, p. 241.

591 'We look at her as a franchise': *RS*, 23 August 1990.

592 'we correct pseudo-singers' pitch': *RS*, 4 February 1993.

593 'Rock and roll is now': *RS*, 19 December 1985.

593 'When Bono, at the Grammies': Steyn, *Broadway Babies Say Goodnight*, p. 226.

594 'We've returned an upturned iceberg': *Q*, May 1987.

594 'There was a time when music': *RS*, 10 November 1983.

595 'All the advertising has been directed': *RS*, 16 June 1994.

595 'We gotta always cross-promote': *Vibe*, August 1999.

595 'I started waking up': ibid.

595 'Whoever put my shit on the Internet': Alderman, *Sonic Boom*, p. 114.

596 'Music should be free, anyway': *Vibe*, August 1994.

596 'The Internet's completely over': mirror.co.uk, 5 July 2010.

597 'Digital distribution means': Alderman, *Sonic Boom*, p. 4.

600 'With iTunes, it's not stealing': Isaacson, *Steve Jobs*, p. 403.

600 'Not having a tangible item': *The Joy of the Single*, BBC4 (TV), 2012.

600 'It's possible the past 10 years': pitchfork.com, 24 August 2009.

601 'With vinyl, the aesthetic': quoted in Fisher, *Politics of Post 9/11 Sound*, p. 41.

605 'listening at top volume': quoted in Johnson, *Dark Side of the Tune*, p. 169.

606 'These people haven't heard heavy metal': bbc.co.uk, 20 May 2003.

Chapter 30:
Blurred Lines

609 'There are so many old things': quoted in *Guardian*, 4 April 2014.

609 'I can't imagine someone': *American Heritage* October–November 1981.

610 'Rock 'n' roll is out of date': *DM*, 8 September 1956.

611 'perpetuates your adolescence': *NME*, 22 November 1975.

613 'Nobody's done a death album': *NME*, 9 October 1976.

615 '[The 90s] was full of music': *Guardian*, 25 February 2011.

617 'Latin culture gets recycled': *Spin*, October 1999.

617 'prison escapes, massacres': Grillo, *El Narco*, p. 170.

618 '*MTV Jams* has made R&B': *Vibe*, November–December 1993.

618 'Eminem raps like a girl': *Vibe*, June 1999.

619 'Many African youths': *Vibe*, August 1997.

620 'I love Eminem': *Vibe*, June 1999.

621 'Can one artist or group': *Vibe*, August 1995.

623 'popped up like some kind': *Guardian*, 14 November 2013.

623 'It's important to me': Vibe, September 1999.

623 'People always ask me': *RS*, 27 May 1999.

624 'Rock has to absorb': *RS*, 14 December 1995.

624 'In America now, Skrillex': *Guardian*, 3 August 2012.

624 'Huge chunks [of the top 40]': *Guardian*, 29 December 2012.

627 'Dance music now *is* pop music': internationalmusicsummit.com, May 2012.

Select Bibliography

Abbott, Lynn, with Doug Seroff: *Out of Sight: The Rise of African-American Popular Music 1889–1895* (Jackson: University Press of Mississippi, 2002)

Alderman, John: *Sonic Boom: Napster, P2P and the Future of Music* (London: 4th Estate, 2001)

Allen, Ray, and Lois Wilcken (eds): *Island Sounds in the Global City: Caribbean Popular Music & Identity in New York* (Urbana: University of Illinois Press, 2001)

Alvarez, Luis: *The Power of the Zoot: Youth Culture and Resistance during World War II* (Berkeley: University of California Press, 2008)

Anderson, Mark, and Mark Jenkins: *Dance of Days: Two Decades of Punk in the Nation's Capital* (New York: Akashic Books, 2003)

Andrews, Maxene, and Bill Gilbert: *Over Here, Over There: The Andrews Sisters and the USO Stars in World War II* (New York: Zebra, 1993)

Apter, Jeff: *Never Enough: The Story of the Cure* (London: Omnibus Press, 2005)

Arthur, Max: *When This Bloody War Is Over: Soldiers' Songs of the First World War* (London: Piatkus, 2002)

Baade, Christina L.: *Victory through Harmony: The BBC and Popular Music in World War II* (New York: Oxford University Press, 2012)

Baddeley, Gavin: *Goth Chic: A Connoisseur's Guide to Dark Culture* (London: Plexus, 2002)

Bane, Michael: *White Boy Singin' the Blues: The Black Roots of White Rock* (London: Penguin, 1982)

Barrios, Richard: *A Song in the Dark: The Birth of the Musical Film* (New York: Oxford University Press, 1995)

Beaumont, Mark: *The King of America: Jay-Z* (London: Omnibus Press, 2012)

Behr, Edward: *Thank Heaven for Little Girls: The True Story of Maurice Chevalier's Life and Times* (London: Hutchinson, 1993)

Belafonte, Harry, with Michael Schnayerson: *My Song* (Edinburgh: Canongate, 2012)

Benatar, Pat, with Patsi Bale Cox: *Between a Heart and a Rock Place: A Memoir* (New York: !t books, 2011)

Bergmaier, Horst J. P., and Rainer E. Lotz: *Hitler's Airwaves: The Inside Story of Nazi Radio Broadcasting of Propaganda Swing* (London: Yale University Press, 1997)

Bergreen, Laurence: *As Thousands Cheer: The Life of Irving Berlin* (New York: Penguin, 1991)

Berlin, Edward A.: *Ragtime: A Musical and Cultural History* (Berkeley: University of California Press, 1980)

Berlin, Edward A.: *King of Ragtime: Scott Joplin and His Era* (New York: Oxford University Press, 1994)

Berrett, Joshua: *Louis Armstrong & Paul Whiteman: Two Kings of Jazz* (New Haven: Yale University Press, 2004)

Berry, Chuck: *The Autobiography* (London: Faber & Faber, 1988)

Best, Curwen: *Barbadian Popular Music and the Politics of Caribbean Culture* (Rochester: Schenkman Books, 1999)

Best, Curwen: *Culture @ the Cutting Edge: Tracing Caribbean Popular Music* (Kingston: University of the West Indies Press, 2004)

Bindas, Kenneth J.: *Swing, That Modern Sound* (Jackson: University Press of Mississippi, 2001)

Bloch, Peter: *La-Le-Lo-Lai: Puerto Rican Music and its Performers* (New York: Plus Ultra, 1973)

Bower, Tom: *Sweet Revenge: The Intimate Life of Simon Cowell* (London: Faber & Faber, 2012)

Bradley, Adam, and Andrew DuBois (eds): *The Anthology of Rap* (New Haven: Yale University Press, 2010)

Bradley, Lloyd: *Sounds Like London: 100 Years of Black Music in the Capital* (London: Serpent's Tail, 2013)

Bret, David: *The Real Gracie Fields: The Authorised Biography* (London: JR Books, 2010)

Brewster, Bill, and Frank Broughton: *The Record Players: DJ Revolutionaries* (London: DJhistory.com, 2010)

Broadcasting in Everyday Life (London: British Broadcasting Corporation, 1939)

Broonzy, William, and Yannick Bruynoghe: *Big Bill's Blues* (London: Cassell, 1955)

Broughton, Viv: *Black Gospel: An Illustrated History of the Gospel Sound* (Poole: Blandford Press, 1985)

Budds, Michael J. (ed.): *Jazz and the Germans: Essays on the Influence of*

'Hot' American Idioms on 20th Century German Music (Hillsdale: Pendragon Press, 2002)

Burton, Humphrey: *Leonard Bernstein* (New York: Anchor Books, 1995)

Butler, Mark J.: *Unlocking the Groove: Rhythm, Meter and Musical Design in Electronic Dance Music* (Bloomington: Indiana University Press, 2006)

Calt, Stephen: *I'd Rather Be the Devil: Skip James and the Blues* (New York: Da Capo, 1994)

Cantwell, Robert: *Bluegrass Breakdown: The Making of the Old Southern Sound* (Urbana: University of Illinois Press, 1984)

Carney, Court: *Cuttin' Up: How Early Jazz Got America's Ear* (Lawrence: University Press of Kansas, 2009)

Cash, Johnny, with Patrick Carr: *Cash: The Autobiography* (New York: HarperSanFrancisco, 1997)

Castro, Ruy: *Bossa Nova: The Story of the Brazilian Music that Seduced the World* (Chicago: A Cappella Books, 2000)

Chanan, Michael: *Repeated Takes: A Short History of Recording and its Effects on Music* (London: Verso, 1995)

Chang, Jeff: *Can't Stop Won't Stop: A History of the Hip-Hop Generation* (London: Ebury Press, 2007)

Charles, Ray, with David Ritz: *Brother Ray* (New York: Da Capo Press, 2004)

Clapton, Eric, with Christopher Simon Sykes: *Eric Clapton: The Autobiography* (London: Century, 2007)

Clayson, Alan, and Spencer Leigh (eds): *Aspects of Elvis* (London: Sidgwick & Jackson, 1994)

Cliffe, Peter: *Fascinating Rhythm* (Baldock: Egon Publishers, 1990)

Clover, Joshua: *1989: Bob Dylan Didn't Have This to Sing About* (Berkeley: University of California Press, 2009)

Cohen, Harvey G.: *Duke Ellington's America* (Chicago: University of Chicago Press, 2010)

Cohen, Rich: *The Record Men: The Chess Brothers and the Birth of Rock & Roll* (London: Profile Books, 2005)

Cohen, Stanley: *Folk Devils and Moral Panics: The Creation of the Mods and Rockers* (Oxford: Martin Robertson, 1980)

Collier, James Lincoln: *The Reception of Jazz in America: A New View* (Brooklyn: Institute for Studies in American Music, 1988)

Cooper, Daniel: *Lefty Frizzell: The Honky-Tonk Life of Country Music's Greatest Singer* (New York: Little, Brown, 1995)

Cope, Julian: *Copendium* (London: Faber & Faber, 2012)

Coward, Noël: *The Lyrics of Noël Coward* (London: Methuen, 2002)

Crosby, David, with Carl Gottlieb: *Since Then* (New York: Berkley Books, 2006)

Crosland, Margaret: *A Cry from the Heart: The Biography of Edith Piaf* (London: Arcadia Books, 2002)

Crouch, Kevin and Tanja: *Sun King: The Life and Times of Sam Phillips* (London: Piatkus, 2008)

Currie, Tony: *The Radio Times Story* (Tiverton: Kelly Publications, 2001)

Dawson, Jim: *The Twist: The Story of the Song and Dance That Changed the World* (Winchester, MA: Faber & Faber,1995)

Delmore, Alton: *Truth is Stranger Than Publicity: Alton Delmore's Autobiography* (Nashville: Country Music Foundation, 1977)

Dewe, Mike: *The Skiffle Craze* (Aberystwyth: Planet, 1998)

Echols, Alice: *Hot Stuff: Disco and the Remaking of American Culture* (New York: W.W. Norton & Co., 2010)

Eisenberg, Evan: *The Recording Angel: Explorations in Phonography* (New York: McGraw-Hill, 1987)

Ellis, Royston: *The Big Beat Scene* (York: Music Mentor, 2010)

Emery, Ralph, with Tom Carter: *Memories: The Autobiography of Ralph Emery* (New York: Pocket Books, 1992)

Epstein, Daniel Mark: *Nat King Cole* (New York: Farrar, Straus and Giroux, 1999)

Escott, Colin, with Martin Hawkins: *Good Rockin' Tonight: Sun Records and the Birth of Rock 'n' Roll* (New York: St Martin's Press, 1991)

Evanier, David: *Roman Candle: The Life of Bobby Darin* (Emmaus: Rodale, 2004)

Ewen, David: *Panorama of American Popular Music* (Englewood Cliffs: Prentice-Hall Inc., 1957)

Faith, Adam: *Poor Me: A Candid Self-Portrait* (London: 4-Square/Souvenir Books, 1961)

Farrell, Gerry: *Indian Music and the West* (New York: Oxford University Press, 1997)

Feldman, Christine Jacqueline: *We Are the Mods: A Transnational History of a Youth Subculture* (New York: Peter Lang, 2009)

Fidelman, Geoffrey Mark: *First Lady of Song: Ella Fitzgerald for the Record* (New York: Citadel Press, 1996)

Firestone, Ross: *Swing, Swing, Swing: The Life and Times of Benny Goodman* (London: Hodder & Stoughton, 1993)

Fisher, John: *George Formby* (London: Woburn/Futura, 1975)

Fisher, Joseph P., and Brian Flota (eds): *The Politics of Post 9/11 Music: Sound, Trauma and the Music Industry in the Time of Terror* (Farnham: Ashgate, 2011)

Fong-Torres, Ben: *The Hits Just Keep On Coming: The History of Top 40 Radio* (San Francisco: Backbeat, 1998)

Fowler, David: *Youth Culture in Modern Britain, c. 1920–c. 1970* (London: Palgrave Macmillan, 2008)

Fox-Strangways, A. H., with Maud Karpeles: *Cecil Sharp* (London: Oxford University Press, 1933)

Frame, Pete: *The Restless Generation* (London: Rogan House, 2007)

Freedland, Michael: *Al Jolson* (London: Abacus, 1975)

Fritz, Jimi: *Rave Culture: An Insider's Overview* (Chemainus: Small Fry Press, 1999)

Gammond, Peter (ed.): *Duke Ellington, His Life and Music* (London: Phoenix House, 1958)

Garratt, Sheryl: *Adventures in Wonderland: A Decade of Club Culture* (London: Headline, 1999)

Geijerstam, Claes af: *Popular Music in Mexico* (Albuquerque: University of New Mexico Press, 1976)

Gelatt, Roland: *The Fabulous Phonograph 1877–1977* (London: Cassell, 1977)

Gelly, Dave: *Stan Getz: Nobody Else But Me* (San Francisco: Backbeat, 2002)

Giddins, Gary: *Bing Crosby: A Pocketful of Dreams: The Early Years 1903–1940* (New York: Little, Brown, 2001)

Gioia, Ted: *The Imperfect Art: Reflections on Jazz and Modern Culture* (New York: Oxford University Press, 1988)

Glasper, Ian: *The Day the Country Died: A History of Anarcho Punk 1980–1984* (London: Cherry Red Books, 2006)

Godbolt, Jim: *All This and 10%* (London: Robert Hale, 1976)

Godbolt, Jim: *A History of Jazz in Britain 1919–50* (London: Northway Publications, 2010)

Goldman, Albert: *Disco* (New York: Hawthorn Books, 1978)

Gottlieb, Robert, and Robert Kimball (eds): *Reading Lyrics* (New York: Pantheon Books, 2000)

Greene, Victor: *A Passion For Polka: Old-Time Ethnic Music in America* (Berkeley: University of California Press, 1992)

Grillo, Ioan: *El Narco: Inside Mexico's Criminal Insurgency* (London: Bloomsbury, 2011)

Groom, Bob: *The Blues Revival* (London: Studio Vista, 1971)

Grudens, Richard: *Star Dust: The Bible of the Big Bands* (Stonybrook: Celebrity Profiles Publishing, 2008)

Guralnick, Peter: *Last Train to Memphis: The Rise of Elvis Presley* (London: Little, Brown, 1995)

Halberstadt, Alex: *Lonely Avenue: The Unlikely Life and Times of Doc Pomus* (London: Jonathan Cape, 2007)

Hall, Fred: *Dialogues in Swing: Intimate Conversations with the Stars of the Big Band Era* (Ventura: Pathfinder Publishing, 1989)

Hamilton, Marybeth: *In Search of the Blues: Black Voices, White Visions* (London: Jonathan Cape, 2007)

Hamm, Charles: *Putting Popular Music in its Place* (Cambridge: Cambridge University Press, 1995)

Hancock, John: *Benny Goodman: The Famous 1938 Carnegie Hall Concert* (Shrewsbury: Prancing Fish Publishing, 2009)

Harker, Dave: *Fakesong: The Manufacture of British 'Folksong' 1700 to the Present Day* (Milton Keynes: Open University Press, 1985)

Harris, Charles K.: *How to Write a Popular Song* (Chicago: self-published, 1906 [1897])

Heath, Ted: *Listen to My Music: An Autobiography* (London: Frederick Muller, 1957)

Hechinger, Grace and Fred M.: *Teen-Age Tyranny* (London: Gerald Duckworth, 1964)

Hernandez, Deborah Pacini, Héctor Fernández-L'Hoeste, and Eric Zolov (eds): *Rockin' Las Americas: The Global Politics of Rock in Latin/o America* (Pittsburgh: University of Pittsburgh Press, 2004)

Heylin, Clinton (ed.): *The Penguin Book of Rock & Roll Writing* (London: Viking, 1992)

Hill, Donald R.: *Calypso Calaloo: Early Carnival Music in Trinidad* (Gainesville: University Press of Florida, 1993)

Hopkins, Jerry: *Elvis* (London: Abacus Books, 1974)

Isaacson, Walter: *Steve Jobs* (London: Little, Brown, 2011)

Jasen, David A., and Trebor Jay Tichenor: *Rags and Ragtime: A Musical History* (New York: Seabury Press, 1978)

Johnson, Bruce, and Martin Cloonan: *Dark Side of the Tune: Popular Music and Violence* (Farnham: Ashgate, 2009)

Jordan, Matthew F.: *Le Jazz: Jazz and French Cultural Identity* (Urbana: University of Illinois Press, 2010)

Kaplan, James: *Frank: The Making of a Legend* (London: Sphere, 2010)

Katz, David: *Solid Foundation: An Oral History of Reggae* (London: Bloomsbury, 2003)

Katz, David: *Jimmy Cliff: An Unauthorised Biography* (London: Macmillan Signal, 2011)

Katz, Mark: *Capturing Sound: How Technology Has Changed Music* (Berkeley: University of California Press, 2004)

Katz, Mark: *Groove Music: The Art and Culture of the Hip-Hop DJ* (New York: Oxford University Press, 2012)

Kelly, Sarah: *Teen Idols* (New York: Pocket Books, 2002)

Kenney, William Howland: *Chicago Jazz: A Cultural History 1904–1930* (New York: Oxford University Press, 1993)

Kirby, David: *Little Richard: The Birth of Rock 'n' Roll* (New York: Continuum, 2009)

Kirn, Peter (ed.): *Keyboard Presents: The Evolution of Electronic Dance Music* (Milwaukee: Backbeat Books, 2011)

Krivine, J.: *Juke-Box Saturday Night* (London: New English Library, 1977)

Lahickey, Beth (ed.): *All Ages: Reflections on Straight Edge* (Huntington Beach: Revelation Books, 1997)

Laird, Tracey E. W.: *Louisiana Hayride: Radio and Roots Music along the Red River* (New York: Oxford University Press, 2005)

Lanza, Joseph: *Elevator Music* (London: Quartet, 1995)

Larkin, Philip: *All What Jazz: A Record Diary 1961–68* (London: Faber & Faber, 1970)

Laurie, Peter: *The Teenage Revolution* (London: Anthony Blond, 1965)

Lauterbach, Preston: *The Chitlin' Circuit and the Road to Rock 'n' Roll* (New York: W.W. Norton & Co., 2011)

Leader, Zachary (ed.): *The Letters of Kingsley Amis* (London: HarperCollins, 2001)

Leigh, Spencer: *Everyday: Getting Closer to Buddy Holly* (London: SAF, 2009)

Leslie, Peter: *Fab: The Anatomy of a Phenomenon* (London: MacGibbon & Kee, 1965)

Leslie, Peter: *A Hard Act to Follow: A Music Hall Review* (New York: Paddington Press, 1978)

Letts, Don, with David Nobakht: *Culture Clash: Dread Meets Punk Rockers* (London: SAF, 2007)

Lewis, Jerry Lee, with Charles White: *Killer!* (London: Century, 1993)

Lloyd, A. L.: *Folk Song in England* (London: Lawrence & Wishart, 1967)

Lombardo, Guy, with Jack Altshul: *Auld Acquaintance: An Autobiography* (Garden City: Doubleday, 1975)

Mabey, Richard: *The Pop Process* (London: Hutchinson Educational, 1969)

Macan, Edward: *Rocking the Classics: English Progressive Rock and the Counterculture* (New York: Oxford University Press, 1997)

Maggin, Donald L.: *Dizzy: The Life and Times of John Birks Gillespie* (New York: HarperEntertainment, 2005)

Malins, Steve: *Depeche Mode: A Biography* (London: Andre Deutsch, 1997)

Malone, Bill C.: *Singing Cowboys and Musical Mountaineers* (Athens: University of Georgia Press, 1993)

Mann, William J.: *Hello Gorgeous: Becoming Barbra Streisand* (London: The Robson Press, 2012)

Manuel, Peter: *Popular Musics of the Non-Western World* (New York: Oxford University Press, 1988)

Manuel, Peter: *Caribbean Currents: Caribbean Music from Rumba to Reggae* (Philadelphia: Temple University Press, 1995)

Margolick, David: *Strange Fruit: Billie Holiday, Café Society and an Early Cry for Civil Rights* (Edinburgh: Canongate, 2001)

Martland, Peter: *Recording History: The British Record Industry 1888–1931* (Lanham: Scarecrow Press, 2013)

McCarthy, Albert: *The Dance Band Era* (London: Spring Books, 1974)

McGee, David: *B.B. King: There Is Always One More Time* (San Francisco: Backbeat, 2005)

McGowan, Chris, and Ricardo Pessanha: *The Brazilian Sound: Samba, Bossa Nova and the Popular Music of Brazil* (New York: Billboard Books, 1991)

McKagan, Duff: *It's So Easy and Other Lies* (London: Orion, 2011)

Mendl, R. W. S.: *The Appeal of Jazz* (London: Philip Allen & Co., 1927)

Miller, James: *Almost Grown: The Rise of Rock* (London: Arrow Books, 2000)

Moore, Carlos: *Fela: This Bitch of a Life* (London: Omnibus Press, 2010)

Morrell, Brad: *Nirvana & the Sound of Seattle* (London: Omnibus Press, 1996)

Murray, Albert: *Stomping the Blues* (London: Quartet, 1978)

Murray, Charles Shaar: *Boogie Man: The Adventures of John Lee Hooker in the American Twentieth Century* (Edinburgh: Canongate, 2011)

Murray, Mitch: *How to Write a Hit Song* (London: B. Feldman & Co., 1964)

Murrells, Joseph: *The Book of Golden Discs* (London: Barrie & Jenkins, 1978)

Myrie, Russell: *Don't Rhyme for the Sake of Riddlin': The Authorized Study of Public Enemy* (New York: Grove Press, 2008)

Nelson, Stanley R.: *All About Jazz* (London: Heath Cranton, 1934)

Ogren, Kathy J.: *The Jazz Revolution: Twenties America and the Meaning of Jazz* (New York: Oxford University Press, 1989)

Oliver, Paul: *Blues Off the Record* (Tunbridge Wells: The Baton Press, 1984)

Oliver, Paul: *Barrelhouse Blues* (New York: BasicCivitas Books, 2009)

Osbourne, Ozzy: *I Am Ozzy* (London: Sphere, 2009)

Ospina, Hernando Calvo: *Salsa! Havana Heat: Bronx Beat* (London: Latin American Bureau, 1995)

Parsonage, Catherine: *The Evolution of Jazz in Britain, 1880–1935* (Aldershot: Aldgate, 2005)

Payne, Jack: *This Is Jack Payne* (London: Sampson Low, Marston & Co., 1932)

Perrone, Charles A., and Christopher Dunn (eds): *Brazilian Popular Music and Globalization* (New York: Routledge, 2002)

Peterson, Oscar: *A Jazz Odyssey* (New York: Continuum, 2002)

Petkov, Steve, and Leonard Mustazza (eds): *The Frank Sinatra Reader* (New York: Oxford University Press, 1995)

The Picture Show Annual 1929–1934 (London: *Picture Show* magazine, 1928–1933)

Pollack, Howard: *George Gershwin: His Life and Work* (Berkeley: University of California Press, 2006)

Poschardt, Ulf: *DJ Culture* (London: Quartet Books, 1998)

Pugh, Martin: *We Danced All Night: A Social History of Britain between the Wars* (London: The Bodley Head, 2008)

Rau, Rutherford: *Stars Off the Record* (London: Eldon Press, 1955)

Redhead, Steve (ed.): *The Clubcultures Reader: Readings in Popular Culture Studies* (Oxford: Blackwell, 1998)

Ribowsky, Mark: *The Supremes* (Cambridge, MA: Da Capo Press, 2009)

Rijff, Ger (ed.): *Long Lonely Highway: A 1950s Elvis Scrapbook* (Ann Arbor: Pierian Press, 1987)

Roach, Martin: *Take That Now and Then: The Illustrated Story* (London: HarperCollins, 2009)

Robb, David (ed.): *Protest Song in East and West Germany since the 1960s* (Rochester: Camden House, 2007)

Rodgers, Nile: *Le Freak* (London: Sphere, 2011)

Rombes, Nicholas: *A Cultural Dictionary of Punk 1974–1982* (New York: Continuum, 2009)

Roth, David Lee: *Crazy from the Heat* (London: Ebury Press, 1997)

Russell, Tony: *Blacks, Whites and Blues* (New York: Stein & Day, 1970)

Russell, Tony: *Country Music Records: A Discography, 1921–1942* (New York: Oxford University Press, 2004)

Rust, Brian: *The Complete Entertainment Discography from the mid-1890s to 1942* (New Rochelle: Arlington House, 1973)

Rust, Brian: *The American Dance Band Discography 1917–1942* (2 vols) (New Rochelle: Arlington House, 1975)

Rust, Brian: *Jazz Records 1897–1942* (2 vols) (New Rochelle: Arlington House, 1978)

Rust, Brian, and Sandy Forbes: *British Dance Bands on Record: 1911 to 1945* (Harrow: General Gramaphone [sic] Publications, 1987)

Ryback, Timothy W.: *Rock around the Bloc: A History of Rock Music in Eastern Europe and the Soviet Union* (New York: Oxford University Press, 1990)

Sanjek, Russell: *American Popular Music and its Business: The First Four Hundred Years* (3 vols) (New York: Oxford University Press, 1988)

Savage, Jon: *England's Dreaming: Sex Pistols and Punk Rock* (London: Faber & Faber, 1991)

Savigliano, Marta E.: *Tango and the Political Economy of Passion* (Boulder: Westview Press, 1995)

Scannell, Paddy, and David Cardiff: *A Social History of British Broadcasting. Vol. 1 1922–1939: Serving the Nation* (Oxford: Basil Blackwell, 1991)

Schafer, William J., and Johannes Riedel: *The Art of Ragtime: Form and Meaning of an Original Black American Art* (New York: Da Capo, 1977)

Schuller, Gunther: *Early Jazz: Its Roots and Development* (New York: Oxford University Press, 1968)

Schuller, Gunther: *The Swing Era: The Development of Jazz 1930–1945* (New York: Oxford University Press, 1989)

Schwartz, Roberta Freund: *How Britain Got the Blues: The Transmission and*

Reception of American Blues Style in the United Kingdom (Aldershot: Ashgate, 2007)

Self, Geoffrey: *Light Music in Britain since 1870: A Survey* (Aldershot: Ashgate, 2001)

Self, Philip: *Guitar Pull: Conversations with Country Music's Legendary Songwriters* (Nashville: Cypress Moon, 2002)

Shapiro, Nat, and Nat Hentoff (eds): *Hear Me Talkin' to Ya: The Story of Jazz by the Men Who Made It* (Harmondsworth: Penguin, 1962)

Sharp, Cecil: *English Folk-Song: Some Conclusions* (London: Novello & Co., Simpkin & Co., 1907)

Shaw, Arnold: *The Rock Revolution* (New York: Macmillan, 1969)

Shaw, Artie: *The Trouble with Cinderella: An Outline of Identity* (New York: Da Capo, 1979)

Siegel, Carol: *Goth's Dark Empire* (Bloomington: Indiana University Press, 2005)

Simon, George T.: *Glenn Miller and His Orchestra* (London: W. H. Allen, 1974)

Smith, Kathleen E. R.: *God Bless America: Tin Pan Alley Goes to War* (Lexington: University of Kentucky Press, 2003)

Spaeth, Sigmund: *A History of Popular Music in America* (London: Phoenix House, 1948)

Spence, Simon: *The Stone Roses: War and Peace* (London: Viking, 2012)

Steele, Tommy: *Bermondsey Boy* (London: Penguin, 2007)

Stewart-Baxter, Derrick: *Ma Rainey* (London: Studio Vista, 1970)

Steyn, Mark: *Broadway Babies Say Goodnight: Musicals Then and Now* (London: Faber & Faber, 1997)

Stock, Mike: *The Hit Factory: The Stock, Aitken & Waterman Story* (London: New Holland, 2004)

Sublette, Ned: *Cuba and its Music: From the First Drums to the Mambo* (Chicago: Chicago Review Press, 2004)

Sudhalter, Richard M.: *Lost Chords: White Musicians and Their Contribution to Jazz, 1915–1945* (New York: Oxford University Press, 1999)

Sudhalter, Richard M.: *Stardust Melody: The Life and Music of Hoagy Carmichael* (New York: Oxford University Press, 2002)

Suisman, David: *Selling Sounds: The Commercial Revolution in American Music* (Cambridge, MA: Harvard University Press, 2009)

Sullivan, Randall: *Untouchable: The Strange Life and Tragic Death of Michael Jackson* (London: Grove Press, 2012)

Sweet, Matthew: *The West End Front: The Wartime Secrets of London's Grand Hotels* (London: Faber & Faber, 2011)

Tannenbaum, Rob, and Craig Marks: *I Want My MTV: The Uncensored Story of the Music Video Revolution* (New York: Plume, 2012)

Taylor, D. J.: *Bright Young People: The Rise and Fall of a Generation: 1918–1940* (London: Chatto & Windus, 2007)

Taylor, Timothy D., Mark Katz, and Tony Grajeda (eds): *Music, Sound and Technology in America* (Durham: Duke University Press, 2012)

Teachout, Terry: *Pops: The Wonderful World of Louis Armstrong* (London: JR Books, 2009)

This England's Book of British Dance Bands from the Twenties to the Fifties (Cheltenham: This England Books, 1999)

Thomas, Bob, with Fred Astaire: *Astaire, the Man, the Dancer* (London: Weidenfeld & Nicolson, 1985)

Thompson, John J.: *Raised by Wolves: The Story of Christian Rock & Roll* (Toronto: ECW Press, 2000)

Thornton, Sarah: *Club Cultures: Music, Media and Subcultural Capital* (Cambridge: Polity, 1995)

Tosches, Nick: *Dino* (London: Vintage, 1999)

Troitsky, Artemy: *Tusovka: Who's Who in the New Soviet Rock Culture* (London: Omnibus Press, 1990)

Tucker, John: *Suzie Smiled . . . The New Wave of British Heavy Metal* (Church Stretton: Independent Music Press, 2006)

Udo, Tommy: *Brave Nu World* (London: Sanctuary, 2002)

Vail, Ken: *Lady Day's Diary: The Life of Billie Holiday 1937–1959* (Chessington: Castle Communications, 1996)

Vail, Ken: *Count Basie: Swingin' the Blues 1936–1950* (Lanham: Scarecrow Press, 2003)

Vernon, Paul: *A History of the Portuguese Fado* (Aldershot: Ashgate, 1998)

Wald, Elijah: *Escaping the Delta: Robert Johnson and the Invention of the Blues* (New York: Amistad, 2004)

Wald, Elijah: *How the Beatles Destroyed Rock 'n' Roll: An Alternative History of Popular Music* (New York: Oxford University Press, 2009)

Waller, Maurice, and Anthony Calabrese: *Fats Waller* (London: Cassell, 1977)

Walser, Robert: *Running with the Devil: Power, Gender and Madness in Heavy Metal Music* (Hanover: Wesleyan University Press, 1993)

Weber, Eugen: *The Hollow Years: France in the 1930s* (London: Sinclair-Stevenson, 1995)

Weingarten, Christopher R.: *It Takes a Nation of Millions to Hold Us Back* (New York: Continuum, 2010)

Whitall, Susan: *Fever: Little Willie John* (London: Titan Books, 2011)

Whitburn, Joel: *Pop Memories 1890–1954* (Menomenee Falls: Record Research Inc., 1986)

White, Charles: *The Life and Times of Little Richard, the Quasar of Rock* (London: Pan Books, 1985)

White, George R.: *Bo Diddley: Living Legend* (Chessington: Sanctuary, 1995)

White, H. Loring: *Ragging It: Getting Ragtime into History (and Some History into Ragtime)* (New York: iUniverse, 2005)

Wilder, Alec: *American Popular Song: The Great Innovators 1900–1950* (New York: Oxford University Press, 1990)

Willens, Doris: *Lonesome Traveller: The Life of Lee Hays* (New York: W. W. Norton & Co., 1988)

Williams, Andy: *Moon River and Me: A Memoir* (London: Weidenfeld & Nicolson, 2009)

Winstantley, Russ, and David Nowell: *Soul Survivors: The Wigan Casino Story* (London: Robson Books, 2003)

Wolfe, Charles K.: *Tennessee Strings: The Story of Country Music in Tennessee* (Knoxville: University of Tennessee Press, 1981)

Woods, Fred: *Folk Revival: The Rediscovery of a National Music* (Poole: Blandford Press, 1978)

Wren, Christopher S.: *Johnny Cash: Winners Got Scars Too* (London: Abacus, 1974)

Yang, Mina: *California Polyphony: Ethnic Voices, Musical Crossroads* (Urbana: University of Illinois Press, 2008)

Young, William H. and Nancy K.: *Music of the Great Depression* (Westport: Greenwood Press, 2005)

Zeldin, Theodore: *France 1848–1945: Taste and Corruption* (Oxford: Oxford University Press, 1980)

This book was also informed by the research I undertook for my previous books, notably *Are You Ready for the Country*, *There's a Riot Going On*, *You Never Give Me Your Money* and *The Man Who Sold the World*, each of which includes its own lengthy bibliography.

Among the newspapers and magazines consulted specifically for this project were *Action, African Music, American Music Lover, The American Record Guide, Beat Instrumental, Billboard, Black Music, Blackshirt, Boyfriend, Buffalo Courier-Express, Cash Box, Charlotte Observer, Cheetah, Church Times, Collier's, Commercial Appeal, Country Music People, Cowboy Songs, Crawdaddy, Cream, Creem, Crescendo, Da Capo, Daily Express, Daily Mail, Daily Mirror, Daily Sketch, Daily Worker, Datebook, Deejay & Radio Monthly, Detroit Free Press, Disc [and Music Echo], Down Beat, Ebony, Edison Phonograph Monthly, Esquire, Evening Standard, Fabulous, The Face, Fascist Week, Flower Scene, The Forty-Fiver, Fusion, The Gramophone, The Guardian, Hi Fi/Stereo Review, High-Fidelity, Hit Parader, Honey, Ink, International Times, Jazz & Pop, Jazz Journal, Jazz Monthly, Jazz Music, Jet, Keyboard, Let It Rock, Life, Melody Maker, Memory Lane, Memphis Press-Scimitar, Mersey Beat, Metronome, The Mod's Monthly, Mojo, The Music Seller, Music Week, National Lampoon, Negro Digest, The New Musical Express, The New York Times, The Phono Trader and Recorder, The Phonograph Monthly Review, Pickup, Popular Science Monthly, Punk Magazine, Q, Radio Pictorial, Radio Times, Rave, Record Collector, Record Mail, Record Mirror, Record Retailer, Records Magazine, R'nB Scene, Rolling Stone, St Paul Globe, Saturday Evening Post, Shreveport Times, Sideburns, Smash Hits, Sniffin' Glue, Soul Underground, Sounds, Spin, Spins & Needles, Tacoma News Tribune, Talking Machine News, Teen Magazine, Teen Set, Tiger Beat, The Times, Town, Uncut, Vancouver Province, Vanity Fair, Variety, Vibe, Vibrations, The Village Voice, Vintage Light Music, The Voice, Vox, The Washington Star, Who Put the Bomp, The Wire* and *Zigzag*.

Index

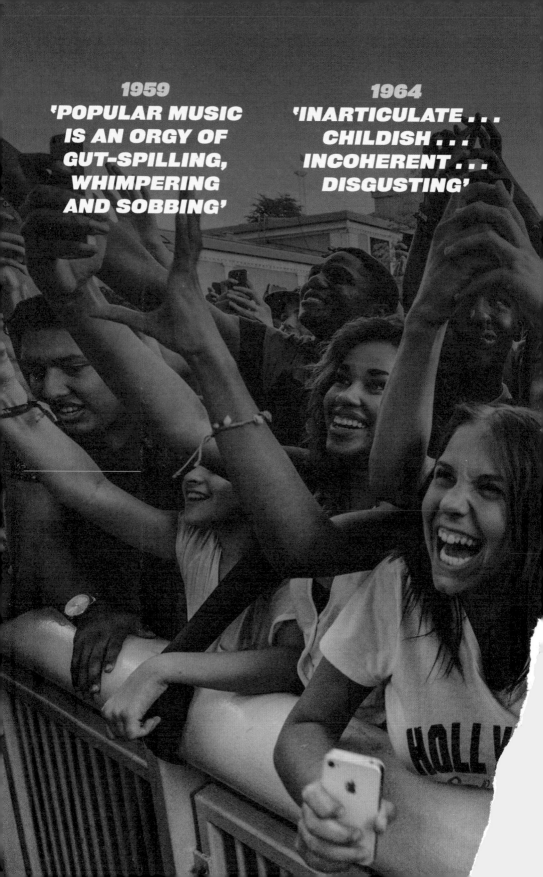

1959
'POPULAR MUSIC
IS AN ORGY OF
GUT-SPILLING,
WHIMPERING
AND SOBBING'

1964
'INARTICULATE . . .
CHILDISH . . .
INCOHERENT . . .
DISGUSTING'